WORSHIP AND ETHICS

Worship and Ethics

A Study in Rabbinic Judaism

Max Kadushin

GREENWOOD PRESS, PUBLISHERS
WESTPORT, CONNECTICUT

Library of Congress Cataloging in Publication Data

Kadushin, Max, 1895-
Worship and ethics.

Reprint of the ed. published by Northwestern University Press, Evanston, Ill.
Includes bibliographical references and index.
1. Worship (Judaism). 2. Jewish way of life. 3. Rabbinical literature--History and criticism. I. Title.
[BM656.K3 1978] 296.4 77-18849
ISBN 0-313-20217-6

Reprinted in 1978 by Greenwood Press, Inc.,
51 Riverside Ave., Westport, Conn. 06880

Printed in the United States of America

To

P.K. and C.G.K.

Preface

In rabbinic Judaism worship and ethics are cultural phenomena. Each individual has his own personal experiences in both spheres, but what make the experiences possible are the values of society. Theories depicting the individual as the creative rebel who overcomes the bonds of routine and inertia with which the tribe would enslave him certainly do not apply to rabbinic Judaism, and in essence probably to no religion. Such theories willy-nilly must use terms like worship, repentance, or love, terms and ideas provided by the tribe, by society.

Worship and ethics are closely associated in rabbinic Judaism. The creative agency which developed both spheres is Halakah, the rabbinic law, and their close association is likewise largely due to Halakah. The aim of this book is to describe how Halakah, working with the value concepts of the folk as a whole, enables the individual to achieve religious experience.

What are rabbinic value concepts? They are rabbinic terms such as Torah, miẓwah (a religious commandment), charity, holiness, repentance, man. Such terms are noun forms, but they have a different character than other types of terms or concepts. These terms are connotative only, and hence are not amenable to formal definition. Again, they refer to matters which are not objects, qualities, or relations in sensory experience. Their function is to endow situations or events with significance. These value concepts are related to each other not logically but organismically. This means that the value concepts are not deduced from one another and that they cannot be placed in a logical order. Instead, the coherence or relatedness of the value concepts is such that they interweave dynamically. This entire theory will be further discussed and illustrated here when the ethical concepts are taken up.

I wish to acknowledge my profound indebtedness to the late

Professor Louis Ginzberg and יבלח״א to Professor Saul Lieberman. For the elucidation of many of the rabbinic texts bearing on this study, I have used Dr. Ginzberg's *A Commentary on the Palestinian Talmud*,[1] and Dr. Lieberman's edition of the Tosefta, his commentary there,[2] and his *Tosefta Ki-Fshuṭah, A Comprehensive Commentary on the Tosefta*.[3] These works are invaluable and they represent what is undoubtedly the greatest modern contribution to the critical study of rabbinic sources.

Contents

WORSHIP AND ETHICS

CHAPTER I

Introduction

A. Rabbinic Worship and Halakah

Rabbinic worship is personal experience and yet it is governed by Halakah, law. Were Halakah merely a set of rules, procedures intended to win divine favor, rabbinic worship would be at most an external art, not a personal experience. But the personal experience of an individual is never raw experience. On the one hand, it is unique and always something newly achieved; on the other hand, to be intelligible at all, what has been achieved must have a form of some kind, a form supplied to the individual by the society of which he is a member. Forms of that kind, which are flexible enough to allow full scope to the individual's temperament and originality and yet which are shared by all other individuals of his society, are value concepts. Even the simplest experience of worship is impossible unless it is literally informed by a value concept. The halakic rules make the experience of worship possible by calling into play the various value concepts which can be associated with worship.

The rabbinic designation for the sacrificial worship in the Temple is ʻabodah—literally "work," "service." The same word is also used by the rabbis as a common designation for berakot (benedictions), the ʻAmidah or the Eighteen Berakot said daily in the morning, afternoon and evening, the Ḳeri'at Shemaʻ (the recitation of the Shemaʻ), and *talmud Torah* (study of Torah). Since all these are things to be said by the individual wherever he may be, to designate them as ʻabodah is to say that they are acts of nonsacrificial worship. All these acts have a certain character in common. Every one of them represents an experience wherein there is felt to be a manifestation of God in one manner or another. Furthermore, in all of them that manifestation of God is conveyed by a value concept.

Halakah calls into play the various value concepts which can be associated with worship and does so in a number of ways. For one thing, it designates the occasions for worship, many of which would otherwise have been stimuli to worship only for especially sensitive individuals. Among those occasions, for example, is the morsel of bread we are about to eat or the water we are about to drink—commonplace, ordinary things which Halakah points to as manifestations of God's love, *middat raḥamim*, and hence to be acknowledged as such in a berakah. Again, in a more complex experience, the experience of holiness, Halakah brings into play not only the concept of *middat raḥamim* but also those of *ḳedushah* (holiness) and miẓwot (commandments). Once more, it is Halakah which enables Ḳeri'at Shema' to evoke the concepts of *malkut Shamayim* (kingship of God) and *talmud Torah* (study of Torah). Several of these concepts convey what are felt to be manifestations of God. At the same time, however, other concepts are also given expression in the experience of worship. How can that be?

A value concept is represented by a conceptual term. But the conceptual term in itself is merely connotative, suggestive. Value concepts take on content only when they are combined in a statement or a situation. We may illustrate this point with the example of the concept of *malkut Shamayim*. "As it combines with other concepts, *Malkut Shamayim*, we learned, signifies that God's dominion is everywhere, that God will ultimately be recognized as King by the whole world, that it negates basically the dominion of the Nations of the World over Israel, that it is acknowledged after experiencing God's love or mercy, that it immediately implies the observance of the *Miẓwot*. Had we found it necessary to cite more passages, we should have drawn forth more ideas implicit in the concept of *Malkut Shamayim*."[1] The content of any particular rabbinic value concept is, therefore, a function of the entire complex of concepts as a whole. If every rabbinic concept depends for its meaning upon all the rest, then all the concepts together constitute an organismic whole.

A prime characteristic of the organismic complex is the potential simultaneity of the value concepts. "It is as if the whole complex were constantly at trigger-point, ready to pour forth *all* its concepts on any occasion or situation. In saying this we are saying no more than that the complex is organic, of one piece. Each situation has focused upon it the whole organic complex, and the concepts that are concretized in that situation represent the maximum possible concretization of the whole organic complex."[2] What always limits the actualization of the whole complex are the particular conditions imposed by a specific situation, and here Halakah displays another role. It ensures that within the limits imposed by the specific situation the maximum number of value concepts will be actualized—in other words, that the value complex will, so to speak, exploit to the full all the possibilities of a situation. For example, when ten men are present, a *ẓibbur*, the delegate of the *ẓibbur* says certain berakot, known as Birkot 'Abelim, in a house of mourners. One of the berakot addresses itself to the mourners with moving words of comfort, words more moving certainly than those generally at the command of men on these occasions, although it is also incumbent upon individuals, during the days of mourning, to comfort the mourners as best they can. Halakah has taken such cognizance of this situation that a berakah, an act of worship, is also an act of *gemilut ḥasadim* (lovingkindness). An ethical concept has been given expression in an experience of worship.

The organismic coherence of the value concepts makes ethical concepts *possible* elements of an experience of worship. What makes them *actual* elements of the experience of worship is Halakah.

B. Ethical Concomitants and Motifs in Worship

There is no rabbinic definition of worship. To identify the various forms of nonsacrificial worship, it is necessary simply to ascertain those things to which the rabbis applied the concept of 'abodah. True, all the forms of rabbinic worship have a common character, all of them being experiences wherein there is felt to be a manifestation of God, but 'abodah can also refer to pagan worship, worship that for the rabbis does not have this character.

Similarly, to designate what today we call the ethical sphere, the rabbis employ the concept of *derek ereẓ* (literally, "the way of the world") without defining that term. Possessing a number of aspects or phases, *derek ereẓ* is broad enough to include an extremely wide range of human acts and attitudes, but these very phases prevent *derek ereẓ* from being an amorphous concept. In fact, one of the phases consists of concepts which further differentiate among human acts or attitudes, concepts which the rabbis recognized as being common to mankind in general—*raḥamim* (love or compassion), *din* (justice), *ẓedaḳah* (charity), *gemilut ḥasadim* (acts of lovingkindness), *shalom* (peace), *'emet* (truth) and the like. These are among the concepts in which great emphatic trends of the value complex rise to expression—the emphasis on love, the emphasis on the individual, and the emphasis on universality.

Rabbinic worship has ethical concomitants and is filled with ethical motifs. An instance of an ethical concomitant in worship is the berakah mentioned above, in which the mourners are addressed with words of comfort, a berakah characterized as *gemilut ḥasadim.* Another berakah which is *gemilut ḥasadim*, one in a parallel series of berakot, the Birkot Ḥatanim, is recited at a wedding. In that berakah the delegate of the assembled *ẓibbur* recites a prayer for the bride and groom, beginning with, "O make these beloved companions greatly rejoice." Here are acts of worship where the whole act is also characterized as *gemilut ḥasadim*, an act engaged in for the benefit of others. In these instances the ethical concomitant is really more than a concomitant. What is said is both an act of worship and an ethical act.

In the Birkat ha-Miẓwot the ethical concomitant is an element in the act of worship. This berakah, which is said before fulfilling a miẓwah and which points to the significance of such an act, embodies a number of concepts, one of them being *ḳedushah*. The concept of *ḳedushah* connotes the imitation of God in acts of *ẓedaḳah* (charity) and *gemilut ḥasadim* and the abstention from cardinal sins; hence, when the individual says the berakah and fulfills the miẓwah he also dedicates himself to this ethical imitation of God. The ethical concomitant now is only an element in an entire experience, for the experience of *ḳedushah* is also informed with the concepts of miẓwot, *middat raḥamim* and berakah; nevertheless, since the ethical concomitant is a constituent element of a unitary experience, it makes the entire experience one that is character building, a source of moral energy. An experience in which a person dedicates himself to the imitation of God in deeds of *ẓedakah* and *gemilut ḥasadim* and to refraining from cardinal sins is an experience charged with ethical motive power.

Rabbinic worship endows the individual with a larger self. When the individual is bidden today to identify himself with humanity, there is an implicit assumption that ordinarily he does not feel himself to be so identified. In rabbinic worship, it is not a matter of the individual being *identified* with humanity but of his being *associated* with humanity. Self-identity is never lost—it is a primary factor of the rabbinic experience of worship—but the individual feels himself to be associated with unspecified others. This happens when one of the concepts embodied in a berakah, especially in the closing formula, is the concept of man, a value concept which has a connotation of both universality and love. The term itself is mentioned in the Fourth Berakah of the daily 'Amidah, a berakah acknowledging God's love in granting man knowledge and discernment. The concept of man is embodied, however, in a number of acts of worship—for example, in other berakot of the 'Amidah, in the First Berakah of the grace after meals, in the berakot on the various kinds of food, in the berakah on the light of the day. When saying these berakot, the individual feels himself to be a representative of man. More technically and more accurately, by being expressed through the concept of man the individual's self-awareness is now conceptualized, with the result that the individual retains awareness of his self-identity while feeling himself to be associated with unspecified others. Similarly, in other acts of worship, the individual's self-awareness is conceptualized through the concept of Israel. It is in acts of worship, then, that the ethical implications of man and of Israel are apprehended in living, experiential contexts. Indeed, what is here an ethical concomitant of worship is probably seldom a matter of actual experience outside of worship, even when an individual does wish to identify himself with humanity.

It is hardly necessary to point out that the emphatic trends mentioned earlier are expressed in the ethical concomitants of worship. But an emphatic trend, the emphasis on love, is also present as an ethical motif in most berakot, namely, when the emphasis on love is given expression in the concept of *middat raḥamim*, God's love. *Middat raḥamim* is obviously not a concept of *derek ereẓ*, human morality, but it is most certainly an ethical concept. Primarily a concept which conveys a felt manifestation of God, its embodiment in berakot also has an effect on the ethical life of man, since it is an ethical concept and one which strengthens the emphatic trend on love.

Our purpose has been to call attention to specific ethical concomitants and motifs in worship. We have therefore not included here the commitment in Ḳeri'at Shema', which is a commitment to the miẓwot in general. A knowledge of Torah is a knowledge as well of the ethical life in all its details, and the study of Torah, accordingly, has its specific ethical concomitants.[3]

The great fault with modern representations of rabbinic ethics is the assumption that the true approach to ethics is the philosopher's approach. Rabbinic ethics has been forced into the framework of Kantian ethics, even by some who find fault with others on that score. In line with the philosophers' view that ethics must exhibit an ultimate criterion, it is customary to represent this or that rabbinic statement as consisting of an ultimate ethical criterion. It is no wonder, therefore, that the crucial role of the ethical concepts has been all but overlooked. Thus, to give an extreme example, works dealing with rabbinic ethics fail to consider the concept of *derek ereẓ* at all. Eminent scholars even go so far as to claim there is no such thing as rabbinic ethics. The rabbis, they say, do not discriminate between ethical acts and other miẓwot; and one writer declares—mark the philosophic approach!—that the rabbis "had no notion of a rationalistic ethics, still less of an intuitive ethics."

In view of all this, there is need for a more authentic representation of rabbinic ethics. Our first task, it seems to us, ought to be an endeavor to meet that need. We regard ethics not as a system thought out by a philosopher but as a pattern of concepts developed by society.

C. Interrelation of Halakah and Haggadah

"Haggadah and Halakah are so closely related because both are concretizations of the value-concepts—Haggadah in speech, Halakah in law and action."[4] This close relationship does not, of course, obliterate the fact that Haggadah and Halakah do constitute two different categories.* Each haggadic interpretation is a unit in itself, a complete entity. Only through certain forms of composition, art-forms, are these essentially independent statements brought together and made into larger wholes.[5] In contrast, a halakah is not an independent entity. There is an implicit nexus between the halakot, a nexus which becomes more and more explicit as the result of logical procedures—classification and discursive reasoning; classification in the Mishnah and discursive reasoning in the Talmud.[6] A haggadic idea is grasped not step by step but as a unitary whole; it is an expression of organismic thought. On the other hand, a halakah, although embodying a value concept, to a certain extent requires the step-by-step procedures of logical thought for its formulation.

Because Halakah and Haggadah embody the same value complex, the two categories are not mutually exclusive but interrelated. Halakah is reflected in the Haggadah, numerous haggadot taking for granted specific halakot. According to the Haggadah, to cite a single illustration, Joseph not only acted according to the fifth, sixth, seventh, and eighth commandments but also observed certain regulations regarding the slaughtering of animals.[7] Occasionally, too, a halakah involves a haggadah. For example, the Mishnah[8] requires that a warning must be given to witnesses in capital cases, and that warning includes an interpretation of Genesis 4:10 which is also found elsewhere as an independent haggadic statement.[9] Ginzberg has called attention to this interrelation of Haggadah and Halakah. He pointed out that the halakic difference between two versions of an opinion held by R. Joḥanan b. Zakkai is indicated by the respective haggadot employed in those versions.[10]

Halakah governs rabbinic worship. It determines not only the occasions and the forms of the various acts of worship but the content of the acts as well. Like other halakot, acts of worship, too, are taken for granted in the Haggadah, as in the well-known haggadah which associates the 'Amidah† with the patriarchs. But rabbinic worship has an especial affinity with the Haggadah. An idea in a berakah may also be a teaching in a haggadah—for example, the

* Haggadah consists of religious and ethical teaching and is nonjuristic in character.

† A unit of nineteen benedictions (originally eighteen), recited in the morning, afternoon, and evening, and said standing.

idea in the First Berakah of the grace after meals that God feeds the whole world, or the idea in the Birkat ha-Miẓwot that Israel is sanctified through the miẓwot. A haggadah may even reflect an experience of worship. One instance is the haggadah alluding to Ḳeri'at Shema' as being a call and a response, a call to which Israel responds by "testifying" for God; another is the haggadic teaching that to be holy Israel must imitate God in acts of *ẓedaḳah* and *gemilut ḥasadim*, a teaching that reflects the experience of *ḳedushah* initiated by the Birkat ha-Miẓwot. Besides, the concepts which in rabbinic worship convey or interpret manifestations of God—such as God's love and *malkut Shamayim*—were made all the more vivid by being frequently embodied in the Haggadah, and hence were all the more warmly apprehended in acts of worship.

Haggadah made vivid the value concepts as a whole, nurtured and cultivated them; Halakah put those concepts into practice, concretized them in daily living. Haggadah and Halakah are interrelated, but that interrelation is especially marked in two spheres. One is the sphere of rabbinic worship; the other is a sphere associated with rabbinic worship, that of rabbinic ethics.[11]

D. Organismic Thought in Halakah

Haggadah is organismic thought par excellence. Each haggadic statement is an independent entity, so that Haggadah has to employ forms of literary composition in order to make larger entities out of what are essentially discrete statements. Moreover, each haggadic statement is not only an independent entity; it is an organismic entity as well. A haggadah usually embodies not one but several value concepts in combination, concepts interlacing in a single idea.[12] The haggadah on the imitation of God, for example, embodies in a single idea the concepts of God's love, *ḳedushah*, *ẓedaḳah*, *gemilut ḥasadim*, and Israel. No less characteristic of organismic thought is the point of departure for a haggadic idea. Such an idea, being a discrete entity and not a link in a logical chain of ideas, needs a stimulus, a point of departure, and that stimulus is usually a biblical text. Even this characteristic of Haggadah is completely consonant with organismic thought. A biblical text is a nondetermining stimulus, for it can set off any number of haggadic interpretations.[13]

The nexus in Halakah means that the halakot are not independent entities. The implicit nature of that nexus, however, is never completely overcome. Logical procedures, although making the nexus more and more explicit, do not succeed in achieving for Halakah a completely rigid, logical structure. The fact is that Halakah, despite the nexus, also possesses some of the characteristics of organismic thought. Thus, just as in the case of a haggadic idea, an act governed by Halakah, too, concretizes a number of value concepts in combination, a characteristic of Halakah particularly evident in acts of worship. Even the simplest form of an act of worship, for example, a form typified by the berakah on bread, embodies at least two concepts; the concept of God's love and that of berakah. But an act governed by Halakah does not, by reason of embodying a number of concepts, convey its meaning in stages; rather, by very reason of the value concepts embodied, the act is an organismic whole, a unitary entity, again just as in the case of a haggadic idea. This is perhaps most apparent in such instances as those of the Birkot Ḥatanim and Birkot 'Abelim. Here an act as a whole is interpreted by two concepts at once, that of berakah and that of *gemilut ḥasadim*; the meaning of the act is conveyed not by these concepts severally but by both together.

A feature of organismic thought is the role played by emphasis. Emphasis is not achieved in any one manner. It may consist of stressing one concept over against another, both in Haggadah and in Halakah. In one haggadic statement, for example, the plea is made that Israel survive lest Torah disappear; in another statement, as an answer to a direct question, Israel is given precedence over Torah.[14] An emphatic trend, however, represents not this type of emphasis but one that is due to repetition, the emphasis now being the result of a repeated effect produced by a number of different value concepts. In any particular haggadah or halakah several types of emphasis may be present simultaneously and so re-enforce each other.

The stressing of one concept rather than another is still another type of emphasis. Ḳeri'at Shema' is an act of worship whereby a person accepts upon himself the kingship of God, but the Ḳeri'at Shema' is also study of Torah. This dual character of the Ḳeri'at Shema' allows the time for reciting the Shema' to be associated with *talmud Torah* in one halakic statement, and in another with the acceptance of *malkut Shamayim*. In the one statement the stress is on the concept of *talmud Torah*, whereas in the other it is on the concept of *malkut Shamayim*. An instance in which one concept is stressed over against another has to do with the 'Amidah, an act of worship which is characterized both as 'abodah and as tefillah, prayer. Here, on a certain issue, R. Joḥanan stressed the concept of tefillah as against that of 'abodah.

Emphasis is a valuational mode which does not rule out what is not emphasized. This is especially true in Halakah. The emphasis on love does not mean that there are not other occasions when the several concepts of justice are concretized. Even when one concept is stressed over against another, the concept not stressed remains relevant: R. Joḥanan's rule (see p. 128, below) stresses the concept of tefillah as against that of 'abodah, yet this does not affect the idea that, even in this case, the 'Amidah is a reminder of the daily communal sacrifice in the Temple, i.e., of 'abodah. Of all the types of emphasis, however, the stressing of one concept rather than another is least exclusive of the concept not stressed: Ḳeri'at Shema' is both the acceptance of *malkut Shamayim* and study of Torah no matter whether, in regard to the time for the recital, one concept is stressed rather than the other.

It is this type of emphasis which allows the rabbis to regard ethical acts as miẓwot and yet to discriminate them from other miẓwot, to be sensitive in the fullest degree to the particular ethical quality informing such an act. We must first of all recognize that an ethical act is interpreted or grasped by two concepts at once, by the concept of miẓwot and by an ethical concept. A striking example is an act of *ẓedaḳah* (charity), an act which is often referred to by the term miẓwah. Now all acts which are miẓwot are to be preceded, according to a rule in the Tosefta and the Yerushalmi,* by the Birkat ha-Miẓwot; nevertheless, this rule is not applied when it comes to ethical acts. Omitting the Birkat ha-Miẓwot does not, of course, change their character and make them acts which are not miẓwot, but it does result in stressing the ethical concept embodied

* The Tosefta is a collection of laws parallel to the Mishnah. The Jerusalem Talmud was developed in Palestine and compiled about 400 C.E., in contradistinction to the Babylonian Talmud, which was developed in Babylon and compiled about 500 C.E. These will be referred to throughout as "Yerushalmi" and "Babli," respectively.

in each particular act rather than the concept of miẓwot. Attention is focused on the special circumstances of the particular act, on the human relationships involved in the act, in a word, on the particular ethical implication of the act. We are saying no more than that they who possess the concepts of *ẓedaḳah* and *gemilut ḥasadim*, concepts which are drives, are obviously motivated by these concepts to perform acts of *ẓedaḳah* and *gemilut ḥasadim*, and that, since these are ethical concepts, they are fully aware of the ethical character of such particular acts.

Discrimination of ethical acts from other miẓwot comes to the fore when there is a conflict of miẓwot. For example, the rule is that a high priest must avoid all contact with a corpse since that would make him "unclean"; yet, because of *kebod ha-beriyyot*, the honor of mankind, he is required to attend to the burial of a *met miẓwah*, the corpse of one whose relatives are not known. There is an emphasis here on an ethical concept by making the act embodying it an overriding miẓwah. An ethical concept has been stressed, but not against the concept of miẓwot.

One characteristic of organismic thought in Halakah is only partly similar to organismic thought in Haggadah. The point of departure for a haggadic idea, as we have said, is a nondetermining stimulus. An act governed by Halakah, too, must have a point of departure: the stimulus for the berakah on bread is the bread about to be eaten, and the stimulus for an act of *ẓedaḳah* is the physical need of another person. But an act governed by Halakah, although an organismic entity, is not an idependent entity, and this is reflected in the stimulus. An independent entity is something which is not predictable, and its stimulus accords with this feature. On the other hand, an organismic act governed by Halakah *is* predictable, else there is no Halakah. Its stimulus, therefore, can only be a determining stimulus.[15]

E. Normal Mysticism and the Common Man

There is an experience of God in an act of rabbinic worship. To the individual who says a berakah, God seems so near that he addresses God with the pronoun "Thou," just as he would address a person facing him. "Thou" is the only word which can express the sense of God's nearness, yet the feeling of God's nearness is obviously different from anything the individual may feel when he addresses a fellow human being with the same pronoun. When God is addressed with the word "Thou," the content of the experience remains unrevealed. The fact is that, so far as nonsacrificial worship is concerned, there is no rabbinic concept which connotes the content of the experience of God's nearness, no way of communicating that experience even by suggestion. It is a wholly private experience and hence a form of mysticism. At the same time, the pronoun "Thou" gives some indication of the kind of mysticism this is. The word does enable the individual to address God, so that this entirely private experience, while not communicable, is not altogether inexpressible. Certainly at one point, therefore, this kind of mysticism is not completely outside the realm of normal experience.

In prayer, too, there is the experience of God's nearness, for in a prayer, as in a berakah, God is likewise addressed with the pronoun "Thou." A prayer, however, though thus related to worship, is not in itself worship; it differs from worship because it is solely a petition, a *baḳḳashah*, not a berakah. A prayer usually consists of a petition for a specific manifestation of God's love not yet experienced but only hoped for. A berakah is usually an acknowledgment of such a manifestation, of something which has just taken place or else which is felt as still taking place. In a prayer we have the only valuational experience wherein not all the concepts involved are concretized. The concept of *baḳḳashah* is concretized, and that enables the individual to experience God's nearness, but the hoped-for manifestation of God's love has not yet been experienced; a prayer, a *baḳḳashah*, is thus an experience, but an incomplete experience. On the other hand, a berakah is an element in a complete, unitary experience. The other element in this unitary experience is the stimulus for the berakah, and that stimulus most often consists in an event or a situation which is interpreted as a manifestation of God's love, *middat raḥamim*. For example, the stimulus for the berakah on bread, as we pointed out at the end of the previous section, is the bread about to be eaten.

Related to the experience of God are not only the concepts of berakah and *baḳḳashah* (or tefillah) but also a large number of other concepts in the value complex: *middat raḥamim*, *middat ha-din* (God's justice), *malkut Shamayim*, Torah, miẓwot, *ḳedushah*, *ḳiddush ha-Shem* (sanctification of the Name), *teshubah* (repentance), *biṭṭaḥon* (trust in God), *'emunah* (trust especially in God's promise). These concepts have to do, each in its own way, with the experience of God and this means that the experience of God is to a degree communicable. Furthermore, these concepts are elements of the organismic complex, enmeshed with all the other concepts in the complex; notice, for example, that ethical acts are also miẓwot. A number of concepts which have a factor in common represent an emphatic trend, and the experience or awareness of God is therefore an emphatic trend of the organismic complex. In other words, the experience of God is an aspect of the normal valuational life, just as the other emphatic trends are aspects of the normal valuational life. The concepts relating to the experience of God are accordingly neither philosophical ideas nor philosophically inspired—nor have they any philosophical implications unless we force them into a framework that adds nothing, pragmatically, to the experience of God itself. When we spoke of the ethical concepts we were obliged similarly to indicate they are not ideas in a philosophical system.

Partly communicable and partly noncommunicable, this dual character of the experience of God is especially evident, once again, in acts of worship. A berakah interprets an event or situation as a manifestation of *middat raḥamim*, yet while saying the berakah the individual has a consciousness of God's nearness which is not communicable. When reciting the Ḳeri'at Shema', the individual accepts "the yoke of *malkut Shamayim*" through a meditative act whereby he makes God "King above and below and in the four directions of the world." To the degree to which this experience is communicable it is expressed in the term *malkut Shamayim* and in the figure of "above and below and in the four directions," but the experience as a whole wherein God is made king is private, noncommunicable. That experience requires *kawwanah* on the part of the individual, a state of mind completely personal. It is devotion of the heart and concentration on the ideas involved in the Shema'. The rabbinic experience of God presents a paradox, the kind of paradox which, as has often been said, is a feature of the spiritual life. Rabbinic experience of God is personal, mystical experience which is nevertheless mediated by concepts that are elements of the normal valuational life. We have, therefore, called the rabbinic experience of God normal mysticism.

Normal mysticism is not infrequently accompanied by changes, for the time being, in the psychological constitution of the individual. We have observed how in some acts of worship the individual achieves a larger self. More striking is the change that occurs, during the recitation of several berakot, in the individual's consciousness of time, the past and the future coalescing with the present. Certain events ordinarily conceived as having taken place in the past or as bound to take place in the future become events that are felt to be experienced in the present.

An act of rabbinic worship is filled with an experience of God. The occasion, the form, even the verbal expression of an act of worship, are governed by Halakah and therefore represent the product of the rabbis. On the other hand, the concepts informing the experience and the normal mysticism which the concepts mediate are not the product of the rabbis but are inherent in the culture of the folk. The concepts relating to the experience of God are an aspect of the normal valuational life, that is to say, of the valuational life of the people as a whole. These value concepts are folk concepts. They offer irrefutable evidence that normal mysticism was the experience of the common man, not only of the rabbis.

The capacity for normal mystical experience on the part of the common man was a basic characteristic of rabbinic Judaism. It made possible, in the sphere of worship, a remarkable interaction between the rabbis, who were the spiritual and intellectual leaders, and the folk. True, without the forms developed by the rabbis the life of worship would no doubt have been very limited. The rabbis tell of a brief berakah on bread recited by Benjamin, the shepherd; and other berakot equally simple must have been evoked spontaneously by the folk. But it is unlikely that the meditative acts of worship would have arisen, and still less likely that acts of worship would have had ethical concomitants without the Halakah on these matters developed by the rabbis. At the same time, these more subtle acts of worship would not have been possible had the folk at large lacked the capacity for normal mysticism.*

* In a later chapter we shall find that the same interaction between the rabbis and the folk also took place in the sphere so closely associated with that of worship, the ethical sphere.

Men differed, of course, in their capacity for normal mysticism. Some of the rabbis themselves, on their own admission, could not achieve *kawwanah* at certain times. This was doubtless true of many common men as well. Nevertheless, the fact remains, as evidenced in the numerous value concepts relating to the experience of God, that normal mysticism was a steady factor in the valuational life of the people as a whole.

CHAPTER II

Rabbinic Ethics

A. The Problem of Morality

Philosophers have oversimplified and, paradoxically, overtheorized the problem of morality and ethics. They oversimplify the problem when they attempt to find a single, universal criterion for morality, whether it be Aristotle's ultimate of well-being, or Kant's categorical imperative, or Bentham's hedonic calculus. Each of such criteria is a test to determine whether an action is truly ethical or moral, and a test only. The individual is left to struggle by himself with what is really the major task, or rather an endless series of tasks. He alone must analyze every situation confronting him—often an urgent, immediate situation—and he alone must find his way to a solution conforming to the ultimate criterion. As a tool to be used in the resolution of human problems, with all their variety and complexity, the ultimate criterion itself is of little help. It has oversimplified those problems.

The fact is, of course, that men do not and cannot make the moral life one long and dreary process of intellectual analysis of situations and problems. Were a man to ponder over every situation, he would have neither time nor will to act at all. There would be only moral stagnation. Moral acts have an emotional, not only a mental aspect, are propelled by inner drives. In directing men to what is primarily an intellectual process, the ultimate criterion oversimplifies the problem of morality and is rendered quite futile as well.

At the same time the universal criterion has overtheorized the problem of morality and ethics. A universal criterion acts as a test in the resolution of moral situations, as we have said. But it also acts as a definition of morality or ethics. Deeds in accord with the criterion are ethical; deeds not in accord are not ethical. Was there no genuinely moral life before any of these definitions was formulated? But if moral life obtained—as obviously it did—men must have been able to distinguish a moral from an immoral act without these definitions to guide them. Apparently, then, the moral life is altogether possible without definitions of morality. In that case, can we not perhaps assume that men act "intuitively" in accord with a definition of morality? Yet if men are not automatons, they must be aware of these intuitions and aware that they are ethical intuitions. Men, in other words, can be aware of the sphere of morality without benefit of definitions of morality. The universal criterion not only oversimplifies morality; it overtheorizes it by attempting to give an abstract definition of morality.

The problem of morality emerges from the foregoing discussion as a threefold one. The first part is concerned with the variety and complexity of the moral life. Since men do not employ an intellectual criterion as a guide, how do they cope with its variety and subtlety? Second, what is the character of the emotional drives that propel men to moral acts? Third, how is it possible for men to have an awareness of morality without having a definition of morality?

A consideration of rabbinic ethics will supply the answers to these and kindred questions. Rabbinic ethics is not the product of philosophic reflection but of a historically evolved tradition. It has to do with the moral life of a people to whom that tradition has given character and continuity over many centuries. It is concerned with day-to-day issues, takes account of social, economic, and political factors, and affects the relations of individual to individual. This is true, of course, of other historically evolved traditions as well; thus we shall be able occasionally to cull from studies of other groups such illustrative material as may suit our purpose.[1]

B. Ethical Value Concepts

The variety of the moral life is spelled out in rabbinic literature in terms of a moral vocabulary. It is a large vocabulary, containing not only terms for matters recognized as ethical or moral, but also for things recognized as immoral. In the one category are such terms as *'emet*[2] (truth), *shalom*[3] (peace), *ẓedaḳah*[4] (charity), *'anawah*[5] (humility); in the other, such terms as *shefikut damim*[6] (murder), *zenut*[7] (unchastity), *gezel*[8] (robbery), *sheḳer*[9] (falsehood). Most of the terms given here are used in the Bible as well as by the rabbis.[10]

When we go on to distinguish between the meanings of related terms in the ethical vocabulary, we get a further impression of complexity, of subtlety. *Ẓedaḳah* (charity) and *gemilut ḥasadim* (deeds of lovingkindness), for example, are terms closely allied in meaning. They can be interchanged,[11] for both have the connotation of love.[12] Nevertheless, the rabbis do discriminate between *gemilut ḥasadim* and *ẓedaḳah* on the basis of actual practice. *Ẓedaḳah* involves an expenditure of money, *gemilut ḥasadim*, of money or personal service; the former has for its object the poor; the latter, both the poor and the rich: the former can have reference only to the living, the latter, both to the living and the dead.[13] Similarly, *'alub* (submissive, lowly, humbled) and *'anaw* (meek, kind, forgiving) are also kindred words and may be used interchangeably,[14] yet each has its own distinctive connotation.[15]

An ethical or moral term refers to a complete act, a complete event, or a situation as a whole. A robbery, for instance, involves a number of things: a definite thing taken, definite circumstances when the event took place, definite individuals. The event may be described in minute detail, so far as all these matters are concerned, and yet, unless the idea of "robbery" is conveyed, the event as a whole will not be communicated. We may say, then, that a moral term unifies a situation or an act. Because a moral term or idea has this unifying function, the moral idea is integral to the event, is an essential element in the situation.

But how does the moral idea act as the integrating agent? Without the moral idea, what do the details lack? What makes each of them merely a disparate element even if we name them all? What is missing is the meaning of the act. When a moral idea unifies an act or situation it gives significance to it. The significance conveyed is to be found in the moral term itself; that is to say, the moral term is a value term. Every moral or immoral act is a value act, the valuation being none other than the moral idea integrating the act and thus conveyed by the act. The moral life is a succession of value acts; it is a life of valuation, full of significance, or rather, in view of the large number of moral terms or ideas, a life full of significances.

The moral life is varied and subtle because the significances of its value ideas are varied and subtle.

We can now see why there is no need for an ultimate criterion as a test for every human act. The ultimate criterion would invest a human act with meaning; it would make us aware of the bearing of an act. But that is exactly what the value ideas do, and without the necessity of continually weighing and pondering, and so hampering all action. Every act charged with a moral idea is filled with significance, and what is more, with a particular significance. If awareness of the implication of our acts is a *desideratum*, we have it here in the awareness of the particular significance of any given act; and we are aware of the particular significance because it is conveyed by a particular term or moral idea.

The value idea gives significance to the act as a whole. It is not something isolated in any detail of the act, but it is something conveyed by the whole act. The same value idea is conveyed, however, by any number of acts or situations. There are, happily, many acts of charity, many instances of lovingkindness, and, unhappily, also many exhibitions of arrogance and many acts of robbery. A moral term like *ẓedaḳah* or *gezel* is a generalization standing for one act or for any number of acts; yet can we say that when we are confronted by an instance of charity or robbery, we stop to analyze and thus draw forth the general idea from the concrete act? Obviously not, for the act would not be an integrated value act, its significance would not register at all without the general idea or the concept to start with. What, then, is the relation of the general idea in all these instances to the concrete act? The general idea, the concept, or as we now can say, the value concept, was there to start with. The act is a concretization of the value concept. If the value concept does not refer to any one specific detail of the act, that does not mean that it has no concrete application. On the contrary, the act as a whole embodies the value concept, so to speak. The act as a whole, carrying its particular significance, possesses that significance because it embodies, concretizes a value concept. Nor would the value concept exist without any concrete applications.

This does not mean that the value concept does not exist apart from its concretizations. What we wish to emphasize is that the value concept functions through its concretizations. There is the value term itself, and the conceptual term is of paramount and absolute importance. The term stands for the concept, and without the term there would be no concept. Here we encounter what is no doubt one of the chief characteristics of the value concept—the paramount importance of the value term, the conceptual term itself. The value concept does not stand for any concrete object or relationship that is conveyed to us through our senses. The word "tree," for example, stands for certain objects in our sensory experience. We could, conceivably, substitute a new word for the term "tree" and have the new word stand for the same objects. Definite, concrete objects have the effect of rendering the conceptual term for them of secondary importance, so long as we do have *a* conceptual term. We demonstrate the validity of all this when we say "car" instead of "automobile," or "fiddle" instead of "violin." Again, an abstract concept that is defined also has a certain definite character: it has a definition; and here, too, the particular term used is a secondary matter, for it is the definition that is of prime importance. We could use any other word in place of "gravity" and still convey the same idea—so long as we continued to imply by it our present definition, or rather equation for gravity. The abstract value concept, however, is in rabbinic literature never given a definition. Even when a distinction is drawn between *gemilut ḥasadim* and *ẓedaḳah*, there is no formal definition of either concept, no general statement or formula defining either concept. The value concept depends for its life, one may say, on the term itself. Here the conceptual term is of primary importance.

A term that is not made explicit, either through sensory experience or through a definition, can be only connotative, suggestive. The abstract value concept is therefore merely connotative or suggestive. Nevertheless, it is a potent concept for it seldom remains abstract. The value concept is embodied most often in an act and we are then conscious of a concretization of the concept; we get an impression of definiteness, of concreteness, fully as strong as that of any sense experience. Indeed, the value concept has unified the details of sense experience into an act or situation.

What is the relation between the abstract value concept and the concrete act? The abstract value concept in itself, we have said, is connotative or suggestive. Upon closer view, we see that the value concept is indeterminate and that it becomes determinate in an act or situation or event. Were a value concept to remain indeterminate for long, it would die, for connotation alone is too indefinite, too fragile in its content to persist. A value concept lives in its concretizations, each concretization being a fresh and unique expression of the concept.

The value concept is kept vital through its concretizations; but what induces the concretization of the concept? The answer is that a value concept has its own drive toward concretization. The value concept is a dynamic concept that is least dynamic when it merely interprets an event or situation, and yet here, too, the indeterminate concept is made determinate in a situation. When we see one man helping another, that situation spells out to us *gemilut ḥasadim*; we interpret the situation and thus concretize the concept merely by having witnessed the event. Now, despite the idea element in it, this interpretation is not an intellectual act. The valuation here is warm and emotional, and this implies a degree of involvement, of participation on the part of the witness to the act.

It is no wonder, therefore, that the value concept can—and so often does—really involve us in action, that it has the force of a genuine emotional drive. To keep to our illustration, we shall cite a halakic concretization of the concept of *gemilut ḥasadim* or of *ẓedaḳah*. A rabbinic ordinance,[16] in consonance, no doubt, with the practice of the rabbis, sets the desirable amount[17] to be given to the poor as a fifth of one's property or profits;[18] on the other hand, it also sets up that amount as the maximum,[19] for otherwise a person might himself become an object of charity.[20] One version of this ordinance stresses its restraining character,[21] and hence there must have been a need for making the restraining feature as forceful as possible. It would almost seem as if the propensity the law sought to curb had the drive of a natural impulse, certainly in a group large enough to warrant legislation, and we would not be altogether wrong if we so regarded the drive possessed by the concept of charity in that society. Indeed, an instance is given in this connection of a Tanna* who had actually divided all his property among the poor,[22] or who had been prevented from doing so.[23]

* An authority quoted in the Mishnah or in the Baraitot, the Baraitot being traditions and opinions related to the Mishnah but not embodied there.

The drive toward concretization is a property only of the positive value concepts. There are negative value concepts, too, concepts that connote a negative valuation, and which thus stigmatize immoral acts. Such concepts have a drive away from concretization. Again our examples are taken from the Halakah, foı if it is the practice of the folk we look for, we shall find it reflected in one way or another in the Halakah. *'Azzut panim* (brazenness) is, of course, a negative value concept. According to Rabbah, a debtor will surely not brazen it out before his creditor, and will therefore not deny his indebtedness completely.[24] An important detail of legal procedure, taking an oath, rests on this observation, an observation that is manifestly the fruit of long experience. *'Azzut panim*, then, possessed a negative drive strong enough to affect a man's actions in business affairs, even to his own detriment. The strongest negative drives of the folk were those associated with *shefikut damim* (murder), *gilluy 'arayot* (incest), and *'abodah zarah* (idolatry). A famous halakah declares that, in order to save his life, a man may yield on other matters but never on these three, under any circumstances;[25] and this ordinance, enacted during a most critical period,[26] can only represent a crystallization in law of the profoundest feelings of the people as a whole.*

If the value concepts represent drives, positive or negative, then they constitute a vital aspect of a man's personality. They are not merely motives, for these may be short ranged. They are dynamic elements of personality, focal points in a continuous process of valuation, primary factors in the experience of significance. A rich personality has many and varied experiences of significance, or more technically, a valuational life governed by a large number of value concepts. A moral act, therefore, involves other concepts besides

* The negative concepts, and in fact the value concepts in general, do not all have the same force or drive. Some are weaker than others. Furthermore, opinions on the strength or weakness of a drive may differ widely, doubtless as the result of differences in observation or experience. Thus, in *Gittin* 81b, a mishnah is interpreted as meaning that Bet Hillel regards it as a presumption that a man does not want to make his intercourse with a woman one of prostitution, and that Bet Shammai's presumption is that he does want to. (Of the two early tannaitic schools of interpretation, Bet Shammai tends to be the more rigorous.) Reflected here are divergent judgments on the strength of the negative drive associated with the concept of *zenut* (unchastity, prostitution) (see, however, Maimonides' view in Hilkot *Gerushin* X.19).

those embodied in it. Although a moral act is the direct concretization of a particular value concept, it constitutes, in fact, the projection of a personality informed by many value concepts. Thus it is not a single emotional drive that propels a man to a moral act, but his entire personality. Any particular valuational drive, any value concept, is but a constituent of an individual's personality, and hence the other value concepts also contribute to the concretization of a concept, even if indirectly.

The value concepts are concretized in acts, situations, or events by the individual who is moved to act or who interprets situations and events. But where does the individual take them from? The value concepts are terms in the common vocabulary of groups, and the individual acquires the value terms just as he acquires his general vocabulary, that is, from childhood on. Society supplies the indeterminate value concepts, and the individual makes them determinate in acts or situations. Were society and the individual two separate and distinct entities, it would still be impossible to assign a specific concretization of a value concept either wholly to the one or wholly to the other; but the fact is that society and the individual cannot even be set up one against the other.[27] "The individual is formative of the society, the society is formative of the individual."[28] These considerations ought to make us aware once more of how abstract ethical theories oversimplify the moral life. Since society and the individual both share in any concretization of a value concept, the division between autonomous and heteronomous acts[29] is hardly a valid one. In fact, this division is an oversimplification, a logical dichotomy that ignores socio-psychological facts.

C. The Role of Emphasis

One of the problems of the moral life is its complexity, and this complexity is due to the variety and sheer number of the value concepts. An ultimate criterion would, in theory, simplify the moral life, to be sure, but it would do so by ignoring the role of the value concepts; it would thus oversimplify. How do men in daily life and practice cope with the complexity of the moral life?

The moral life is characterized by great emphatic trends. In rabbinic ethics there can be distinguished an emphasis on love, an emphasis on the individual, and an emphasis on universality. We shall, first, endeavor to establish the presence of these trends; second, we shall try to indicate how the emphatic trends simplify the moral life without thereby eliminating any of the value concepts.

Although an emphatic trend is not something that the rabbis have actually named for us in so many words, it is nonetheless something easily discernible. It is, indeed, more than discernible, for a genuine emphatic trend practically forces itself on our attention. It is a repeated effect produced by a number of distinct but related value concepts. Thus, in the concepts of *ẓedaḳah*, *gemilut ḥasadim*, *'ahabah* (love),[30] and *raḥamim* (compassion),[31] we recognize an emphasis on love, for each of them connotes love in one way or another. Among these concepts, *gemilut ḥasadim* stands primarily for acts of love and personal service to individuals,[32] but there are also other concepts that emphasize the individual, as we shall soon see. Another group of value concepts—man, the world, *bereshit* (that which was made during the first six days of creation)—have in common a connotation of universalism.[33]

In no case is a conceptual term mentioned here merely synonymous with another conceptual term. As we have shown elsewhere, a rabbinic value term always represents a concept having a distinctive character of its own, and differing in some respects from any other rabbinic value concept.[34] What we have, then, is a repeated effect produced by a number of related but different value concepts, all exhibiting a common general quality or trend; in other words, an emphatic trend has risen to expression in those concepts.

Deeper examination of the value concepts reveals further evidence of the presence of these emphatic trends. Rabbinic laws are based in great measure on biblical laws, and haggadic statements are usually interpretations of biblical texts.[35] This is to say that the foundation of both Halakah and Haggadah is the Bible. We might, therefore, expect a conceptual term of the Bible to retain its meaning or connotation when used by the rabbis as well. Instead, rabbinic usage is different from biblical in regard to many biblical terms, and the new meanings are clearly influenced by the rabbinic emphatic trends. A striking illustration is the term *ẓedaḳah*. Words formed from the root *ẓdḳ*, as found in the Bible, have a common ground in the idea of "right," but *ẓedaḳah* in rabbinic usage, as we have observed, refers to acts of charity and has the wider connotation of love. Even when the word occurs in a biblical verse, it is very often interpreted by the rabbis as referring to charity or love.[36]

Further instances of the difference between rabbinic and biblical usage reflect the presence of the other emphatic trends. The word "Israel" in the Bible is a collective noun; in rabbinic literature it also designates the members of the people individually.[37] In the Bible, the word *goy* means "nation," is a collective noun, and is applied both to Israel and to other nations, whereas in rabbinic usage it refers to the individual non-Jew.[38] *'Olam* in the Bible refers to "time"; in rabbinic literature it means "world."[39] The *ger* in the Bible is a resident alien, but the *ger* in rabbinic literature is a convert.[40] When the change in usage makes room for, or designates, the individual, as is the case with Israel and *goy*, there is obviously an emphasis on the individual; and when the change spells a wider, more universalistic idea, as is the case with *'olam* and *ger*, it clearly reflects a trend toward universality. Again, even when these words occur in biblical verses, the rabbis often interpret them in accordance with their new usage.[41]

We must recognize one thing more. The emphatic trends are not mutually exclusive. A concept expressive of love may also emphasize the individual, as we noticed in the example of *gemilut ḥasadim*. *Ger* reflects the trend toward universality, but it also stresses the individual; and that is likewise true of the concept of man. In the moral life the presence of one emphatic trend does not eliminate the others. This is the same as saying, of course, that the *concepts* expressive of the trends are not eliminated.

The emphatic trends simplify the moral life, yet without damage to its richness or variety. Simplification is achieved by stressing a common element in various concepts, not by eliminating those concepts. Nor does one emphatic trend imply the exclusion of the others, but rather the contrary. A concept belonging to the orbit of one emphatic trend may also belong to the orbit of another, and hence be a factor in the coalescence of the trends. The emphatic trends, in fine, are dependent on the value concepts.

Frequently we are made aware of an emphatic trend through an arresting statement or a law. "There are times," says Resh Laḳish, "when the neglect of Torah is its establishing."[42] Rashi rightly takes

Torah here to refer to the study of Torah and the general statement to mean that there are times when one ought to interrupt one's study, namely, in order to take part in a funeral escort or in a wedding procession (acts of *gemilut ḥasadim*).[43] A paradoxical statement, it calls attention to the importance of acts of lovingkindness, and it makes us aware of an emphasis on love. Emphasis on kindness and compassion made also for breadth of compassion. Kindness is not to be confined to human beings: "It is forbidden a man to eat before he has given food to his animal."[44]

We become aware of the emphasis on the individual too, through a striking statement or law. "The individual prays and God hears his prayer," and hence "a man ought not to say, 'I am not worthy to pray for the Temple and for the land of Israel' "[45]—that is, even though he feels himself not qualified to pray for these things, implying as they do the redemption of all Israel.[46] The emphasis on the individual is no less striking in ethical relationships. A group is not permitted to save itself by handing over any individual to be dishonored or killed. If Gentiles threaten to violate an entire group of women unless the women themselves deliver up one from among them to be violated, the law in the Mishnah states: Let them all be violated, "but let them not deliver up a single soul of Israel."[47] Again, if Gentiles threaten to kill an entire group of men unless the men themselves deliver up one from among them to be killed, the law in the Tosefta states: Let them all be killed, "but let them not deliver up a single soul of Israel."[48] The "Gentiles" here are marauders or soldiers, and both passages apparently reflect a period of disorder and strife.

A statement in the Sifra declares that "even a Gentile who studies the Torah [or who practices the Torah][49] is like the high priest," the proof-text being, "Which, if a *man* do, he shall live by them" (Lev. 18:5).[50] To emphasize this teaching, the statement further interprets other biblical verses to the effect that in each case the verse refers not to "priests, Levites and Israelites," but either to mankind, the righteous Gentile, or to the righteous in general. For example, II Samuel 7:19 is rendered to mean, "This is the Torah of mankind," and Isaiah 26:2 as, "Open ye the gates that a righteous Gentile keeping faithfulness may enter in."[51] The same statement is found in the Talmud,[52] however, without the corroborative interpretation of verses that makes it so emphatic, and the discussions there tend to limit or even nullify what is left of it. In other words, the trend toward universalism encountered some resistance, probably because of frequent persecution of the Jews.

We have presented here an instance of how the trend toward universalism is expressed in a statement, and of the resistance encountered by that trend; our illustration reflects both. But the prevalence of universalism as an emphatic trend is not to be determined by ascertaining whether there are more passages on one side or on the other, for the basic elements of the ethical life, propulsive yet subtle, are the value concepts. A genuine emphatic trend is primarily a repeated effect produced by a group of value concepts, and the emphatic trend toward universalism is just such a repeated effect. Indeed, as we have shown elsewhere, the very structure of the value concepts reflects the trend toward universalism: ". . . the very structure of the rabbinic value-concepts necessitates the concept of 'the righteous of the Nations of the World.' "[53] A statement, if it is a striking one, does call attention to an emphatic trend, but the trend is established by a group of value concepts, not by a number of statements.

The trend toward universalism manifests itself, among other ways, in the recognition of non-Jewish legal institutions. As given in the Mishnah, a law declares valid writs or documents signed by Gentile witnesses and confirmed by Gentile officials.[54] One authority extends this law even to bills of divorcement and writs of manumission,[55] despite the religious implications of these documents,[56] and there is a report that this is the opinion, not only of R. 'Aḳiba, but of the *Ḥakamim* (scholars) as well.[57] Such recognition of Gentile institutions, Alon says,[58] was entirely voluntary. There is thus a whole class of cases in which the rabbis voluntarily made Gentile institutions competent under Jewish law. Embodied in this law is the concept of *din*, a concept with universalistic connotations, as we shall see later.[59]

All these statements and laws are expressions of emphatic trends. But they are primarily concretizations of value concepts, and in every instance the value concept involved itself belongs to the orbit of an emphatic trend. An emphatic trend rises to expression in a particular value concept, and when the value concept, charged in that manner, is made concrete in statements or laws, the statements or laws, too, will often reflect the same trend. Conversely, no matter how emphatic a statement may be, it can only be an expression of a particular emphatic trend, and no more. It will be a concretization of a value concept belonging to the orbit of an emphatic trend.

If we have established the presence of emphatic trends, have we not also apparently established the presence of intuitive morality? An emphatic trend, as we have said, is not something that the rabbis have actually indicated for us in so many words. Nevertheless, men do feel in accordance with it and act in accordance with it. Are they not moved, therefore, by a kind of intuition? Let us remember that every act, every statement, informed by an emphatic trend is a concretization of a value concept. At the basis of every action is not an intuition but a concept, a connotative idea, not mere feeling alone. A value concept is not submerged when it is part of an emphatic trend that includes other concepts as well. On the contrary, its effect is heightened. An emphatic trend, in fine, has primarily to do with the functioning of the value concepts concerned, and is not something that displaces them.

D. Devices for Emphasis

Our contention is that rabbinic literature does not contain all-inclusive, general ethical principles, nor was there any attempt to formulate such principles. Some modern scholars, it is true, do claim that a number of rabbinic statements are general ethical rules. Their conclusion is, we believe, the result of a tendency to look for an ultimate criterion and is not warranted by the rabbinic statements themselves. A passage in the Sifra reads as follows: " 'And thou shalt love thy neighbor as thyself' [Lev. 19:18]— R. 'Aḳiba says: This is a comprehensive rule in the Torah [*kelal gadol ba-Torah*]. Ben 'Azzai says: 'This is the book of the generations of man; (in the day that God created man, in the likeness of God made He him)' [Gen. 5:1]—this is a more comprehensive rule [*kelal gadol mi-zeh*]."[60] *Kelal gadol* is a halakic term, and it does not mean that a principle so designated is the most important or the most inclusive or the most comprehensive; it apparently means, rather, that a rule so designated is *more* inclusive than another rule.[61] Our passage is no exception.

As used by R. 'Aḳiba here, the term means that the rule, "Thou shalt love thy neighbor as thyself," is more inclusive or more comprehensive than some other rules also stated in the Torah, the very rules, perhaps, that are given in the first half of the verse (vs. 18) and in the verse immediately preceding (vs. 17). We can now understand more readily Ben 'Azzai's dictum—a dictum, be it noticed, in which the comparative, "more comprehensive," is used, and not the superlative. Ben 'Azzai sees implied in Genesis 5: 1 a more comprehensive rule than the one explicitly stated in Leviticus 19: 18.[62]

Neither of these rules, then, is an ultimate criterion. Each is an emphatic statement, to be sure, and not only an emphatic but also an arresting statement. We have just studied other striking or arresting statements, however, and found them to be expressions of emphatic trends. We shall find that this is true of R. 'Aḳiba's and Ben 'Azzai's statements as well. Both statements, we must add, are to be taken as representing rabbinic rather than biblical thought, despite the fact that the rules quoted are biblical verses. When a verse is given a certain character by the rabbis, even if it be only a matter of emphasis, the new character is, in effect, a rabbinic interpretation.

A statement expressive of an emphatic trend has the following characteristics: the statement is a concretization of a value concept; the concept involved belongs to the orbit of an emphatic trend—that is to say, the concept belongs to a group of concepts which have an element in common and hence produce a repeated effect; the statement is striking enough to make us aware of the emphatic trend. All of these characteristics are exemplified by R. 'Aḳiba's statement: " 'And thou shalt love thy neighbor as thyself' [Lev. 19: 18]—this is a comprehensive rule in the Torah." That statement is a concretization of the value concept of *'ahabah*, love, and *'ahabah* is a conceptual term not only in the Bible but in rabbinic usage as well.[63] Again, as we saw above, *'ahabah* is one of a number of concepts, each of which has its own particular connotation, but also connotes love; it is thus a concept belonging to the orbit of an emphatic trend. Finally, the words, "this is a comprehensive rule in the Torah," focus attention on our verse as against other verses or rules, and they make us acutely aware of the sentiment the verse contains, the sentiment of love.

Ben 'Azzai wishes to make his statement even more emphatic: " 'This is the book of the generations of man; (in the day that God created man, in the likeness of God made He him)' [Gen. 5:1]—this is a more comprehensive rule." The concept involved here is "man," a biblical term, but as used by the rabbis it is one of a group of concepts that emphasize universalism. We have noticed before, however, that the emphatic trends are not mutually exclusive, so that, for example, a concept reflecting the trend toward universalism may also stress the individual. Indeed, in a version of Ben 'Azzai's statement, it is the individual that is stressed, the following being added: "For thou shalt not say, 'Since I have been despised let my neighbor be despised with me.' R. Tanḥuma said: 'If thou actest so, know Whom thou dost despise—in the likeness of God made He him.' "[64] The concept involved in this additional statement, too, is none other than man—only now the emphasis is on the individual rather than on universalism. Moreover, the verse here is not necessarily associated with the individual: elsewhere the verse, "For in the image of God made He man" (Gen. 9:6) is made to refer, apparently, to mankind.[65]

What do these statements of R. 'Aḳiba and Ben 'Azzai convey? Modern scholars have attempted to draw certain implications from the statements, to formulate principles of ethics and conduct ostensibly inherent in them, to distinguish between a principle inherent in the one statement as against that of the other;[66] in a word, to make these statements explicit and precise. If the scholars differ in their interpretations,[67] however, it is because the rabbinic statements do not lend themselves to such treatment. In fact, Ben 'Azzai's original statement is, strictly speaking, not anything as definite as a rule at all, but a suggestive verse, a verse made more suggestive by Ben 'Azzai's emphasizing it as more important than Leviticus 19:18.

The two rabbinic statements were not put forth either as new or as definitive statements. So far as the elements of the statements are concerned, they represented nothing new to the people of the time. The biblical verses pointed out were familiar to those people. Nor were these biblical verses made the criteria for a new post-biblical ethic informing personal conduct and law. The people already possessed a new pattern of ethical value concepts, concepts rooted in the Bible, dynamic concepts that acted as drives in personal conduct and in the formulation of laws. Among them were the very concepts embodied in the two statements—*'ahabah* (R. 'Aḳiba) and man (Ben 'Azzai). Not even the emphatic trends expressed in the two statements were new to the people. The statements simply express, as we have noticed, already existing emphatic trends.

Just because the elements of the two statements were all familiar to the people, the statements themselves could be meaningful and effective. Being expressions of emphatic trends, they acted primarily as reminders of those emphatic trends and strengthened them. That is why it does not matter so much if a statement is not pointed, if it is not actually stated as a rule. R. 'Aḳiba's statement is a rule whereas Ben 'Azzai's statement is not; yet the latter is no less effective or moving. Indeed, even R. 'Akiba's statement, although a rule in form, is not a halakic rule; it does not point to any specific act. We are not dealing, then, with specific or concrete rules, but simply with reminders of emphatic trends.

Kelal gadol (comprehensive rule), the term used by both R. 'Aḳiba and Ben 'Azzai, turns the biblical verses they selected into emphatic statements. The term is admirably suited for this purpose. It is a halakic term for indicating greater scope or inclusiveness, yet here it does not refer to halakic matters. *Kelal gadol* is thus used here as a device for calling attention to the verse selected, for stressing that verse.

There is another device for calling attention to an ethical idea or statement. Sometimes an idea is emphasized by making the claim, in one way or another, that it amounts to the entire Torah. The claim is, of course, a trope, a hyperbole, for there are obviously other things, too, to be found in the Torah. The claim is a device, and an effective one, whereby a statement so characterized becomes an emphatic statement.

The Torah, says R. Simla'i, begins and ends with *gemilut ḥasadim* (deeds of lovingkindness); and as proof he cites Genesis 3:21 (which tells of how God clothes the naked) and Deuteronomy 34:6 (which tells that He buried the dead).[68] This statement is, in effect, a lesson concerning *gemilut ḥasadim*, and it implies that the entire burden of the Torah consists in that lesson. A later version strengthens this implicit claim by adding the idea that the middle of the Torah, too, teaches that lesson.[69] Why has there been no outright claim?

Because the purpose of the hyperbole has already been achieved, attention has been drawn to *gemilut ḥasadim*, and the statement as a whole is already an emphatic statement. What is recalled in the statement is the emphasis on love, for *gemilut ḥasadim* is one of a group of concepts that have love as a common connotation.[70]

An outright claim is made in Hillel's famous statement. To the Gentile who asked to be taught the entire Torah while he stood on one foot, Hillel said: "What is hateful to yourself, do not do to your fellow. That is the entire Torah; the rest is explanation. Go and learn."[71] The words, "What is hateful to yourself, do not do to your fellow" are in the vernacular Aramaic,[72] and they stand out, therefore, against the rest of the passage, which is in Hebrew; this is also the case in the other version of the story where R. 'Aḳiba is the authority instead of Hillel.[73] What we have here is a characteristically terse maxim of the folk, and it is to be found elsewhere in cognate literatures.[74] As to the claim itself—"That is the entire Torah"—it is a teaching device, a hyperbole no different from the one we have just examined. Leaving altogether out of account prayers and even ethical matters such as punishment for crimes, at best this statement can refer only, as Rashi says, "to most of the mizwot."[75]

Hillel's maxim is a negative form of the teaching in Leviticus 19:18, "And thou shalt love thy neighbor as thyself." Later Jewish authorities regarded it as equivalent to that verse;[76] indeed, it is incorporated in the Targum Jonathan on that verse. Furthermore, the value concept embodied in the maxim is none other than *'ahabah* (love), the concept embodied in the biblical verse. By means of the claim or hyperbole attention is called to the maxim, and the statement as a whole thus becomes an emphatic statement. It is an emphatic statement serving as a reminder of the already existing emphasis on love.[77]

An emphatic trend which we spoke of in Chapter I is the emphasis on the experience of God. This emphatic trend, too, is reflected in emphatic statements, and again it is the hyperbole or claim that makes the statements emphatic. In fact, the same form is used, a particular biblical verse being characterized as central to, or a summary of the Torah as a whole. Bar Ḳappara makes such a claim for the following verse: "In all thy ways acknowledge [literally, know] Him, and He will direct thy paths" (Prov. 3:6). He speaks of this verse as "the small section on which all essentials of the Torah depend";[78] but he makes no attempt to relate "the essentials of the Torah" to the verse, nor does he tell us what these essentials are. His characterization of the verse can, therefore, be only a hyperbole which draws our attention to the verse, and which thus emphasizes the experience of God that the verse reflects. A more elaborate statement of the same kind has as its author R. Simla'i who, we may remember, is also the author of another "hyperbole-claim" statement cited earlier in this section. R. Simla'i taught: Six hundred and thirteen miẓwot were given to Moses; David reduced them to eleven (Ps. 15), Isaiah to six (Isa. 33:15), Micah to three (Micah 6:8), Isaiah again to two (Isa. 56:1), Amos to one—"Seek Me and live" (Amos 5:4).[79] R. Naḥman declared that it was Habakkuk who reduced them to one—"But the righteous man shall live by his faith" (Hab. 2:4).[80] Here, again, there is no attempt to demonstrate that Amos 5:4 or Habakkuk 2:4 is either basic or equivalent to all the miẓwot. The elaborately formulated claim only emphasizes the verses chosen, especially the ultimate one, the verse reflecting the experience of God. In the statements of both Bar Ḳappara and R. Simla'i, the same emphatic trend has been recalled and strengthened.

All of the statements given here have a distinctive feature in common. That distinctive feature is their form. In every instance, an idea or biblical verse is presented and the claim is made, in one fashion or another, that it is the epitome of the entire Torah, or else that it is a comprehensive rule in the Torah. In no instance, however, is there any attempt whatsoever to substantiate the claim; the claim remains, in fact, but a teaching device. As a teaching device, it calls attention to the idea or verse presented.

Does each of these statements, taken individually, perhaps represent an attempt at presenting a single ethical criterion, a single basis for ethics? Surely not, for the verse or idea pointed to is only suggestive, and not a definite rule. Moreover, the verse or idea was already familiar to the people, and the concept embodied in the verse was already a dynamic factor in their daily lives. If the verse or idea is merely suggestive and if it was not in any sense new to the people, pointing to it can only mean stressing it, making it emphatic. That is exactly what we have tried to demonstrate in the case of each statement presented here. Each individual statement in this section is an emphatic statement, not an ultimate criterion.

The emphatic statements are not to be taken simply as isolated ideas or rules struck off by a few great men. On the contrary, the emphatic statements issue out of the entire background of rabbinic thought and the direction taken by them was not essentially new. The emphatic statements expressed already existing emphatic trends —the emphasis on love, on universality, on the individual, on the experience of God. The emphatic statements, each in its own way, recalled and strengthened and reinforced the emphatic trends; and that is why they were so suggestive and effective. They were charged, so to speak, with the energy of the emphatic trends. Although a similar effect was also achieved by emphatic statements lacking this form, as we saw in the preceding section, the form made the emphasis much stronger.

CHAPTER III

The Sphere of Ethics and Morality

A. The Phases of *Derek Ereẓ*

The rabbis, as we have just observed, establish no ultimate criterion for morality. This is tantamount to saying that the rabbis have no definition of morality and ethics.[1] How can the rabbis have an awareness of morality and ethics, then, if they lack such a definition? We are faced here with a problem presented by all ethical traditions that are nonphilosophical. So far as the rabbinic tradition is concerned, that problem is resolved by a study of the various phases of the rabbinic concept of *derek ereẓ*.[2]

In one of its phases, *derek ereẓ* refers to phenomena or modes of behavior common to all of mankind. Normal sex behavior is *derek ereẓ*.[3] "Man's purposeful direction of his daily activities toward practical and useful ends is also *derek ereẓ*"—his work or business activity, his effort to make a livelihood for himself.[4] To recognize that these are universal human traits or activities does not require any wide experience of the world; they are matters of common observation. On the other hand, sometimes what is characterized as *derek ereẓ* is the shrewd conclusion of a man versed in the ways of the world. Such observations as the following, for example, are called *derek ereẓ*: "When a man gets angry in his house, he fixes his eyes upon the person of least importance";[5] when a man is young he is given to singing songs, when he is older he is given to telling proverbs, when he is old he is given to saying, "All is vanity."[6]

On the basis of these examples, how can we classify *derek ereẓ*? What kind of concept is it? Common observation teaches that certain forms of behavior are characteristic of and may be expected of mankind. Labor is *derek ereẓ*; but it is also *derek ereẓ* to expect that when a man builds a house, he does so in order to store fruit, furniture, and other things in it, and not to destroy it by fire; or when he plants a vineyard he does so in order to have grapes and wine, and not just to fill it with weeds.[7] Our concept thus implies both observation and predictability, and these implications are perhaps contained in the literal meaning of the conceptual term—"the way of the world" (or, "of the land"). Are we not, then, dealing with a concept akin to a scientific concept, since the latter, too, directs observation and makes for predictability? Furthermore, it is not only to obvious instances that our concept directs observation. Those shrewd conclusions as to a man when he is angry, or as to the three stages of a man's life, bespeak not only wide experience but close observation. We are not suggesting, of course, that *derek ereẓ* is a scientific concept. In order to be definite and exact a scientific concept depends upon a formal definition, whereas *derek ereẓ* is an undefined concept. We can say, nevertheless, that *derek ereẓ*, with respect to the phase we have discussed here, is a popular, quasi-scientific concept.[8]

Another phase of the concept refers to matters of practical wisdom. The following statements are introduced with the phrase, "the Torah taught you *derek ereẓ*": A man should not put all his property in one corner;[9] if a man wishes to build a ship that will stand in the harbor (i.e., remain afloat), let him make its width one-sixth its length, and its height one-tenth its length;[10] if a field has brought forth thorns, it is well to sow it with wheat, and if it has brought forth sour grapes, it is well to sow it with barley.[11] Predictability is a factor in this phase of *derek ereẓ*, too, for it is assumed that these teachings, with the authority of the Torah behind them, are sound. Again, although now no longer directed to new instances, observation is a factor as well, since the teachings call for confirmation from experience. This phase of *derek ereẓ*, therefore, may likewise be regarded as quasi-scientific.

Yet in this phase something has been added—a note of obligation. If a matter of *derek ereẓ* is also a teaching of the Torah, it is expected that a person will heed that teaching. When you go on a journey, arrive and leave in the daytime, says the Mekilta, giving instances of how "the patriarchs and the prophets conducted themselves in accordance with [this principle of] *derek ereẓ*;" and concluding with the admonition that if the patriarchs and the prophets did so, "who went to do the will of Him Who spake and the world came to be," all the more ought "the rest of mankind."[12] The phase of *derek ereẓ* containing practical wisdom thus also contains moral overtones, overtones ranging from sound advice to straight admonition.[13]

We have depicted two phases of the concept of *derek ereẓ*. Each phase has an area of its own, the first covering traits or modes of behavior common to all of mankind, whereas the second is limited to definite matters of practical wisdom. With regard to terminology, however, these conceptual phases are not distinguished from each other. Neither conceptual phase has a name of its own, and the term *derek ereẓ* stands for either phase. Nevertheless, the second phase does have a feature not possessed by the first phase. Statements belonging to it are introduced with the words, "the Torah taught you *derek ereẓ*," and hence the second phase is not only an aspect of *derek ereẓ* but also of Torah.

This second conceptual phase thus is not altogether nameless; it is called *derek ereẓ*. Since it is an aspect of Torah, and since it is also symbolized by a term or name, we may speak of it as a subconcept of Torah. A subconcept is an aspect of a concept, but it is also identified by its own name. In this case, definite matters of practical wisdom are identified as *derek ereẓ*; they are also identified as Torah; this phase of *derek ereẓ*, therefore, is a subconcept of Torah.[14]

Still another phase of the concept of *derek ereẓ* refers to good manners. Such teachings, too, are frequently inferred from biblical texts and introduced by the formula, "the Torah taught *derek ereẓ*." " 'And Moses reported the words of the people unto the Lord' [Exod. 19:18]: was there any need for Moses to report? The Torah, however, taught *derek ereẓ*: Moses came and reported back to Him that sent him."[15] " 'And the Lord called unto Moses and spoke to him' [Lev. 1:1]: why did calling precede speaking? The Torah taught *derek ereẓ* [namely], that one should not say anything to his fellow without having first called him."[16] "['Where is Sarah, thy wife?']—the Torah taught *derek ereẓ* [namely], that one must inquire after the health of his hostess."[17]

Rules of good manners are not limited to those deduced from biblical texts, nor are they always specifically designated as *derek ereẓ* in their rabbinic sources. There are, for example, post-talmudic collections of rabbinic statements and anecdotes to which the name "*Derek Ereẓ*" has been given;[18] and much of the material there presented belongs to the sphere of good manners, as Higger has shown.[19] Similarly, statements belonging to other phases of *derek ereẓ*, as well, are often not specifically designated as *derek ereẓ* by the rabbis. Yet, as Friedmann has pointed out—and correctly—the many rabbinic prescriptions on the ways to maintain bodily health, and kindred matters do, in fact, belong to Hilkot *Derek Ereẓ*;[20] or, according to our scheme here, to the phase referring to practical wisdom.

Like *derek ereẓ* as practical wisdom, *derek ereẓ* as good manners is a subconcept of Torah—"the Torah taught *derek ereẓ*." Now, however, it is no longer a matter of sound advice at all but purely of admonition. By the same token, the term *derek ereẓ* in this third phase does not refer to anything quasi-scientific. Here the factors of observation and predictability play no role whatsoever; a person is enjoined to act in a certain way not because it will lead to success or ward off a danger, but simply because it is the proper way to act. The term *derek ereẓ* now means, apparently, that acts of this kind are incumbent upon all of mankind, that they ought to be "the way of the world."

There is a fourth phase to the concept of *derek ereẓ*. In this phase are the matters which, the rabbis say, are essential to the existence of mankind, matters that have, thus, a crucial character.

Ẓedaḳah (charity) and *gemilut ḥasadim* (deeds of lovingkindness) are called *derek ereẓ*. The people of Israel who lived in the days of the First Temple, though often idol-worshippers, nevertheless had *derek ereẓ* in them. "And what was that *derek ereẓ* that was in them? *Ẓedaḳah* and *gemilut ḥasadim*."[21] Furthering peace among men and refraining from talebearing are characterized as *derek ereẓ*;[22] and so, too, is refraining from taking anything illegitimately, "fleeing from the *gezel*."[23] The principle that testimony is to be accepted only from an actual eyewitness to an event, and not from him who merely heard of it from even a trustworthy person, is also referred to as *derek ereẓ*;[24] in this case, *derek ereẓ* has to do with law and justice, with *din*,[25] and also, of course, with truth.[26]

The concepts here designated as *derek ereẓ* are grouped together, as we shall now see, in various rabbinic statements. What the rabbis say about these concepts as a group constitutes the nature of these concepts. Some of the rabbinic statements, it is true, depict other concepts—not specifically designated as *derek ereẓ*—as also having the same character. But this only means that the concepts which are designated as *derek ereẓ* do not exhaust what we have called the fourth phase of *derek ereẓ*; all the concepts mentioned that are thus grouped together and given the same character belong to that fourth phase. We noticed above that matters belonging to other phases of *derek ereẓ*, as well, are often not specifically designated as *derek ereẓ*.[27]

"The world [*ha-'olam*] endures [קים] because of three things," says R. Simeon ben Gamaliel, "because of truth, because of justice [law], and because of peace."[28] A later source speaks of four things whereby civilization is established—charity, justice (law), truth, and peace.[29] Are these things modes of behavior common to all of mankind, just as the traits in the first phase of *derek ereẓ* are common to all of mankind? They are, indeed, common to mankind in the round, but the idea is also present that were they lacking, society or civilization would not exist. Furthermore, the rabbis speak of human traits, some of them hardly uncommon, because of which "the world is destroyed." "Because of eight things is the world destroyed: injustice in the courts [על הדינין], idolatry, incest, murder, *ḥillul ha-Shem* [the profanation of God's Name], because of foul things a person utters, arrogance, and the evil tongue [scandal-mongering], and some say also because of covetousness."[30] These things, too, are modes of human behavior, but behavior that a person should refrain from. The modes of behavior given here, then, are in a different category from those in the first phase. Whereas the first phase is descriptive only, here the rabbis insist on the necessary character of the "four things," and on the dangerous character of the "eight things."

In the Sifra, an early source, and in several parallels, there occurs the following passage: "'Mine ordinances [*mishpaṭai*] shall ye do' [Lev. 18:4]. Those are the things that are written in the Torah, which, had they not been written, it stands to reason that they should have been written [בדין היה לכתבן]; for example, [ordinances in respect to] theft and incest and idolatry and blasphemy and murder. Had they not been written, it stands to reason that they should have been written."[31] A whole class of laws is here apparently depicted as being affirmed by man's reason. Moreover, man could have learned certain moral qualities from the animals. Had the Torah not been given, says R. Joḥanan, we might have learned decency (*ẓeni'ut*) from the cat, refraining from theft (*gezel*) from the ant, chastity from the dove, sexual manners from the rooster.[32]

By using the phrase, "it stands to reason," or by saying that proper behavior might have been "learned" from the animals, the rabbis are not pointing to social utility as a basis for ethics. That idea is found in medieval Jewish philosophy and it is applied there at least to a segment of the moral life, but the idea is not rabbinic. Yehudah Ha-Levi speaks of "rational laws" and of "social laws" as being indispensable in the conduct of every human society;[33] "even a band of robbers must have justice among themselves, for if not, their association could not last."[34] On the basis of our passage in the Sifra, Maimonides says that *mishpaṭim* (ordinances) are commandments the utilitarian purpose of which (תועלתם) is clear to everyone.[35] Albo says that to prevent quarrels, every society must administer justice; that it must maintain order so as to give protection against murder, theft, robbery, and the like; and that this order "the wise men call natural law."[36] All such theories of social utility more or less imply that justice, truth, and so on are fruits of reason, that they are products of "practical wisdom."[37] "Practical wisdom" always posits a utilitarian end. The end may be social utility, or it may apply only to an individual in a specific situation, as is true of our second phase of *derek ereẓ*. The rabbis, however, posit no end whatever, specific or otherwise. Phrases like "it stands to reason" must not lead us to *supply* the "reason."

What the rabbis have in mind becomes evident when we examine the second part of the passage in the Sifra. There are other matters in the Torah, besides those things that "stand to reason." There are laws in the Torah (designated in Lev. 18:4 as *ḥukkotai*) against which the evil *yeẓer* and the nations of the world raise objections (משיבין עליהם)—the laws against eating pork and against wearing garments of linsey-woolsey, the law of *ḥaliẓah* (see Deut. 25:5–14), the law of the cleansing of the leper, the law of the scapegoat.[38] The objections raised against these laws are not stated, nor need they be, so far as the contrast between these laws and the laws that "stand to reason" is concerned. On the one hand are laws "written in the

Torah, which, had they not been written, it stands to reason that they should have been written"; on the other, are laws against which the evil *yeẓer* and the nations of the world raise objections. Obviously the contrast is between the laws which the nations of the world and Israel possess in common and those that Israel alone possesses. The former, then, are universal laws—"for example, [laws about] theft and incest," etc. "It stands to reason" simply refers to the fact that those things are universal. They are characteristic of man as man. Further, there are things so universal as to be found distributed even among various animals, and although not all of them are found together in any one animal, man might have learned them, in order to be man, from the different animals.

It has been assumed that the contrast drawn by the passage in the Sifra is between ethics and ritual.[39] But do the nations raise objections against the ritual laws as such? If so, why do they not object to rites that are really typical and frequent, to sacrifices and festivals? Sacrifices and festivals, however, are the kind of rites practiced by the nations as well; they are universal institutions. What the nations and the evil *yeẓer* question are rites that appear peculiar because they are found only in Israel. The contrast, then, is not between ethics and ritual, but between laws that are universal and laws possessed by Israel alone.

Yet the nations practiced idolatry. How, then, could the rabbis have seemed to imply that the nations negated idolatry?[40]

The idea of social utility is not contained in the other rabbinic statements either. When the rabbis tell of three things because of which the world endures, or of four things whereby civilization is established, they are not ascribing to these things any social utility. When we assign to ethics a utilitarian role, we tend to reduce ethics to something neutral, to a means to an end, to mechanics, as it were. In our rabbinic statements, on the contrary, the object is, patently, to extol justice, truth, peace, and charity. These are virtues not because they have social utility; they are virtues in their own right. Moreover, they are virtues of such importance that without them mankind would not be civilized, nor be fit to endure.[41] Nor need we only surmise that it is the intention of the rabbis to extol the "four things" as virtues. The same passage also says that "because of eight things is the world destroyed," and it enumerates the wicked men who, because they engaged in these things, "were uprooted from the world." If the passage condemns the "eight things" as vices, it must also extol the "four things" as virtues.

All of the concepts grouped together in these various statements have a common character. Not only do the groupings overlap, but the statements grouping the concepts all contain the same idea. All of the statements declare, in one way or another, that the concepts are common to mankind and that without them, man cannot be; in one case, the concepts are "things" man must refrain from doing, else he cannot be. In other words, the rubric *derek ereẓ*, the way of the world, applies here as well,[42] but with a somewhat different connotation. What we have here is the fourth phase of *derek ereẓ*. It connotes that there are certain positive matters, common to all mankind, that man must do, and that there are negative matters he must refrain from doing. Between this fourth phase of *derek ereẓ* and the third phase, good manners, there is kinship, but in this fourth phase the mandatory element is far, far stronger.

In one important respect the fourth phase differs from all the other phases of *derek ereẓ*. We described the first three phases of the concept on the basis of rabbinic usage, but that was the only guide we had. The rabbis themselves do not specifically classify them. Here, however, the phase—to use our terminology—has been made by the rabbis; it is they who group the concepts, and they group them by means of statements which underscore the character of those concepts. The character of this phase is literally the character ascribed by the rabbis to the concepts of the phase.

Another distinction, with even greater implications, must likewise be evident by now. The rabbis group "three things," "four things," "eight things," "things" which "stand to reason." What are these "things"? They are, in each case, concepts—justice, peace, charity, truth, theft, and so on. They are generalizations, abstract ideas that give meaning to concrete situations and events. In contrast to these lists of concepts, the first three phases of *derek ereẓ* are concerned, by and large, with specific acts or situations, and the generalizing term there is *derek ereẓ* alone. Now, if the rabbis use such terms as "justice" or "charity" in describing events or acts, they obviously have an awareness of justice or charity as such. Further, they are also aware of the character of justice and charity. These things, these concepts, they say, are characteristic of man as man; without them there would be no society or civilization. In short, the concepts of justice and charity and theft give meaning to *specific events*; and the concept of *derek ereẓ*, in turn, gives character to the other concepts, to the concepts of justice, charity, and the like.

Justice and charity and the other universal concepts give meaning to specific events; as value concepts, they also constitute emotional drives, and are concretized in laws. The concept of *derek ereẓ* is, therefore, almost displaced in this phase by the universal concepts. There are many passages, however, in which the rabbis definitely associate the universal concepts with the concept of *derek ereẓ*. Those passages indicate that the universal concepts are classifications of *derek ereẓ*, or subconcepts of *derek ereẓ*.[43]

In ascribing a certain character to concepts like justice and charity, are not the rabbis establishing a definition of ethics and morality? A definition enables one to recognize new instances that conform to the definition and deliberately to seek out such new instances.[44] Had the rabbis ascribed social utility to such concepts as justice and charity, they would, indeed, have posited a definition, vague though it would have been; we should then have been directed, at least, to look for further instances of social utility. But the rabbis do no more than extol the positive ethical concepts and warn against the negative ones. The character which the rabbis ascribe to the ethical concepts does not constitute, then, a definition of ethics and morality.[45]

Nevertheless, had the rabbis given a definite list of the ethical concepts, such a list might have served as a definition. But there is no definite list. When the rabbis speak of "things" which "stand to reason," how do they introduce them? By the phrase, "for example." When they do group the concepts by means of numbers, one group consists of "three things" and another of "four things." The lists of ethical concepts, then, also do not constitute a definition of ethics and morality.

Finally, there is still another phase of the concept of *derek ereẓ*. It consists entirely of ethical rules and concepts, although a number of these rules may also have to do with good manners. We should, therefore, place this phase between the third phase, good manners, and the fourth phase, that which refers to universal ethical concepts.

This final phase of *derek ereẓ*, like all the other phases except the first, is a subconcept of Torah as well.[46] "The Torah taught you *derek ereẓ*—[namely] that the bridegroom does not enter the bridal chamber until the bride has given him permission."[47] "The Torah taught you *derek ereẓ*"—namely, that a man travelling in a land not his own, instead of eating of the sustenance he brings with him, must put that aside and buy from the local storekeeper to the latter's profit.[48] In these instances, what is enjoined is not courtesy alone, but ethical behavior. Again, in the following statement, what is given is not only a rule of hospitality but what amounts to a law of *ẓedaḳah*. "The Torah taught you *derek ereẓ*"—a man must take care of his relative for a month.[49]

There is no real line of demarcation between manners and morals. A collection of rabbinic statements and anecdotes to which the name "*Derek Ereẓ*" has been given, and which has been referred to above,[50] tells a story that may serve as an illustration. R. Simeon, the son of Eleazar, was once riding leisurely on an ass along the lake shore when he came upon a man there who was exceedingly ugly. " 'Wretch!' R. Simeon called to him, 'How ugly are thy deeds! How ugly are the children of our father Abraham!' 'What can I do?' the man answered, 'Go and tell this to the Artisan who made me!' " The story goes on to relate that R. Simeon thereupon pleaded with the man to forgive him, and the man did forgive, but only after the townspeople also pleaded, and only on condition that R. Simeon would "not act in this manner again."[51]

The same tractate, avowedly teaching *derek ereẓ*, presents rules that are solely ethical halakot and that are definitely beyond the sphere of manners. Often such halakot are not only rules of *derek ereẓ* but concretizations of other value concepts as well. According to our text, for example, a person is forbidden to say to a seller in the market place, " 'How much do you charge for this article?' when he does not intend to buy," and the reason given here is that he thereby raises false hopes in the seller.[52] Precisely the same prohibition is found in the Mishnah—"He must not say, 'How much do you charge for this article?' when he does not intend to buy";[53] and now the question of the pretended buyer is cited as an instance of *'ona'ah* by means of words—*'ona'at debarim*, a wrong or injury done by means of words.[54] Our text and the Mishnah give the selfsame reason for the halakah; our text merely indicates what *'ona'ah* consists in, specifically in this case. The halakah here is thus a concretization of both *derek ereẓ* and *'ona'ah*. Indeed, if concepts like *gemilut ḥasadim* and others of the same sort represent classifications of *derek ereẓ*—that is, are subconcepts of *derek ereẓ*—then *'ona'ah*, too, is a subconcept of *derek ereẓ*.

Similarly, other matters prohibited by our text are not only violations of *derek ereẓ*, but are stigmatized as acts with a taint of robbery, "a manner of *gezel*."[55] A person must not give his friend new wine to drink, telling him that it is old wine, "for this is a manner of *gezel*."[56] Again, a person selling wine to ass-drivers—that is, to a caravan—should not say (to his helpers), " 'Remove this wine and give that wine,' for this is a manner of *gezel*."[57] Apparently, in this instance also, it is not a case of perpetrating an actual fraud, for that would definitely be *gezel*, not "a manner of *gezel*."

With regard to the concepts of the fourth phase, the rabbis say that not only are they common to all mankind, but that without them civilization would not exist. No such claim is made with regard to the rules included in the final phase. Enjoined or else prohibited in the final phase are acts on which, so to say, the fate of the world does not depend, and yet which do fall within the sphere of ethics. The final phase is thus sufficiently distinguishable from the fourth phase to have some individuality of its own. Nevertheless, the fourth phase does have a tendency to absorb the final phase. Certain acts are stigmatized as "a manner of *gezel*," and *gezel* itself is in the fourth phase; the rule which enjoins proper sexual behavior on the part of the bridegroom is not only a rule of good manners but of universal moral behavior;[58] a rule of hospitality toward a poor relation amounts to a law of *ẓedaḳah*. But it is thus also evident that the fourth phase has a relationship with the third phase, the phase of good manners, as well.

We can now, at last, address ourselves to the question posed at the beginning of this section: Do the rabbis have an awareness of ethics and morality as such, despite having no definition or ultimate criterion for ethics or morality? The answer is that not only do they have this awareness, but they also outline the *sphere* of ethics and morality. The concept of *derek ereẓ* expresses their awareness of morality and ethics, and the phases of *derek ereẓ* adumbrate the sphere of morality and ethics.

In all the phases of the concept except the first, the connotation of *derek ereẓ* is morality and ethics. No one can question the fact that the fourth phase deals with morality and ethics. The fourth phase refers to the concepts which, according to the rabbis, are common to all mankind, and without which, the rabbis also say, civilization would not exist. But is the sphere of morality limited to this crucial kind of morality? Are there not other areas as well? We find that this fourth phase tends to absorb another phase without, however, actually being identical with it; the "absorbed" phase apparently thus refers to ethical acts which are not crucial. We find, again, that the fourth phase, crucial morality, is also related to good manners. Moreover, these three phases are all subconcepts of Torah —"the Torah teaches *derek ereẓ*." If the three phases are all *derek ereẓ*, and furthermore, are all subconcepts of Torah, then if *derek ereẓ* connotes morality in the one phase, it must do so in the other phases as well, and especially so if these three phases are related to one another. On the other hand, we find that the phase of practical wisdom is not related to these three, and that it is nonetheless a subconcept of Torah. *Derek ereẓ* here, too, connotes morality, but of a more indirect kind, and the note of admonition or obligation is stronger in some cases than in others.

The term *derek ereẓ* does not necessarily point to any one phase of *derek ereẓ*. One source declares that *derek ereẓ* preceded Torah by twenty-six generations,[59] meaning that the world practiced *derek ereẓ* in the twenty-six generations before the Torah was given on Sinai. Another source has God saying that He gave the Torah in order that men might study it and "learn from it *derek ereẓ*."[60] *Derek ereẓ* is used in these passages in a general sense, and refers patently to moral behavior.

Do the phases represent a hierarchy of ethical behavior? Are they gradations of the moral life in which one phase contains higher or more urgent moral demands than another phase? To the extent that there is a hierarchy in the moral life, it is the Halakah that establishes such a hierarchy, and not the phases of *derek ereẓ*. A phase of *derek ereẓ* is not a unit, so far as the moral implications or consequences of the act it refers to are concerned. The phase of practical wisdom, for example, contains sound advice as to investments, but it also contains urgent admonitions and rules concerning personal safety and the proper rearing of children. The phase which refers to universal human concepts places among them not only theft but also murder. Further, the phases themselves are not altogether separable: there is no real demarcation between manners and morals, and the fourth phase tends to absorb the final phase. The phases are the result of the effort to concretize the concept of *derek ereẓ* in as many ways as possible, rather than an attempt to establish an ethical hierarchy.

Like all value concepts, *derek ereẓ* is a dynamic concept and has a drive toward concretization. The phases are the means whereby the sphere of the concept is continually being extended. Even the proper way to rehabilitate a field has a moral implication of some kind—"the Torah taught you *derek ereẓ*." To be sure, here (and in similar instances) the note of obligation contained in the teaching is a faint one, whereas in other teachings belonging to the same phase, the phase of practical wisdom, the admonitory tone is emphatic.[61] Faint or emphatic, the note of obligation is there. The teaching with the fainter note of obligation or admonition is no less a concretization of *derek ereẓ* than the teaching with the emphatic note.

We have thus far left out of consideration the first phase of *derek ereẓ*, the phase referring to phenomena or modes of behavior common to all of mankind. This is the only phase of *derek ereẓ* which is not a subconcept of Torah—there is hardly room for admonition with respect to matters set down as sheer human phenomena. The first phase is thus merely descriptive and not admonitory. What has this descriptive phase to do with the other phases, all of which are admonitory?

The first phase is purely descriptive, certainly, and yet it contains a number of traits that are not morally neutral. Modes of behavior are included in this phase which are always either moral or immoral. Normal sexual behavior, for example, is a basic form of human behavior; but it is always either moral, as when there is no incest[62] and the proprieties are observed, or else immoral, as in the case of incest. The same thing is true of another mode of human behavior—work or business activity. It is immoral even if it is but tainted with *gezel*; otherwise it is moral.[63] These modes of behavior, then, have immediate moral implications, positive or negative, and it is only when moral implications are put aside that the traits wear a neutral aspect. Further, there are traits which are not moral but even so are characteristic of man. Among these is that of the angered head of the family "fixing his eyes upon the person of least importance." We, too, tend to speak of such a trait as "all too human."[64]

Since this phase of *derek ereẓ* refers to general human phenomena, it is natural that it should also include phenomena that have no moral implications. Rapid success (literally, ascent) and rapid decline (literally, descent) are not according to *derek ereẓ*;[65] the opposite, therefore, is according to *derek ereẓ*. Attending to natural functions is *derek ereẓ*.[66] Using a synecdoche—"an ox" for "oxen," "an ass" for "asses" (Gen. 32:6)—is *derek ereẓ*, for it is the way men speak.[67] These and other morally neutral phenomena can be included in the first phase because that phase is merely descriptive and not admonitory. Yet even in the phase which is purely descriptive, many of the human phenomena there included are not, in fact, morally neutral. The first phase is, therefore, not incompatible with the other phases of *derek ereẓ*: it represents, on the contrary, an extension of the concept.

The first phase of *derek ereẓ* includes only general human phenomena. General physical or natural phenomena are represented by another concept; *sidre bereshit*, "orders of *bereshit*," for which there is also an alternate term, *sidre 'olam*, "orders of the world." That concept, as we have pointed out elsewhere, is a quasi-scientific concept.[68] In that respect, it is like both the first and second phases of *derek ereẓ*.[69]

The quasi-scientific character of the first and second phases of *derek ereẓ* limits, to some degree, its effectiveness as a value concept. To function freely, a value concept must be free from admixture with any other type of concept, must be a pure *value* concept.[70] Being simply descriptive, the first phase designates as *derek ereẓ* phenomena that have no moral implications whatever; moreover, being nonadmonitory, it naturally ignores the moral implications of matters that are not morally neutral; and again, since this phase is concerned with observations concerning human nature, it can include, as well, traits that are not moral at all. At the very least, therefore, the concept must have been at times ambiguous.[71]

Similarly, the second phase, too, sometimes weakened *derek ereẓ* as a value concept. Practical wisdom may lead to sound advice rather than to outright admonition. There were occasions, as we have just seen, when the note of obligation was only faint, and this despite the formula, "the Torah taught you *derek ereẓ*." The effectiveness of the formula was bound to be weakened when the admonitory tone was not emphatic.

Flaws notwithstanding, *derek ereẓ* remains an effective value concept on the whole. The weak first phase is, after all, only an extension of the concept, and usually the second phase is quite emphatic in its admonitions. All the other phases are purely valuational, not quasi-scientific. Furthermore, what we have called subconcepts of *derek ereẓ*, concepts such as *din*, *ẓedaḳah*, or *'ona'ah*, are also value concepts in their own right and hence are not affected by the limitations of *derek ereẓ*.

The limitations of the concept of *derek ereẓ* are another indication that the term *derek ereẓ* does not define the universal ethical concepts. *Din*, *ẓedaḳah*, and the other ethical concepts have a common ground in *derek ereẓ*, are subconcepts of *derek ereẓ*. Nevertheless, the concept of *derek ereẓ*, by pointing to these subconcepts as matters characteristic of man, does not define them, for *derek ereẓ* has, in addition, a quasi-scientific, morally neutral phase and that phase, too, refers to matters characteristic of man.

The concept of *derek ereẓ* does two things at the same time. It expresses awareness of morality and ethics, and through its phases, it also limns the sphere of morality and ethics. In thus exercising a dual function *derek ereẓ* is by no means unique. As depicted here, *derek ereẓ* is not more complex than other rabbinic concepts. There are other rabbinic concepts which are similarly constituted, and they, too, exercise a dual function—that is to say, every concept which possesses conceptual phases not only expresses a valuational idea, but it also indicates, through its phases, the range of that idea.[72] *Derek ereẓ* is actually no more complex than any other concept having conceptual phases. What gives the impression of complexity is simply the fact that *derek ereẓ* has an unusually large number of conceptual phases.[73]

The concept of *derek ereẓ* gives to morality and ethics a much wider scope than that ordinarily envisaged by modern man.

Charity and justice and love and truth and all the rest of the virtues are *derek ereẓ*, but so are other matters which we usually do not think of as within the scope of morality. If those other matters are called to our attention, however, do we not recognize that they have moral implications? To lose the savings of a lifetime through a rash investment in a single venture is no small matter, and hence warning against it does have a moral implication. Manners imply, at the very least, considerateness. The moral sphere expands as we begin to reflect upon it.

Modern scholars have failed to recognize how wide indeed is the scope of rabbinic morality and ethics; as a result, they find it difficult to convey the meaning of *derek ereẓ*. Thus Bacher says that *derek ereẓ* has to do "not with matters of religion, and also not with matters of morality, but refers to the wide circle beyond them, to the habits of men, to social manners, to day-to-day life."[74] But the province of morality is precisely day-to-day life, and that includes the manners and customs of society. One of the great achievements of the rabbis is so to enlarge the sphere of morality, by means of the concept of *derek ereẓ*, as to include within that sphere acts that are undramatic and commonplace, the very acts that form the texture of daily living.

Most of the examples of *derek ereẓ* cited by Bacher himself[75] afford just so many instances of everyday morality. Some of them are rules of practical wisdom: a person ought not to accustom himself to meat—that is, not develop a need for expensive food;[76] those who are about to start on a journey ought to be alert (that is, not tarry or dally);[77] a person who is ill ought to cease working and seek a cure.[78] There are also rules of good manners: Moses reported back to Him Who sent him (a rule to be followed by all agents);[79] if a person wishes to speak to one of two men who happen to be together, he must not tell the other man to go away, but rather draw the former off and speak with him.[80] Prayer, too, must not be devoid of good manners: petitions to God ought always to be preceded by words of supplication.[81]

The scope of morality cannot be delimited or defined. Like all value concepts,[82] *derek ereẓ* is never defined; nor do the various phases, taken together, constitute a definition of *derek ereẓ*. In the first place, except for the fourth phase, the phases have not been designated as such by the rabbis; they are our own constructs, based on rabbinic usage, and are intended only as helpful guides. Second, the phases themselves are not closed and static, but remain open and dynamic. When the rabbis list concepts of the fourth phase, those concepts are given as "examples," and hence the list is not definitive. The other phases are even less definitive. They consist of rules and laws called forth by the circumstances of daily life, and not only of those already crystallized in the tradition. Can there be a point, therefore, at which a phase may be regarded as closed? Can there be a fixed limit to the phase, let us say, of practical wisdom, to the rules having to do with long-range moral effects? The concept of *derek ereẓ* is a dynamic concept, as we have said, and this means that, in rabbinic experience, there are no set boundaries to the moral life. The moral life is not, for the rabbis, contained in any definitive rule or in any formula.

The scope of the moral life, we repeat, cannot be described by a formula, not even by the formula "between a man and his fellow man." That phrase, or its equivalent, is used by the rabbis in one context and in one context only, and it is not a general designation for ethics or morality. However the statements in which the phrase occurs may differ in expression, the context in those statements is always the same, namely, the sins forgiven and the sins not forgiven by God. "For sins that are between a man and God, the Day of Atonement brings forgiveness; for sins that are between a man and his fellow man, the Day of Atonement brings no forgiveness until he has conciliated his fellow man."[83] " 'He will show thee favor' [Num. 6:26]—in matters that are between you and Him; 'He will not show favor' [Deut. 10:17]—in matters that are between you and your fellow man."[84] " 'And acquitting' [Exod. 34:7, *we-naḳḳeh*] —in matters that are between you and Him; 'He will not acquit' [*ibid.*, *lo' yenaḳḳeh*]—in matters that are between you and your fellow man."[85] We may say, indeed, that not only the context but the idea in these statements remains the same. A phrase limited to a specific context and to a particular idea cannot be regarded as a general classification.

In point of fact, the scope of morality includes much else besides "matters between a man and his fellow man." There are moral rules and admonitions with regard to the safety and welfare of one's own person, such as the rule that when going on a journey a person must arrive and leave in the daytime, or the admonition to a person who is ill to cease working and seek a cure. A man's general outlook, his affirmative or negative attitude toward life, is a moral matter. The rabbis condemn the man who wearies of life, of "the good life in this world," and after adding a parable in which a subject wished to leave in the midst of a feast given him by the king, stigmatize such behavior as not being *derek ereẓ*.[86]

Within the scope of the concept of *raḥamim* (compassion), the rabbis include not only human beings but also animals. On the basis of Leviticus 22:27–28, for example, they say that just as God has compassion on mankind, so has He compassion on the animals, and Deuteronomy 22:6 enables them to conclude that "just as the Holy One blessed be He bestowed His compassion [*raḥamim*] on beasts," so also has He compassion on fowl.[87] Again, according to rabbinic legend, Moses' tenderness toward Jethro's flock which he was herding demonstrated his fitness to lead Israel, so that God said: "Thou takest compassion [*raḥamim*] on a flock belonging to a man of flesh and blood! As thou livest, thou shalt pasture Israel, My flock."[88] These instances prove that the term *raḥamim* refers to compassion for animals as well as for human beings. Most often, however, there is no need to mention the abstract value-term; the concept is embodied in a concretization, whether the latter be a midrashic interpretation or a halakah.[89] Numerous halakot are thus concretizations of the concept *raḥamim*, as it applies to animals, even though these halakot do not contain the conceptual term itself.[90]

In still another and more striking respect, the scope of rabbinic morality cannot be limited to relations "between a man and his fellow man." Idolatry and blasphemy are patently "sins between a man and God." Nevertheless, the rabbis group idolatry and blasphemy together with theft, incest, and murder.[91] We found that these negative concepts, negative because they represent things men must refrain from doing, are among a group of concepts, some positive and some negative, which the rabbis regard as characteristic of man in general, and which constitute what we have called the fourth phase of *derek ereẓ*.

By placing the negative concept of idolatry among the concepts characteristic of mankind in general, the rabbis certainly suggest that non-Jews, too, rejected idolatry. Where did the rabbis see non-Jews who rejected idolatry and accepted the other moral laws as well? They had in mind, undoubtedly, the "fearers of Heaven," the many non-Jews who rejected idolatry, and who also practiced the other moral laws, but who were not actually proselytes.[92] Among such non-Jews, very likely, were those "who raised objections" to the laws against eating pig and against wearing garments of linsey-woolsey, and to several other laws, the objectors being, apparently, of various nationalities and representatives, so to speak, of the nations of the world.[93] We ought to add that the rabbis were also well aware of the genuine virtues to be found in Gentile society itself, and that they took occasion to extol these virtues.[94]

Rejection of idolatry by non-Jews in rabbinic times was, then, far from uncommon, and this affected the scope of rabbinic ethics. It permitted the rabbis to name idolatry, and blasphemy too, as negative concepts characteristic of man in general, alongside such other negative concepts as theft and murder, and thus to include idolatry and blasphemy in the scope of *derek ereẓ*, "the way of the world."

A proper evaluation of the rejection of idolatry cannot be made at this time. In later discussions we hope to show that the relationship to God is at the very center of the moral life, and that this relationship is expressed through concepts which have vast moral implications. Rejection of idolatry was thus an indispensable condition of the moral life. The morality and practice of the "fearers of Heaven" constituted a confirmation of the rabbis' own moral experience. Rejection of idolatry and the practice of morality proved to be bound up with each other. But is not rejection of idolatry a matter "between man and God"? How can we say, then, that either this formula or the formula "between a man and his fellow man" is a hard and fast category?[95]

B. The Interaction of the Rabbis and the Folk

The development of rabbinic morality and ethics is a social phenomenon. Rabbinic morality developed as a result of the interaction between the rabbis as an intellectual class and the folk in general; and that interaction was possible because the rabbis, although trained in the academies, were bound up with the life of the people as a whole and did not constitute a separate professional class.[96] The concept of *derek ereẓ*, and its subconcepts as well, were elements of the culture of the folk in general, for they were terms in the common vocabulary.[97] What, then, was the contribution of the rabbis?

Can we say that it was the task of the rabbis, through their teachings and halakot, to make it possible for the people to concretize the concepts of morality? Unmodified, this statement is unjust to the common people. An abstract value concept does not exist for long apart from its concretizations,[98] nor are abstract ideas the métier of the common people. There certainly were occasions when the common people concretized a moral concept without any guidance from the rabbis: on the other hand, it is hard to imagine what the moral pattern might have been without the rabbis, even assuming the existence of the valuational terms, a very doubtful assumption. Social interaction is always intricate and subtle, and the interaction of the rabbis with the folk was no exception.

The role of the folk predominates in the first phase of *derek ereẓ*, doubtless for the very reason that this phase is only an extension of the concept. Everybody can recognize that normal sexual behavior, engaging in work or business, and attending to natural functions are universal human modes of behavior; such observations are clearly those of the folk. An observation such as the one on the use of a synecdoche, however, is an academic observation.

When it comes to the other phases of *derek ereẓ*, the ethical phases proper, the role of the rabbis grows increasingly larger, although the role of the folk is still to be discerned. In the second phase, there are rules of practical wisdom which are patently common-sense rules of the folk, but which the rabbis reinforce by declaring them also to be teachings of Torah[99]—rules like not putting all your property in one corner, and that you must arrive and leave in the daytime. Where practical wisdom has to do with long-range effects, as in the warning against accustoming a child to expensive food,[100] the rules apparently originate with the rabbis. The phase of good manners, too, has unquestionably a folk background, but again, the delicacy and refinement so characteristic of many of its rules bespeak a tutored and cultivated class; rules like those telling a bridegroom not to enter until the bride has given permission, or a traveler to buy from the local storekeeper, or what to do when a person wishes to speak to one of two men who happen to be together.

The fourth phase, as we may remember, is the only one given a distinctive feature by the rabbis themselves, the other phases being distinguished from each other only through rabbinic usage. What we have called the fourth phase consists of concepts which the rabbis regard as universal, since the rabbis relate them, in one way or another, to mankind as a whole—positive concepts such as truth, justice, peace, and charity, and negative concepts such as theft, murder, incest, and idolatry. These concepts are, by and large, emotional drives, matters of the heart, and that is one reason, no doubt, why the rabbis regard them as universal. At a first glance, therefore, the fourth phase may appear as one in which the role of the folk predominates. But it is precisely here, in the realm of positive and negative moral drives, that a society depends on its most gifted members. Justice and laws, for example, have always been the concern of some of the best minds of every people; peace became a vivid ideal when envisioned by prophets and poets; charity was not left to the whim of the individual but was embodied in institutions; there is no need to add examples of how the intellect has canalized the emotional drives. It is no wonder, then, that so much of the Halakah, and even a larger portion of the Haggadah, is concentrated on the fourth phase of *derek ereẓ*. Of course, had the emotions of the folk not been engaged, the work of the rabbis would have been futile. Without the training, guidance, and laws of the rabbis, however, what could the folk have done?

The universal concepts are always mediated by a particular culture. We recognize today that every culture imparts to a universal concept a special quality, overtones of significance that the concept does not have elsewhere. "Patience," for instance, has overtones for the Siamese it does not have for us, according to Kroeber. " 'Patience' . . . involves calm circumspection and acting with worldly wisdom; it gives peace as well as success. Patience is really self-control over disturbing emotion, and leads to a species of self-reliance."[101] Kroeber calls attention earlier to differences in form even among kindred cultures. "There is an Italian, a French, a British pattern or form of European civilization."[102]

The rabbis refined and enriched the universal ethical concepts, especially the concept of love. Instead of having a single concept, "love," they have a number of conceptual terms—among them being *'ahabah, raḥamim, ẓedaḳah,* and *gemilut ḥasadim.* Each of these terms has its own connotations; and since the terms are not defined, their connotations can be expressed verbally only in teachings or laws. Rabbinic law did not stifle love, as some have asserted. On the contrary, rabbinic law sensitized a man to occasions for expressing love through action. Formal modes of concretization, laws, enabled a person to recognize occasions for concretizing the concept of deeds of lovingkindness,[103] for example. The many laws and the multiplicity of moral concepts went together; the laws were the concretizations of the concepts. To deny that the multiplicity of moral cencepts gave morality a wide range and made for moral depth and sensitivity is to deny the potency of any value concept.

In the fifth phase, the phase associated with universal morality but not identified with it, the role of the rabbis predominates. Only the spiritual leaders could take it upon themselves to stigmatize as "a manner of *gezel*" acts that are not *gezel* in themselves. The concept of *'ona'ah*, like all value concepts, was doubtless a folk concept, but it was the rabbis who, so to say, built up that concept. Rabbinic law decided what constitutes *'ona'at mamon*, a fraudulent business transaction, both in regard to objects which have ordinary market value and in regard to objects that do not.[104] *'Ona'at mamon* is one aspect of the concept. The other is *'ona'at debarim*, an instance of which was given above,[105] but which connotes any injury done by means of words, such as reminding anyone of his past misdeeds, shaming anyone in public, or causing a woman to shed tears.[106] Only men of sensitivity and insight could have depicted the occasions of *'ona'at debarim*.

The interaction between the folk and the rabbis was an extraordinary phenomenon. It was a continuous interaction between a society and its ethical leaders, a process in which the ordinary man was often raised to the level of the gifted man.[107]

The universal concepts are concretized in laws, and many tractates of the Mishnah are devoted to these laws. These laws were taught in the academies, as were the other laws of the Mishnah. But besides the Mishnah, there were also nonofficial collections of rules and laws, among them collections known as Hilkot *Derek Ereẓ*.[108] Such collections of Hilkot *Derek Ereẓ* were not part of the official and regular studies of the academies.[109] The term *derek ereẓ* thus seems to apply only to the rules in Hilkot *Derek Ereẓ*, and not to the universal concepts concretized in laws of the Mishnah.

It remains true, nevertheless, that the universal concepts are a phase of *derek ereẓ*. They are classifications of matters that are also *derek ereẓ*. In an extra-mishnaic collection of rules and laws called *Tosefta Derek Ereẓ*, an entire chapter consists of laws of *'arayot* (incest, forbidden marriages), laws that are also found in the official texts.[110] *'Arayot*, a universal concept, hence constitutes a classification of matters designated also as *derek ereẓ*. We have called attention earlier to other passages in which the rabbis indicate that universal concepts are classifications under, or subconcepts of, *derek ereẓ*.

A law in the Mishnah or Talmud which is a concretization of a universal concept is also a concretization of *derek ereẓ*, but it is a halakah and not merely a guiding rule. Indeed, the Mishnah contains other halakot of *derek ereẓ*, as well. For example, a law with respect to *'ona'at debarim*, a concept of the fifth phase of *derek ereẓ*, is a mishnaic law, as we noticed above. We therefore must conclude again that there is no dichotomy between the laws of the Mishnah on the one hand, and concretizations of *derek ereẓ*, on the other. Many laws of the Mishnah are concretizations of *derek ereẓ*, and among such mishnaic laws are the concretizations of the universal concepts.

Is it possible to have awareness of morality and ethics without having an ultimate criterion for morality? Is it possible, in other words, to have an awareness of morality without recourse to a formal definition of morality? In this chapter we have shown that the rabbis had a most profound awareness of what is moral or ethical, that they even adumbrated the sphere of morality, and that all this was achieved without recourse to a formal definition or an ultimate criterion. It was achieved through a concept, that of *derek ereẓ*.

The concept of *derek ereẓ* gives to morality a scope and a range larger than that of any system of philosophic ethics. Included in that scope are not only the concepts of "crucial morality" but commonplace acts, and every possible occasion of moral significance.

Not contained in any formula, nor governed by any definition, the scope of rabbinic ethics and morality cannot be delimited.

Rabbinic morality is not simply a folk product. It is the product of the interaction between a society and its best minds, the product of the continuous interaction between the folk and the rabbis.

CHAPTER IV

The Experience of Worship

A. Berakah—An Act of Worship

At every turn, the rabbis saw manifestations of *middat raḥamim*,[1] God's love, and of *middat ha-din*,[2] God's justice. By means of these concepts and their subconcepts,[3] the rabbis interpreted the national catastrophes and calamities of their own times,[4] and events in the lives of individuals as well.[5] More illuminating, however, are the instances of God's love or of His justice to be found in rabbinic interpretations of the narratives of the Bible. There the rabbis not only add details, but often supply entire incidents or stories in order to make these concepts more vivid,[6] and—be it noted—also to emphasize God's love.[7] Through such interpretations of Scripture, the rabbis taught the folk at large to see manifestations of God's love and justice everywhere.

The concepts of God's love and justice are usually embedded in the interpretations. That is to say, when the rabbis interpret an event as a manifestation of God's love or of His justice, they seldom employ the conceptual term itself; rather, the concept is embodied in the interpretation. Various passages, for example, depict disasters that befell Israel as punishments of God: the first Exile, the scattering of the Ten Tribes, the destruction of the Temple, the degrading servitude to Rome.[8] In none of these passages does the conceptual term itself, *middat ha-din*, occur. Instead, the concept has been, so to speak, embedded in the interpretation.

What we have just described is a prime characteristic of a value concept. It is only a value concept that is usually embodied in an interpretation of an event, as we have observed in Chapter II. The value concept, since it is embodied in an event, is integral to the event; indeed, it integrates all the definite, concrete details of that event into a single, unitary entity. But the event, we must remember, has been interpreted by the value concept. When this takes place, the concept not only integrates the details of the event but gives them meaning, as well. An event embodying a value concept is a unitary entity fraught with significance.[9]

We can now classify the concepts of God's love and God's justice. They are value concepts, integrating happenings into unitary entities and endowing the integrated events with significance. When they interpret events they act very much in the same way as do the concepts of human morality, the subconcepts of *derek ereẓ*.

But the subconcepts of *derek ereẓ*, such as *gemilut ḥasadim* or *ẓedaḳah*, not only interpret events; they also possess a drive toward concretization of the concepts impelling a person to act.[10] This can hardly be the case, of course, with the concepts of God's love and justice. All that a person can do, apparently, is to interpret in their light events that have happened. The concepts of human morality seem to have, so far as human action is concerned, more vitality than do the concepts of God's love and of His justice.

A consideration of the main features of Jewish worship, however, tells another story. The concepts of God's love and God's justice utilize drives toward concretization, but in their own manner.

The simplest form of Jewish worship is a "short berakah"[11]—that is, any berakah in which reference is made to only a single matter.[12] "Blessed [or praised] art Thou, O Lord our God, King of the world, Who bringest forth bread from the earth"[13] is an example of a short berakah. Simple in form, it contains only the formula "Blessed art Thou, O Lord our God, King of the world" and an appositive clause in which reference is made to a single matter, bread. The berakot on other foods have the same pattern.[14]

A berakah by itself is merely a literary form. To be a genuine religious expression, to be worship, it must be stimulated by an occasion in the life of the individual. A berakah not called forth by an occasion, "an unnecessary berakah," is so far from being worship as to be stigmatized as the taking of God's name in vain.[15] Thus, if no bread is eaten, saying the berakah on the eating of bread is obviously uttering "an unnecessary berakah." On the other hand, when that berakah precedes the actual eating of a morsel of bread, its recitation constitutes true worship.[16] So intimately related is the occasion to the berakah that the specific character of the berakah most often corresponds to the occasion.

The recitation of the berakah and its occasion form a unitary entity, a total event or situation. When the berakah corresponds to the occasion, the berakah interprets the occasion; in that case, any irrelevant interruption by word or deed breaks the association between the interpretation and the occasion[17] and destroys the unitary entity. The halakah here guards against destroying what is not merely a unitary entity, but a value experience, for there are value concepts embedded in a berakah. Holding to our example, the bread assumes significance when we are conscious that it is a concretization of God's love—"Who bringest forth bread from the earth"—and this consciousness is deep enough to move us to an expression of gratitude to God, an expression that is a berakah, worship. The concepts of God's love and berakah have, so to speak, cut a unitary event out of the flow of daily life, an event which includes not only the reciting of the berakah but also ordinary acts, the breaking of bread,[18] the eating of the first morsel.[19] A commonplace thing and ordinary acts in daily life have now become a unitary entity full of significance.

Any valuational experience, as we have said, must be a unitary entity. Every berakah, of whatever type, must be an element in that entity. The berakah we have just discussed, and all the berakot of that type, are joined to commonplace things, to daily foods and to ordinary daily acts. Normal occurences, happenings of the now and the everyday, become occasions for worship.

A unitary entity charged with significance always bears the imprint of personality. (We came to this conclusion in an earlier work when we discussed the kinship between Haggadah and poetry.[20] A poem expresses an aesthetic insight of an individual, while a haggadic statement expresses a valuational insight of an individual; in both cases there is an expression of individuality, of personality.)[21] Now, we have just seen that when a berakah is recited, that berakah is an element in a unitary entity charged with significance. Here we have a unitary entity which not only "bears the imprint of personality," as in a haggadic statement, but which almost palpably molds and enlarges the individual.

Again we illustrate with the berakah on bread. To the individual who is about to recite that berakah, the bread represents a manifestation of God's love both for mankind in general and for himself in particular. Having naturally his own need in mind, he regards himself as a recipient of God's bounty and an object of God's love; nevertheless, he thanks God for His bounty to all mankind—"Who bringest forth bread from the earth." When the individual recites the berakah, therefore, he does so as a member of society. This is the view taken by R. Levi in a reason he gives for reciting a berakah of this type. Upon reciting the berakah, says R. Levi, the individual is permitted to have, as a member of society, what up to that moment had belonged solely to God. Before the berakah, "the earth is the Lord's and the fullness thereof" (Ps. 24:1), but after the berakah, "the earth hath He given to *the children of men*" (Ps. 115:16).[22]

As in all value experiences, the recitation of the berakah engages the personality of the individual, varying in depth of significance as individuals vary in depth of personality, and in accordance, too, with circumstances; now, however, the sheerly personal experience is enlarged by an awareness on the part of the individual that he is a member of society, and the personal experience thus becomes one with vast social import. Without minimizing the character of the occasion as a personal experience, the recitation of the berakah has the effect of bringing to consciousness society at large.

Everything associated with a berakah, as well as the berakah itself, is in the sphere of Halakah,[23] and the unitary entity characterized by the berakah on bread is an example of the creative power of that sphere. The berakah embodies the concept of God's love, of His universal love, in the appositive clause, "Who bringest forth bread from the earth," an idea reaffirmed in general terms in the First Berakah after the meal by the words, "Who feedest the whole world."[24] Now, the Haggadah as well teaches that "the Holy One Blessed be He feeds the whole world,"[25] and the appositive clause of the berakah on bread is thus but a more specific form of a haggadic teaching. Halakah, therefore—not only Haggadah—embodies value concepts and has to do with teachings and ideas. But Halakah does more than teach. Out of a commonplace event it makes an occasion for a personal experience of God's love, attaches to that experience social import, and provides expression for that experience in worship.

As a rule, berakot embody the concept of God's love, being expressions of gratitude for manifestations of that love. A berakah is also said, however, at the loss of a near relative (e.g., one's father),[26] at evil tidings,[27] at serious damage to one's property;[28] and this berakah, praising "the true Judge,"[29] embodies the concept of God's justice. A man who has so often seen manifestations of God's love must now see, in his personal tragedy and loss, a manifestation of God's justice; nor is that enough, but he must also thank and praise Him. "A man is duty bound to give thanks for the evil just as he gives thanks for the good. . . . Whatever be the measure He metes out to thee, be thou exceedingly thankful to Him."[30] This is a statement in the Mishnah. Another tannaitic source, after repeating the statement and enlarging upon it with an exhortation to be "beautiful in *pur'anut* (punishment)," adds that a man ought to rejoice in *yissurim* (chastisements) more than in "the good," for *yissurim* cause his sins to be forgiven.[31] The evil that befalls a man, it would seem, may be interpreted not only as *pur'anut*, punishment or retribution, but also as *yissurim*, chastisements sent by God out of love.[32]

The concepts of God's love and God's justice connote experience of God, and are thereby distinguished from the concepts of human love and human justice. Further, both the concept of God's love and that of His justice possess aspects which human love and human justice do not have. *Yissurim*, for example, may be regarded as aspects of God's love,[33] and vicarious atonement is one of the aspects, or subconcepts, of God's justice.[34]

At the same time, it is also true that there is little to distinguish the conceptual terms for God's justice and love from the conceptual terms for human justice and love. Literally, *middat ha-din* simply means "the quality of justice," and *middat raḥamim* "the quality of love," and it is only in usage that these terms are primarily associated with God's justice and with God's love;[35] indeed, occasionally the terms are used with respect to human justice[36] and to human love.[37] Even the faint linguistic distinction between the two sets of concepts is sometimes lacking, the single word *din* standing both for God's justice[38] and for human justice, and the single word *raḥamim* both for God's love and human love. *Din* and *raḥamim*, therefore, are not wholly to be distinguished from *middat ha-din* and *middat raḥamim*. But *din* and *raḥamim* are concepts which belong to the fourth phase of *derek ereẓ*, the phase of universal human morality, as we saw in the preceding chapter; if these concepts connote morality then so do *middat ha-din* and *middat raḥamim*.

The ways in which the rabbis depict God's love also indicate that for them it was a moral experience. They depict God's love as *ẓedaḳah* (charity, love) and *gemilut ḥasadim* (deeds of lovingkindness), and these concepts, again, belong to the fourth phase of *derek ereẓ*, the phase of universal human morality. According to a passage in the Talmud, God "did *ẓedaḳah*" to Israel in scattering them among the nations, for, being now scattered, they could not all be destroyed by any one nation;[39] whilst a passage in the Midrash has it that one-third of the day God "does *ẓedaḳah* and feeds and sustains and provides for the whole world,"[40] a statement more than reminiscent of the First Berakah after the meal. Similarly, acts of God told of in Genesis 3:21 and in Deuteronomy 34:6 are designated by the rabbis as *gemilut ḥasadim*, and in several berakot God is praised as *Gomel Ḥasadim*, or "he who does deeds of lovingkindness."[41] The rabbis regard *ẓedaḳah* and *gemilut ḥasadim*, we know, as elements of universal human morality; if they also employ these concepts in telling of God's love, it can be only because an event experienced as a manifestation of God's love was, for them, a moral experience.[42]

In a unitary entity characterized by a berakah, at least two concepts usually are concretized, namely, berakah and either the concept of God's love or, far less frequently, the concept of God's justice. Here the concepts are concretized in Halakah, and such concretizations are markedly different from concretizations in Haggadah. A happening may or may not prove to be a stimulus for a concretization of a concept in Haggadah; in Halakah, the stimulus (bread, for example) is a steadily repeated occasion for the concretization of the concepts of berakah and God's love. An interpretation in Haggadah does not call for an action; in the Halakah, the interpretation of the occasion, the berakah, often does call for an act, such as the eating of bread. In Haggadah, the statement embodying the concepts is itself the unitary entity, a literary entity; in Halakah, the statement embodying the concepts, the berakah, is itself only an element in the situation as a whole, and the unitary entity is not a literary but an experiential entity.

Of the two concepts embedded in an experiential entity characterized by a berakah, the concept of berakah alone possesses a genuine drive toward concretization. With respect to the concepts of God's love and His justice, a man can act only as an interpreter, designating an event or occasion as a manifestation either of God's love or else of His justice. Here, however, we have a unitary entity, and the berakah, the interpretation, is not separable from the occasion. When there is an occasion, the value concept of berakah impels a man to recite a berakah, just as on certain occasions the value concept of *ẓedaḳah* impels a man to an act of *ẓedaḳah*. But a berakah interprets an occasion to be a manifestation of God's love or of His justice. The drive toward concretization of the concept of berakah results, therefore, in steadily repeated interpretations of the concepts of God's love or justice—in what almost amounts to their steady concretizations.

Jewish worship, in its simplest form, is an element in a unitary entity consisting of a berakah and the occasion for reciting it. It is praise of God at the same time that there is an experience of God's love or, sometimes, of His justice—an experience which is akin to that of human love or justice and hence a moral experience. In that experience there is an awareness of the self as an object of God's love, but an awareness of the self that includes society as well.

B. The Role of Form in Worship—Birkat ha-Mazon

The Birkat ha-Mazon, grace after meals, consists of four berakot. "The order of the Birkat ha-Mazon is as follows: The First Berakah is Birkat ha-Zan ['Who feedest']; the Second is Birkat ha-'Areẓ ['the Land']; the Third is '[Who] buildest Jerusalem'; the Fourth is 'Who art good and doeth good.' "[43] Although cited in rabbinic literature, as in this baraita and elsewhere,[44] these berakot are not given there in full.[45] In the course of our discussion, therefore, we shall present or quote from these four berakot as they are given in *Siddur R. Saadia Gaon*,[46] "the oldest prayer book available to us."[47]

Akin to the berakah on the eating of bread which interprets a specific, concrete occasion, the First Berakah similarly interprets a specific occasion, a meal. "Blessed [or praised] art Thou, O Lord our God, King of the world, Who feedest [us and] the whole world with goodness, with grace, with lovingkindness and with mercy. Blessed [or praised] art Thou, O Lord, Who feedest all."[48] In this berakah, the food which has been eaten is taken to be a manifestation of God's lovingkindness, and once more a commonplace event has thus been invested with significance. But the berakah is, of course, more than just an interpretation of the meal: reciting the First Berakah after eating a meal is an act of worship; the meal has been the occasion and the stimulus for worship, and this is reflected in the interpretation of the meal as a manifestation of God's love. To put it differently, when the First Berakah is recited after eating, the meal and the recitation of the berakah constitute a unitary entity in time, and the meal, as the occasion for the berakah, is then an element in an integrated religious experience. By the same token, the recitation of the First Berakah is an expression, through worship, of the experience of God's love represented by the meal.

In this instance, too, it is the Halakah itself which indicates that we have to do with a unitary entity. The association between the meal and the Birkat ha-Mazon must not be broken. The Birkat ha-Mazon ought to be said at the place where one has eaten the meal.[49] A man who is about to leave the place where he has eaten in order to speak to a friend (even if it be no further than to the door), ought first to say the Birkat ha-Mazon.[50]

Primarily, the association is not between the meal and the entire Birkat ha-Mazon but, as we have just indicated, between the meal and the First Berakah. It is the First Berakah alone that actually corresponds to the occasion. Indeed, since the unitary entity of meal and berakah is an experiential entity, the meal stimulating a man to say a berakah in gratitude for it, the meal and any berakah called forth by it constitute a unitary entity. A shepherd by the name of Benjamin, before a scant meal of a piece of bread "wrapped around" (with some herbs possibly), said in vernacular Aramaic, "Blessed is the Master of this bread,"[51] and the Talmud declares that brief berakah to be an equivalent also of the First Berakah if said after the meal.[52] Benjamin's berakah is equivalent to the First Berakah because the one as well as the other is called forth by the meal and interprets it to be a manifestation of God's love.[53] Of course, there is also a marked difference between the two berakot. An individual reciting the First Berakah has in mind not himself alone but "the whole world,"[54] whereas there is no such enlargement of the self when he recites the shepherd's berakah.

Worship of the kind we have been describing is not possible without an occasion or stimulus. Such worship consists of two elements—a thing or an event experienced as a manifestation of God's love (or justice) and the expression of that experience in a berakah praising and thanking God. The berakah interprets the occasion, but it is not, so to say, an explanation; the recitation of the berakah is itself an element in the situation, giving it character. Here is an experiential, unitary entity, not two successive states of experience, and so the recitation of the berakah enhances and heightens the original apprehension of God's love touched off by the occasion. At the same time, through the recitation of the berakah, the very apprehension of the self is enlarged, and the individual has a sense of kinship with society, with the whole world. Worship is thus a moral experience not only because it is an experience of God's love or of His justice, but also because it engenders an awareness of, and a sense of kinship with, the whole world.[55]

The experiential entity characterized by the First Berakah is partly phenomenal and partly literary: the occasion is a phenomenon while the berakah is a literary form. Another literary form, often employed elsewhere in the liturgy, enables this original experience of worship to become an impetus in its own right to a further act of worship, the Second Berakah, and the religious experience represented in the latter, an impetus for still a third act of worship, the Third Berakah. An actual concrete experience of God's love, a phenomenal experience, here initiates the chain of religious experiences; it is now possible for the first act of worship to be an impetus to a second and, in turn, for the second, a nonphenomenal experience, to be an impetus to still another act of worship. Again, when a religious experience gives rise to another religious experience, we have a conceptual continuum. Since the initial experience was a concretization of God's love, the successive experiences in the chain must also be concretizations of God's love. An integral factor in an act of worship, this more inclusive form in addition helps to create successive acts of worship.

A prime characteristic of this more inclusive form is "the berakah which is joined to the immediately preceding berakah."[56] The

Second Berakah of the Birkat ha-Mazon is of that kind.[57] "We thank Thee, O Lord our God, because Thou didst give as a heritage unto us a desirable, good and ample Land [of Israel], a covenant and Torah, life and food; and for all these we thank Thee and bless [or, praise] Thy Name forever. Blessed art Thou, O Lord, for the Land and for the food."[58] No opening formula—"Blessed art Thou," etc.—marks this berakah, but only a closing formula, and that is the distinguishing feature of "a berakah which is joined to the immediately preceding berakah."[59] Some say that the closing formula of the "immediately preceding berakah" serves also "as a sort" of opening formula for the berakah which follows;[60] accordingly, "Blessed art Thou, O Lord, Who feedest all," the closing formula of the First Berakah, serves also as a sort of opening formula for the Second Berakah. These and other halakic details reflect an experience of worship more subtle than those we have already studied.

No concrete phenomenon or other vivid occasion touches off the Second Berakah; that is why it does not have an opening formula. Instead, it begins with a meditation. A meditation by itself, however, is hardly equivalent to a phenomenal stimulus. In order to become an experience of worship, the meditation must start with an impetus toward worship, and that impetus is supplied by the First Berakah. Concretized there are the concepts of God's love and berakah, and these concepts proceed to inform the meditation which follows. Nor do we have here a departure from other types of valuational experience. Every value experience is strongly affected by the one preceding it.[61] We can now see why the Second Berakah is "a berakah that is joined to the immediately preceding berakah," and how it is that the closing formula of the immediately preceding berakah can be regarded as a sort of opening formula for the Second Berakah.

A meditative experience of worship requires more of a person than a phenomenal experience of worship. A phenomenal experience of worship can be achieved even by a man untutored in Halakah—witness the brief berakah in the vernacular uttered by Benjamin the shepherd. When it comes to a meditative experience of worship, however, the guidance of the Halakah is indispensable, and so the rabbis have formulated a number of rules with respect to the Second Berakah. The Halakah indicates the subject of the meditation, namely, the land. Thanksgiving (הודאה) is to be said both at the beginning and at the end of the meditation,[62] obviously to ensure direction to the meditation. In this "berakah of the Land," a person ought to say the words "a desirable, good and ample Land,"[63] a phrase conveying the biblical delight in the land.[64] One authority teaches that the covenant (of Abraham) should be mentioned (for the covenant is linked with God's promise of the land);[65] another declares that Torah should be mentioned (for the Bible speaks of the land as reward for Torah).[66] In this wise does the Halakah endeavor to build up an apprehension of God's love as manifested in the heritage of the land.[67]

A general rule requires that the idea mentioned immediately preceding the closing formula be also contained in the formula itself;[68] in our case, and in most berakot, this rule simply requires that the closing formula refer to the subject of the meditation.[69] "Blessed art Thou, O Lord, for the Land and for the food."[70] The closing berakah thus both expresses and enhances the particular expression of God's love built up in the meditation. Meditation and berakah constitute a unitary entity, an experience achieved by the individual now in his role as one of the people of Israel.

Both the phenomenal and the meditative experiences of worship demand of the individual a deliberate focusing of the mind. But there were other factors, we must not forget, that encouraged and made possible this focusing of the mind. The rabbis and the people they taught were always eager to find fresh manifestations of God's love and God's justice. The concept of berakah had the effect of sensitizing the individual to such manifestations in his own life and so to see in them occasions for worship. In a phenomenal experience, to focus the mind, therefore, was simply to be aware of the occasion. In a meditative experience such as the Second Berakah, what corresponds to the occasion had to be built up, and hence required a greater mental effort; but here, too, the initial impetus had been supplied, after all, by the First Berakah.

The Third Berakah is likewise a meditative experience developed in accordance with the Halakah. A person must not fail to include the phrase "the kingship of the house of David."[71] On the opening and closing phrases, there are various opinions. R. Sheshet says, "If he begins with 'Have mercy upon Israel, Thy people,' he closes with '[Who] savest Israel,' and if he begins with 'Have mercy upon Jerusalem,' he closes with '[Who] buildest Jerusalem' "; while R. Naḥman says, "Even if he begins with 'Have mercy upon Israel,' he closes with '[Who] buildest Jerusalem.' "[72] As support, R. Naḥman cites and interprets Psalm 147:2; [when] "the Lord doth build up Jerusalem, He gathereth together the dispersed of Israel."[73] The Palestinian version began with "O comfort us," and closed with "[Who] comfortest His people in the building of Jerusalem."[74] The full text of the Third Berakah in Saadia's *Siddur* reads: "Have mercy, O Lord our God, upon us, upon Israel, Thy people, and upon Jerusalem, Thy city, and upon Thy Temple, and upon Thy dwelling place, and upon Zion, the abiding place of Thy glory, and upon the great and holy house that was called by Thine own Name; and mayest Thou restore the kingship of the house of David to its place in our days, and build Jerusalem speedily. Blessed art Thou, O Lord, [Who] buildest Jerusalem. Amen."[75]

Does not this entire berakah seem to contradict what we know about the basic character of a berakah? We have recognized that a berakah is an expression of gratitude for a manifestation of God's love. Indeed, the meditation in the Second Berakah explicitly begins with thanksgiving for a specific manifestation of God's love. In contrast, the meditation in the Third Berakah seems hardly to be a meditation at all. It begins with such phrases as "have mercy," or "O comfort us"; that is to say, it begins with a supplication or petition, *baḳḳashah.*[76] Surely a supplication is not equivalent to a meditation of thanksgiving. But there are also other peculiarities. The closing formula, the berakah itself, is always an affirmation, and so it is here. But how can a petition lead directly to an affirmation? Further, the affirmation here is in the present tense, and this is true of every version—"[Who] buildest Jerusalem," "[Who] savest Israel," "[Who] comfortest." How can a petition, necessarily referring to the future, close with a berakah referring to the present?

What appear to be peculiarities in this berakah, however, are really the characteristics of a special type of berakah, other examples of which are found in the 'Amidah. The supplication has for its theme the days of the Messiah, the future era when "the kingship of the house of David" will be restored, when Jerusalem and the Temple will be rebuilt, when "the dispersed of Israel will be gathered together." It is this theme that marks off this berakah as belonging to a special type. As we have concluded elsewhere, the concept of the days of the Messiah and the other concepts of the hereafter associated with it are not pure value concepts but rabbinic dogmas.[77] They possess a degree of specificity which the value concepts, being indeterminate, do not have: A value concept is only suggestive or connotative, whereas the rabbinic dogmas point to specific events:[78] in the case of the days of the Messiah, to the restoration of the house of David, to the ingathering of the Diaspora, and to the building of Jerusalem. The petition in the Third Berakah, then, has to do with a rabbinic dogma. It is a petition concerning an event believed to be a future certainty and a supplication that this event take place "in our days."

But the petition is also informed by a value concept, the concept of *'emunah*. "*'Emunah* has the connotation of general faith or trust in God, general in the sense that it does not necessarily imply reliance on God for security or personal welfare."[79] Often such trust in God is related to faith in His promise or word.[80] Now the theme of the petition is a preordained event, a promise of God; hence dwelling upon that event evokes *'emunah*, complete, unbounded trust in God, a trust so unaffected by present circumstances as to create a sense of the promise being fulfilled "in our days." The situation has thus a meditative aspect; that is why it closes with "Who builds Jerusalem" in the present tense, a phrase affirming and enhancing something quite like a meditative experience, an "as if" experience.

The rabbis link *'emunah* with berakot of this type, including one which is practically identical with the Third Berakah of the Birkat ha-Mazon in a comment on Psalm 31:24.[81] They extol Israel by applying to them the text, "the Lord preserveth the faithful (*'emunim*)." For they (i.e., the people of Israel) say, "Blessed [art Thou, O Lord] Who quickenest the dead," though the resurrection of the dead has not yet come; they say, "Redeemer of Israel," though they are not yet redeemed; they say, "Blessed [art Thou, O Lord,] Who buildest Jerusalem," though Jerusalem is not yet built. The Holy One Blessed be He says, "Israel was redeemed for only a little while and then went back into servitude, and [yet] they have faith [*ma'aminim*] in Me that I shall redeem them in a time to come!"

The Third Berakah is an experiential entity which embodies a number of concepts. It owes its impetus to the Second Berakah,[82] and hence, like that berakah, it embodies the concept of God's love. Unlike the Second Berakah, however, the specific manifestation of God's love is something petitioned for rather than something which has occurred, and the petition consists in a plea for the restoration of the house of David and for the building of Jerusalem, specific events summed up in the concept of the days of the Messiah. Since those events are matters of dogma and hence felt to be preordained events, the thought of them evokes trust in God, *'emunah*, an unbounded trust that finally gives the individual the assurance that the events are indeed taking place in the present. At the end, when gratitude is uttered in the closing berakah for the building of Jerusalem, the entire berakah, petition and all, has the vividness of a meditative experience; once more we see that the meditation or the occasion and their expression in a berakah are not successive states but constitute a unitary entity. Of course, being a unitary entity, the experience both affects and is affected by the personality of the individual, although now it is an experience of the individual in his role as a member or representative of the people of Israel.

In the form characterized by "the berakah which is joined to the immediately preceding berakah," we have a dynamic form which makes it possible for an impetus to be given toward a new meditation, that is, toward a new experiential entity. It is an elastic form. Since it is a form that consists of a series of unitary entities, any one of which, once achieved, is complete in itself, the series may close with any new entity, and yet there need be no given limit to the successive experiences. Traditions may well differ, therefore, as to the closing of a series of this kind, and there are indeed two such differing traditions regarding the closing of the Birkat ha-Mazon. At one time, undoubtedly, the Birkat ha-Mazon closed with the Third Berakah, for early tannaitic sources speak of three berakot after a meal.[83] Other tannaitic statements tell also of a Fourth Berakah[84] which, apparently beginning with a meditation[85] and closing with "Who hath bestowed upon us all good,"[86] was thus a berakah that was "joined to the immediately preceding berakah."[87] Since the closing formula embodied the concept of God's love, this berakah, as we should expect, held to the conceptual continuum.

The Halakah did establish a Fourth Berakah, not one "which is joined to the immediately preceding berakah," but one which has an opening formula: "Blessed art Thou, O Lord our God, King of the world, O God, our Father, our King, our Creator, our Redeemer, O King Who art good and doeth good, Who many a time, day by day, doeth good unto us, and Who wilt ever bestow upon us grace and lovingkindness and relief and mercy and all good."[88] A berakah with an opening formula is usually related to an occasion of some kind and, according to both the Jerusalem and the Babylonian Talmud, this berakah was established when "the slain of Bettar," after the disastrous revolt of Bar Kokeba, were permitted to be buried.[89] The berakah as established, Albeck points out, is similar to the one on hearing good tidings;[90] it also contains, however, phrases from the original version of the Fourth Berakah ("wilt bestow") and from the First Berakah ("grace, lovingkindness, mercy"). In any case, however the berakah arose, it is an acknowledgment of God's love solely in general terms.[91]

We can discern now another feature of the form we have been studying. Under special circumstances it permits deviations or departures from the pattern. Unlike the Second and Third Berakot, the Fourth Berakah, as established by the Halakah, has no meditation, and yet the experiential character of the pattern as a whole is not impaired. Each an embodiment of the concept of God's love, the first three berakot have a cumulative effect, an effect which, in this instance, enables the Fourth Berakah to be the culmination of the preceding berakot. The impact of the first three berakot takes the place of a meditation, as it were, and the Fourth Berakah, as finally established, is the response to that impact. The Fourth Berakah is truly the climax of the Birkat ha-Mazon, an experience of worship achieved as the result of preceding acts of worship, a profound acknowledgment of God's love and mercy in themselves rather than as manifested in any specific thing or manner.[92]

Characterized by the rabbis as "the berakah which is joined to the immediately preceding berakah," the form exemplified by the Birkat ha-Mazon allows the individual to achieve successive experiences of worship. The series begins with a berakah called forth by a specific manifestation of God's love, a phenomenal experience which the berakah both interprets and enhances, the occasion for the berakah and the berakah itself being a unitary experiential entity. This experience of worship imparts an impetus toward a new experiential entity; a nonphenomenal, meditative experience of God's love, built up in accordance with Halakah and having its own response of gratitude in a berakah. In the Birkat ha-Mazon, the Second Berakah, in its turn, imparts an impetus toward another meditative experience of worship, and there are still longer chains of successive meditative experiences of this kind in the liturgy. Since every experience in the series, once achieved, is complete in itself, the series may close with any new entity; in other words, the form as such sets no limit to the series. On the other hand, although each experiential entity is a unit in itself, the successive berakot do have a cumulative effect, so that when a berakah, under special circumstances, deviates from the form, the cumulative effect of the preceding berakot overcomes the deviation and maintains unimpaired the experiential character of the pattern as a whole. An example is the manner in which the cumulative effect of the preceding berakot overcomes the deviation of the Fourth Berakah of the Birkat ha-Mazon.[93]

C. The Shema'—Worship, Commitment, and Study

We have thus far discussed berakot, the initial occasions for which are phenomenal experiences. However, the occasion for a berakah may also be a more complex experience. Further, there is a liturgical act which is at once worship, self-commitment, and study. These features of worship and liturgy are to be found in the Ḳeri'at Shema' and its berakot.

Although the Shema' is composed of two separate passages from Deuteronomy (6:4–9 and 11:13–21) and, following them, a third from Numbers (15:37–41), the proper recitation of the Shema', Ḳeri'at Shema', makes of those three passages a unitary entity. When the Shema' is recited, the several passages in their prescribed order convey certain logically related commitments and so the passages constitute, in that respect, a logical unit. Doubtless because the Shema' was taken to be a logical unit, a person reciting it was not permitted to reverse the order of the passages, according to the Tosefta.[94] But the Shema' is a unitary entity not alone by virtue of possessing an internal unity. Preceded and followed by berakot, it is nevertheless, authorities say, independent of these berakot.[95] Despite its position in the liturgy, the Shema' is thus held to be a complete entity in its own right.

The first section of the Shema' (Deut. 6:4–9) has to do with the acceptance upon oneself of the kingship of God, and the second section (Deut. 11:13–21) with commitment to the miẓwot. In the sequence of these passages as recited in the Ḳeri'at Shema', R. Joshua b. Ḳorḥah sees a logical relationship: "so that a person shall first accept upon himself the yoke of the kingship of Heaven [God], and after that accept upon himself the yoke of miẓwot."[96] Acceptance of the kingship of God takes place when reciting the first verse of the first section: "Hear, O Israel, the Lord our God, the Lord is One," a verse which implies also the negation or exclusion of idolatry (*'abodah zarah*);[97] acceptance of "the yoke of miẓwot" takes place when reciting the first verse of the second section: "And it shall come to pass if ye shall hearken diligently unto My commandments which I command you this day."[98] Commitment to God's commandments necessarily must follow, and not precede, acceptance of God's sovereignty. In the opinion of R. Simeon b. Yoḥai, the sequence of the passages in the Shema' is due to another series of commitments, again of a necessarily successive character, namely, commitments to learn Torah, to teach it, and to practice it.[99] According to the Talmud, R. Simeon agrees with R. Joshua but merely offers an additional reason for the sequence.[100] The recitation of the Shema' hence consists of accepting commitments which logically follow upon each other, the logical coherence of the commitments making of the recitation a single act, a unitary entity.

Ḳeri'at Shema' is a liturgical act in which the acceptance of God's kingship is followed by the commitment to the miẓwot. The rabbis stress this conjunction between the two commitments not only with respect to Ḳeri'at Shema', however, but when interpreting several other biblical passages. Thus, in an interpretation of the Ten Commandments, they emphasize the successive character of the two commitments by a parable telling of a king of flesh and blood who, upon entering a province, was advised by his attendants to issue decrees to the people but who refused to do so until the people should accept his kingship. " 'For if they will not accept my kingship they will not accept my decrees'. Likewise, God said to Israel: 'I am the Lord thy God, Who brought thee out of the land of Egypt. . . . Thou shalt have no other gods' [Exod. 20:2–3]. He said to them, 'I am He Whose kingship you accepted upon yourselves in Egypt'; [and when] they said, 'Yes,' He continued, 'Now just as you accepted My kingship upon yourselves, accept [now] My decrees'— 'Thou shalt have no other gods before Me' [*ibid.*]."[101] Following upon this interpretation is a similar one by R. Simeon b. Yoḥai on a different passage: " 'I am the Lord your God,' which is said further on [Lev. 18:2] means: 'I am He Whose kingship you accepted upon yourselves at Sinai'; [and when] they said, 'Yes, yes,' He continued, 'You have accepted My kingship, accept [now] My decrees—'After the doings of the land of Egypt', etc. [*ibid.*, v.3]."[102] R. Simeon's teaching here, incidentally, is patently at one with R. Joshua's teaching on the Shema'.

Both *malkut Shamayim*, the kingship of God, and miẓwot, commandments of God, since they convey significance, are value concepts. Now, value concepts have an organismic and not a logical coherence; a value concept depends for its meaning upon the integrated value complex as a whole, and its idea content expands and grows as it interweaves with the other value concepts. Concepts that are logically related are defined concepts, whereas abstract value concepts are indeterminate and merely connotative.[103] To all this *malkut Shamayim* and miẓwot prove to be no real exception, notwithstanding the logical coherence of the passages of the Shema', for the two concepts are not permanently interlocked. Each of them combines and interweaves with the other value concepts so vividly, indeed, as to illustrate the very process of organismic integration.[104] True, there are occasions which exhibit a logical relation between value concepts, but important as these occasions are, they are too few to imperil the general organismic process.[105]

To accept the kingship of God is to achieve a meditative experience of God. A meditative religious experience, one that does not arise out of an actual phenomenal occasion is, we recognized, achieved by most men only with the aid of halakic rules or guides. Thus, after the first verse of the Shema' a response is inserted, an early practice surely, since in both the Mishnah and the Tosefta it appears as the established rule.[106] Evidently consisting originally of the phrase "Blessed is His glorious Name forever" (after Ps. 72:19), Finkelstein has pointed out, the response was changed to "Blessed is the Name of His glorious Kingship forever" in order, as Finkelstein says, "to emphasize the Kingship of God."[107] There are also instructions regarding the utterance of the first verse of the Shema', the declaration or affirmation of God's kingship. The last word in the affirmation, *'eḥad* (אחד), is to be lengthened[108] so as to permit the utterance to be a meditative experience,[109] and a rule given by R. Ḥiyya bar 'Abba indicates the character of that experience. When R. Ḥiyya noticed that R. Jeremiah greatly prolonged the word, he said, "When you have made Him King above and below and in the four winds [i.e., directions] of heaven, you need do no more."[110] In the Yerushalmi, the same incident is reported with R. Ze'ira in place of R. Ḥiyya, and the rule there says that it is sufficient "to make Him King in heaven and on earth and in the four winds of the world."[111]

Acceptance of *malkut Shamayim*, the kingship of God, is the end, the rules being but helpful guides in achieving this experience. It was the custom of the men of Jericho to omit the response after saying the first verse of the Shema', according to R. Judah, and the rabbis did not prohibit their doing so.[112] Had the acceptance of *malkut Shamayim* depended on the insertion of the response, it is inconceivable that the rabbis would have permitted them to omit it. Apparently the men of Jericho had been accustomed to accept God's kingship in Ḳeri'at Shema', doubtless from early times, without inserting the response, and the rabbis were aware of that. Similarly, R. Jeremiah obviously had an approach of his own with respect to the meditative experience different from that of R. Ḥiyya.[113]

Experience of God is never raw experience but an experience mediated by a concept. In the case of a berakah, the mediating concept is usually *middat raḥamim*, God's love. Here the concept is *malkut Shamayim*, and its scope is larger than that of *middat raḥamim*. Whereas the concept of God's love is solely interpretive, endowing an event or occasion with significance, the significance achieved in accepting *malkut Shamayim* goes beyond interpretation of this or that event to an interpretation of the world as a whole. Acceptance of *malkut Shamayim* usually consists in making "Him King in heaven and on earth and in the four directions of the world." The individual who accepts God's kingship thus interprets the world itself to be a manifestation of that kingship. This interpretive act is also a commitment. The individual commits himself to loyalty and obedience, loyalty implying a negation of idolatry[114] and obedience implying a readiness to observe the miẓwot or commandments.[115] In this entire experience, the individual acts both on his own private behalf and, at the same time, as a representative of the world.

Acceptance of miẓwot in this commitment is but implied. That is why the rabbis teach that another commitment ought to follow in which there is explicit acceptance of "the yoke of miẓwot." In the priests' service in the Temple, the commitments were made still more explicit. Preceding the recitation of the three sections of the Shema' was the recitation of the Ten Commandments, says a mishnah formulated toward the close of the Temple era;[116] and the Ten Commandments, in addition to representing the miẓwot in their own right, also represent, in the tannaitic tradition, Israel's acceptance at that cataclysmic moment in their history of the same commitments as those contained in the Shema'.[117] It was felt, indeed, that the reading of the Ten Commandments together with the Shema' ought to be the daily practice of the people at large,[118] and in fact there were several attempts to establish such a practice[119] during the amoraic period in Babylon, one being as late as in the generation of R. 'Ashi. The desire not to seem to give support to sectarians prevailed, however, for it was the ardent contention of sectarians that the Ten Commandments alone were given to Moses on Sinai;[120] later, this precedent prevailed, too, against all the Babylonian attempts to attach the Ten Commandments to the Shema'.[121] But the tradition that the Ten Commandments made explicit what was implicit in the Shema' was maintained, nevertheless. R. Ba' declares in a halakic context that the Ten Commandments are integral to the Shema',[122] containing the same theme;[123] and R. Levi, interpreting the sections of the Shema' haggadically, shows how they contain (or hint at) every one of the Ten Commandments.[124]

Complete devotion of the mind and heart, unwavering focusing of attention, are required if the commitments of the Shema' in all the richness of their connotations are to be matters of genuine experience. Some authorities insist that the whole Shema' be recited with this kind of sustained concentration, else it must be repeated. "He that reads the Shema' must direct his heart—שיכוין את לבו."[125] On the other hand, R. Me'ir, obviously reckoning with the powers of the ordinary man, declares that only the first verse of the Shema' need be recited with "direction of the heart—כוונת הלב," and this rule became the final halakah.[126] Naturally, the rest of the Shema', too, even according to the least demanding view, must not be read mechanically.[127]

We have tried to suggest by words like "attention," "devotion," and "concentration" something of what the rabbis mean in this connection by the term *kawwanah*, a word just quoted both in verbal and nominal forms.[128] In the context here, *kawwanah* refers to the great commitments and inward experience in Ḳeri'at Shema', and elsewhere it similarly refers to profound inward experiences. But it also occurs in other discussions by the rabbis on the Shema', and there it is used in a more limited sense, namely, in the sense of one's being aware during the recital of the Shema' that he is observing a miẓwah.[129] The concept of *kawwanah* thus possesses at least two phases.[130] We shall accord it fuller consideration in due course.

The inward experience in Ḳeri'at Shema' is an experience of God. As in manifestations of *middat raḥamim* and *middat ha-din*, the experience of God here, too, is brought to man through the medium of a concept, the concept of *malkut Shamayim*. The concept does not intervene between God and man; it merely canalizes the experience of God, enabling that experience now to have the whole wide world for its setting and making the individual himself conscious of a cosmic status and of a high, indeed the highest duty. In other words, here the experience of God is at once man's experience of God's kingship, his awareness of God's kingdom, and his apperception of his own role in that kingdom. All these things are accomplished when a man "directs his heart" in reciting the Shema'.

Ḳeri'at Shema', like a berakah, is worship; in fact, when the rabbis characterize Ḳeri'at Shema' as worship, they do so by employing the same verse (Exod. 23:25)[131] by which they characterize a berakah as worship.[132] In the case of a berakah we found that an experience of worship is a unitary entity in which there is experience of God. These are also the characteristics of Ḳeri'at Shema'. Acceptance of *malkut Shamayim* is an experience of God, and this experience is achieved in the recital of discrete passages of the Bible that in the Shemaʿ are felt to be logically related and sensed as elements of a unitary entity.[133]

Besides being a liturgical act, Ḳeri'at Shemaʿ is study of Torah, and this function of Ḳeri'at Shemaʿ is stressed no less than its liturgical function. The term Ḳeri'at Shemaʿ itself indicates that the recital of the Shemaʿ is the study or reading of Scripture, for the root קרא refers specifically to scriptural study.[134] By reciting the Shemaʿ a man fulfills the minimum that is required by the duty to study Torah.[135] A man who does no more than recite Ḳeri'at Shemaʿ morning and evening, says R. Joḥanan in the name of R. Simeon b. Yoḥai, already fulfills the charge, "This Book of the Torah shall not depart out of thy mouth, but thou shalt meditate therein day and night" (Josh. 1:8).[136] Because the study of Torah and Ḳeri'at Shemaʿ are thus of a piece— "one matter," as Ginzberg puts it—the rabbis interpret "and ye shall teach them [to] your children" to refer to Ḳeri'at Shemaʿ.[137] Again, in another discussion, Ḳeri'at Shemaʿ is not only identified as study of Torah but both are put on the same plane, these ideas being needed to account for R. Simeon b. Yoḥai's practice of not interrupting his study even for Ḳeri'at Shemaʿ.[138] This was a divergence from the general rule, but that rule itself emphasizes Ḳeri'at Shemaʿ as study of Torah. When the rabbis say that it is an obligation upon each individual to recite the Shemaʿ "with his own mouth," the basis of that obligation is study of Torah.[139]

The dual function of Ḳeri'at Shemaʿ is an instance of organismic thought in the Halakah. As a liturgical act, Ḳeri'at Shemaʿ embodies the concept of *malkut Shamayim*, whereas as recital of Scripture it embodies the concept of *talmud Torah*. Neither function is an alternative function; that is why the berakah preceding and anticipating the Shemaʿ refers to both functions of the Shemaʿ and embodies both concepts.[140] Actually, Ḳeri'at Shemaʿ itself embodies not only these concepts but others, among them the concept of miẓwot, and is thus a halakic example of how a number of value concepts may be combined in a single act. Elsewhere we saw that this feature of organismic thought is typical of the Haggadah,[141] and earlier in this chapter we found it also to be a characteristic of all berakot (p. 68).[142]

In organismic thought, the same situation may be interpreted in various ways and this occurs when a situation is interpreted by different value concepts.[143] Further, a situation embodying several value concepts may give rise to various interpretations, the interpretation now depending upon the emphasis placed on one rather than on another of these concepts.[144] This characteristic of organismic thought is not confined to Haggadah but is to be found in Halakah as well. It is exhibited by halakic discussions or statements bearing on mishnaic rules with respect to the Shema', rules telling when the period for recital begins in the evening[145] and when in the morning.[146] In one such discussion, it is assumed that the Shema' is recited because it is study of Torah. "Why are these two passages recited every day?" asks the Yerushalmi.[147] Although referring to the Shema', the Yerushalmi poses the problem of "these two passages" as if they were discrete passages and quite as if other passages might not be recited instead;[148] the concept implicit here, therefore, is not acceptance of *malkut Shamayim* but study of Torah. R. Simon's reply, "Because they [the two passages] contain [speak of] 'lying down' and 'rising up,' "[149] likewise relates to study of Torah. The verses to which he points, Deuteronomy 6:7 and 11:19, enjoin study of Torah, to be engaged in "when thou liest down and when thou risest up," that is, at night and at dawn,[150] every day. The time for reciting the Shema' is, then, in this statement directly associated with study of Torah. Other authorities, however, associate the time for reciting the Shema' in the morning with the acceptance of *malkut Shamayim*. By saying the 'Amidah after Ḳeri'at Shema', they teach, a man thus first accepts God's kingship and then stands in prayer, and thus also, since the Shema' is to be recited at dawn, the 'Amidah will be said after dawn, which is proper.[151]

Emphasis on one concept rather than on another may, in Halakah, make for divergence in practice. R. Simeon b. Yoḥai's practice, already mentioned, is a case in point. When he was engaged in study, he did not interrupt it even for Ḳeri'at Shema' because, the explanation is, Ḳeri'at Shema', too, is study of Torah.[152] The emphasis on Ḳeri'at Shema' as study of Torah made, in this instance, for a divergence from the general practice.

Ḳeri'at Shema' has, then, a dual character, being both an act of worship and study of Torah. It could not have this dual character were the proper study of Torah in general solely an intellectual activity.

"Just as the 'Abodah of the altar is called 'abodah, so is Study [of Torah] called 'abodah."[153] By characterizing study of Torah as 'abodah, worship,[154] the rabbis are saying that the proper study of Torah is a mystical experience, an experience wherein there is felt to be a manifestation of God in some manner. What this experience ought to be is made explicit in a comment on the words, "*This day* they came into the wilderness of Sinai [Exod. 19:1]" (emphasis supplied). "When you study Torah, do not regard them [the words of the Torah] as old but as though [the] Torah were given you this day."[155] Similarly: " 'All the statutes and the ordinances which I set before you *this day*' [Deut. 11:32]—let them be as beloved of you as though you received them from Mount Sinai this day, be as conversant with them as though you heard them this day."[156] These statements are not just exhortations. If study of Torah is indeed 'abodah, then the person who is studying the laws of the Torah has an experience akin to that of hearing them from God here and now, an experience as though he is receiving those laws "this very day." The phrase "this day" in Deuteronomy 6:6 again conveys to the rabbis the same message. That verse—"and these words which I command thee this day"—is interpreted to mean that they ("these words") must not be regarded as an old edict which no one minds, but as a new one which everyone is eager to read.[157] Since each edict or law is a unitary entity, the study of Torah as an act of worship may consist of the study of one law or of many.

In study of Torah as worship, a dogma practically loses its character as dogma and becomes, instead, a personal experience. The dogma is *mattan Torah*,[158] now so transformed that it can be referred to only by phrases like "as though you received" or "as though you heard." We called attention to such transformations of dogma when we discussed the Birkat ha-Mazon, and we shall take note of further instances in subsequent discussions.

Ḳeri'at Shema' is a call and a response whereby Israel can testify that God alone is King.[159] That is how ענה בי in Micah 6:3 is interpreted in a midrash at the beginning of a passage found in a number of sources. " 'O My people, what have I done unto thee? And wherein have I wearied thee? Testify for Me [ענה בי]'—said R. 'Aḥa': Testify for Me and receive reward, but if you will not testify you will be punished."[160] Further on in the same passage is another, closely related midrash on the same verse, Micah 6:3, in which Ḳeri'at Shema' is designated as God's edict. "'And wherein have I wearied thee?'—[It may be compared] to a king who sent his edict [פרוסדונגמא] to a province. What did the people of the province do? They stood on their feet and uncovered their heads, and read it with awe and with fear, with trembling and with agitation. [But] thus did the Holy One blessed be He say to Israel: This Ḳeri'at' Shema' is My edict [פרוסדיגמא]; I did not cause you to be wearied, and I did not tell you to read it standing on your feet and with uncovered heads, but 'when thou sittest in thy house, and when thou walkest in the way' [Deut. 6:7]."[161] This midrash is quoted in *Seder R. Amram Gaon*, and the Gaon prefaced it with the statement, "Every time a man recites the Shema' he ought to regard it as a new edict —כפרוזדגמא חדתא."[162] But in what sense can Ḳeri'at Shema' be characterized as an edict? Furthermore, what are the words in Micah 6:3 which can be taken to mean that the verse refers to Ḳeri'at Shema'? We need only continue with the verse being interpreted, however, to recognize that the edict is "testify for Me" and that it refers to the call in Ḳeri'at Shema' to testify to God's kingship. By the same token, the words "testify for Me" are taken to mean that the verse refers to Ḳeri'at Shema'.

Study of Torah is itself an act of worship. Only if this is recognized can the Ḳeri'at Shema' as an act of worship be accounted for. Only because the Ḳeri'at Shema' is really a special instance of the study of Torah can the particular act of worship take place which constitutes compliance with the edict contained in the Shema'.[163]

Several rabbinic sources indicate, it seems to us, that acceptance of *malkut Shamayim* through study of Torah was not limited to Ḳeri'at Shema'. A tannaitic source teaches that the words of the Torah as a whole can lead the individual to accept upon himself the kingship of Heaven, if they are studied and reflected upon. Commenting on Deuteronomy 32:29, the Sifre says: "Had Israel reflected upon [נסתכלו] the words of the Torah that was given them, no nation or kingdom would have had dominion over them. And what did it say to them? Accept upon yourselves the yoke of the kingship of Heaven, and exceed [הכריעו] one another in fear of Heaven, and act toward one another with deeds of lovingkindness."[164]

All of the charges here are directed to the individual, as is evident specifically in the last two; all of them must represent ideals and reflect practices of the rabbis' own day. Now, how does the Torah admonish the individual to be God-fearing and to engage in deeds of lovingkindness? Obviously through the medium of its texts, which the individual is bidden to reflect upon, that he may draw forth from them their full implication. This must also be the way, therefore, in which the individual is to carry out the behest to accept upon himself the yoke of the kingship of Heaven. He is to do so as he recites a text which teaches or implies upon reflection acceptance of *malkut Shamayim*. The scholars were, of course, better qualified and also had more occasion to identify such texts than the folk in general. A passage in praise of the learned links their acceptance of *malkut Shamayim* with their daily study of Torah.[165]

We saw above that, according to the rabbis, other scriptural passages besides Ḳeri'at Shema' refer to the acceptance of *malkut Shamayim* and commitment to the miẓwot. These passages are the Ten Commandments (Exod. 20:2 ff.) and Leviticus 18:2 ff.[166] Exodus 20:2–3 is interpreted as follows: "He [God] said to them [Israel], 'I am He Whose Kingship you accepted upon yourselves in Egypt;' [and when] they said, 'Yes,' He continued, 'Now, just as you accepted My Kingship upon yourselves, accept [now] My decrees.'" A very similar interpretation is given by R. Simeon b. Yoḥai to Leviticus 18:2–3. Most likely these interpretations are projections in Haggadah of the daily acceptance of *malkut Shamayim* through Ḳeri'at Shema'; at the same time, however, the scriptural passages so interpreted may well have taught acceptance of *malkut Shamayim* and commitment to the miẓwot here and now. Certainly the Ten Commandments carried such an implication. Coupling the first statement there—"I am the Lord thy God"—with the third commandment, the rabbis teach that he who is accustomed to swear in vain or falsely does not accept upon himself the full kingship of God (מלכות שמים שלמה), and he who is not thus accustomed does accept upon himself the full kingship of God.[167] Indeed, the tradition persisted that the Ten Commandments contained the same themes as the Ḳeri'at Shema', a tradition probably going back to the priests' service in the Temple where the Ten Commandments were recited preceding the Ḳeri'at Shema'.[168]

Not only the Shema' and the Ten Commandments referred, in accordance with rabbinic interpretation, to the acceptance of *malkut Shamayim* and commitment to the miẓwot, but other scriptural texts as well. This is borne out by R. Simeon b. Yoḥai's interpretation of Leviticus 18:2–3. The Sifre seems to indicate that the scholars, at least, sought out texts of that kind, and that these texts, "when reflected upon," gave them additional opportunities to accept *malkut Shamayim* and to commit themselves to the miẓwot.

D. The Berakot of the Shema'

In the morning liturgy the berakah immediately preceding the Shema' begins as follows: "With abounding love hast Thou loved us, O Lord our God. Great and exceeding compassion hast Thou had for us. O our Father, our King, for our father's sake, who trusted in Thee, and whom Thou didst teach the statutes of life, be also gracious to us and teach us."[169] In *Siddur R. Saadia Gaon* the text is slightly different, but there, too, the idea is expressed that God has loved us and has had compassion for us "and taught us the statutes of life," the statement closing with the plea that He continue in this wise to be gracious to us.[170]

This berakah, second in the order of the berakot which precede the Shema', is called in the Babli (the Babylonian Talmud), because of the opening words, 'Ahabah Rabbah.[171] The Yerushalmi, however, calls it Birkat Torah.[172] That name, according to Elbogen, corresponds with the content of the berakah which, he says, consists of thanksgiving for the giving of Torah.[173] But the berakah takes for granted that God gave the Torah. The concept embedded in the berakah is study of Torah, not the giving of Torah, the thought being that God teaches us now, and at all times, by means of the words of the Torah and that the very understanding of the Torah is a gracious gift from God. When we study Torah, and understand what we study, it is God himself Who is our Teacher: "Thou didst teach the statutes of life"; "Be gracious to us and teach us"; and further on, "Enlighten our eyes in Thy Torah, and let our hearts cleave to thy miẓwot."[174] When we study and acquire knowledge of Torah, therefore, we are the objects of God's "abounding love." Precisely the same idea is expressed in the parallel berakah said before the Shema' in the evening: "With everlasting love Thou hast loved the house of Israel, Thy people; Torah and miẓwot, statutes and judgments hast Thou taught us."[175] In each case, the berakah immediately before the Shema' begins with giving thanks to God for teaching us Torah and for the knowledge gained through study, both of which are felt to be manifestations of God's love.[176] Anticipating th recital of the Shema', this section of the berakah stresses that aspect of Ḳeri'at Shema' which constitutes study of Torah.

A statement in 'Ahabah Rabbah also anticipates the recital of the Shema' as an acknowledgment of *malkut Shamayim*. Our version of that statement amplifies slightly the one in *Siddur R. Saadia Gaon*, which reads: כי בנו בחרת מכל עם ולשון וקרבתנו לשמך להודות לך וליחדך.[177] Let us consider, for a moment, the last phrase of this statement. Elsewhere we have demonstrated that מודים אנחנו לך in the 'Amidah refers to the acknowledgment of God, and that this phrase is linked in rabbinic literature with the acceptance of *malkut Shamayim*;[178] moreover, the two ideas are explicitly linked in the long berakah after the Shema' in the phrase: הודו והמליכו ואמרו וכו׳.[179] Acknowledgment of God is similarly linked with the acceptance of *malkut Shamayim* in the phrase, להודות לך וליחדך, except that now, in the word וליחדך, there is a particular reference to the Shema'. The section of the berakah which precedes the whole statement, and which consists of a plea for the restoration of Israel, varies greatly in the different versions, and that fact, as well as the content of the section, indicates that it is a later interpolation.[180]

Let us now consider the first phrase of the statement—כי בנו בחרת מכל עם ולשון. The idea here does not contain a rabbinic concept of the chosen people, for there is no such rabbinic concept. Always, without exception, a rabbinic value concept is represented in rabbinic literature by a substantive; that is, by a conceptual term which can abstract and classify. But the idea present here is not represented by a conceptual term in rabbinic literature, and that means that it is always tied to another idea which does possess a conceptual term. Here it is tied to the concept of *malkut Shamayim*, the emphasis being on that concept and not on our having been chosen. We thank God because He has permitted us or enabled us to acknowledge His kingship.

Furthermore, as used in the liturgy, the verb בחר in the present tense always signifies "to take delight in," "to love," rather than "to choose." In the daily berakah after the recital of the psalms,[181] for example, the word הבוחר cannot possibly mean that God has chosen the psalms from among other writings;[182] likewise, in the berakah before the Hafṭarah that word certainly does not convey the idea that God has chosen the Torah from among other possible Torot. The words הבוחר בעמו ישראל, at the end of 'Ahabah Rabbah, can only mean, therefore, that God loves or takes delight in Israel, a meaning that seems to be corroborated by the text in *Siddur R. Saadia* which does not have the redundant באהבה.[183] Although the idea is similar to that of the closing formula of the parallel berakah in the evening, the wording here expresses gratitude for God's love in enabling us both to study Torah and to acknowledge His kingship.[184]

'Ahabah Rabbah, unlike the berakot we discussed above, is not occasioned by a phenomenal experience. This berakah is called forth by an act yet to be performed by the individual, the very anticipation of the act being an experience in itself. In anticipating the act of study, the individual feels that God Himself is the teacher, and in anticipating the acceptance of *malkut Shamayim* he has a sense of a high privilege being conferred by God; and both anticipations blend in a single berakah of gratitude for God's love in a unitary experience of worship. Notwithstanding allusions to Israel's past in this berakah, it is the individual who has this experience of worship—the individual in his role as a representative of Israel. In early times, according to Ginzberg, the individual most likely recited the Shema' and its berakot immediately upon arising in the morning[185] and hence by himself and not with the community at prayer.

Formally, the berakah just before the Shema' and the berakah just after it are not independent berakot, since they do not have an opening formula. Indeed, they are constituents of a chain of berakot, the first of which, as we shall see, is touched off by a phenomenal experience and does have an opening formula; that is why, no doubt, the Yerushalmi gives the berakot adjacent to the Shema' as instances of berakot "joined to the preceding berakah."[186] On the other hand, the Tosefta certainly implies that these berakot are not "joined to the preceding berakah," and later authorities stress that implication.[187] This view, it seems to us, takes cognizance of the orientation of these berakot, for both 'Ahabah Rabbah and the berakah following the Shema' are oriented to the Shema', and it is that orientation, rather than their position in the chain of berakot, which determines their character. In fact, there is a rabbinic rule to the effect that the successive order of the berakot of the Shema' is not mandatory, the rule itself being based on the practice of the priests in the Temple who said 'Ahabah Rabbah alone before the Ten Commandments and Ḳeri'at Shema'.[188] Our point is that, although 'Ahabah Rabbah and the berakah following the Shema' are constituents of a chain of berakot, their real character derives from their association with the Shema'.

'Emet we-Yaẓẓib, the berakah following the Shema', is at once oriented to the Shema' and a meditative experience in its own right. Ideas of the Shema' are given a new turn in the berakah.

Rules of the Halakah enable the individual to achieve a meditative experience in this case, too. "He who recites the Shema' in the morning," states a baraita in the Yerushalmi, "ought to make mention of (להזכיר) the Exodus from Egypt in 'Emet we-Yaẓẓib. Rabbi [Judah the Prince] says, 'He ought to make mention there of the Kingship [of God] [*malkut*].' Others say, 'He ought to make mention of the division of the Red Sea and the plague of the first-born.' R. Joshua b. Levi says, 'He ought to make mention of all these [matters] and ought to say [at the end], Rock of Israel and his Redeemer.' "[189] As Lieberman has indicated, there was a period when it was not yet the established practice to specify the division of the Red Sea and the plague of the first-born,[190] apparently because, we should say, they are only details of the Exodus itself. The idea-content of the meditative experience had to do with the Exodus and with *malkut*.

The impetus to recall the Exodus from Egypt in the berakah is given by the last verse in the third paragraph of the Shema': "I am the Lord, your God, Who brought you out of the land of Egypt, to be your God" (Num. 15:41). This is to be inferred from the baraita just quoted. In mishnaic times, the third paragraph of the Shema' was recited only in the morning and not in the evening;[191] accordingly, the baraita states that he who recites the Shema' in the morning ought to make mention of the Exodus, the inference being that when the third paragraph is not recited, there is no reason to make mention of the Exodus in the berakah.[192]

If we turn now to the berakah itself, we find that the Exodus is referred to not only explicitly but, in fervent words, by implication. The Exodus is an event the significance of which is conveyed by the concept of *ge'ullah*, redemption. Phrases which contain only forms of the root of the conceptual word *ge'ullah* refer to the Exodus merely by implication, but they are phrases which are highly connotative and charged with significance: גואלנו גואל אבותינו and גאל ישראל or צור ישראל וגואלו.[193] Specific references to Egypt, too, contain forms of the conceptual word, as in ממצרים גאלתנו.[194] We may say, then, that, although the Exodus is recalled in the Shema', it is the berakah which expresses the significance of the Exodus; and this was probably already the case in very early times, for Ginzberg has shown that the first statement in the baraita goes back at least to the period of the schools of Shammai and Hillel.[195] Incidentally, since the Exodus is an instance of *ge'ullah*, the connotation of *ge'ullah* is redemption from servitude or oppression, and not, as some modern writers would have it, redemption from sin.

The idea of *malkut*, too, is given a new turn in the berakah. *Malkut* as a technical term, Ginzberg points out, may refer to God either as King of the world or as King of Israel, and he adds that, both in the morning and the evening, what the berakah after the Shema' speaks of is the sovereignty of God over Israel.[196] That berakah also indicates, however, that it is the acceptance of *malkut Shamayim* which gives rise to the fresh awareness of God's kingship over Israel. "*'Emet*, it is true," declares the berakah, thus first affirming the experience of Ḳeri'at Shema', "it is true: the God of the world is our King, the Rock of Jacob."[197] On the other hand, there is now an emphasis on the idea of God as the Protector of Israel, the Rock of Jacob, and hence an emphasis on the concept of God's love rather than on that of *malkut Shamayim*.

In the berakah after the Shema', the redemption from Egypt is felt to be an event which took place in the individual's own day, and not only an event of the remote past. "True it is," the individual says, "that Thou art indeed the Lord our God, and the God of our fathers, our King, King of our fathers, our Redeemer, the Redeemer of our fathers."[198] In the text as given in *Siddur R. Saadia*, there is almost a demarcation between the event as an experience of the present and the event as a happening in the past: גואלינו וגאל את

אבותינו.[199] There is indeed so strong an awareness of the redemption, so poignant a sense of the event as a present actuality, that in the evening berakah references to details of the Exodus are couched in the present tense: העושה לנו נסים וכו׳.[200] We have here, then, a meditative experience which is extraordinarily vivid.

The belief that God brought Israel out of Egypt, we have demonstrated elsewhere, is a rabbinic dogma.[201] A rabbinic dogma is a matter of belief, not a matter of personal experience, a belief that an event did take place or will take place. Often, however, the dogma is mitigated by the endeavor to render the event of the past, imaginatively, a matter of personal experience. The Passover Seder is such an attempt, its theme being, in the words of the Passover Haggadah, that "in every generation, a man is duty-bound to look upon himself as though he personally had gone out of Egypt."[202] But this quotation from the Passover Haggadah and from the Mishnah[203] is not just the theme of the Passover Seder; it is a halakah, and it is stated in general terms. It reflects a meditative experience on the part of the individual, not at the Passover Seder alone, but one which is achieved every day in the berakah after the Shema', except that now the background is different. In place of the imaginative reliving of the Exodus through the cumulative effect of the Passover Seder, the consciousness of God as King, Protector, and Redeemer of Israel rises now out of the previous experience of Ḳeri'at Shema'.[204]

In subject-matter, the First Berakah in the series is entirely unrelated to Ḳeri'at Shema'. It has not only a closing formula, as do the other two berakot, but also an opening formula. Thus in the morning it opens with "Blessed art Thou, O Lord our God, King of the world, Who formest light and createst darkness, Who makest peace and createst all things";[205] and it closes with "Blessed art Thou, O Lord, Who formest the lights."[206] Already given in the Talmud,[207] the statements here are in consonance with the following phrase in the berakah, likewise, in the main, found in the Talmud, although in quite a different context: "[And in His goodness, He] renews the Creation every day continually."[208] What is expressed in all these statements is the feeling on the part of the individual who witnesses the sunrise that God creates anew every day the light of the day. The sunrise, which is a phenomenal experience, is interpreted by the berakah to be a manifestation of God's love, a present act of God's, as it were, the occasion and the berakah together constituting a unitary, experiential entity. Once more a daily event is, through a berakah, charged with significance; and once more, through that same act of worship, the individual is given a sense of kinship with the whole world, a kinship again expressed in yet another phrase: "Who in lovingkindness givest light to the earth and to them that dwell thereon."[209]

The connection between this berakah and Ḳeri'at Shema' is really only a temporal one. Sunrise marks the beginning of the period for the recitation of Ḳeri'at Shema' in the morning, as we have seen above,[210] but the sunrise is itself an element in an integrated experience of worship. Ḳeri'at Shema' and its berakot can be recited, therefore, only after the berakah on the lights has already been said. When the Shema' was recited before sunrise, however, as was done by the priests in the Temple, there was no occasion to say the berakah on the lights at that time, but only the berakah immediately preceding the Shema'.[211] Of course, it is true that ordinarily the berakah on the lights is recited as the first of a series, and this practice is, no doubt, the basis for the view that the berakot adjacent to the Shema' are instances of berakot "joined to the preceding berakah."[212]

There is reference in this berakah, also, to the Messianic redemption—a petition which consists of the phrase, "O cause a new light to shine upon Zion."[213] Saadia objects to this phrase on the ground that, as ordained by the *Ḥakamim*, the theme of the berakah is simply the light which we have every day, and he therefore omits the phrase in his *Siddur*.[214] His stricture as to the mention of a future redemption thus applies only to this berakah.[215] We have noticed, however, that petitions for redemption in the other berakot of the Shema' are later additions,[216] and Ginzberg points out that, originally, none of the berakot of the Shema' contained any reference to a future redemption.[217] Nevertheless, if we hold that the berakah on the lights has a single theme, we have to account for the presence of the Ḳedushah in this berakah. Saadia does include it here in his order of public worship,[218] although he omits it in his section on the individual's worship, for another reason.[219]

The berakot of the Shema' are formally constituents of a single series. They can be taken as members of the same series because, ordinarily, the berakah on the lights, the Yoẓer, precedes the others;

moreover, the berakot do present a conceptual continuum, since each of them is an acknowledgment, in one way or another, of God's love. But the conceptual continuum is not a basic one, for the Yoẓer does not impart an impetus to the berakah adjacent to the Shema'. Ḳeri'at Shema' represents a new experience, only temporally associated with the Yoẓer, an experience so profound and moving as to give rise to a berakah before and after it. Before Ḳeri'at Shema', the anticipation of studying Torah and at the same time of accepting upon oneself the kingship of God becomes itself a religious experience, and the individual is moved to thank God for enabling him to study Torah and for permitting him to acknowledge *malkut Shamayim*. When the Shema' has been said, the recitation gives rise to another experience, a meditative experience, in which the individual, guided by the Halakah, comes to regard the redemption from Egypt as an event of his own day. Ḳeri'at Shema' and the berakot associated with it are, in a sense, a continuous religious experience.

CHAPTER V

The Daily Tefillah ('Amidah)

A. The Conceptual Continuum in the Tefillah

In Palestine the Daily Tefillah, in the second century C.E., consisted of eighteen berakot,[1] and thus "Eighteen" (*Shemoneh 'Esreh*) came to be a common designation not only for the Daily Tefillah, but also for the Tefillah on the Sabbath and festivals, even though on those occasions the Tefillah consists of fewer berakot. Conforming to the practice of Babylon, however, the Daily Tefillah now has nineteen berakot, not because another was added there, but because Babylon kept to the very early practice of not combining the Fourteenth and Fifteenth Berakot, whereas in Palestine these two Berakot were made into a single berakah.[2] Of these berakot, the first three and the last three are characterized by the rabbis as "praise of God [*Maḳom*]," and the "middle" berakot as referring to "the needs of men."[3] Because the middle berakot contain petitions, the Eighteen Berakot as a whole are designated as *ha-Tefillah*, the Prayer.[4] In fact, the word tefillah, prayer, became so closely associated with the Eighteen Berakot that it was used as warrant for regarding other words in biblical texts as referring to these berakot, among such other words being the term 'Amidah.[5]

In the days of the Second Temple—as a controversy between the schools of Shammai and Hillel indicates—the six berakot characterized as "praise" were already the fixed elements of every Tefillah.[6] Two in the last group of berakot, indeed, were originally part of the Temple service itself.[7] Undoubtedly, therefore, the Tefillah was ordained by the Men of the Great Synagogue, as the rabbis explicitly say.[8] On the other hand, the Talmud also records that Simeon Ha-Paḳoli arranged the Eighteen Berakot in their successive order "before R. Gamaliel at Jabne."[9] The sources are not contradictory, however, as Ginzberg has pointed out, but only tell of different stages in the development of the Tefillah, the berakot not having had the present order until Simeon so arranged them.[10] Lieberman also draws the conclusion that before Jabne it had been permitted to enlarge the Tefillah by saying more than the Eighteen Berakot.[11] Moreover, arranging the berakot must have involved a general editing of them, although in a manner which still left the wording of the berakot not entirely fixed. Numerous variants in the texts of the early versions testify to the fluid character of the berakot for centuries after the tannaitic period, so far as the wording was concerned.

A conceptual continuum results from the form of the Tefillah, a form through which the berakot express a series of successive experiences.[12] The form of the Tefillah allows one concept, God's love, to be carried over from one berakah to the next. Beginning with, "Blessed art Thou, O Lord our God and God of our Fathers, God of Abraham, God of Isaac and God of Jacob, the great, mighty and awesome God, the most high God," and closing with, "Blessed art Thou, O Lord, the Shield of Abraham,"[13] the First Berakah, designated in the Mishnah as 'Abot (Fathers or Patriarchs),[14] is the only one in the series which has both an opening and a closing formula. Every berakah which follows is "a berakah which is joined to the immediately preceding berakah," and hence has only a closing formula. A meditative, nonphenomenal experience of worship, and in that respect not like the First Berakah either in the Birkat ha-Mazon or in the berakot of the Shema', 'Abot represents an experience of God's love that imparts an impetus to a further act of worship and the latter, in turn, imparts an impetus to still another act of worship, and so on.[15] There need be no given limit to such a series, as we saw in an earlier section, for each berakah is a unitary entity in itself;[16] that is why the Tefillah could consist, at various times, of more than eighteen berakot or of fewer. What needs explanation is, essentially, not the length of the series in the Tefillah, but rather the occasion for the Tefillah. What kind of an occasion can it be that gives rise to a nonphenomenal, meditative religious experience, the experience expressed in 'Abot? The answer involves other aspects of the Tefillah and we shall come to it in due course.

A berakah in the Tefillah may embody other value concepts beside the concept of God's love. For example, the Fifth Berakah, closing with "Who delightest in *teshubah* [repentance]," fuses the concepts of God's love and *teshubah*; and the Sixth, closing with, "Who dost abundantly [i.e., again and again] forgive," fuses the concepts of God's love and forgiveness.[17] In these and many similar instances, the presence of other concepts in a berakah only emphasizes God's love, and the conceptual continuity is, therefore, also emphasized all the more. This cannot be said now of the Third and of the Twelfth Berakot; in both of these, the inclusion of other concepts not present in those berakot originally tends to weaken the conceptual continuum.

The Third Berakah, Ḳedushat ha-Shem,[18] consists, in the Palestinian version, of a brief statement (the first four words of which are given in the Sifre)[19] on the holiness of God and the berakah closes with "Blessed art Thou, the holy God."[20] The statement "Holy art Thou and awesome is Thy Name, and there is no God beside Thee"[21] does not attempt to express any specific experience. We shall see later that a vivid awareness of God's holiness involves the presence of at least ten Jews: a *parhesya'* in the case of a heroic act of *ḳiddush ha-Shem*, and a *ẓibbur* in the case of a liturgical act of *ḳiddush ha-Shem*.[22] If it does not relate to an actual experience, however, the Third Berakah, in its Palestinian version, does make a fitting close to the series of berakot here "in praise of God." This Third Berakah is thus bound with the first two meditative experiences even though it is not a meditative experience in itself. What is more, it does not interrupt the conceptual continuum. The concept of *ḳedushah*, holiness, has an association with God's love, and that association is reflected in the Third Berakah on New Year and on the Day of Atonement. On those days the Palestinian version is recited, but with the addition of the proof-text "And the Lord of hosts is exalted in judgment, and the holy God is sanctified in *ẓedaḳah*" (Isa. 5:16).[23] This verse was chosen not only because the first half was taken to refer to the "ten days between New Year and the Day of Atonement," the days when God "is exalted in judgment,"[24] but also because the second half goes on to speak of God's charity or mercy at that very period of judgment, for according to the rabbis, *ẓedaḳah* stands for charity or love in this verse,[25] and indeed in almost every verse in which the word occurs.[26] The holy God is made holy, sanctified in His charity at judgment. In the brief Palestinian version, a version to which no other concept has been added, the concept of holiness in the Third Berakah has, then, an association with God's love, since the verse, as the rabbis interpret it, only carries out the holiness theme of the berakah.[27]

Finkelstein has called attention to the difference in the Third Berakah between the Palestinian version and the non-Palestinian versions. He rightly concludes that, since the Palestinian version contains no reference to the Ḳedushah and the others do contain such references, the Ḳedushah was not part of the Third Berakah when the Palestinian version was formulated and that the others are later versions formulated after the Ḳedushah had been inserted.[28] We must add, however, that the non-Palestinian versions differ in a striking manner from each other as well; they differ in the character of their references to the Ḳedushah. In the version where the reference consists of וקדושים בכל יום יהללוך, "And holy beings praise Thee daily," reciting the Ḳedushah was regarded as simply telling of the praise of the angels; whereas in the version where the reference consists of ולנצח נצחים קדושתך נקדיש, the words קדושתך נקדיש correspond to נקדש את שמך, the words with which the whole section on the Ḳedushah begins, and both these phrases alike refer to the Ḳedushah as an act of worship and as an act of *ḳiddush ha-Shem*.[29] After the Ḳedushah was attached to the Third Berakah, there apparently was a period when the Ḳedushah was not an act of worship in itself but merely an enlargement of the Third Berakah, an addition to the original statement on God's holiness in the berakah, telling by means of biblical verses of how the angels praise God by reciting, "Holy, holy," etc.; it is this enlargement of the berakah which is reflected in the version containing the phrase "and holy beings praise Thee daily." But the Ḳedushah also crystallized into an act of worship in itself, an act of *ḳiddush ha-Shem* (as we shall see in the next chapter), and in time a reference to that act of *ḳiddush ha-Shem* was put into the Third Berakah itself. This berakah was thereby given a character which makes it different from all the other berakot of the Tefillah. All the other berakot express various aspects of God's love; the concept of *ḳiddush ha-Shem* expressed in the Third Berakah does not refer to an act by God but to an act by man. It is only the cumulative effect of the preceding berakot which overcomes this break in the conceptual continuum.[30]

Except for phrases added later, the Twelfth Berakah, like the rest, was formulated in the period of the Second Temple. It contains a petition for the uprooting of "the arrogant kingdom [מלכות זדון]"—an epithet for Rome, and earlier for Syria, as Ginzberg has shown.[31] Proof that this petition was the principal theme of the berakah is to be found in the closing formula of the old Palestinian version, for that formula consisted only of the words "Blessed art Thou, O Lord, Who dost subdue the arrogant (מכניע זדים)."[32] When the era of "the arrogant kingdom" is over, the age of perfect justice and peace will begin, the days of the Messiah or the world to come, and hence not God's justice alone is the concept embodied here but God's love as well. True, the petition and the berakah have reference only to the prelude of the new and perfect world order, but the prelude necessarily implies the sequel, and this is made evident in the Tefillah of Rosh ha-Shanah. In a prayer there, the phrase "when Thou makest the arrogant government [ממשלת זדון] to pass away from the earth" is followed directly by the statement "and Thou, O Lord, shalt reign, Thou alone, over all Thy works."[33] Evident, too, in that prayer is the fusion of God's love and His justice: "Then shall the righteous see and be glad; the upright shall exult and the pious rejoice in song, and iniquity shall close its mouth, and all wickedness shall be wholly consumed like smoke, when Thou makest the arrogant government to pass away from the earth."[34] What is implicit in the Twelfth Berakah of the Daily Tefillah is but given explicit expression in the prayer on Rosh ha-Shanah. Both contain the same idea; and not only the striking expression "the arrogant kingdom [or government]" which is common to both but, more especially, the closing formula of the Twelfth Berakah, bears witness that this idea was the theme of the Twelfth Berakah from the very beginning.

The petition of the berakah was expanded, however, to include references to Jewish separatists and to *minim*, sectarians.[35] If these dissident groups, among them some of the Judeo-Christian sects, were placed in a category with Rome as enemies of Israel, it was because they had demonstrated their antagonism to the nation as a whole in the period following the destruction of the Temple and denied Israel's belief in a national redemption.[36] The feeling against them expressed itself at Jabne when Samuel the Little, at the behest of R. Gamliel, formulated the berakah against the *minim*, a formulation which, as Lieberman explains, really meant amending the existing berakah so as to have it make specific mention of the *minim*.[37] A concept was thus inserted into the berakah which had not been present there before, the concept of *minim*. When this added concept was emphasized it became the major theme of the berakah.

On that score Palestine differed from Babylon. In Palestine, the *minim* were only an incidental theme in the berakah; in Babylon, on the other hand, they became, in effect, the major theme. Ginzberg shows that the very manner of referring to the Twelfth Berakah is indicative. In the Yerushalmi, it indicates that the main theme of the berakah is "subduing the arrogant," while in the Babylonian Talmud it indicates that the theme of "subduing the arrogant" is secondary to that of the *minim*.[38] Again, in the various versions of a Midrash on the Tefillah, the haggadot on the Twelfth Berakah have for their theme (as Ginzberg points out) enemies of Israel, "the arrogant," and never the *minim*,[39] and that Midrash, he demonstrates, is of Palestinian origin.[40]

The insertion of the *minim* into the Twelfth Berakah did not inevitably make for a break in the conceptual continuity, but it did make such a break or interruption possible. There was no interruption so long as the added concept remained an incidental theme, and this was the case in Palestine. On the other hand, when the added concept is emphasized and made the major theme of the berakah (as was the case in Babylon) the chain of experience inherent in the Tefillah is broken, and only the cumulative effect of the preceding berakot overcomes the break in the conceptual continuum.

We have left for the last, in this discussion of the Twelfth Berakah, the consideration of two halakot: a halakah in the Yerushalmi and a related halakah in the Babylonian Talmud. A baraita in the Yerushalmi states that a leader who has omitted two or three berakot in the Tefillah is not made to go back and say them "*except* when he has not said, 'Who quickenest the dead' [the Second Berakah], or 'Who dost subdue the arrogant' [the Twelfth Berakah], or 'Who buildest Jerusalem' [the Fourteenth Berakah], [for] I conclude he may be a *min*."[41] A suspicion of being a *min* thus attaches not just to him who has omitted the Twelfth Berakah but to a person who has omitted any one of the three berakot named here; the berakot are mentioned in accordance with their order in the Tefillah and the phrase "I conclude he may be a *min*" follows the last berakah named, the Fourteenth, and hence must refer to the omission of any one of these berakot. Evidently, then, the three berakot have a character in common. Furthermore, since each can become a means for testing whether the leader is a *min*, the character which is common to all of them must have to do with rabbinic dogma. Now we found, in an earlier discussion, that the concept of the days of the Messiah and the other hereafter concepts are not pure value concepts, but are rabbinic dogmas which possess a degree of specificity which the value concepts do not have, pointing to such specific events as the ingathering of the Diaspora and the building of Jerusalem.[42] This explains why the berakot named in the baraita relate to rabbinic dogma. Specific events indubitably constitute the themes of the Second and Fourteenth Berakot, future events pointed to by hereafter concepts. Those berakot involve rabbinic dogma because they embody not only the concept of God's love but also concepts of the hereafter, the days of the Messiah or the world to come. That is likewise true of the Twelfth Berakah for, as we saw, its major theme is the uprooting of "the arrogant kingdom," a specific event of the future which is the prelude to the days of the Messiah or the world to come. When the baraita speaks of the Twelfth Berakah, it refers, as do similar references in the Yerushalmi, to the original, major theme of the berakah.

The halakah in the Babylonian Talmud declares that if the leader has omitted (טעה) any of the berakot of the Tefillah he is not removed, but if it be the "Birkat ha-Minim he is removed, [for] we apprehend lest he be a *min*."[43] Here, as in the Yerushalmi, the apprehension is lest a *min* be the leader in the Tefillah, but otherwise the halakot are different. By naming no berakot other than the Twelfth, the Babylonian halakah reveals that, unlike the Yerushalmi, its ground for apprehension is something other than the leader's omission to say berakot embodying concepts concerning the hereafter. It is simply a matter of the *min* having given himself away by omitting the berakah which contains a prayer for the destruction of his sect, and that is why he is to be removed forthwith. Once again the

Babylonian Talmud has made the added concept of the *minim* the major theme of the Twelfth Berakah.

A Yelammedenu (a homily beginning with an inquiry regarding a halakah) passage combines the halakah in the Yerushalmi with the Babylonian halakah and also contains an idea not found in either. We may divide the passage, for the purpose of analysis, into three parts. In the first part, which largely employs the phraseology of the Babylonian halakah, only the Birkat ha-Minim is named, but now the leader who omits it is to be made to go back to the berakah, as the Yerushalmi teaches.[44] The passage continues with an idea not expressed in either the Yerushalmi or the Babylonian halakah: "And he is to recite it even against his will. And why do we make him go back? We apprehend lest he be a *min*; if he indeed holds a heretical doctrine, [by reciting the berakah] he utters a curse against himself to which the congregation responds, 'Amen.' "[45] A statement then follows which is reminiscent of the Yerushalmi but which mentions only the Fourteenth Berakah: "And so, too, he who has not said 'Who buildest Jerusalem' is made to go back [for] we apprehend lest he be a *Kuti* [Samaritan]."[46] The first and the last parts of the passage are palpably post-talmudic; the first part because it utilizes the crystallized halakot of *both* the Yerushalmi and the Babylonian Talmud, and the last part because it reflects a development of the post-talmudic period. Instead of completing the list given in the Yerushalmi, the last part of the Yelammedenu passage names only the Fourteenth Berakah and makes no mention of the Second, "Who quickenest the dead," and yet *Masseket Kutim*, a Palestinian (Yerushalmi) treatise,[47] indicates that the *Kutim* not only refused to acknowledge Jerusalem but also denied the quickening of the dead,[48] the dogma in the Second Berakah; if, therefore, the Yelammedenu gives as a test for a *Kuti* the recitation of the Fourteenth Berakah alone, the passage must have been composed in the post-talmudic period when the Samaritans had come to accept the dogma of the quickening of the dead.[49] Indeed, the entire passage is post-talmudic, the middle part as well, for the middle part is based on the first part, giving a reason for the halakah stated in the first part.

The Yelammedenu passage depicts the Twelfth Berakah, when uttered by a *min*, as a curse directed against himself. This is an idea which is not to be found either in the Babylonian halakah or in the Yerushalmi. According to the former, the leader suspected of being a *min* is to be removed and hence he is not to be permitted to say the Twelfth Berakah at all. According to the Yerushalmi, the leader is suspected of being a *min* if he has omitted the Second, the Twelfth, or the Fourteenth Berakah; in that case he must go back and say whichever of these three he has omitted. All three are tests of a *min* because all three contain dogmas, embodying the concepts of the days of the Messiah or the world to come. No distinction is made in the Yerushalmi between these berakot, and the Twelfth Berakah is not singled out as different in kind from the others, as a berakah which is a denunciation. Nevertheless, although only the Yelammedenu passage depicts this berakah as a denunciation, we need not conclude that the idea is altogether post-talmudic. It may have been an interpretation already placed upon the berakah in talmudic times—not by the rabbis, to be sure, but by the folk.[50] Be that as it may, we do find such an interpretation of the berakah by post-talmudic authorities, some of whom clearly take it for granted that the term Birkat ha-Minim is a euphemism for ḳilelat (denunciation of) ha-Minim.[51]

B. Prayer, Berakah, and the Self

Tefillah, we noticed in the preceding section, is a word which stands for both the 'Amidah and for prayer in general.[52] Tefillah also applies more specifically to the middle section of the 'Amidah, the section that follows the berakot of praise. This the rabbis indicate when, in support of their statement that the petitions of the Tefillah ought to be preceded by praise of God, they interpret *rinnah** in I Kings 8:28 to be *tehillah*, praise, and then say that the word tefillah which follows *rinnah* in that verse means *baḳḳashah*, petition or request.[53]

Prayer is petition of a special kind. To pray is "to beseech compassion" from God—*le-baḳḳesh raḥamim*.[54] Thus the rabbis declare, "Anyone who can beseech compassion for his fellow and does not beseech is called a sinner," and they cite as proof I Samuel 12:23: "Far be it from me that I should sin against the Lord by ceasing to

* Literally, "song," hence praise. Usually translated "cry."

pray [*le-hitpallel*] for you."[55] Just as the word Tefillah stands for the entire 'Amidah, so also does the Talmud characterize the Tefillah itself as *raḥame*,[56] referring by that word alone to the beseeching of compassion from God.[57] A tefillah, then, is the beseeching of compassion from God, an appeal to His *middat raḥamim*, to His love or mercy.

But the 'Amidah has a dual character. Not only does the section of praise consist of berakot, but every petition in the 'Amidah concludes with a berakah and hence the term "Eighteen Berakot" as a designation for the daily 'Amidah.[58] It is not our purpose, at present, to account for the rabbinic nomenclature: we are simply pointing out that the designations for the 'Amidah reflect its dual character of tefillah and berakah.

Between a berakah and a prayer there is a fundamental distinction. A berakah refers to something which has already taken place, or else to something felt as taking place in the present. On the other hand, a prayer or petition refers to something which one hopes will take place. R. Ze'ira makes this distinction between a berakah and a prayer when he contrasts a phrase in the Ḳiddush of the Sabbath, the Ḳiddush being a berakah, with a similar phrase in the Tefillah of the Sabbath. The Ḳiddush contains the phrase "Who has sanctified us by Thy miẓwot," whereas the Tefillah contains the phrase "O sanctify us by Thy miẓwot." Why? Because the Tefillah is "the beseeching of compassion."[59]

Every petition in the 'Amidah closes with a berakah. Yet a petition is tefillah, beseeching God for a particular manifestation of His love or compassion. On the other hand, a berakah, we repeat, is usually an expression of gratitude for a particular manifestation of God's love, a manifestation experienced either in some phenomenal manner or through meditation; the berakah itself is an element in that experience, interpreting and enhancing it. On the surface, therefore, a petition which closes with a berakah appears to contain a basic contradiction: something which has not been experienced is prayed for and apparently immediately afterwards it is acknowledged in gratitude as something that has already been experienced. There is no contradiction, however. What is necessary now is a clearer apprehension of a psychological factor we have spoken of before: namely, the larger self and its role in the consciousness and experiences of the individual. It is the larger self which is expressed in prayers and berakot relating to needs men have in common. In the prescribed prayers and berakot, private needs are by no means ignored but the greater emphasis is placed on the common needs.

A prayer or berakah in which the individual refers to himself in the first person singular expresses a private need. This is the case, for example, in the following prayer to be said by a person upon entering a town: "May it be Thy will, O Lord my God, that I enter in peace [לשלום]."[60] Similarly, again speaking in the first person singular, the individual, after having entered the town safely, is to say, "I thank Thee, O Lord my God, that Thou hast enabled me to enter in peace. May it likewise be Thy will to bring me forth in peace."[61] In like vein, and once more employing the first person singular, the individual is to thank God after having come forth from the city, and is also to say a prayer for his safe return home.[62] Part of a section dealing with prayers and thanksgiving of the same personal character,[63] the halakot just cited have Ben 'Azzai as authority and very likely reflect a period of Roman violence and lawlessness. We must add that the phrases of thanksgiving here, although not containing a berakah formula, nor even the root *brk*, are regarded as berakot; they are referred to as such when the texts or the variants introduce them with the word "*mebarek*," "says a berakah."[64]

In contradistinction to these prayers and berakot, the entire 'Amidah, including the petitions, is recited in the first person plural. The needs mentioned in the petitions are common needs, either those of mankind in general or of the whole people of Israel: knowledge and understanding, repentance, forgiveness by God, health, good crops, and the rebuilding of Jerusalem, to mention several. Because they relate to common needs, the "middle" berakot, those containing petitions, are designated at one place in the Yerushalmi as "the needs of men [צרכן של בריות]."[65] But the Tannaim, Ginzberg has pointed out, usually designate the middle berakot as "his needs [צרכיו]"[66]—that is, the needs of the individual. Now these needs relate to mankind as a whole or to Israel as a people. Not only are they not private needs, but at the moment of prayer they may not even be relevant to the individual, as is the case, for example, of the person in good health when he is reciting the Eighth Berakah with its petition for recovery from illness. Again, the Tenth Berakah is called "the Ingathering of the Exiles,"[67] and it closes with "Who gathereth the dispersed of His people, Israel" (after Is. 56:8), yet it was, of course, recited in Palestine as well as in the Diaspora. How is it that the individual can regard common needs as "his needs," even when they are not at the time his own needs at all?

The concept of man, its near alternate, *'olam* (world),[68] and the concept of Israel are value concepts. They do not represent external objects, basically, but are concepts of valuational experience and hence, their concretizations, like all concretizations of value concepts, are expressions of the self. Ordinarily the awareness of the self is not conceptualized, and even when expressed, must rely on the pronouns "I" and "my"; the concepts of man and Israel, however, have the special quality of supplying in their concretizations the awareness of the self with conceptual expression. On such occasions, the self is enlarged: a person is both himself and at the same time man, all men, or himself and all Israel. When, for example, after a meal, a man thanks God for feeding "the whole world," he refers, in his experience of worship, not just to "the whole world" but to himself as well. Similar in character are the petitions and berakot of the 'Amidah, except that they are more subtle expressions of the larger self. Not an actual experience, but the sheer knowledge of a common need of man is now the occasion for an individual's petition and he regards the common need as his need. Once more the awareness of the self is an awareness of the larger self. The pronoun used in those petitions and berakot is the first person plural, the plural standing not for a given number of individuals but for himself and all men, for man. We may put the entire matter more simply but not altogether correctly by saying, as we did earlier, that, when reciting such berakot, the individual senses himself to be a representative of man or of Israel.

The problem of the larger self is a fundamental problem, but a consideration of the 'Amidah may at least illumine some aspects of it. The key to the problem is to be found in the way the pronouns "we" or "us" are used by the individual. Ordinarily, when the individual says "we" he refers to himself and other individuals. Self-awareness, at such times, implies that the individual is also aware of other individuals. But this is not the case when the larger self comes into play. Then the word "we" as used by the individual refers to himself and, it is true, to others but not to others as individuals. The "others" are now undifferentiated; they are man or Israel, or any group within man or Israel, again not as individuals, but as man or Israel having, for the time, a distinguishing characteristic. For example, when the individual uses "we" or "us" in the petition of 'Ahabah Rabbah, the berakah before the Shema', he refers at that moment to himself and others, the "others" here being all of Israel. When, however, he says "we" and "us" in the petition for recovery from sickness, he is referring to himself and to man as characterized by sickness, to the undifferentiated group of men who are sick.[69] This is not identification of himself—if he is well—with those who are sick. On the one hand, the sick are not particular individuals with whom he can identify himself, and on the other, he is bound, on such an occasion, to be conscious of his own good health. The larger self allows an individual to be aware, poignantly aware, that there are others who are sick; the awareness is so strong that he associates himself with them, though at the same time retaining his self-identity. It is precisely in a petition of this kind, a petition not relevant to the individual qua individual and yet one in which he says "we" and "us", that the character of the larger self is best revealed. Self-identity is retained and the material circumstances of the individual have not changed; nevertheless, the self has become larger, more inclusive: large enough to include indefinite others and a consciousness of their needs.

There is no loss of self-identity either, even when the "others" are all men or all Israel. When reciting 'Ahabah Rabbah, for instance, the individual associates himself with all Israel in anticipating the recital of the Shema', but there can be no loss of self-identity. Acceptance of *malkut Shamayim* is incumbent upon each individual, and the commitments involved are personal commitments. The experience demands *kawwanah*, something in which no other individual can have a share. In anticipating this experience, the individual associates himself with all Israel but completely retains his self-identity. "We" and "us" in 'Ahabah Rabbah are expressions of the larger self.

We have noticed that the rabbis designate the 'Amidah as tefillah, "the beseeching of compassion" from God. A petition in the

'Amidah is no less a whole-souled prayer for a particular manifestation of God's compassion than is a prayer concerning a private need. Indeed, so completely in keeping with the character of true prayer are the petitions in the 'Amidah that a petition there reflects changing needs. The petition of the Ninth Berakah, the Mishnah says, is to include a prayer for rain,[70] and the insertion of this prayer, according to a baraita, is to depend "upon the nature of the seasons and upon the nature of the localities."[71]

Because they embody the concept of man or of Israel, the petitions in the 'Amidah are more than just petitions, however. They act as meditations, as well, being meditations of one type in petitions embodying the concept of man and largely of a second type in those embodying the concept of Israel. Petitions of the first type, those referring to the common needs of man, are, besides prayers, reminders to the individual that here and now man possesses the very things prayed for—that is, such a petition reminds the individual that there is a group within man, an undifferentiated group and not a given number of men, which at this moment possesses the thing prayed for. But to possess a thing which has been prayed for is to possess a gift from God, and hence the individual now says a berakah, thanking God for a particular manifestation of His love or compassion. The petition for a common need culminates in a meditative experience—an experience in which the individual, becoming aware of a manifestation of God's love, expresses that awareness in a berakah which itself enhances the experience.[72]

Although the individual associates himself in these petitions with others, that association, let us remember, is always with undifferentiated others. He associates himself with man, not with any definite group of men. Not being differentiated as individuals, the others may now be man with this distinguishing characteristic, now man with some other characteristic. Thus, in the petition for the recovery of the sick, the individual associates himself with man as characterized by illness, whereas in the berakah at the end of that petition he associates himself with man as characterized by being healed. The Fourth Berakah, again, is an instance, apparently, in which both petition and berakah involve the same "others." Here, before the petition, the individual recites an ascription which explicitly names man as the recipient of God's favor: "Thou favorest *'adam* [man] with knowledge, and teachest *'enosh* [another word for man] understanding."[73] In the petition, which employs the first person plural, he prays for "knowledge, understanding and discernment," (since these may fail man at any moment unless given anew by God)[74] and in the berakah he thanks God Who is "the gracious Giver of knowledge."[75] But the others in the petition may well include the witless, and if so, the others there are simply man, and not man as characterized by understanding or knowledge.

What has been called here the larger self is, essentially, the individual's awareness of a relationship between himself and others. In this consciousness of relationship, the awareness of the self is a stable element, for the individual always retains his self-identity in petitions and berakot. The awareness of others, on the contrary, is an unstable element: the others, we have just observed, may have now one character and now a different character. In fact, since the others may be either man or Israel, a petition may embody the concept of Israel whereas the berakah in which the petition culminates may embody the concept of man. For example, the petition in the Fifth Berakah reads: "Cause us to return, O our Father, to Thy Torah; draw us near, O our King, unto Thy service, and bring us back in complete repentance to Thee [before Thee]";[76] and "us" here manifestly refers to Israel, since Israel alone possesses the Torah. This petition, however, culminates in the following berakah: "Blessed art Thou, O Lord, Who delightest in [or, accepts] repentance";[77] but now the reference is to all who repent, to man as distinguished by repentance, for God accepts everyone who repents, Jew or Gentile.[78]

Sometimes the early Palestinian version of such a culminating berakah refers to man, and the later Babylonian version refers, instead, to Israel. That is the case with the Nineteenth Berakah, the early Palestinian version reading "Who makest peace"[79] where the Babylonian version reads "Who blesseth His people Israel with peace."[80] In all the versions, however, the petition of this berakah refers to Israel, for the petition takes its departure from the priests' blessing (Num. 6:24–26) preceding it, and the blessing itself is introduced in the verse immediately preceding with the words "On this wise ye shall bless the children of Israel."[81] Again, the Eighth Berakah concludes in the early Palestinian version with "Who healest the sick,"[82] and in the later Babylonian version with "Who healest the sick of His people Israel";[83] but in this case, the petition of the berakah has no specific reference to Israel and therefore we have every reason to assume that, in the early Palestinian version, petition and culminating berakah are of a piece, and hence that petition, as well as the berakah, refer to man.

In a previous section we found that the recitation of a berakah is an element in a moral experience, since a berakah interprets an event or situation as being a manifestation of God's love, and God's love is characterized as *raḥamim*, *ẓedaḳah*, and *gemilut ḥasadim*, all moral or ethical concepts.[84] When a berakah is recited, therefore, the scope of morality is made to extend beyond the range of purely human relations; not only that, but the individual's entire moral life is thereby strengthened, for any concretization of a moral concept, even if it consists simply of an interpretation of an event by the individual, in some degree strengthens that moral concept's very drive toward concretization.

A berakah in which the individual associates himself with man is a moral experience in a double sense. Besides interpreting a situation or a phenomenon as a manifestation of God's love, it calls into play a concept, man, which has moral implications with respect to human relations. At times, to be sure, the word "man" is no more than a description of a biological species, but at other times it has, on the contrary, a universalistic, valuational connotation.[85] *'Adam*, man, say the rabbis, "is a term of love, and a term of brotherhood, and a term of friendship"; [86] similarly, to call Ezekiel "the son of man" (Ezek. 2:1) is tantamount to calling him "the son of upright people, the son of righteous people, the son of those who do deeds of *gemilut ḥasadim*."[87] Statements such as these, conveying the moral connotations of the concept of man, are concretizations of the concept in Haggadah, in speech. When man is one of the concepts embodied in a berakah, it is again, of course, concretized in speech, yet not in speech alone; it is now a factor in a moral and emotional experience in which the dominant feeling is gratitude for a manifestation of God's love, and the moral implications of the concept of man are thus apprehended in a living rather than a literary context. An individual reciting a berakah in which he associates himself with man becomes aware not only of God's love but of a relationship to all men, a relationship "of love, of brotherhood, of friendship." We have here another instance of the organismic integration of concepts, another example of how a number of value concepts may combine in a unitary yet many-toned experience.[88]

Most of the berakot of the 'Amidah in which the individual associates himself with Israel embody concepts of the hereafter, the days of the Messiah or the world to come; these berakot represent a fusion of such concepts with the concept of God's love. Several berakot of this type we have already discussed: the Second Berakah ("Who quickenest the dead"), the Twelfth Berakah ("Who dost subdue the arrogant"), and the Fourteenth Berakah ("Who buildest Jerusalem").[89] By reason of the hereafter concepts which they embody all three berakot, we saw, have to do with rabbinic dogma. Concepts of the hereafter are not pure value concepts, for instead of being only suggestive or connotative, they point to specific events, events that, it is believed, will take place in the future; in fine, a hereafter concept represents a rabbinic dogma.[90]

What is true of the berakot just mentioned is also true of other berakot in the 'Amidah. Specific events regarded as certain to take place in the future constitute the themes of the Seventh Berakah (the redemption of Israel), the Tenth (the ingathering of the exiles), the Eleventh (the restoration of the judges, i.e., the Sanhedrin),[91] the Fifteenth (the flourishing of the sprout of David),[92] and the Seventeenth (the dwelling of the *Shekinah* in Zion and restoration of the Temple service).[93] All these future events are subsumed under the concept of the days of the Messiah or the world to come. Furthermore, these particular events of the future relate to the restoration of Israel and to that of the Temple in Jerusalem. When the individual recites petitions and berakot having those events as themes, therefore, the pronouns "us" and "we" mean that he now associates himself with Israel.[94]

Such petitions and berakot have a distinctive character of their own. We depicted that character when we dealt with the Third Berakah of the Birkat ha-Mazon, a berakah which is practically identical, in R. Saadia's version, with the Fourteenth Berakah of the 'Amidah.[95] A rabbinic comment on Psalm 31:24—"The Lord preserveth the faithful [*'emunim*]"—we found, indicates that still another concept is embodied in these berakot, the concept of *'emunah*. "They say: Who quickenest the dead, though the resurrection of the dead has not yet come; they say: Redeemer of Israel, though they are not yet redeemed; they say: Who buildest Jerusalem, though Jerusalem is not yet built. The Holy One Blessed be He says: Israel was redeemed for only a little while and then went into servitude, and [yet] they have faith [*ma'aminim*] in Me that I shall redeem them in a time to come."[96] *'Emunah* connotes faith or trust in God's word or promise, and the preordained events referred to in the 'Amidah, being matters of dogma, are taken as so many promises of God.[97] This is not to say that the petitions having these preordained events as their themes are not whole-souled petitions; on the contrary, the promised events are profoundly longed for and the petitions express that longing. What the embodied concept of *'emunah* does is to make of these petitions, even as they are being uttered, a meditative experience as well. So unbounded is the trust in God that present circumstances for the moment fade away and there is a pervasive consciousness that the promised event is indeed taking place right now. These meditative experiences culminate, therefore, in berakot employing the present tense: "Who gatherest the dispersed of His people Israel"; "Who buildest Jerusalem."

Rabbinic dogmas are concerned with events which, in a literal sense, are beyond the range of an individual's experience, but which become, especially during the recitation of the pertinent berakah, something akin to experience. "In the berakah after the Shema', the redemption from Egypt is felt to be an event that has taken place in the individual's own day, and not only as an event of the remote past."[98] Similarly, the closing formula of both berakot on the Torah uses the present tense—"Who givest the Torah"—thereby expressing the feeling that the Torah is being given "this day."[99] Now, sober reflection upon these events certainly did not place them literally within the range of the individual's experience. Rabbinic injunctions to recollect those events, it must be noticed, qualify the duty to recollect them with the phrase "as though"; "as though he [the individual] personally had gone forth out of Egypt";[100] and with respect to *mattan* (the giving of) *Torah*, "as though you received them [the statutes and ordinances] from Mount Sinai this day" and "as though you heard them this day."[101] In sober discussion of the 'Amidah, likewise, the promised events were regarded as imminent, but certainly not as a present reality.[102] It is primarily in berakot, acts expressing and enhancing religious experience, that these things, events ordinarily depicted as having taken place in the past and promised events of the future, take on the character of contemporary happenings. Events that are matters of dogma, of belief, lose their dogmatic character and become matters of personal experience. They become personal experiences, however, when the individual associates himself with Israel, for this is the case with all berakot having such events as themes.

These berakot help us to realize that, although berakot are in the category of Halakah, they also have a character of their own. In halakic discussions of the promised events of the future, or of the Exodus from Egypt and the giving of Torah, there is a clear awareness of future and of past, and the categories of time are not to the slightest degree obliterated. Haggadah, too, holds fast to the categories of time. In contrast, a berakah tends to interpret an event or situation as, in some sense, a present experience of God, and the other categories of time, when not obliterated in a berakah, always implicate the present.[103] Not being entirely subject to the categories of time, an experience expressed in a berakah has thus a mystical character, a character which we shall describe as "normal mysticism" when we take up the general problem of the rabbinic experience of God.

The Thirteenth Berakah was already in tannaitic times a composite of several berakot. From the Tosefta it is apparent that although originally there was a berakah in the 'Amidah concerning the *zeḳenim*, elders, and another berakah concerning the *gerim*, proselytes, the two were soon combined by expanding the petition in the former to include *gerim*.[104] A baraita in the Yerushalmi records a somewhat different tradition, namely, that the berakah on *zeḳenim* and the one on *gerim* should be included in "the Trust (*Mibṭaḥ*) of the *ẓaddiḳim* (righteous)";[105] this can only mean that the petition in the Thirteenth Berakah ought to refer not only to the *ẓaddiḳim* but also to the *zeḳenim* and to the *gerim*, the *ẓaddiḳim* being taken here as the major theme of the berakah.[106] In *Siddur R. Saadia Gaon*, the berakah reads as follows: "Towards the righteous and the pious and the true proselytes, may Thy mercies be stirred, O Lord, our God; and grant a good reward unto all who trust in Thy Name, and may they not be put to shame. Blessed art Thou, O Lord, the Stay and Trust of the righteous."[107]

Ẓaddiḳim, *zeḳenim*, *gerim*, and similar terms in the texts of the berakah are all value concepts.[108] A *ẓaddiḳ* may also be a *ḥasid* (pious),[109] and a *ger* may likewise be a *ẓaddiḳ*; hence such terms do not designate groups but are valuational characterizations of individuals. A person who prays for the welfare of these individuals does so, however, not because he may happen to know some of them, but because all of them are of especial concern to him when, as now, he associates himself with all Israel. That association is either explicitly expressed or else simply alluded to in the different versions of this berakah; in *Siddur R. Saadia* it is implied in the additional plea for "a good reward unto all who trust in Thy Name," but in the other versions it is expressed explicitly—as in our present version which adds to that plea "and set our portion with them," and as in the early Palestinian version which reads "and grant us a good reward."[110] "Us" refers to the person reciting the berakah and to the "undifferentiated others" with whom he is now associated, whereas the *ẓaddiḳim*, the *gerim*, etc., are the differentiated others who are the burden of the petition.

As given in the Yerushalmi, the closing formula of the berakah, we noticed, is "the Trust (*Mibṭaḥ*) of the *ẓaddiḳim*." Obviously God is also the Trust of the *zeḳenim*, the *gerim*, and all the others mentioned in the petition. He is, indeed, the Trust of all Israel, of "all who trust in Thy Name." The closing formula mentions the major theme of the berakah, the *ẓaddiḳim*, but in affirming that God is the Trust of the *ẓaddiḳim* it also affirms, by direct implication, that He is the Trust of all Israel. In fine, when the individual closes the berakah with the phrase "the Trust (*Mibṭaḥ*) of the *ẓaddiḳim*" he is expressing, as well, his own heart-felt trust in God. Embodied in that phrase is the concept of *biṭṭaḥon*, a term which connotes reliance on God for welfare and security,[111] and which is, therefore, to be distinguished from the kindred concept of *'emunah*, the trust in God's word or promise.

An expression of *biṭṭaḥon*, however, need not be only the culmination of a petition for welfare and security. Reliance on God is an abiding consciousness and hence may be expressed in a berakah of praise alone, one that does not contain a petition. Such an expression of *biṭṭaḥon* is the First Berakah in the 'Amidah, a berakah in which that concept is fused with the concepts of God's love and *'Abot* (Patriarchs). Being the First Berakah it has an opening as well as a closing formula,[112] and yet, because the concepts are fused, the berakah is a unitary entity. The two formulas are dependent on each other for their full meaning. In consonance with the opening formula, "Blessed art Thou, O Lord our God and God of our Fathers, God of Abraham, God of Isaac and God of Jacob," the closing formula praises God as "the Shield of Abraham" (in accordance with Gen. 15:1) and thus gives pre-eminence to the first Patriarch.[113] But if "Shield" as a metaphor for God's protecting love refers back to "God of Abraham," it also refers back to the phrase "our God and God of our Fathers"—God protected the Patriarchs and He protects us now, as well. Insofar as the First Berakah relates to the individual's own experience, therefore, it expresses gratitude for God's protection here and now; in other words, it is an expression of *biṭṭaḥon*.[114] This theme of *biṭṭaḥon* is emphasized in the Palestinian version by the phrase "our Shield and the Shield of our Fathers, our Trust (*Mibṭaḥenu*) in every generation,"[115] a phrase that immediately precedes the closing formula. In our version the same idea is expressed by the words "O King, Helper, Savior,[116] and Shield," words that, again, immediately precede the closing formula. The term "the Shield of Abraham" in the closing formula hence implies, at least, God's protection in the present, too. We ought to add that the section in our version affirming that God remembers the deeds of the Patriarchs and that He is bringing a redeemer to their children's children is not even hinted at in the Palestinian version; the themes of this section are not integral to the berakah.[117]

Biṭṭaḥon is, indeed, an abiding consciousness, but it will not become a crystallized experience without an occasion of some sort. That occasion, however, need be no more than a reminder and the occasion for the First Berakah, we shall see, is precisely of such a character.

The Tefillah or 'Amidah makes high demands upon the individual. In the first place, there must be the awareness on the part of the individual of a relationship between himself and others, but this in itself presents no difficulty when the concepts of Israel and of man are elements of the common value complex. Moreover, the very idea that one is saying the Tefillah also contributes to this expression of the larger self, as we can see from the "short Tefillah." This short Tefillah consists of a single petition which culminates in the berakah "Blessed art Thou, O Lord, Who hearkenest unto prayer," the closing formula of the Sixteenth Berakah. The short Tefillah is to be said instead of the regular Tefillah when a person journeys in dangerous territory.[118] The danger is limited to the individual, yet in the various formulations of the petition for safety the individual associates himself with the people of Israel: "Save, O Lord [הושע השם], Thy people, Israel";[119] or "Hearken to the prayer of Thy people, Israel";[120] or "Thy people's needs are many. . . . May it be Thy will, O Lord our God, that Thou give to each one according to his needs."[121] Despite the particular danger to which he is exposed, the individual prays not for personal deliverance but for the people as a whole; he is, after all, saying what constitutes the Tefillah in these circumstances, and that very idea makes his personal need subordinate. 'Abaye later put into words what had long been the general view when he said, "A person ought always to associate himself with the *ẓibbur* [community]."[122]

A major difficulty, however, is the length of the regular Tefillah. True, the conceptual continuum which unites all the berakot enables a person to carry over the experience of God's love from berakah to berakah. On the other hand, that experience was made difficult to achieve when the Tefillah was recited from memory by the effort to recollect the correct phrases, and the longer the Tefillah, the greater the difficulty. The early Tannaim differed, therefore, with respect to the recitation of the Daily Tefillah by the individual, there being no difficulty, of course, when it was recited at the synagogue service by the leader.[123] As against Rabban Gamaliel, who holds that the individual ought to recite the full Eighteen Berakot every day, R. Joshua says, "the substance [or an abstract, מעין] of the Eighteen" and R. 'Aḳiba says, "if the Tefillah is fluent in his mouth" he ought to recite the full Eighteen, but if not, the substance of the Eighteeen.[124] Ginzberg has demonstrated that the statements of R. Joshua and R. 'Akiba relate to everybody and not only to him who is at the time harassed or distracted.[125] R. Joshua holds that the individual may, if he wishes,[126] recite merely an abstract of the Tefillah every day, but R. 'Aḳiba evidently holds that only if it is difficult for the individual to recollect the full Tefillah ought he to recite an abstract. With respect to the abstract itself, Rab taught that it is to consist of "the end of each and every berakah," including the closing formula of each of them, while Samuel taught that the middle section is to be condensed and made into one berakah but that the first three and the last three berakot are to be recited in full.[127]

Keeping to a fixed text over a long period of time likewise makes a heartfelt Tefillah difficult. Reciting the same words day after day doubtless results in fluency, but it may also result in saying the Tefillah mechanically and by rote. The individual who fulfills R. 'Aḳiba's requirement and who recites the Tefillah fluently may simply be reciting it in this way. R. Eliezer hence takes issue here with R. 'Aḳiba and with him alone, as Lieberman shows conclusively.[128] When R. Eliezer says, "He who makes his Tefillah *ḳeba'*, his Tefillah is not supplication,"[129] he means by *ḳeba'*, accordingly, keeping to a fixed text of the Tefillah over a long period of time.[130] This interpretation is borne out by the statements in the Yerushalmi which follow upon R. Eliezer's dictum. R. 'Abbahu in the name of R. Eleazar explains the dictum as merely a warning that reciting the Tefillah should not become as casual as reading a secular document—that is to say, *ḳeba'* does not mean that one must change the text of the Tefillah every day but that the same text must not be kept to over a long period of time. R.'Aḥa' in the name of R. Jose declares that one should say something new in the Tefillah every day; R. Eleazar said a new Tefillah every day—that is, he changed the text of the middle part, which is supplication, every day; and R. 'Abbahu said a new berakah every day—that is, he changed a text in the berakot "of praise" daily, as well.

If we take *ḳeba'* in R. Eliezer's dictum to refer to "any fixed form" and thus interpret the dictum to mean that the individual must not employ any fixed form at all when he is saying his Tefillah, we are forcing R. Eliezer into a contradiction; a fixed form of the short Tefillah was formulated by R. Eliezer himself.[131] But it can hardly be supposed that R. Eliezer objects to form as such. Were that so, he would disapprove, too, of all the berakot, of any formulated berakah.

Actually, his dictum, it seems to us, implies just the opposite. When he says that the Tefillah must be supplication he can only be referring to the *petitions* of the Tefillah; if these are not heartfelt, we take him to be saying, the formulated culminating berakot[132] are not heartfelt and consequently the Tefillah as a whole does not represent an experience. He points to a difficulty, one that is inherent in the nature of a prescribed liturgy. To overcome the difficulty by eliminating the forms, however, is to do away with the possibility of profound spiritual experiences, the nurture and expression of a rich variety of value concepts, the cultivation of the larger self.

An individual's prayer which wells out of his own immediate or special need, all must grant, is heartfelt. But such a prayer does not merely "well out" of one's need; to pray at all, an individual must have the assurance that God is near, and that He hearkens to prayer. Now, the berakot of the Tefillah can bring not only the assurance but the experience of God's nearness and the experience, too, that He answers prayer. It was the practice, therefore, to attach personal petitions to the Tefillah, or else to insert them, and that practice surely testifies that the saying of the Tefillah was not a matter of rote. Rather, it brought the individual a genuine experience, an experience which enabled him to give voice to his own personal need.

A baraita rules that a person may "say words" after the Tefillah,[133] these "words" being, as Lieberman points out, thanksgivings and supplications.[134] The rule given here raises no problem, since what is added by the individual comes at the end of the Tefillah and thus does not affect the conceptual continuum of the berakot. But another baraita states that a man may insert a petition for his own needs in "Who hearkenest unto prayer," the Sixteenth Berakah,[135] and the Amoraim, while acknowledging this statement, nevertheless go further and say that he may insert a petition for a particular need toward the close of any relevant berakah.[136] Those who hold that insertions of this kind are permissible feel, we assume, that such personal petitions are entirely incidental to a berakah and so do not interrupt the conceptual continuum. In any case, we may draw the same conclusion from all these halakot; namely, that the experience achieved in saying the Tefillah helped to evoke nonformalized private prayer.

C. The Occasions for the Tefillah

The First Berakah of the Tefillah is an expression of *biṭṭaḥon*, of reliance on God.[137] *Biṭṭaḥon* is an abiding consciousness; it enables a man to initiate and carry through his daily enterprises and also to meet adversity. Nevertheless, *biṭṭaḥon* remains implicit unless it is meditated upon and put into words, as in a berakah. When expressed in a berakah, *biṭṭaḥon* becomes a unitary meditative experience, and such a unitary meditative experience is the First Berakah. But every berakah needs a stimulus of some sort, an occasion, and hence the First Berakah, too, needs an occasion. Since *biṭṭaḥon* is an abiding consciousness, the occasion here, however, need be only a reminder.[138] True, the reminder is for the recital of the Tefillah as a whole, but the Tefillah is a series of berakot united in a conceptual continuum, and the reminder directly recalls, therefore, the first of that series, the First Berakah.

Certain periods of the day are the reminders for saying the Tefillah. The Mishnah rules that the Tefillah is to be said at three different periods of the day. According to the *Ḥakamim* (a group of scholars), it may be said in the morning until midday and in the afternoon "until the evening,"[139] whereas the evening Tefillah has no fixed time (*ḳeba'*).[140] Asking, "Why did they state [i.e., in the Mishnah] that the morning Tefillah [may be recited] until midday," and repeating a similar question with regard to the afternoon Tefillah, the Tosefta supplies an explanation for the rules of the Mishnah. The morning Tefillah may be said until midday, explains the Tosefta, because the communal sacrifice of the morning (שחר) was offered until midday and the afternoon Tefillah, Minḥah, may be said until the evening because the communal sacrifice of the afternoon (בין הערבים) was offered until the evening.[141] It was because there was no communal sacrifice in the evening that there is no fixed time (*ḳeba'*) for the evening Tefillah which, consequently may be said at any time during the night.[142] But the Amoraim interpret this rule, too, in such fashion as to establish further the time-correspondence between the daily sacrifices and the Tefillah. R. Tanḥuma interprets the rule to mean that the time for the evening Tefillah corresponds to the time for the all-night consumption of the limbs and fat pieces on the altar,[143] and a supplementary interpretation in the Babli takes the rule to be also in accord with the opinion that the saying of the evening Tefillah is an optional matter.[144] The Mishnah itself, however, makes no mention of the correspondence in time between the daily sacrifices and the Tefillot, although it certainly takes such correspondence for granted.[145]

For a moment let us digress to draw attention to the implication of the view that saying the evening Tefillah was an optional matter. Such a view clearly implies that the Tefillah was not strictly a mode of communal worship but rather a mode of worship for the individual; were it primarily a mode of communal worship, at no time could the saying of the Tefillah be something left altogether to the individual.[146] The same implication is present in the wide latitude of time for the evening Tefillah given in the Mishnah.

As the occasions for the Tefillah, the designated periods of the day differ from every other occasion that serves as the initiating stimulus for a series of berakot. In all the other instances of a conceptual continuum, the First Berakah interprets the initial stimulus or occasion and the occasion becomes thereby an element in the total unitary experience expressed by the First Berakah. We observed this to be the case in the First Berakah of the Birkat ha-Mazon, a berakah which interprets the meal just eaten as a manifestation of God's bounty and love;[147] and again in the case of the First Berakah of the berakot of the Shema', a berakah which interprets the light of the new day as a manifestation of God's love.[148] Now, the designated periods of the day are likewise related to common phenomena. They constitute the three common divisions of the day: the morning, when the sun is in the east; noon, when the sun is at the zenith; the evening, when the sun is in the west. The occasions for the Tefillah, then, are none other than phenomena in common experience. Indeed, R. Samuel b. Naḥman declares that it is because of these three changes in the position of the sun every day that a man ought to say the Tefillah three times every day.[149] But the identical Tefillah is said at all three periods of the day,[150] and hence the First Berakah cannot be an interpretation of each one of them in turn. Being factors of common experience, however, the periods of the day can act as reminders to recite the Tefillah, if the First Berakah is of such a character that merely a reminder will suffice. Since the First Berakah embodies the concept of *biṭṭaḥon*—an abiding consciousness—a reminder is altogether sufficient for the berakah to become a meditative experience.

In the days of the Temple, an era of sacrificial worship, the present order of the first three berakot, beginning with 'Abot, had already become an established tradition.[151] This indicates that the occasion for the Tefillah was not, in fact, the daily communal sacrifice; had it been, the First Berakah would certainly have referred to the sacrifices. Correspondence in time between the daily communal sacrifices and the saying of the Tefillah implies, therefore, not that the communal sacrifice is the occasion for the saying of the Tefillah, but, on the contrary, that the saying of the Tefillah is to be a reminder of the communal sacrifice—and this, even in the days of the Temple.

A comparison of the statements in the Mishnah and the Tosefta cited above leads to the same conclusion. We noticed that the Mishnah, although taking for granted the correspondence in time between the daily sacrifice and the saying of the Tefillah, makes no mention of that fact. Why? Because the Mishnah states a rule with respect to the reminders for saying the Tefillah and the matter of the time-correspondence does not add anything to the rule itself. The Tosefta, on the other hand, bases its statement on the rule in the Mishnah and adds a reason for that rule: namely, the time-correspondence between the saying of the Tefillah and the daily sacrifice. But what halakic bearing does this statement have? What does the Tosefta actually add? Surely the statement in the Tosefta does not mean simply to reaffirm the halakah in the Mishnah, a halakah which the statement quotes. If the Tosefta teaches anything new, it cannot be something with regard to reminders for saying the Tefillah but with regard to recollecting the daily sacrifices. The Mishnah states a rule with regard to reminders for saying the Tefillah; the Tosefta adds to this rule the halakah that saying the Tefillah is to be a reminder of the daily communal sacrifices.[152]

Rabbinic statements implying a correspondence between the Tefillah and the sacrifices do not refer to any correspondence in subject-matter. That is evident when we examine, for example, the statements of R. Joshua b. Levi and R. Jose b. R. Ḥanina as given in *Berakot* 26b and the discussion there. R. Joshua says that the Tefillot were ordained "as against" (*keneged*) the daily communal sacrifices, but in support of this statement the Talmud brings the passage of the

Tosefta on the correspondence of the time of the Tefillot to that of the daily sacrifices.[153] R. Joshua's view that the Tefillah corresponds to the daily communal sacrifice is thus supported only by the baraita as to the correspondence in time. R. Jose makes no reference to the sacrifices at all. He says that the *'Abot* (Patriarchs) ordained the Tefillot, and in support of that statement the Talmud brings a baraita to the effect that Abraham ordained the Tefillah of the morning, Isaac that of the afternoon, and Jacob that of the evening.[154] Later, in order to harmonize R. Jose's statement with the Tosefta, the Talmud explains R. Jose to mean that the Tefillot were ordained by the *'Abot* but that the rabbis attached the Tefillot (אסמכינהו) to the sacrifices.[155] Even in the statement as amended, then, the content of the Tefillah as whole is one thing and the connection with the sacrifices quite another. Similarly, in all the versions of the various statements given here[156] and in other statements on the number, the time, or the form (Eighteen Berakot) of the Tefillot,[157] the daily sacrifices are not connected with the subject-matter of the Tefillah as a whole.

D. Worship in the Heart

'Abodah as worship refers either to the sacrificial worship in the Temple, or else pejoratively to the manner of worshipping any idol; in either case, the worship consists of actions of some kind.[158] But the rabbis extended the scope of 'abodah as proper worship, the worship of God, to include berakot and the Tefillah, the acceptance of *malkut Shamayim* and study of Torah; in other words, they developed forms of nonsacrificial worship.

Berakot are characterized as 'abodah in a rabbinic interpretation of a biblical verse and through a halakah. The berakot on bread and on water are equated with 'abodah in an interpretation of Exodus 23:25.[159] A halakah states that just as an offensive-looking or ill-smelling priest is unfit to participate in the 'Abodah (of the Temple), so ill-smelling hands make one unfit to say the berakah[160] and thus the Birkat ha-Mazon, most likely, is in this halakah equated with 'abodah.[161]

Directly associated with the daily communal sacrifices by reason of correspondence in time, the Tefillah is characterized as 'abodah in a far more emphatic manner than is any other form of nonsacrificial worship. In the halakah just cited, the berakah is characterized as 'abodah by being made analogous to the 'Abodah of the Temple, but there is no direct connection between the two. The Tefillah, however, is directly connected with the 'Abodah of the Temple; it is connected with the 'Abodah not only through the halakah which makes of the Tefillah a reminder of the 'Abodah, but also through related halakot—through the halakot that permit the evening Tefillah to be said at any time during the night since it is not a reminder of the 'Abodah, and that, for the same reason, make recitation of the evening Tefillah an optional matter.[162] Stemming from a correspondence in time, these halakot imply that the Tefillah and the 'Abodah are of a piece, a much more emphatic manner of characterizing the Tefillah as 'abodah than by the method of analogy. What the halakot can only imply, R. Joshua states more explicitly when he says that the Tefillot were ordained "as against" the daily communal sacrifices; it is a statement characterizing the Tefillah as 'abodah but which is supported, again, by reference to the time-correspondence between the two.[163]

A famous passage in the Sifre not only characterizes the Tefillah as 'abodah but indicates the distinction between the Tefillah and sacrificial worship. Taking Deuteronomy 11:13 as saying "to love the Lord your God and to worship Him [*le 'abedo*] in all your hearts," the Sifre declares that "to worship Him in all your hearts" can refer only to the Tefillah, since the sacrificial worship takes place not in the heart of the individual [but on the altar], and the passage closes (after adducing further proof from Ps. 141:2 and Dan. 6:11, 21) with the statement "just as the 'Abodah of the altar is called 'abodah, so the Tefillah is called 'abodah."[164] A version of the passage is found in the Yerushalmi and there the Tefillah is specifically designated as '*abodah ba-leb*, worship in the heart.[165] The passage in the Sifre and its variants say in so many words that the Tefillah is 'abodah, but that it is nonsacrificial worship. Despite the time-correspondence and despite halakot which connect the Tefillah with the sacrificial worship, the Tefillah—by reason of its content—is to be distinguished from sacrificial worship.

It is unlikely that any form of nonsacrificial worship, including the Tefillah, was explicitly referred to as 'abodah before the cessation of the sacrificial worship. Each form of nonsacrificial worship has its own name, such as berakah or tefillah, and that name, being a value concept, is a sufficient characterization of the form. After the Temple was destroyed, however, and sacrificial worship was no longer possible, the nonsacrificial forms of worship were felt to be, in a sense, surrogates for the sacrificial worship and it was for that reason, apparently, that they were also characterized as 'abodah. Being the reminder of the daily sacrifices, "of one piece" with 'abodah, the Tefillah was especially singled out as the surrogate for the sacrifices. Simply to characterize the Tefillah as 'abodah, therefore, was not enough and the Tefillah was further related to the daily sacrifices, as we shall see immediately, by being invested with their character and function. But the rabbis could not have equated the Tefillah and the other matters with 'abodah, even at a later time, had these things not already been from the very beginning, i.e., in the days of the Temple as well, forms of nonsacrificial worship.

In addition to being a reminder of the daily communal sacrifices because of their time-correspondence, the Tefillah was conceived, after the destruction of the Temple, as being itself an offering given in place of those sacrifices. The afternoon Tefillah, Minḥah, is designated, according to R. Samuel b. Naḥman, "a pure oblation" in Malachi 1:11, where it is depicted as a pure oblation (*minḥah*) which is offered to God everywhere, in every land.[166] Further, the Tefillah acts as a surrogate for other Temple sacrifices as well. Hosea 14:3 was interpreted to mean: We render in place of bullocks the words of our lips, the Tefillah;[167] and this interpretation cannot refer to the daily communal sacrifices, for the latter were lambs, not bullocks.

By a play on the word *kebes*, lamb, Bet Shammai taught that the daily communal sacrifices, consisting of lambs (Num. 28:3), "press down" the iniquities of Israel, whereas Bet Hillel, also playing on the same word, taught that these sacrifices "wash off" the iniquities.[168] Bet Hillel's metaphorical teaching is tantamount to saying that the daily sacrifices atone for Israel's sins, an idea elaborated by R. Judan b. R. Simon who declares that the morning sacrifice atoned for the sins committed at night and the evening sacrifice for the sins committed during the day.[169] Another source describes the atoning function of the two daily sacrifices by calling them two daily intercessors or advocates.[170] When R. Joshua says that the Tefillah was ordained "as against" the daily sacrifices,[171] he apparently suggests that the Tefillah, acting as a surrogate, likewise has an atoning function. Similarly, when the rabbis speak of the Tefillah (of Minḥah) as recited "in place of the sacrifice,"[172] they evidently imply that this Tefillah, like the sacrifice, has an atoning function. Indeed, Hosea 14: 3 once more is taken to mean that the Tefillah is a surrogate for all sacrifices of atonement, the verse being interpreted as follows: When the Temple was standing we brought a sacrifice in atonement, but now we have only the Tefillah.[173]

The concepts of 'abodah and tefillah interpret the same entity. They illustrate, but in a singular manner, how, in an organismic complex, different value concepts may interpret the same act or entity. In this section the rabbinic statements and the halakot we have cited are concretizations of the concept of 'abodah; and it is to be noticed that such statements and halakot embodying the concept of tefillah as well are based on one thing, namely, the time-correspondence between the Tefillah and the daily communal sacrifices. In all the previous sections, however, we discussed the content and form of the Tefillah and found that the many halakot cited there were concretizations of the concepts of tefillah and berakah. The concepts embodied in the content and structure of the Tefillah, therefore, are those of tefillah and berakah; in that respect the Tefillah is like all other instances of organismic thought wherein the concepts involved are embodied in the content.[174] That is not the case when the concept of 'abodah interprets the Tefillah as a sacrifice; we then have the singular instance in which a value concept interpreting an act is not involved in the content of that act.

In an organismic complex, sometimes one concept is stressed above another concept, and sometimes the stress is the other way around.[175] According to a tannaitic interpretation of Deuteronomy 12: 5, the prophets and *zekenim* ordained that Israel recite the Tefillah three times every day and thus say, "Restore Thy *Shekinah* to Zion and the order of Thy 'Abodah to Jerusalem, Thy city."[176] Here the concept of 'abodah is distinctly stressed above that of tefillah. Yet, in a statement containing similar phrases, tefillah is expressly stressed above 'abodah. Moses foresaw, say the rabbis, that the Temple would be destroyed and the bringing of the first fruits would cease, and he therefore ordained that Israel recite the Tefillah three times every day, "for the Tefillah is dearer to God than all the good deeds and all the sacrifices."[177] "The Tefillah," says R. Eleazar simply, "is greater than the sacrifices."[178]

'Abodah and tefillah are posed against each other in a halakic discussion.[179] On the one hand, the Tefillah (of Minḥah) is "in place of sacrifice" and hence ought not to be said later than the designated time of the sacrifice; on the other hand, it is *raḥame*, the beseeching of compassion from God, and, therefore, ought to be said whenever one wishes to do so. R. Joḥanan ruled that the principle applying in the case of a sacrifice—"When its day has passed, the sacrifice of the day is void"—does not apply here, and that when one has forgotten to say the Tefillah of Minḥah at its designated time it may be said later. What primarily characterizes the Tefillah is its content.

Besides the berakot on bread and water, the Birkat ha-Mazon, and the Tefillah, there are also other matters which are designated by the rabbis as 'abodah: Ḳeri'at Shema'[180] and study of Torah.[181] Like Ḳeri'at Shema', study of Torah can be made an occasion for the experience of God and, in fact, Ḳeri'at Shema' is only a special instance of study of Torah.[182] When these matters are characterized as 'abodah, the term 'abodah can refer only to nonsacrificial worship. But what is the distinctive character of nonsacrificial worship? We have found that in the act of saying a berakah before eating a morsel of bread an individual expresses his awareness of God's love, and that the berakah enhances that awareness. This is likewise true of the act of saying a berakah on water. In each case, the berakah and the occasion for reciting it constitute a unitary entity, an integral experience of God's love. Essentially, the Birkat ha-Mazon and the Tefillah also represent unitary experiences of God's love, although here that concept connects a series of berakot, all of which, after the First Berakah, are meditative experiences of God's love. Acceptance of *malkut Shamayim* through Ḳeri'at Shema' and the study of Torah involves an altogether different experience, but once more a unitary experience of God is achieved—this time as the result of meditating upon and studying an integrated literary entity. These various experiences are characterized as 'abodah because they have a character in common, each of them representing a unitary experience of God mediated by a concept.

If this is the distinctive character of nonsacrificial worship, then every berakah may be characterized as 'abodah, for every berakah represents a unitary experience of God mediated by a concept. True, the rabbis do not designate every berakah as 'abodah, but that is because no purpose was to be served by doing so. Nothing is actually added when a berakah is characterized as 'abodah: no special function is assigned to it, nor is it otherwise distinguished from the berakot in general. It was enough to designate a few berakot as 'abodah in order to establish the idea that all berakot were to be regarded as nonsacrificial worship, as surrogates for the worship in the Temple, and the few chosen are those that are said most often.

Nonsacrificial worship is normal mysticism. We shall discuss normal mysticism at some length in Chapter VII; in order to compare nonsacrificial with sacrificial worship, however, we must indicate how the various forms of nonsacrificial worship exhibit characteristics of normal mysticism. In a berakah the experience of God is mediated, usually, by the concept of God's love, and sometimes by that of God's justice, but these concepts are very much akin to almost parallel concepts informing universal human morality, akin, that is, to normal human experience.[183] Moreover, among the very berakot specifically designated as 'abodah are berakot which are joined to commonplace things, daily acts; normal occurrences being thus occasions for worship.[184] In Ḳeri'at Shema' the experience of God is mediated by the concept of *malkut Shamayim*, the experience being a meditative one in which the individual makes "Him King above and below and in the four winds of heaven."[185] Instructions enabling a person to achieve this experience are intended for the people as a whole, for the normal man, and are not directions aiming toward visions or locutions.[186] Nonsacrificial worship is normal mysticism, religious experience which is not isolated from normal human experience, mystical experience which does not involve such sensory phenomena.

Sacrificial worship of God can take place only in the Temple at Jerusalem. Some tannaitic sources assume that the pilgrims who came to the Temple on the festivals could experience there *gilluy Shekinah*, a revelation of God in some visible manner.[187] The *Ḥakamim* of the Mishnah reject that assumption, however, and their view is reflected in both Talmuds as well.[188] According to the general view it seems, therefore, that a pilgrim who "stood by" his sacrifice as it was being offered in the Temple had no experience of *gilluy Shekinah*, and, by the same token, neither did the representatives of the people as a whole who "stood by" as the daily communal sacrifices were being offered.[189] All agree, however, that in the future sacrificial worship will be associated with *gilluy Shekinah*. The petition quoted above, "Restore Thy *Shekinah* to Zion and the order of Thy 'Abodah to Jerusalem," reflects the assumption that when the 'Abodah will be restored, *gilluy Shekinah* will also be restored at the Temple.[190]

Since the rabbis firmly believed that ultimately the 'Abodah would be restored to Jerusalem, they obviously regarded the Tefillah as having a sacrificial character only for the time being. Because of the time correspondence, the Tefillah serves now as a reminder of the daily communal sacrifices, but basically it is in itself not a sacrifice. Sacrificial worship of God is associated with *gilluy Shekinah*, whereas the Tefillah, like the berakot and Ḳeri'at Shema', is nonsacrificial worship or normal mysticism.

CHAPTER VI

The Element of Community in Worship

A. Aspects of *Kiddush ha-Shem*

The rabbinic term for community is *ẓibbur*. It is a concept of relationship, referring to the group as a corporate entity, a collectivity, in contradistinction to the individual member. Since the contradistinction holds whether the *ẓibbur* be large or small, the word *ẓibbur* may stand either for the entire people or for a local community. When the rabbis speak, for example, of "the sacrifices of the *ẓibbur*,"[1] they refer to the Temple sacrifices brought in behalf of the entire people;[2] on the other hand, when they speak of the *ẓibbur* at prayer, they definitely refer to a local community.[3]

Being a concept of relationship, *ẓibbur* is a cognitive concept.[4] In concrete valuational situations, cognitive concepts are fused with value concepts,[5] and *ẓibbur* is a cognitive concept often fused with the value concept of Israel. When the word *ẓibbur* is used, the value concept of Israel is made concrete, embodied in a living human group. Thus, when the word *ẓibbur* is applied to Israel as a whole, the Talmud indicates, it excludes those who are no longer living.[6] When the word is applied to a local community, it is used in so concrete a sense as to refer, frequently, to a face-to-face group.[7]

We must, however, distinguish between a mere aggregate of individuals and a *ẓibbur*. A *ẓibbur* is a corporate entity, that is to say, it has a character which is often expressed in corporate acts. A corporate act is an act which, as a unitary entity, is performed by the *ẓibbur* but in which the individual members participate in definite and varied ways. Further, despite only sharing in the preformance of the act, each individual has an experience of the act as a whole. On the other hand, when the word *ẓibbur* is used without any reference to a corporate act, the word refers to Israel as a whole or to the community as a whole—to either as a corporate entity which is not differentiated into particular individuals.

In the case of the "sacrifices of the *ẓibbur*," participation by all the members of the *ẓibbur*, meaning by all Israel, was obviously not possible, and could therefore only be symbolized. Present at these daily Temple sacrifices were weekly representatives of the people of Israel as a whole—priests, Levites, and laymen,[8] and these representatives "stood by" the sacrifice as it was being offered.[9] To stand by a sacrifice was a duty laid upon the person bringing the sacrifice;[10] the representatives were thus deputies, agents acting in behalf of all the living members of the people.[11] The point is that the deputies consisted of representatives of all three divisions of Israel, so that symbolically the entire people participated.

In nonsacrificial worship, the type of worship we are discussing in this chapter, acts of communal worship require a face-to-face group. We shall see how, in a number of such acts, the face-to-face *ẓibbur*, in the very process of a corporate act, brings to its members a vivid awareness of God's holiness. The *ẓibbur* enables the individual to achieve an experience of worship he could not otherwise have achieved.

A corporate act of worship bringing to the individual a consciousness of God's holiness is a concretization of *ḳiddush ha-Shem*. Now *ḳiddush ha-Shem* involves not only an act itself but the effect which the act produces upon others, and these two factors are not readily apparent in an act of worship, precisely because it is a corporate act. When *ḳiddush ha-Shem* is not an act of worship, however, the two factors are obvious, as the following halakah indicates. Even to save his life, declares R. Ishmael, a Jew must not commit an act of idolatry in public, *be-farhesya'*, for it says, "Ye shall not profane My holy Name, but I will be hallowed among the children of Israel" (Lev. 22:32).[12] The verse here speaks of profaning the Name, *ḥillul ha-Shem*, and of hallowing the Name, *ḳiddush ha-Shem*, the act in either case, according to R. Ishmael's interpretation, being *be-farhesya'*, "among the children of Israel." Another baraita teaches that "among the children of Israel," taken in conjunction with

Numbers 16:21, refers to the presence of at least ten Jews, and so the Talmud defines *be-farhesya'*, "in public," to mean an act which is beheld by at least ten Jews.[13]

From the halakah just cited we can apprehend the significance of *ḳiddush ha-Shem*. *Kiddush ha-Shem*, we learn, consists of an act which produces a consciousness of God's holiness in the beholders, since it is "among the children of Israel" that the hallowing of the Name of God occurs. Obviously the heroic act and the effect which that act produces have something in common. The heroic act, whatever else it may be, is an ultimate acknowledgment of God. Its effect, therefore, on the beholders, must be a concurrence with, almost a participation in, that acknowledgment. There is a consciousness of God's holiness in the beholders because the martyr, through his heroic act, demonstrates his own consciousness of God's holiness.[14]

Further, the halakah helps us to differentiate between corporate acts on the one hand, and acts which require what is merely an aggregate of individuals, on the other. A heroic act of *ḳiddush ha-shem* takes place *be-farhesya'*—that is, in the presence of at least ten Jews. An act of corporate worship, we shall see, also requires at least ten Jews. In a corporate act, however, every individual present is an active participant, and hence the ten constitute a *ẓibbur*. On the other hand, the individuals beholding a heroic act of *ḳiddush ha-Shem* are not active participants in that act, and hence are only a public, a mere aggregate of individuals. A corporate act of *ḳiddush ha-Shem* in worship is the act of a *ẓibbur*, whereas a heroic act of *ḳiddush ha-Shem* is the act of an individual which takes place *be-farhesya'*, in public. This is not to say, of course, that "the public" can be dispensed with. *Be-farhesya'* is a requisite if the act of martyrdom is to be *ḳiddush ha-Shem*, an act that produces a consciousness of God's holiness in fellow-Jews.[15]

Ḳiddush ha-Shem is not limited to an act of martyrdom on the part of a Jew and to the effect of such an act upon its Jewish beholders. Among the other aspects of *ḳiddush ha-Shem* is one in which a righteous act by a Jew toward a Gentile elicits from the Gentile an acknowledgment of the God of the Jews, albeit a qualified acknowledgment, and this aspect of *ḳiddush ha-Shem*, too, has a bearing on corporate worship. Stories on this aspect of *ḳiddush ha-Shem* are found in the Yerushalmi, some having a circumstantial character and some being evidently folk tales. There is a circumstantial character, for example, to the story of R. Jonathan and his Roman neighbor. It tells how R. Jonathan, before deciding a case dealing with property infringement, first corrected a similar infringement of his own against the property of his Roman neighbor, and how the Roman, impressed by R. Jonathan's integrity, thereupon exclaimed, "Blessed is the God of the Jews!"[16] A story with a folk-tale quality is the one about R. Samuel b. Sisraṭai and the empress.[17] R. Samuel had found a jewel belonging to the empress and, having heard it proclaimed that the finder would be rewarded should he return it within thirty days, and be decapitated should he return it after that time, R. Samuel returned the jewel after thirty days. When the empress asked him his reason for the delay, he replied that it was in order to make evident that what he did was not out of "fear of thee, but out of fear of God [*Raḥamana'*]"; whereupon the empress declared, "Blessed is the God of the Jews!" In a similar tale, 'Abba' 'Osha'yah likewise returns to the empress her lost ornaments and jewelry,[18] but the moral of this story is more subtle. Here the empress says that these articles belong to the finder, adding that she has other such things which are more valuable. 'Abba' 'Osha'yah replies, however, "The Torah has decreed we must return [the valuables]," and once more the response is, "Blessed is the God of the Jews!" Another story regarding the return of a lost jewel has to do with Simeon b. Shaṭaḥ.[19] To ease his daily labor his pupils bought a donkey for him from a Sarḳi (a member of a trading tribe), and found a pearl hanging from its neck. Simeon ordered his pupils to return the pearl, and when they demurred, he said to them, "Do you think Simeon b. Shaṭaḥ is a barbarian? Simeon b. Shaṭaḥ would rather hear [the Sarḳi say], 'Blessed is the God of the Jews' than have all the wealth of this world."[20] (There is still another story on the same theme in this collection, also with Gentiles exclaiming, "Blessed is the God of the Jews!")[21]

These stories in the Yerushalmi undoubtedly reflect a dominant attitude of the Jews during much of the rabbinic period. The Jews were very anxious to have the Gentiles acknowledge God, incomplete as that acknowledgment had to be by persons who still remained Gentiles. Simeon b. Shaṭaḥ's statement, though perhaps apocryphal, does indicate how keenly leading scholars felt on this matter. In like manner, the stories about R. Samuel and 'Abba' 'Osha'yah reflect numerous less dramatic occasions when there was *ḳiddush ha-Shem* as a result of a righteous act by a Jew toward a Gentile. But all the stories, and not only the folktales, reflect something else as well. In all the stories, the Yerushalmi has the Gentiles, in every instance, make the same declaration, "Blessed is the God of the Jews," and this declaration identifies the incident as an instance of *ḳiddush ha-Shem*. Actually, however, "Blessed is the God of the Jews" is a declaration which does not commit the Gentile at all. What suggests an acknowledgment of God here is the form of the declaration, the form being very reminiscent of a berakah. We shall find, indeed, that there is a genuine berakah which consists solely of an acknowledgment of God, and that this berakah is part of a corporate act of worship. The declaration or formula placed in the mouths of the Gentiles reflects that berakah. In other words, the berakah associated with *ḳiddush ha-Shem* was already so well known that a formula resembling it identified acts of another type as acts of *ḳiddush ha-Shem*. All this does not mean that a new type of *ḳiddush ha-Shem* emerged, but only that the literary formula which identified that type presupposed an actual berakah consisting solely of an acknowledgment of God.[22]

B. Baraku

Ḳiddush ha-Shem in noncorporate acts is always an outcome of a specific situation. Even when *ḳiddush ha-Shem* is avowedly sought for, as in the story of Simeon b. Shaṭaḥ or in that of R. Samuel, the act of *ḳiddush ha-Shem* is made possible because of a specific situation. *Ḳiddush ha-Shem* in corporate acts, that is, in acts of worship, likewise is an outcome of a situation, namely, the presence of a *ẓibbur*. A *ẓibbur* is not deliberately formed for the purpose of making a corporate acknowledgment of God. An acknowledgment of God under such circumstances would undoubtedly tend to be something contrived and artificial. A *ẓibbur* is formed in the first instance to enable the individual to engage in certain acts of worship incumbent upon him as an individual.[23] There is thus a *ẓibbur* to start with. Because a *ẓibbur* had already been formed, it could also engage in a corporate act of *ḳiddush ha-Shem*.

A mishnah, *Megillah* IV.3, gives a list of the occasions requiring the presence or the participation of at least ten Jews. First in that list is the public recitation of the Shema', but it is described as פורסין את שמע, a phrase to which many different meanings have been variously assigned.[24] On the basis of the evidence in other tannaitic passages,[25] however, there can be little doubt that the phrase refers to a kind of responsive recitation, the leader reciting the first part of a verse in the Shema' and the *ẓibbur* apparently repeating that part and completing the verse.[26] The public recitation of the Shema' was, therefore, a corporate act; that is, an act in which every member of the *ẓibbur* was an active participant. It had to be a corporate recital, we should say, for the simple reason that in early tannaitic times the Shema' was known by many only imperfectly. Calling attention to the baraita (*Berakot* 47b) which defines an *'am ha-'areẓ* (one who is ignorant and negligent of the law) as one who does not recite the Shema', Ginzberg points out that there were Jews who could not recite the Shema',[27] and that this was especially true in Galilee until toward the close of the tannaitic period.[28] The corporate recital enabled the untutored to join in Ḳeri'at Shema' and was a pedagogic device as well, by means of which they could learn the Shema'.[29]

But there is also a corporate act associated with the Shema' and its berakot, and with another occasion named in the mishnah, the public reading of the Torah, to which the mishnah makes no explicit reference. It is an act of worship so simple as to require almost no previous training at all, and it embodies the concept of *ḳiddush ha-Shem*. This corporate act of worship the Gemara assumes to be the one referred to in the mishnah, probably for several reasons. In the first place, the rabbis of the Talmud, as we have demonstrated elsewhere, always endeavor to establish, or rather to make explicit, the nexus inherent in the laws;[30] here they posit *ḳiddush ha-Shem* as the uniting principle which several of the occasions mentioned in the mishnah have in common. Moreover, *ḳiddush ha-Shem* actually does relate to those occasions because they do make possible corporate acts of *ḳiddush ha-Shem*. Second, certain acts of worship, including the corporate recital of the Shema',[31] are not intrinsically corporate in character—that is, the act need not be corporate but may be accomplished by the individual in private; yet the mishnah does not qualify its statement that not less than ten be present on, or participate in, the various occasions listed. The presumption is, therefore, that the mishnah lists only those acts of worship which are intrinsically of a corporate character, and that is precisely the category to which belong such acts of worship as constitute *ḳiddush ha-Shem*.

The uniting principle adduced in the Gemara is a maxim-like interpretation of verses employed by the rabbis to elucidate the concept of *ḳiddush ha-Shem*.[32] In this interpretation *ḳiddush ha-Shem* consists of acts of worship, for the maxim teaches that words which are acts of *ḳiddush ha-Shem* may not be said (at worship) by less than ten.[33] What these acts of worship are is not specified in this passage of the Gemara because they are presumed to be specified in the mishnah; they are, however, named or referred to or discussed by Rashi and other commentaries on the passage, commentaries which reflect an authentic tradition. Rashi names the Ḳaddish, Baraku and, by inference, the Ḳedushah,[34] and we shall see that it is just these acts of worship, and no others, which constitute *ḳiddush ha-Shem*. Asheri refers to "Baraku and Ḳaddish," as occasions when an individual says "a word involving *ḳedushah*" and thus "sanctifies the Name among 'ten.'"[35] Elsewhere in the Talmud itself, an authority characterizes the Ḳedushah by the very maxim and the supporting verses which the Talmud here employs for the interpretation of the mishnah.[36] Finally, *Masseket Soferim*, a post-talmudic tractate, in a section which is practically a quotation of the mishnah, asserts that Ḳaddish and Baraku may not be said in the presence of "less than ten."[37] The acts of worship constituting *ḳiddush ha-Shem* are thus Baraku, the Ḳaddish, and the Ḳedushah.

Baraku is associated, in the synagogue service, with Ḳeri'at Shema'. Because there were Jews who could not recite the Shema' by themselves in early tannaitic times, the recitation of the Shema' was made the act of a *ẓibbur*, one of whom functioned as the leader. The leader also recited, in behalf of the *ẓibbur*, the berakot which precede and follow the Shema',[38] again doubtless because of the untutored in the *ẓibbur*. But the presence of the *ẓibbur* makes possible still another act of worship, one that constitutes *ḳiddush ha-Shem*. Before engaging in the berakot preceding the Shema', the leader says, "Bless ye [*baraku*] the Lord Who is blessed," and the rest of the *ẓibbur* responds with, "Blessed is the Lord Who is blessed for ever and ever."[39] Unlike Ḳeri'at Shema' and its berakot, this act of worship is intrinsically of a corporate character, for it is an act which no individual can accomplish in private. When the leader calls on the others to bless or acknowledge God, he merely initiates the act of hallowing God's Name, the act itself being accomplished when the others actually do acknowledge God. True, since the leader issues the call and hence initiates the act, he is regarded as the one who sanctifies God's Name—witness Asheri's reference to him above; nevertheless, there is no *ḳiddush ha-Shem* until the others respond. Being thus intrinsically corporate, this act of worship remained the act of a *ẓibbur* even when Ḳeri'at Shema' and its berakot ceased to be so.

The response of the *ẓibbur*, "Blessed [*baruk*] is the Lord Who is blessed forever and ever," is a berakah. Although a berakah is usually couched in a formula, Ginzberg has pointed out that there are also instances when a berakah is to be recognized as such by virtue of the idea it expresses.[40] We observed an instance of this type, above, in the berakah of Benjamin the shepherd,[41] and we have another clear instance in the response to Baraku—"Blessed is the Lord." Does not a berakah, however, always express a specific experience of God? What experience of God does the berakah in Baraku reflect?

A berakah which is the response of a *ẓibbur* reflects experience of God, but it is a berakah *sui generis*.[42] The *ẓibbur* consists of individuals to whom God's love is made apparent, through berakot, many times every day. Each berakah expresses and enhances a specific experience of God's love. A berakah which is the response of the *ẓibbur*, however, voices an awareness of God rising not out of a specific experience but out of all of them, an awareness of God Whom the individuals experience on so many different occasions, and in so many different ways, every day. Even a corporate act of worship may reflect a specific experience; it is only in a corporate act of *ḳiddush ha-Shem* that a *ẓibbur* gives expression to an encompassing awareness of God—in a word, to a consciousness of God's holiness itself. In such an act of worship a *ẓibbur* achieves what no individual can achieve. It confirms the personal experience of God by every individual in the *ẓibbur*. If it is to do so in a berakah, that berakah must express a general consciousness of God.[43]

To express this consciousness, the corporate act of worship can have recourse only to general ideas—here to the idea that God is "blessed for ever and ever," and in the Ḳedushah, as we shall find, to the idea that God is everywhere. A corporate act of *ḳiddush ha-Shem* consists, accordingly, of an acknowledgment of God in general terms, although such an acknowledgment can only emerge out of many specific experiences of God. Nor should we be misled into thinking that the general ideas in the acknowledgment contain philosophic implications. The acknowledgment is a berakah, and the general idea, too, is introduced with a form of *baruk*. What is expressed is a consciousness of God which rises out of many and repeated experiences, and not a philosophic abstraction. The abstract terms attempt to express a sense of the holiness of God, an awareness of God not restricted now to any single experience of God.[44]

Baraku and its response are associated also with the public reading of the Torah, another matter listed in *Megillah* IV.3 as requiring the presence of not less than ten. To arrive at the nature of this association, however, we must first describe some features of the public reading of the Torah.

Public reading of the Torah takes place at the services in the morning and at Minḥah on the Sabbath and on fast days; on Monday, Thursday, and on the festivals, only in the morning.[45] Depending on the occasion, from three to seven (or more) are called up to read from the Torah.[46] The reading in later times was done by a man skilled in the practice, although in early times, when the sections were shorter, each of those called up read his own section.[47] According to the Mishnah, a berakah before beginning the reading of the Torah was recited by the first man to read, and another berakah was recited by the last man upon the completion of the entire reading;[48] but it later became the custom for every man called up to recite both berakot, the one before and the other after the reading of his particular section.[49]

The public reading of the Torah is a corporate act on the part of the *ẓibbur* as a whole. Not only do men from the *ẓibbur* participate by being called up to the Torah and by reciting the berakot, but the rest of the *ẓibbur* too is involved. The *ẓibbur* responds with "Amen" to each berakah on the Torah, and the reader must not begin to read until this response has been completed;[50] the members of the *ẓibbur* must refrain from talking during the reading, even to discuss a point of Halakah;[51] it is forbidden for anyone to leave while a section is actually being read.[52] Since it thus involves the *ẓibbur* as a whole, the public reading of the Torah is a corporate act; further, as we shall now see, it is an act which is intrinsically corporate. Manifestly, public reading of the Torah is public instruction, but it is also more than that; the berakot indicate that it is part of an experience of worship. Detailed halakot as to the writing and as to the preparation of the parchment of the scroll to be used for public reading[53] again imply that this reading is not simply public instruction. Such a scroll of the Torah, moreover, is highest in the hierarchy of holy objects.[54] Public reading of the Torah on Sabbaths and festivals, and on several other occasions, goes back, say the rabbis, to an ordinance of Moses.[55] All this is sufficient to demonstrate that participation in public reading of the Torah is something different from an individual's study of Torah. We may say, then, that public reading of the Torah is not merely a corporate act on the part of the *ẓibbur*, but is one which is intrinsically corporate in character.

The berakot on the Torah are an essential feature of this corporate act.[56] The berakah preceding the reading is, in some respects, akin to 'Ahabah Rabbah.[57] Like 'Ahabah Rabbah, it is an anticipatory berakah, called forth by an act yet to be performed. Like 'Ahabah Rabbah, once more, it contains the idea of "the chosen people," the idea now being expressed in the phrase "Who has chosen us from all the peoples."[58] Here, however, this nonconceptualized idea is tied to the concept of *mattan* (the giving of) *Torah*, for the full phrase reads, "Who has chosen us from all the peoples and has given us His Torah," and the emphasis now is on the concept of *mattan Torah*, a concept already concretized in the very selection about to be read. That selection, as it is read, is felt to represent a gift from God, and so when the reading is over another berakah is recited, similar to the first and expressing and enhancing this experience.[59] The corporate act is a unitary act of worship, beginning with a berakah on the Torah, continuing with the reading of a section of the Torah felt to represent a gift from God, and closing with another berakah on the Torah.

But this unitary act of worship does not stand alone. Immediately before reciting the first berakah on the Torah, the man who has been called to the Torah says the Baraku and the rest of the *ẓibbur* replies with the response.[60] The association between Baraku and the first berakah on the Torah is so early as to have been taken for granted in tannaitic times.[61] Nevertheless, there is no integral relation between Baraku and the first berakah on the Torah—for one thing, because the first berakah begins a unitary entity in its own right, and for another, because Baraku constitutes an act of *ḳiddush ha-Shem*, whereas the act of public reading of the Torah, as has been remarked by post-talmudic authorities,[62] does not. The association of Baraku with the public reading of the Torah is entirely due to the circumstance that the public reading of the Torah is intrinsically a corporate act, an act which the individual cannot engage upon alone. Because a *ẓibbur* is present for the reading of the Torah, a corporate act of *ḳiddush ha-Shem*, the Baraku, can precede the reading.[63]

C. The Ḳaddish

The Ḳaddish is a corporate act of *ḳiddush ha-Shem*, and its response is very similar to the one in Baraku. From various statements in rabbinic literature, it is evident that the Ḳaddish was associated originally with public lectures by the rabbis having Haggadah as the subject matter.[64] At the end of such lectures, if there were at least ten men present, there would take place a corporate act of worship. The leader, most likely the lecturer himself, would say, "May His great Name be magnified and sanctified [*we-yitḳaddash*] in the world which He hath created according to His will, and may He make His kingship recognized ["His kingship to reign"—וימליך מלכותיה] during your life and during your days, and during the life of all the house of Israel, speedily and at a near time and say ye, Amen."[65] This part of the Ḳaddish is a prayer by the leader that in the lifetime of his hearers God's Name may be sanctified "in the world": that is, that the whole world may acknowledge God, which means also that His kingship will be recognized by all.[66] The entire idea in this prayer, including the words "magnified and sanctified" which epitomize it, stems from Ezekiel 38:23: "And I will magnify Myself and sanctify Myself, and I will make Myself known in the eyes of many nations; and they shall know that I am the Lord."[67]

When the people say "Amen" to this prayer, as they are bidden to do, they are naturally reminded that they themselves ought to acknowledge God here and now. Immediately after saying "Amen," therefore, they add, "Blessed be His great Name forever and ever."[68] Almost identical with the berakah in Baraku, this statement, too, is an acknowledgment of God in general terms and is a berakah in content, if not in form. Prayer and response now constitute a corporate act of *ḳiddush ha-Shem*,[69] and hence the rubric "Ḳaddish," taken from the second epitomizing term, *we-yitḳaddash*. Since the act of *ḳiddush ha-Shem* has been consummated by the response, the rest of the paragraph is probably a later addition, as indeed its partly Hebrew, partly Aramaic character seems to indicate. The Ḳaddish proper—that is, the prayer and the response—are in Aramaic, for the Ḳaddish came at the end of lectures to the Aramaic-speaking public.[70]

Later it became the practice to recite the Ḳaddish at public worship at the end of each section of the liturgy, and public worship as a whole thus came to be an occasion for acts of *ḳiddush ha-Shem*. A conjunction of two separate acts of *ḳiddush ha-Shem* occurs at the morning service when Baraku is preceded by Ḳaddish, a conjunction so striking that it was repeated at the end of that Tefillah ('Amidah) for possible latecomers, according to *Masseket Soferim*.[71] Providing for similar circumstances, Rashi too says that latecomers can have Baraku recited, preceded by the Ḳaddish.[72] Actually, however, Ḳaddish before Baraku is by no means an introduction to Baraku, but, as post-talmudic authorites have declared, is rather a corporate act of *ḳiddush ha-Shem* which closes the first section of the liturgy at public worship.[73] Originally, then, the presence of the folk at public lectures, and hence the presence of a *ẓibbur*, provided an occasion to say the Ḳaddish, and later the very presence of the *ẓibbur* at worship likewise provided occasions for reciting the Ḳaddish; in both developments the recital of the Ḳaddish is the outcome of an occasion,[74] something which is true of all acts of *ḳiddush ha-Shem*. Since in rabbinic literature the Ḳaddish is associated with public lectures, it is obviously not associated with the list given in *Megillah* IV.3.

D. The Ḳedushah

After the public recital of the Shema', and so conforming to the order in the liturgy, *Megillah* IV.3 lists the recital of the Tefillah or

'Amidah by the "deputy of the *ẓibbur*"[75]—that is, by the leader—as another act requiring not less than ten. Repeated by the leader at the synagogue service in behalf of those who knew the Tefillah only imperfectly,[76] the Tefillah becomes a corporate act when the *ẓibbur* as a whole responds with "Amen" to each berakah.[77] Since the individual can recite it privately, however, even the reciting of the Tefillah aloud[78] is not an act of worship which is intrinsically corporate.

When the leader, in repeating the Tefillah, reaches the Third Berakah, which is called Ḳedushat ha-Shem,[79] and which has for its theme, as the name implies, the holiness of God, there takes place, according to an express declaration, a corporate act of *ḳiddush ha-Shem*, the Ḳedushah.[80] Like other liturgical acts of *ḳiddush ha-Shem*, the Ḳedushah here consists essentially of two parts. The first is a declaration of intention to "extol and sanctify Thee" (נעריצך ונקדישך) as do the holy seraphim,[81] or, in a simpler version, to "sanctify Thy Name in the world" as it is sanctified in heaven.[82] Specifically stressed in *Masseket Soferim*,[83] this declaration is the introduction to the Ḳedushah proper, and is said by the *ẓibbur* and then repeated by the leader.

In all the versions, the conclusion of the declaration of intention introduces the Ḳedushah proper with the words, "As it is written by Thy prophet, 'And one called unto another and said.' . . ." This quotation of the opening phrase of Isaiah 6:3 concludes the introduction to the Ḳedushah. Now the Ḳedushah itself begins, the *ẓibbur* picking up the verse precisely where the leader has left off: "Holy, holy, holy is the Lord of hosts; the whole world is full of His Glory." But the Trisagion ("thrice-holy") does not close the Ḳedushah. To these words of the seraphim in heaven, according to the Ḳedushah, there is an antiphonal response by other celestial beings, and this response is a phrase in Ezekiel 3:12. The leader refers to these beings and introduces the antiphonal response after the Trisagion has been recited by the *ẓibbur* by saying, in the simple version, "Those over against them say, 'Blessed [*baruk*].' " The *ẓibbur* now responds with the whole phrase from Ezekiel 3:12, "Blessed [*baruk*] is the Glory of the Lord from His place."[84] Only the verses presented here (Isa. 6:3 and Ezek. 3:12) are germane to the Ḳedushah; the verses which now follow these are later additions.

We are led to this conclusion not alone by a consideration of the various ways in which the particular verses are introduced or connected,[85] but by the character of the Ḳedushah as a midrashic interpretation.

A midrashic interpretation, we have demonstrated elsewhere, is always a unitary entity,[86] and the Ḳedushah is fundamentally a midrashic interpretation. Two verses (Isa. 6:3 and Ezek. 3:12) are brought together and so interpreted that they become integral elements of a new idea, an idea that would not be complete were either of the verses omitted. In Scripture, each of these verses has for its context a description of a mystical experience of God on the part of a prophet, a phenomenal experience in which celestial beings utter praise of God; in Isaiah, the celestial beings are six-winged seraphim, and in Ezekiel, they are, apparently, the *ḥayyot* and *'ofannim* (the "living creatures" and "wheels" of Ezek. 1:5 ff. and 1:15 ff.).[87] In the Ḳedushah, not only is the praise in Ezekiel 3:12 made an antiphonal response to the praise in Isaiah 6:3, but both verses are taken as embodying the same rabbinic concept. Both verses, in speaking of "the Glory of God," use a form of the word *Kabod*, and that word in rabbinic usage is a term for God limited to *gilluy Shekinah*—that is, to visual or auditory revelations of God.[88] Does God, then, reveal Himself to the celestial beings? He does not, as a comment by the leader in the Musaf Ḳedushah tells us. After the praise of seraphim, the leader says, "His *Kabod* [meaning God] fills the world,[89] [yet] His servitors [the *ḥayyot*] ask one another, 'Where is the place of His *Kabod*?'"[90] Because the question has been raised, there must be an affirmation, an acknowledgment of God, and this acknowledgment, emphasizing the presence of God by mentioning "His place," is made by the *ḥayyot* and *'ofannim* themselves in the form of a berakah. In other words, it is necessary for the *ḥayyot* to acknowledge the presence of God because neither they who carry the Throne see Him, nor by implication, do the seraphim who are more distant, even though the latter know and proclaim that God may reveal Himself anywhere. The Ḳedushah thus integrates the aforementioned verses into a midrashic interpretation which concretizes the concept of *gilluy Shekinah*, and which teaches that God is everywhere and that the scene of His revelation may be anywhere, any place, in the world.[91] The verses in the

Ḳedushah which at present follow the praises of the seraphim and the *ḥayyot*, however, do not embody the concept of *gilluy Shekinah*, are not integral elements of the midrashic interpretation,[92] and hence can only be later additions.

In its declaration of intention, "We will sanctify Thy Name," the introduction characterizes the Ḳedushah which follows it as an act of *ḳiddush ha-Shem*. The declared intention is realized when the *ẓibbur* recites a berakah[93] affirming that God is everywhere, and hence a berakah which consists of a general acknowledgment of God. Moreover, as in the other corporate acts of *ḳiddush ha-Shem*, this liturgical act, too, takes place because a *ẓibbur* has already been formed, this time because of the need to hear the repetition of the 'Amidah or Tefillah by the leader. On the other hand, there is an aspect to the Ḳedushah which makes it different from what we have come to regard as a corporate act of *ḳiddush ha-Shem*. An act of *ḳiddush ha-Shem* has, as background, experience of God on the part of the individuals of the *ẓibbur*, specific and daily experience. The Ḳedushah in the 'Amidah, however, does not arise out of such a background. It is, after all, only a representation of the angels' praises, and hence its sanctification of God is conceived to be, in the very declaration of intention, but an act which imitates that of the angels.[94]

In the early amoraic period authorities still differed as to whether or not the Ḳedushah in the 'Amidah was to be regarded as a corporate act of *ḳiddush ha-Shem*. The question is a halakic one, and is an instance of how a value concept depends on the Halakah for concretization. It is a halakic question because it involves a decision as to whether the individual may recite the Ḳedushah in the 'Amidah by himself or whether he may not. As inferred in the Talmud, R. Joshua b. Levi, a Palestinian, says he may not, whereas R. Huna', a Babylonian, says he may, and the Talmud goes on to cite R. 'Adda' b. 'Ahabah, a countryman and contemporary of R. Huna', who not only agrees with R. Joshua b. Levi but who also characterizes the Ḳedushah as *dabar shebi-ḳedushah*—that is, as a corporate act of *ḳiddush ha-Shem*.[95] According to Ginzberg, it is not possible that the text here contained, originally, any reference to R. Joshua b. Levi or to any other Palestinian.[96] The fact remains, however, that R. Huna' does not regard the Ḳedushah as intrinsically a corporate act.

At that period, therefore, the Ḳedushah in the 'Amidah could not have been preceded by a declaration of intention characterizing the Ḳedushah as a corporate act of *ḳiddush ha-Shem*.[97]

The only form of the Ḳedushah in which no extraneous verses were added to the midrashic interpretation is the Ḳedushah of the Yoẓer (the first of the two benedictions preceding the Shema'). Now it is true that a good many literary embellishments crept into the Yoẓer in the course of time, and that these vary from version to version.[98] But it is also true that the Ḳedushah proper has remained intact and furthermore, that the idea introducing the Ḳedushah is the same in all the versions. It is merely necessary to disengage the idea from the embellishments.

The introduction relates the Ḳedushah to the theme of the berakah in the Yoẓer. Found in all the versions, the phrases "[Who] createst holy ones" (בורא קדושים) and "[Who] formest ministering angels" (servitors—יוצר משרתים) continue the theme of the berakah with the very words, יוצר and בורא, employed in the berakah itself. Moreover, just as the present tense of these verbs in the berakah implies a renewed creation every day, an implication made explicit there,[99] so does it imply, in the phrases on the angels, the daily creation of new angels. Again, in all the versions the introduction concludes with a statement leading directly to the Ḳedushah proper to the effect that the angels say the Ḳedushah in unison.* These elements, which all the versions have in common, are constituents of a single

* See Baer, *op. cit.*, pp. 78 f. The key phrase in the concluding statement is וכלם מקבלים . . . ונותנים רשות זה לזה; see the notes, *ibid.*, p. 79. From the sources cited there, *Targum Jonathan* on Isa. 6:3 and *Tanḥuma*, *Ẓaw*, par. 13, it is evident that מקבלים refers to "receiving permission from one another," and this accords with the phrase that follows, "and give permission to one another"; this receiving and giving permission to each other to say the Ḳedushah meant that the angels said it in unison. But our present text is certainly not clear. How was it possible to receive עול מלכות שמים, the yoke of the kingship of Heaven, "from one another"? The entire idea is even more difficult. The yoke of the kingship implies positively acceptance of miẓwot and negatively the denial of idolatry, as we have seen; and what have the angels to do with either? The early liturgy had, undoubtedly, a far more simple introduction. Very likely what we have in *Targum Jonathan* and in the *Tanḥuma* is not the *source* of the introduction in the Yoẓer (although Rashi on Isa. 6:3 says that it is), but on the contrary, it is part of the actual introduction itself, taken bodily from the early liturgy. Usually a midrashic interpretation, though only stimulated by a biblical text, retains the tense of the biblical text, but that is not the case here. Whereas Isa. 6:3 is in the past tense, *Targum Jonathan*

idea, as the parallels to that idea in rabbinic literature demonstrate. Such parallels contain the idea that angels who say *shirah* (i.e., the Ḳedushah)[100] are created every day.[101]

Despite the similarity in theme between the berakah of the Yoẓer and the introduction to the Ḳedushah, the Ḳedushah unquestionably represents an addition—although an early addition—to the Yoẓer. The berakah is called forth by the sunrise; it interprets the light of the new day as a manifestation of God's love, and the occasion and the berakah together are an integrated unitary entity. Meditation brings the Ḳedushah into the context of the Yoẓer, to be sure, but only as something additional, and hence as something which is not alluded to either in the opening or in the closing formula of the berakah.[102] Yet, if the Ḳedushah has been inserted into the Yoẓer, it is also completely in consonance with it. The Yoẓer depicts the world as being created anew every day by God; the Ḳedushah, in its rabbinic interpretation, depicts God as being everywhere in that world. It was a problem, however, how to demarcate the Ḳedushah, which is praise of God, from its introduction which, though necessary, is only narrative. This problem was solved, it would seem, by R. Judah who, the Tosefta reports, singled out the verses of the Ḳedushah (Isa. 6:3 and Ezek. 3:12) and said them together with the leader out loud, the rest of the Yoẓer being said apparently by the leader alone.[103] Incidentally, the embellishments in the Yoẓer, too, probably stem in part from the later endeavor to render the narrative in the introduction, as well, a means of praising God.

---

reads: ומקבלין דין מן דין ואמרין, an act in the present tense, and hence referring to a daily act such as is depicted in an introduction forming part of the Yoẓer. In the *Tanḥuma*, more of the old liturgical introduction is given, though it is interrupted by some explanatory material. Beginning with the phrase in *Targum Jonathan* but now in mishnaic Hebrew, the introduction here contains also the idea that the angels say the Ḳedushah in unison: [וקרא זה אל זה ואמר] נוטלין רשות זה מזה . . . פתחו כולם כאחד ועונין וכו׳ The word פתחו means to begin, and it should, of course, read פותחין to conform with נוטלין and עונין, which are in the present tense. The word עונין means to recite in a loud voice (see below, n. 103, the reference to the ראבי״ה). Moreover, a phrase in *Targum Jonathan* on Ezek. 3:12—דמשבחין ואמרין—also presupposes the Ḳedushah, most likely that of the Yoẓer. The entire phrase is something which has been added by the *Targum Jonathan*. Again, whereas the preceding verbs of the verse are given in the past tense, and so in accordance with the Hebrew, this phrase is in the present tense. We have here, evidently, part of the introduction to the second verse of the Ḳedushah.

The Ḳedushah of the Yoẓer is not *dabar shebi-ḳedusha*—at least it was not such in the tannaitic period. From the account in the Tosefta, it is clear that the *ẓibbur* did not say the verses in the Ḳedushah together with the leader and that originally only R. Judah did so. At that time, apparently, it was felt that the Ḳedushah in the Yoẓer was of a piece with the narrative, rather than an entity in itself, and R. Judah did no more than to bring the Ḳedushah into bolder relief.

Recital of the Ḳedushah in the Yoẓer, including the introduction, is ordained by the Halakah. We might suppose, therefore, that the events pictured in the Ḳedushah and in its introduction, events depicted in a section of prescribed liturgy, are matters of dogma. But rabbinic dogmas, we have shown elsewhere, are few in number, and the events spoken of in the Yoẓer are not among them.[104] Far from being dogma, the Ḳedushah in its setting here is only one among a number of divergent representations in rabbinic literature of the *shirah* (song) of the angels.* It is difficult for the modern man to recapture the category of thought and feeling which permits divergent and even contradictory concretizations of the same value

* According to the Yoẓer, the angels "continually declare the Glory of God and His holiness," whereas a baraita in *Ḥullin* 91b states that they say it only once a day, or once a week, or once a month, or once a year, or once in seven years, or once a Jubilee, or "once in the world." *Targum Jonathan* on Isa. 6:3 interprets the Trisagion ("holy, holy, holy") to mean that God is holy in the highest heavens and upon the earth, and forever and ever. Another source interprets it to mean that mankind (הבירויות) do not see Him, that the ministering angels do not see Him, "that even the *ḥayyot* carrying His throne do not see the *Kabod*" (*Seder Eliahu*, ed. Friedmann, p. 163). The same source also states that two rows of angels sanctifying God say the Trisagion from the rising of the sun until its setting, and from the setting of the sun till its rising they say, "Blessed be," etc. (*ibid.*, and pp. 34, 84, 156, 193). According to the Talmud in *Ḥullin* 91b–92a, however, three groups of angels say the Trisagion, one group saying, "Holy," the second saying, "Holy, holy," and the third group saying the entire Trisagion and finishing the verse; and it also states that the '*ofannim* say, "Blessed be," etc. It is not likely that the *merkabah* hymns were intrinsically related to the Ḳedushah. "All these hymns end with the *trishagion* of Isa. 6:3 and are therefore *Ḳedushah*-hymns. In many of them, however, this refrain is introduced quite artificially and without any reference to the text of the hymn itself" (G. G. Scholem, *Jewish Gnosticism, Merkabah Mysticism, and Talmudic Tradition* [New York, 1960], p. 21, n. 2). A comparison between the interpretation of the Trisagion in *Targum Jonathan* to Isa. 6:3 and the use of the Trisagion in Christian liturgy has been made by Mann, "Changes in the Divine Service," etc., *Hebrew Union College Annual*, IV, 263 f. See also his discussion there of the Ḳedushah de-Sidra', pp. 267–277.

concept—in this case, the value concept of *ḳiddush ha-Shem*. We have described it in earlier works as the "category of significance," and also as "indeterminacy of belief."[105] Belonging to this category are the events portrayed in the Ḳedushah and its introduction, notwithstanding their halakic framework. Indeed, they afford an instance of the interrelation of Halakah and Haggadah.

The Ḳedushah of the Yoẓer is earlier than that of the 'Amidah and, with respect to the liturgy, is the original Ḳedushah.[106] It was inserted early in the tannaitic period, for by the time of R. Judah it was already an integral part of the liturgy. Not on that account alone, however, do we hold it to be earlier than the Ḳedushah of the 'Amidah. In the Yoẓer, the Ḳedushah is made continuous with the berakah of the Yoẓer, as we have noticed; in the 'Amidah, it so obviously interrupts the berakot that it must have been inserted after the berakot were established, and inserted for a specific purpose. In the Yoẓer, the two verses of the Ḳedushah are seen to be elements of an integrated midrashic interpretation; in the 'Amidah, other verses follow the midrashic interpretation, verses which can only be later additions to the original Ḳedushah, since they are not integrated with the midrashic interpretation.[107] Decidedly a later composition, too, is the introduction to the Ḳedushah of the 'Amidah; although the midrashic interpretation itself is in accord with a tannaitic tradition,[108] the idea in this introduction is distinctly not in line with tannaitic statements on the same theme. While the introduction, in effect, declares that Israel will imitate the angels by saying the *shirah* of the angels, tannaitic sources state that Israel says *shirah* all the while (בכל שעה), whereas the ministering angels say *shirah* less often, opinions here ranging from *shirah* once a day to once in time;[109] that Israel mentions God's Name after two words, evidenced in the Shema', and the angels only after three, evidenced in the *shirah*;[110] that the angels do not say *shirah* until after Israel has said [the Shema'];[111] and that all these things indicate that Israel is more beloved of God than the ministering angels.[112] The introduction to the Ḳedushah in the 'Amidah appears, therefore, to be non-tannaitic and a later addition. In fact, we found above that it was not in the Ḳedushah during the period of the early Amoraim.[113]

First, then, the Ḳedushah came to be an integral part of the Yoẓer, and only subsequently was it also inserted into the Third Berakah of the 'Amidah. Since the introduction to the Ḳedushah in the Yoẓer is associated with the theme of the Yoẓer, and since that theme, the creation of the new day, is irrelevant to the Third Berakah of the 'Amidah, the midrashic interpretation alone was inserted there. In other words, the Ḳedushah in the 'Amidah originally consisted merely of: (*a*) the second part of Isaiah 6:3, (*b*) a reference to the *ḥayyot*,[114] and (*c*) the last part of Ezekiel 3:12, these being the sole elements of the midrashic interpretation and sufficient to convey a complete rabbinic idea, a unitary thought. But now a change began to take place in the character of the Ḳedushah. Recited without its introduction in the Yoẓer, the Ḳedushah in the 'Amidah took on an independent character, and the biblical verses, while recognized as the praises of the angels, also became more clearly a means of worship in themselves. It was possible, moreover, to regard them as being intrinsically a means of corporate worship, for the folk, having undoubtedly followed the example of R. Judah,[115] continued to say the verses out loud when they were made part of the 'Amidah, so that, as far as the action of the *ẓibbur* was concerned, the Ḳedushah resembled corporate acts of *ḳiddush ha-Shem* already established. The berakah in the Ḳedushah, a berakah expressing a general acknowledgment of God, completed the resemblance. In the early amoraic period, accordingly, some held that the Ḳedushah in the 'Amidah was a corporate act of *ḳiddush ha-Shem*, *dabar shebi-ḳedushah*, although there was also a contrary opinion.[116] Of course, when the declaration of intention was added, the Ḳedushah in the 'Amidah definitely assumed the character of *dabar shebi-ḳedushah*.

Several circumstances enable us to surmise the reason for the insertion of the Ḳedushah into the 'Amidah. It was at first recited in the 'Amidah only on the Sabbath and on the festivals, and even then, only at the Shaḥarit service. In Palestine the Ḳedushah in the 'Amidah was limited to these occasions until well into geonic times.[117] Now the Fourth Berakah on the Sabbath and on the festivals, the Ḳedushat ha-Yom, refers to the hallowing of the day, either of the Sabbath or of the festival, while the theme of the berakah which precedes it—that of the Third Berakah—is Ḳedushat ha-Shem, the holiness of God. To differentiate between these two aspects of the concept of *ḳedushah*, something especially necessary because the

Ḳedushat ha-Shem was so brief,[118] the Ḳedushah, with its vivid representation of the holiness of God, was inserted into the Third Berakah. Since in the tannaitic (and early amoraic) period, the 'Amidah as a whole was not recited on Friday night,[119] the first opportunity to differentiate between the Ḳedushat ha-Shem and the Ḳedushat ha-Yom occurred at the Shaḥarit service (the morning liturgy), and hence the practice of reciting the Ḳedushah in the Shaḥarit 'Amidah. It was not inserted into the other 'Amidot of the day since its quasi-pedagogic function had already been fulfilled, and it was not inserted into the week-day 'Amidah since that 'Amidah naturally does not contain the Ḳedushat ha-Yom. Because it was said only on certain occasions, the Ḳedushah in the 'Amidah was thereby accentuated and the *ẓibbur*, who recited it aloud, were all the more likely to regard it as *dabar shebi-ḳedushah*.

Geonic sources and cognate material, adduced and interpreted by Ginzberg, reveal how the hegemony of Babylon in the geonic period further affected the character of the Ḳedushah in the 'Amidah and determined the occasions when that Ḳedushah was to be recited. Babylonian mystics had provided an introduction to the Ḳedushah in the 'Amidah, the כתר formula, and had inserted the Ḳedushah, together with that formula, into every 'Amidah, on week-days as well.[120] The Palestinians were obliged to accept the Babylonian practices but they divested the Ḳedushah of the mystical *merkabah*★ idea.[121] In place of the Babylonian formula, they employed the introduction characterizing the Ḳedushah as *ḳiddush ha-Shem* and as an act whereby Israel engages in the practice of the angels.[122] It seems likely, therefore, that the Ḳedushah in the 'Amidah did not have the Palestinian introduction either until the geonic period; and if that was indeed the case, the introduction, by putting into words what had hitherto been left uncrystallized, gave the Ḳedushah an imitative character which it had not originally possessed.[123]

E. Berakot as *Gemilut Ḥasadim*

A passage in the Midrash tells of occasions when a person acting as deputy of a *ẓibbur* thereby performs an act of *gemilut ḥasadim*.[124] Those occasions are the public recitation of the Shema', the recital

★ The "chariot" of Ezek. 1:4 ff., relating to theosophic speculations.

of the Tefillah by the leader, the recital of the Birkat Ḥatanim (benedictions said at a wedding), and the recital of the Birkat 'Abelim (benedictions said at a house of mourning); he who is the deputy of the *ẓibbur* on any of these occasions performs an act of *gemilut ḥasadim* when the others in the *ẓibbur* do not know how to serve as the deputy or leader.[125] A corporate act of *ḳiddush ha-Shem* is never, under any circumstances, an act of *gemilut ḥasadim*, for it is never done in behalf of others. None of the acts named here, therefore, is an act of *ḳiddush ha-Shem*.

A berakah which is part of a corporate act of *ḳiddush ha-Shem* is, in fact, altogether different from any other berakah. It consists solely of a general acknowledgment of God, and hence it does not embody, as do all the other berakot, the concept of God's love or that of His justice. A corporate act of *ḳiddush ha-Shem*, furthermore, is intrinsically corporate in character, but this feature is possessed by a number of other corporate acts as well. Thus, of the acts named in the midrash referred to above, Birkat Ḥatanim and Birkat 'Abelim are, we shall soon see, intrinsically corporate in character, although, as we have noticed, the public recitation of the Shema' and the recital of the Tefillah by the leader are not. All four acts are in the list of things enumerated in *Megillah* IV.3 as requiring the presence of "not less than ten."[126]

Birkat 'Abelim consists of a series of berakot said in the presence of mourners, and Birkat Ḥatanim, of a series of berakot said at a wedding.[127] These two series, Lieberman has shown, were once closely related: the halakot on the one series largely corresponded with the halakot on the other, and the form of the one series largely paralleled the form of the other. Birkot 'Abelim were said first in the synagogue or in the open place of the town (רחבה), and were repeated in the house of the mourners, where they were said during the first two days (not necessarily in conjunction with a meal);[128] similarly, Birkot Ḥatanim were said first at the *ḥuppah* (i.e., at the wedding) and were repeated in the home of the groom (*bet ḥatanim*), again not necessarily in conjunction with a meal.[129] On each of those occasions three berakot were said, the series in the Birkat 'Abelim and the series in the Palestinian version of Birkat Ḥatanim each containing three berakot.[130] When Birkat 'Abelim was said after a meal during the first two days of mourning, the three berakot were so combined with Birkat ha-Mazon that the result was a special form of the Birkat ha-Mazon for mourners.[131] For all the remainder of the seven days, however, the only one of these berakot retained together with its closing formula as a substitute for a regular berakah in the Birkat ha-Mazon was that which closed with "Who comfortest His people in His city";[132] and similarly, the only berakah of the Birkat Ḥatanim which was said after a meal during all the seven days was that which closed with "Who makest His people joyful in His city."[133]

The parallelism between Birkat 'Abelim and Birkat Ḥatanim thus, in a degree, extended to the actual phraseology. We have just pointed out one instance. Another is the phrase, "Who hast formed man," which was at one time part of the First Berakah of the Birkat 'Abelim as well as part of the First Berakah of the Birkat Ḥatanim.[134]

All these halakic and literary similarities stem from an unusual conceptual kinship between the two sets of berakot. Both Birkat 'Abelim and Birkat Ḥatanim contain berakot which are concretizations of *gemilut ḥasadim*,[135] berakot representing acts of *gemilut ḥasadim* that are incumbent upon the *ẓibbur* as a whole. Other acts of *gemilut ḥasadim* are often conditioned by the wealth or superior position or skill possessed by the benefactor: that is to say, are acts on the part of an individual.[136] In the midrash cited above, we had an example of such a benefactor in the person who serves as the leader in a corporate act of worship when none of the others can serve in that capacity. At the same time, this very midrash also indicates that Birkat Ḥatanim and Birkat 'Abelim themselves have to do with acts of *gemilut ḥasadim*, and that these acts require a *ẓibbur*. It speaks of ten who gathered to enable a bride to be married and of ten who gathered in the house of a mourner (to comfort him), and in both instances the act which required the presence of the ten was the saying of the appropriate berakot.[137]

Comforting mourners was a deed of lovingkindness incumbent not only on the friends of the mourners[138] but also on the *ẓibbur* as a whole. Pointing to the role of the *ẓibbur* are the place where the Birkat 'Abelim is first said and the content of the Second and Third Berakot. Birkat 'Abelim is first said in the synagogue or in the open square of the town, the meeting places of the *ẓibbur*, and this can only mean that the saying of these berakot is incumbent on the *ẓibbur* as a whole. But if Birkat 'Abelim is to be a means of comforting the mourners, it must contain words of comfort addressed directly to them. Such is precisely the case with the Second Berakah of Birkat 'Abelim. Characterized as relating to the mourners, it begins by addressing them as "our brethren, who are worn out and crushed by this bereavement," continues with phrases of comfort, the burden of the berakah, to the effect that "such is the path from the Six Days of Creation," and concludes with, "Our brethren, may He Who comforteth [בעל הנחמות] comfort you—Blessed art Thou, O Lord, Who comfortest mourners."[139] This is indeed a peculiar berakah, for it begins not by addressing itself to God, as is true of berakot and prayers generally, but to the mourners.[140] It is not intended to be a berakah in the usual sense, however. What we have here is a statement and a berakah combined—a statement of comfort addressed to the mourners, and then a brief prayer and a berakah. Said in the first instance by the *ẓibbur* in the synagogue, or rather by the deputy on behalf of the *ẓibbur*, the words of comfort together with the prayer and the berakah constitute an act of *gemuilt ḥasadim* on the part of the *ẓibbur* as a whole.

The Third Berakah of Birkat 'Abelim complements the Second. Characterized as relating to the comforters, it addresses them directly, describes them as those who engage in deeds of lovingkindness, and after a prayer that they be rewarded, concludes with the berakah, "Blessed art Thou, O Lord, Who rewardest the good deed [משלם הגמול]."[141] This is a counterpart of the Second Berakah, for the Third, too, begins by addressing itself not to God but to men—this time to the comforters. The comforters are members of the *ẓibbur* who, having just performed an act of *gemilut ḥasadim* by means of the Second Berakah, are addressed by the deputy, now not in his capacity as a deputy but as an individual. The Third Berakah complements the Second Berakah: it refers to the Second, designates the Second as an act of *gemilut ḥasadim*, reflects the same situation as does the Second: that of the *ẓibbur* as a whole comforting the mourners. Since this act is incumbent upon the *ẓibbur* as a whole—witness the locale of the act, the synagogue—the act is intrinsically corporate in character. When the act was repeated in the house of the mourners, the character of the act had already been established and hence Birkat 'Abelim requires "not less than ten."

Birkat 'Abelim was a conceptual continuum. The First Berakah closed with, "Blessed art Thou, O Lord, Who quickenest the dead," but it also possessed, according to Rashi, an opening formula: "Blessed art Thou, O Lord, our God, King of the world, the great God," etc.[142] Every berakah which followed, in contradistinction to the First, had a closing, but no opening formula, and thus was "a berakah which was joined to the immediately preceding berakah." The occasion for the First Berakah was an event which the other berakot in the series reflected as well, namely, the death of a member of the community. Such an event called forth a berakah with the same closing formula as that of the Second Berakah of the Tefillah, a formula embodying the concept of God's love and the rabbinic dogma of *teḥiyyat ha-metim*, the resurrection of the dead.[143] The verbs in the formula were in the present tense because, like the other hereafter concepts, the resurrection was felt to be a promise of God, and the trust in God, *'emunah*, made resurrection seem like a present reality.[144] As in every series of this kind, the concept of God's love was carried over from one berakah to the next; nor was that conceptual continuum broken when the mourners were addressed at the beginning of the Second Berakah and the comforters at the beginning of the Third, for there were other unifying factors that overcame those interruptions. All the berakot in the series were united because, in one way or another, they were concerned with the same event and, in addition, the Third Berakah, as a complement of the Second, was continuous with the Second.[145]

Although an element in a conceptual continuum, the Second Berakah was an act of *gemilut ḥasadim* rather than a berakah of the usual character. The First Berakah expressed a religious experience on the part of the *ẓibbur*, an experience evoked by the death of one of its members. But the Second Berakah did not express a specific religious experience on the part of the *ẓibbur* despite the berakah formula at the end. Just as both the statement of comfort and the prayer which followed it referred to the mourners, so did the berakah at the end refer to the mourners. It is also possible that the berakah at the end referred to mourners in general, but in any case, though said by the deputy in behalf of the comforters, this berakah did not include the comforters at all. Unlike the berakot in the Tefillah and other berakot, the berakah here did not employ the first person plural[146] either in the prayer or in the berakah at the end, but only the second person plural and the third person plural. We must conclude, therefore, that the berakah formula expressed, not a specific religious experience, but at best, only generalized experience. The Third Berakah, on the other hand, may well have represented felt, specific experience, since it was said by the deputy as an individual, and since he was at the same time one of the comforters.

The parallelism exhibited by Birkat Ḥatanim and Birkat 'Abelim is due to their conceptual kinship. Like comforting mourners, to gladden the bride and the groom is a deed of lovingkindness and again, one that is incumbent not only on the friends[147] but also on the *ẓibbur* as a whole. Here, too, this role of the *ẓibbur* is indicated by the circumstances under which Birkat Ḥatanim was first said, and especially by the content of one of the berakot.

In Palestine, as we noticed, Birkat Ḥatanim was said first at the *ḥuppah* and was repeated in the home of the groom (*bet ḥatanim*);[148] the wedding, accordingly, was not held in the home. It was held, undoubtedly, in the presence of the *ẓibbur*, for he who said the berakot was the *ḥazzan*, a paid official of the *ẓibbur*.[149] The *ẓibbur* as a whole engaged in an act of *gemilut ḥasadim* when, through the *ḥazzan* as deputy, it prayed for the bride and groom. "O make these loved companions greatly to rejoice, even as of old Thou didst gladden Thy creature in the Garden of Eden—Blessed art Thou, O Lord, Who makest bridegroom and bride to rejoice."[150]

There is a striking contrast between this act on the part of the *ẓibbur* and the acts of *gemilut ḥasadim* toward the bride and groom on the part of individuals. Individuals, among them the scholars, would sing bridal songs, praising the bride as being beautiful and graceful, or would dance and at the same time perform feats of jugglery to amuse her, and one scholar even carried the bride on his shoulder as he danced.[151] In contrast, the act of *gemilut ḥasadim* performed by the *ẓibbur* is a religious act, consisting of a prayer which closes with a berakah. Incumbent on the *ẓibbur*, said first in the presence of the *ẓibbur* as a whole by the *ḥazzan* of the *ẓibbur* acting as its deputy, Birkat Ḥatanim was thus originally an intrinsically corporate act. As with Birkat 'Abelim, the character of Birkat Ḥatanim was established by the context in which those berakot were said in the first instance. Wherever Birkat Ḥatanim is said, therefore, it requires not less than ten.

In Babylon, Birkat Ḥatanim consisted of the seven berakot we say to this day, whereas in Palestine it consisted of but three berakot, the full text of which has been lost.[152] The berakah we quoted is the Fifth Berakah in the Babylonian series, not counting the berakah on wine, the use of wine here being optional.[153] It seems to us, nevertheless, that in this Fifth Berakah we have either the original Third, and last, Berakah of the Palestinian series, or else one very much like it; and that, indeed, the Fifth Berakah closes a series of three berakot which, again, either represent the original Palestinian series or else are berakot in every way similar.

The two berakot preceding the Fifth read seriatim as follows:[154] "Blessed art Thou, O Lord our God, King of the world, Who hast formed man in his [man's] image, in the image [and] likeness of his form,[155] and hast prepared unto him, out of his very self [ממנו], a perpetual fabric [בנין עדי עד, i.e., woman][156]—"Blessed art Thou, O Lord, Creator of man" (Third Berakah); "May she who was barren [Zion] be exceeding glad and exult, when her children are gathered within her in joy—Blessed art Thou, O Lord, Who makest Zion joyful in her children" (Fourth Berakah). Now the Third Berakah begins with the identical phrase with which the First Berakah in the Palestinian series also began[157] and is very similar in content and style to a Palestinian morning berakah.[158] The closing phrase of the Fourth Berakah, furthermore, is certainly reminiscent of the closing phrase of the only berakah in the Birkat Ḥatanim said in Palestine after a meal during all the seven days.[159] Such a relationship to Palestinian berakot indicates that the Third and Fourth Berakot, though found in the Babli, are not purely Babylonian. This is also true, most likely, of the Fifth Berakah, for it is associated with the two preceding berakot in a unitary series characterized by a conceptual continuum.

We base our remarks on the conceptual continuum in this series upon Rashi's interpretation.[160] Since it opens the series of the three berakot having to do with the occasion—the marriage itself—the Third Berakah has both an opening and a closing formula, while the Fourth and Fifth, being dependent berakot, have, each of them, only a closing formula. The theme of the Third Berakah is the manifestation of God's love in the creation of man, and that idea is so phrased as also to relate the present marriage to that of the first man and woman, and to convey the thought of the permanence of mankind as well.[161] Included, too, in the closing formula—"Blessed art Thou, O Lord, Creator of man"—is the gratitude felt by the members of the *ẓibbur* that they themselves were created by God. The Fourth Berakah begins with a prayer for the restoration of Zion in accordance with the rabbinic emphasis on Psalm 137: 5–6: "If I forget thee, O Jerusalem. . . . If I set not Jerusalem above my chiefest joy"; and closes with a berakah in which the restoration of Zion is represented as taking place in the present. This type of berakah, we have so often noticed, reflects an "as if" experience, for the prayer is in effect a meditation, and the meditation on what is regarded as a promise of God results in the feeling that the restoration is taking place right now.[162] Like the Fourth, the Fifth and last Berakah in this series of three similarly begins with a prayer and closes with a berakah, and now the prayer is for the happiness of the bride and groom. But the berakah here, "Who makest bridegroom and bride to rejoice," a berakah said by the *ẓibbur* through its deputy, does not express a specific experience of the *ẓibbur*, a present experience, and all that we said about the Second Berakah in Birkat 'Abelim applies equally to this berakah. The rejoicing of the bride and groom is an experience which is theirs alone, one in which the *ẓibbur* cannot share. At best, the berakah expresses, as in the case of the Second Berakah of Birkat 'Abelim, not a specific religious experience of the *ẓibbur*, but only generalized experience. Both berakot alike are acts of *gemilut ḥasadim* rather than berakot of the usual character. We must add, however, that the Fifth Berakah, like its parallel, does not altogether lose its character as a berakah. All of the three berakot, including the Fifth, are elements in a conceptual continuum, wherein the concept of God's love is carried over from one berakah to the next, and all of them have reference, in one way or another, to the same event.[163]

A berakah embodies a number of other concepts, not only that of berakah. It usually embodies the concept of God's love, or else that of God's justice, and frequently, as in the Tefillah and Birkat ha-Mazon, the concept of man; all of these are moral or ethical concepts, though those of God's love and God's justice are interpretive only. A berakah is thus an instance of how "a number of value concepts may combine in a unitary yet many-toned experience."[164] A distinction is to be drawn, however, between the role of berakah and that of the other concepts in any berakah. The term berakah alone usually designates the act as a whole. The act as a whole is a concretization of the concept of berakah; although other concepts are also concretized when the act is performed, the other concretizations are concomitant concretizations. In other words, when a berakah is said, an act of worship takes place and such an act of worship usually carries with it ethical concomitants.

But Birkat 'Abelim and Birkat Ḥatanim, while designated by name as berakot, are also designated as *gemilut ḥasadim*.[165] They are called *gemilut ḥasadim* because in each series there is one berakah which is an act of *gemilut ḥasadim* as well. So far as these two berakot are concerned, the concretization of *gemilut ḥasadim* is not simply a concomitant of the act of worship; the ethical concept, in fact, so predominates that the character of these berakot is different from that of all others, and instead of expressing felt, specific religious experiences, they express generalized experience. Because in both cases, the berakot in the series are not only integrated but are all related to the same event, the entire series is designated as *gemilut ḥasadim*.

Birkat 'Abelim and Birkat Ḥatanim demonstrate to what degree worship can implicate ethics. It is possible for a berakah to be also an act of *gemilut ḥasadim*, and to stamp with this dual characterization an entire series of berakot. On the other hand, it is also possible for a berakah to be an act of worship alone, and to have no ethical concomitants at all—as we noticed in the berakot of *ḳiddush ha-Shem*.[166] Both extremes are acts of worship which are intrinsically corporate.

F. Birkat ha-Zimmun

Birkat ha-Zimmun is an act of worship incumbent on three (or more) men who have eaten a meal together,[167] an act which, on such occasions, precedes Birkat ha-Mazon.[168] When the company consists of at least three and fewer than ten, one of them acting as leader says, "We will bless [*nebarek*] Him of Whose bounty we have eaten," and the others respond with, "Blessed [*baruk*] is He of whose bounty we have eaten and by Whose goodness we live."[169] The response is then repeated by the leader.[170]

The response is a berakah, for the act as a whole is designated in the Tosefta[171] and in the Talmud[172] as Birkat ha-Zimmun; moreover, the response begins with "*baruk*" and is introduced in the call with the word "*nebarek*." We have here a berakah, therefore, similar in several respects to the berakah in Baraku. Like the latter,[173] the berakah in Birkat ha-Zimmun is not couched in the formula of a berakah and, again like the berakah in Baraku, it is a berakah said in response to a call. So far as form is concerned, Birkat ha-Zimmun as an act of worship thus strongly resembles Baraku, a corporate act of *ḳiddush ha-Shem*. It is even likely that at one time, the leader's call in Birkat ha-Zimmun was the same as the call in Baraku.[174]

Nevertheless, Birkat ha-Zimmun is not a corporate act, much less a corporate act of *ḳiddush ha-Shem*. A corporate act requires a *ẓibbur*, the presence of at least ten men, whereas here the minimum is three. Besides, the berakah in Birkat ha-Zimmun is not a general acknowledgment of God, as is the berakah in an act of *ḳiddush ha-Shem*,[175] but one that is related to an event, the meal just eaten, and one that embodies the concept of God's love—"Of Whose bounty we have eaten and by Whose goodness we live." We can only conclude that Birkat ha-Zimmun represents a special case, that it is an act of worship which is a group act but not a corporate act.

If the group consists of ten men, the leader is to say, "We will bless our God of Whose bounty," etc., and the rest of the group is to respond with, "Blessed be our God of Whose bounty," etc.[176] Birkat ha-Zimmun is hence now to include the Name of God,[177] and, accordingly, *Megillah* IV.3 lists among the acts requiring "not less than ten" the inclusion of the Name of God in the Zimmun. It is not *derek ereẓ* (*'oraḥ 'ar'a*, in the Aramaic), says the Gemara in accounting for this inclusion, to mention the Name of God when there are less than ten present.[178] That statement applies, of course, to a group act only, and it thereby implies a distinction between a group act and one that may be taken to be an act of a *ẓibbur*.

In passing, it is well to recognize that no single principle unites all the matters which are listed in *Megillah* IV.3 as requiring "not less than ten." The Gemara accounts for some of the acts of worship named there on the ground of *ḳiddush ha-Shem*, as we saw earlier in this chapter, and here the Gemara accounts for another act of worship on the ground of *derek ereẓ*. If a principle other than *ḳiddush ha-Shem* is explicitly stated to be the ground for having not less than ten in an act of worship, we certainly have no right to assume that such an act is also *ḳiddush ha-Shem*. Moreover, an act listed as among those requiring not less than ten is by no means necessarily an act of *ḳiddush ha-Shem*. Birkat 'Abelim and Birkat Ḥatanim are definitely not acts of *ḳiddush ha-Shem*, let alone the matters in the list which are not acts of worship at all.[179]

The question is: Does Birkat ha-Zimmun change its character when there are ten and become an act of corporate worship, an act of a *ẓibbur*, or does it always retain its special character and remain an act of merely a group, no matter how large the group comes to be? Bearing on this question are statements in *Berakot* VII.3, a mishnah which is interpreted by both the Babli and the Yerushalmi in much the same way. According to the Babli,[180] the mishnah contains two opposing opinions: on the one hand, the opinion of R. Jose, who teaches that the larger the size of the gathering, the more numerous are to be the epithets for God in Birkat ha-Zimmun, the wording depending on whether the gathering is that of three, ten, a hundred, a thousand, or ten thousand; and, on the other hand, the opinion of R. 'Aḳiba, who teaches that Birkat ha-Zimmun is to remain the same "whether there are ten or ten myriads."[181] The Yerushalmi says, in effect, much the same thing as the Babli except that, according to the Yerushalmi, the opinion that Birkat ha-Zimmun is to remain the same "whether there are ten or ten myriads" is that of the *Ḥakamim*.[182]

On the basis of these interpretations, it appears that, according to R. 'Aḳiba or the *Ḥakamim*, Birkat ha-Zimmun is no longer a group act when there are ten but an act of worship intrinsically corporate in character. Like other corporate acts of worship, no matter how many are present providing there are at least ten, the wording remains the same. Indeed, R. 'Aḳiba,[183] as the Babli interprets him, by offering Baraku as an analogy and thus equating Birkat ha-Zimmun with another intrinsically corporate act of worship, actually identifies Birkat ha-Zimmun as a corporate act of worship when there are ten or more present. The Yerushalmi does so also, but by indicating that the ten or more constitute a *ẓibbur*.[184] R. Jose's view, however, is otherwise. Since he teaches that the formula changes in accordance with the size of the gathering, he must hold that ten or more do not constitute a *ẓibbur* in the case of Birkat ha-Zimmun. He maintains, we take it, that because Birkat ha-Zimmun is merely a group act when there are three, it always possesses that character. This view allows any berakah which is a response by a *ẓibbur* to have a consistent, distinctive character. Such a berakah is a general acknowledgment of God, an act of *ḳiddush ha-Shem*. A berakah that is a general acknowledgment of God confirms the past and varied experiences of God of the individuals who compose the *ẓibbur* reciting that berakah. In contrast, the berakah of Birkat ha-Zimmun expresses a specific experience of God which the individuals reciting the berakah have just had in common.

Even in a corporate act, there must be an expression of the individual, of each and every member of the *ẓibbur* engaged in the act. A corporate act requires not only that ten or more must be present, but that each and every man present must act. This is just as true when the deputy acts on behalf of the *ẓibbur* as when the members of the *ẓibbur* themselves say a berakah.

When a deputy acts on behalf of the *ẓibbur*, every member of the *ẓibbur* is to respond, "Amen."[185] What that response implies is especially evident when the act is not intrinsically corporate, as in Birkat ha-Mazon[186] and in the Tefillah.[187] Since such acts are incumbent on the individual in any case, and may be accomplished by him in private, the deputy acts not for the *ẓibbur* as a whole but for each individual in the *ẓibbur*, and it is as though the individual himself has said the berakah when he responds, "Amen." "Amen" cannot have a different implication even when it is a response in acts intrinsically corporate, as in Birkat 'Abelim and Birkat Ḥatanim. Acts of *ḳiddush ha-Shem* are a class by themselves, for in these acts each member of the *ẓibbur* himself says the berakah. According to R. Jose's teaching, however, there is one act resembling the act of a *ẓibbur*, Birkat ha-Zimmun, in which the individual has an even larger role; the very form of that act, in his opinion, depends on the number of individuals who participate.

CHAPTER VII

Worship as Normal Mysticism

A. From *Gilluy Shekinah* to Normal Mysticism

There are verses in the Psalms in which the psalmist speaks of having had a visual, sensory experience of God in the Sanctuary, or else in which he expresses the expectation or hope of having such an experience. "So have I beheld Thee [חזיתיך] in the Sanctuary, to see Thy strength and Thy glory."[1] "I shall behold [אחזה] Thy face in righteousness; I shall be satisfied, when I awake, with Thy likeness."[2] "My soul thirsteth for God, for the living God: 'When shall I come and see the face of God?' "[3] A visual experience of God is, in rabbinic terminology, an experience of *gilluy Shekinah* (revelation of God), a term which stands also for other sensory experiences of God.[4]

The rabbis, too, say that *Shekinah* "dwelt" or "rested" (*sharetah*) in the Tabernacle and in the First Temple.[5] In other words, they regarded the Tabernacle and the First Temple as locales of *gilluy Shekinah*. With respect to the Second Temple, opinions differed, some holding that *Shekinah* did not,[6] and others holding that *Shekinah* did,[7] dwell there. In an early controversy between the Sadducees and the Pharisees, the halakah taught by the Sadducees implies that in the Holy of Holies there is permanent and steady *gilluy Shekinah*, whereas the halakah taught by the Pharisees seems to imply that *gilluy Shekinah* may take place there, not that it necessarily will occur.[8] Ultimately at the basis of these various statements and halakot is the association of *gilluy Shekinah* with the sacrificial worship of the Temple, an association reflected in the petition "Restore Thy *Shekinah* to Zion and the order of Thy 'Abodah to Jerusalem."[9] Some tannaitic sources even assume, if our interpretation is correct, that there was *gilluy Shekinah* at the time a sacrifice was being offered; they assume that the pilgrim to the Temple on the festivals could, apparently, experience *gilluy Shekinah* when he stood by his sacrifice as it was being offered.[10] But whatever the opinion held with regard to *gilluy Shekinah*—that it occurred at the sacrificial service, or that it occurred only occasionally and then in the Holy of Holies—everybody felt that *gilluy Shekinah* and the sacrificial service at the Temple were ultimately associated. Everybody felt that the sacrificial service took place in, so to speak, the proximity of God, a proximity that, when all conditions were fulfilled, would be made visibly manifest.

As we saw in a preceding chapter, nonsacrificial forms of worship had already been developed in the days of the Second Temple; and these acts of worship were designated by the same word as designates the sacrificial worship of the Temple—'abodah.[11] The new forms of worship, in which there is no *gilluy Shekinah*, were called for, it seems to us, by the rabbinic value complex which had crystallized during the days of the Second Temple. The concept of *gilluy Shekinah* is not fully compatible with this value complex as a whole. "Standing for the revelation of God to human senses, particularly the sense of sight, it represents a mixture of the valuational and the cognitive, and it is therefore not a pure value-concept."[12] The rabbinic value complex called for acts of worship fully in consonance with the character of the value complex as a whole; moreover, it called for acts of worship in which as many value concepts as possible would be given expression. We are saying no more than that it is in the very nature of institutions to express the dominant character and the content of the value complex of the folk.

Although not a pure value concept and therefore restricted in its application,[13] *gilluy Shekinah* is nonetheless a component part of the value complex. It is a concept that connotes the experience of God's nearness, albeit in a visual and sensory manner. Now the awareness of God's nearness is also an element in the experience of God involved in the Tefillah and in the berakot, nonsacrificial forms of worship. In this awareness there is no *gilluy Shekinah*, no sensory experience and so, of course, the concept of *gilluy Shekinah* is not concretized in these acts. Nevertheless, a relationship between the nonsensory experience and *gilluy Shekinah* is certainly discernible: in both there is awareness of God's nearness and in both God is external to man. The new forms of nonsacrificial worship were developed not only in accordance with the dominant character of the value complex but were also affected by the concept of *gilluy Shekinah*. Indeed, the dominant character of the value complex doubtless also shaped, to a degree, the character of the concept of *gilluy Shekinah* itself.

Different as is nonsacrificial from sacrificial worship, there is nevertheless a link between them, and that link is the Tefillah. There is a time correspondence between the saying of the Tefillah and the offering of the daily communal sacrifices in the Temple, the Tefillah being thus a reminder of the daily communal sacrifices. The Tefillah was ordained "as against" those sacrifices. After the destruction of the Temple, the Tefillah, as their surrogate, like them atones for Israel's sins. The Tefillah is "in place of the sacrifice." All these matters, which we have discussed earlier,[14] tend to give the Tefillah the character of a sacrifice. On the other hand, the Tefillah is obviously nonsacrificial worship, for it consists of berakot. Furthermore, its sacrificial character is only temporary. Related to the daily sacrifices, yet itself nonsacrificial worship, the Tefillah constitutes a link between sacrificial and nonsacrificial worship.

Practices accompany the saying of the Tefillah which can only be reminiscent of an experience of *gilluy Shekinah*. They point to the special character of the Tefillah as a surrogate for the daily communal sacrifice, for they derive from the association of the sacrifices with *gilluy Shekinah*, and hence themselves constitute a link between *gilluy Shekinah* and awareness of God without visual experience. A person saying the Tefillah is to face and to direct his heart toward Jerusalem, the Temple, and the Holy of Holies;[15] if he cannot determine the proper direction, he is simply to direct his heart toward the Holy of Holies.[16] At the beginning and at the end of the First Berakah ('Abot) one is to bow, and again at the beginning and the end of the Eighteenth Berakah (Hoda'ah)[17]—the bowing at the First Berakah being apparently an obeisance in greeting, and the bowing at Hoda'ah being an obeisance accompanying מודים אנחנו לך, "We acknowledge Thee."[18] Although these obeisances suffice for an ordinary person, they are not enough for those of exalted rank. According to one version of a tradition, the high priest is to bow at the end of every berakah, and the king, at the beginning and at the end of every berakah, while another version requires the latter practice of the high priest and directs the king to kneel throughout the Tefillah.[19] After a person has recited the Tefillah, he steps back three steps, bowing and inclining his head to his left and then to his right.[20] The background of these practices is the association of the sacrificial worship (for which the Tefillah is a surrogate) with *gilluy Shekinah*. "He who is reciting the Tefillah (*ha-mitpallel*) ought to regard himself as though *Shekinah* were in front of him, as it says, 'I have set the Lord always before me' " (Ps. 16: 2).[21] Rashi applies this talmudic dictum to the practice at the leave-taking,[22] but it is no less applicable to the other practices accompanying the recital of the Tefillah.

Since there is no *gilluy Shekinah* when the Tefillah is recited, these practices but express and accentuate the awareness of God's nearness. "Can you have a God nearer than that?" ask the rabbis in telling of how God hears even a whispered Tefillah.[23] The rule forbidding one to raise his voice when reciting the Tefillah[24]—a rule which teaches how to express in a practice the awareness of God's nearness—is thus quite in consonance with all the other rules and practices as to the reciting of the Tefillah. All of them teach how to express in various practices the awareness of God's nearness.

A berakah is an acknowledgment of God's love in a living context. Such a living context is provided by the occasion for the berakah, the occasion and the berakah which interprets it combining to form a unitary, experiential entity. We have characterized this as an experience of God mediated by the concept of God's love, *middat raḥamim*, but we can now better appreciate what the experience of God in these contexts implies. The berakah formula expresses not only an awareness of God's love in a particular situation but also awareness of God's nearness. "Blessed art Thou, O Lord," are the words of the berakah formula, and these words, as Rab teaches, accord with the verse "I have set the Lord always before me" (Ps. 16: 2).[25] When the individual addresses God with the words of the berakah, he feels that God is before him, and hence he can use the pronoun, "Thou." Other than by some such figure of speech, there is no way to express the nonsensory awareness of God's nearness. That kind of awareness has not been conceptualized. To convey the idea of God's nearness, therefore, the rabbis often use *Shekinah*, the name for God which is part of the term *gilluy Shekinah*, the conceptual term which connotes the visual experience of God's nearness.[26]

Just as the Tefillah involves the awareness of God's nearness, so does the berakah. The same verse, Psalm 16:2, accords with the individual's experience when he says a berakah as when he recites the Tefillah. The fact is that the Tefillah consists of berakot; it is a particular form of the type of worship represented by a berakah.

This type of worship is normal mysticism. It is mystical because awareness of God's nearness is a mystical experience—experience that is not conceptualized and hence private, not communicable to others. And because awareness of God's nearness is not an experience that can be conveyed to others, it cannot be demonstrated or proved. On the other hand, it is no more questioned by the individual than is the experience of the self, another noncommunicable experience. Awareness of God's nearness is, indeed, as steady and on-going an experience as the awareness of the self. At worship and on some other occasions, awareness of God's nearness becomes more acute, quite as the awareness of the self is more acute at some times than at others.

Nonsacrificial worship is not exclusive mysticism, however, but *normal* mysticism.[27] Awareness of God when reciting the Tefillah or saying a berakah is, to a certain degree, communicable, primarily by means of the concepts of God's love, *middat raḥamim*, and God's justice, *middat ha-din*. These concepts are not only terms in the common vocabulary of the folk, elements of ordinary speech, but are also very much akin, as we have noticed,[28] to the parallel concepts of universal, human morality. Awareness of God, though a mystical experience because actual awareness of His nearness is not communicable, is at the same time a normal experience because awareness of His love and His justice *is* communicable. Experience of God in a nonsacrificial act of worship is, in fact, marked by a paradox. Awareness of God's nearness, the noncommunicable factor, is then made more acute than ordinarily by the awareness of God's love, a communicable factor. Of course, the value concepts in an act of worship are not limited to those of God's love and, sometimes, God's justice, and when other value concepts are involved as well, concepts such as *biṭṭaḥon* or Torah, they enrich the entire experience of worship.

Normal mysticism enables a person to make normal, commonplace, recurrent situations and events occasions for worship. The food he eats, the water he drinks, the dawn and the twilight are joined to berakot acknowledging God's love. These daily commonplace situations are not only interpreted in the act of worship as manifestations of God's love, but they arouse in the individual, in the same act of worship, a poignant sense of the nearness of God.

Antecedents of the normal mysticism of the rabbinic period are to be found in the Bible and particularly in the Psalms, where the nearness of God, God's justice and His love are recurrent themes. The nearness of God expressed in the berakah formula accords, as the rabbis taught, with "I have set the Lord always before me" (Ps. 16:2). The First Psalm is entirely devoted to the theme of God's justice. He whose "delight is in the law of the Lord" is rewarded, for "he shall be like a tree planted by streams of water," whereas the wicked are punished and are "like the chaff which the wind driveth away"; and the psalm closes with, "For the Lord regardeth the way of the righteous, but the way of the wicked shall perish." The Twenty-third Psalm tells of both God's love and His nearness. "The Lord is my shepherd; I shall not want. . . . Yea, though I walk through the valley of the shadow of death, I will fear no evil, for Thou art with me; Thy rod and Thy staff, they comfort me." Even the use of the word *baruk* (blessed) in an acknowledgment of gratitude for God's love is biblical: "Blessed [*baruk*] is the Lord, Who hath not given us as a prey to their teeth" (Ps. 124:6). Indeed, the berakah formula itself—"Blessed art Thou, O Lord"—is a clause in Psalm 119:12.

But *middat raḥamim* (God's love), *middat ha-din* (God's justice) and berakah, the noun forms, are not biblical terms. They are rabbinic terms, and this means that the ideas for which these terms stand were fully crystallized only in the rabbinic period. Represented by abstract terms, terms which may be used to abstract and classify, the rabbinic concepts are more applicable than the nascent concepts which were their biblical antecedents.[29] What is more, as elements in the common vocabulary, they can be employed by the ordinary man, and not only by the gifted, temperamentally sensitive man. Thus, everybody can now make even commonplace things significant, let alone matters like the giving of Torah, by interpreting them as manifestations of God's love. The new development is most strikingly exemplified, however, by the rabbinic concept of berakah. That concept's drive toward concretization impels everybody, the gifted and the ordinary alike, to make of anything interpreted as a manifestation of God's love a stimulus for an act of worship.

In one respect, we ought to add, the normal mysticism of the rabbis does not represent a new development, but remains altogether the same as in the Bible. Nonsensory awareness of God's nearness is conceptualized neither in the Bible nor in rabbinic literature.

We discussed earlier another form of nonsacrificial worship, Ḳeri'at Shema', as a special instance of the study of Torah.[30] In Ḳeri'at Shema', the individual accepts upon himself God's kingship and commits himself to His miẓwot. Normal mysticism in this experience does not involve awareness of God's nearness but a sense of His kingship and an awareness that the entire world is His kingdom. Acceptance of *malkut Shamayim*, God's kingship, is in this mystical experience accomplished by a meditative act, an act whereby the individual makes God "King above and below and in the four directions of the world." Here, too, normal mysticism is marked by a paradox. A communicable aspect of the experience is expressed in the term *malkut Shamayim*, and in the figure of "above and below and in the four directions" which makes that term more definite, yet the experience as a whole wherein God is made King is private, noncommunicable. That experience requires *kawwanah*, "direction of the heart," on the part of the individual, a state of mind completely personal and noncommunicable.[31]

In Haggadah, acceptance of *malkut Shamayim* and commitment to the miẓwot are associated with *gilluy Shekinah*. When God reminded Israel that they had accepted His kingship in Egypt, according to one passage, they replied, "Yes," whereupon He continued, "Now, just as you accepted My kingship upon yourselves, accept [now] My decrees—'Thou shalt have no other gods before Me' [Exod. 20:3]."[32] Here God first demands confirmation by Israel that they accepted *malkut Shamayim*, and then He demands of them acceptance of His decrees, the Ten Commandments. This portrayal of an auditory manifestation of *gilluy Shekinah* is a projection in Haggadah of the acceptance of *malkut Shamayim* and of the miẓwot as experienced in Ḳeri'at Shema'.[33] There is no suggestion of *gilluy Shekinah*, however, in the actual experience of Ḳeri'at Shema' itself.[34] That experience is normal mysticism.

Although *malkut Shamayim* is a rabbinic term, the concept has an antecedent in the Bible—for example, "The Lord reigneth" (Pss. 93:1, 97:1, and 99:1). But the rabbinic term, an abstract term, enables the individual now to abstract the idea from biblical statements, to meditate on the idea and to transmute its implications, the kingship of God and commitment to the miẓwot, into a fresh emotional experience. Miẓwot, on the other hand, is already used in the Bible as a conceptual term—for example, "This miẓwah which I command thee this day" (Deut. 30:11); "And remember the miẓwot of the Lord" (Num. 15:39). Yet, as we shall see in the next chapter, when used by the rabbis, miẓwot, too, has a new connotation which is at times distinctly moral.[35] To *kawwanah* as a rabbinic term, we shall give separate treatment in a later section of this chapter.

Elements of the experience of worship are factors in the valuational life of the individual not only in conjunction with acts of worship. By being interpreted as a manifestation of God's love or God's justice, every event acquires significance, an event in the individual's own life, as well as an event in the contemporary world or in the nation's history.[36] In any heartfelt prayer and in repentance, there is an acute awareness of God's nearness. Occasions for performing miẓwot, many of them of an ethical character, are frequent. Precisely because the elements of normal mysticism occur in numerous other contexts besides that of worship, the mystical experience of worship itself can only be characterized as normal mysticism.

In each instance, however, something is added in the context of worship. Since a berakah refers to a personal experience, the experiential quality of the concept of God's love and God's justice is accentuated there. Recital of the Tefillah brings a more acute awareness of God's nearness than does a private prayer, so that it became the practice to attach purely personal petitions to the Tefillah.[37] In accepting *malkut Shamayim*, commitment to the miẓwot may indeed be only a general commitment; nevertheless, that entire, exalting experience, a daily orientation to one's duties and opportunities, adds its sanction to every specific miẓwah to be performed.

Acts of worship, we have noticed, call into play the larger self.[38] Ordinarily, the awareness of the self is not conceptualized, and even when expressed must rely on pronouns such as "I" or "my." But in the acts of worship, by and large, the awareness of the self is conceptualized through the concept of man or that of Israel, and this is achieved by the individual without loss of his self-identity. There is an enlargement of the self in a living, experiential context. A person is both himself and man, all men, or himself and all Israel. When awareness of the self is conceptualized in an act of worship, the individual associates himself with others, with undesignated, undifferentiated others. It is not a matter of identifying himself with others for, on the one hand, the individual always retains his self-identity[39] and, on the other hand, the "others" with whom he associates himself are not specified individuals. In sum, the larger self is, essentially, the individual's awareness of a bond, a relationship, between himself and others. All this does not mean that no room is left for the ordinary self. Not only may purely private petitions be attached to the Tefillah, but there are even forms of berakot of an entirely personal character.[40]

For the larger self, events ordinarily depicted as having taken place in the past or conceived as certain to take place in the future assume the character of contemporary happenings.[41] In halakic discussions of the Exodus from Egypt and the giving of Torah, or of the promised events of the future, past and future are never, to the slightest degree, obliterated. Haggadah, too, holds fast to the categories of time. When, however, the larger self is called into play in berakot, in acts of worship, these events of the past and the promised events of the future lose their orientation in time, and they are apprehended, instead, as manifestations of God's love in the present. Such a psychological phenomenon cannot be characterized as other than mystical. Since, however, it is not accompanied by visions or locutions, it can only be a phenomenon of normal mysticism.

B. Interrelation of Worship and Ethics

In the course of our discussions thus far, a number of ethical concomitants of worship have come to light, some of which we designated as such[42] and others which we did not.[43] In fact, rabbinic worship implicates ethics to such a degree that some berakot are themselves acts of *gemilut ḥasadim*.[44] We can now demonstrate that rabbinic worship as a whole implicates ethics, that rabbinic worship is interrelated with the great emphatic trends of ethics and morality: namely, with the emphasis on love, the emphasis on universality, and the emphasis on the individual.[45]

In worship there is the experience of God, an experience mediated by concepts, and there is also the awareness of the self, usually conceptualized but also sometimes unconceptualized. Again, worship consists of specific acts, such as the saying of specific berakot or the acceptance of *malkut Shamayim*. Each emphatic trend is interrelated, in some manner, with all of these aspects of worship. That is most clearly discernible, perhaps, with respect to the emphasis on love. There is an emphasis on love in the experience of God because the great majority of the berakot concretize the concept of God's love. Awareness of the self is conceptualized through the concept of man and that concept, we saw, has the connotation of love. Specific berakot in Birkat Ḥatanim and Birkat 'Abelim constitute acts of *gemilut ḥasadim*, deeds of lovingkindness.

We found above that the emphatic trends tend to coalesce.[46] In worship that tendency is especially to be discerned in the way the emphasis on universality coalesces with the other emphatic trends. Emphasis on universality rises to expression in the concept of *malkut Shamayim*, God's kingship, a kingship of absolutely universal scope. Yet that kingship is to be accepted twice daily by each individual, and by him alone. Further, the same concepts emphasizing love also emphasize universality. God's love is universal and is manifested to all mankind.[47] The concept of man not only has the connotation of love but also that of universality.

The emphasis on the individual is particularly noticeable when we consider the specific acts of nonsacrificial worship. In contrast to the daily communal sacrifice, which was "the sacrifice of the *ẓibbur*," the Tefillah, although the surrogate for that sacrifice, is intrinsically not a corporate act but one that is incumbent upon the individual. Most of the other berakot, too, are to be said by the individual. Even in those nonsacrificial acts that are intrinsically corporate, every individual has his particular role, and we have just spoken, also, of the stress laid on the individual in the acceptance of *malkut Shamayim*.

We may put the entire matter in another way. The many acts of worship employ a large number of value concepts—not only those already mentioned here but numerous others, such as *'olam* (world), Israel, *ger* (proselyte), *zaddik* (righteous man), *rasha'* (wicked man), *ge'ullah* (redemption), *bittaḥon* (trust), *teshubah* (repentance), *shalom* (peace), to give only a partial list. Since the value concepts are organismically interrelated, the emphatic trends rise to expression in the sphere of worship just as they do in the other spheres of valuational experience. Indeed, various acts of worship employ, among other concepts, the very concepts which enabled us to describe the emphatic trends in our earlier discussion. Because the value concepts are organismically interrelated, acts of worship are not only experiences in normal mysticism but acts which are fraught with ethical concomitants and motifs. It is no wonder, therefore, that some acts of worship, as we shall see in the final chapter, have profound implications for personal morality.

The prophets exhibit a negative attitude toward sacrificial worship. Isaiah includes prayer as well in his condemnation: "Yea, when ye make many prayers, I will not hear" (Isa. 1:15). Did the rabbis, in developing the forms of nonsacrificial worship, go contrary to the message of the prophets? Before an answer can be given, that message itself must be stated, and stated correctly. Of modern writers, Yehezkel Kaufmann alone, it seems, has plumbed to the depth of that message and his presentation alone is free from ideological anachronisms.

Classical prophecy teaches that God requires morality and ethical sensitivity of man, and not worship. "I hate, I despise your feasts, and I will take no delight in your solemn assemblies. Yea, though ye offer Me burnt-offerings and your meal-offerings, I will not accept them; neither will I regard the peace-offerings of your fat beasts. . . . But let justice well up as waters, and righteousness as a mighty stream. Did ye bring unto Me sacrifices and offerings in the wilderness forty years, O house of Israel?" (Amos 5:21–25).[48] "For I desire mercy [*ḥesed*; lovingkindness], and not sacrifice, and the knowledge of God rather than burnt-offerings" (Hosea 6:6, and cf. *ibid.*, 4:1 f.).[49] "To what purpose is the multitude of your sacrifices unto Me? saith the Lord; I am full of the burnt-offerings of rams, and the fat of fed beasts; and I delight not in the blood of bullocks, or of lambs, or of he-goats. . . . Wash you, make you clean, put away the evil of your doings from before Mine eyes, cease to do evil. Learn to do well; seek justice, relieve the oppressed, judge the fatherless, plead for the widow" (Isa. 1:11–17).[50] "Wherewith shall I come before the Lord, and bow myself before God on high? Shall I come before Him with burnt-offerings, with calves a year old?. . . . It hath been told thee, O man, what is good, and what the Lord doth require of thee: only to do justly, and to love mercy [*ḥesed*], and to walk humbly with thy God" (Micah 6:6–8).[51]

At the same time, many details of the Temple cult and worship, far from being negated by the prophets, are taken entirely for granted by them. Cultic matters, in fact, sometimes figure in their utterances in a positive manner. Amos speaks of the land of the Gentiles as "an unclean land" (Amos 7:17), and he regards it as a sin that the Nazarites were given wine to drink (*ibid.*, 2:11).[52] When Hosea speaks of "the Lord's land," "the house of the Lord," "the feast of the Lord" (Hosea 9:3–5), he thereby designates these matters as sacred in his eyes, too, and not only in those of the folk, for he also prophesies, "I will drive them out of My house" (*ibid.*, v. 15).[53] Isaiah, too, regards the Temple as the house of the Lord. In his very reproof, he says, "Who hath required this at your hand, to trample My courts?" (Isa. 1:12); the Temple stands in the center of his vision of universal justice and peace (*ibid.*, 2:2–4); the entire background of his vision in 6:1 ff. is the Temple and its cult—the song of the seraphim, the cloud of incense, the altar, the tongues, the ritual of cleansing.[54] The Temple and the worship in the Temple are likewise sacred matters to Jeremiah. He underscores his reproof when he says, "Yea, in My house have I found their wickedness" (Jer. 23:11); the Temple is God's throne of glory: "Thou throne of glory, on high from the beginning, thou place of our sanctuary" (*ibid.*, 17:2); he prophesies that the vessels of "the house of the Lord" will, in the end, be "restored to this place" (*ibid.*, 27:22); he tells of the glad events of the future, of chants and offerings of thanksgiving "in the house of the Lord" (*ibid.*, 33:11); he declares, "Neither shall there be cut off unto the priests the Levites a man before Me to offer burnt-offerings, and to burn meal-offerings, and to do sacrifice continually" (*ibid.*, v. 17), and he speaks of "the Levites the priests" as "My ministers" (*ibid.*, vv. 21–22).[55] How is this positive attitude of the prophets toward the Temple and toward worship to be reconciled with their even more forceful negative stand on worship?

First of all, we must recognize that sacrificial worship in Israel was utterly different, in conception, from pagan worship.[56] Pagan cultic worship is magical and mythological. In pagan religions the cult has an intrinsic value. The fate of the gods themselves depends on it. This basic pagan conception of cult and worship is not even alluded to by the prophets. They apparently need do no more than remind the people that God has no need for food and drink, and therefore has no need for sacrifices, an idea explicitly expressed in Psalm 50:8–13. To be sure, the prophets thereby argue against a widespread pagan idea, but their argument does not touch on the magical and mythological core at the center of all the forms of pagan worship. They inveigh neither against totemistic sacrifice, an ancient form of pagan folk worship, nor against other ideas of pagan worship, the ideas informing cult and sacrifice in Egypt, Babylon, and Canaan, the civilizations of which constituted the cultural milieu of Israel. In Egypt, cult and sacrifice were based on the idea of the death of the gods and their rebirth, and the food was the magical-mystical crystallization of the power of the god and his life; in Babylon, the sacrifice meant mystical strengthening of the divine powers in their war against the demons, and the sacrifice was similarly conceived in Canaan. But in the prophets' denunciations of the views of the folk on worship, not one of these ideas is mentioned. We can only conclude, hence, that in the religion of the folk, too, there was no mystical and mythological conception of sacrificial worship.[57] Their assumption was that God does not need the sacrifice, and the prophets' light mockery—"to what purpose?"—was sufficient to bring that assumption to the fore as something which was self-evident. If the prophets went beyond the folk, it was partly due to the ideas which they received from the folk.

The prophets insisted that only morality and ethics have intrinsic value and this idea was the prophetic innovation.[58] It is neither a metaphysical idea nor a "humanistic" one. According to the prophets, God requires morality and ethical sensitiveness of man: lovingkindness, justice, righteousness, truth, humility. It is this sphere alone that man shares with God, for the qualities of God are lovingkindness and justice. What of sacrificial worship? That, too, was ordained by God as an act of lovingkindness toward man; it is a symbol of God's love and His covenant with man, for God Himself has no need of sacrifices and offerings. Had man proved himself morally worthy, his sacrificial worship would have been acceptable to God. When Jeremiah declares that the people "have not attended unto My words," and therefore, "your burnt-offerings are not acceptable, nor your sacrifices pleasing unto Me" (Jer. 6:19–20), there is the inference that the offerings and sacrifices would have been "acceptable" and "pleasing" had the people "attended unto My words." The negative attitude of the prophets toward sacrificial worship is always associated with denunciations of the immorality of those who bring the sacrifices, the immorality consisting, in the main, of those violations of social ethics so often found among all peoples to this day—perversion of justice, bribery, oppression of the poor, exploitation, cynicism, lying, fornication, and so on. Such violations of ethics and social morality on the part of those who bring offerings to God make of those offerings a travesty. On the other hand, the same prophets occasionally refer to the cult and the Temple in a positive manner because they regard the cult, too, as ordained by God.

For all their depth and passion, the prophets did not crystallize into a conceptual term their awareness that morality constitutes a sphere in itself. This was achieved in rabbinic thought where, as we have seen, the term *derek ereẓ* refers to ethics and morality as a whole. Rabbinic thought, in this regard, developed out of the prophets.[59] Nor is that the only development in rabbinic ethics which goes back to the prophets. Deriving from the emphasis of the prophets on the ethical sphere are the great emphatic trends of the rabbinic value complex: the emphasis on love, universality, and individuality, an emphasis which sometimes found expression in a new ethical concept, as in *gemilut ḥasadim*. Even the prophets' implication that man shares with God the ethical sphere is reflected in rabbinic thought. The rabbis teach that man ought to imitate God, "to walk in the ways of Heaven," and the imitation of God is to consist primarily in the imitation of God's lovingkindness—mercy, compassion, graciousness, patience, forbearance.[60] It goes almost without saying that when there is a conflict of laws in the Halakah, the ethical is given right of way.[61]

In accord with this rabbinic emphasis on the ethical sphere, an emphasis deriving from the prophets, are the acts of nonsacrificial worship. Interrelated with ethics, these acts of worship not only give expression to the great ethical trends but also embody a large number of ethical concepts. The berakot and the other acts of worship thus have the effect of sensitizing the individual, during the experience of worship, to the ethical sphere.[62]

The rabbis' interpretations of sacrificial worship enable us better to recognize the point at which the rabbis do diverge from the prophets. Like the prophets, the rabbis, too, declare that God does not need the sacrifices, that "there is no eating and drinking for Him"; indeed, sometimes the rabbis marshal argument after argument in support of that teaching.[63] In keeping with the view of the prophets, also, is the rabbinic teaching that the sacrifices are ordained by God, and are for man's benefit, not for God's.[64] Again, the rabbis are at one with the prophets when they negate the belief that the sacrifices can be a means of propitiating God.[65] The rabbis certainly diverge from the prophets, however, when they also interpret the sacrifices symbolically. Drawing their lessons from the less costly as opposed to the more costly sacrifices, and from other aspects of the sacrificial ritual, the rabbis find in these things calls to repentance, good deeds, study of Torah, deep humility, and a sense of sin.[66] According to these interpretations, sacrificial worship, like nonsacrificial worship, is interrelated with ethics. At this one point, then, the rabbis differ from the prophets, even though in other respects the rabbis' teachings concerning sacrificial worship are much the same as those of the prophets.

If the rabbis differ at this one point from the prophets, it does not mean that they failed to absorb the message of the prophets. The contrary is true. Just because they absorbed the basic teaching of the prophets as to the primacy of the ethical sphere, the acts of nonsacrificial worship developed by the rabbis are fraught with ethical concomitants and ethical motifs. The rabbis were able to develop such new forms of worship because, we make bold to say, they had a conceptual advantage over the prophets. The awareness that morality constitutes a sphere in itself was not expressed by the prophets in a conceptual term, and they could present that idea only by placing specific moral matters on one side and sacrificial worship on the other. The rabbis crystallized and gave expression to the message of the prophets. In *derek ereẓ* they possessed a term referring to ethics and morality as whole, and they had no need to present morality and worship as contrasts. They could, therefore, take heed of the emphasis of the prophets on morality and give it expression in worship as well as in other fields.[67]

C. What Normal Mysticism Is Not

"Normal mysticism" is a descriptive term only,[68] calling attention to certain phenomena in rabbinic worship. Instead of enumerating these phenomena when we have occasion to discuss them as a whole, we epitomize them either by the term "normal mysticism" or else by that of "religious experience." Normal mysticism is the term used when we wish to stress the idea that the religious experience of the rabbis was associated with ordinary daily living, since the term "mysticism" by itself usually designates a far different type of religious experience.

A brief comparison of these two types of religious experience, of mysticism with what we have called normal mysticism, will serve to bring into bolder relief several features of normal mysticism. Such a comparison is all the more in place because it is often assumed that actual religious experience, the experience of God, is limited to mysticism in the accepted usage of the word. On the other hand, the character of rabbinic religious experience is obscured when it is described in terms which seem to us inadequate or incorrect, and it is well to deal with these matters, as well.

In her brilliant work on mysticism, Evelyn Underhill characterizes mysticism as "the art of establishing [man's] conscious relation with the Absolute."[69] "Union with the Divine" is a quest; the goal is not to be achieved without strenuous search, and the Mystic Way itself is constituted of various states or phases.[70] It is only in the final state that union is achieved, a state in which "the Absolute Life is not merely perceived and enjoyed by the Self, as in Illumination, but is one with it":[71] a state, in other words, of "communion between the soul and the Absolute," when "a mysterious fusion of divine and human life takes place."[72] Before such fusion or communion can take place, the Self must "surrender itself, its individuality, and its will, completely."[73] The Self is remade: the mystic life "abolishes the primitive consciousness of selfhood, and substitutes for it a wider consciousness; the total disappearance of selfhood in the divine, the substitution of a Divine Self for the primitive self."[74] From "this ineffable meeting-place, which is to the intellect an emptiness, and to the heart a fulfillment of all desire, . . . the normal self is separated by all the 'unquiet desert' of sensual existence."[75] But the Self can "become detached from the 'things of sense' " by purgation—that is, by discipline and mortification, fasting and solitude.[76] Complete surrender of selfhood, "self-naughting," occurs, however, in the process of a "passive purgation," a process accomplished in the soul "whether she will it or no."[77]

At some points mysticism and normal mysticism seem to converge, yet at these points, too, more is dissimilar than similar. Mysticism seems to have something in common with normal mysticism when we are told that for "the primitive consciousness of selfhood" mystic life substitutes "a wider consciousness." This statement reminds us of those occasions at worship when the individual associates himself with Israel or with mankind, occasions when he posseses a larger self, "a wider consciousness." That enlargement of the self is possible psychologically because the self is less an entity than a continuous process making for an entity; the self can be enlarged because it is not static.[78] But mysticism speaks an altogether different language when it characterizes selfhood as "primitive" and says that it is subject to "substitution." More, we see that "a wider consciousness" means one thing when it refers to the association of the individual with mankind and an entirely different thing when it refers to "a conscious relation with the Absolute." At this point, too, another parallel between mysticism and normal mysticism breaks down: the obliteration of the categories of time. In normal mysticism, we may remember, there are occasions when the categories of past and future are obliterated and only the present is retained. Since mysticism is union with the Absolute, however, all the categories of time are obliterated in an experience felt to partake of eternity rather than of time. In normal mysticism, the present is retained because what is experienced is an event, and an event can be experienced only in the present. Furthermore, these events (such as the Exodus from Egypt and certain promised events of the future) to be events at all, must normally be oriented in time: that is, when not experienced in worship, they must either be regarded as having taken place in the past or else assumed to be events of the future; and they are indeed so oriented when not experienced in acts of worship.

There is no "self-naughting" of any kind in normal mysticism, and neither is there purgation. Association with Israel and with man is nothing other than self-awareness conceptualized in the concepts of Israel and of man. In such relationships with Israel and with man, self-awareness is never lost, for the individual always retains his self-identity.[79] The general prevalence of value concepts in normal mysticism makes, in fact, for the opposite of "self-naughting." Value concepts, we noticed in an earlier chapter, not only constitute a vital aspect of a man's personality, but project, whenever concretized, his entire personality, his own particular individuality. When, therefore, in an act of worship, an individual interprets a situation by means of value concepts (among which there is always the concept of God's love or God's justice), he expresses at the same time his own individuality. By the same token, the prevalence of value concepts in normal mysticism makes for the opposite of purgation. Instead of detaching a man from "the things of the senses," religious experience, through the concepts of God's love, *nes* and berakah, makes of the things of the senses, in themselves ordinary and commonplace, things fraught with significance.[80]

Since they make for self-expression, not for "self-naughting," rabbinic acts of worship are emphatically not a means of communion or fusion with the divine. On the contrary, God is felt to be other than the self—"Blessed art *Thou.*" Even in *gilluy Shekinah* there was no communion. *Gilluy Shekinah* is a concept connoting a sensory awareness of God's nearness, but it does not connote fusion or communion with Him. Sacrificial worship as described in the Bible, too, was not communion, modern theories to the contrary notwithstanding.[81] Kaufmann once again brings us back to what the Bible itself has to say. The sacrifices referred to in the modern theories, the *shelamim*, were eaten "*before* the Lord," and not *with* the Lord (see Deut. 12:7, 18; 14:23, 26; 15:20; 27:7); further, it is not required that a sacrifice to God be brought out of the tithes, yet any person eating the tithe, and even drinking "the wine or strong drink" bought with the money of the tithe, is likewise spoken of as eating "before the Lord" (*ibid.*, 14:26).[82] "Before the Lord" can only be, therefore, an expression implying nearness to God, as Kaufmann says,[83] an implication very similar to the connotation of *gilluy Shekinah*. Communion is no more a biblical idea that it is a rabbinic idea. It is the central idea of the mystery cults, where "the characteristic rite is sacramental—an act of communion and reunion with the daemon."[84] What is experienced in all the forms of Jewish worship considered here is not communion but God's nearness.[85] Conceptualized in *gilluy Shekinah*, the awareness of God's nearness remains unconceptualized, as we have seen, in normal mysticism.

Although not conceptualized, and hence not an experience that can be conveyed to others, nonsensory awareness of God's nearness is not entirely ineffable. In the total experience of worship represented by a berakah, the berakah itself expresses an awareness of a manifestation of *middat raḥamim*, God's love. Normal mysticism is marked by a paradox, we pointed out earlier in the chapter, awareness of God's nearness, the noncommunicable factor being made acute in the total experience of worship by the consciousness of God's love, a communicable, conceptualized factor.[86] Thus, also with respect to ineffability, normal mysticism is different from mystical union with the divine, that "ineffable meeting-place which is to the intellect an emptiness."

Awareness of God's nearness is not to be confused with the idea of God's immanence, an error made by some modern writers. "God is not external to anyone, but is present in all things, though they are ignorant that He is so," says Plotinus in telling of God's immanence.[87] The mystic, accordingly, is able to discover a " 'divine' essence or substance, dwelling at the apex of a man's soul."[88] Especially in keeping with the idea of communion, the doctrine of God's immanence may also imply the idea of "the Creative Logos."[89] It is almost unnecessary, by now, to point out that all such ideas are contradicted by the experience of normal mysticism, and indeed, by that of *gilluy Shekinah* as well. In both there is awareness of God's nearness, and in both God is felt to be entirely external to man.[90]

Underhill tells us that "we can gauge something of the supernormal vitality" of the great mystics by the magnitude of what they accomplished in a practical way, and that "the things done" by them "are hardly to be explained unless these great spirits had indeed a closer, more intimate, more bracing contact than their fellows with that Life 'which is the light of men.' "[91] Normal mysticism is not limited to the few who have special gifts of temperament. It is the experience of the ordinary man as well as of the gifted man; rather, it is the experience of the gifted man which has also become the experience of the ordinary man. The effectiveness of normal mysticism, too, can be gauged by "the things done," but these practical results of normal mysticism can only be in the field of morality and ethics, a field cultivated by normal mysticism.

As a term professing to represent the Jewish experience of God, "monotheism," so widely used today, is certainly inadequate and may be misleading. The term is inadequate because it does not distinguish between the Jewish experience of God and a cult such as that of Aten in Egypt which, as Albright justly remarks, "was a true monotheism."[92] The term may be misleading when it fosters nonrabbinic interpretations of rabbinic statements. If Judaism can be equated with monotheism, then it ought to be possible to relate philosophical ideas of monotheism to biblical and rabbinic texts; we must remember, however, that when medieval Jewish philosophers attempted to do this very thing, they had to employ the method of allegorical interpretation, a completely arbitrary method.[93]

In polytheism, worship of a deity centered around a concrete object, usually an image. A particular image might be regarded as only *a* manifestation of a deity, but this consideration by no means interfered with the worship of the image itself. Thus, an Egyptian text declares, "Honor [the] god in his way, [honor] him who is made of precious stones and formed of copper, just as water takes the place of water," and the meaning seems to be that, although the image made of precious stones and copper is only temporary and will be replaced by another image, another manifestation, "as water takes the place of water," the present image itself is to be honored and worshiped.[94] The particular image plays so great a cultic role that, among the Romans, one image of a deity may be superior to another image of the same deity, depending on the locale. "The cult-titles of this Jupiter, Optimus Maximus, the best and the greatest, seem to raise him to a position not only far above his colleagues, but above all other Jupiters in Latium or elsewhere, and presumably above all other deities. They thus suggest a deliberate attempt to place him in a higher position than even the Jupiter Latiaris of the Mons Albanus, whose temple had been rebuilt in the same period."[95] On the other hand, as can here be seen, making one representation of a deity "the best and the greatest" is perfectly compatible with the idea that other representations of the deity worshiped elsewhere—that is to say, other images—are also manifestations of that deity. Similarly, Ishtar and Adad were worshiped in many different places in Mesopotamia, and the same was true of Baal and Anath in Canaan.[96] "As a result of this phenomenon," says Albright, "we find in Canaanite an increasing tendency to employ the plural *'Ashtarôt*, "Astartes," and *'Anatôt*, "Anaths," in the clear sense of 'totality of manifestations of a deity.' "[97] The plural forms also indicate, however, that the various representations of a deity in as many different localities were all regarded as manifestations of the deity; conversely, without such representations or images, it would not have been possible to worship the same deity in different localities.

An image, then, was not an incidental matter in polytheism but an essential element in worship. The image was felt to be a manifestation of a deity. Images made it possible to worship the same deity in different localities. Placing a specific image in a specific locality could be a means of making that particular manifestation of a deity "the best and the greatest." Polytheism did allow for the view that "the domain of a high god is universal," and even for a monotheistic view in which "Marduk of Babylon is successively identified with a whole list of male deities," or in which "all the important deities are listed successively as parts of the body of Ninurta."[98] Nevertheless, it is obvious that, according to these views too, the images of the various deities listed are also to be worshiped, so that, as far as worship was concerned, polytheism was not affected by these views.

Monotheism was established for a brief period in Egypt as a solar monotheism, "with the solar formula, 'who rejoices on the horizon in his quality [literally, name] as light which is in the solar disk.' "[99] The sun-god himself cannot be separated from his "quality," from the light which is in the solar disk, and the worship of the sun-god thus involves the worship of an object, the sun. The association of the sun with the sun-god is even closer, apparently, than the one between a deity and any particular image of it.

There can be no gainsaying that the worship of images or of sundry concrete things is a characteristic element of polytheism, be the other elements in polytheism what they may. Similarly, there can be no gainsaying that the worship of Aten involves the worship of the sun itself. All such worship, including specifically the worship of the sun and the moon and other heavenly bodies,[100] the rabbis stigmatized as *'abodah zarah*, strange and abhorrent worship. Now the Halakah provides for the avoidance of any possible contact with *'abodah zarah*,[101] but that is not all. The negation of *'abodah zarah* is actually an aspect of an experience of worship. Acceptance of *malkut Shamayim* when reciting the first verse of the Shema' implies also the negation or exclusion of *'abodah zarah*.[102] The monotheism of the rabbis (and of the Bible, as well), demands the exclusion of the faintest taint of idolatry, and we wash away that fact when we put Judaism and idolatrous religions in the same category.

Philosophic monotheism may be either theistic or pantheistic. A nonrabbinic interpretation is placed on the first verse of Ḳeri'at Shema' as a result of associating rabbinic monotheism with philosophical theism. The first of the three sections of Ḳeri'at Shema' is Deuteronomy 6:4–9, and that is followed by the second section, Deuteronomy 11:13–21, which in turn is followed by the third section, Numbers 15:37–41. According to Maimonides, "The section beginning, 'Hear, O Israel' [Deut. 6:4–9] is recited first because it sets forth the duties of acknowledging the Unity of God, loving Him, and studying His words [מפני שיש בה צווי על ייחוד השם ואהבתו ותלמודו]."[103] Maimonides has here interpreted the acceptance of the kingship of God to mean the acknowledging of the unity of God, for the commentaries all take it for granted that the source of the statement is *Berakot* II.2,[104] where the reason for first reciting "Hear, O Israel" (Deut. 6:4–9) is declared to be "so that a person shall first accept upon himself the yoke of the kingship of Heaven [God], and after that accept upon himself the yoke of mizwot."[105] For Maimonides and for other medieval authorities affected to a lesser degree by medieval philosophy, this interpretation was undoubtedly a valid one;[106] the fact remains, however, that it *is* an interpretation and that for the ordinary man it over-intellectualizes what is primarily a mystical experience.

Moreover, the interpretation has led to a basic misconception. In 'Ahabah Rabbah, which is the berakah preceding the recital of the Shema', the phrase להודות לך וליחדך anticipates the acceptance of *malkut Shamayim* through the recital of the Shema'. It refers to the acknowledgment of God and links that acknowledgment with the acceptance upon oneself of God's kingship by the recitation of the Shema'.[107] Influenced by the notion, however, that the first verse of the Shema' teaches the idea of the unity of God, modern translators have so misunderstood the phrase as to make it say, "That we might give thanks unto Thee and proclaim Thy unity."[108] Acceptance of *malkut Shamayim* has thus been transformed into the proclamation of God's unity, a proclamation of a form of philsophic monotheism.

Philosophic pantheism, too, is monotheism, as in Stoic thought where God is conceived as the all-pervading Soul of the world or as the creative Reason of the world. Stressing unduly in several rabbinic passages what we call "auxiliary ideas,"[109] modern scholars often point to such passages as expressions of the Stoic doctrine that God is the Soul of the universe.[110] But this brings us back to the doctrine of the immanence of God, and we have already seen how that doctrine runs counter to the rabbinic experience of God. In this case, rabbinic texts have been misinterpreted because no differentiation was made between pantheistic monotheism and rabbinic monotheism. Once more as a representation of the rabbinic experience of God, the term "monotheism" was definitely misleading.

D. *Kawwanah*

The term *kawwanah* is used in several different ways in rabbinic literature, ways which are closely related yet which are to be distinguished from each other. These various aspects of the concept of *kawwanah* constitute fairly distinct conceptual phases.

One phase of the concept is to be found chiefly in the context of worship, and in that phase *kawwanah* connotes devotion, concentration, the sustained focusing of attention. This was exemplified in an earlier chapter when we discussed Ḳeri'at Shema'. By reciting the first verse of the Shema' "with direction of the heart—כוונת הלב,"

the individual accepts upon himself "the yoke of *malkut Shamayim*, the kingship of God."[111] To aid the individual in this meditative experience there is also the rule that when saying *'eḥad*, the last word in the verse, the individual is to make God king "above and below and in all the four directions."[112] *Kawwanah* here is associated with the concept of *malkut Shamayim*; by directing his heart or mind the individual achieves the experience of accepting "the yoke of *malkut Shamayim*," and it is the concept of *malkut Shamayim* which gives that experience its idea-content. But to limit the need for *kawwanah* to the first verse of the Shema', as R. Me'ir does, could only be the result of reckoning with the limited powers of the ordinary man.[113] According to the opinion of other authorities, the whole of the Shema' must be recited with *kawwanah*, sustained concentration,[114] and this opinion means that a person must attempt to achieve not only the experience of accepting upon himself *malkut Shamayim* but that of accepting upon himself "the yoke of the miẓwot" as well.[115] Although both R. Me'ir's teaching and that of the other authorities stress the need for *kawwanah*, the other authorities refer to an experience in addition to the one referred to in R. Me'ir's teaching. *Kawwanah*, then, does not point to the actual content of these experiences. It is characteristic of this phase that, while *kawwanah* is a necessary element in an experience of worship, the content of such an experience is not given in the concept of *kawwanah* but in the other concepts which are involved in that experience.

As we shall soon see, rabbinic teachings concerning *kawwanah* in the saying of the Tefillah or in the recitation of the berakot, the other forms of worship, likewise usually have to do with *kawwanah* in the sense of concentration or the sustained focusing of attention. Once more, as in Ḳeri'at Shema', *kawwanah* is a necessary element in these experiences of worship but does not determine the content of those experiences. Both the Tefillah and the berakot embody the concept of God's love and it is that concept which, concretized in one specific experience after another, largely gives such experiences their idea-content.

At the same time that we recognize the role of the other concepts in the various forms of worship, however, we must by no means relegate *kawwanah* to an inferior role. *Kawwanah* in this phase amounts to nothing less than the deliberate cultivation of an inward experience. True, the other concepts involved in an experience of worship determine its idea-content, but it is *kawwanah* which makes any experience of worship possible at all. In other words, without conveying the idea-content of an experience of worship, *kawwanah* is as large a factor in such an experience as concepts which do express the idea-content.

A person saying the Tefillah ought to "direct his heart": that is, say the Tefillah with *kawwanah*.[116] A man's mood at the time, however, may make it impossible for him to concentrate. One authority teaches, therefore, that a man ought to gauge himself, when the time for prayer comes, as to whether he can "direct his heart" or not, and if he feels that he cannot, he ought not to say the Tefillah;[117] while another authority, in a similar vein, declares that he whose mind is unquiet (at the time for prayer) ought not to say the Tefillah.[118] From still another passage in the Talmud, the inference is to be drawn that he who says the Tefillah without "directing his mind" is to repeat the Tefillah and say it with *kawwanah*,[119] an inference made by Maimonides who adds, "A Tefillah said without *kawwanah* is no Tefillah."[120]

Kawwanah in the saying of the Tefillah does not mean only the awareness of performing a miẓwah, as may be the case with the recital of Ḳeri'at Shema',[121] but refers to concentration on the ideas of the Tefillah. That is borne out by the passages just cited and by other statements and practices. "He who says the Tefillah must direct his heart in all of them [all the berakot], but if he is unable to direct his heart in all of them, he must at least direct his heart in one."[122] "He whose dead lies [unburied] before him is exempt from Ḳeri'at Shema' and from [saying] the Tefillah,"[123] the reason being, as Ginzberg shows, that under these circumstances a person cannot direct his heart.[124] Again, artisans working on a precarious perch, such as a tree-top, are not permitted to say the Tefillah since, as Rashi explains, "The Tefillah is *raḥame* [the beseeching of compassion from God] and needs *kawwanah*."[125] When R. Eliezer declares, "He who makes his Tefillah *ḳeba'*, his Tefillah is not supplication,"[126] his objection to *ḳeba'*, manifestly, is on the ground that it makes *kawwanah* in the supplications of the Tefillah impossible. In fact, various practices are recorded which are intended to avoid *ḳeba'* and these are patently just so many attempts to keep the ideas of the Tefillah fresh, as an aid to *kawwanah*; this is especially evident in the practice of changing the text of the berakot "of praise" daily, and not only that of the supplications.[127] On the other hand, R. Ḥanina b. Dosa, according to a story told about him, achieved the acme of concentration while keeping, apparently, to a fixed text of the Tefillah. It is told of him that though once a serpent stung him while he was saying the Tefillah, he did not even pause because, as he explained later, his mind had been so concentrated on the Tefillah that he had felt no sting.[128] There are men, however, who are not able to concentrate at all unless they can at least hear the words of the Tefillah. To him who could not direct his heart were he to say the Tefillah in a whisper, it is, therefore, permitted to make his voice heard.[129] In all the texts quoted or cited here, *kawwanah* in the saying of the Tefillah can only refer to concentration on the ideas of the Tefillah, and we shall find that *kawwanah* has the same connotation also in those texts on the Tefillah we shall have occasion to discuss later.*

With respect both to Ḳeri'at Shema' and the Tefillah there are, as we have just seen, rules requiring that they be said with *kawwanah*, with concentration. These rules are necessary because neither the Shema' nor the First Berakah of the Tefillah interprets specific occasions. Certain periods of time constitute the occasions for

* *Kawwanah* in the sense of concentration is associated not only with tefillah as worship (the 'Amidah) but also with tefillah as prayer in general, and hence with personal or private prayer and petition. Thus, according to R. Me'ir, when one of two men in the same mortal danger has been saved and the other has not, the reason is that the one who has been saved had prayed with *kawwanah* and therefore his prayer was answered, whereas the other had not prayed with *kawwanah* and therefore his prayer was not answered (*Rosh ha-Shanah* 18a, and Rashi, *ad loc.*). There is a view, too, that the very ability to have *kawwanah* in the Tefillah is an indication that one's petition will be answered—see 'Abba Saul's statement in *Tos. Berakot* III.4, ed. Lieberman, p. 12, and the versions and variants there, and see *Tos. Kif.*, I, 29, top; apparently, then, so far as the petition is concerned, that relates to specific desires or needs of an individual. In specific personal petitions, however, there lurks the danger that the consciousness of saying them with *kawwanah* may make of them not true prayers at all, and the rabbis warn against that danger. They declare that if one is long at prayer and expects his petition to be answered because he has said it with *kawwanah*, his petition will not be answered, and indeed, he will be punished instead. (See *Berakot* 32b and Tosafot *ibid.*, *s.v.* כל; *Berakot* 55a and Rashi, *ad loc.*; *Rosh ha-Shanah* 16b and Tosafot *ibid.*, *s.v.* ועיון.) When *kawwanah* passes over into theurgy, we no longer have true prayer. עיון תפלה applies both to true prayer and to improper prayer (see the remarks in Tosafot) because the sheer effort at concentration is characteristic of both.

(reciting) the Shema' and the Tefillah, and since those occasions serve only as reminders, they do not determine the actual content of either form of worship. In other words, these forms of worship are not directly stimulated by external occasions, and the experience of worship in both is entirely a matter of *kawwanah*, of concentration upon ideas.

When a berakah interprets a specific occasion, however, *kawwanah* is not a matter of concentration upon an idea alone. In such cases, the occasion constitutes the stimulus for the berakah. Saying a berakah of that kind with *kawwanah*, therefore, is largely a matter of focusing attention upon the occasion or stimulus for the berakah; hence rules concerning *kawwanah* in the saying of such berakot consist of rules calculated to make a person more aware of the occasions for those berakot. For example, there are two different berakot for the fruit of trees and for the fruits of the earth, the one on the fruit of trees calling attention to its occasion by the words "Who createst the fruit of the trees," and the one on the fruits of the earth, including vegetables, calling attention to its occasion by the words "Who createst the fruit of the earth."[130] These rules are given in an anonymous statement in the Mishnah but other tannaitic authorities discriminate further between the occasions. Maintaining that the berakot to be said ought to vary in accordance with the species,[131] R. Judah disagrees with the anonymous opinion and states that the berakah on vegetables ought to be "Who createst the various kinds of herbs";[132] similarly, and holding to the same principle, the Tosefta has a different berakah in each case for seeds, for herbs, and for vegetables which are not herbs.[133] Far from being "legalism," such refinements are, on the contrary, examples of how focusing attention on the specific occasion makes for *kawwanah* in the saying of the berakot. When a person has to select a berakah in order to interpret an occasion, his attention is called to the specific character of the occasion, and the occasion then becomes all the more a stimulus for the berakah—that is, all the more poignant a factor in a religious experience.

A berakah and its occasion constitute a unitary experiential entity, as we have observed before, but that is true only when a person directs his heart. "In all the berakot," says the Gaon R. Samuel b. Ḥofni, "the person saying the berakah ought to direct his heart in regard to what he is saying the berakah for, from the beginning of the berakah."[134] This rule, too, reflects experience. When a person directs his heart from the beginning of the berakah, saying the berakah has the effect of enhancing the experience of God's love as manifested in the occasion for the berakah.

Kawwanah in worship, though referring to concentration upon ideas, is not intellectual concentration. Those ideas express emotional experiences, religious experiences. As we have observed so often, the idea in a berakah refers to an experience of God's love, the ideas in the Tefillah, to a chain of such experiences, and the ideas in the Shema', to the acceptance of God's kingship. The ideas here embody value concepts, and through *kawwanah* those value concepts are concretized in fresh experiences. Because *kawwanah* itself is a value concept, it can be an integral element in all these experiences.

A consideration of a passage in Sifre Deuteronomy, par. 335 (ed. Friedmann, p. 140b) will help us to recognize the difference between intellectual concentration and *kawwanah*. The passage declares that a man's eyes, heart, and ears "ought to be directed to the words of the Torah"; continuing, by quoting Ezekiel 44: 5, "Son of man, set thy heart, and behold with thine eyes, and hear with thine ears all that I say unto thee concerning all the ordinances of the house of the Lord", the passage underlines its initial statement with the lesson, "If in the case of the Temple which could be seen by the eyes and measured by the hand, eyes, heart and ears must be directed, how much more so, in the case of the words of the Torah which are as mountains hanging on a hair." Concentration, as advocated in this passage, is intellectual concentration, the subject matter being at once difficult and fine-spun—"as mountains hanging on a hair." Nor is the emphasis on the heart (mind), the eyes, and the ears accidental, for in intellectual concentration just these organs were involved since attention was focused either on a book or on a lecture. In contrast, *kawwanah* does not refer to an intellectual problem at all, but to an experience or an act.

All of this may very well be reflected in the difference between the form of the root *kwn* indicating intellectual concentration and the one which indicates *kawwanah*. In the passage we have just considered, the verb is passive: "ought to be directed" (מכוונים). When *kawwanah* is referred to, however, the verb is active: "ought to direct his heart" (לכוין את לבו). The noun *kawwanah* itself, furthermore, is formed from the active verb, not from the passive. At the same time, it must not be forgotten that both *kawwanah* and the form indicating intellectual concentration derive from the same root, *kwn*, and hence that they are, to some degree, related.

In the phase of *kawwanah* we have just discussed, *kawwanah* refers to concentration upon the ideas in acts of worship. Although *kawwanah* is a necessary element in all such acts, the specific character of an act of worship is determined not by *kawwanah* but by the ideas concentrated on. In that respect, this phase of *kawwanah* represents a departure from the usual manner in which a value concept functions, for as a rule a value concept embodied in an act determines, at least as one of several such concepts, the specific character of that act. There is, however, another phase of the concept, another connotation of *kawwanah*, that of intention, which either by itself determines the specific character of an act, or else does so in combination with other value concepts.

Halakah has given the phase of *kawwanah*, which connotes intention, wide and varied application. We shall cite several examples. A person engaged in an act of formal acquisition must not merely intend to perform the formal act, such as making a furrow in the field, but must intend to acquire the object in question;[135] in marriage, cohabitation is not sufficient, but both parties must intend marriage;[136] in *ḥaliẓah*, the act of taking off the shoe (Deut. 25:9) must be performed with the intention of *ḥaliẓah* on the part of both the man and the woman concerned, else the *ḥaliẓah* is not valid.[137] A writ of divorce is valid only if it is written with the intention of using it for a particular, specified woman.[138] In vows, the bearing of the vow is determined not only by the actual words uttered but also by the intention of the person when he makes the vow.[139] It is this phase of *kawwanah*, too, which is involved in the question as to whether miẓwot must be performed with *kawwanah*, and we shall shortly take up that topic.

Higger distinguishes between *kawwanah* as intention and *maḥashabah* (having an idea in mind) by pointing out that the latter refers to a future act, the execution of which is indefinite.[140] *Maḥashabah* also refers to instances of an intention which may be expressed in words. That usage of the term is to be found in cases of sacrificial offerings,[141] but it is not limited to those instances.[142]

Kawwanah possesses still another conceptual phase. In that phase, *kawwanah* refers to the deliberate cultivation of an inward experience, and is in that regard similar to the conceptual phase we discussed first: the phase in which *kawwanah* refers to concentration upon ideas. Now the inward experience, a meditative experience, is not something that can be expressed in words or ideas but is sheer experience of God, for the moment unconceptualized and hence not communicable at all. Were such an experience of God, unmediated as it is by any concept, an experience complete in itself, it would not have been possible in normal mysticism. But it is not a unitary experience for, as we shall see, it is always associated with another experience, one that is expressible in a concept. What starts out as altogether incommunicable mysticism soon becomes an experience in normal mysticism.

A mystical experience of God is associated with the Tefillah. It was the practice of the pious men of former generations (*ḥasidim ha-rishonim*) before saying the Tefillah, to wait for an hour "in order to direct their heart to God."[143] Their practice was to direct their hearts to God, yet that experience but prepared them to say the Tefillah. A brief experience of a similar character takes place when the individual, as he is about to say the Tefillah, faces Jerusalem and directs his heart toward the Temple and the Holy of Holies—that is, toward the *Shekinah*.[144] The orientation is not primarily just a physical orientation, but a means of cultivating an acute awareness of God's nearness, of His immediate presence.[145] The practice derives, we have tried to indicate, from the association of *gilluy Shekinah* with the sacrifices in the Temple, the Tefillah being a surrogate for the sacrifices;[146] moreover, there is the rule that they who are unable to determine the proper direction need but direct their hearts toward "their Father Who is in heaven."[147] Here what begins as incommunicable mysticism almost immediately becomes normal mysticism: the sheer experience of God's presence leads directly to the awareness of God's love as expressed in the conceptual continuum of the Tefillah.

In the haggadot found in *Rosh ha-Shanah* III.8, a physical orientation is likewise represented to be a means of cultivating an awareness of God's near presence. This mishnah interprets Exodus 17:8–13 to teach that "when Israel looked upward and subjected their heart to their Father Who is in heaven,"[148] they prevailed, and that when they did not, they were slain in battle; similarly, continues the mishnah, but now interpreting Numbers 21:4–9, "When Israel looked upward and subjected their heart to their Father Who is in heaven," they were healed (of the serpents' bites), and if not, they decayed.[149] Now these haggadot immediately follow a halakah dealing with *kawwanah* in the performance of a miẓwah, the halakah and the haggadot being juxtaposed, as Bertinoro has pointed out, because both have to do with *kawwanah*.[150] The phrase "when Israel looked upward . . ." embodies, therefore, the concept of *kawwanah*. But this phrase, whatever else it contains, refers to an act, a physical orientation, an orientation which is thus akin to the one required before saying the Tefillah; indeed, the phrase resembles a statement made with regard to the Tefillah—"He that says the Tefillah ought to direct his heart upward (למעלה)."[151] Looking upward is represented in these haggadot as an act of orientation informed by *kawwanah*, and hence as an act which made for an experience of God's immediate presence.

For the meaning of the remainder of the phrase—"and subjected their heart to their Father Who is in heaven"—the word "subjected," משעבדין, is decisive. To say that the Israelites subjected their hearts to God is to say that they acknowledged in their hearts the kingship of God.[152] The need in both cases for such an acknowledgment of God's kingship is supplied by the respective backgrounds of the haggadot. According to an oft-repeated rabbinic tradition, derived from Exodus 17:8, Israel was obliged to do battle with Amalek in punishment for having sinned and for having neglected the study of Torah and the doing of miẓwot,[153] while in the passage on the serpents, the Bible itself says, "And the people spoke against God, and against Moses" (Num. 21:5).* These haggadot speak, then, of an experience which begins as an incommunicable awareness of God's immediate presence but which becomes an experience mediated by a concept, the concept of *malkut Shamayim*, God's kingship.

The juxtaposition of the halakah and the haggadot confirms what we have been saying here, namely, that the various aspects of *kawwanah* are phases of a single concept. In *Rosh ha-Shanah* III.7,

* In relating that the Israelites subjected their hearts to God, the haggadot tell us that they now acknowledged God's kingship and were no longer rebellious.

the Mishnah declares that, "If one was passing behind a synagogue, or if his house was near a synagogue, and he heard the sound of the *shofar* or the reading of the *megillah*, if he directed his heart, he fulfilled his obligation, but if not, he did not fulfill his obligation—even though the one heard and the other heard, the one directed his heart but the other did not direct his heart."[154] *Kawwanah* as described in this halakah refers to intention, for by the words "directing the heart" the Mishnah here means having the intention to fulfill the miẓwah regarding the hearing of the *shofar* or the miẓwah of the reading of the *megillah*. The Mishnah so far, however, has only stated the law. In order to extol *kawwanah*, therefore, the Mishnah places the two haggadot on *kawwanah* right after this halakah; by implication, *kawwanah* as described in the halakah too is extolled, even though *kawwanah* there refers to the intention to observe a miẓwah and not, as in the haggadot, to the cultivation of an experience of God's immediate presence. In all these phases of *kawwanah*, a man "directs his heart" or his mind, and hence all these phases possess a character in common. That common character permits the rabbis to use *kawwanah* as a single concept despite the fact that the very instances they refer to at any given time embody different phases of the concept.

Somewhat expanded, the same halakah is given in the Tosefta.[155] There *kawwanah* is extolled in a statement which is connected with the halakah itself, yet there, too, the general concept is employed in much the same manner as in the Mishnah. The halakah in the Tosefta concludes by stating, "All depends upon the direction of the heart,[156] as it says, 'Thou wilt direct their heart, Thou wilt cause Thine ear to attend' [Ps. 10:17], and it [also] says, 'My son, give Me thy heart and let thine eyes observe My ways' [Prov. 23:26]." But the first verse quoted here, although referring to " the direction of the heart," to *kawwanah*, is not directly related to the halakah in this passage, and consequently the passage gives no clue as to how this verse, Psalm 10:17, is to be interpreted. It is in another tractate of the Tosefta that this verse is interpreted, and there the verse is taken by 'Abba Saul to mean that when the individual has *kawwanah* in the saying of the Tefillah, he is thereby given an indication that his petition will be answered.[157] Once more *kawwanah* as described in the halakah is extolled by implication; whereas the halakah deals with instances of *kawwanah* as intention, the verse quoted in the halakah and extolling the efficacy of *kawwanah*, according to rabbinic interpretation, refers to *kawwanah* in the saying of the Tefillah, and thus to concentration on ideas. *Kawwanah* is again used as a single concept despite the fact that the instances involved embody different phases of the concept.

Found in several contexts is the teaching "it matters not whether much or little, if only a man directs his mind [or, heart] to Heaven," but that teaching has no reference either to a preparatory experience or to a physical act of orientation. The original setting of the statement is a mishnah (and a baraita) which teaches that so long as a sacrifice is offered with the proper intention—that is, to God—it matters not whether the sacrifice be a bullock, or only a bird, or even a meal-offering.[158] A different meaning is conveyed by the statement, however, when the rabbis detach the statement from its context in the Mishnah and quote it in connection with the study of Torah. R. Eleazar was ill and R. Joḥanan went to visit him. Finding R. Eleazar weeping, he asked, "Why do you weep? If it is because you have not studied as much Torah as you wished, we have learned in the Mishnah, 'It matters not whether much or little, if only a man directs his heart to Heaven.' "[159] The same statement is again applied to the study of Torah in the famous passage in which the rabbis of Jabneh compare their work with that of the non-scholars.[160] What can the teaching, "it matters not whether much or little, if only a man directs his heart to Heaven," mean in these contexts? We take it to mean that, besides being an intellectual activity,[161] study of Torah ought to be a mystical experience. A man has such mystical experience when he feels that what he is acquiring through study is being taught him at that very moment by God; in other words, on these occasions *mattan Torah* is not merely a dogma, an event in the past, but is felt as a present reality.[162] "It matters not whether much or little"—the experience is the same—"if only a man directs his heart to Heaven." Experience of God is here mediated by the concepts of study of Torah and *mattan Torah*.

Although the concepts of God's love and His justice are value concepts, they differ from most other value concepts in that they only interpret events or occasions.[163] What enables these concepts to be factors in day-to-day living are the berakot, or rather the halakot concerning the berakot, for those halakot call attention to the daily occasions which can be interpreted as manifestations of God's love. The question remains, however, whether such habitual interpretations can always constitute genuine experience of God's love, even with the aid of the berakah formula. This problem comes to the fore in the rabbinic views on *kawwanah*.

The material adduced in our discussions so far assumes that every individual can experience what we have called normal mysticism. There is the teaching, for example, that a man ought to gauge himself, when the time for saying the Tefillah has come, as to whether he can "direct his heart" or not;[164] obviously, the assumption is that generally an individual can "direct his heart." Again, to recall another example, it is assumed that artisans working on a precarious perch cannot have *kawwanah*, and hence the rule is that they are not permitted to say the Tefillah;[165] that rule, too, obviously also assumes that under proper circumstances, all men, artisans included, can have *kawwanah*.

But some scholars declare that, even if they try, they do not have *kawwanah* when saying the Tefillah. A scholar who admits to never having had *kawwanah* relates that on one occasion he did make an attempt, but only found himself debating in his mind as to who preceded whom in appearing before the king, a high Persian dignitary or the Exilarch.[166] Similarly, another scholar relates that he found himself counting flying birds.[167] A third scholar states that he is grateful to his head, since it bows of itself at "*Modim*" ("We acknowledge," the beginning of the Eighteenth Berakah).[168] From these examples it is apparent that rabbinic scholarship did not always go hand in hand with a capacity for normal mystical experience; untutored artisans may have had that capacity whereas some eminent scholars may have lacked it. Nevertheless, we must also recognize that the entire development of normal mysticism was largely the outcome of the experience of the scholars as a whole. Were it not for the rabbis, there would have been no Halakah, no perception of the occasions for religious experience, no permanent means for the cultivation and expression of normal mysticism.

If some scholars found *kawwanah* difficult, then this must have been all the more true of the many who were not scholars. There must have been a segment of the folk in general that found *kawwanah* difficult to achieve or who could not achieve it at all. This segment of the folk had its champions among the rabbis, especially among the Amoraim. Despite numerous rules and statements emphasizing *kawwanah*, sometimes opinion is divided on whether this or that thing "requires *kawwanah*." In such instances, the negative opinion certainly implies no objection to people having *kawwanah*; it simply states the case for those for whom *kawwanah* is difficult. Thus, when R. Jose holds, in the Yerushalmi, that the berakot of the Shema' require *kawwanah* and the anonymous opinion has it that they do not require *kawwanah*,[169] the negative opinion certainly implies no objection to the saying of these berakot with *kawwanah*. The negative opinion here simply does not impose *kawwanah* as a requirement for everybody, thereby taking into account those for whom it would be too stringent a requirement.[170]

In the Babli, this division of opinion has crystallized into two opposing general principles—a positive principle, "Miẓwot require *kawwanah*,"[171] and its negative, "Miẓwot do not require *kawwanah*."[172] According to the proponents of the positive principle, by the words "directing the heart," the Mishnah always means having the intention to fulfill a particular miẓwah,[173] and that is the way we have interpreted these words above, when we discussed *Rosh ha-Shanah* III.7; according to the proponents of the negative principle, however, by those words the Mishnah means having the intention merely of hearing the blowing of the *shofar*, or hearing the reading of the *megillah*, or reading the Shema', as the case may be, but not in order to fulfill a particular miẓwah.[174] The difference between the two views, it is to be noted, is not with regard to intention as such, but rather with regard to the *scope* of the intention. According to the negative view, for example, the Mishnah requires a person to have the intention only of blowing the proper sounds on the *shofar*, whereas, according to the positive view, the Mishnah goes further and requires that it be the intention to blow those sounds on the *shofar* because it is a miẓwah to do so.[175] Similarly, according to the negative view, the Mishnah requires a person to have the intention only of reading the Shema', an intention whereby just mechanical reading is excluded, whereas, according to the positive view, a person must have the intention of reading the Shema' in this manner because it is a miẓwah to do so.[176] Hence the intention to fulfill any particular miẓwah includes the intention to perform the required act in a particular manner. The proponents of the negative principle cannot possibly object, therefore, to the performance of such an act with the intention of fulfilling a miẓwah. They simply do not make it a requirement for everybody to have that kind of *kawwanah*, since for many it would be too stringent a requirement.[177] (In the next chapter we shall see that *kawwanah* in miẓwot, too, is associated with normal mystical experience.) A discussion in the Babli on certain details of the Passover Seder relates the two opposing principles to differences in view between tannaitic sources.[178] Apparently, already in tannaitic times, some authorities took a less rigorous stand on *kawwanah*.[179]

All the phases of *kawwanah* have a character in common. This is reflected, as we saw above, in the term "directing the heart [or, mind]," a term employed by the rabbis in regard to every phase of *kawwanah*. The term itself is biblical, despite a formal grammatical difference in the verb. "And direct your hearts unto the Lord" (I Sam. 7: 3); "A generation that directed not their heart [to God]" (Ps. 78: 8);[180] "If thou direct thy heart [to Him]" (Job 11: 13);[181] "Neither as yet had the people directed their hearts unto the God of their fathers" (II Chron. 20: 33).[182] The concept of *kawwanah*, then, has a biblical antecedent.

But the abstract noun *kawwanah* is rabbinic, not biblical. This means that the rabbinic concept possesses connotations which its biblical antecedent does not have, something also true of *middat raḥamim*, *middat ha-din*, and *malkut Shamayim*.[183] Indeed, *kawwanah* is often integrated with those three concepts. One of the connotations of *kawwanah* is concentration on the ideas in worship—that is to say, concentration on one or another of these value concepts. *Kawwanah* may also be associated with study of Torah, and in this phase, according to our interpretation, the dogma of *mattan Torah* also enters into the experience. The organismic character of the value concepts enables *kawwanah* to be integrated with other concepts as well, however. As we saw specifically when we studied the relation of *kawwanah* to miẓwot, *kawwanah* has in those instances the connotation of intention. Finally, there is a phase of *kawwanah* which refers to sheer, unconceptualized experience of God. Were that experience anything but a preparatory one, it would not have been possible in normal mysticism.

CHAPTER VIII

Miẓwot, Ethics, and Holiness

Since it is not our intention to present here all the various types of berakot, we shall discuss in this last chapter only the Birkat ha-Miẓwot, a berakah which directly affects the moral life. Embodied in the Birkat ha-Miẓwot are the concepts of miẓwot (commandments) and *ḳedushah* (holiness). Before dealing with the berakah itself we must discuss, therefore, some aspects of the concepts of miẓwot and *ḳedushah*.

A. The Concept of Miẓwot

According to the rabbis, the miẓwot of the Torah consist not only of the commandments or laws which are explicitly given in the written Torah, the Bible, but also of laws derived from the Bible and found in the oral Torah.[1] To identify all the laws implied in the Torah remains a problem, however. Although the rabbis employed definite hermeneutic rules, the thirteen *middot*, in deriving laws from the Torah, the textual methods and approach are quite the same when they designate a verse as merely *'asmakta*, "support," for a nonbiblical law.[2] What criterion, therefore, will enable us to distinguish between a biblical basis for a law and an *'asmakta*? Maimonides states that laws derived by the thirteen *middot* are to be regarded as biblical only if the rabbis themselves declare them to be so. Naḥmanides, on the other hand, brings proof to the contrary, namely, that all matters derived by means of the thirteen *middot* are to be regarded as biblical unless the rabbis characterize a derivation as an *'asmakta*.[3] Obviously, if these great authorities could differ so radically, there is not always a clear demarcation between laws regarded as rabbinic and laws regarded as implicit in the Bible.

To be sure, in the famous statement by R. Simla'i cited earlier,[4] the miẓwot "delivered unto Moses on Mount Sinai" are characterized as fixed in number, the number being six hundred and thirteen. Again, however, Naḥmanides differs from Maimonides and others who based their lists of laws, or codes, on that number. To quote Schechter: "Nachmanides questions the whole matter, and shows that the passages relating to this enumeration of laws are only of a homiletical nature, and thus of little consequence. Nay, he goes so far as to say, 'Indeed the system how to number the commandments [miẓwot] is a matter in which I suspect all of us [are mistaken] and the truth must be left to him who will solve all doubts.' "[5]

The point we are making is that there is no clear demarcation between the laws felt to be implied in the Bible and laws that are purely rabbinic. But a word ought to be added with regard to what appears to be the vast number of the miẓwot in any case. To quote Schechter once more: "Even a superficial analysis will discover that in the times of the Rabbis many of these commandments were already obsolete, as, for example, those relating to the arrangements of the tabernacle and to the conquest of Palestine; whilst others concerned only certain classes, as, for instance, the priests, the judges, the soldiers and their commanders, the Nazirites, the representatives of the community, or even one or two individuals in the whole population, as, for example, the king and the high priest. Others, again, provided for contingencies which could occur only to a few, as, for instance, the laws concerning divorce or levirate-marriages. The laws, again, relating to idolatry, incest, and the sacrifices of children to Moloch, could hardly be considered as coming within the province of the practical life of even the pre-Christian Jew."[6] Schechter concludes by saying, "A careful examination of the six hundred and thirteen laws will prove that barely a hundred laws are to be found which concerned the everyday life of the bulk of the people."[7]

The rabbinic dogma of *mattan Torah*, the giving of Torah, includes within its scope the oral as well as the written Torah. After stating that Moses learned the Mishnah or oral Torah directly from God, a baraita tells of how Moses taught the oral Torah to Aaron, and then to the sons of Aaron, and then to the elders and then to the people as a whole.[8] Another tannaitic passage refers specifically to the mizwot, declaring that all the mizwot were ordained at Sinai, and not only the general principles but the details as well.[9]

As we have pointed out elsewhere,[10] the concept of Torah modifies the dogma, of *mattan Torah*. Torah was, quite like the other value concepts, an indeterminate concept which was made determinate when concretized in new laws and in new interpretations. It is the concept of Torah rather than the dogma of *mattan Torah* which endows Midrash with divine sanction, even with divine origin, and Midrash consists of what is avowedly the work of the rabbis, namely, the interpretation of the Bible together with the laws resulting from the interpretation.[11] " 'But if ye will not hearken unto Me' [Lev. 26:14]—if ye will not hearken unto the Midrash of the *Ḥakamim*."[12] If mizwot recognized as derived from the Bible by the rabbis themselves are nevertheless characterized as mizwot of God, it was not necessary always to make a clear demarcation between laws regarded as implied in the Bible and laws acknowledged to be essentially rabbinic.

Sometimes, indeed, the rabbis taught that "the words of the *Ḥakamim*," the purely rabbinic laws, are more "weighty" than "the words of the Torah." The legislative authority of the rabbis is usually based on Deuteronomy 11:17: "According to the Torah which they shall teach thee, and according to the judgment which they shall tell thee, thou shalt do; thou shalt not turn aside from the sentence which they shall declare unto thee, to the right hand nor to the left."[13] A tannaitic comment on "thou shalt not turn aside from the sentence which they shall declare unto thee," after stating that this phrase refers to the tradition handed down from one man to another, adds: "Weighty [חמורים] are the words of the *Ḥakamim*, for he who transgresses their words is like him who transgresses the words of the Torah—indeed, the words of the *Ḥakamim* are more weighty than the words of the Torah, for among the latter there are light and weighty [mizwot], whereas the words of the *Ḥakamim* are all weighty."[14] Now this statement, and others in a similar vein,[15] do not altogether agree with the Halakah, for in the Halakah "the words of the Torah" are often applied with greater strictness than "the words of the *Ḥakamim*." For example, a doubtful case in a matter of biblical law is decided in accordance with the stricter practice, whereas a doubtful case in a matter of rabbinic law is decided according to the lenient practice.[16] But when the rabbis say that "the words of the *Ḥakamim* are more weighty" they are not referring to this or that principle. They are expressing their feeling of reverence for rabbinic law in general, a feeling as profound as their reverence for biblical law.[17]

Do the rabbis, however, actually characterize as miẓwot of God laws that are acknowledged to be purely rabbinic? Here authorities differ. In *Yebamot* II.3–4, the phrase *'issur miẓwah*, is applied to certain marriages (incest of second degree) prohibited by rabbinic law, and 'Abaye interprets the word miẓwah here to mean that "it is a miẓwah to obey the words of the *Ḥakamim*."[18] The same idea is more fully stated in the Yerushalmi on our mishnah: "It is a miẓwah of the Torah to obey the words of the *Soferim* [i.e., *Ḥakamim*]."[19] According to both statements, apparently, the phrase in *Yebamot* II.3–4 refers to Deuteronomy 11:17: "Thou shalt not turn aside," etc., and the rabbinic laws are thus associated with miẓwot of God, albeit indirectly. Alon thinks it likely that by miẓwah here the Mishnah itself has in mind *miẓwat Zeḳenim* (elders = *Ḥakamim*), and he cites passages containing this term.[20] The term *miẓwat Zeḳenim*, we ought to add, certainly indicates that the rabbinic laws are to be regarded as distinct from "the words of the Torah,"[21] as does likewise the term, *'aberah de-rabbanan*.[22] Even so, there is a passage, with versions elsewhere, which explicitly teaches that *miẓwot Zeḳenim* are to be associated with "words of the Torah," although again by virtue of Deuteronomy 11:17. "A man ought not say, 'I shall not fulfill *miẓwot Zeḳenim* since these are not [miẓwot] of the Torah.' The Holy One Blessed be He says to him: No, My son, but fulfill thou all that they decree, for it says, 'According to the Torah which they shall teach thee' [Deut. 11:17]."[23] The passages adduced in this paragraph, then, relate the rabbinic laws or ordinances to the miẓwot of the Torah by means of the biblical law in Deuteronomy 11:17, and hence do no more than to associate rabbinic law with "the words of the Torah."

But there are also authorities who go much further, and who deliberately and unmistakably characterize rabbinical ordinances as miẓwot of God. They do so in their wording of the Birkat ha-Miẓwot on matters that are nonbiblical. As given in the Yerushalmi, Rab's wording of the berakah on the Ḥanukkah light reads: "Blessed art Thou, O Lord our God, King of the world, Who has sanctified us by His miẓwot, and commanded us concerning the miẓwah of kindling the light of Ḥanukkah."[24] Although a rabbinical ordinance (מדבריהם), as the discussion in the passage itself brings out, the kindling of the Ḥanukkah light is twice characterized in this berakah as a miẓwah of God—first implicitly in the general formula, and again explicitly in the phrase "And commanded us concerning the miẓwah." The same passage[25] also allows us to see how a form of the Birkat ha-Miẓwot which only associates a rabbinical ordinance with the miẓwot of God differs from the form which characterizes that ordinance to *be* a miẓwah of God. On the first day of Sukkot, both R. Joḥanan and R. Joshua b. Levi in reciting the berakah on the *lulab* (palm frond) said, "And commanded us concerning the taking of the *lulab* [על נטילת לולב]"; on the rest of the days, however, since the taking of the *lulab* on those days (elsewhere than in the Temple) was a rabbinical ordinance, R. Joshua changed the formula to say, "and commanded us concerning a miẓwah of the *Zeḳenim* [על מצות זקנים],"[26] whereas R. Joḥanan retained on those days, too, the formula of the first day. Another version, after stating that R. Joḥanan agrees that the taking of the *lulab* after the first day is a rabbinical ordinance, gives as the reason for his practice the following interpretation: " 'The words of the wise [*Ḥakamim*] are as goads . . . they are given from One Shepherd' [Koheleth 12: 11]—the words of the Torah and the words of the *Ḥakamim* are given from One Shepherd."[27]

When a person is about to fulfill a miẓwah with *kawwanah*, he has a heightened awareness of a relationship between himself and God. The miẓwah, he feels, represents a communication which has been directed to him by God. In such an experience, the particular miẓwah which the individual is about to perform is not merely a practice transmitted to him by previous generations but is a command from God here and now. Such an experience, in other words, belongs in the category of normal mysticism.

This mystical experience of the rabbis is reflected in rabbinic literature in various ways. By saying or implying that the individual heard the miẓwah at Sinai, some statements, so to speak, transport the individual to Mount Sinai and thus relate an occasion in the present to the dogma of *mattan Torah*, a dogma positing an event in the past. For example, the rabbis, in purely halakic contexts, speak of a miẓwah as something "on which he [the individual] is sworn from Mount Sinai."[28] Again, in reference to the thief, the Mekilta says, "[His] ear had heard, 'Thou shalt not steal' [Exod. 20:13], and yet he went and stole."[29] Such statements certainly accord with the well-known haggadah that the souls of those who were not yet born were present at Sinai,[30] yet it is hardly possible that the halakic statements were based entirely on the haggadah. Both the halakic statements and the haggadah reflect, it seems to us, the consciousness of the rabbis as they were about to perform a miẓwah—namely, that the miẓwah was given to them directly by God, and hence they associated that consciousness with the dogma of *mattan Torah* itself.

We noticed that Rab and R. Joḥanan, in their berakot, designate rabbinical ordinances as miẓwot of God, but that R. Joshua b. Levi, in his berakah, designates a rabbinical ordinance as a miẓwah of the *Zeḳenim*. A difference so basic can only imply a difference in experience, Rab and R. Joḥanan having the consciousness, as they pronounce the berakah, that such a miẓwah is given them now directly by God, a consciousness not possessed by R. Joshua b. Levi. Haggadot reflect this difference in experience. There is a baraita, for example, which relates the rabbinical ordinances directly to the whole dogma of *mattan Torah* and calls them miẓwot which are to be instituted in the future. It declares that the covenant was made not only with those who stood at Mount Sinai but also with the generations to come (not mentioning souls at all), and with the *gerim* who would be converted in the future; and it adds that the covenant was made not only with respect to the miẓwot received "from Mount Sinai," but also with respect to miẓwot to be instituted in the future, such as the reading of the *megillah*, meaning, with respect to rabbinic ordinances as well.[31] On the other hand, there is also the haggadah, as we have seen, which designates the rabbinical ordinances as *miẓwot Zeḳenim* and which, while associating them with "words of the Torah," does so indirectly and by virtue of Deuteronomy 11:17.

In an earlier work we show that when the rabbis speak of acknowledging God, they refer to experience of God, and that when they speak of denial of God, or of one "who denies the root," they refer to willful rebellion against God, to willful rejection of Him on the part of one who had known, had experienced Him.[32] Now the rabbis say that no one transgresses a miẓwah "until he denies the root," applying that phrase in a number of instances: to him who denies the Ten Commandments, to him who deals falsely with his neighbor "in a matter of deposit," to him who utters slander, to him who lends money on interest.[33] If the rabbis assume denial of God to be a condition for the transgression of a particular miẓwah, it can only be because for them the fulfillment of a miẓwah involves an experience of God.

To fulfill a miẓwah with *kawwanah*, a person must have the consciousness that the particular miẓwah he is performing has been given him directly by God. Many, apparently most, of the rabbis retained this consciousness even when about to fulfill a rabbinical ordinance. Making for this attitude, we may safely say, was the awareness that much of what was regarded as biblical law was itself the work of the rabbis. There were others, however, who found that, while they could associate avowedly rabbinical ordinances with biblical law, they could do so only indirectly.

Miẓwot is a conceptual term which is found in the Bible, but once more it is a term whose rabbinic connotations differ from the biblical. In the Bible, while the word often refers to commandments of God,[34] it also refers, as Greenberg has shown, to the commands or admonitions of a king, parent, or teacher, or those of "any other superior."[35] In rabbinic literature, the tendency is to limit the term to the miẓwot of God, even *miẓwot Zeḳenim* being either characterized as, or associated with the miẓwot of God.[36] But the rabbinic concept possesses another connotation as well. We shall notice that the rabbinic concept of miẓwot sometimes has a moral or ethical connotation.

B. Miẓwot and the Ethical Concepts

In this section we shall discuss several ways in which the ethical concepts dealt with in earlier chapters[37] interweave with the concept of miẓwot. We shall find that these ways of interweaving relate to the role of emphasis in organismic thought.

Most often, an ethical concept is associated with the concept of miẓwot in such fashion that both interpret an act or a situation as a whole. This is true even when the word miẓwah itself has an ethical connotation, the connotation of *ẓedaḳah*. Men are described as doers of miẓwah, meaning doers of *ẓedaḳah*,[38] and a plea for charity may often be phrased as, "Give me miẓwah."[39] Miẓwot likewise can connote charity, as in the halakah in the Yerushalmi which limits what a man may give away in miẓwot.[40] But though miẓwah and miẓwot may thus, in many instances, connote *ẓedaḳah*, that connotation does not displace the primary meaning of miẓwot. In the very passage of the Yerushalmi just cited, the discussion there indicates that charity is a miẓwah in the same sense as are the other miẓwot; indeed, the Tosefta declares that *ẓedaḳah* and *gemilut ḥasadim* are equal in importance to all the [other] miẓwot taken together.[41] An act of charity, in fine, is interpreted by two concepts at once: the concept of *ẓedaḳah* and the concept of miẓwot.

"The Sons of Noah," or mankind in general, were given, the rabbis say, seven miẓwot, and they are: To institute law and justice (*dinin*), not to blaspheme God (*birkat ha-Shem*) and not to worship idols (*'abodah zarah*), not to commit incest (*gilluy 'arayot*), murder (*shefikut damim*), or robbery (*gezel*), and not to eat the meat of a living animal.[42] We have here a formulation of what we have recognized above to be the rabbinic category of universal ethics.[43] Acts of incest, murder, and robbery, when designated as such, are thereby interpreted by negative ethical concepts, and when they are characterized as violations of miẓwot they are interpreted by the concept of miẓwot as well. To eat the meat of a living animal is to violate a miẓwah but it is also the opposite of the ethical concept of *raḥamim*, the scope of which includes animals.[44] The one positive miẓwah in the list is the instituting of law and justice, and that is characterized by the term *dinin*, an ethical value concept. If the rabbis include in the list also matters relating to God, it is because, as we shall see later, the relationship to God was a primary factor in their ethical consciousness.

In another formulation of universal ethics, the rabbis say, "Because of eight things is the world destroyed: Because of *dinin*, idolatry, incest, murder, profanation of the Name (*ḥillul ha-Shem*), because of foul things a person utters, arrogance (*gassut ruaḥ*), scandal-mongering (*lashon ra'*), and some say also because of covetousness."[45] This list contains, in addition to most of the matters mentioned in the other formulation, more acts or types of acts, the names for which constitute negative ethical concepts. But all the matters here are also designated, by implication, as violations of miẓwot, the concept of miẓwot being embodied in the statement. "Because of eight things is the world destroyed" contains the concept of God's justice;[46] by the same token, the statement also embodies the concept of miẓwot, for when God rewards, it is for the performance of a miẓwah, and He punishes when a miẓwah has been violated.[47] A statement in the Mishnah similarly embodies the concepts of God's justice and miẓwot, but now there is posited God's reward for refraining from unethical conduct. Pointing to Deuteronomy 12:23–25, verses which prohibit the eating of the blood of a slaughtered animal "that it may go well with thee and with thy children after thee," the Mishnah draws the following lesson: If a man receives reward for refraining from eating blood, something a man loathes, all the more will he receive reward, he and his generations after him, for refraining from *gezel* and *'arayot* (forbidden marriages), things which he may desire or covet.[48] Acts of *gezel* and *'arayot* are then interpreted not only by the negative ethical concepts which designate these acts but also by the concept of miẓwot embodied in the statement.

Acts prohibited by a biblical verse are, of course, governed by a negative miẓwah. When such acts are also designated by a negative ethical concept, they are being interpreted both by an ethical concept and by the concept of miẓwot. Acts of *'ona'ah* are a case in point, and these acts are of two kinds: *'ona'at mamon* and *'ona'at debarim*. *'Ona'at mamon* refers to certain instances of fraud or over-reaching in business transactions,[49] acts prohibited according to rabbinic interpretation, in Leviticus 25:14: "And if thou sell aught unto thy neighbor, or buy of thy neighbor's hand, ye shall not wrong [*'al tonu*] one another."[50] The last part of the verse is practically repeated in verse 17: "And ye shall not wrong [*we-lo' tonu*] one another, but thou shalt fear thy God"—and since verse 17 makes no reference to "money" the rabbis say that it refers to *'ona'at debarim*, injury or wrong through words.[51] Among the many instances given of *'ona'at debarim* are those of merely pretending to buy an article, saying to a person who has repented, "Remember your former deeds," or to a proselyte, "Remember the deeds of your fathers";[52] and saying, after the manner of Job's friends, to a person who is afflicted or ill or has buried his sons, "Remember, I pray thee, who ever perished, being innocent, or where were the upright cut off," etc. (Job 4:6 f.).[53] It is proved in various ways that *'ona'at debarim* is worse than *'ona'at mamon*. The former is the greater wrong, says one authority, since the verse prohibiting it adds, "But thou shalt fear thy God," whereas the verse prohibiting *'ona'at mamon* does not do so.[54] The former affects the man himself, the latter (only) his property, says another.[55] Still another points out that *'ona'at mamon* can be made good but *'ona'at debarim* cannot.[56]

From the discussion in the last paragraph it is patent that acts of *'ona'ah* were interpreted both as violations of miẓwot of the Torah and as unethical acts, the unethical quality of the acts being designated as *'ona'ah*. But we have also adduced material bearing on the role of the ethical term. Those who have dealt with the ordinances or rules on *'ona'ah* found in the Mishnah and the Talmud have recognized that these ordinances constitute a remarkable foliation and development of the biblical precepts underlying them.[57] What has apparently altogether escaped attention, however, is the tremendous role played by the rabbinic term *'ona'ah*, the conceptual term itself, the noun-form. Thus, Lazarus, while evidently approving of the rabbinic term *'ona'at mamon* as an expression of the idea in Leviticus 25:14, regards *'ona'at debarim*, the rabbinic term expressing the idea in Leviticus 25:17, as "a rather infelicitous term";[58] and this, after he himself had demonstrated that the biblical *lo' tonu* defies consistent translation.[59] The fact is that the rabbinic word *'ona'ah*, too, defies translation into a modern idiom. *'Ona'ah* is a rabbinic concept which has as its antecedent the biblical *lo' tonu*. Because the rabbinic concept is represented by an abstract conceptual term, a classifying noun-form, *'ona'ah*, the range of the rabbinic concept is much wider than that of its biblical antecedent,[60] the rabbinic concept including within its scope such widely different matters as fraud in a business transaction and a husband causing his wife to shed tears.[61] Both *'ona'at mamon* and *'ona'at debarim* are sub-concepts of *'ona'ah*, aspects of *'ona'ah*.

If *'ona'ah* is not translatable, there is a reason for that. So far as the individual instances of *'ona'ah* are concerned, these can, of course, be described in any modern idiom. What modern idioms cannot do, since they lack equivalents for *'ona'ah*, is to unify all these instances, to give them all a similar significance, to interpret them as a whole. There is simply no modern ethical concept which can designate at the same time such diverse matters as fraud and *Schadenfreude*.

'Ona'ah is a striking example of what an ethical concept does when it designates an act. By designating an act, the ethical concept not only classifies it but gives significance to the act as well. More correctly, the significance is not given to the act but is inherent in it, since the ethical concept, being a value concept, is embodied in the act.

Certain miẓwot themselves, that is, the laws apart from the acts enjoined or prohibited by the laws, may be characterized, and hence interpreted, by means of an ethical concept. The verses, "Whether it be cow or ewe, ye shall not kill it and its young both in one day" (Lev. 22: 28) and "If a bird's nest chance to be before thee . . . thou shalt not take the dam with the young," etc. (Deut. 22: 6 f.) are interpreted in several rabbinic sources to mean that God has compassion on the animals. From Leviticus 22: 27 f. those sources conclude that just as God has compassion on mankind so He has compassion on the animals, and from Deuteronomy 22:6 f. that "just as the Holy One blessed be He has bestowed His compassion [*raḥamim*] on beasts" so also has He compassion on fowl.[62] *Targum Jonathan* on Leviticus 22: 28, in the spirit of this teaching, renders that verse as follows: "O My people, ye Children of Israel, just as I am compassionate in heaven, so be ye compassionate on earth: cow or ewe, ye shall not kill it and its young both in the same day."[63] When this law is observed, *Targum Jonathan* says in effect, a man is both performing a miẓwah and acting with *raḥamim*, compassion.

In all of the instances so far cited, both an ethical concept and the concept of miẓwot interpret an act or a situation as a whole. Acts so interpreted have a dual significance, a phenomenon of interpretation fairly common in organismic thought where a situation usually embodies several concepts.[64] Thus, in addition to the concept of miẓwot and an ethical concept, an act may also embody the concept of the sons of Noah, a concept which is practically an alternative to the concept of man, and the act has thereby been given a universal significance. Similarly, when an element in the interpretation is the concept of God's justice, that concept adds its own significance to the interpretation of the act as a whole. When two value concepts interpret an act as a whole, therefore, the several concepts do not contradict but supplement each other. Organismic interpretation usually endows an act with a significance that is many toned.

Usually when an act as a whole is interpreted by two concepts at once, neither of the concepts is stressed above the other. But this form of organismic interweaving of concepts is by no means the sole form. One of the concepts interpreting a situation as a whole may be stressed on one occasion, and the other on another occasion; in the case of the Shema', for example, at one time the study of Torah is stressed, and at another time the acceptance of *malkut Shamayim*.[65] It is also possible to stress one concept as against the other, as does that halakah on the saying of the 'Amidah which stresses the concept of tefillah as against the concept of 'abodah.[66] Organismic thought allows room for differences in temperament, in point of view and in circumstances. On the one hand, organismic thought makes for rich significance by allowing full play to all the value concepts embodied in a situation; on the other hand, by permitting now one concept to be stressed and now another, organismic thought allows room for the predilections of the individual and for special circumstances.

We have presented a number of illustrative instances in which an act is interpreted at the same time both by the concept of miẓwot and by an ethical concept, and in which neither concept is stressed above the other. We shall soon see that the association between the two concepts is not lost even if one of them should be stressed. At present, however, we wish to indicate that when the idea of God's command is emphasized by the concept of *gezerot*, *gezerot* may exclude an ethical concept. *Gezerot* and miẓwot are closely related, so closely related that the verb *ẓwh* is sometimes used in connection with the word *gezerah*, as Albeck has shown.[67] *Gezerot* refers, therefore, to commands or decrees, and often to the commands or decrees of God.[68]

Taking issue especially with *Targum Jonathan*, R. Jose b. Bun ('Abun), a Palestinian Amora, characterizes Leviticus 22:28 and

Deuteronomy 22:6 f. as *gezerot* of God. He says that those who declare that the qualities of the Holy One Blessed be He consist (primarily) of mercy or love (שעושין למדותיו של הקב״ה רחמים), "do not do right," and then he adds, "Those who translate [Lev. 22:8], 'O My people, ye Children of Israel, just as I am compassionate in heaven, so be ye compassionate on earth: cow or ewe, ye shall not kill it and its young both in the same day [*Targum Jonathan* to Lev. 22:8],' do not do right, for they render the *gezerot* of the Holy One Blessed be He [to be] mercy."[69] The basis for this statement is the rule in the Mishnah that if a man says in the Tefillah, "Thy mercy extends to a bird's nest," he is to be silenced;[70] the rule here forbids including in the Tefillah any plea wherein the law in Deuteronomy 22:6 f. is interpreted as an evidence of God's mercy.[71] The term *gezerot* (of God) in R. Jose b. Bun's statement, therefore, refers both to the law in Leviticus 22:28 and to the law in Deuteronomy 22:6 f. As a characterization of those laws, *gezerot* implies so strong an emphasis on the idea of God's command as to exclude other considerations. If the organismic complex allows room for such emphasis on that idea, however, it also allows room for the interpretation to which R. Jose objects, an interpretation of Leviticus 22:28 and Deuteronomy 22:6 f. discussed a few pages back. That is why, despite R. Jose's explicit objection, *Targum Jonathan*'s rendering was retained by the rabbis. Incidentally, R. Jose b. Bun's comment on the rule in the Mishnah does not represent a consensus, for other interpretations of that rule are also given.[72]

When a law is characterized as a *gezerah* of God, the idea of God's command is so strongly emphasized as often to exclude either an ethical concept or else some other matter. R. Jose b. Bun designates certain laws as *gezerot* of God in order that they may not be taken as embodying the ethical concept of *raḥamim*. R. Eleazar b. Azariah, a Tanna, uses the verb *gazar* to emphasize the idea of God's command, likewise in order to exclude something.[73] "A man should not say, 'I have no desire to wear a garment of mixed stuff, I have no desire to eat pig's meat, I have no desire for forbidden sexual connections'; but [he should say], 'I do have the desire, [but] what shall I do, since my Father Who is in heaven has so decreed [*gazar*] for me.'" This teaching R. Eleazar finds in the proof-text, "I have set you apart from the peoples, that ye should be Mine" (Lev. 20:26), a text which enables him also to conclude his teaching with the following statement: "[A man] thus [both] keeps himself aloof from the transgression and accepts upon himself *malkut Shamayim* [the kingship of God]." This concluding statement is overlooked by modern writers critical of R. Eleazar's teaching. To obey a law solely because it is felt to be a *gezerah* of God is not obedience in a spirit of arid formalism, as they would have it. Such obedience, instead, is accompanied by a religious experience, the acceptance of *malkut Shamayim*.[74]

There are points in common between this passage which we shall call B, and another passage in the Sifra cited earlier,[75] which we shall call A. Mentioned in both passages are the laws against eating pig's meat and wearing garments of mixed stuff; Rashi in his glosses on a version of A also designates the laws there as *gezerot*.[76] Furthermore, the context in A implies that those laws are possessed by Israel alone. In B a similar thought is conveyed by the proof-text, "I have set you apart from the peoples," a verse relating, according to R. Eleazar b. Azariah, to distinctive laws which set Israel "apart from the peoples." Finally, the *gezerot* in A, too, exclude something, although only as a means of drawing a contrast. As against the universal laws mentioned there—laws in the Torah which other peoples possess as well—are *gezerot*, laws which are *not* universal but which are possessed only by Israel.

We shall cite one more instance. The law in Numbers: 19 ordains that persons who had in some manner been in contact with the dead and a house in which a death had occurred be purified by the ashes of a red heifer in water. That law is introduced with the words, "This is the statute [*ḥuḳḳat*] of the law" (Num. 19:2). On the basis of these words, R. Joḥanan b. Zakkai declares, "A dead person does not make unclean nor does the water purify, but it [i.e., the law] is a *gezerah* of the King of the kings of kings."[77] By designating the law here as a *gezerah* of God the idea of God's command is so strongly emphasized as to exclude the thought that contact with the dead makes a person intrinsically unclean or that the water of the red heifer has an intrinsic power of purification.[78]

When the term *gezerah* is used so as to emphasize the idea of God's command, it often excludes something, including an ethical concept, as these examples demonstrate. On the other hand, we saw that the concept of miẓwot is often associated with ethical concepts, so much so that the words miẓwah and miẓwot may also connote *ẓedaḳah*. We shall now see that there are statements or principles which do stress the concept of miẓwot, but that even in such instances the association between miẓwot and the ethical concepts is not lost.

"Greater is he who does because he is commanded," says R. Ḥanina in regard to miẓwot, "than he who does without being commanded."[79] In several passages this statement definitely emphasizes the concept of miẓwot as against ethical concepts, and yet the association between miẓwot and the ethical concepts is not really lost. As an answer to the question of how far one must go in *kibbud 'ab wa-'em*, honoring father and mother, a story is told of a Gentile in Ashkelon by the name of Dama b. Netinah who refused a fabulous profit because he did not wish to disturb his sleeping father; God rewarded him when a red heifer was born in his herd for which he asked and received the sum he had felt obliged to refuse while honoring his father.[80] After telling this story, one of the sources in the Babli adds: "And R. Ḥanina said, If he who does without being commanded thus [is rewarded by God], he who does because he is commanded is all the more [certain to be rewarded]—for R. Ḥanina said, 'Greater is he,' " etc.[81] Nevertheless, it remains true, first, that *kibbud 'ab wa-'em* is both a miẓwah and an ethical concept; second, that, according to the rabbis, when God rewards, it is for the performance of a miẓwah;[82] and that, hence, in this story which tells of a reward for an act of *kibbud 'ab*, the association between miẓwot and ethical concepts is not lost. This conclusion holds with respect to another instance where R. Ḥanina's principle is applied. When God saw that the sons of Noah did not keep the seven miẓwot which they had accepted on themselves, He made those miẓwot no longer mandatory, so that even if the sons of Noah do observe them the reward is only that given to him who does without being commanded, for R. Ḥanina said, "Greater is he," etc.[83] Here, too, an element of reward nevertheless remains, and hence here, too, there remains an association between miẓwot and ethical concepts.[84] (We must add that statements of R. Ḥanina's principle occur only in the Babli.[85] A better version of the story about Dama ben Netina is found in the Yerushalmi,[86] and that version contains neither R. Ḥanina's remark nor his principle.)

A principle enunciated by Raba stresses the idea of God's command inherent in miẓwot, although the stressing is achieved through an implication. The miẓwot, he says, were not given (to Israel) as a means of enjoyment,[87] a statement which calls forth Rashi's gloss, "But were given for a yoke on their necks."[88] Raba's principle is a legal principle and it means that legally the observance of the miẓwot is not considered enjoyment, rather than that such observance ought not to bring enjoyment.[89] The principle is applied to matters such as blowing the *shofar*[90] and sitting in the *sukkah*.[91] In a discussion on the *'erub*,* this principle is also applied, however, to going to a house of mourning and going to a wedding feast,[92] acts of *gemilut ḥasadim*.[93] Here we have a principle which stresses the idea of God's command, yet one which maintains the association between miẓwot and the ethical concepts.

According to Lazarus' interpretation,[94] Raba's principle is a general ethical idea which has been restricted by its halakic application. He declares that Raba's statement "originally and in much earlier times had a wider meaning," that it was "directed against the hedonist view of life." He goes on to say, "The pleasure derived from the fulfilment, especially from the glad fulfilment, of commands had probably become an Epicurean subterfuge, which the ethical spirit of the Rabbis desired to render unavailing, so that men might fulfil duty for its own sake. Here, as in so many cases, the Kantian conception of duty and its contrariety to inclination suggests itself." But where, we ask, is the motive of "duty for its *own* sake" to be found in Raba's principle? On the contrary, the principle plainly says that the miẓwot were "given," and it does not say that they were given for their own sake. A philosophical, non-rabbinic criterion for ethics has here been read into a rabbinic text. Lazarus also misinterprets the principle when, according to him, "'the expression is restricted to its legal sense." He limits the halakic application to "the use of an object in the execution of a ceremonial law." A rabbinic text is always misconstrued when given a philosophical interpretation.[95]

* The establishment, before the Sabbath, of a symbolical domicile by an individual at some point within the limit of permitted locomotion on the Sabbath, in order that he might go beyond that limit on the Sabbath for the purpose of performing a mizwah.

The concept of miẓwot, we have found, is often associated with ethical concepts. Acts as a whole may be interpreted at the same time by both the concept of miẓwot and an ethical concept, for in the organismic valuational process not one, but several concepts may be embodied in an act or in a situation. The organismic process, however, also allows one concept occasionally to be emphasized over another; there are thus some statements or principles which primarily emphasize the concept of miẓwot, sometimes even as against the ethical concepts. Nevertheless, in these instances as well, the association between miẓwot and the ethical concepts is maintained; it is only when the idea of God's command is expressed through the concept of *gezerot* that an ethical concept may be excluded.

An act as a whole may be interpreted by both the concept of miẓwot and by an ethical concept, and yet be an act in which the ethical concept is emphasized. This occurs when such an act is regarded as a miẓwah that supersedes the other miẓwot, as an overriding miẓwah. A well-known instance is the saving of a life on the Sabbath, the principle in the Mishnah being that the Sabbath is to be superseded when the danger to life is possible or even uncertain.[96] The rule applies, of course, to all the other miẓwot, not to the Sabbath alone.[97] It is a rule which enjoins acts prompted by *raḥamim*, compassion,[98] as against the observance of other miẓwot.

Nor are the ethical concepts emphasized only when it is a question of saving a life. A high priest or a Nazarite is not permitted to attend to the burial of even near relatives, since any contact with a corpse makes him ritually unclean, yet he is required to attend to the burial of a *met miẓwah*, the corpse of one whose relatives are not known.[99] Were he both a high priest and a Nazarite and, furthermore, on his way to slaughter his paschal lamb (which cannot be eaten if a person is unclean), attending to the burial of a *met miẓwah* supersedes all.[100] An overriding miẓwah, the obligation concerning a *met miẓwah* is imposed, the Talmud says, because of *kebod ha-beriyyot*, the honor of mankind,[101] that is to say, because of an ethical value concept. Similarly, acts of *gemilut ḥasadim* may be overriding miẓwot: A baraita teaches that the study of Torah is to be interrupted for the sake of participating in a funeral escort or in a wedding procession.[102]

All these instances are, of course, prime examples of the association between the concept of miẓwot and the ethical concepts.

A bond unites the rabbis with the prophets, as was observed in the previous chapter.[103] Further evidence of that bond is the parallel between the prophets' interpretation of acts and the rabbinic interpretation. The prophets, feeling themselves to be messengers of God, have, of course, a different approach and their ethical vocabulary, too, is somewhat different from that of the rabbis. Nevertheless, despite these differences, the parallel is close enough to enable us to use rabbinic concepts in order to describe the prophets' message. A few verses will suffice as illustrations: "It hath been told thee, O man, what is good and what the Lord doth require of thee: Only to do justice [*mishpaṭ*], and to love mercy [*ḥesed*], and to walk humbly with thy God" (Micah 6:8). Acts designated by the ethical concepts of *mishpaṭ* and *ḥesed* are acts which "the Lord doth require of thee," that is to say, they are miẓwot of God. "Thus hath the Lord spoken, saying: Execute justice [*mishpaṭ*], and do [acts of] mercy [*ḥesed*] and compassion [*raḥamim*] every man to his brother" (Zech. 7:9). This verse similarly allows us to characterize as miẓwot of God actions designated by the ethical concepts of *mishpaṭ*, *ḥesed*, and *raḥamim*. Hosea 4:2 refers to acts designated by negative ethical concepts and verse 3 embodies the concept of God's justice—"Swearing and lying, and killing, and stealing, and committing adultery! They break all bounds and blood toucheth blood. Therefore doth the land mourn, and every one that dwelleth therein doth languish."

C. *Kedushah* and the Moral Life

Kedushah is a complex concept. Not only is it composed of phases, like other concepts studied here, but the phases themselves are complex. Besides, it also possesses a subconcept in *ḳiddush ha-Shem*, several aspects of which were discussed in Chapter VI.

One phase of *ḳedushah* refers to a sphere in which it is sensed as a mystical quality of certain objects, days, and persons. If these are felt to possess a mystical quality it is because they are regarded as being God's own, as belonging to God in a special sense. That sphere of *ḳedushah* is conceived, furthermore, as consisting of various hierarchies of *ḳedushah*, each hierarchy being arranged in an ascending order of things designated as *ḳedushot*. At the same time, in a number of instances, though not in all, this mystical quality results from human acts, acts of a kind which in other contexts have no such mystical association. We shall exemplify these matters as briefly as we may.

"There are ten *ḳedushot*," says the Mishnah, and it then proceeds to describe the particular hierarchy of holy areas, beginning with the lowest, the Land of Israel, and ascending to the highest, the Holy of Holies.[104] In a version of this tannaitic tradition, the Land of Canaan is declared to be holier than Trans-Jordan, the reason being that "the Land of Canaan is fit for the House of the *Shekinah*," whereas Trans-Jordan is not.[105] Another tannaitic source affirms that "the *Shekinah* does not reveal itself outside the Land,"[106] a statement which refers to God's communications to the prophets. The reason for the holiness of the Land of Israel, such statements indicate, is that only there are there forms of *gilluy Shekinah*. The hierarchy of the holy areas relates to the closeness of those areas to the Holy of Holies, the locus of *gilluy Shekinah* in the Temple.[107]

Related to the hierarchy of holy areas is that of the sacrifices and the tithes. The highest grade in this hierarchy is designated as *ḳodshe ḳodashim*, the most holy.[108] Among such sacrifices or offerings are those which are to be eaten by the priesthood, but only by the males and only "inside of the enclosures [literally, curtains]."[109] Lower than this grade are the sacrifices designated as *ḳodashim ḳallim*, that is, sacrifices holy in a lesser degree.[110] A common characteristic of the various kinds of sacrifices placed in this category is that all of them may be eaten in any part of the city of Jerusalem.[111] The area where the sacrifice or offering is to be eaten is thus one of the factors bearing on the gradations in this particular hierarchy, the wider area indicating a lower degree of holiness. That criterion is reflected in the *ḳodashim ḳallim* taken by themselves. The first-born of the clean cattle is to be eaten by the priests only, whereas the tithe of cattle may be eaten by any person, and yet, because both may be eaten in any part of Jerusalem they are in the same category, that of *ḳodashim ḳallim*.[112] On the other hand, the grade of *ḳodshe ḳodashim*, restricting as it does the eating of such sacrifices as may be eaten to male priests, indicates that another factor has a bearing on the gradations in this hierarchy, namely, whether the holy thing be among the *mattenot kehunah*,[113] the gifts or prerogatives of the priesthood. Both *ḳodshe ḳodashim* and *ḳodashim ḳallim* are, of course, offered in the Temple, although here, too, a distinction is made between the two grades with respect to the place where they are to be slaughtered.[114]

Included in the *mattenot kehunah* are *ḳodshe ha-gebul*, the holy things, such as *terumah*, the priest's share of the crop, and *ḥallah*, his share of dough, which are set apart and consumed outside the Temple and Jerusalem.[115] A passage in the Sifre, stressing the idea that the *ḳodshe ha-gebul* are included in *mattenot kehunah*, but also distinguishing between the *ḳodshe miḳdash*, the offerings in the Temple, and *ḳodshe ha-gebul*, identifies *ḳodshe ha-gebul*, practically in so many words, as the third grade in the hierarchy below *ḳodashim ḳallim*. To all three, to *ḳodshe ḳodashim*, *ḳodashim ḳallim*, and *ḳodshe ha-gebul*, the passage applies the same formula: לגזור דין ולכרות להם ברית, a formula referring to God's confirmation of Aaron in the priesthood as against Koraḥ, and to areas where these various grades of holy things may be eaten and indicating by whom they may be eaten.[116] Since that formula is applied to all three grades, all of them are thereby characterized as *mattenot kehunah*. But the formula is applied seriatim —first to *ḳodshe ḳodashim*, then to *ḳodashim ḳallim*, then to *ḳodshe ha-gebul*.[117] Since we know that *ḳodshe ḳodashim* is the highest grade in the hierarchy and that *ḳodashim ḳallim* is the second grade, *ḳodshe ha-gebul* must, therefore, be the third grade. Again, as we have said, the passage demarcates between the offerings in the Temple and *ḳodshe ha-gebul*.[118] Since all the holy things mentioned here are *mattenot kehunah*, the demarcation can only mean that *ḳodshe ha-gebul* are lowest in the grades of *mattenot kehunah*, in other words, that they are the third grade in the hierarchy.

Having given the *terumah* to the priest and the first tithe to the Levite, a man must then set aside *ma'aser sheni*, the second tithe,[119] every year in the sabbatical period except the fourth and the sixth, when the tithe was given to the poor.[120] In conformity with Deuteronomy 14:22 ff., *ma'aser sheni* was to be consumed by the owner and his family in the city of Jerusalem. Designated in Scripture as holy, according to the Tannaim,[121] it cannot be higher than the fourth grade in the hierarchy, since the first three consist of *mattenot kehunah.* Concerning the fourth year's fruits of a young tree (Lev. 19:24), Bet Hillel and Bet Shammai differ, Bet Hillel coupling them with *ma'aser sheni*,[122] and Bet Shammai obviously regarding them as of a lower grade of holiness.[123] The first tithe, however, was not taken to be holy by most of the rabbis.[124]

Kodshe ḳodashim, ḳodashim ḳallim, ḳodshe ha-gebul, ma'aser sheni, and the fourth year's fruits of a young tree or vineyard, it was felt, all possessed the quality of *ḳedushah*, holiness. It was this felt quality alone that distinguished those things from the rest of their kind with which they had originally been intermingled, that marked off those things as being something other, something different. The quality of *ḳedushah* was thus a purely mystical quality, so much so that it could neither be described nor demonstrated. This did not mean that the sense of *ḳedushah* was weak. On the contrary, the sense of *ḳedushah* was so strong that it made possible an awareness of ascending grades. In turn, that hierarchical order almost gave to *ḳedushah* a character of substantiality, since some things were felt to possess more of *ḳedushah* than others. Now these things became *ḳedushot*, by and large, when they were dedicated to God, but no element of theurgy whatsoever was involved in the manner whereby either sacrifices or the things which were set apart became peculiarly God's own. According to an anonymous statement in the Mishnah, a sacrifice is to be slaughtered with certain ideas in mind, among them the idea that it is being dedicated to God.[125] R. Jose declares, however, that it is a proper sacrifice even if it is slaughtered with no idea in mind.[126] Again, when a person sets apart *terumah*, he is to say, "*Terumah* to God";[127] on the other hand, it is also enough if he only has such an idea in mind and utters nothing at all.[128] Theurgy is obviously out of the question in the halakah stated by R. Jose, but the other halakot likewise have nothing to do with theurgy.

In all the halakot here, we are dealing with intention, *maḥashabah* or *kawwanah*,[129] whether the intention is expressed in words, or consists of an idea in the mind, or is indicated simply by an act.[130] The intention whereby a thing is made holy is akin to the instances of intention mentioned in Chapter VII, section D—the intention required, for example, on the part of a person who performs an act of acquisition, or the intention required in a writ of divorce.[131] Indeed, in consecutive statements, authorities differing with respect to intention in the redemption of *ma'aser sheni* differ also with regard to intention in the matter of handing a writ of divorce to a woman,[132] evidently because intention in the one instance is analogous to intention in the other. The manner whereby any particular holy thing acquired its character was akin to the manner in which a number of nonholy things acquired their specific character. If the character of these nonholy things was not determined by theurgy, neither was the character of the holy things so determined.

The hierarchy of holy days, as we have indicated elsewhere, consists, in descending order, of the Sabbath, the Day of Atonement, Rosh ha-Shanah, the Three Festivals, and the intermediate days of the Festivals.[133] In the mishnaic period and for some time afterward, the first day of every month was established by a proclamation of the *bet din*, the court,[134] upon the evidence of witnesses that they had seen the new moon. As a result, it was the *bet din* that determined when the holy days would fall,[135] except, of course, for the Sabbath which is fixed. The holy days are, to be sure, "the appointed seasons of the Lord" (Lev. 23:4), but they assume that character only when they are proclaimed as such by Israel: "If ye proclaim them, they are My appointed seasons, but if [ye do] not [proclaim them] they are not My appointed seasons."[136] Distinguishing between the Sabbath and the other holy days, a tannaitic statement specifically relates the holiness of the other holy days to the decision of the *bet din*. Whereas the Sabbath has been determined by God—"But on the seventh day is a Sabbath of solemn rest holy to the Lord" (Exod. 35:2)—"the holiness of the 'appointed seasons' [קדושת מועדות] is given over [מסורה] to the *bet din*."[137] The holiness of a day is not associated, therefore, with theurgy. The Sabbath simply recurs regularly every seventh day. Although the holiness of the other days depends upon the decision of a court,[138] that decision is based on the evidence of witnesses as to the recurrence of a natural monthly phenomenon; hence, in the final analysis, the holiness of the other days, too, depends upon regular recurrences. In fact, the law is that if the first appearance of the new moon has not been seen, there is no proclamation by the court, and the month just past becomes a "full month" of thirty days.[139]

Halakah makes the holy days distinctive. It does so by prescribing acts through which the individual himself is to make the days holy, and these acts are of an entirely normal character. The *Mekilta de Rabbi Simon* speaks of such acts in commenting on the verse, "Remember the Sabbath Day to make it holy [לקדשו]" (Exod. 20:8).[140] "Remember" refers to remembering the Sabbath by reciting the Ḳiddush over a cup of wine, while "to make it holy" means that the Ḳiddush is to be recited, in the first instance, on the Sabbath Eve.[141] According to another interpretation, "remember" means to remember the Sabbath every day by designating the successive days of the week as "the first day in the Sabbath, the second day in the Sabbath," and so on until the sixth day, the designation for that day being, "the eve of the Sabbath."[142] The Sabbath Day is to be made holy by being made festive: " 'To make it holy'—with what are you to make it holy? With food and with drink and with clean clothes," so that your meals and clothes may be different on the Sabbath from what they are on week-days;[143] and the same rule is applied to the Festivals.[144] More than in any other way, however, the holy days are distinguished by the individual abstaining from work on those days. "Make it holy by [refraining from] the doing of work."[145] The gradations in the hierarchy of holy days are established, in large measure, by the halakot which prohibit anything classified as "labor." In the main, the holier the day, the more inclusive is the category of prohibited "labors."[146]

On the hierarchy of holy objects we need not enlarge here, for we have dealt with aspects of it at some length in an earlier work.[147] In descending order, that hierarchy consists of a *Sefer Torah* (a scroll of the Pentateuch), *tefillin* (four specified passages from the Pentateuch on parchment), *mezuzot* (two specified passages from the Pentateuch on parchment), *sefarim* (scrolls of Prophets and *Ketubim* [from Psalms to Chronicles]), a synagogue.[148] Failure to conform with but a single one of the many rules for the writing of a *Sefer Torah* and for the preparation of its parchment is enough to disqualify it,[149] and similar rules apply to the making of *tefillin* and *mezuzot*.[150] A number of those rules have to do with *kawwanah*, intention, and one rule in particular reminds us of *kawwanah* in the case of sacrifices and of tithes:[151] names of God in a *Sefer Torah*, *tefillin*, and *mezuzot* must be written with *kawwanah*, that is, each name must be written with the idea in mind that it refers to God.[152] Basically, however, the holiness of a *Sefer Torah* and of *tefillin* and *mezuzot* must derive from the dogma of *mattan Torah*, the belief that the Pentateuch was given by God.[153] We infer this because *sefarim* are but a degree less holy than *mezuzot*, and the holiness of *sefarim* can be accounted for only on the ground that Prophets and *Ketubim* are associated with that dogma.[154] The synagogue derives its holiness simply from its specified use as a house of prayer.[155] Neither the dogma, a matter of belief alone, nor the mere use of a building, involves theurgy.[156]

At first sight, the *ḳedushah* of persons, too, seems to present a firm hierarchical order. The highest grade of *ḳedushah* is that of the *kohanim*, the priests. Their *ḳedushah* derives from the *ḳedushah* of Aaron: "Who has made us holy with the *ḳedushah* of Aaron";[157] as descendants of Aaron they were given the *mattenot kehunah*, the holy things which priests alone are permitted to eat.[158] The other groups in Israel are holy also; for example, a child born to converts after they have been converted, says a mishnah, is born "in *ḳedushah*."[159] Between the *ḳedushah* of the priests and that of all other groups, however, the demarcation is so strong that even the Levites, so far as levitical impurity is concerned, are classified together with the Israelites.[160]

But this demarcation was challenged. It was in conflict, Alon has demonstrated, with a contrary tradition regarding both the obligation of levitical purity and the holiness of persons.[161] That contrary tradition insisted that *ḥullin*, ordinary food, be eaten in levitical purity;[162] by the same token, the contrary tradition tried to extend the *ḳedushah* of the priests to all Israel.[163] This view is epitomized in a brief passage cited by Alon. It is a passage that insists on "the washing of the hands" before eating *ḥullin*, and it concludes with, "Not to the priests alone was *ḳedushah* given, but to all—to the priests and to the Levites and to the Israelites."[164] Doubtless because most people found it too difficult to observe all the laws of levitical purity in their everyday life, the demarcation remained;[165] nevertheless, the contrary tradition did prevail with respect to a number of laws.[166] Among them is the practice of "the washing of the hands" before a meal,[167] a practice specifically informed by the idea that the *ḳedushah* of the Israelite is like that of the priest.

Since one value concept can be stressed as against another in the process of their organismic integration, the rabbinic value complex allowed room both for the demarcation between the priests and the

people and for the opposition to that demarcation. In the demarcation, the concept of *kehunah* was stressed as against the concept of
Israel,[168] whereas in the opposition to the demarcation, the concept
of Israel was stressed as against that of *kehunah*.[169] The opposition
to the demarcation, however, was not limited to laws and statements
involving those concepts alone. It also called upon and stressed, as
against the concept of *kehunah*, the concept of Torah, although now
the opposition to the demarcation is more explicit on some occasions
than on others. "A *mamzer* [bastard] who is a *talmid ḥakam*
[learned] precedes a high priest who is an *'am ha-'areẓ* [un-
learned]."[170] "Torah is greater than the *kehunah* and than the *malkut*
[kingship], for the *malkut* is acquired through thirty qualifications
and the *kehunah* through twenty-four, but Torah is acquired through
forty-eight things," etc.[171] The knowledge and practice of Torah
renders one who is not a priest "worthy to offer up a burnt-offering
upon the altar."[172]

Ḳedushah as concretized in a hierarchical order is only one phase of
the concept. In another phase *ḳedushah* is inseparable from personal
conduct and, instead of connoting a hierarchical order, has several
connotations of its own, a complex of connotations. In this phase,
ḳedushah means the holiness acquired through the observance of the
miẓwot; it means the imitation of God in deeds of lovingkindness
and in like matters; it means separation or refraining from the
cardinal sins: murder, sexual sin, and idolatry.[173] But deeds of
lovingkindness and refraining from specific sins are themselves
miẓwot. The several connotations of this phase of *ḳedushah* are
interconnected, interrelated, as is the case in general with the different
phases of a concept. Indeed, the various connotations of *ḳedushah*
in this phase may themselves be viewed as phases of *ḳedushah*.

Ḳedushah is acquired through fulfilling the miẓwot. " 'Ye shall
be holy' [Lev. 19:2]—that refers to the holiness [conferred by] all
the miẓwot."[174] " 'Be holy' [Num. 15:40]—for as long as you
fulfill the miẓwot you are sanctified, but if you neglect them, you
will become profaned."[175] "With every new miẓwah which God
[*ha-Maḳom*] issues to Israel He adds to them *ḳedushah*."[176]

This phase of *ḳedushah* seemingly has some elements in common
with the phase wherein *ḳedushah* connotes a hierarchical order, but
only apparently so. Thus, we have noticed that when *ḳedushah*

connotes a hierarchy, *ḳedushah* is felt to be a mystical quality which almost possesses the character of substantiality. Something quite similar seems to be conveyed by the statement, "With every new miẓwah which God issues to Israel He adds to them *ḳedushah*." But another statement, in like manner apparently attributing substantiality to *ḳedushah*, enables us to recognize that now this mystical quality has a moral implication. The angels, says R. 'Abin ('Abun), were given only one *ḳedushah*, since as heavenly beings they are not subject to the evil *yeẓer*, whereas earthly beings, men, because they are subject to the evil *yeẓer*, were given two *ḳedushot*, and "would that they might stand up with [the help of] two *ḳedushot*."[177] The mystical quality remains, but now, so far as it relates to man, it implies the moral strength to withstand temptation.[178]

In hierarchical *ḳedushah*, what is holy is regarded as belonging to God in a special sense, as being God's own. Now, however, a similar idea is given an entirely different turn; in fact, the idea is inverted. Because Israel belongs to God in a special sense it is incumbent upon them, obligatory for them, to be holy. " 'Ye shall be holy, for I, the Lord, am holy' [Lev. 19:2]— 'Ye shall be holy'—why? Because I am holy, for I have attached you to Me, as it is said, 'For as the girdle cleaveth to the loins of a man, so have I caused to cleave unto Me the whole house of Israel' [Jer. 13:11]."[179] The same point is made in a passage which Schechter renders as follows: "Another Rabbi remarked, 'God said to Israel, Even before I created the world you were sanctified unto me; be ye therefore holy as I am holy'; and he proceeds to say, 'The matter is to be compared to a king who sanctified [by wedlock] a woman unto him, and said to her: Since thou art my wife, what is my glory is thy glory, be therefore holy even as I am holy.' "[180] The import of the command, "Be holy," must not escape us. That command marks a vital difference between hierarchical and nonhierarchical *ḳedushah*. Rather than just a mystical quality alone, *ḳedushah* is now something which must be achieved through effortful personal conduct. To achieve holiness is obligatory upon Israel because they are God's own and God is holy. It follows, therefore, that only when the individuals in Israel are holy men are they indeed God's own. The verse "And ye shall be holy men unto Me" (Exod. 22:30) is interpreted by R. Ishmael to say, "When you are holy men, then you are Mine."[181] How Israel is to achieve holiness is not stated in these passages. But we already know that Israel achieves holiness through the miẓwot, and we shall soon see how such efforts to achieve holiness are profoundly affected by the idea that God is holy.

To demonstrate that the *kedushah* acquired through the fulfillment of the miẓwot differs from hierarchical *kedushah* we have shown that what appear to be elements in common between these two phases of *kedushah* are only seemingly in common. At one point, nevertheless, these two phases of *kedushah* are completely congruent. The act whereby a holy thing in hierarchical *kedushah* is made holy is at the same time an act that is a miẓwah, and hence also belongs to the nonhierarchical phase of *kedushah*. Now we have recognized that such an act, often merely expressing intention, is entirely devoid of theurgy. In other words, the only type of miẓwah which could possibly have had theurgical associations is definitely nontheurgical, for there is no question of theurgy at all with regard to the rest of the miẓwot. The *kedushah* achieved through fulfilling the miẓwot is throughout, therefore, nontheurgical. Instead, it is an experience in normal mysticism, an experience of a close relationship with God, so close that passages can tell of how God has attached Israel to Himself, and of how Israel was "sanctified unto" God even before the creation of the world. Such an experience of relationship can take place, of course, only when a miẓwah is fulfilled with *kawwanah*. Indeed, *kawwanah* in this connection, we have noticed, itself implies an awareness of a relationship with God, a consciousness that a particular miẓwah is a communication by God here and now.[182]

There is a phase of *kedushah* which does not have even an apparent resemblance to any element in hierarchical *kedushah*. Schechter has called this phase or aspect of *kedushah* the imitation of God.[183] " 'Ye shall be holy, for I the Lord am holy' [Lev. 19:2]. These words are explained by the ancient Rabbinic sage Abba Saul to mean 'Israel is the *familia* [suite or bodyguard] of the King [God], whence it is incumbent upon them to imitate the King.' "[184] Another statement by Abba Saul tells of the nature of this imitation. "*I and He*, that is, like unto him [God]. As he is merciful and gracious, so be thou [man] merciful and gracious."[185] Similarly, a passage in the Sifre teaches: "As the Holy One blessed be He is called merciful and gracious, so be thou merciful and gracious, giving free gifts to all; as the Holy One blessed be He is called righteous, so be thou righteous; as the Holy One blessed be He is called loving [*ḥasid*], so be thou loving."[186] An obligation rests upon Israel to imitate God in these ways because they are His *familia*, and they must, therefore, like Him be holy. The close relationship of Israel with God is expressed in other metaphors as well, and once more that relationship is given as the reason for the imitation of God. God, according to the rabbis, investigated within Himself, and found eleven qualities, those mentioned in Psalm 15:2 ff.: "He that walketh uprightly, and doeth charity [צדק]," etc. And He asks of Israel nothing but that they imitate these eleven qualities, basing His request on the ground that "ye are My children and I am your Father, ye are My brothers and I am your Brother, ye are My friends and I am your Friend, ye are My beloved and I am your Beloved."[187]

A motive behind an act of charity or a deed of lovingkindness may be the imitation of God. "The profession of the Holy One blessed be He is the practice of charity and deeds of lovingkindness, and Abraham who will command his children and his household after him 'that they shall keep the way of the Lord' [Gen. 18:19] is told by God, 'Thou hast chosen My profession.' "[188] A famous statement in Soṭah 14a specifies the deeds of lovingkindness in which a man ought to imitate God. Schechter renders that passage as follows: "Walk in the attributes of God (or rather make his attributes the rule for thy conduct). As he clothes the naked [Gen. 3:21], so do thou clothe the naked; as he nurses the sick [Gen. 18:1], so do thou nurse the sick; as he comforts the mourners [Gen. 25:11], so do thou comfort the mourners; as he buries the dead [Deut. 34:5], so do thou bury the dead."* To do charity and to perform these deeds of lovingkindness, as we know, are miẓwot.

* Schechter, *Aspects*, pp. 202 f. See also A. Marmorstein, *Studies in Jewish Theology* (London, 1950), pp. 113 f. The following is taken from a cento formed by E. Hatch (*The Influence of Greek Ideas on Christianity*, ed. F. C. Grant [New York, 1957], p. 155) of passages from Epictetus: "Every one of us may call himself a son of God. Just as our bodies are linked to the material universe, so by virtue of reason our souls are linked to and continuous with Him, being in reality parts and offshoots of Him. He Himself is within us, so that we are His shrines, living temples and incarnations of Him. We and He together form the greatest and chiefest and most comprehensive of all organizations. If once we realize this kinship, no mean or unworthy thought

Besides standing for the imitation of God by man, *kedushah* in this phase also has the connotation of love. Whether related to God or to attitudes and acts of man in imitation of God, holiness in this context refers only to acts and attitudes which express love.[189] But in another context, too, *kedushah* is associated with God's love. In the 'Amidah for New Year and the Day of Atonement, the Third Berakah closes with Isaiah 5:16, since that verse, as interpreted by the rabbis, contains the idea that God is sanctified in His charity at judgment. The verse was taken as saying, "And the Lord of hosts is exalted in judgment, and the holy God is sanctified in *zedakah*."[190] In view of the connotation of love in the context of the imitation of God, such an added association of *kedushah* with God's love indicates that *kedushah* is among the concepts in which the emphasis on love rises to expression. The question is, however, under what circumstances does this phase of *kedushah* emerge, for the concept of *kedushah* may also refer to hierarchical *kedushah*. We shall attempt to answer that question in the next section.

There remains one more phase of nonhierarchical *kedushah* to be considered. Because that phase is posed against acts designated as *tum'ah* [defilement], we must first touch on several matters concerning the concept of *tum'ah*.

Tum'ah is the obverse of the concept of *kedushah*. When *tum'ah* refers to levitical impurity it is the obverse of hierarchical *kedushah*, and that relationship manifests itself, among other ways, in a certain similarity of structure. Like hierarchical *kedushah*, this type of *tum'ah* too possesses hierarchical orders.[191] The structural similarity, however,

---

of ourselves can enter our souls. The sense of it forms a rule and standard for our lives. If God be faithful, we also must be faithful: if God be beneficent, we also must be beneficent. If God be highminded, we also must be highminded, doing and saying whatever we do and say in imitation of and union with Him." In Epictetus' view, the imitation of God is the result of coming to the recognition that "our souls are . . . in reality parts and offshoots" of God; that is to say, the imitation is due to a proper knowledge of the universe, to a rational or intellectual factor. According to the rabbis, as we shall see in the next section, it is in an emotional experience, the mystical experience of *kedushah*, that the individual dedicates himself to the imitation of God. Of course, the rabbis would be unalterably opposed to the idea expressed by Epictetus that the human being is an incarnation of God. That notion leads him also to say, "We and He together form the greatest and chiefest and most comprehensive of all organizations." Such a statement would strike the rabbis as being extremely presumptuous, to put it mildly.

serves only to emphasize the antithetical character of the two concepts. Thus, in the case of *ḳedushah*, a person must act in such fashion that a higher degree is achieved if possible, and not a lower;[192] in the case of *ṭum'ah*, on the other hand, it is ordinarily not permitted to allow a thing already levitically unclean to become *ṭum'ah* of a higher degree.[193] At the same time, the prohibitions relating to *ṭum'ah* apply only to the Temple, the sacrifices, and the *terumot* and *ma'aser sheni*, but not to *ḥullin*, ordinary food; hence a person is permitted to eat and drink *ḥullin* that is levitically impure.[194]

But there is also *ṭum'ah* which is nonhierarchical. On the basis of biblical verses, a passage in the Sifra[195] specifically designates three acts as *ṭum'ot*—the *ṭum'ah* of *'abodah zarah*, the verse being, "To defile My sanctuary, and to profane My holy Name" (Lev. 20:3), and referring to the worship of Moloch; the *ṭum'ah* of *gilluy 'arayot*, the verse being, "That ye do not any of these abominable customs, which were done before you, and that ye defile not yourselves therein" (*ibid.*, 18:30), and referring to adultery and prohibited sex relations; the *ṭum'ah* of *shefikut damim*, the verse being, "And thou shalt not defile the land which ye inhabit, in the midst of which I dwell" (Num. 35:34), referring to murder. In each instance, the verse employs a verb with the root *ṭm'* (defile), thereby allowing the rabbis to draw the conclusion that the act referred to is *ṭum'ah*. As Tosafot says, those acts are not "real *ṭum'ah*" but are simply alluded to in the Bible linguistically as *ṭum'ah*.[196] What the rabbis characterize here as *ṭum'ah* is not hierarchical *ṭum'ah* but the three cardinal sins.[197] In other words, *ṭum'ah* here is moral *ṭum'ah*.

When posed against nonhierarchical or moral *ṭum'ah*, *ḳedushah* connotes the idea of separation from moral *ṭum'ah* or abstention from such acts. That idea is contained in a rabbinic comment on Leviticus 19:2: "Speak unto all the congregation of the children of Israel, and say unto them: Ye shall be holy; for I the Lord your God am holy." The comment paraphrases this verse as follows: "The Holy One blessed be He said to Moses, 'Say to the children of Israel: My sons just as I am separated [פרוש], so be ye separated [פרושין]; just as I am holy, so be ye holy.' "[198] An interpretation in the Sifra likewise paraphrases "Ye shall be holy" as "Be ye separated."[199] These rabbinic renderings of Leviticus 19:2 relate that verse to what immediately precedes it, namely, to the chapter in Leviticus containing a catalogue of the prohibited sexual relations.[200] All the prohibited sexual connections there, "all the *'arayot*," are characterized in the Sifra on Leviticus 18:30 as *ṭum'ah*.[201] In this context, then, *ḳedushah* means abstaining from all the prohibited sexual connections, these things being *ṭum'ah*. That is also the connotation of *ḳedushah* in rabbinic interpretations of Exodus 19:6 and Leviticus 20:26. To quote Schechter:[202] "The Rabbis interpret the verse, 'And ye shall be unto Me a kingdom of priests and a holy nation' (Exod. 19:6) with the words, 'Be unto Me a kingdom of priests separated from the nations of the world and their abominations.'[203] This passage must be taken in connection with another, in which, with allusion to the scriptural words, 'And ye shall be holy unto Me . . . and I have severed you from other people that you should be Mine' (Lev. 20:26), the Rabbis point to the sexual immorality which divides the heathen from Israel."[204] Schechter goes on to say that "the notion of impurity is further extended to all things stigmatized in the Levitical legislation as unclean, particularly to the forbidden foods."[205] Except for the forbidden foods, however, what is stigmatized as unclean in levitical legislation is treated by the rabbis as hierarchical *ṭum'ah*. Even with regard to the forbidden foods, a rabbinic statement deliberately refers to nonhierarchical *ṭum'ah* and then to hierarchical *ṭum'ah*, and unless we distinguish between the two, the statement is confusing.[206]

Every precaution was taken to preclude the remotest contact with idolatry, as is evident from the tractate *'Abodah Zarah*. In this anxiety to be "separated" from the least suggestion of idolatry, apparently some individuals practiced precautions of their own. R. Menaḥem b. Sim'ai went so far as never to look at the figures stamped on the silver coins, and that was reason enough for R. Joḥanan to refer to him as "the descendant of holy men."[207]

The idea of "separation" from sin was naturally not limited to the sins designated as *ṭum'ah*. A mishnah uses the same verb (פורש), for example, not only in reference to abstaining from *'arayot*, but also in reference to abstaining from eating blood and to abstaining from *gezel*.[208]

Ṭum'ah is the obverse of nonhierarchical *ḳedushah* just as it is the obverse of hierarchical *ḳedushah*, and yet the resemblance between the two phases of *ḳedushah* is, once more, only apparent. In the first place, nonhierarchical *ḳedushah* is not posed against "real *ṭum'ah*" but against the cardinal sins, moral *ṭum'ah*. That difference, furthermore, makes for a basic difference in the attitudes engendered by the respective phases of *ḳedushah*. Hierarchical *ḳedushah* does not rule out all possible contact with "real *ṭum'ah*," a person being permitted to eat *ḥullin* which is levitically unclean. On the other hand, nonhierarchical *ḳedushah* connotes complete separation from moral *ṭum'ah*. To imitate God by being "separated" can only imply that Israel is thus separated from moral *ṭum'ah* and made undefiled. The imitation here does not consist of acts, as in the imitation of God's love, but only of separateness.

This phase of *ḳedushah* differs from hierarchical *ḳedushah* in another respect as well. At times it does not have *ṭum'ah* as its obverse at all. When *ḳedushah* connotes separateness it connotes self-restraint. The rabbis can therefore extend the concept of *ḳedushah* to include self-control in matters that are not moral *ṭum'ah*—to restraint in licit sexual relations and also to other forms of self-control or self-discipline. "Hallow thyself in what is permitted to thee," say the rabbis.[209] They employ the idea of holiness in the same way when they speak of the man who "hallows himself" in the marriage bed.[210] Asceticism as such, however, is regarded as *ḳedushah* only by R. Eleazar, the other authorities even disagreeing with him when he calls the Nazarite holy by reason of the Nazarite's abstention from wine.[211]

We can now see how closely interrelated are the various phases of nonhierarchical *ḳedushah*. The phase in which *ḳedushah* means the holiness acquired through the fulfillment of the miẓwot is inseparable from the other two phases. Imitation of God refers to specific acts of *ẓedaḳah* and *gemilut ḥasadim*, acts that, for a man, are miẓwot. Separateness is the withdrawal from the three cardinal sins, moral *ṭum'ah*, and from the forbidden foods, all of which matters are negative miẓwot. The mystical quality inherent in nonhierarchical *ḳedushah*, we noticed, implies moral strength to withstand temptation, and we can now recognize the relevance of that implication. Such moral strength is called upon when the temptation is to withhold from an act of kindness or to surrender to an immoral desire. In the next section we shall discuss the occasions in which all these phases of *ḳedushah* come to the fore.

Despite its dependence on the Bible, the rabbinic concept of *ḳedushah* has definite characteristics of its own. But the problem of the relation to the Bible involved here is a very complex one, requiring an extended discussion. It will suffice now to point to several matters that are solely rabbinic. Stressing the concept of Torah as against that of *kehunah* (priesthood); the phase of *ḳedushah* in which the imitation of God consists of doing *ẓedaḳah* and *gemilut ḥasadim*; the extension of the concept of *ḳedushah* to include self-restraint even in matters legally permitted—all these are purely rabbinic.

Thus far we have discussed phases of the concept of *ḳedushah*—connotations of the concept which do not possess abstract conceptual terms of their own but which are all represented by the term *ḳedushah*. *Kiddush ha-Shem*, however, is a subconcept of *ḳedushah*, an aspect of *ḳedushah* sufficiently crystallized to be represented on its own account by a conceptual term. Although we dealt with concretizations of *kiddush ha-Shem* in Chapter VI, we are only now in a position to indicate its relation to the concept of *ḳedushah*.

Kiddush ha-Shem means, literally, hallowing God's Name. There is *kiddush ha-Shem* in a heroic act of martyrdom before a *parhesya'* (ten or more Jews);[212] in a righteous act by a Jew toward a Gentile which elicits the response, "Blessed is the God of the Jews";[213] in the corporate act of worship consisting of the Baraku and its response,[214] and in several other corporate acts of worship.[215] Since these are acts of *kiddush ha-Shem*, presumably they are acts whereby God's Name is hallowed. But these are acts which call forth an explicit or, in the case of the *parhesya'*, an implicit acknowledgment of God. In what sense is God's Name hallowed when an acknowledgment of God is called forth?

A general acknowledgment of God is associated with the denial of idolatry. The concurrence of the *parhesya'* with the martyr's denial of idolatry is therefore tantamount to an acknowledgment of God on their part. Idolatry is also negated, however, by the concept of *ṭum'ah*. We must remember that idolatry is *ṭum'ah*, and that *ṭum'ah* is the obverse of *ḳedushah*. An idol itself is an original cause of an entire order of hierarchical *ṭum'ah*.[216] A person or thing in physical contact with an idol thereby becomes unclean,[217] and similarly a person who has entered the house of an idol and benches brought into that house become unclean.[218] *Ṭum'ah* here constitutes a denial, the strongest denial possible, that whatsoever is worshiped other than God is a deity. To acknowledge God is to affirm that it is God alone Who is holy. God's Name is "hallowed," therefore, when an act calls forth an explicit or implicit acknowledgment of God. An acknowledgment of God is an affirmation of the *ḳedushah* of God.

In the struggle against idolatry, the people of Israel as a whole were pitted against the Gentile world. This, it seems to us, is reflected in the character of these acts of *ḳiddush ha-Shem*. The general acknowledgment of God is always by the *ẓibbur* or by the *parhesya'*, that is, by the community.[219]

Ḳiddush ha-Shem is a rabbinic term, but the concept has, as in all such instances, its biblical antecedent.[220] The difference between the rabbinic concept and its biblical antecedent, however, is striking, as Avraham Holtz has shown in a recent study.[221] According to the Bible, whereas the people of Israel have the power to profane the Name of God, it is God alone Who can sanctify His Name. Most of the aspects of *ḳiddush ha-Shem*, including *ḳiddush ha-Shem* in a *parhesya'* and in a *ẓibbur*, are thus purely rabbinic.

D. The Experience of *Ḳedushah*

A miẓwah is performed with *kawwanah*, we saw, when the individual feels that the miẓwah represents a communication which has been directed to him by God. "In such an experience, the particular miẓwah which the individual is about to fulfill is not merely a practice transmitted to him by previous generations, but is a command from God here and now."[222]

During the process of performing a miẓwah with *kawwanah*, a person has an experience of *ḳedushah*. It is a mystical experience and yet, being normal mysticism, it is in some degree describable. The miẓwah as a communication from God is felt to be a priceless privilege. Having been given that privilege, the individual has a consciousness, not of union with God, but of belonging to God, of being God's own. At the same time, this entire emotional experience is pervaded through and through with a sense of dedication. The individual dedicates himself to imitate God in acts of *zedakah* and *gemilut hasadim* and to abstain from moral *tum'ah.* A mystical experience is thus also a source of moral energy, and the more often the experience occurs the greater will be the latent ethical motive power; in other words, experiences of *kedushah* are character-building experiences. It will be noticed, of course, that in describing the mystical experience of *kedushah* we have simply set down the rabbinic ideas already discussed in the previous section, the ideas concerning the *kedushah* of the mizwot, the nonhierarchical phase of *kedushah.* Those rabbinic ideas can only reflect the actual experience of that phase of *kedushah.*

An experience of *kedushah* is always associated with an act of worship. The consciousness that the mizwot are a priceless privilege evokes a berakah, an expression of gratitude for God's love as manifested in the conferring of that privilege. The berakah here, however, embodies not only the concepts of God's love and berakah, but also those of *kedushah* and mizwot. Again, as in all berakot, one of the elements of the experiential entity consists of an occasion, the occasion now being an act about to be performed or a holy day. But here the occasion has a dual role; not only is it the stimulus for the berakah but it also serves as a reminder of the mizwot in general. We shall shortly take up the Birkat ha-Mizwot, the berakah said when the occasion is an act about to be performed, leaving perhaps for future consideration the Kedushat ha-Yom and the Kiddush, berakot said when a holy day is the occasion.

The concept of *kawwanah* is a factor in the experience of *kedushah*, as much a factor as any of the other concepts involved. Nevertheless, like *kawwanah* in the other forms of worship,[223] the concept of *kawwanah* here, too, is not a constituent of the idea content of the experience. *Kawwanah* is a factor in the experience as a whole solely by virtue of making the concept of mizwot a vital factor, the result being that the concept of mizwot, and not that of *kawwanah*, is a constituent of the idea content. The question is whether, for those who cannot achieve *kawwanah*, the concept of mizwot has any meaning at all. In the Babli, we saw above,[224] the division of opinion on this matter crystallizes into two opposing general principles—a positive principle ("mizwot require *kawwanah*") and a negative principle ("mizwot do not require *kawwanah*"). The proponents of the negative principle obviously feel that the concept of miẓwot retains a certain meaning even for those who cannot achieve *kawwanah*. The latter can at least have the intention of observing the miẓwot, can have the intention of hearing the blowing of the *shofar*, or of hearing the reading of the *megillah*, or of reading the Shema', as the case may be. Probably, in one way or another, this intention of fulfilling a miẓwah may at times be an element in an experience of *ḳedushah*, but an element in a correspondingly weak experience. Only the positive principle—"miẓwot require *kawwanah*"—accords with a morally energizing experience of *ḳedushah*.

E. Birkat ha-Miẓwot

Acts designated as miẓwot include acts ordained by the rabbis, as we pointed out in the first section of this chapter. The berakah on the kindling of the Ḥanukkah light cited there is hence typical of the Birkat ha-Miẓwot, even though the act referred to in that berakah is a rabbinic ordinance. "Blessed art Thou, O Lord our God, King of the world, Who has sanctified us by His miẓwot, and commanded us to kindle the light of Ḥanukkah."[225] Up to and including "and commanded us [*weẓiwwanu*]," the formula remains the same for all the Birkot ha-Miẓwot, and only the words which follow refer to this or the other specific act. (Some of these specific acts are referred to by a verb,[226] as here, and others by a gerund.)[227]

The rule is that the Birkat ha-Miẓwot is to precede the act which is the occasion for the berakah.[228] This rule is called for so that the recitation of the berakah together with the act may constitute a unitary entity. The berakah is an expression of gratitude for the privilege of having been given a command here and now by God—"and commanded us," as the berakah declares. A consciousness of the command naturally must precede the fulfillment of the command. But the consciousness of the command continues to inform also the fulfillment of the miẓwah otherwise the performance itself would lack *kawwanah*. There is no break in mood from the moment the berakah is begun until the command has been fulfilled;[229] that is to say, the recitation of the berakah and the act which follows constitute a unitary experience. As the plural "us" in the berakah indicates, that experience engages the larger self. Once again the individual associates himself with all of Israel whilst retaining his own self-identity.[230]

Kawwanah encompasses every detail of the act enjoined by the miẓwah. Even the quality of the object employed in such an act can express *kawwanah*. Interpreting ואנוהו in Exodus 15:2, R. Ishmael says, "And is it possible for [a man of] flesh and blood to make lovely his Creator? But [it means] I will be lovely to Him in [performing] miẓwot: I will make before Him a lovely *lulab*, a lovely *sukkah* [booth], lovely *ẓiẓit* [fringes], lovely *tefillin*."[231] The concept of *kawwanah* is integrated in this statement with that of *hiddur miẓwah* (doing a miẓwah in the handsomest way).[232]

In contradistinction to the last part of the berakah and its reference to a specific miẓwah, the words, "And Who has sanctified us by His miẓwot," speak of the miẓwot in general. These words, too, nevertheless relate to the act about to be performed, since what they say has relevance, at the moment, to that particular act. Nor should the past tense in which the phrase is couched lead us to think otherwise. The phrase conveys several things, all of them associated with *kedushat miẓwot*, the holiness conferred by miẓwot.[233] One of the ideas implied by the phrase is that God adds *kedushah* to Israel with every new miẓwah which He issues to them,[234] an idea referring to the individual who fulfills any given miẓwah, as Maimonides says.[235] To the individual about to fulfill a miẓwah, therefore, the phrase "And Who has sanctified us by His miẓwot," past tense and all, suggests an experience of *kedushah*; indeed, the past tense encourages him by reminding him of past experiences of that kind. In any case, the phrase certainly relates to the particular miẓwah in which he is engaged. The other ideas conveyed by the phrase—*kedushah* as the imitation of God in acts of love and *kedushah* as abstaining from moral *tum'ah*—suggest to the individual, in like manner, the moral idea content in the hoped-for experience of *kedushah*.

According to a view in the Yerushalmi, a berakah (i.e., the Birkat ha-Miẓwot) ought to be said at the fulfilling of every miẓwah,[236] and the same rule, somewhat differently worded, is found in the Tosefta as an anonymous statement.[237] This rule, on the face of it, would seem to apply to ethical acts too since, as we saw in the last chapter, ethical acts are also characterized as miẓwot.[238] A medieval authority, on the ground that a berakah ought to be said when observing any of the positive miẓwot, did go so far as sometimes to say the Birkat ha-Miẓwot when he gave charity and on similar occasions.[239] One of the earlier commentators on the Yerushalmi properly adds that this was not the general practice.[240] Obviously the rule in regard to saying a berakah when fulfilling any of the miẓwot was not meant to be taken literally; it is probably a way of declaring that a berakah ought to be said at every possible occasion.

There are, in fact, occasions when the Birkat ha-Miẓwot is said and occasions when it is not said. In a *responsum*, R. Joseph Ibn Plat[241] points out that there is no one general reason which accounts for all the various occasions when the berakah is not said, but that such occasions are to be accounted for on the basis of various principles. Among the principles he adduces is one that, we should say, may apply to many ethical acts, namely, the principle that the berakah is not said when the act depends upon the acquiescence of others, for example, in the case of charity, upon the acquiescence of the recipient of charity. We are here concerned, however, not so much with the principles adduced as with Ibn Plat's approach to the problem. As a general proposition, it appears, the berakah should normally be said (a general principle quite in accord with the rule in the Yerushalmi and the Tosefta), but there are many exceptions, each exception being due to special circumstances.[242]

When it comes to ethical acts, each separate ethical act, it seems to us, constitutes an exception by virtue of its own special circumstances. In an ethical act, there is a certain emotional undercurrent or a degree of tension peculiarly its own, apart from its being a miẓwah. Were such acts subject to the Birkat ha-Miẓwot, the concept of miẓwot would be stressed as against the ethical concept which also qualifies or interprets the act, and the act would then in large part lose its own peculiar character. Instead, therefore, the ethical concept is stressed, and the stressing is achieved by omitting the berakah. All such acts are prime examples of ethical concepts being stressed rather than the concept of miẓwot, other examples of which we noticed before.[243] At the same time, of course, these acts are miẓwot as well. In an organismic complex, as we have so often observed, more than one concept may be embodied in a concretization, although one concept may be stressed rather than another.

We ought not to conclude this section without some discussion of an approach which is different from the one we have utilized. Maimonides lays down the general rule that the Birkat ha-Miẓwot is said before all acts commanded by the miẓwot which are "between a man and God,"[244] and hence he implies, as the *Kesef Mishneh* adds, that the berakah is not said when the act is required by a law which is in the category of "between a man and a fellow-man,"[245] another general rule. The making of a "railing," *ma'aḳeh*, required by a law seemingly "between a man and his fellow-man,"[246] is nevertheless given by Maimonides in the selfsame paragraph as an example of the acts requiring a berakah. There are two opposing traditions as to whether *ma'aḳeh* requires a berakah,[247] and Maimonides doubtless had his reasons for his opinion; if so, however, besides his general rule other factors were to be taken into consideration. Furthermore, there are acts required by laws which are obviously in the category of "between a man and God," and yet those acts do not call for a berakah; such acts, for example, as are required by the laws in Exodus 12:13.[248] There are exceptions, it would seem, to Maimonides' general rules, for taking other considerations into account is only a way of indicating that those general rules do not always apply.

When ethical acts are described by a general formula, and that general formula is the same for all ethical acts, no recognition whatsoever is given to the particular character possessed by each and every ethical act. On the other hand, a value concept, being merely connotative and not a formula, has meaning only so long as it is concretized in a particular act. Conversely, when stress is laid upon the ethical value concept embodied in an act, there is also full awareness of the circumstantial, particular character of that act.

Notes to Preface

1. L. Ginzberg, *A Commentary on the Palestinian Talmud* (New York, 1941).

2. S. Lieberman, *The Tosefta, The Order of Zera'im* (New York, 1955).

3. S. Lieberman, *Tosefta Ki-Fshuṭah, A Comprehensive Commentary on the Tosefta* (New York, 1955).

Notes to Chapter I

1. M. Kadushin, *The Rabbinic Mind* (New York, 1952), p. 23. This book will hereafter be referred to as *RM.*

2. M. Kadushin, *Organic Thinking* (New York, 1938), p. 194. This book will hereafter be referred to as *OT.*

3. "The Efficacy of Torah," *OT*, pp. 68 ff., especially pp. 72 f.

4. *RM*, p. 11.

5. *RM*, pp. 59 f., 62 f., 68.

6. "Halakah and Its Nexus," in *ibid.*, pp. 89 ff.

7. *OT*, p. 98, where other examples are also cited. How extensively Halakah is reflected in Haggadah is apparent from the long list of such haggadot in the Index to Ginzberg's *Legends of the Jews* (Vol. VII, pp. 200 f.), a list running to several columns.

8. *Sanhedrin* IV. 5.

9. *Bereshit R.* XXII.9, ed. J. Theodor (Berlin, 1912), p. 216, and the sources in the note there.

10. L. Ginzberg, "Commentary to Ḳiddushin" (mimeographed, 1932), p. 142. Cf. Rashi on Exod. 21:6 in his *Commentary on the Pentateuch.*

11. "*Derek Ereẓ,*" pp. 117 ff.; "Charity and Deeds of Lovingkindness," pp. 131 ff.; "Ethical Dicta," pp. 140 ff. (all cited from *OT*).

12. *Ibid.*, pp. 192 f.

13. *RM*, pp. 113 ff., 132.

14. M. Kadushin, *The Theology of Seder Eliahu* (New York, 1932), p. 25.

15. In mishnaic times there was, however, wide divergence in law, an organismic characteristic (*RM*, pp. 93 f.).

Notes to Chapter II

1. See Chap. III, nn. 101–02, below.

2. *'Abot* I.18, V.7, VI.6; *Yer. Sanhedrin* XI, 30c; and *passim.*

3. *Pe'ah* I.1; *Yebamot* XV.1; *'Abot* I.12; and *passim.*

4. *'Abot* II.7; *Ḳiddushin* IV.5; *Baba Ḳamma* X.1; and *passim.*

5. *Soṭah* IX.15; *'Abot* VI.1; *'Arakin* 16b; and *passim.*

6. *'Abodah Zarah* II.1; *'Abot* V.9; *Tosefta Pe'ah* I.2; and *passim.*

7. *Yebamot* VI.5; *Ketubbot* V.1; *Soṭah* IX.13; and *passim.*

8. *Giṭṭin* V.8; *Makkot* III.15; *Shabbat* 32b; and *passim.*

9. *Rosh ha-Shanah* II.8; *Sanhedrin* XI.5; *Shebuot* 21a; and *passim.*

10. Only *shefikut damim* (the abstract form) is solely rabbinic.

11. M. Kadushin, *Organic Thinking* (New York, 1938), pp. 138–139. This book will hereafter be referred to as *OT*.

12. *Ibid.*, pp. 132 f., 136 f., and the references in the notes. On *ẓedaḳah*, see also M. Kadushin, *The Rabbinic Mind* (New York, 1952), p. 297, and the notes and references there. This book will hereafter be referred to as *RM*.

13. *Sukkah* 49b. Parallels: *Tos. Pe'ah* IV.19, ed. S. Lieberman (New York, 1955), pp. 60 f.; *ibid.*, *Yerushalmi*, I.1, 15b–c; *Kohelet R.* VII.2.
According to Maimonides, Hilkot *'Ebel* XIV.7, there is a gradation in *gemilut ḥasadim* itself, comforting the mourners taking precedence over visiting the sick—see Lieberman, *Tosefta Ki-Fshuṭah*, I (New York, 1955), p. 191.

14. *OT*, pp. 148 f.

15. *'Alub* has the connotation not only of humility but of humiliation; see M. Jastrow, *A Dictionary of the Targumim, The Talmud Babli and Yerushalmi, and the Midrashic Literature* (New York, Berlin, and London, 1926), p. 1080, *s.v.* עלוב.

16. *Yer. Pe'ah* I.1, 15b. See n. 19 below.

17. This is the way Maimonides seems to interpret the ordinance; see his *Mishneh Torah*, Hilkot *Mattenot 'Aniyyim* VII.5.

18. Yer. *Pe'ah*, *loc. cit.*; the first time a fifth of the principal and after that a fifth of the profits.

19. *Ibid.* R. Gamaliel cites this ordinance to R. Yeshebab who had divided all his property among the poor. The term miẓwot here, therefore, refers to charity. See *Midrash Debarim Rabbah*, ed. S. Lieberman (Jerusalem, 1940), p. 36, n. 10.

20. *Ketubbot* 50a.

21. *Ibid.*, and parallels.

22. Above, n. 19.

23. *Ketubbot* 50a. Here in one report the Tanna is not named and in another he is R. Yeshebab.

24. *Baba Meẓi'a* 3a, bottom, and parallels: אין אדם מעיז פניו.

25. *Sanhedrin* 74a. R. Ishmael permits private, but not public avowal of idolatry, to save one's life and this holds, apparently, with respect to other matters as well (on the basis of his proof-text). See also *Sifra*, *Aḥare* (on Lev. 18:5), ed. I. H. Weiss (Vienna, 1862), 86b.

26. H. Graetz, *History of the Jews* (Hebrew translation by S. P. Rabinowitz) (Warsaw 1898), II, 254 f.

27. *RM*, pp. 1–8.

28. A. N. Whitehead, *Religion in the Making* (New York, 1926), p. 87.

29. M. Lazarus attempts to depict Jewish ethics on the basis of this Kantian principle,

and he calls it "the principle of Jewish ethics"; see his *Ethics of Judaism*, Part I (English translation, Philadelphia, 1900), pp. 107 ff., especially pp. 132 f., 137 f., and 157 f. He can do so only by a free, homiletic interpretation of biblical verses and rabbinic dicta; see, for example, *ibid.*, pp. 14 f., 64, 117, 122 f., 128, 137 f., 158; (on p. 159, and earlier on p. 17 where the source is given, the important כאלו, "as if," is omitted—"as if he becomes a partner of God"); p. 278 f. Nevertheless, Lazarus makes a very valuable contribution. He emphasizes the awareness on the part of the rabbis of the ethical sphere, their great sensitiveness to moral and ethical problems of the individual and society, something that later writers have obscured by the insistence on a "logic of revealed religion" or similar ideas. A fine exposition and evaluation of Lazarus' work is given in Julius Guttman, הפילוסופיה של היהדות (Hebrew translation, Jerusalem, 1951), pp. 314 f.

30. Below, p. 243, n. 63.

31. *Bereshit R.* VI.5, ed. J. Theodor (Berlin, 1912), p. 44, and the parallels there; *Bemidbar R.* XX.1; and elsewhere.

32. *OT*, p. 137, and p. 304, n. 227.

33. *RM*, pp. 150 f.

34. *Ibid.*, pp. 38 f.

35. *Ibid.*, pp. 114–30.

36. See, for example, the interpretation of II Samuel 8:15 in *Sanhedrin* 6b.

37. *RM*, p. 55 and n. 8. The plural *Yisre'elim* is also found (*'Erubin* VI.1, *'Abodah Zarah* IV.11).

38. *RM*, pp. 40 f.

39. *Ibid.*, pp. 293 f.

40. *Ibid.*, pp. 291 f.

41. Illustrations will be found in nn. 37–40 on these terms.

42. *Menaḥot* 99a–b. Parallels: *Shabbat* 87a; *Yebamot* 62a; *Baba Batra* 14b; and see also the next note.

43. Rashi *ad loc.*; also Rabbenu Gershom *ad loc.* "The neglect of Torah" is a technical expression referring to neglect of the study of Torah: see *Tos. Shabbat* VII (VIII).5; *ibid.*, 32b; and *passim*.

The general statement is: פעמים שבטולה של תורה זהו יסודה. This is followed by an interpretation of Exod. 34:1 according to which God commends Moses for having broken the Tablets. The interpretation is not in consonance with the general statement. The latter says, "There are times" (plural), whereas the interpretation is concerned with a single occasion only, and one to which there is no parallel. Again, the idiom or technical term always refers to "neglect of the study of Torah," whereas if applied to the interpretation it would have to mean something more drastic and not refer to study at all. Furthermore, in the textual parallels only the interpretation is found, and not the general statement. The idea in the interpretation is also found in *Yer. Ta'anit* IV.8, 68c, in a substantially different form, and with a Tanna, R. Ishmael, as its author. The general statement is, then, really discrete. It contains the idea given by Rashi which is borne out by the baraita in *Ketubbot* 17a (*Megillah* 3b, 29a) where the same idiom is used. See also *'Abot de R. Nathan*, ed. S. Schechter (Vienna, 1887), Version A, Chap. IV, pp. 9a, f. and n. 16 and the references there; Version B, Chap. VIII, p. 11b.

44. *Berakot* 40a; *Giṭṭin* 62a. The proof-text is Deut. 11:15, where food "for thy cattle" is mentioned first.

45. *Mekhilta D'Rabbi Simon b. Jochai*, ed. J. N. Epstein and E. Z. Melamed (Jerusalem, 1955), p. 211; ed. D. Hoffmann (Frankfurt a. M., 1905), p. 151.

46. See G. Alon, תולדות היהודים בארץ ישראל (Tel Aviv, 1952), I, 329, citing this passage.

47. *Terumot* VIII.12. See the commentaries; also the next note.

48. *Tos. Terumot* VII.20, ed. Lieberman, p. 148, and the parallels. The passage continues with a qualifying statement, and concludes with the opinions of R. Judah and R. Simon, each of whom also specifies conditions. See Lieberman's commentary, *ad loc.* See also his *Tosefta Ki-Fshuṭah, ad. loc.*, where he discusses all the views and various later interpretations, and also to what extent the opinions in the Tosefta concur. He points out there (I, 420) that in the case of the women, no "guilty" one was specified at all, since it was a matter of sheer lust, whereas the Tosefta speaks of a case where one of the men had angered the Gentiles, but the latter did not know exactly who had done so.

49. See S. Abramson, לשוננו, קובץ מיוחד (Jerusalem, 1954), p. 63; cf. *ibid.*, pp. 64 f.; *OT*, pp. 29 f., p. 272, n. 76.

50. *Sifra, Aḥare* XIII.12, ed. Weiss, 86b. The proof-text there stresses the value concept *man*.

51. *Ibid.*

52. *Baba Kamma* 38a; *Sanhedrin* 59a; *'Abodah Zarah* 3a. The correct reading in all three references here is, very likely, not R. Me'ir but R. Jeremiah, as in the passage of the Sifra; see Abramson, *op. cit.*, p. 63, n. 1.

53. *RM*, p. 28, and see the discussion there on pp. 27 f. See also M. Kadushin, "Aspects of the Rabbinic Concept of Israel," *Hebrew Union College Annual*, XIX (1946), 60 and especially pp. 83–87, where we show how the element of universality acts as a check on the element of nationality.

54. *Giṭṭin* I.5. Lieberman points out that the Tosefta, *ibid.*, I.4, agrees with the Mishnah here according to the readings in the Vienna MS and other early sources; see his *Tosefeth Rishonim*, II, 69. The Erfurt MS may have been affected by the discussion in the Talmud.

55. *Giṭṭin* I.5.

56. והא לאו בני כריתה נינהו—*ibid.*, 10b, in regard to non-Jewish witnesses on a writ of divorce.

57. *Tos. Giṭṭin* I.4—again the same readings as those referred to in n. 54 above; *ibid.*, 11a.

58. Alon, *op. cit.*, p. 347, quoting Gulack. See Alon's remarks on these Gentile institutions, p. 346. His interpretation of the Tosefta passages is apparently based on the Erfurt MS.

59. See below, p. 43. Mark the dictum by Samuel in the Talmud here (*Giṭṭin* 10b): *dina' demalkuta' dina'*.

60. *Sifra Kedoshim* to Lev. 19:18, ed. I. H. Weiss (Vienna, 1862), p. 89b. For the inclusion of the latter part of Gen. 5:1, see the comment of R. Abraham b. David of Posquières here. A parallel is found in *Yer. Nedarim* 41c, and a version in *Bereshit R.* XXIV, end, ed. J. Theodor (Berlin, 1912), pp. 236 f.; see Theodor's note there which cites additional references in regard to the inclusion of the latter part of Gen. 5:1.

61. See the discussion in *Shabbat* 68a. The discussion there deals with the *comparative scope* of particular rules, despite the mention of "punishment," as can be seen from the instances taken up. Maimonides, however, in his commentary on the Mishnah (*ad Shabbat* VII.1), does stress "punishment"; and Edeles (*ad Shabbat* 68a, *s.v.* ודע), remarking on this contradiction to the discussion in the Talmud, offers a harmonization.

62. We can explain the widespread view that our Sifra passage contains principles intended as "the most important" (Jastrow, *op. cit.*, *s.v.* כלל גדול), or as "the most comprehensive" (G. F. Moore, *Judaism in the First Centuries of the Christian Era* [Cambridge, 1927], I, 446; II, 85), only on the ground that we are so prone today, as we have said, to look for an ultimate criterion.

63. Some instances of the conceptual term *'ahabah* in rabbinic usage are: *'Abot* V.16; *Tos. Berakot* III.7; *ibid.*, *Shabbat* VII (VIII).12; *Baba Meẓi'a* 84a; *Sanhedrin* 61b; *ibid.*, 105b; *'Abot de R. Nathan*, ed. Schechter, Version B, Chap. XXXVII, p. 49a.

64. *Bereshit R.* XXIV, end, ed. Theodor, pp. 236 f., and Theodor's notes there. See *Mekilta* (ed. J. Lauterbach [Philadelphia, 1933]), II, 291 f., where the same idea is associated—implicitly—with our verse; and see also *Tos. Sanhedrin* IX.7, *Sanhedrin* 46b, and the parallels cited in Lieberman, *Tosefeth Rishonim*, II, 159–60 (and see also Rashi's *Commentary on the Bible ad* Deut. 21:23—his explanation of the word קללת). It may well be that the version in *Bereshit R.* XXIV, end, with its additional statement, was affected by such prevalent tannaitic interpretations.

65. *'Abot* III.14, with R. 'Aḳiba as authority; *'Abot de R. Nathan*, Chap. XXXIX, ed. Schechter, p. 59b, with R. Me'ir as authority. The passage speaks first of man, then of Israel. This is how the passage is taken by *Tosefot Yom Ṭob ad 'Abot* III.14, although he also adds there some extraneous matters.

66. See W. Bacher, *Agadot ha-Tannaim* (2d ed.; Jerusalem and Berlin, 1922) (Hebrew trans.), I, Part 2, 131, n. 3, where the view of Weiss is also given, and refuted; and see also Theodor, *loc. cit.*, who has still a different view. A recent interpretation is that of Alon, *op. cit.*, p. 332, where Ben 'Azzai is regarded as the proponent of the absolute love of man as against R. 'Aḳiba who is regarded as the proponent of a realistic ethic of equality which is also love of man; and where there is even an attempt to make R. 'Aḳiba's principle apply to his stand on another occasion.

67. See the preceding note.

68. *Soṭah* 14a. On the connotation of *gemilut ḥasadim*, see above, p. 21.

69. *Tanḥuma*, ed. S. Buber (Wilna, 1885), I, 43b (*Wayyera*, par. 4), and the references and notes there. This is a later version because: (*a*) the idea that the lesson is to be found in the middle of the Torah is placed last, is tacked on; (*b*) the version has now a formal midrashic introduction and this introduction is a duplication; and (*c*) most of the proof-texts and the interpretations in the body of the statement are drawn from other midrashic sources. All this is true, as well, of the smoother variant of this version found in *Yalḳuṭ Shime'oni*, Psalms, par. 702, except for (*a*).

70. Above, p. 27.

71. *Shabbat* 31a.

72. דעלך סני לחברך לא תעביד. On Aramaic as the vernacular, see G. Dalman, *Die Worte Jesu* (Leipzig, 1930), I, 1 ff.

73. *'Abot de R. Nathan*, ed. Schechter, Version B, Chap. XXVI, p. 27a: מה דאת סני לגרמך לחברך לא תעביד. The rest of the passage here is commentary and a later addition; see Bacher, *op. cit.*, I, Part 1, 3, n. 3.

74. See the references in Theodor's note in his edition of *Bereshit R.*, p. 237.

75. Rashi *ad Shabbat* 31a, *s.v.* דעלך סני.

76. See the authorities cited in Theodor, *loc. cit.*

77. Similar in character, although not an ethical injunction, is the statement that "the entire Torah" has for its purpose "the ways of peace" (*Giṭṭin* 59b). The claim is worded exactly as in Hillel's statement—כל התורה כולה. Here, too, it can be meant only as a hyperbole; in the selfsame passage, for example, the holiness of the priests is related to its basis in the Torah, and the concept of holiness has connotations that *peace* does not have. *Shalom* (peace) does have a connotation of love—see *'Abot* I.12; *Ketubbot* 8a. This statement also, then, is an emphatic statement, recalling and strengthening the emphasis on love.

78. *Berakot* 63a—שכל גופי תורה תלוין בה. Prov. 3:6 embodies the concept of God's love: "He will direct my paths."

79. *Makkot* 23b–24a; *Tanḥuma*, ed. Buber, *Shofetim*, V, 16b, par. 10.

80. *Makkot* 24a. "Faith" is *'emunah*, and the latter concept in a rabbinic setting or interpretation has the connotation of trust in God (*RM*, p. 42).

Notes to Chapter III

1. Above, p. 19.

2. An analysis of *derek ereẓ* is given in M. Kadushin, *Organic Thinking* (New York, 1938 [to be referred to hereafter as *OT*]), pp. 117–30, and we shall draw on some of our conclusions there. The present study, however, is a more inclusive discussion of the concept.

3. *Ibid.*, p. 117.

4. *Ibid.*, pp. 118 f.

5. *Mekilta*, ed. J. Z. Lauterbach (Philadelphia, 1933), II, 129, and the parallels there.

6. *Canticles R.* I.10, end—see מתנות כהונה.

7. *OT*, p. 118.

8. On quasi-scientific concepts, see the discussion and examples in M. Kadushin, *The Rabbinic Mind* (New York, 1952 [to be referred to hereafter as *RM*]), pp. 147–49.

9. *Bereshit R.* LXXVI.3, ed. J. Theodor and C. Albeck (Berlin, 1927), p. 899. The teaching is drawn from Jacob in Gen. 32:8–9.

10. *Bereshit R.* XXXI.10, ed. J. Theodor (Berlin, 1912), p. 282, and the notes there. The teaching is drawn from the proportions of Noah's ark in Gen. 6:15.

11. *Pesiḳta de R. Kahana*, ed. S. Buber (Lyck, 1868), p. 98b; *Tanḥuma, Re'eh*, par. 15. The teaching is drawn from Job 31:40.

12. *Mekilta*, ed. H. S. Horovitz and J. A. Rabin (Frankfurt am Main, 1928), p. 38 and the references there; ed. Lauterbach, I, 86, and n. 4 there. The passage is a comment on a phrase in Exod. 12:22 and is introduced by the term ללמדך, "to teach you."

13. The note of admonition is usually present where "practical wisdom" has to do with long-range effects. "The Torah taught you *derek ereẓ*—[namely] that a man

ought not to accustom his son to meat and wine," (i.e., he ought to train his son so that the child would not develop a need for expensive food); *Ḥullin*, 84a. The other instances of *derek ereẓ* given there are admonitions of the same nature; see Rashi, *ibid.*, *s.v.* אלא בחזמנה. Another well-known example is in *Tos. Soṭah* VII.20 (*ibid.*, 44a): "The Torah taught *derek ereẓ*"—A man should first buy a house and then buy a field and then get married.

14. On subconcepts and conceptual phases, see also *RM*, pp. 16–17.

15. *Mekilta*, ed. Horovitz and Rabin, pp. 209–10.

16. *Yoma* 4b; cf. *Numbers R.* XIV.35.

17. *Baba Meẓi'a* 87a. The inference is from the dots over some of the letters of the word *'elaw*, "to him," in Gen. 18:9—"And they said unto him, 'Where is Sarah, thy wife?' " On the dotted places in the Bible, see S. Lieberman, *Hellenism in Jewish Palestine* (New York, 1950), pp. 43–46, and the references in n. 43 there.

18. See *The Treatises "Derek Erez,"* ed. M. Higger (New York, 1935); and compare *Massektot Ze'irot*, ed. M. Higger (New York, 1930). In his Introduction (Hebrew) to the latter, Higger presents a study of the various ways in which the term *derek ereẓ* is used in rabbinic literature; although that analysis differs from ours, we have found both his study and the lists given there decidedly helpful.

19. See Higger's Introduction I (English) to *The Treatises "Derek Erez."*

20. M. Friedmann, *Pseudo-Seder Eliahu Zuta* (Vienna, 1904), Introduction I (Hebrew), p. 5, bottom.

21. *OT*, p. 120.

22. *Leviticus R.* IX.3, ed. M. Margulies (Jerusalem, 1953), p. 178, and the notes there.

23. *Deuteronomy R.* V.2, in *Midrash Debarim Rabbah*, ed. S. Lieberman (Jerusalem, 1940), p. 96.

24. *Exodus R.* XLVI.1—"Moses made *derek ereẓ* known to Israel." The version in *Midrash Haggadol on Exodus*, ed. M. Margulies (Jerusalem, 1956), p. 689, has: "[Moses] taught *derek ereẓ* to Israel."

25. On the meaning of the word, see M. Jastrow, *Dictionary* (New York, Berlin, and London, 1926), *s.v.* דין II.

26. "Woe unto the men who testify to what they had not seen!" in both versions.

27. The very nature of the value concept is such that the concept is *embedded* in a situation or statement; that is why, in contrast to the concepts referring to perceived things and to defined concepts, the value concepts are so often used without employing the value term. The instances of *derek ereẓ* where the term itself is not used as a designation only illustrate this trait of the value concept. For an analysis and explanation of this phenomenon, see *RM*, pp. 3–4, 52, 54, 59–60, 111.

28. *'Abot* I.18. For the rendering here, see Bertinoro *ad. loc.* The proof-text from Zech. 8:16 is a late addition (see H. L. Strack, *Pirqe Aboth* [Leipzig, 1915], p. 12 [Hebrew] and the notes there). It is obviously, too, not a proof-text at all, for it does not actually cover the statement of R. Simeon that the world exists or is preserved by these three things.

Bertinoro also calls attention to the difference between our statement and *'Abot* I.2; in our statement, *'olam* refers to mankind, not to the cosmos (see also *RM*, pp. 150 f.), and hence the "three things" are traits of mankind in general. For a different reading and rendering, see below, p. 246, n. 41.

29. *Seder Eliahu*, ed. M. Friedmann (Vienna, 1900), p. 74—העולם מתישב. (The term "ישוב העולם" is the nearest equivalent to our term 'civilization' "; L. Ginzberg's note in M. Kadushin, *The Theology of Seder Eliahu* [New York, 1932], p. 186, n. 99. This book will hereafter be referred to as *TE*).

30. *Seder Eliahu*, *loc. cit.* The passage continues with an enumeration of those "who were uprooted from the world" because of these things. On *ḥillul ha-Shem*, see *TE*, pp. 64 f.

31. *Sifra, Aḥare*, par. 9, ed. I. H. Weiss (Vienna, 1862), p. 86a; *Yoma* 67b (*Yalḳuṭ Shime'oni*, Leviticus, par. 587)—דין הוא שיכתבו. For examples of דין or בדין as used here, see Ben Yehuda, *Thesaurus*, II, p. 928b.

32. *'Erubin* 100b. The rooster first gains the consent of the hen. See Rashi *ad loc.*

33. Yehudah Ha-Levi, *Kuzari*, II, 48. He distinguishes there between התורות האלהיות, divine laws, and התורות המנהגיות והשכליות, social and rational laws; among the rational laws, however, is acknowledgment of God's goodness.

34. *Ibid.*

35. *Mishneh Torah*, Hilkot Me'ilah, end; *Moreh Nebukim* III, 26. In his *Commentary to the Mishnah, Introduction to 'Abot*, Chapter VI, Maimonides places incest not among *mishpaṭim*, as our texts do, but among *ḥuḳḳim* (and that is why, apparently, he also gives "forbidden intercourse" as an example of "transgressions against God"; see Hilkot *Teshubah*, II.9). As has been remarked by the מסורת הש״ם on *Yoma* 67b, this must have been in accordance with the texts as Maimonides had them. There is a passage in *Midrash ha-Gadol* to Gen. 26:5, ed. M. Margulies (Jerusalem, 1947), p. 447, in which *ḥukkotai* is said to refer to incest, but the passage itself *may* be a reflection of Maimonides' view. On the relation of Maimonides to the *Midrash ha-Gadol*, see *Mekilta D'Rabbi Simon b. Joḥai*, ed. J. N. Epstein and E. Z. Melamed (Jerusalem, 1955), Introduction, p. 54.

36. Joseph Albo, *Sefer ha-'Iḳḳarim*, I, 5, ed. I. Husik (Philadelphia, 1929), p. 72—דת טבעית.

37. According to Albo, *ibid.*, natural law may be the product of a wise man or a prophet—מסודרת מחכם או מנביא.

38. *Sifra, loc. cit.* Some of the readings in the parallel, *Yoma* 67b, give a longer list; see *Diḳduḳe Soferim ad loc.* Cf. also *Pesiḳta de R. Kahana*, ed. Buber, 38b–39a.

39. See, for example, C. G. Montefiore, *Rabbinic Literature and Gospel Teachinng* (London, 1930), p. 194. Incidentally, the word בדין is entirely misinterpreted there; see the reference above, n. 31.

40. Below, p. 57. On the entire passage, see below, p. 212.

41. A rendering of *'Abot* I.18 contained in a passage in *Deuteronomy R*. V.1 not only supports our contention but makes it even more emphatic. *'Olam* is taken there not as mankind, but as "cosmos"; the reading is not קים, endures, but עומד, stands; and hence justice, peace, and truth are the three legs on which the world stands. "If you pervert justice, you cause the world to shake, since justice is one of its legs" (notice the reading מגלגל in *Deuteronomy R.*, ed. Lieberman, *op. cit.*, p. 95). Here it is not mankind but the entire created world that rests, in a mystical sense, on the virtues.

42. See how *ẓedaḳah*, *gezel*, etc. are designated as *derek ereẓ* (above, p. 42).

43. Subconcepts are also concepts in their own right, and are treated as such (*RM*, p. 16).

44. *OT*, p. 190.

45. See also below, p. 53.

46. "Practical wisdom" and "good manners" are subconcepts of Torah (see above, pp. 41, 42). The fourth phase is depicted as consisting of "things that are written in the Torah."

47. *Leviticus R.* IX.6 (end); ed. Margulies, p. 185. For the versions and parallels, see the note there and also the note at the beginning of the section on p. 182 there.

48. *Tanḥuma, Ḥukkat*, 12.

49. *Bereshit R.* LXX.14; ed. Theodor and Albeck, p. 813, and the parallels there.

50. Above, p. 245, n. 18.

51. "Pirke Ben Azzai," in *The Treatises "Derek Erez,"* pp. 166 f. For the many parallels, see *ibid.*, p. 165, n. 2 (I have utilized here the felicitous translation of Judah Goldin, *The Fathers According to Rabbi Nathan* [New Haven, 1955], pp. 169 f.).

52. *Ibid.*, p. 228. On שמשביח דעתו של מוכר, see the comment of R. Abraham b. David *ad Sifra, Behar, Perek* IV, ed. Weiss, *op. cit.*, p. 107d, *s.v.* ר׳ יהודה. His reference there to a "Tosefta" is a reference to our text. In our text, a person asks "grain-sellers" the price of an article (*ḥefeẓ*)! See the next note.

53. *Baba Meẓi'a* IV.10. Our text has been affected by this Mishnah. Originally, the halakah of our text dealt specifically with grain merchants, just as the halakah immediately preceding it deals specifically with wine merchants (see below, n. 57). The mishnaic phrase, however, had evidently become a cliché, and was used as such—compare R. Judah's statement in the passage of the *Sifra* cited in the preceding note with his statement as given in *Baba Meẓi'a* 58b.

54. *Baba Meẓi'a* IV.10, and *ibid.*, 58b. On *'ona'ah* as an ethical concept, see below, p. 207 f.

55. "Pirke Ben Azzai," in *The Treatises "Derek Erez,"* p. 227—דרך גזל.

56. *Ibid.*, pp. 226 f.

57. *Ibid.*, p. 227.

58. Above, p. 44 and n. 32 there.

59. *Leviticus R.* IX.3, ed. Margulies, p. 179.

60. *Seder Eliahu*, p. 56. See also *OT*, pp. 70, 73, and 126 f., for similar statements on *derek ereẓ* in this source. Cf., also, p. 248 below, n. 71, and especially the reference to *Numbers R.* XIII.15.

61. In regard to the manner of rehabilitating a field, for example, the admonitory tone is limited to the expression, "it is well to" (יפה) (see references on p. 40). Compare this with the emphatic tone in the teaching that when one goes on a journey he ought to arrive and leave in the daytime.

62. Incest is one of the negative concepts of the fourth phase, see above, p. 43.

63. Here there is another consideration as well. Not only is work a moral activity, when there is no taint of *gezel*, but it is also highly laudatory. See, for example, the many laudatory statements on work in *'Abot de R. Nathan*, ed. Schechter, Version B, Chap. XXI, pp. 22b f. In R. Eliezer's statement there, a contrast is drawn between work and *gezel*. On the rabbis' favorable attitude to business activity, see *OT*, p. 119. On the other hand, the rabbis voice disapproval when work or business crowds out study of Torah, and sometimes even advise reducing it to a minimum in favor of study; see, for example, *'Abot* IV.10.

64. The rabbis urge that a man be humble in his relations with others "and even more so" in relations with members of his household (*The Treatises* "*Derek Erez*," p. 90, Hebrew); and never to lose one's temper in one's house (*Ta'anit* 20b). Similar statements are found in *Midrash Tehillim*, ed. S. Buber (Wilna, 1891), 214b, *Giṭṭin* 6b, and elsewhere.

65. *Mekilta de R. Simeon*, ed. Epstein and Melamed, *op. cit.*, p. 108; ed. D. Hoffmann (Frankfurt am Main, 1895), p. 95.

66. *Yer. Berakot*, IX, 14b; cf. *Pesiḳta de R. Kahana*, ed. Buber, p. 104a—R. 'Abbahu's statement.

67. *Tanḥuma*, ed. Buber, *op. cit.*, I,82b; "he spoke [in the manner of] *derek ereẓ*." The synecdoche in Gen. 32:6 is lost in translation. An example given in the comment here is retained in the English "[the] cock crowed."

68. *RM*, pp. 147–149.

69. The concepts of *derek ereẓ* and *sidre 'olam* (or *sidre bereshit*) are not interchanged, even when they impinge on each other. The correct text in *Pesiḳta R.*, ed. M. Friedmann (Vienna, 1860), p. 84b, as can be seen from its parallel in *Midrash ha-Gadol* to Exodus, ed. Margulies, p. 246 (see n. 6 there), is: "the water [comes] from above them, and the bread from beneath them [i.e., from the earth]." This is designated *derek ereẓ* because the point of reference is man; but even so, this use of the term is very unusual. See the longer and earlier version in *Exodus R.* XXV.6, where the term is not used at all. Compare *Mekilta* II, p. 102, where the same idea is spoken of as a change in natural order.

In *Bereshit R.* XXXII.11, there is no reference to *derek ereẓ* in the correct text; see *ibid.*, ed. Theodor, p. 294.

70. *RM*, pp. 143 ff. on the generally consistent dichotomy of value concepts and cognitive concepts; *ibid.*, pp. 162 f. on *nes* and *sidre bereshit*; *ibid.*, pp. 232 ff. on *gilluy Shekinah*; *ibid.*, pp. 261 f. on *bat ḳol*.

71. Following are several instances where the commentators differ as to the meaning of *derek ereẓ*: "Everyone that is occupied with [שישנו] Bible, Mishnah, and *derek ereẓ* will be slow to sin" (*Ḳiddushin* I.10). Some take *derek ereẓ* here to refer to "work" or "occupation" and so make the statement equivalent to *'Abot* II.2 (see C. Albeck, *Commentary to Seder Nashim* [Jerusalem and Tel Aviv, 1955], p. 413); Maimonides, and following him Bertinoro, in their commentaries on the Mishnah, take it to refer to social behavior and ethics. "If there is no Torah, there is no *derek ereẓ*; if there is no *derek ereẓ* there is no Torah" (*'Abot* III.17). On this statement, see *OT*, p. 130, and the references there. The ambiguity of the concept sometimes results in different interpretations of the same mishnah even in rabbinic literature. *Derek ereẓ* in *'Abot* II.2 is interpreted as meaning "work" or "occupation" in *'Abot de R. Nathan*, ed. Schechter, Version B, p. 35b and in *Koh. R.* to *Koh.* 7:11, whereas in *Numbers R.* XIII.15 it is interpreted as meaning good deeds (cited by Albeck, *Commentary to Neziḳin*, p. 495). See also Judah Goldin, *The Living Talmud* (New York, 1957), pp. 81 f.

72. Examples of concepts which have conceptual phases are: God's justice (*middat ha-din*), with two conceptual phases—the justice due the individual and corporate justice (*RM*, p. 17); Torah, which has the phase of the efficacy of Torah (*ibid.*); *nes*, with two conceptual phases—*nes* involving spectacular things, such as changes in *sidre bereshit*, and *nes* not involving spectacular things (*ibid.*, pp. 159–162).

73. *Derek ereẓ*, as we have seen, has five phases, whereas other concepts cited (see preceding note) have only two.

74. W. Bacher, ערכי מדרש (Hebrew translation, Tel Aviv, 1923), p. 18, *s.v.* דרך ארץ.

75. *Loc. cit.*, and n. 3 there.

76. *Sifra*, *'Aḥare*, *Perek* XI, ed. Weiss, p. 84c, and the notes and references there.

77. *Mekilta*, ed. Friedmann, p. 7a.

78. *Ibid.*, p. 83a, and n. 24 there (this is apparently directed against those who would not seek a cure, but only rely on prayer; see *Berakot* 60a, bottom, and Rashi *ad loc.*).

79. *Ibid.*, p. 63a; ed. Horovitz and Rabin, pp. 209–10.

80. *Sifre Numbers*, ed. M. Friedmann (Vienna, 1864), p. 27b, and the note there; ed. H. S. Horovitz (Leipzig, 1917), p. 100, and the note there.

81. *Sifre Numbers*, ed. Friedmann, p. 28b, top. There remain two more references cited by Bacher to be accounted for. Both are concerned with the descriptive phase of *derek ereẓ*. (*a*) It is a phenomenon of history ("a trait prevalent in all generations") that he who smites Israel will himself in the end be smitten, and the prime example is Amalek (*Mekilta*, ed. Friedmann, p. 54b–55a). Here the phenomenon depicted is itself not *derek ereẓ* but an aspect of God's justice. By drawing the proper inference "from Amalek" we arrive, according to the rabbis, at a characteristic of human history and hence of man in general; it is this element of repetition in man's history that constitutes *derek ereẓ*, for the other traits of mankind are also characterized by the element of repetition, of predictability. (*b*) R. Ishmael in *Sifre Deut.* (ed. Friedmann, p. 80b), commenting on Deut. 11.14 ("and thou shalt gather in thy corn, and thy wine, and thine oil"), says that Torah speaks here of *derek ereẓ*; and here the term refers to a person's occupation or livelihood (see Rashi on the parallel in *Berakot* 35b). See also above, p. 247, n. 63. The use of the term in these passages demonstrates again that the descriptive phase of *derek ereẓ* is not morally neutral.

82. Above, pp. 22–24.

83. *Yoma* VIII.9. Parallels and versions: *Sifra*, ed. Weiss, pp. 83a–b; *Pesiḳta R.*, ed. Friedmann, p. 185a; *Tanḥuma*, ed. Buber, I, p. 52a, and the notes there. Cf. *Yer. Nedarim* IX.41b, where the phrase "matters that are between him and God" does occur in another context, but not the "ethical formula."

84. *Sifre Zuṭṭa*, ed. Horovitz, p. 248 (cf. *Rosh ha-Shanah*, 17b).

85. *Ibid.*

86. *OT*, p. 122.

87. *Deut. R.* VI.1, ed. Lieberman, p. 103; cf. *Lev. R.* XXVII.11, ed. Margulies, p. 644 f.

88. *Exod. R.* II.2. See L. Ginzberg, *Legends of the Jews*, II (Philadelphia, 1913), 301. R. Judah the Prince, who was punished because he failed to take compassion on animals, and then was cured when he did take such compassion, quotes Psalm 145:9, "And His compassion is on all His works" (*Bereshit R.* XXXIII.3, ed. Theodor, p. 305, and the note and references there).

89. See above, p. 245, n. 27.

90. See the laws and interpretations given in Greenstone's article, "Cruelty to Animals," in the *Jewish Encyclopedia*, IV, pp. 376 ff. Many of the rabbinic laws represent interpretations or generalizations of biblical laws, as can be seen there. The rabbis maintain that the duty of relieving the suffering of animals is a biblical

injunction (צער בעלי חיים דאורייתא); cf. *Baba Meẓi'a* 32b; *Shabbat* 128b. R. Jose the Galilean, however, holds that it is a rabbinic principle (*Baba Meẓi'a* 33b; cf. *Shabbat* 154b). On kindness to animals, see above p. 29.

91. See above, pp. 43 f. *Ḥillul ha-Shem*, too, a form of blasphemy, is among the eight things because of which "the world is destroyed" (*ibid.*, p. 43, and Ginzberg's remark in *OT*, p. 300, n. 147).

92. See the material in S. Liebermann, *Greek in Jewish Palestine* (New York, 1942), pp. 77 ff., and especially pp. 81 f. There are *goyim*, Gentiles, who do not forget God and are righteous (*RM*, p. 41). On non-Jews "cancelling" an idol, see *ibid.*, p. 197.

93. There was even the term גרי אומות העולם as designation for a category of semi-proselytes (non-Jews) (Lieberman, *op. cit.*, p. 84).

94. Lieberman, *op. cit.*, pp. 76 f.

95. Maimonides regards "between a man and God" and "between a man and his fellow man" as basic general categories. When it comes to the actual organization of the laws in his Mishneh Torah, however, he does not employ these categories, but fourteen divisions of a different character; nor is his later endeavor to superimpose the two categories on the fourteen divisions very successful, since, as he says, a part of his third division deals with matters "between a man and his fellow man," and the other part concerns matters "between a man and God." He says, too, that "between a man and God" consists of matters that in the long run and indirectly also lead to matters that are "between a man and his fellow man." See his *Moreh Nebukim*, Part III, Chap. 35.

96. "The Rabbis and the Folk," *RM*, pp. 84 f. It is true that toward the end of the second century and later, the rabbinic class was more and more crystallized as a class apart. There was a tendency to free the rabbis from taxes, and there were perhaps even attempts to ensure succession to their sons. See Alon, *op. cit.*, II, 142 f.

97. Above, p. 26.

98. *Ibid.*, p. 24.

99. The phrase, "the Torah taught you *derek ereẓ*" does not introduce an actual commandment. The phrase does introduce, therefore, an *'asmakta*, "support." On *'asmakta*, see *RM*, pp. 124 f.

100. See above, p. 244, n. 13.

101. A. L. Kroeber, *Anthropology* (New York, 1948), pp. 589 f. In the rabbinic tradition, patience is associated with humility (see above, p. 248, n. 64).

102. *Ibid.*, p. 316.

103. Some of these formal ways of concretization, as well as the distinction drawn between this concept and charity, are to be found above, pp. 20–21, and n. 12 there.

104. The subject of *'ona'ah* is taken up in *Baba Meẓi'a* IV.3 ff.

105. See above, p. 48.

106. *Baba Meẓi'a* 58b–59a.

107. This was true in other spheres as well (see *RM*, pp. 211 f., and n. 36 there).

108. *Iggeret R. Sherira Gaon*, ed. B. Lewin (Haifa, 1921), p. 47, and I. H. Weiss, *Dor Dor We-Dorshaw* (4th ed.; Wilna, 1904), II, 222. See also above, p. 42.

109. *Berakot* 22a—R. Judah and his pupils.

110. *The Treatises "Derek Erez,"* pp. 265 ff., and the references there.

Notes to Chapter IV

1. On these conceptual terms, see M. Kadushin, *The Rabbinic Mind* (New York, 1952 [to be referred to hereafter as *RM*]), pp. 215 ff.

2. *Ibid.*

3. *Ibid.*, p. 15.

4. See M Kadushin, "Aspects of the Rabbinic Concept of Israel," *Hebrew Union College Annual*, XIX (1946), 85 f.

5. M. Kadushin, *The Theology of Seder Eliahu* (New York, 1932), pp. 172–76 (to be referred to hereafter as *TE*).

6. M. Kadushin, *Organic Thinking* (New York, 1938 [to be referred to hereafter as *OT*]), p. 222.

7. *Ibid.*, p. 225. When they interpret events of their own day as well, the rabbis often emphasize God's love. Thus Israel's dispersal is interpreted as an act of God's love. It was an act of charity, of love (*ẓedaḳah*) on God's part to have scattered Israel among the nations (*Pesaḥim* 87b), a statement which means, as the passage goes on to indicate, that God has assured Israel's survival since thus they cannot "all be destroyed" by any one nation. This statement has often been taken by modern writers to mean that Israel has a mission to the nations, a gross misinterpretation. See Edeles' comment, *ad loc.*, and his reference to a related passage in *'Abodah Zarah* 10b.

8. See the sources referred to in the article mentioned above in n. 4.

9. See also the characteristics of the value concept depicted above, pp. 22 ff.

10. See above, pp. 24 ff.

11. *Yer. Berakot* I.8, 3d; R. Judan's statement.

12. L. Ginzberg, *Commentary on the Palestinian Talmud*, I (New York, 1941), 178, 199; and S. Lieberman, *Tosefta Ki-Fshuṭah*, (New York, 1955), I, 7, *s.v.* שאמרו להאריך.

13. *RM*, p. 168 and n. 1 there.

14. *Berakot* VI.1–4. On these being short berakot, see *Tosefta Berakot*, I. 3 6–7, ed. Lieberman, p. 3, and see his *Tos. Kif.*, *ad loc.*, p. 9, n. 40. Cf. also the baraita in *Berakot* 46a, bottom.

15. *Berakot* 33a.

16. *Yer. Berakot* VII.1, 11a; *Yer. Megillah* IV.1, 75a (with R. Nathan as the authority in both references); *Berakot* 48b (with R. Isaac as the authority). The proof-text is: "And ye shall *serve* the Lord your God" (Exod. 23:25); and hence this berakah is service ('abodah), worship.

17. *Berakot* 40a, and Tosafot, *ibid.*, *s.v.* הבא מלח.

18. *Ibid.* 39b, and Tosafot, *s.v.* והלכתא.

19. *Yer. Berakot* VI.4, 10a, toward the bottom.

20. *RM*, pp. 113 f.

21. *Ibid.*

22. *Berakot* 35a–b. See Tosafot, *ibid.*, *s.v.* כאן לאחר ברכה, as to these verses being used in actual custom.

In *Tos. Berakot* IV.1 (and parallels), ed. Lieberman, p. 18, there is the related idea that, since "the earth is the Lord's and the fulness thereof" (Ps. 24:1), the individual who partakes of anything in this world without reciting a berakah is guilty of *me'ilah*, of diverting a sacred thing to a secular use; in this view, a berakah redeems what is partaken of, from its status as a holy thing; see Lieberman, *op. cit.*, I, *ad loc.*, 55. But this reason leaves out of account altogether the role of the individual as a member of society which is implicit in the berakah itself.

23. See above, p. 4.

24. See S. Baer, סדר עבודת ישראל (Roedelheim, 1868), p. 554.

25. *Berakot* 10a; *'Abodah Zarah* 3b.

26. *Berakot* 59b (a baraita).

27. *Berakot* IX.2.

28. *Yer. Berakot* VI.3, 10c.

29. See the three preceding references.

30. *Berakot* IX.5, ed. C. Albeck (Jerusalem and Tel Aviv, 1957), p. 32, and the note there.

31. *Sifre Deut.* on Deut. 6:5, ed. M. Friedmann (Vienna, 1864), pp. 73a–b.

32. *Ibid.*, p. 73b. A proof-text is: "For whom the Lord loveth He correcteth, even as a father the son in whom he delighteth" (Prov. 3:12).

33. It is a subconcept both of God's love and of God's justice. There are rabbinic concepts which share in two grounds simultaneously; see *RM*, pp. 28 f.

34. *RM*, p. 218.

35. On the association of *middat raḥamim* with the Tetragrammaton and *middat ha-din* with *'Elohim*, see *ibid.*, pp. 216 f.

36. For example, *Tos. Yebamot* IX.3; *Tos. Baba Ḳamma* IX.2.

37. For example, *Bemidbar R.* XX.1.

38. For example, *Bereshit R.* XXXIX.6, ed. J. Theodor (Berlin, 1912), pp. 368–9.

39. *Pesaḥim* 87b. See above, p. 251, n. 7.

40. *TE*, p. 38.

41. גומל חסדים: *Berakot* 60b, in the last berakah of the series there upon arising in the morning, dressing and so on; it is also in the "short" berakah to be recited upon recovering from illness or deliverance from peril, as given in *Berakot* 54b, both in the editions and MSS, but the codists have a different version and that version is given in the *Prayer Book*; see *Diḳduḳe Soferim, ad loc.*; and it is also in the "long" berakah with which the 'Amidah begins (see Baer, *op. cit.*, pp. 87 f., *Seder R. 'Amram Gaon*, ed. A. L. Frumkin (Jerusalem, 1912), I, p. 117b, and *Siddur R. Saadia Gaon*, ed. I. Davidson and others (Jerusalem, 1944), p. 18 [in the text]).

42. Other aspects of this moral experience are discussed below, pp. 112 f.

43. *Berakot* 48b.

44. *Tos. Berakot* VI (VII).1, ed. Lieberman, p. 32 and the references there.

45. This is true not only of the Birkat ha-Mazon but, in Ginzberg's words, of all "the principal prayers." "We know for certain that the principal prayers, for instance the *'Amidah* and the Benedictions of the *Shema'*, were in use at least as far back as the first century before the Common Era. Yet in the entire talmudic-midrashic literature, extending approximately from the second to the sixth century, one does not find a single principal prayer in full. . . . These prayers are cited only by initial words or have at most a sentence quoted from them. This mode of quoting surely proves the

more or less fixed character of these prayers, the assumption being that the sequel was in everyone's memory. One must not however be misled by this in concluding that at that period prayer books were in existence. The contrary may be proved by the Talmuds and has been done so by as early an authority as the Italian scholar, R. Zedekiah degli Mansi (*Shibbale ha-Leket*, p. 12) seven hundred years ago." L. Ginzberg, "Saadia's Siddur," *Jewish Quarterly Review*, N.S., XXXIII, 315 f.

46. N. 41, above.

47. Ginzberg, *op. cit.*, p. 328. He points out there that Saadia's *Siddur* has reached us in a more authentic form than that of R. Amram. "R. Amram's work has reached us in such a form that only in very rare cases are we in a position to recognize its original contents. Of course, it is not our opinion that Saadia's Siddur reached us exactly as it left his hands . . . yet with all the omissions, additions and faulty readings, one is safe in stating that on the whole the *Siddur* reached us in a fairly good state."

An essay by Louis Finkelstein, "The Birkat Ha-Mazon" (*Jewish Quarterly Review*, N.S., XIX, No. 3, 211 ff.), is devoted to the reconstruction of the original text and to the various versions of the Birkat ha-Mazon. His conclusion is "that the earliest of extant forms is not that of Palestine as recovered from the Genizah, but that of Seder R. Saadia" (*ibid.*, p. 224).

48. *Siddur R. Saadia Gaon*, p. 102. "Us and" were evidently not in the text originally; see the textual note. "The Holy One, Blessed be He, feeds the whole world" is a haggadic cliché found in *Berakot* 10a and *'Abodah Zarah* 3b.

49. This is taken for granted both by Bet Shammai and by Bet Hillel in *Berakot* VIII.7, for they differ only in case one had not said it at the place he had eaten. See Maimonides, *Mishneh Torah*, Hilkot *Berakot* IV.1.

50. See *Tos. Berakot* IV.20, ed. Lieberman, p. 25, and his comment there; and see his *Tos. Kif.*, I, 71 f., where he discusses the entire literature on this baraita. He suggests there that by הפליג the baraita refers especially to the diversion of attention through a long conversation. "Even if it be no further than to the door" seems to be an opinion held by Maimonides alone; see his Hilkot *Berakot* IV.3, and R. Abraham b. David of Posquière's comment there.

51. *Berakot* 40b (see both references to the *Tur* on the margin).

52. *Ibid.* Rab is the authority who regards this berakah as halakically valid, and the Talmud, in order to make it consistent with Rab's view that a berakah must mention the name of God, has the berakah read, "Blessed be the Merciful [רחמנא], Master of this bread." On the practice in Palestine, see Lieberman, *Tos. Kif.*, I, 60.

53. This is taken as a matter of course by the Talmud, for it asks, "What does he [Rab] teach us?" (*Berakot*, *loc. cit*). We ought to add that the answer to this question is: "Even though he [the shephered] said it in the secular vernacular."

54. Above, p. 66.

55. "World" is practically equated with the concept of man, an ethical concept connoting brotherhood; see *RM*, pp. 150 f. Worship as an expression of the larger self is a topic which we shall discuss at some length when we take up the Daily 'Amidah.

56. ברכה הסמוכה לחברתה; *Berakot* 46a, end; *Tos. Berakot* I.9, ed. Lieberman, p. 3. "Conceptual continuum" was first used by Charles Kadushin in an unpublished paper.

57. *Berakot* 49a.

58. *Siddur R. Saadia Gaon*, p. 102.

59. See above, n. 56.

60. See Tosafot to *Pesaḥim* 104b, *s.v.* חוץ and Ginzberg, *Commentary*, I, 193. Rashi, however (to *Pesaḥim, loc. cit.*), takes the berakah with the opening formula to be sufficient for all the rest, and so also does Rashbam, who uses Rashi's phraseology.

61. *RM*, p. 190. The point is also made there that "the valuational events in an individual's life are unitary but not isolated."

62. *Berakot* 49a.

63. *Ibid.*, 48b.

64. A "desirable land" (Jer. 3:19); "a good and ample land" (Exod. 3:8).

65. *Berakot* 48b and Rashi *ad. loc.* Rashi supplies the biblical verses, undoubtedly from a tradition; see the Yerushalmi referred to in the next note.

66. *Ibid.* and Rashi, *ad loc.* In *Yer. Berakot* I.9.3d, the reward of the land for Torah is adduced from Ps. 105:44–45.

67. Rab and R. Ḥisda', and probably others too, did not feel the need to practice all these rules; see Lieberman, *Tos. Kif.*, I, 38, *s.v.* ר' יוסי. We also noticed above (p. 253, n. 52) that Rab was satisfied with a brief berakah. But there was also very likely another factor. Finkelstein (*op. cit.*, p. 229 and n. 37 there) points out "that the insertion of the Covenant and the Torah was made by authorities of the second century," probably as a "reaction to the persecutions to which the Jews were exposed on their account." Some of the rabbis apparently did not feel that these latter-day insertions were actually integral to the meditation; see Ginzberg, *Commentary*, II, 155, beginning at וכבר.

68. See Samuel's rule in *Pesaḥim* 104a, and the text as given in R. Ḥananel (and in other early authorities). See *Diḳduḳe Soferim, ad loc.*

69. Tosafot to *Pesaḥim* 104a, *s.v.* מאי בינייהו.

70. *Berakot* 49a. According to the rule there, the closing formula must refer to only one thing, and "for the Land and for the food" seems to violate that rule. The explanation there is that the phrase means "the Land that gives forth food," and hence that the principle is not violated.

71. *Berakot* 48b and 49a. See Ginzberg, *Commentary*, II, 155 and n. 33 there.

72. *Berakot* 49a. R. Sheshet thus upholds the view of R. Jose (*ibid.*) despite the dictum of R. 'Abba (Rab).

73. *Ibid.* and Rashi, *ad loc.*

74. See Lieberman, *Tos. Kif.*, I, 52 (top), and *ibid.*, nn. 69 and 70. He regards "Have mercy" as the older version. "When Jerusalem was destroyed, they substituted 'comfort' for 'Have mercy' "; *ibid.*, n. 69. Finkelstein suggests "that the prayer for Jerusalem was composed during the Maccabean struggle when the Temple and the Altar, the importance of both of which is emphasized in the earliest form of this prayer, were under the control of the heathen" (*op. cit.*, pp. 221 f., and the references there).

75. *Siddur R. Saadia Gaon*, p. 102. See Finkelstein, *op. cit.*, p. 233, on the tautology here.

76. See Tosafot to *Berakot* 48b, *s.v.* ומתחיל; also *Ṭur 'Oraḥ Ḥayyim*, par. 188, and its source quoted in the Bet Joseph to *ibid.*, par. 187.

77. *RM*, pp. 361 ff.; on the days of the Messiah, pp. 362 f.

78. *Ibid.*, pp. 365 f. On the special character of the hereafter concepts, see *ibid.*, p. 364. The rabbinic dogmas are also not pure dogmas, nor do they constitute a creed; see *ibid.*, pp. 366 f.

79. *Ibid.*, p. 42. *'Emunah* does *not* mean belief in the existence of God. See the discussion there. An example of *'emunah* is the farmer sowing and expecting to harvest; see Tosafot to *Shabbat* 31a, *s.v.* אמונת (see also *Midrash Tehillim* to Ps. 19:8, ed. S. Buber [Wilna, 1891], p. 86a, which ought to be corrected accordingly). E. Hatch, in *The Influence of Greek Ideas on Christianity*, ed. F. C. Grant (New York, 1957), pp. 310 ff., describes how "the word Faith came to be transferred from simple trust in God to mean the acceptance of a series of propositions, and these propositions, propositions in abstract metaphysics."

80. See, for example, the passage on *'emunah* in the *Mekilta*, ed. H. S. Horovitz and J. A. Rabin (Frankfurt am Main, 1928), pp. 114 f. Notice that *'emunah* there is interchanged with *'amanah*, the common term for "trust." The word *'emunah*, too, is also used for trust or faith in men; see Jastrow, *Dictionary* . . . (New York, Berlin, and London, 1926), *s.v.* אמונה.

81. *Midrash Tehillim*, ed. Buber, p. 120b. Cf. the references there. The passage refers to berakot of this type in the 'Amidah, one of which is the Fourteenth Berakah of the Daily 'Amidah. The closing formula of that berakah—"Blessed art Thou, O Lord, Who buildest Jerusalem"—is the same as the closing formula of the Third Berakah of the Birkat ha-Mazon.

82. It is "a berakah which is joined to the immediately preceding berakah," that is, to the Second Berakah: see *Berakot* 49a.

83. *Berakot* VI.8; *Tosefta*, *ibid.*, IV.6, 7, 15 (*Berakot* 37a). The saying of "Amen" by the individual who himself recites the Birkat ha-Mazon (see the text above, p. 74) also indicates that the Third Berakah closed the series; see *Berakot* 45b, Rashi, *ad loc.*, and Maimonides, *Hilkot Berakot*, I.17. The prayer of thanksgiving in the Didache, which many scholars say was written shortly after the destruction of the Second Temple, is another indication, as has been shown by K. Kohler (*Jewish Encyclopedia*, IV, 587) and especially by Finkelstein (*op. cit.*, pp. 213 f.). Alon (מחקרים בתולדות ישראל, I [Tel Aviv, 1957], pp. 286–90) tentatively suggests that on the basis of the material in the Didache, the Second Berakah of the Birkat ha-Mazon was originally the first of the three berakot (*ibid.*, p. 290). But the First Berakah obviously must refer to the meal, else the meal does not serve as an occasion for a berakah at all; therefore, the present order is without question the original order. Further, it is not coincidental that the *second* section of the Thanksgiving in the Didache contains the phrase "for all these we thank Thee," a phrase which is found in the *Second* Berakah.

84. *Tos. Berakot* VI(VII).1, ed. Lieberman, p. 32, where all the other sources are given. The four berakot are a series derived from Deut. 8:10 and thus are "from the Torah."

85. *Ibid.* I.7, ed. Lieberman, p. 3, and the discussions and references in Lieberman, *Tos. Kif.* I, 10, *s.v.* היה חותם.

86. שגמלנו כל טוב; see the discussion in Lieberman, *Tos. Kif.*, I, 101, *s.v.* הטוב והמטיב.

87. See Tosafot to *Berakot* 49a, *s.v.* מאן. The point made here is that if the Fourth Berakah is also "from the Torah", it is similar in form to the preceding berakot. See also Lieberman, *loc. cit.*, as to R. Ishmael's view.

On a possible other version of this berakah, see below, p. 256, n. 91.

88. *Siddur R. Saadia Gaon*, pp. 102 f.

89. *Berakot* 48b, and parallels; *ibid., Yer.*, I.8, 3d.

90. Albeck, *Commentary on Berakot*, Introduction, p. 10 (the berakah on good tidings; *Berakot* IX.2).

91. The berakah "Who art good and doeth good" is said not only when hearing of good tidings but on other occasions as well; see *Berakot* 59b. It is quite possible that there were several versions of the original Fourth Berakah and that one of them had as its closing formula "Who art good and doeth good"; in that case, the berakah as established simply retained this phrase too.

92. From the viewpoint of those who regard the Fourth Berakah as "from the Torah," it is so closely related to the preceding berakot as to be "a berakah, which is joined to the immediately preceding berakah," and this despite the fact that it has an opening formula (Rashi to *Berakot* 49a, *s.v.* ומאן דאמר).

93. For variations in this type of berakah, see below, pp. 100, 102.

94. See *Tos. Berakot* II.4, and Lieberman, *Tos. Kif.* I, 15–16.

95. *Yer. Berakot* II.1, 4a—זאת אומרת שאין ברכות מעכבות, and see Ginzberg, *Commentary*, I, 225–227, where he also explains that this is the view of Resh Laḳish as well (*ibid.*, pp. 165 f.) in *Yer. Berakot* I.8, 3c. See also *Ṭur 'Oraḥ Ḥayyim*, par. 60.

96. *Berakot* II.2. "Heaven" is an appellative for God; see *RM*, p. 204. On the third section of the Shema', see Lieberman, *Tos. Kif.* I, 12, *s.v.* מזכירין, and *RM*, p. 359 and the note there.

97. *Sifre* on Num. 15:39, ed. H. S. Horovitz (Leipzig, 1917), p. 126.

98. See Albeck's comment on *Berakot* II.2, and the reference there to *Sifre* on Deut. 11:13.

99. *Sifre* on Num. 15:39, ed. Horovitz, *loc. cit.* In the parallel in *Berakot* 14b, R. Simeon b. Yoḥai introduces his argument with the term בדין, "it stands to reason."

100. *Berakot* 14b.

101. *Mekilta*, ed. Horovitz and Rabin, p. 222.

102. *Ibid.* For an analysis of this and the preceding reference, see *RM*, p. 21.

103. Above, pp. 23 f.

104. *RM*, pp. 18–21, 23 (*malkut Shamayim*); *OT*, pp. 110 f. (miẓwot).

105. For a haggadic example, see *OT*, pp. 208 f. Genuinely interlocking concepts are the "hereafter concepts," but they are beliefs, dogmas, rather than value concepts; even so, they exhibit some flexibility (see *RM*, pp. 347 [on dogmas], and pp. 364 f.).

106. *Pesaḥim* IV.8, and *Tosefta, ibid.*, II(III).19, ed. Lieberman (New York, 1962), pp. 156 f. See also Lieberman, *Tos. Kif.*, IV (New York, 1962), 541 f.

107. Louis Finkelstein, "The Word פרס," *Jewish Quarterly Review*, XXXIII, No. 1, 36–38. On this response in Temple usage, see also I. Davidson, אוצר השירה והפיוט, II, 75, and *RM*, pp. 212 f. and the notes there. On this response as a berakah, see p. 275, n. 43. M. Friedmann, in a long note in his edition of *Sifre Deut.*, pp. 72b–73a, says that originally the Ḳeri'at Shema' was made an element of the Temple ritual in order to include the study of Torah in that ritual. It was only after Herod, whose kingship the people resented, that the idea of the acceptance of God's kingship was added to the Shema'; this idea harked back "to the words of the prophet Samuel who said, 'But the Lord your God is your King' [I Sam. 12:2]." Friedmann also implies in this connection that God's rule meant to the Jews a negation of any human

sovereignty or rule. But the acceptance of God's kingship negates idolatry and not human rule as such (see above, p. 79). Moreover, we shall soon see that the acceptance of God's kingship in Ḳeri'at Shema' does not depend, as Friedmann would have it, on the insertion of the response. Again, unless Ḳeri'at Shema' had already meant to the people the acceptance of *malkut Shamayim*, the change in the response so as to emphasize God's kingship would have been meaningless. We shall find, indeed, that there is an association between the acceptance of God's kingship and the study of Torah itself.

108. *Berakot* 13b; *ibid.*, *Yer.*, II.1, 4a.

109. See Ginzberg, *Commentary*, I, 230, *s.v.* צריך. See also Edeles on *Berakot* 13b, *s.v.* כיון.

110. *Berakot* 13b.

111. *Ibid.*, *Yer.* II.1, 4a bottom.

112. See above, p. 256, n. 106.

113. See Edeles, *loc. cit.*, who takes R. Jeremiah's approach to be that of the individual mystic as against R. Ḥiyya's, which was meant for the people as a whole.

114. See above, p. 79.

115. Notice especially the parable in the Mekilta passage cited above, p. 80; "For if they will not accept My kingship, they will not accept My decrees."

116. *Tamid* V.1. On the formulation of this tractate, see J. N. Epstein, מבואות לספרות התנאים (Jerusalem, 1957), pp. 27–31.

117. See above, p. 80. R. Phineas b. Ḥama, an Amora, even declares that at Sinai God began with, "Hear, O Israel: 'I am the Lord thy God,' " and that Israel answered, "The Lord our God, the Lord is One," and that Moses thereupon uttered the response, "Blessed" etc. (*Deut. R.* II.22). There was a widespread tradition also that in the Ten Commandments the entire Torah was included (see the supplementary notes in C. Albeck's edition and *Commentary on Ḳodashim* [Jerusalem and Tel Aviv, 1956], p. 428, top). The Ten Commandments preceded the Shema' in the service because they precede in the Bible; notice the question raised with regard to the sections of the Shema' itself in Tosafot on *Berakot* 14b, *s.v.* למה קדמה.

118. *Yer. Berakot* I.8, 3c, and *ibid.*, *Babli*, 12a. See also Rashi, *ibid.*, *s.v.* בקשו.

119. *Berakot* 12a.

120. *Yer. Berakot* I.8, 3c, and Ginzberg, *Commentary*, I, 166. As against the sectarians, mark the "widespread tradition" mentioned in note 117 above.

According to Ginzberg, the statement that the sections on Balak and Balaam ought to be recited daily was also an attempt to offset "the contention of the sectarians," some of whom claimed that these and other sections were not written by Moses but added later; and hence this statement is given here in connection with that on the Ten Commandments. R. Eleazar's interpretation, he feels, is in accordance with this view. See the entire discussion in his *Commentary*, I, 167.

121. *Berakot* 12a.

122. הן הן גופה של שמע; *Yer. Berakot* I.8, 3c.

123. Ginzberg, *op. cit.*, I, 166.

124. *Yer. Berakot, loc. cit.*; שעשרת הדברות כלולין בהן. See also *Deut. R.*, ed. Lieberman, p. 69 and the references there in n. 6.

125. *Tos. Berakot* II.2, ed. Lieberman, p. 6. See *idem, Tos. Kif.*, I, 15, *s.v.* שיכוין, on the sense in which this word is used here, and see also the next comment there. Cf. *Berakot* 13b. "Else it must be repeated" is evident from R. Judah's differing opinion. R. Josiah's view in the second baraita in *Berakot* 13b is similar to the anonymous opinion in the Tosefta here; see Ginzberg, *op. cit.*, I, 233.

126. *Berakot* 13b.

127. Even revising the text is classed as mechanical reading; *ibid.*, 13a. See below, p. 197.

128. The nominal form is here in the construct state. But it is also used in reference to the commitment and experience of the Shema' in the absolute state; כונה. For example, *Yer. Berakot* II.1, 4a, bottom (in a baraita); *ibid.*, 4b, top; *ibid., Babli*, 13b (R. Josiah).

129. Ginzberg, *op. cit.*, p. 228, *s.v.* נישמעינה. In *Berakot* II.1, and as discussed *ibid.*, 13a, it is used in the limited sense. See Lieberman, *Tos. Kif.*, *loc. cit.*

130. Ginzberg (*loc. cit.*) cites medieval authorities who called attention to these phases.

131. *Baba Ḳamma* 92b; *Baba Meẓi'a* 107b. It is linked with the Tefillah.

132. See above, n. 16.

133. On the Shema' as a unitary entity, see above, pp. 78 ff.

134. *OT*, p. 39. Miḳra', the word used for Scripture in general, stands for Ḳeri'at Shema' in *Berakot* II.1.

135. Ginzberg, *Commentary*, II, 133.

136. *Menaḥot* 99b. Similarly, *Midrash Tehillim*, ed. Buber, p. 8b, the proof-text here being Ps. 1:2; according to Ginzberg (*op. cit.*, I, 136), we ought to read "R. Simeon" for "R. Joshua."

137. *Yer. Berakot* III.3, 6b, and Ginzberg, *op. cit.*, II, 133. Daughters are in this halakic statement excluded from study of Torah, but *Nedarim* IV.3 speaks of teaching "his sons and daughters Scripture"; compare also *Soṭah* III.4 and the controversy there. See also *Tosefot Yom Ṭob* on *Nedarim* IV.3. The Mishnah, ed. W. H. Lowe (Cambridge, 1883), p. 86a (Yerushalmi) does not read "and daughters."

138. *Yer. Berakot* I.5, 3b, and Ginzberg, *op. cit.*, I, 136 f., *s.v.* וזהו שינון: because he is at the same time engaged in the study of Torah, he need not interrupt that study for Ḳeri'at Shema', which is also study of Torah.

139. *Yer. Berakot* III.3, 6b, and Ginzberg, *op. cit.*, II, 178.

140. See below, p. 90.

141. *OT*, pp. 192 ff., where a theory in explanation of this phenomenon is developed.

142. See above, pp. 68, 76.

143. *RM*, pp. 73 f.: the instances of the Exodus from Egypt and the crossing of the Red Sea.

144. *OT*, p. 197, the instances of Israel and Torah and prophecy among the Gentiles; see also the instances of Israel and Torah in *TE*, p. 25.

145. *Berakot* I.1. The statement in this mishnah refers to all priests (see Albeck's remarks in his *Commentary on Berakot*, p. 13 and p. 325 f.).

146. *Berakot* I.2.

147. *Yer. Berakot* I.8, 3c. The third passage (Num. 15:37–41) was not read at night even in the time of the Amoraim (see Lieberman, *Tos. Kif.* I, 12, *s.v.* מזכירין).

148. Ginzberg, *Commentary*, I, 162 (top).

149. *Yer. Berakot* I.8, 3c.

150. Ginzberg, *op. cit.*, I, 73 and cf. p. 63. Workingmen started their work at dawn.

151. *Tos. Berakot* I.2, ed. Lieberman, pp. 1 f., and *idem*, *Tos. Kif.*, I, 3. Besides the parallels, see the references there; *Yer. Berakot* II.3, 4c top and I.1, 2d bottom; see also Ginzberg's remarks referred to there (*Commentary*, I, 119).

152. See above, p. 84, and the note there.

153. *Sifre* to Deut. 11:13, ed. Friedmann, p. 80a. See also *Bereshit R.* XVI.5, ed. Theodor, p. 149, and the notes there.

154. On the term 'abodah as worship, see below, p. 124.

155. *Pesiḳta de R. Kahana*, ed. S. Buber (Lyck, 1868), p. 107a.

156. *Sifre Deut.*, ed. Friedmann, p. 87a, and the references there.

157. *Ibid.*, p. 74a, and the note there. A slightly different version is found in *Pesiḳta de R. Kahana*, ed. Buber, p. 102a, where the verse interpreted is Deut. 26:16 ("This day," etc.). The word for edict there is פרוזדוגמא.

158. *RM*, pp. 348 ff.

159. The call is "Hear, O Israel," and the response (the testimony) is "The Lord, our God, the Lord is One." The verse is taken as call and response in *Sifre Deut.*, ed. Friedmann, p. 72b (and see *Debarim R.*, ed. S. Lieberman [Jerusalem, 1940], p. 67, and the references in n. 4 there), the response of Jacob's sons; and again in *Deut. R.* II.22, the response of Israel to God (see above, n. 117).

160. *Lev. R.* XXVII.6, ed. M. Margulies (Jerusalem, 1956), p. 633, and the references there. See Margulies' n. 2 there, in which he rightly takes this "testifying" as referring to "Ḳeri'at Shema' which is testimony to *malkut Shamayim*." The latter part, "but if you do not," etc., is clearer in the version in *Tanḥuma*, *'Emor*, 10, and we adopted that version here.

161. *Ibid.*, p. 637, and see the notes there.

162. *Seder R. Amram Gaon*, ed. Frumkin, I (ירושלים, תרע"ב), 105a. In this edition the words דלא מטרח עלן follow here, but they are not found in the Sulzberger MS, which Marx described as the best of all the MSS of the Seder (see D. Hedegard, *Seder Amram Gaon* [Motala, 1951], p. 26 [Hebrew] and p. xxi). Moreover, those words are also not found in this quotation from the Seder given in *Ṭur 'Oraḥ Ḥayyim*, par. 61 (beginning). They were added by a copyist who attempted to explain thereby what the edict consisted of.

163. For Finkelstein's view of Ḳeri'at Shema', see his article, "The Word פרס," *Jewish Quarterly Review*, XXXII, No. 4, 378 ff., and the subsequent article quoted above, n. 107.

164. *Sifre* to Deut. 32:29, ed. M. Friedmann (Vienna, 1864), p. 138b. For שמי read שמים. In the proof-text (Deut. 32:29), the rabbis take זאת to refer to the Torah, as they do elsewhere, e.g., *Pesiḳta R.*, ed. Friedmann, 191b, where the warrant for taking the word to refer to Torah is Deut. 4:44, and so also in the examples given by Theodor, *Bereshit R.*, p. 57, bottom.

165. *Seder Eliahu*, ed. Friedmann, p. 97, and *TE*, p. 61, n. 153.

166. See above, pp. 79 f.

167. *Seder Eliahu*, ed. Friedmann, p. 132, and *TE*, p. 60, n. 151, and notice also the version in the *Yalkuṭ*, cited by Friedmann, *loc. cit.*, n. 13. Cf. also *Lev. R.* XXXIII.6, ed. Margulies, p. 770, and the reference there.

168. See above, p. 82.

169. *Daily Prayer Book*, ed. and trans. S. Singer (London, 1890), p. 39; Baer, *op. cit.*, p. 80.

170. *Siddur R. Saadia Gaon*, pp. 13 f.: ותלמדנו חקי חיים כן תחננו. See the note there, p. 13, on אהבת עולם.

171. *Berakot* 11b.

172. *Ibid.*, *Yer.*, I.8, 3c.

173. I. Elbogen, תולדות התפלה והעבודה בישראל (Jerusalem–Berlin, 1924), p. 20. Kol Bo has a similar view, and also connects the First and the Second Berakot of the Shema' in a way we can only regard as homiletical; see the quotation in the note in Baer, *loc. cit.*

174. *Daily Prayer Book*, ed. and trans. Singer, pp. 39 f.; Baer, *loc. cit.*

175. Singer, p. 96; Baer, *op. cit.*, p. 164; and so also, with a minor variation, in *Siddur R. Saadia Gaon*, p. 26.

176. On knowledge of Torah, and study itself, as gifts from God, see *OT*, pp. 45 f.

177. *Siddur R. Saadia Gaon*, p. 14; see also Singer, p. 40, and Baer, p. 81.

178. *RM*, pp. 343–346. Lieberman has pointed out in a private communication that: מודים אנחנו לך, פירושו מודים אנחנו בך, and he called attention to the many examples in J. N. Epstein, מבוא לנוסח המשנה (Jerusalem, 1948), pp. 1110–1119.

179. See *RM*, pp. 346 f., where we show that הודו here cannot mean "They gave thanks."

180. It is so regarded by L. Zunz, הדרשות בישראל (Hebrew translation) (Jerusalem, 1947), ed. C. Albeck, p. 180, and the reference in n. 45; and by Elbogen, *op. cit.*, pp. 20 f. See also L. Ginzberg, *Geonica*, I (New York, 1909), 128, n. 1, where he says, "It is hardly possible that the insertion of the *Geullah* could go back to the Talmudic time."

181. Baer, *op. cit.*, p. 75.

182. E. Garfiel, *The Service of the Heart* (New York, 1958), p. 154.

183. *Siddur R. Saadia Gaon*, *loc. cit.*

184. In *RM*, pp. 52 ff., we depict the ideas that are not represented by conceptual terms as "auxiliary ideas," and on pp. 56 f. there we give more examples of בחר as "love." When we come to discuss the Daily 'Amidah, we shall also indicate how it is possible for the berakah here to be apparently the culmination of a prayer, a petition. The pertinent paragraphs are below, pp. 110 f.

185. Ginzberg, *Commentary*, I, 171.

186. *Yer. Berakot* I.8, 3d; so also Rashi, with regard to the berakah after the Shema' (*Berakot* 46b, top).

187. *Tos. Berakot* I.9, ed. Lieberman, p. 3, and *idem*, *Tos. Kif.*, I, 10 f.

188. See *Berakot* 11b–12a. Compare *ibid.*, *Yer.*, I.8, 3c, and Ginzberg's discussion, *op. cit.*, I, 165, 168.

189. *Yer. Berakot* I.9, 3d. Cf. *Tos. Berakot* II.1, ed. Lieberman, p. 6, and *idem*, *Tos. Kif.*, *ad loc.*

190. Lieberman, *Tos. Kif.*, I, 14, *s.v.* מכת.

191. *Berakot* II.2, end and Lieberman, *Tos. Kif.*, I, 12, *s.v.* מזכירין, and also his reference to Ginzberg there.

192. On surrogates for the third section of the Shema' in the evening, see Ginzberg's view in *RM*, p. 359, n. 80. On the early date of the initial statement in the baraita, see below, next paragraph.

193. See Singer, *op. cit.*, pp. 43 f.; Baer, *op. cit.*, pp. 85 f.

194. See the references in the preceding note.

195. Ginzberg, *op. cit.*, I, 215.

196. *Ibid.*, I, 216, *s.v.* ר' אומר.

197. *Siddur R. Saadia Gaon*, p. 15; *Siddur R. Amram*, ed. Frumkin, I, 210; (Singer, *op. cit.*, p. 42; Baer, *op. cit.*, p. 84): אמת אלהי עולם מלכנו צור יעקב.

198. Singer, *op. cit.*, pp. 42 f.; Baer, *op. cit.*, p. 84.

199. *Siddur R. Saadia Gaon*, p. 16.

200. Singer, *op. cit.*, p. 99; Baer, *op. cit.*, p. 166; *Siddur R. Saadia Gaon*, p. 27.

201. *RM*, pp. 358 f.

202. *Ibid.*, pp. 360 f., and the notes there.

203. *Ibid.* D. Goldschmidt regards it as a baraita originally; see his סדר הגדה של פסח (Tel Aviv, 1947), p. 10.

204. It was only in geonic times that there was inserted in 'Emet we-Yaẓẓib a petition for a future redemption and this was done without the sanction of the Geonim; in fact, a geonic responsum declares explicitly that a petition here is out of place, since the berakah refers only to the Exodus. (See Ginzberg, *Geonica*, I, 128, and II, 89, 91. On p. 89 there, note especially Ginzberg's brief discussion on the various versions. In *Siddur R. Saadia Gaon*, p. 16, again, there is no petition.)

205. Singer, *op. cit.*, p. 37; Baer, *op. cit.*, p. 76. It is given in the Talmud: see *Berakot* 11b, top; the phrase "Who formest light," etc., is from Is. 45:7, except that "evil" there has been changed to "all things," since the latter is felt by the rabbis to be a more favorable term (לישנא מעליא).

206. Singer, *op. cit.*, p. 39; Baer, *op. cit.*, p. 79. This too is given in the Talmud; see *Berakot* 12a.

207. See the two preceding notes.

208. Singer, *op. cit.*, p. 37; Baer, *op. cit.*, p. 76; and see *Ḥagigah* 12b. On מעשה בראשית, here rendered (though not adequately) as "the Creation," see *RM*, pp. 35 f., and n. 4 on p. 36.

209. Singer, *loc. cit.*; Baer, *loc. cit.* Finkelstein regards this berakah and others of a similar universalistic nature as having been ordained by the Men of the Great Synagogue (and hence pre-tannaitic); see his הפרושים ואנשי כנסת הגדולה (New York, 1950), p. 72; see also p. 56 and the notes there.

210. See above, p. 85.

211. See above, p. 92.

212. *Ibid.* and Ginzberg, *Commentary*, I, 191.

213. Singer, *op. cit.*, p. 39; Baer, *op. cit.*, p. 79.

214. *Siddur R. Saadia Gaon*, p. 37 and n. 6 there.

215. He has a petition for the future redemption in 'Ahabah Rabbah (*ibid.*, p. 14).

216. See above, p. 90, and n. 180; and p. 261, n. 204.

217. L. Ginzberg, *Geonica*, I, 128.

218. See *Siddur R. Saadia Gaon*, pp. 36 f. R. Sherira Gaon, who disagrees with Saadia's view, finds Saadia inconsistent here (see אוצר הגאונים, ed. B. Lewin, I [Haifa, 1928], Part I, 33).

219. *Siddur R. Saadia Gaon*, p. 13, and the note there.

Notes to Chapter V

1. The successive order of the Eighteen Berakot was established in the time of R. Gamaliel of Jabne: see the baraita in *Berakot* 28b and *Megillah* 17b, and see *Berakot* IV.3. See also L. Ginzberg, *A Commentary on the Palestinian Talmud* (New York, 1941), I, 322; III, 277. We shall soon discuss the implications of the baraita.

2. *Tos. Berakot* III.25, ed. S. Lieberman (New York, 1955), pp. 17 f., and the parallels and references there, and see S. Lieberman, *Tosefta Ki-Fshuṭah* (New York, 1955), I, 53–55. See also Ginzberg, *op. cit.*, I, 335, 337; III, 277–279.

3. *Yer. Berakot* II.4, 4d; cf. *Berakot* 34a.

4. It is so designated, for example, in the reference in the preceding note. Actually, two of the last three berakot, although characterized as "praise," contain petitions like the middle berakot.

5. *Ibid.*, *Yer.*, IV.1, 7a. Cf. *Sifre* to Deut. 3:23, ed. M. Friedmann (Vienna, 1864), p. 70b. The latter reference indicates that, while tefillah in a technical sense refers to the 'Amidah, its basic meaning is petition, that is, prayer in the sense of petition. It is used in that sense elsewhere also, for example, in *Berakot* IX.3–4.

6. See *Tos. Rosh ha-Shanah* II (IV).17, ed. S. Lieberman (New York, 1962), 320 f., and see also S. Lieberman, *Tosefta Ki-Fshuṭah*, V (New York, 1962), 1062.

7. L. Finkelstein, "The Development of the Amidah," *Jewish Quarterly Review*, N.S., XVI, No. 1, 38–41. See the entire article in that volume, pp. 1–43, and in *ibid.*, No. 2, pp. 127–170, for a detailed and suggestive treatment of the history and text of the 'Amidah. On the text of the berakot, see also J. Elbogen, תולדות התפלה והעבודה בישראל (Jerusalem and Berlin, 1924), pp. 34 ff.

8. *Berakot* 33a; cf. *Yer. Berakot* II.4, 4d, and Ginzberg, *op. cit.*, I, 327 f.; and see also Finkelstein, *op. cit.*, pp. 2 ff.

9. See the references above, n. 1.

10. Ginzberg, *op. cit.*, I, 322.

11. Lieberman, *Tos. Kif.*, I, 53. This conclusion is based on a statement in *Megillah* 18a.

12. On the conceptual continuum and on the form, see above, pp. 71 f. (Birkat ha-Mazon); 95 f. (berakot of the Shema').

13. S. Baer, *Seder 'Abodat Yisra'el* (Roedelheim, 1868), pp. 87 f., and the notes there on p. 88; S. Singer, *The Daily Prayer Book* (London, 1890), p. 44. What we have just quoted of the First Berakah lacks but a few words in order to be the original form of that berakah; we need only complete the phrase "the most high God" with "Maker of heaven and earth," so that the whole phrase from Gen. 14:19 precedes the closing formula (see Ginzberg, *op. cit.*, IV, pp. 177, 182 f. See also *ibid.*, pp. 179 f., as to the very early date of this berakah).

14. *Rosh ha-Shanah* IV.5. The Second Berakah is designated there Geburot, and the third, Ḳedushat ha-Shem.

15. See above, p. 71 f., for a detailed discussion of this form.

16. Above, pp. 76 f., 77 f.

17. On the text of these berakot, see Elbogen, *op. cit.*, p. 38; Singer, *op. cit.*, p. 46.

18. On the name, see above, n. 14.

19. *Sifre Deut.*, par. 343, ed. Friedmann, 142b.

20. See Elbogen, *op. cit.*, p. 37, and the references there.

21. קדוש אתה ונורא שמך ואין אלה מבלעדיך; see Finkelstein, "La Kedouscha et les Bénédictions du Schema," (Paris 1932, offprint from *Revue des Études Juives*), pp. 3 f., and the notes there.

22. These matters are taken up in the next chapter.

23. Baer, *op. cit.*, p. 386. He refers in the notes to *Pirḳe de R. Eliezer*, XXXV, end, where the verse is incorporated with the berakah. Ginzberg, *op. cit.*, III, pp. 21 f. gives this among a number of Palestinian practices which are followed now only during the period of New Year and the Day of Atonement, although they were practiced in Palestine originally in the course of the entire year.

24. *Berakot* 12b—R. Eleazar.

25. *Pirḳe R. Eliezer*, *loc. cit.*, and Luria, *ad loc.*; and see *Targ. Jonathan* to this verse; *Tanḥuma*, *Ḳedoshim*, par. 1, end; *Debarim R.* V.6.

26. M. Kadushin, *The Rabbinic Mind* (New York, 1952), pp. 40 f. (to be referred to hereafter as *RM*).

27. Ginzberg, *op. cit.*, IV, 200, says that in Yannai's *Ḳerobot* for New Year the content of the Third Berakah is צדקה ומשפט, and that it closes with תוגבה במשפט ותוקדש בצדקה, this line referring, as he points out, to Is. 5:16: "And the Lord of Hosts is exalted in judgment, and the holy God is sanctified in *ẓedaḳah*."

We find that the lines just preceding the one quoted by Ginzberg read as follows (*Maḥzor Yannai*, ed. I. Davidson [New York, 1919], p. 30):

מכון כסאך שתה חסד וצדקה
חלילה לך מעשות משפט בלי צדקה.

Yannai thus takes *ẓedaḳah* to be lovingkindness and charity and, accordingly, he interprets the proof-text in the Third Berakah as declaring that God is made holy, sanctified, in His charity at judgment. See also Ginzberg, *op. cit.*, IV, p. 239, and the *piyyuṭ* he quotes there.

28. Finkelstein, *loc. cit.*

29. On the Ḳedushah, see below, p. 142 ff., where we also deal with the problem of the introductory phrase.

30. We had an instance above, p. 77, of a deviation from the conceptual pattern, a deviation also overcome by the cumulative effect of the preceding berakot.

Ginzberg's theory in the fourth, and posthumous, volume of his *Commentary*—which appeared after our discussion on the Third Berakah had been written—may be summarized as follows: While it is true that the version of קדוש אתה found in the Sifre is Palestinian and is the oldest version (p. 196), it was probably only the Galilean practice (p. 172); the version of אתה קדוש, which is the Diaspora version, was originally, however, a Judean practice, and hence was probably the original version (pp. 172, 196 f.); the version of לדור ודור is geonic and was originally said only by the leader in the Tefillah (pp. 175 f., 197, 201 f., 203). This brief summary does not do justice, of course, to the many points of interest in Ginzberg's treatment; see pp. 196 ff.

31. See Ginzberg, *op. cit.*, III, 280 f., and the sources referred to there.

32. See Ginzberg, *op. cit.*, I, 324; III, 280 f.

33. Baer, *op. cit.*, p. 386, and the notes.

34. *Ibid.*; Singer, *op. cit.*, p. 239. In the same prayer, earlier: "May all creatures prostrate themselves before Thee, and may all of them form a single band to do Thy will with a perfect heart."

35. See the text of this berakah in Finkelstein, "The Development of the Amidah," *ibid.*, No. 2, p. 156. On *minim*, see the discussion in G. Alon, תולדות היהודים בארץ ישראל בתקופת המשנה והתלמוד (Tel Aviv, 1952), I, 180 ff.

36. Alon, *op. cit.*, pp. 191 f.

37. Lieberman, *op. cit.*, I, p. 54. There can be no doubt that the berakah so amended was the Twelfth Berakah, although in *Tos. Berakot* III.25 it is referred to as the one "on the separatists" (פרושין—see Lieberman, *loc. cit.*, and his reference to Finkelstein). That only means that the Twelfth Berakah had already been amended before to include mention of "separatists." See also I. Davidson, אוצר השירה והפיוט, II, 192 f.

38. Ginzberg, *op. cit.*, III, 284.

39. *Ibid.*, pp. 284 f.

40. *Ibid.*, pp. 249 f.

41. *Yer. Berakot* V.3, 9c—אני אומר מין הוא. This halakah constitutes a confirmation of the point made above, p. 98, regarding the number or limit of the berakot in a conceptual continuum. The leader is not ordinarily made to go back, for each berakah is a unitary entity in itself (but see Ginzberg, *op. cit.*, IV, 276). The Second Berakah, according to Ginzberg, originally did not contain the dogma of *teḥiyyat ha-metim*, resurrection. In *Rosh ha-Shanah* IV.5 this berakah is designated as Geburot, which is another form for Nissim (*ibid.*, p. 155). The berakah was thus not established originally because of the sectarians who denied the doctrine of resurrection; only in the course of time did the berakah of Geburot become that of *teḥiyyat ha-metim* (*ibid.*, pp. 164, 184). Originally, Geburot had but one theme, namely, God's *geburot* in saving Israel from their enemies; late in the period of the Second Temple, both the *geburot* of rain and of resurrection were added, the latter because of the aforementioned sectarians (*ibid.*). When these additions were made, the closing formula was changed to "Who quickenest the dead" (*ibid.*, pp. 167, 190). In the berakah itself all references to resurrection are post-talmudic except the one in the phrase "[Thou] sustainest the living with lovingkindness [and] quickenest the dead" (*ibid.*, pp. 187, 193). Other expressions there are likewise additions (*ibid.*, pp. 165, 184 f., 187, 188, 196).

42. Above, pp. 74 f. and the notes there.

43. *Berakot* 29a, and see *Diḳduke Soferim, ad loc.* We have stated the halakah in accordance with the rendering in *Ṭur 'Oraḥ Ḥayyim*, par. 126 (beginning).

44. *Tanḥuma, Wayyiḳra'*, par. 2; *ibid.*, ed. S. Buber (Wilna, 1885), III, 2a.

45. *Ibid.*—שאם יהא בו צד מינות.

46. *Ibid.* A *Kuti*, Samaritan, is not a *goy* (see *RM*, p. 41, and the note there).

47. M. Higger, *Seven Minor Treatises* (New York, 1930), Introduction, p. 6 (with a reference to Ginzberg, *Geonica* (New York, 1909), I, p. 73, n. 1), and p. 7 (Hebrew).

48. "Masseket Kutim," Chap. II, Higger, *op. cit.*, p. 67. See also Abraham Geiger, המקרא ותרגומיו (Hebrew) (Jerusalem, 1949), p. 85, n. 1.

49. On the doctrine of the resurrection in the Samaritan liturgy, see A. Cowley in *Jewish Encyclopedia*, X, 674a, bottom.

50. Some of the Church Fathers (Justin, Epiphanius, and Jerome) declare that three times a day, at their prayers in their synagogues, the Jews curse Jesus and the Christians (cf. H. Graetz, *Geschichte der Juden* [Leipzig, 1866], IV, 434 f.). This may refer to the Twelfth Berakah, but such a view could not have been transmitted by those who knew the berakah well, the learned.

51. See *Ṭur 'Oraḥ Ḥayyim*, par. 126, who, however, also quotes and interprets the halakah of the Yerushalmi, a quotation to which *Bet Joseph* objects because it disagrees with the Babylonian halakah. *Bet Joseph*, too, paraphrases the pupils of R. Jonah who designate the Twelfth Berakah as a denunciation and thereby distinguish between that berakah and the Second. The view of the codists is probably reflected in a late MS of the Yelammedenu passage as given in *Tanḥuma*, ed. Buber, *loc. cit.*, which contains the phrase ברכת קללת המינין—see n. 22 there. A number of scholars hold the view that the Twelfth Berakah, as formulated in the time of R. Gamaliel at Jabne (see above, p. 101 f.) was a new berakah and was not merely edited but composed at that time. Among them are Elbogen (*op. cit.*, pp. 31 f.), and Albeck (in Zunz, הדרשות בישראל (Jerusalem, 1947), pp. 480 f. n. 35).

52. Above, p. 97 and n. 5.

53. *Tos. Berakot* III.6, ed. Lieberman, p. 13, and the parallels and references there; and see Lieberman, *Tos. Kif.*, I, 30 f. I Kings 8:28 begins with ופנית אל תפלת עבדך, a phrase which is amplified, according to this interpretation, in the words: לשמע אל הרנה ואל התפלה. *Rinnah* is interpreted as *tehillah* by comparison with Ps. 33:1.

54. *Tos. Baba Ḳamma'* IX.29, ed. M. S. Zuckermandel and S. Lieberman (2nd ed; Jerusalem, 1937), p. 365; *Berakot* 34b; *Shabbat* 67a; *ibid.*, 151b; *Baba Batra* 91b; *Deut. R.* VII.11; and *passim*.

55. *Berakot* 12b.

56. *Berakot* 20b; *ibid.*, 26a; *Soṭah* 33a.

57. In explaining the halakah on the Tefillah in *Berakot* III.3, the Yerushalmi says, "In order that each and every one should beseech compassion for himself," while the Babli (*Berakot* 20b) merely says, "For it is *raḥame*," and, as Ginzberg has pointed out (*Commentary*, II, 151 f.), both are saying the same thing. Ginzberg also shows (*ibid.*, III, 149 f.) that Rashi deleted from the explanation in *Berakot* 20b all but the words "for it is [or, they are] *raḥame*" in accordance with his opinion that the Tefillah is a rabbinical ordinance.

58. Above, p. 97 and n. 1.

59. *Pesaḥim* 117b, and Rashbam, *ad loc.* Raba's statement there, preceding that of R. Ze'ira, is not a clear instance, for the Palestinian version has ונגואלו, and therefore implies a present experience (see above, p. 93). For the Ḳiddush, see Baer, *op. cit.*, p. 198, and for the Tefillah, see *ibid.*, p. 188.

60. יהי רצון מלפניך ד׳ אלהי; *Tos. Berakot* VI (VII).16, ed. Lieberman, pp. 37 f., and the parallels cited there. On "town" (כרך), see Albeck's remarks in his edition of *Seder Nashim* (Jerusalem and Tel Aviv, 1955), p. 356.

61. מודה אני לפניך; *Tos. Berakot, loc. cit.*

62. *Ibid.*

63. *Ibid.*, VI (VII).17, ed. Lieberman, p. 38, and the parallels.

64. See Lieberman, *Tos. Kif.*, I, 118, *s.v.* מתפלל, and p. 119, *s.v.* מברך. We take it that *mitpallel* is used because of the tefillah, petition, ordained by the halakah, and that *mebarek* is used because of the berakah ordained by the same halakah.

65. *Yer. Berakot* II.2, 4d.

66. Ginzberg, *op. cit.*, III, 356 f. He cites *Tos. Berakot* III.6 (ed. Lieberman, p. 13); the baraita in *Berakot* 31a (see Rashi, *ad loc.*, *s.v.* יכול ישאל); the baraita having one version in *'Abodah Zarah* 7b and another in *Yer. Berakot* IV.4, 8b, the versions containing different halakot. On the baraita in the Tosefta, see Lieberman, *Tos. Kif.*, I, 30 f.

67. *Megillah* 17b.

68. *RM*, pp. 150 f.

69. On this berakah as referring to man, see below, p. 111 f.

70. *Berakot* V.2.

71. *Ta'anit* 14b, ed. Malter (ed. minor; Philadelphia, 1928), pp. 97 f. The rendering is Malter's. See also Elbogen, *op. cit.*, p. 39.

72. Outside of the 'Amidah, this description holds also for practically all the prayers culminating in berakot which have Israel as the "others." An instance is the prayer-meditation in 'Ahabah Rabbah, which is discussed above, pp. 89 ff.

73. The ascription is of Babylonian origin, but is very early—see Ginzberg, *op. cit.*, III, p. 346; cf. Elbogen, *op. cit.*, pp. 37 f.

74. See *Seder Eliahu*, ed. M. Friedmann (Vienna, 1900), p. 70: "Were wisdom, understanding, knowledge and discernment taken away from them [men], they would be accounted as the cattle or beasts or birds." Notice that the identical words of the berakah, "wisdom, understanding," etc., are here, as it were, commented on. On "wisdom" in this berakah, see Elbogen, *loc. cit.*

75. The phrase חונן הדעת is in *Berakot* V.2.

76. Baer, *op. cit.*, p. 90, and the notes, and see also Elbogen, *op. cit.*, p. 38. On the basis of *Yer. Berakot* II.4, 4d, Ginzberg suggests that the ancient form was: "Accept our repentance (רצה בתשובתנו), and 'Turn Thou us unto Thee, O Lord, and we shall be turned; renew our days as of old' [Lam. 5:21]" (*op. cit.*, I, 324 f.). In this ancient version, too, "us" refers to Israel.

77. Elbogen, *loc. cit.* On "Who accepts" for הרוצה, see in the version of the petition given in the preceding note.

78. The repentance of the "men of Nineveh" is spoken of in *Ta'anit* II.1 as the classic example of what repentance should consist in: "Of the men of Nineveh it is not said:

And God saw their sackcloth and their fasting, but [Jonah 3:10]: 'And God saw their works, that they turned from their evil way.' " Elsewhere the rabbis speak of the equal acceptance by God of all who repent, "whether among Israel or among the nations," as a *middah*, rule (see M. Kadushin, *The Theology of Seder Eliahu* [New York, 1932]), p. 125. "Blessed art Thou, O Lord, Who hearkenest unto prayer" of the Sixteenth Berakah also refers, obviously, to man, and this point is stressed in the petition of the berakah as found in *Seder R. Amram*—see Elbogen, *op. cit.*, p. 44.

79. See the notes and references in Baer, *op. cit.*, p. 103; Elbogen, *op. cit.*, p. 48; Ginzberg, *op. cit.*, III, 250.

80. Elbogen, *loc. cit.*

81. "Unto us" (עלינו) in the first part of the petition refers to Israel, and *Siddur R. Saadia Gaon*, ed. I. Davidson and others (Jerusalem, 1941), p. 19, does not have there any other reference to Israel.

82. Ginzberg, *op. cit.*, III, 250, and the reference there; cf. *ibid.*, I, 323.

83. Elbogen, *op. cit.*, p. 39.

84. Above, pp. 67 f.

85. *RM*, pp. 150 f., where this matter is discussed; cf. *OT*, p. 137. The word *'adam* in rabbinic thought is solely a conceptual term, so much so that Adam himself is not designated as Adam by the rabbis but as "The First *'adam* [man]"—אדם הראשון. See, e.g., *Gen. R.* VIII.1, 4, 5, 15.

86. *Leviticus R.* II.8, ed. M. Margulies (Jerusalem, 1953), p. 46, and the notes there.

87. *Ibid.* Up to this point the connotations, drawn forth in this midrash refer to "the son of man," and from this point on to "the son of Buzi" (Ezek. 1:3) (see Margulies, *ibid.*, note).

88. There is no berakah in the entire 'Amidah which does not present an instance of the organismic integration of concepts. Attention has been called above (p. 84) to examples elsewhere.

89. Above, pp. 101 ff.

90. See especially *ibid.*, pp. 102 f.

91. Originally the petition here consisted solely of "Restore our judges as at first and our counsellors as at the beginning"; that is the text in *Siddur Saadia*, p. 18, which does not have the later additions. This berakah was formulated when the Sadducees controlled the Sanhedrin. On all this, see Ginzberg, *op. cit.*, III, 326 f.

92. On this berakah, see above, p. 97, and the references in n. 2 there.

93. This berakah had its origin in the Temple service, and the references to the restoration of the Service were added after the Destruction (see Finkelstein, "The Development of the Amidah," *Jewish Quarterly Review*, N.S., XVI, No. 1, pp. 38 ff., and Elbogen, *op. cit.*, pp. 44 f.). Originally, as can be seen from the material cited by Elbogen and Finkelstein, the closing formula of this berakah read: שאותך ביראה נעבוד; and this reading, in contrast to the present version, indicates how the early rabbis refrained from using the concept of *gilluy Shekinah* when it came to actual religious experience (see *RM*, pp. 235, 238 ff.).

94. The Second Berakah refers not to Israel alone but also to the righteous among the Gentiles (see G. F. Moore, *Judaism in the First Centuries of The Christian Era* [Cambridge, 1927], II, 386 [corrected in *ibid.*, III (Cambridge, 1930), 205] where R. Joshua and the halakah as formulated by Maimonides are cited).

95. Above, pp. 73 ff.

96. Above, pp. 75 f.

97. On this, see above, p. 75, and especially the notes there. *'Emunah*, as we said there, does not mean belief in the existence of God. That meaning is not rabbinic but was given the word in medieval philosophy.

98. Above, p. 93 f.

99. On the dogma of *mattan Torah*, see *RM*, pp. 348 ff., especially p. 351; on the berakot, see below, p. 140. See also the discussion above, p. 86.

100. Above, p. 94.

101. *RM*, p. 351.

102. They were indeed felt to be imminent, yet no more than that. R. Joshua b. Levi, in positing a logical order for the berakot in the 'Amidah, declares that the successive order of "the middle berakot" from the Seventh Berakah onward is due to the way these "needs" will be successively fulfilled in the future, from the redemption and onward (see *Yer. Berakot* II.4, 4d, and in Ginzberg, *op. cit.*, I, pp. 322–324, 326 f.). Similarly, the Babli accounts for the position of the Ninth Berakah by referring it to the future and linking it with "the Ingathering of the Exiles." (See *Megillah* 17b and Ginzberg's stricture, *ibid.*, p. 323. On the textual problems of the similar statement in the Yerushalmi, see *ibid.*, pp. 333 f.)

103. A good example is the First Berakah on the Torah which reads: "Who hast chosen us from all peoples and hast given us Thy Torah," with both verbs here in the past tense, and which closes with: "Who givest the Torah," in the present tense. (On the idea of "chosen" in this berakah, see below, p. 140.) For an example of implication of the present, see below, p. 117.

104. *Tos. Berakot* III.25, ed. Lieberman, p. 18, and *Tos. Kif.*, I, 54. He takes the term פליטת סופריהם to be among the early terms.

105. *Yer. Berakot* II.4, 5a; *ibid.*, IV.3, 8a, and the other parallels in *Tos. Berakot*, ed. Lieberman, p. 17.

106. That *ẓaddiḳim* is the major theme is also apparent from *Megillah* 17b and Yer. *Berakot* II.4, 5a.

107. *Siddur R. Saadia Gaon*, p. 18; cf. Singer, *op. cit.*, p. 48.

108. See Baer, *op. cit.*, p. 95, for explanations of these terms.

109. *RM*, pp. 39 f., and the notes there.

110. Elbogen, *op. cit.*, pp. 41 f.

111. *RM*, p. 43.

112. Above, p. 98.

113. See the statement of R. Simeon b. Laḳish in *Pesaḥim* 117b.

114. Cf. Ginzberg, *Commentary*, IV, 121.

115. Elbogen, *op. cit.*, p. 35. According to Ginzberg, the phrase was added—*ibid.*, p. 183.

116. As the context indicates, this word refers not to salvation but to safety, security, in the present.

117. See Elbogen, *loc. cit.* (Incidentally, the statement in Tosafot to *Berakot* 49a referred to by Elbogen here in n. 37 means that since the Shemoneh Esreh does not have a "kingship" formula, all the berakot in the series go back, "are joined," to

the First Berakah in the evening service, אל חי וקים, which does begin with the formula; the statement does not mean that the Berakah of 'Abot closed with those words, as Elbogen would have it. Tosafot goes on to say that "God of Abraham" is equivalent to the "kingship" formula.) (On this section as not being integral to the berakah, see also Ginzberg, *ibid.*, pp. 184, 192.)

118. *Berakot* IV.4 and *Tos. Berakot* III.7, ed. Lieberman, pp. 13 f., and the parallels there.

119. Mishnah *Berakot*, *loc. cit.* See Lieberman's remarks on the Palestinian texts of this petition (*Tos. Kif.*, I, p. 33).

120. *Tos. Berakot*, *loc. cit.*

121. *Ibid.* On this and the preceding reference, see Lieberman, *loc. cit.*, *s.v.* אי' זה, who points out that the Tannaim in the Tosefta, as against R. Joshua in the Mishnah, hold that the short Tefillah consists of only a single berakah. R. Eliezer's petition is different in tone from the others, but there, too, ליריאיך refers to Israel. We did not cite the petition of R. Eleazar, the son of R. Zadoḳ, because it is similar to that of "Hearken", etc.

122. *Berakot* 30a; cited by Lieberman, *loc. cit.* Rashi, *ad loc.*, explains that this refers to the use of the plural in saying the short Tefillah, but adds that the prayer is thereby made more efficacious.

123. On the leader reciting the Tefillah, see below, p. 143.

124. *Berakot* IV.3.

125. Ginzberg, *op. cit.*, III, 237 f.

126. Tosafot to *Berakot* 16a, *s.v.* אפילו.

127. *Berakot* 29a; *ibid.*, *Yer.*, IV.3, 8a; and Lieberman, *op. cit.*, I, 32 f. See also Ginzberg, *op. cit.*, III, 315 ff.

128. Lieberman, *op. cit.*, I, 31 f., and the notes there. R. Eliezer's statement, he points out, properly belongs at the end of *Berakot* IV.3, as it is in the Yerushalmi edition (Venice, 1523), and it has been placed deliberately after R. 'Aḳiba's opinion so as to indicate R. Eliezer's meaning. See also his reference to Ginzberg in n. 13 there.

129. *Berakot* IV.4, but see the preceding note—העושה תפלתו קבע אין תפלתו תחנונים.

130. See Lieberman, *loc. cit.*, on this and on the rest of this paragraph.

131. Above, p. 118, n. 121, and the source there; but cf. Ginzberg, *op. cit.*, III, 354.

132. Notice that R. Eliezer employs, in his short Tefillah, the closing formula of the Sixteenth Berakah; see *Tos. Berakot* III.7.

133. *Tos. Berakot* III.6, ed. Lieberman, p. 13, and the references there.

134. Lieberman, *Tos. Kif.*, I, 31.

135. *'Abodah Zarah* 7b–8a; cf. *ibid.*, *Yer.*, IV.4, 8b. Ginzberg suggests that this halakah is of Babylonian origin (*op. cit.*, III, 360).

136. *'Abodah Zarah* 8a, and Rashi, *ibid.*, *s.v.* מעין כל ברכה.

137. Above, p. 117.

138. We saw in the last section that *biṭṭaḥon* as a meditative experience can also be the culmination of a prayer for security and welfare, and this is the case in the Thirteenth Berakah.

139. This is taken to mean until sunset by Maimonides, Hilkot *Tefillah* III.4.

140. *Berakot* IV.1. The evening Tefillah may be said at any time during the night: see Albeck's commentary on *Zera'im* (Jerusalem and Tel Aviv, 1957), *ad loc.*, and his supplementary note on p. 331; and see Lieberman, *Tos. Kif.*, I, 27, *s.v.* קבע. The morning Tefillah is to be said after dawn (see above, p. 85).

141. *Tos. Berakot* III.1, ed. Lieberman, p. 11. The basic difference between the *Ḥakamim* and R. Judah with respect to the time is in regard to the daily communal sacrifices, and the matter of the time of the Tefillah is but the result of that difference; *idem*, *Tos. Kif.*, I, p. 27, *s.v.* עד פלג.

142. *Yer. Berakot* IV.1, 7b, and Ginzberg, *op. cit.*, III, 30 f.; and see above, n. 140.

143. *Yer. Berakot*, *ibid*; *Bereshit R.* LXVIII.9, ed. J. Theodor and C. Albeck (Berlin, 1927), p. 780; cf. *Berakot* 26b.

144. *Berakot* 27b, and the pupils of R. Jonah, *ad loc.* No *ḳeba'*, as the latter interpret it, refers here to both ideas: to the idea that the Tefillah in the evening is not a matter of fixed duty and to the idea that it is not fixed as to time.

145. See above, n. 141.

146. According to Ginzberg, the opinion that the evening Tefillah was an optional matter was based on custom, for only individuals said it during the Temple days and it was not the common practice at that time (*op. cit.*, III, 170). With regard to the later practice, see *ibid.*, pp. 172 f. On the early practice, see also G. Alon, מחקרים, I (Tel Aviv, 1957), 285.

147. Above, pp. 69 f.

148. Above, p. 94.

149. *Tanḥuma*, *Ḥayye Sarah*, 5. ובמנחה should read ובערבית: see Ginzberg, *op. cit.*, III, 22, and his remarks there. The text in the *Tanḥuma* is the original statement.

150. The Nineteenth Berakah was the same for all the periods of the day until the Middle Ages (see Elbogen, *op. cit.*, p. 48).

151. Above, p. 97. At the offering of the morning sacrifice the priests said a berakah before the 'Abodah and that apparently constituted the one berakah of the Tefillah which they said in the morning (see Ginzberg, *op. cit.*, III, 28, and the note there; cf. Finkelstein (above, p. 267, n. 93).

152. The Musaf on the Sabbath and festivals, too, is a reminder despite its name. The pattern of the Tefillah remains the same, including the First Berakah, and the Musaf sacrifice is mentioned only in the Fourth Berakah, and even so only in the petition. Indeed, Ginzberg (*op. cit.*, III, 434 f.) says it is likely that in the days of the Mishnah, and in Palestine in the amoraic period as well, there was no difference between the Musaf and the other Tefillot, and that the recital of ומפני חטאינו is a Babylonian practice. He inclines to the opinion that in the Temple period there was no separate Musaf Tefillah, but that on days when there was a Musaf sacrifice, some mention of it was added in the single morning Tefillah (*ibid.*, pp. 28 f.).

153. *Berakot* 26b. In the parallel in *ibid.*, *Yer.*, IV.1, 7b, the authority is *Rabbanan* and not an individual, and instead of "ordained as against," the reading is, "They learned the Tefillot from the daily communal sacrifices—The Tefillah of the morning from the sacrifice of the morning," etc. But here, too, the association is only that of the time, for the passage continues, "They did not find what to *attach* the evening Tefillah to," and then it quotes the Mishnah which states that this Tefillah had "no *ḳeba'*."

154. *Berakot, loc. cit.* The parallel in the Yerushalmi, *loc. cit.*, has here also, "They learned the Tefillot" from the Patriarchs, meaning, that those who ordained the Tefillot found support both as to the number and as to the time for the Tefillot in the examples of the Patriarchs (Ginzberg, *op. cit.*, III, 24 ff., 30). On the question of the "baraita," see *ibid.*, p. 25, n. 30, and also *RM*, p. 128.

155. *Berakot, loc. cit.*

156. See *Bereshit R.*, *loc. cit.*, ed. J. Theodor and C. Albeck, pp. 779–80, and the sources quoted in the notes there; and Ginzberg, *loc. cit.*

157. On the number and the time: *Tos. Berakot* III.6 and the parallels, ed. Lieberman, p. 12, and *Tos. Kif.*, I, 29–30 (Daniel); *Tanḥuma, loc. cit.* (the three changes in the position of the sun). On the berakot as being Eighteen in number: *Yer. Berakot* IV.3, 7d–8a, and Ginzberg, *ad loc.*, who also gives and compares the parallels. The association of the "Eighteen" with the building of the Tabernacle is not due to the daily sacrifice, however, as Ginzberg would have it (*op. cit.*, III, 289). The "Eighteen" are the Tefillah and the Tefillah is to be directed toward the Holy of Holies (the Tabernacle), as is explicitly stated in *Berakot* IV.5–6, and as Ginzberg himself emphasizes elsewhere (*ibid.*, p. 377).

158. See *Sanhedrin* 60b. The sacrificial worship in the Temple is עבודת פנים. See also *Mekhilta D'Rabbi Sim'on b. Jochai*, ed. J. N. Epstein and E. Z. Melamed (Jerusalem, 1955), p. 210, and the references there. On actions as "cancelling" an idol, see *RM*, pp. 196 f.

159. Above, p. 65, and the references in n. 16 there.

160. *Berakot* 53b.

161. R. Naḥman, *ibid.*, quotes a baraita as tantamount to the halakah and that baraita has been variously interpreted by the post-talmudic authorities. We have taken the interpretation implied by Tosafot, *ad loc.*, and given in the דרישה to *Ṭur 'Oraḥ Ḥayyim*, par. 181, and also given in Rashi as printed with Alfasi, *ad loc.*

162. Above, p. 122, and n. 144 there.

163. Above, p. 123. Our remarks here apply as well to the parallel cited in n. 153, above.

164. *Sifre* on Deut. 11:13, ed. M. Friedmann (Vienna, 1864), p. 80a. Moore (*Judaism*, II, pp. 217 f.) errs in taking this passage and a number of others to refer to prayer in general and in doing so obliterates the rabbinic distinction between *baḳḳashah*, petition or prayer in general, and 'abodah, worship. See also below, p. 272, n. 176.

165. *Yer. Berakot* IV.1, 7a, and see Ginzberg, *op. cit.*, III, p. 3. On the basis of our discussion here, the concluding statement in the Sifre is not an addition, and the Yerushalmi simply has a somewhat different version. See also the version in *Ta'anit* 2a, ed. H. Malter (ed. major; New York, 1930), p. 3, and the other parallels referred to there.

166. *Tanḥuma, Aḥare*, par. 9; *ibid.*, ed. S. Buber, par. 14, pp. 34b–35a. מקטר in Mal. 1:11 is related to the קטורת, incense, of the Minḥah of the evening. Proofs are Ps. 141:2 and I Kings 18:36. See Albeck's discussion in his note on p. 331 in his edition of *Zera'im*, *s.v.* ר׳ יהודה.

167. *Pesiḳta de Rab Kahana*, ed. S. Buber (Lyck, 1868), p. 165b—R. 'Abbahu.

168. *Pesiḳta Rabbati*, ed. Friedmann, p. 84a; *Pesiḳta de Rab Kahana*, ed. Buber, p. 61b; and the notes in both. Buber quotes from the 'Aruk a Yelammedenu variant in which Bet Shammai says that the daily sacrifices "press down" the sins "and *Yom Kippur* comes and atones." Cf. *Rosh ha-Shanah* 17a—R. Eliezer, and see R. Ḥananel, *ad loc.*

169. *Pesikta Rabbati*, ed. Friedmann, p. 84b, and the references and notes there; *Pesikta de R. Kahana, loc. cit.* R. Judan makes this statement in support of his midrash on Isa. 1:21 which teaches that no man passed the night in Jerusalem stained by a sin. צדק in the verse is taken as צדיק.

170. *Yer. Berakot* IV.1, 7b: שני פרקליטין ליום. In *Tanḥuma, Ẓaw*, par. 13, a similar idea is conveyed in the interpretation of עולה as "ascending ('*olah*) to the Holy One blessed be He and atoning for the iniquities of Israel."

171. Above, pp. 123 f. and the version in the note there. R. Joshua's statement is in general terms and hence includes the characterization of tefillah as 'abodah.

172. *Berakot* 26a.

173. *Tanḥuma*, end *Ḳoraḥ*; *Numbers R.* XVIII.17; see also *Tanḥuma, Wayyishlaḥ*, par. 9. Cf. *Exod. R.* XXXVIII.4.

174. Thus, in the case of Ḳeri'at Shema', given above (pp. 84 f.), the *content* embodies the various concepts. See the next note.

175. Here the characteristic is that of organismic thought in general (*OT*, pp. 197 f.).

176. Lieberman, *Tos. Kif.*, I, p. 30, and the source and note there. The petition is evidently an early Palestinian version of the petition in the Seventeenth Berakah, and is retained in the Musaf of the Ashkenazi rite at the Birkat Kohanim on the Three Festivals. Being a quotation from the Tefillah, this petition, therefore, is direct proof that the word מתפללין in these statements refers to the recitation of the Tefillah and not to prayer in general.

177. *Tanḥuma, Ki Tabo*, beginning; cf. *ibid.*, ed. Buber, V, 23a (see the preceding note).

178. *Berakot* 32b.

179. *Ibid.*, 26a.

180. Above, p. 83, and the note there.

181. Above, p. 86.

182. See the discussion above, p. 87.

183. Above, pp. 67 f.

184. Above, p. 65.

185. Above, p. 81.

186. Above, p. 257, n. 113.

187. *RM*, pp. 239 ff.

188. *Ibid.*, pp. 242 ff.

189. See the discussion below, p. 132.

190. The *Shekinah* dwelt in the Tabernacle and in the First Temple (*RM*, p. 226). Cf. also *ibid.*, p. 253, nn. 130 and 131.

Notes to Chapter VI

1. For example, *Yoma* I.7; *Zebaḥim* XIV.10. Notice that the *ẓibbur* stands in contradistinction to the individual.

2. L. Finkelstein, *The Pharisees* (2d ed.; Philadelphia, 1940), pp. 282 f., 682 f.

3. *Berakot* 7b–8a; *ibid.*, 27b.

4. In M. Kadushin, *The Rabbinic Mind* (New York, 1952; to be referred to hereafter as *RM*), pp. 151 f., we discussed another concept expressive of relation, the concept of *seder*, and found it to be a cognitive concept. Being a concept of relationship, the word *ẓibbur* does not refer only to "community." It is used in the sense of a heap or a pile: a pile of *ḥameẓ* (*Pesaḥim* 10a), and in the plural, for piles of fruit, piles of coins (*Baba Meẓ'ia* II.2). These usages indicate, once more, that *ẓibbur* is a cognitive term.

5. *RM*, p. 189.

6. *Temurah* 15b: אין הצבור מתים. See the commentaries. This is somewhat qualified in *Horayot* 6a.

7. See, for example, the way *ẓibbur* is used in *Soṭah* 39b.

8. *Ta'anit* IV.2; and see C. Albeck's comments in *Commentary to Mo'ed* (Jerusalem and Tel Aviv, 1952), p. 341, and especially his long note, *ibid.*, pp. 495 f. On the problem of מעמד, see also H. Malter's remarks in his edition of *Ta'anit* (ed. major; New York, 1930), p. 120.

9. *Sifre* on Numbers, *piska'* 142, ed. Horovitz (Leipzig, 1917), p. 188.

10. *Ta'anit* IV.2.

11. *Yer. Ta'anit* IV.2, 67d, where it is also stated that מוכיחין על עצמם שהן שלוחיהן של כל ישראל.

12. *Sanhedrin* 74a (baraita). See above, p. 25 and n. 25 there.

13. *Sanhedrin* 74b, and *Diḳduḳe Soferim ad loc.*; cf. *Sanhedrin* I.6. See also Maimonides, Hilkot *Tefillah*, VIII.5.

14. On how the acknowledgment of God is related to a sense of God's holiness, see below, p. 231 f.

15. The לחם משנה calls attention to the plain statement of the Talmud as to *be-farhesya'*, regardless of how we interpret Maimonides' view. See his gloss on Maimonides, Hilkot *Yesode ha-Torah*, V.4, *s.v.* ואם.

16. *Yer. Baba Batra* II.11, 13c: בריך אלההון דיהודאי.

17. *Yer. Baba Meẓi'a* II.5, 8c.

18. *Ibid.* As given in the text, the story is a fragment, but see the פני משה, *ad loc.*

19. *Ibid.*

20. In the version given in *Deut. R.* III.5 (end), the donkey is bought by Simeon himself, the jewel is immediately returned, and the Ishmaelite says, "Blessed is the Lord, God of Simeon b. Shaṭaḥ."

21. *Yer. Baba Meẓi'a, loc. cit.*—the story of the money found in the wheat.

22. For a general treatment of *ḳiddush ha-Shem* and *ḥillul ha-Shem*, see M. Kadushin, *The Theology of Seder Eliahu* (New York, 1932), pp. 64–71, and *RM*, p. 45, n. 1. See also below, p. 231 f.

23. This is not the case in regard to the public reading of the Torah, but here too, as we shall see, there is a corporate act of *ḳiddush ha-Shem* because of the presence of the *ẓibbur* for the public reading.

24. Albeck, *op. cit.*, Supplements, pp. 502 f., summarizes there the views of both post-talmudic authorities and of modern scholars.

25. *Tosefta Soṭah* VI.3; *Soṭah* 30b (פורם על שמע), a baraita. Cf. also *Mechilta*, ed. Horovitz and Rabin (Frankfurt am Main, 1928), p. 118, and *Mekhilta D'Rabbi Sim'on*, ed. Epstein and Melamed (Jerusalem, 1955), pp. 72 f.

26. L. Ginzberg, *A Commentary on the Palestinian Talmud* (New York, 1941), I, 251 f., and II, 179 and 201 (each individual recited Ḳeri'at Shema'). Albeck, *op. cit.*, *ad Megillah* IV.3, says that the leader recited the first half of a verse and the congregation responded with the second half; but see above, p. 84, as to the obligation upon every individual to recite the Shema' "with his own mouth." L. Finkelstein says that originally the phrase פורס את שמע meant "to promulgate the Shema' "—see his article "The Meaning of the Word פרס," *Jewish Quarterly Review*, N.S., XXXII, No. 4, 387 ff.

27. Ginzberg, *op. cit.*, I, 63.

28. *Ibid.*, I, 70 and n. 75. That is why, he says, they had the custom in Galilee לפרוס על שמע של ערבית בבה״כ קודם תפלת ערבית.

29. See *ibid.*, I, 252, on the words פסוקא and סופר.

30. *RM*, pp. 89–93, especially pp. 92 f.

31. Ginzberg, *op. cit.*, I, 74; II, 277. See also above, p. 91.

32. *Megillah* 23b, and above, p. 132 f. and n. 12 there.

33. *Megillah* 23b—כל דבר שבקדושה לא יהא פחות מעשרה. That דבר in this context means "word" can be seen from Rashi to *ibid.*, 27b, *s.v.* ליכא: שאין אומדים דבר שבקדושה פחות מעשרה. Further, the term שבקדושה must refer in this context to *ḳiddush ha-Shem* because the maxim is derived from "Ye shall not profane My holy Name, but I will be hallowed among the children of Israel" (Lev. 22:32). See also below, n. 35. In another context, דבר שבקדושה is used in connection with the honor due a *kohen*, and there it has a different meaning (see the gloss on the term by R. Asher to *Nedarim* 62a, end).

34. See Rashi on the mishnah in *Megillah* 23b, *s.v.* אין פורסין. When he includes there "the First Berakah before Ḳeri'at Shema' " he does so because of the Ḳedushah in that berakah, as R. Nissim, *ad loc.*, points out. With respect to the meaning of the word פרס itself, Rashi is of two minds, for in *Soṭah* 30b, *s.v.* כסופר, he assigns to it a different meaning, one that R. Nissim (*loc. cit.*) cites in the name of the Ge'onim. The confusion as to the meaning of the word stems of course, from the difficulty of reconciling the mishnah with its interpretation in the Gemara. We may be sure, however, that Rashi would never have stated the halakah regarding Ḳaddish, Baraku, and the Ḳedushah without having a basis for it in tradition.

35. Asheri on the mishnah in *Megillah* 23b: שיאמר הוא דבר שבקדושה הרי הוא מקדש השם בעשרה.

36. *Berakot* 21b.

37. *Masseket Soferim* X.8(7), ed. J. Muller (Leipzig, 1878), p. xviii. See his notes there, p. 150, as to the correct text. The peculiar variant of seven or six men instead of the "ten" has been explained, though, it seems, not explained away; see Tosafot to *Megillah* 23b, *s.v.* ואין, and Asheri, *loc. cit.*

38. According to the Ge'onim, פורסין את שמע refers to the berakot of the Shema', the mishnah laying down the halakah that a person may recite these berakot in behalf of others only when there are "not less than ten" (see R. Nissim, *loc. cit.*). Once more, the halakah is indubitably rooted in tradition, despite the meaning assigned to פרס.

39. Baer, *Seder 'Abodat Yisra'el* (Roedelheim, 1868), p. 76, and the notes. The sources are discussed by Finkelstein ("The Meaning of the Word פרס," p. 394, n. 23). He shows there that the two tannaitic sources, *Berakot* VII.3 and *Sifre Deut.*

306, ed. Friedmann (Vienna, 1864), 132b, take for granted that Baraku and its response are to be recited both before Ḳeri'at Shema' and before the berakah on the reading of the Torah. It seems to us that *Sifre Deut.* 306, also takes for granted that Baraku and the response of the Ḳaddish constitute *ḳiddush ha-Shem*. (On the Zimmun, which, requiring three men and not ten, is not an act of *ḳiddush ha-Shem*, see below, p. 160.) After applying the first part of Deut. 32:3 to Baraku and the second part of that verse to its response, and thus similarly to the response of the Ḳaddish, which is here broken into two parts, the passage tells of *nissim* (miracles) performed by God "in order to sanctify His great Name in the world" and, moreover, applies to these *nissim* Deut. 32:3, the very verse which the rabbis apply in the same passage to Baraku and the response of the Ḳaddish. This would indicate that not only were these corporate acts taken for granted in tannaitic times, but that they were regarded from the very beginning as *ḳiddush ha-Shem*. Notice also above, p. 135, that in those acts of *ḳiddush ha-Shem* in which the Gentiles "acknowledge" the God of the Jews, the formula attributed to them reflects the berakah formula.

40. Ginzberg, *op. cit.*, I, 174 f.

41. Above, p. 70. Ginzberg, *loc. cit.*, cites this example as well as Birkat ha-Zimmun.

42. R. Jose does not make of Birkat ha-Zimmun an exception; see below, pp. 161 f.

43. "Blessed is the Name of His glorious Kingship forever," the response after the first verse of the Shema', although both a berakah and a response and in that respect like the response in Baraku, is otherwise not at all similar to the latter. The response after the Shema' emphasizes the concept of God's kingship (see above, p. 81); it is a berakah reflecting a specific experience, that of accepting the kingship of God. Unlike the response in Baraku, it does not complete an act of *ḳiddush ha-Shem*. That is why it is said by the individual when he recites the Shema' in private.

44. Below, p. 232. R. Joseph Karo seems to have overlooked completely the response to Baraku. In the בית יוסף to *Ṭur 'Oraḥ Ḥayyim*, par. 69, he says that Baraku is a call to say a berakah, and hence that the Yoẓer must be recited, for otherwise a person will appear to be a כופר, a denier of God, since the call to say a berakah was issued and he did not respond to the call. See the דרישה ופרישה, *ad loc.* Elbogen, and others, too, take Baraku to be simply a call to prayer (see J. Elbogen, תולדות התפלה והעבודה בישראל [Tel Aviv and Berlin, 1924], p. 17).

45. Elbogen, *op. cit.*, pp. 107 f., for the details.

46. *Megillah* IV.1–2. See the Mishnah here for the occasions, at that period, when more than the minimum number of men could be called up.

47. Elbogen, *op. cit.*, p. 115. See also L. Zunz, הדרשות בישראל (Hebrew translation, Jerusalem, 1947), pp. 193 f.

48. *Megillah* IV.1, and see Elbogen, *loc. cit.*, for the sources for these berakot.

49. Elbogen, *loc. cit.*

50. *Soṭah* 39b. The rabbis emphasize the importance of responding with "Amen" to a berakah, and some even say, "Greater is he who responds with 'Amen' than he who recites the berakah" (*Berakot* 53b). The one who responds participates, as it were, in the saying of the berakah.

51. *Soṭah* 39a.

52. *Berakot* 8a.

53. See Maimonides, *Mishneh Torah*, Hilkot *Sefer Torah* X.1 for a summary of the twenty things, any one of which disqualifies a scroll for public reading.

54. *RM*, pp. 178 f.

55. See the discussion of this tradition and others in Elbogen, *op. cit.*, p. 108, and see Ginzberg, *op. cit.*, III, 145, n. 168.

56. For the text and rabbinic sources of these berakot, see Baer, *op. cit.*, p. 123, and the notes there and on p. 124; and see also above, p. 114.

57. Above, pp. 89 ff., and mark how this berakah differs.

58. See the discussion of this idea above, p. 90 f.

59. The wording of this second berakah is apparently of later origin: see Elbogen, *op. cit.*, p. 115.

60. Baer, *loc. cit.*

61. Above, n. 39, and the reference there to Finkelstein's illuminating note.

62. Rabbenu Nissim, to *Megillah* 23b, explicitly declares that it is not *dabar shebi-ḳedushah*. The Me'iri, *ad loc.*, does regard it as such, but only because of Baraku: שהרי צריך לומר ברכו.

63. A statement recited before the public reading of the Torah indicates that Baraku and its response are to be taken as constituting an act of worship in itself. The statement reads, "Ascribe, all of you, greatness unto our God, and render honor to the Torah" (Baer, *op. cit.*, p. 123 and the notes there; Singer, *The Daily Prayer Book* (London, 1890), p. 67). "Ascribe, all of you, greatness unto our God" relates to the interpretation of Deut. 32:3 in *Sifre Deut.* par. 306, ed. Friedmann, p. 132b, in which the first part of that verse, rendered as "when I proclaim the Name of the Lord," is applied to the leader saying Baraku, and the second part, "ascribe ye greatness unto our God," to the response by the congregation in the synagogue. The statement before the reading of the Torah is directed to the congregation—"all of you"—and the congregation is thus instructed to do two things: to respond to Baraku and to "render honor to the Torah" as it is being read. Our text of the statement is found in *Seder R. Amram*, ed. A. L. Frumkin (Jerusalem, 1912), I, 154a, and in *Maḥzor Vitry*, ed. S. Hurwitz (Nuremburg, 1923), p. 72, but the statement has a somewhat different form in *Masseket Soferim*, XIV.11. Linked with the public reading of the Torah is the public reading of the lection from the Prophets, the *Hafṭarah*, with its own berakot (see Elbogen, *op. cit.*, p. 117), and hence *Megillah* IV.3 names the *Hafṭarah*, too, as requiring the presence of "not less than ten."

64. D. de S. Pool, *The Kaddish* (2d ed.; New York, 1929), pp. 8 f.

65. Baer, *op. cit.*, pp. 129 f., the text and the notes.

66. *Malkut* is kingship, not kingdom, as in the response to the Shema' (see above, p. 81). If so, then it is not a matter of the establishment of His kingdom but of the recognition of His kingship. As to וימליך, notice "you have made Him King" (דאמליכתיה), *ibid.*, and the reference there.

67. The same verse is used as a proof-text in a passage of the Mekilta, telling that God will punish the wicked nations, and hence make Himself known to them (see *Mekilta*, ed. J. Z. Lauterbach [Philadelphia, 1933] I, 192 f.).

68. After Ps. 113:2. The term לעלם ולעלמי עלמיא is an emphatic term, used in the Aramaic for the Hebrew לעולם ועד. Similar terms are employed in Targum Jonathan and Targum Yerushalmi for לעולם ועד—see the material given by

Finkelstein, "The Meaning of the Word פרס" (XXXIII, No. 1), pp. 36 f., and Kimḥi on Isa. 6:3.

69. See the geonic references to the Ḳaddish as sanctifying God in J. Mann, "Changes in the Divine Service," *Hebrew Union College Annual*, IV, 267, n. 49.

70. See Tosafot to *Berakot* 3a, *s.v.* ועונין, end.

71. See *Masseket Soferim* X.8(7), ed. Muller, p. xviii, and see the notes there, pp. 150, 152.

72. See the reference in n. 34, above.

73. See the authorities quoted by C. L. Ehrenreich in his notes to his edition of *Sefer Abudraham* (Cluj [Klausenberg], 1927), p. 243.

74. There grew up various forms of the Ḳaddish, and that is true of all of them. These later forms add various Aramaic prayers after the original paragraph of the Ḳaddish. On the forms of the Ḳaddish, see Pool, *op. cit.*, pp. 79 ff.

75. The phrase used in the Mishnah is: עוברין לפני התיבה. On that expression, see Elbogen, *op. cit.*, p. 25.

76. *Rosh ha-Shanah* 34b, and Lieberman, *Tosefeth Rishonim* (Jerusalem, 1937), I, 217.

77. See Maimonides, *Mishneh Torah*, Hilkot *Tefillah*, IX. 3, and cf. *ibid.*, VIII.9 and the sources in the commentaries there.

78. In Palestine the Tefillah was recited aloud by the *individuals* at the synagogue service (see Ginzberg, *op. cit.*, III, 16 f., 20 f., and see also *ibid.*, II, 277, n. 2).

79. *Rosh ha-Shanah*, IV.5.

80. For this name see Elbogen, *op. cit.*, pp. 49 f.

81. Baer, *op. cit.*, p. 236, and Elbogen, *op. cit.*, pp. 52 f.

82. Baer, *op. cit.*, p. 89; Elbogen, *loc. cit.*, for this and other forms of the declaration.

83. *Masseket Soferim* XVI.12, ed. Muller, p. xxxi.

84. For the texts, see Baer, *op. cit.*, pp. 89 f., 218, 236 f., and his notes.

85. Elbogen, *op. cit.*, pp. 51–54.

86. *RM*, pp. 59 ff.

87. A. Bertholet, "*Das Buch Hesekiel,*" in *Kurzer Hand-Kommentar zum Alten Testament*, IV, 18, who says that Isa. 6:3 had an influence on Ezek. 3:12, and notice there Luzzatto's suggestion as to the original reading.

88. *RM*, p. 253, n. 131. For *ha-Kabod* as used interchangeably with *Shekinah*, see *ibid.*, p. 74 and n. 36 there. On the concept of *gilluy Shekinah*, see *ibid.*, pp. 228 ff. Targum Jonathan on Ezek. 3:12, instead of the construct, has *Yeḳara'*, the Aramaic for *ha-Kabod*, and so also on *ibid.*, 1:28, 10:4, etc. On the term, see *RM*, pp. 332 f.

89. Mark how in this midrashic comment the rabbinic *'olam* for "world" takes the place of the biblical "the whole earth." On *'olam* as "world", see *RM*, pp. 293 f.

90. This accords with a tannaitic tradition. R. 'Aḳiba says the *ḥayyot* do not see *ha-Kabod* and R. Simeon adds that the angels, too, do not—*Sifra* on Lev. 1:1, ed. Weiss (Vienna, 1862), p. 4a (*Numbers R.* XIV, end), and see *RM*, p. 235, n. 60. Again, according to *Exod. R.* XXIII, end, He is not revealed to the *ḥayyot*, despite their carrying the Throne, and it is the *ḥayyot* who, when the time has come for them to say *shirah* (the song to God), say that they do not know in which place He is, but that in every place where He may be, "Blessed . . . from His place." See

below, p. 148, on the ministering angels. *Pirḳe de R. Eliezer*, IV, end, obviously builds on this earlier tradition, and not very successfully. After saying that the *ḥayyot* proclaim, "Blessed," etc., it adds that Israel "respond[s] and say[s], 'Hear, O Israel. . . .' " Does Israel respond to the angels? See the comment here by R. David Luria, p. 11b, n. 60. This Midrash cannot be dated earlier than the eighth century (see Zunz, *op. cit.*, p. 140).

91. It is hardly conceivable that the two verses would have been brought together without a connecting idea. That idea, as we have seen in the preceding note, is tannaitic, and *Exod. R.* XXIII, end, we think, presupposes the Ḳedushah. A halakah with regard to the connecting idea, *'Ofannim*, is given in *Yer. Berakot* V.3, 9c, and has as an authority R. Joshua b. Levi (see below, n. 93).

92. Above, n. 90, on the failure of the attempt to integrate "Hear, O Israel" with the praises of the angels.

93. In *Yer. Berakot* V.3, 9c, R. 'Abun states that, since the Trisagion (קדושתא) had already been recited by the *ẓibbur* (in the case of the leader who became mute at *'Ofannim*), for the new leader to continue with *'Ofannim* is like having him start with a berakah (כמי שהוא תחלת ברכה). That statement means, it seems to us, that R. 'Abun, and R. Joshua b. Levi whom he quotes, regard "Blessed be," etc. (Ezek. 3:12), as a berakah, for the words ממקום שפסק must refer to *'Ofannim*. Those words are so taken at one point by the Lebush, *'Oraḥ Ḥayyim*, 62. The codists take *'Ofannim* itself to refer to the Ḳedushah of the Yoẓer.

94. This is not true of the Ḳedushah having for its introduction the כתר formula, a formula still retained in the Ḳedushah of the Musaf of the Sephardic rite. That introductory formula, however, changes the entire character of the Ḳedushah. "The conception conveyed by it is the mystical idea that God receives his 'crown' from Israel as from the heavenly host, when they adore him by means of the Trisagion" (Ginzberg, *Geonica* [New York, 1909], I, 132). The mystics referred to here are the *yorede merkabah* (see the reference in *ibid.*, n. 1), and that mystical school was not representative of the rabbinic tradition. The concept of *gilluy Shekinah* has nothing to do with *merkabah* mysticism (*RM*, pp. 260 f.). For the versions of the כתר formula, see A. L. Gordon, *'Oẓar Ha-Tefillot*, I, pp. 728 f. The כתר formula was employed in Babylon in every 'Amidah-Ḳedushah, Ginzberg points out, and "when the other countries yielded to the influence of the Babylonian schools and introduced the קדושת מוסף, they took over the formula כתר with it" (see his *Geonica*, II, 48–49).

95. *Berakot* 21b, and *Diḳduḳe Soferim*, *ad loc.* Without doubt, קדוש is the correct reading but the word probably refers to the Ḳedushah; see, for example, in *Masseket Soferim*, *loc. cit.*

96. See Ginzberg, *Commentary*, III, 438. But see above, n. 93.

97. According to Ginzberg (*Geonica*, I, 130 ff. and II, 48 f.), the Ḳedushah was put into the 'Amidah by the Babylonian mystics, and was accepted in Palestine only under duress. But this influence of Babylon, and of the mystics as well, must be dated as in the geonic period. We deal with the question of the influence of Babylon on the 'Amidah below, pp. 150 f. Finkelstein develops the theory that the Ḳedushah was added to the 'Amidah in Palestine in the second century during the Hadrianic persecutions, and that the Shema' was by then already part of the 'Amidah; see his article referred to above, p. 263, n. 21.

98. Elbogen, *op. cit.*, pp. 18 f. He takes the Ḳedushah here, therefore, to be a late insertion.

99. Above, p. 94.

100. On the *shirah* of the angels being the Ḳedushah, see above, n. 90, and the following note.

101. *Ḥagigah* 14a; *Ḥullin* 91b (where *shirah* is equated to the Ḳedushah), and the commentaries there; *Bereshit R.* LXXVIII.1, ed. Theodor and Albeck (Berlin, 1927), pp. 916 f., and see the references and notes there.

102. Above, p. 94.

103. *Tosefta Berakot* I.9, ed. S. Lieberman, pp. 3 f., and Lieberman, *Tosefta Ki-Fshuṭah* (New York, 1955), I, 11, especially his quotations from the ראבי"ה and his comment on them. See also Ginzberg, *Geonica*, I, 129.

104. See the section on "Rabbinic Dogma" in *RM*, pp. 340 ff.

105. Divergencies and contradictions are inherent in Haggadah because a characteristic of haggadic interpretation is the multiple interpretation of biblical texts (*RM*, pp. 104–107). They are a feature, too, of the category of significance, a category which permits a value concept—in this case, the concept of *ḳiddush ha-Shem*—to have concretizations akin to poetry, a kind of "valuational poetry" (*ibid.*, pp. 112 f., and *OT*, pp. 213–217). On "indeterminacy of belief," see *RM*, pp. 131 ff.

106. This is Ginzberg's opinion and also that of Finkelstein, *op. cit.* Ginzberg, however, maintains that the Ḳedushah in the 'Amidah is "specifically Babylonian" (Ginzberg, *loc. cit.*).

107. Above, n. 90.

108. *Ibid.*

109. *Ḥullin* 91b, a baraita. (For the range of the opinions, see above, p. 148.)

110. *Ibid.* See the following note.

111. *Ibid.*, and *Sifre* on Deut., par. 306, end, ed. Friedmann, p. 132b (*Yalḳuṭ Shime'oni*, par. 542). The Sifre here states that the ministering angels mention God's Name only after Israel has mentioned it in the Shema', and this seems to be an earlier version. *Ḥullin* 91b apparently has expanded on it. See also the version in *Bereshit R.* LXV, ed. Theodor and Albeck, pp. 738 f., and the other versions given in the notes there.

112. *Ḥullin* 91b. Interpretations by R. 'Abin, an Amora of the fourth century who spent part of his life in Babylon, reflect a change in attitude, although Israel is still favored by God as against the angels. Whereas the angels are given one *ḳedushah*, he says, Israel is given two *ḳedushot*, but only because they are exposed to the rule of the evil *yeẓer*. Again, he says, the angels in saying "Holy" three times in the Trisagion make three "crowns" for God, but He gives two of them to Israel. This interpretation has an affinity, certainly, with the כתר introduction (cf. above, n. 94), and yet here Israel is the recipient of the "crowns" made by the angels. Both these interpretations are in *Leviticus R.* XXIV.8, ed. Margulies, pp. 562 f.

113. Above, p. 145 f.

114. The longer forms of the reference to the *ḥayyot* more nearly resemble the one in the Yoẓer and hence are the earlier forms. See also Elbogen, *op. cit.*, p. 53.

115. Above, n. 93. Long before the time of R. 'Abin, the *ẓibbur* recited the verses aloud.

116. Above, p. 145.

117. See Ginzberg, *Geonica*, II, 48 and the sources given there, and 52.

118. On the berakah of the Ḳedushat ha-Shem and also on the changes in it resulting from the insertion of the Ḳedushah, see above, pp. 99 f.

119. Lieberman, *Tos. Kif.*, I, 34, *s.v.* אבא, who concludes that where there was wine (Palestine), a berakah was recited by the leader and that the people did not recite the evening service at all. Where there was no wine (Babylon), this berakah also constituted the Ḳiddush ha-Yom, and he suggests that this may have been its original function, too, where there was wine. See also Ginzberg (*Commentary*, III, 170), who holds it likely that because the people came on Friday evening to hear a scholar lecture, the Friday evening service was instituted before the evening service on weekdays, but that at first the Friday evening service consisted only of a Berakah מעין שבע; cf. *ibid.*, pp. 172 f.

120. Ginzberg, *Geonica*, II, 48 f. and 52.

121. Ginzberg, *ibid.*, and I, 132 f. For the כתר formula and *merkabah* mysticism, see above, n. 94.

122. Ginzberg, *Geonica*, I, 133.

123. "Many of the Geonim, as well as most of the old authorities down to and including Maimonides" held that the Ḳedushah in the Yoẓer, too, is *dabar shebi-ḳedushah*, and Saadia and others of the Geonim therefore formulated abridged versions of the Yoẓer for the individual's worship, versions which omitted the Ḳedushah (see Ginzberg, *Geonica*, p. 130 and the notes there). On Saadia's version, see above, p. 95, and n. 214; and see אוצר הגאונים, ed. B. Lewis (Haifa, 1928), I, Part I, 52 f., for other versions. Rashi was among those who regarded the Ḳedushah in the Yoẓer as an intrinsically corporate act (see above, p. 137 and n. 34 there). Asheri, however, holds the Ḳedushah in the Yoẓer to be part of the narrative (*ad Berakot* 21b and *Megillah* 23b) and so do the pupils of R. Jonah and others; hence the "general practice" is, according to Karo, also for the individual to say this Ḳedushah. See *Ṭur 'Oraḥ Ḥayyim*, par. 59, and *Bet Joseph*, *ad loc.* The Tosefta implies Asheri's view (see above, p. 147).

124. *Leviticus R.* XXIII.4, ed. Margulies, pp. 530 f.

125. *Ibid.* The passage interprets the verse, "as a lily among thorns" (Song of Sol. 2:2), the leader being the "lily" and the others in such a *ẓibbur* being the "thorns."

126. See *Tosefot Yom Ṭob*, *ad loc.*, on תנחומי אבלים, and see also Lieberman, *Tos. Kif.*, I, 49 and *Yer. Pesaḥim* VIII.8, 36b, cited by him there.

127. See the explanations of these terms in Albeck's commentary to the Mishnah, *ad loc.* Birkat Ḥatanim is also said, on occasion, during the seven days of the celebration (Maimonides, Hilkot *Berakot* II.9–10, and the sources in the *Kesef Mishneh* there).

128. Lieberman, *op. cit.*, pp. 49 f. and p. 50, beginning ומסתבר.

129. *Ibid.*, p. 50 and n. 62.

130. *Ibid.*, p. 50. *Ketubbot* 8b gives the texts of four berakot as constituting the series in Birkat 'Abelim, whereas *Tos. Berakot* III.23 gives three as the number. Lieberman suggests that Birkat 'Abelim may once have included a berakah relating to the mourners (the Second Berakah) similar in content to the Fourth Berakah in the Babli.

131. Lieberman, *op. cit.*, pp. 50–53. There were evidently also special forms of Birkat ha-Mazon for *Ḥatanim* (*ibid.*, p. 50, n. 60).

132. *Ibid.*, p. 52.

133. *Ibid.*

134. *Ibid.*, p. 51 and n. 67. In Birkat 'Abelim, one of the versions had as its closing formula מעורר ברחמים יצורים (a phrase referring to the resurrection of the dead) (*ibid.*).

135. *Kohelet R.* VII.7. Here among the deeds of lovingkindness performed by God—הקב״ה גומל חסדים—are Birkat Ḥatanim (Adam and Eve) and Birkat 'Abelim (Jacob). Cf. *Bereshit R.* VIII.13, ed. Theodor, p. 67. On Birkat Ḥatanim as *gemilut ḥasadim*, see *Pirḳe de R. Eliezer*, Chap. XII, end, and on Birkat 'Abelim as *gemilut ḥasadim*, see *ibid.*, Chap. XVII, end, and Luria, *ad loc.*

136. Above, p. 21.

137. *Leviticus R.* XXIII.4, ed. Margulies, pp. 530 f.

138. See, for example, *'Abot* IV.18; *Mo'ed Kaṭan* 21b (within the thirty days); *ibid.*, 28b (the comforting by the four elders); *Yer. 'Abodah Zarah* I.3, 39c (mourners of the Gentiles are to be comforted as well as those of Israel).

139. *Ketubbot* 8b.

140. The peculiarity of this berakah and the one following in Birkat 'Abelim has been noticed by W. Jawitz, מקור הברכות (Berlin, 1910), p. 15. He makes no attempt to account for it, however.

141. *Ketubbot, loc. cit.*

142. *Ibid.*, and Rashi there, *s.v.* האל הגדול.

143. Above, p. 102. On the room for differences of opinion with respect to details of this dogma, see *RM*, p. 362.

144. See discussion above, pp. 113 f.

145. On the fourth berakah of the Babli (*Ketubbot* 8b), see above, n. 130.

146. On such use of the first person plural and its implications, see above, pp. 108 ff.

147. With regard to the groom—*Berakot* 6b (R. Huna'), and with regard to the bride—*Ketubbot* 16b–17a. In Maimonides, Hilkot *'Ebel* XIV.1, gladdening the bride and the groom is among the things designated as *gemilut ḥasadim*.

148. Above, p. 152.

149. *Pirḳe de R. Eliezer*, Chap. XII, end. On the *ḥazzan* or *ḥazan*, see *OT*, p. 283, n. 291.

150. *Ketubbot* 8a; Singer, *op. cit.*, p. 299.

151. *Ketubbot* 17a.

152. Lieberman, *op. cit.*, p. 50 and n. 60.

153. On the wine here being optional, see Maimonides, Hilkot *'Ishut* X.3–4, and the *Maggid Mishneh, ad loc.*

154. *Ketubbot* 7b–8a. Singer, *loc. cit.*

155. See Ginzberg, *Commentary*, III, pp. 228 f. He quotes there a Palestinian morning berakah which begins with "Blessed art Thou, O Lord our God, King of the world, Who hast created [בראת] Adam [אדם הראשון] in his form and in his image [בדמותו ובצלמו]," and he takes בדמותו ובצלמו to refer to man's own form and image as being different from those of the rest of the creatures—an interpretation for which he adduces proof from rabbinic and medieval sources. He also calls attention to the close similarity between this Palestinian berakah and the Third Berakah of our Birkat Ḥatanim. See also the following note.

156. Rashi, to *Ketubbot*, *loc. cit.*, interprets "Who hast formed man" to refer to the groom, and והתקין לו ממנו בנין עדי עד to refer to the bride. These phrases, accordingly, relate at once both to the marriage of Adam and Eve, and to the present marriage, the occasion for the berakot. Such usage is not uncommon in rabbinic literature, and it reflects the idea of corporate personality (*RM*, p. 218 and the references there in n. 70).

157. Above, p. 153.

158. N. 155 above.

159. Above, p. 153.

160. Rashi, *loc. cit.*

161. Above, n. 156, and the reference there to the idea of corporate personality.

162. Above, p. 155, and the reference in n. 144 there.

163. The remaining three berakot given in *Ketubbot* 8a are also to be accounted for. The Second Berakah, as its very wording indicates, is an alternative to the Third. According to R. Ḥananel (cited by Tosafot, *ibid.*, *s.v.* שהכל), the Second Berakah was sometimes not said at all, as reported in the Gemara (*loc. cit.*). Rashi accounts for the Sixth Berakah, and for its having both an opening and a closing formula, by pointing to its usage, for it is the only berakah said on most of the days when no new guest is present. He takes the First Berakah to refer to the assembled folk, a gathering engaged in an act of *gemilut ḥasadim*, and he associates the berakah with the haggadah which tells of the marriage of Adam and of God's performance of such an act of *gemilut ḥasadim* on that occasion.

164. Above, p. 112 f, where the moral connotation of the concept of man is discussed.

165. Above, n. 135.

166. When the act is neither a corporate act of worship nor an act of martyrdom, ethical concepts are concretized in an act of *ḳiddush ha-Shem*. See above, pp. 133 f., where we discuss such an aspect. On the interweaving of other concepts with that of *ḳiddush ha-Shem*, see the examples in *Sifre Deut.*, par. 306, ed. Friedmann, p. 132b (the concept of *nes*) and *TE*, pp. 67 ff.

167. *Berakot* VII.1.

168. Zimmun itself refers to the manner in which Birkat ha-Mazon is said on these occasions, one of the men reciting it and the rest responding, "Amen" (Lieberman, *Tos. Kif.*, I, 100, and references there).

169. *Berakot* 49b–50a (Mishnah and Gemara); and see Maimonides, Hilkot *Berakot* V.2.

170. *Berakot* 46b and Tosafot, *s.v.* להיכן.

171. *Tos. Berakot* VI.1, ed. Lieberman, p. 32, and the sources referred to there. See also Lieberman, *Tos. Kif.*, I, *loc. cit.*

172. *Berakot* 46a, and see Maimonides, *loc. cit.* Notice, too, the expression by R. Jose in *Berakot* VII.3—הן מברכין. Cf., also, Ginzberg, *Commentary*, I, pp. 174 f.

173. Above, p. 138.

174. In *Sifre Deut.*, par. 306, ed. Friedmann, p. 132b, Deut. 32:3 is applied both to Baraku and to Zimmun. If that verse, which is to be rendered in this connection, "When I proclaim the Name of the Lord, ascribe ye greatness to our God," is to relate not only to Baraku but also to Zimmun, then the call in Zimmun, too, must proclaim "the Name of the Lord." R. 'Aḳiba in *Berakot* VII.3 holds that when ten

or more are present, the call in Zimmun is the same as in Baraku, according to the authorities cited in הערות, *ad loc.*, ed. Herzog (Jerusalem, 1945), p. 28a. See also Albeck in his *Commentary to Zera'im*, pp. 336 f. Another verse, Ps. 34:4 is also applied to Birkat ha-Zimmun. See the baraita in *Berakot* 48b (Rabbi), and cf. *ibid.*, 45a, where both verses are given. On Zimmun as also referring to Birkat ha-Zimmun, see Rashi on the mishnah, *ibid.*, *s.v.* שלשה שאכלו, and on the Gemara, *ibid.*, *s.v.* מה"מ.

175. Above, pp. 138 f.

176. *Berakot* VII.3, and Maimonides, *loc. cit.*, V.4.

177. On *'Elohenu*, our God, as a term for God, see *RM*, p. 196, and the following discussion there.

178. *Megillah* 23b; *Berakot* 45b: כיון דבעי לאדכורי שם שמים. *Derek erez* is a decided factor in other acts of worship as well. For example, in the Tefillah, a person must not make petition for "his needs" in the first three berakot, but these berakot must be of praise only, and the reason for that is *derek erez* (*Berakot* 34a). On this phase of *derek erez*, that of good manners, see above, p. 41 f., p. 47.

179. Listed in *Megillah* IV.3 among the matters requiring "not less than ten" are "the standing up and sitting down" of the group returning from a burial, and the valuation of immovable property dedicated to the Sanctuary, and these are not acts of worship at all.

180. *Berakot* 50a—R. Joseph.

181. According to Epstein, the words אחד עשרה ואחד עשר רבוא in *Berakot* VII.3 were added later, and R. Joseph's statement originally was similar in style to the one by R. Joḥanan in the Yerushalmi (see the next note): מבוא לנוסח המשנה, pp. 430 f. Albeck, *loc. cit.*, holds, on the contrary, that these words represent an ancient halakah, and that the mishnah, therefore, contains three opinions: that of the *Ḥakamim*, that of R. Jose, and that of R. 'Aḳiba. See also above, n. 174.

182. *Yer. Berakot* VII.3, 11c—R. Joḥanan.

183. *Berakot* VII.3.

184. *Yer. Berakot*, *loc. cit.* The question is asked here of how the rabbis interpret Ps. 68:27, the verse used by R. Jose in *Berakot* VII.3 as support for his view, and two answers are given—one anonymous and one by R. Ḥanina b. 'Abbahu. The anonymous answer is that the word "assemblies," in the plural, in that verse does not refer, as R. Jose would have it, to the sizes (plural) of the assemblies, but that it is to be understood in a distributive sense, each assembly (singular) being an entity in itself: a *ẓibbur*. R. Ḥanina says that the *ketib* is במקהלת (singular) and therefore the word has reference to an assembly (a *ẓibbur*). In our present text, incidentally, there is no *ketib* for that word. Between this statement and the one in which the view of the *Ḥakamim* is distinguished from that of R. Jose is another passage. That passage deals with different verses as interpreted by different authorities, the interpretations teaching that *'edah*, a congregation, consists of ten, and that the phrase "children of Israel" refers to ten. They are the same verses as are used in the Babli (see above, p. 137, and the notes there) in order to elucidate the concept of *ḳiddush ha-Shem*. Here, however, there is no reference to that concept, and the passage is placed here in order to emphasize that ten are an *'edah*, a *ẓibbur*. The passage is used in *Yer. Megillah* IV.4, 75b, apparently with reference to *kiddush ha-Shem*, though the corresponding section in the Babli is more pointed, and once more in *Yer. Sanhedrin* I.6, 19c, where it is connected with the mishnah being interpreted.

185. On the importance of "Amen", see above, n. 50.

186. Above, n. 168.

187. Above, p. 143, n. 77; also the berakot of the Shema'.

Notes to Chapter VII

1. Ps. 63:3. The Jewish Publication Society version renders it "so have I looked for Thee."

2. *Ibid.*, 17:15, J.P.S. version. בהקיץ, however, may mean "in the waking state."

3. *Ibid.*, 42:3. The Massoretic reading is difficult and וְאֵרָאֶה here is supported by rabbinic interpretations of the very similar phrase in Exod. 23:17; see M. Kadushin, *The Rabbinic Mind* (New York, 1952), p. 240. (To be referred to hereafter as *RM*.) See also the *Commentary on Psalms*, H. P. Chajes (Kiev, 1908), p. 94.

4. See the lengthy discussion of this concept in *RM*, pp. 228 ff.

5. Above, p. 272, n. 190, and the references there.

6. *Yoma* 9b–10a; *ibid.*, 21b (baraita).

7. *RM*, p. 253, n. 131, and Ginzberg, *A Commentary on the Palestinian Talmud* (New York, 1941), III, 395–7.

8. We have discussed details of this controversy in *RM*, pp. 245–49.

9. Above, p. 127, and n. 176 there.

10. The *Ḥakamim* of the Mishnah reject that assumption (see above, p. 129).

11. Above, Chap. V, sec. D.

12. *RM*, p. 238, and see the entire discussion there.

13. See the discussion referred to in the preceding note.

14. Above, Chap. V, secs. C.–D.

15. *Berakot* IV.5, and *ibid.*, 30a: the baraita on "directing the heart" toward the Land of Israel, Jerusalem, and so on. See the Pupils of R. Jonah, *ad loc.*

16. See *Berakot* IV.6, and *Tos. Berakot* III.14–16, ed. S. Lieberman (New York, 1955), pp. 15 f., and see also the discussion of the various sources by Lieberman, *Tosefta Ki-Fshuṭah* (New York, 1955), I, 43 f. The matters involved there are discussed below, p. 192.

17. *Berakot* 34a, bottom—a baraita. On the difference in the practices of Palestine and Babylon, see Ginzberg, *op. cit.*, I, 181 f.

18. "We acknowledge Thee" is a phrase linked in rabbinic literature with the acceptance of God's kingship (see above, p. 90, and on the phrase itself, p. 260, n. 178). A late midrash finds support in Gen. 24:28 for the bowing at these two berakot; see Ginzberg, *loc. cit.*, and see also the Pupils of R. Jonah, *ad loc.*

19. *Berakot* 34a–b. "The greater he is, the more he must humble and lower himself": Rashi, *ad loc.*, *s.v.* כהן גדול.

20. *Yoma* 53b. To your left, "which is the right of the Holy One Blessed be He" (Raba'). See *Ṭur 'Oraḥ Ḥayyim*, par. 123.

21. *Sanhedrin* 22a.

22. Rashi to *Yoma* 53b, *s.v.* לשמאל.

23. *Yer. Berakot* IX.1, 13a.

24. *Tos. Berakot* III.6, ed. Lieberman, p. 12, and see his *Tos. Kif.* I, 30, and the sources there.

25. For the sources and references, see *RM*, p. 208, n. 21, and *ibid.*, p. 209, n. 24. "Blessed art Thou, O Lord" is itself taken from Ps. 119:12.

26. *RM*, pp. 226 f. The name *Shekinah* is sometimes used in contexts of God's nearness only, and sometimes in contexts of *gilluy Shekinah*. See *ibid.*, pp. 253 f., and n. 131 on p. 253.

27. F. von Hügel, *The Mystical Element in Religion* (2d ed.; New York, 1923), II, 283 f. Although describing a type of mysticism which is certainly not normal mysticism, Baron von Hügel emphatically denies that there can be "a specifically distinct, self-sufficing, purely mystical mode of apprehending Reality." See the discussion in *OT*, pp. 237 ff.

28. Above, pp. 67 f.

29. For a more extensive treatment of this topic, in which a number of other concepts are given as well, see "Organismic Development" in *RM*, pp. 288 ff.

30. Above, pp. 78 ff.

31. Above, pp. 82 f.

32. Above, p. 80, where a similar interpretation of Lev. 18:2 is also quoted, but here God reminds them that they had accepted His kingship at Sinai.

33. The first verse in the Shema' is interpreted as a call by God and a response to Him by Israel—see above, p. 86.

34. Above, p. 87.

35. On other examples of similar differences between rabbinic and biblical usage of the same conceptual terms, see above, pp. 27 f.

36. Above, p. 63, and the references there.

37. Above, p. 120.

38. On this entire matter, see above, pp. 107 ff.

39. There are several illustrative examples in the discussion cited in the preceding note. An entire list of such examples is furnished by the berakot on awakening and arising in the morning, and given in *Berakot* 60b. On opening his eyes, a person is to say, "Blessed . . . Who openest the eyes of the blind"; on sitting up, "Blessed . . . Who loosest them that are bound"; on dressing, "Who clothest the naked"; and so on. In most of these berakot, the awareness of the self is conceptualized through the concept of man, and in several, through the concept of Israel. When, however, an individual does not perform one of these acts—e.g., if he has to remain in bed and cannot get dressed—he is not to say the berakah referring to the act. See Tosafot to *Berakot* 60b, *s.v.* כי פרים, and Maimonides, Hilkot *Tefillah*, VII.7–8, which are based on *Megillah* 24b. Retention of self-identity does not permit saying a berakah which cannot refer to the individual qua individual.

40. Above, p. 107.

41. On the topic of this paragraph, see above, pp. 113–115.

42. Above, p. 158 f.

43. *Derek ereẓ* is a factor in several acts of worship; see above, p. 160 and n. 178 there.

Humility is expressed in the obeisances during the Tefillah (above, p. 165 f. and n. 19 there).

44. Above, Chap. VI, sec. E., "Berakot as *Gemilut Ḥasadim*."

45. On these emphatic trends, see above, Chap. II, sec. C., "The Role of Emphasis."

46. See the preceding note.

47. We called attention to that especially when we discussed the berakah on bread, the First Berakah of the Birkat ha-Mazon, and a number of the berakot in the Tefillah. See also p. 285, n. 39.

48. Yehezkel Kaufmann, *Toledot ha-'Emunah ha-Yisre'elit* (Tel Aviv, 1947), III, 71.

49. *Ibid.*, p. 125.

50. *Ibid.*, p. 193.

51. *Ibid.*, p. 282. On Jeremiah, and his particular teaching, see *ibid.*, pp. 443 f.

52. *Ibid.*, pp. 71 f.

53. *Ibid.*, pp. 116 f.

54. *Ibid.*, p. 194.

55. *Ibid.*, pp. 444 f. Kaufmann calls attention to the cultic aspect of the covenant, which made the breaking of the covenant all the more sinful in the eyes of Jeremiah (Jer. 34:15, 18); and to Jeremiah's telling the people to pray (*ibid.*, 29:7, 12).

56. For this paragraph, see Kaufmann, *op. cit.*, I, pp. 603 ff. For a comprehensive treatment, see *ibid.*, pp. 396–416.

57. A criticism leveled against Kaufmann is that he argues, as in this case, from "negative evidence." That kind of criticism harbors an underlying scientific fallacy, as Kroeber indicates. "It cannot be too much emphasized that for probability findings to be worth anything they must be in terms of the total situation. . . . Negative evidence is particularly likely to be overlooked, both by the biased and by the inexperienced. We are so constituted, as primates, that occurrences impress us more than absences. The business of science is to train us in being critical enough to see both positive and negative evidence" (A. L. Kroeber, *Anthropology* [New York, 1948], p. 552).

58. For this paragraph, see Kaufmann, *op. cit.*, III, pp. 79–81, 445, 77.

59. The biblical phrase דרך כל הארץ (Gen. 19:31; I Kings 2:2) is hardly to be taken as the biblical antecedent of the rabbinic concept, despite the similarity of the terms. At most, the biblical phrase points to what we have called the first phase of *derek ereẓ*, the phase referring to phenomena or modes of behavior common to all of mankind, and that is the only phase in which *derek ereẓ* is not a subconcept of Torah (see above, pp. 51 f.). On instances where the rabbinic term has wider and sometimes even different connotations than a similar term or phrase in the Bible, see *RM*, pp. 290–96. Notice there, too, how the rabbinic concept of *ger* has its antecedents in the ideas of the prophets.

60. *OT*, pp. 142 f.

61. *Ibid.*, pp. 109–10, and n. 72.

62. In that respect, the berakot and the other acts of worship have some kinship with the Haggadah, for the Haggadah, too, helps to keep the value concepts vivid, as we have indicated in *RM*, p. 84. The acts of worship, however, are living experience, and so are more effective than Haggadah which is, after all, not experience.

63. *RM*, pp. 315 f.

64. *Ibid.* A striking statement is the passage in *Lev. R.* XXII.8, telling that the sacrifices were given Israel in order to wean them away from idolatry. See *ibid.*, ed. Margulies, pp. 517 f., and the note there. As he indicates, this view has much in common with that of Maimonides, *Guide for the Perplexed*, III, Chaps. 32 and 46. Abarbanel (*Commentary to the Pentateuch*, Introd. to Leviticus), in support of Maimonides' view, points especially to this passage in *Lev. R.*, and he also quotes other rabbinic passages which say that God desires study of Torah rather than sacrifices.

65. M. Kadushin, *The Theology of Seder Eliahu* (New York, 1952), pp. 129 f.

66. *Ibid.*

67. Nonsacrificial worship, in its various forms, was developed after the period of the prophets. From the prophets' attitude toward prayer and fasting as means of supplication, no sound conclusion can be drawn as to what their attitude might have been toward the various forms of nonsacrificial worship. To be sure, the prophets negate prayer and fast-days in the same way as they negate the sacrifices (see Kaufmann, *op. cit.*, III, p. 72; and see also *ibid.*, IV, pp. 141 f., 145 f., and especially n. 129). But prayer, though obviously a religious act and one that is found even among primitive peoples, is not 'abodah, or worship in the rabbinic sense, and neither is fasting. Prayer and fasting are forms of supplication, cries for help, and they are not inherently interrelated with the ethical sphere.

68. The difference between descriptive or analytic terms and organismic value concepts is discussed in *OT*, pp. 250 f. See also *RM*, p. 8.

69. Evelyn Underhill, *Mysticism* (Meridian ed., New York, 1957), p. 81.

70. *Ibid.*, pp. 127 ff., 168 ff.

71. *Ibid.*, p. 170.

72. *Ibid.*, p. 304.

73. *Ibid.*, p. 170.

74. *Ibid.*, p. 417, quoting Delacroix.

75. *Ibid.*, p. 304.

76. *Ibid.*, pp. 169, 201.

77. *Ibid.*, pp. 399, 416. In another work, Miss Underhill describes the ideal of monasticism as being not only "separation from the world," but as the "total oblation of personality" and as "death to self" (*Worship* [New York, 1957], p. 252).

78. *RM*, p. 81.

79. There are even a few instances of religious experience where the larger self is not called forth at all; see above, p. 107.

80. See the discussion in *RM*, pp. 167 f. A degree of asceticism is advocated by the rabbis as a requisite to the study of Torah, but not out of disdain for the flesh; see *OT*, pp. 53 ff.

81. These theories go back to W. Robertson-Smith's interpretation of "peace-offerings," *shelamim*: see his *The Religion of the Semites* (Meridian ed., New York, 1956), pp. 236 ff., especially pp. 239 f., and see also his summary with regard to "sacramental communion," *ibid.*, pp. 439 f.

82. Kaufmann, *op. cit.*, I, 563 ff.

83. *Ibid.*

84. F. M. Cornford, *From Religion to Philosophy* (New York, 1957), p. 112, and see the entire discussion there; cf. Underhill, *Mysticism*, p. 24, n. 1.

85. The idea of communion with God, as expressed in the term *deveḳut*, is a basic idea in Kabbalah and Ḥasidism. "In general Hebrew usage, *Devekuth* only means attachment or devoutness, but, since the thirteenth century, it has been used by the mystics in the sense of close and most intimate communion with God. Whereas in Catholic mysticism, 'Communion' was not the last step on the mystical way . . . in Kabbalism it is the last grade of ascent to God. It is not union, because union with God is denied to man even in that mystical upsurge of the soul, according to Kabbalistic theology. But it comes as near to union as a mystical interpretation of Judaism would allow. . . ." G. G. Scholem, "*Devekuth*, or Communion with God," *Review of Religion*, XIV, No. 2 (January, 1950), 115. See also Scholem's treatment of the idea (*ibid.*, pp.134–39), and in *Major Trends in Jewish Mysticism* (Jerusalem, 1941), p. 121, and *Reshit ha-Kabbalah* (Jerusalem and Tel Aviv, 1948), pp. 114 f. and 142 f. Cf. I. Tishby's view regarding *deveḳut* and *unio mystica* in *Mishnat ha-Zohar*, II (Jerusalem, 1961), 289, n. 69. Tishby also points out that *deveḳut* is definitely a nonrabbinic idea, and he quotes *Ketubbot* 111b and *Soṭah* 14a to prove that the rabbis deny the very possibility of any such phenomenon (*op. cit.*, p. 284 f.).

86. On the communicable and noncommunicable factors in the acceptance of *malkut Shamayim*, see above, p. 169.

87. Underhill, *Mysticism*, p. 99.

88. *Ibid.*, p. 100.

89. *Ibid.*, pp. 28, 101.

90. In *Ta'anit* 11a–b (Malter, ed. minor, pp. 77 f.; ed. major, p. 40), R. Eleazar is quoted as saying, "One should always regard oneself as if the Holy One were within him, for it is said, 'The Holy One in the midst of thee' [Hosea 11:9]." This statement does not teach that God is immanent in man. In the first place, the idea is qualified by the important word כאלו—"as if" or "as though." Notice how this word makes of the idea which it qualifies merely a figure of speech (above, p. 166; and see also p. 240, n. 29). Second, the statement is incidental to the point made in the passage, and this point is simply that man must not afflict himself (see Malter, ed. minor, p. 78, n. 185). On *Shekinah* as not standing for immanence, see *RM*, pp. 255 ff. and 221 f.

91. Underhill, *Mysticism*, p. 414.

92. W. F. Albright, *From the Stone Age to Christianity* (Baltimore, 1940), p. 167.

93. On the difference between philosophic interpretation and rabbinic interpretation, see *RM*, pp. 98–107.

94. Albright, *op. cit.*, p. 137, giving a somewhat different interpretation. There is no evidence, it seems to us, that the text contains an idea which is "close to monotheism." On the contrary, the phrase, "Honor [the] god in his way" implies that the god is to be honored in accordance with his particular mode of worship. This idea is in alignment, it seems to us, with the quotation in H. Frankfort, *Ancient Egyptian Religion* (2d ed.; New York, 1961), p. 24: "And so the gods entered into their bodies of every kind of wood, of every kind of stone, of every kind of clay, of every kind of thing which grows upon him (Ptah), in which they have taken form." Frankfort's view, incidentally, has some points in common with our organismic view. He speaks of "a multiplicity of approaches" and of "a multiplicity of

answers" (pp. 18 f.) and also of "several separate avenues of approach" (pp. 91 f., 121 f.). We have indicated, similarly, that the same situation may be interpreted at one time by one value concept and at another time by a different one. The question is whether the Egyptian "approaches" and "answers" are true concepts; that is, whether they are values crystallized in abstract, general terms.

95. W. Warde Fowler, *The Religious Experience of the Roman People* (London, 1911), p. 238. Fowler believes that "a man or men inspired by a new national feeling" were those who "took advantage of the uncompleted Etruscan temple . . . to settle there a new Jupiter, better and greater than any other, to whom his people would be for ever grateful, and in whom they would for ever put their trust" (*ibid.*, p. 239). Similarly, there were a number of Junos, each Juno—meaning, each local image of Juno—being designated in a special manner (*ibid.*, p. 318 and p. 332, n. 17).

96. Albright, *op. cit.*, p. 161.

97. *Ibid.*

98. *Ibid.*, p. 164 f. At the other extreme is the view that regards a particular statue not merely as a manifestation of the deity but as the deity itself. A scene on a lekythos, or oil jar, "represents Cassandra flying from Ajax and taking refuge at the xoanon [statue of the goddess] of Athene," and a detail in that scene shows that Athene, "statue though she be, is apparently about to move to the rescue" and "has sent as her advance guard her sacred animal, a great snake" (Jane Harrison, *Prolegomena to the Study of Greek Religion* [4th ed.; New York, 1957], p. 305).

99. Albright, *op. cit.*, p. 167.

100. '*Abodah Zarah* 54b: the mishnah and the baraita, where the correct reading in both, changed by the censor, is עבודה זרה. See also *Rosh ha-Shanah* 31a.

101. In the tractate '*Abodah Zarah*.

102. Above, p. 79. The first verse of the Shema' is associated with the martyrdom of R. 'Akiba precisely because it negates emperor-worship. "Iron combs were applied to prevent R. 'Akiba from his recitation." See *RM*, p. 131, note, which refers to an article by Lieberman. In *Gittin* 57b, the same verse is quoted by one of the martyr-brothers as a negation of idolatry. On the versions of the legend, see Gerson D. Cohen, מעשה חנה ושבעת בניה בספרות העברית, offprint from ספר היובל לכבוד מרדכי מנחם קפלן (New York, 1953). He demonstrates that the questions asked by the "king" and the answers given by the brothers, which are to be found only in the rabbinic versions, reflect Roman procedures and martyrs' responses in rabbinic times.

103. Maimonides, *Mishneh Torah*, Hilkot Ḳeri'at Shema' I.2, ed. Hyamson (New York, 1949), p. 94a.

104. See the *Kesef Mishneh* and the other commentaries, *ad loc.*

105. See the discussion above, p. 79.

106. A striking instance is to be found in the long statement by R. Isaiah di Trani the Younger, quoted in שלטי הגבורים to Alfasi, '*Abodah Zarah* 17b. The study of philosophy may lead to heresy, he states there, and he declares that the main aim of the Torah is to teach fear of God and proper conduct. Thus, Moses commanded us he continues, "Hear, O Israel, the Lord our God, the Lord is One." Moses did not say that we are to arrive at knowledge of God through philosophy, "but to believe concerning the Unity in accordance with tradition [אלא להאמין היחוד ע״פ שמועה וע״פ קבלה]." (R. Isaiah relates שמועה, tradition, to שמע.) Opposed as he was to philosophy,

R. Isaiah nevertheless interprets the Shema' to refer to the unity of God. On the other hand, he obviously also understands it "in accordance with tradition," and this can only mean as an acknowledgment of God's kingship. (This point is entirely missed by modern writers referring to R. Isaiah's statement, for they "correct" the text and assume that להאמין היחוד ought to read להאמין ביחוד. See now the text in מעט דבש, הוצאת ד. ששון [Oxford, 1928], p. 47, a book called to my attention by Dr. Saul Lieberman.)

107. Above, p. 90.

108. So Singer, *Prayer Book* (London, 1890), p. 40; others have similar renderings. See also I. Abrahams, *A Companion to the Authorized Daily Prayer Book* (2d ed.; London, 1922), p. xlix.

109. On auxiliary ideas, see *RM*, pp. 52 ff., 220 ff.

110. *Ibid.*, pp. 221 f.

111. Above, pp. 79 and 83.

112. Above, p. 81.

113. Above, p. 83.

114. P. 82 f. and n. 125 there.

115. Above, p. 79 and cf. Ginzberg, *Commentary*, I, 228 (the remark in parentheses).

116. *Tos. Berakot* III.4, ed. Lieberman, p. 12: המתפלל צריך שיכוין את לבו. The parallel in *Berakot* 31a adds לשמים, but this word is not found in the MSS and in the quotations by medieval authorities; see Lieberman, *Tos. Kif.*, I, 28, bottom.

117. *Berakot* 30b—R. Eleazar. A related statement by the same teacher is in *Yer. Berakot* II.4, 5a.

118. *'Erubin* 65a—Rab. R. Ḥanina did not say the Tefillah on a day when he was upset (*ibid.*).

119. *Berakot* 30b.

120. Maimonides, Hilkot *Tefillah*, IV.15 (X.1), and see the *Kesef Mishneh*, *ad loc.*, and his reference to R. Asher.

121. Above, p. 83.

122. *Berakot* 34b, a baraita. "In one" is taken to refer to the First Berakah, 'Abot.

123. *Berakot* III.1.

124. Ginzberg, *Commentary*, II, 34 f. (where he cites *Deut. R.* IX.1), and see also *ibid.*, pp. 54 f.

125. *Berakot* II.4 and Rashi to *ibid.*, 16a, *s.v.* מה שאינן. As to the rule with respect to Ḳeri'at Shema' in this mishnah, see Bertinoro, *ad loc.* On the characterization of the Tefillah as *raḥame*, see above, p. 106.

126. Above, p. 119.

127. Above. See also *Berakot* 29b and Rashi, *ibid.*, *s.v.* מי.

128. *Yer. Berakot* V.1, 9a: שהיה לבי מתכוין בתפילה; *Tos.*, *ibid.*, III.20, ed. Lieberman, p. 17, and the parallels and sources given there; and see also *Tos. Kif.*, I, 46 f.

129. *Berakot* 24b. This does not apply to a person in a congregation, for he might disturb others.

130. *Berakot* VI.1.

131. *Ibid.*, 40a.

132. *Berakot* VI.1. R. Judah does not state here his opinion regarding the berakah on fruits of the earth in general (see Lieberman, *Tos. Kif.*, I, 59).

133. *Tos. Berakot* IV.4, ed. Lieberman, p. 19, and *Tos. Kif.*, *loc. cit.*, *s.v.* ועל ירקות and *s.v.* פרי. See also *ibid.*, *s.v.* אדמה. Lieberman suggests that R. Judah may be disagreeing in this baraita with the statement on שהכל in *Berakot* VI.2; in that case, the latter would refer only to the fruit of trees and the fruits of the earth mentioned in that mishnah and not to "everything," wine and bread included, as the Babli (*Berakot* 12a) assumes, for R. Judah's berakah reads, "Who, by His word, causest the earth to produce."

134. אוצר הגאונים *Berakot*, Part II, p. 75. Nevertheless, as the Gaon goes on to say, a berakah is valid if at least the close refers to the occasion, and he cites *Berakot* 12a, where not only berakot on liquids are mentioned, but also the First Berakah of the Shema'.

135. *Yebamot* 52b; cf. *Baba Batra'* 53b, 54a.

136. *Tos. Ḳiddushin* I.3; cf. *Ḳiddushin* 2b. (Cohabitation was one of the three forms of *ḳiddushin* or betrothal [*Ḳiddushin* I.1; *'Eduyyot* IV.7], but was discouraged by the rabbis.)

137. *Yebamot* 102b, 106a; *Ketubbot* 74a; *Tos. Yebamot* XII.13. This and the two preceding examples are cited by Michael Higger, *Intention in Talmudic Law* (doctoral dissertation) (New York, 1927), pp. 29 ff.

138. *Giṭṭin* III.1; IV.2. Tosafot, *ibid.*, 22b, *s.v.* והאי לאו, indicates how in some particulars divorce and *ḥaliẓah* differ with respect to *kawwanah*.

139. For example, *Nedarim* III.7–9; VIII.6.

140. Higger, *op. cit.*, pp. 19–21.

141. See Rashi *ad Zebaḥim* 41b, *s.v.* כגון שנתן; *ad Menaḥot* 2b, *s.v.* אבל מחשבה. With regard to *piggul* (a sacrifice to be rejected because of a wrong intention in the mind of the officiating priest), see Tosafot *ad Baba Meẓi'a* 43b, *s.v.* החושב, and the references there.

142. An instance of *maḥashabah* is the declaration of the intention to misappropriate a trust (see Tosafot, *Baba Meẓi'a*, and Rashi, *ad loc.* See also *Tosefot Yom Ṭob* to *Baba Meẓi'a* III.12, *s.v.* החושב.

143. *Berakot* V.1: כדי שיכונו את לבם למקום. The mishnah in the Gemara has לאביהם שבשמים. The reference to God, למקום, is not found in the mishnah of the Yerushalmi as given in the printed editions, but the Cambridge MS (ed. Lowe) does have it. See R. Jonah who, in his commentary on Alfasi *ad loc.*, points out that this passage does not refer to *kawwanah* in the saying of the Tefillah.

144. Above, p. 165.

145. As can be seen, too, from the discussion by Lieberman, *Tos. Kif.*, I, 43, *s.v.* סומה, and from the sources quoted there.

146. Above, pp. 165 f.

147. *Tos. Berakot* III.14, ed. Lieberman, p. 15, and the parallels there.

148. כל זמן שהיו ישראל מסתכלים כלפי מעלה ומשעבדין את לבם לאביהם שבשמים.

149. On other tannaitic interpretations of the same passages, see the discussion in *RM*, p. 347 n. 32.

150. Bertinoro on *Rosh ha-Shanah* III.8. See also Edeles' remarks, *ad loc.*

151. *Yebamot* 105b, and see Lieberman, *Tos. Kif.*, *loc. cit.*

152. Witness the term שעבוד מלכיות, "subjection to the empires"—*Berakot* 12b; *ibid.*, 34b, and elsewhere.

153. *Mechilta*, ed. Horovitz and Rabin (Frankfurt am Main, 1928), p. 176, and the parallels and variants referred to in the notes there and in the note on line 12, p. 173.

154. See also translation and discussion of this mishnah in Judah Goldin, *The Living Talmud* (New York, 1957), pp. 30 f.

155. *Tos. Rosh ha-Shanah* III (II).6, ed. Zuckermandel and Lieberman (Jerusalem, 1937), p. 212.

156. אין הכל הולך אלא אחר כוונת הלב.

157. *Tos. Berakot* III.4, ed. Lieberman, p. 12, and the sources there, and see *Tos. Kif.*, I, 29, top. See also above, p. 188.

158. *Menaḥot* XIII.11, and *ibid.*, 110a, where the baraita clearly indicates that the statement refers to having the proper intention; cf. Rashi, *s.v.* לבעל הדין. Cf. also *Zebaḥim* IV.6, ed. Albeck (Jerusalem and Tel Aviv, 1956), p. 22, and the notes there and on p. 355.

159. *Berakot* 5b.

160. *Ibid.*, 17a, and see Rashi, *ad loc.*

161. Above, p. 190.

162. Above, p. 86.

163. Above, p. 69.

164. Above, p. 187.

165. Above, p. 187.

166. *Yer. Berakot* II.4, 5a.

167. *Ibid.*, according to the reading in a Genizah MS (see Ginzberg, *Commentary*, I, 346).

168. *Ibid.*

169. *Ibid.*, II.1, 4a bottom, and Ginzberg, *op. cit.*, I, 227 f.

170. There are several statements on *kawwanah* in the Yerushalmi which only appear to be negative but which are not so in fact. R. Jose's statement in *Yer. Shabbat* I.5, 3a (*ibid.*, *Berakot* I.5, 3b) is not to be taken as though Ḳeri'at Shema' does not require *kawwanah* at all for, as the sequel shows, the first three verses do require *kawwanah* (see Ginzberg, *op. cit.*, I, 125, 128). Similar "negative" statements in *Yer. Berakot* II.5, 5a bottom on *kawwanah* in Ḳeri'at Shema' and the saying of the Tefillah relate to *Parah* VII.9, the question being whether *kawwanah* in these acts of worship constitutes, technically, "diversion of attention"; see Ginzberg, *op. cit.*, I, 356–358.

171. *Berakot* 13a; *Pesaḥim* 114b; cf. '*Erubin* 95b: מצות צריכות כוונה.

172. *Rosh ha-Shanah* 28b; *Pesaḥim*, *loc. cit.*: מצות אין צריכות כוונה.

173. See *Rosh ha-Shanah* 28b.

174. *Ibid.*

175. See *Maggid Mishneh* to Maimonides, Hilkot *Shofar*, II.4, *s.v.* המתעסק, where he distinguishes between *mit'assek̦* (to do something without practical purpose) according to the proponents of the positive principle and *mit'assek̦* according to the proponents of the negative principle.

176. *Berakot* 13a (*Rosh ha-Shanah* 28b), and above, p. 83 and n. 127 there.

177. According to an interpretation of the Pupils of R. Jonah to *Berakot* 12a, *s.v.* אמנם, the proponents of the negative principle hold that in the case of deeds as, for example, the lifting of the *lulab*, the deed serves in place of *kawwanah*, but that when the miẓwah consists solely of an oral act, *kawwanah* is required. R. Joel Sirkis rightly points out in a marginal note, however, that the reading of the Shema' is an oral act and yet that it does not require *kawwanah* according to the proponents of the negative principle. A. J. Heschel, in *God in Search of Man* (Philadelphia, 1956), pp. 317 f., n. 3, refers to the interpretation of the Pupils of R. Jonah just cited. In his view, the issue between the proponents of the two opposing principles is "whether all religious acts should be regarded as analogous to the sacrifice or as analogous to the Deed of Divorce." In the case of sacrifices, "no intention is considered as if there were proper intention," whereas in the case of a Deed of Divorce, "absence of intention invalidates the act." See also the discussion on *kawwanah*, *ibid.*, pp. 314 ff.

178. *Pesaḥim* 114b.

179. Post-talmudic authorities, as well, are divided on the question as to whether miẓwot require *kawwanah*. Alfasi, Asheri (see Asheri to *Rosh ha-Shanah* 28b), and Maimonides in his *Commentary to the Mishnah*, as well as in the *Mishneh Torah* (see *Tosefot Yom Ṭob* to *Sukkah* III.14, *s.v.* מפני), are proponents of the positive principle, but there are other authorities (cited by the *Maggid Mishneh*, *loc. cit.*) who are proponents of the negative principle. Tosafot to *Berakot* 12a, *s.v.* לא, not only emphatically asserts that miẓwot do not require *kawwanah*, but also applies that principle to a person who was passing behind a synagogue and heard the Tefillah and did not have *kawwanah*, an instance *not* given in *Rosh ha-Shanah* III.7, and to which mishnah this statement in Tosafot obviously refers. There was a feeling, too, among some medieval authorities that genuine *kawwanah* was hardly, or rarely, possible in their day. See Tosafot to *Berakot* 17b, *s.v.* רב שישא, and *Ṭur 'Oraḥ Ḥayyim*, par. 101; and see also the commentaries on Maimonides, Hilkot *Ḳeri'at Shema'* IV.7. The *Migdal 'Oz* there calls attention to the contradiction in the stricture by R. Abraham b. David.

180. N. H. Ṭur-Sinai, ספר איוב (Tel Aviv, 1954), p. 119; also Duhm, *Die Psalmen, Kurzer Hand-Commentar zum A.T.* (Leipzig and Tübingen, 1899), p. 202. Cf. *Targum Jonathan* on Ps. 78:8.

181. Ṭur-Sinai, *loc. cit.*

182. In an essay entitled "Kawwana," H. G. Enelow (*Selected Works* [privately printed, 1935], IV, 256 f.), takes other biblical verses as well to be the "foreshadowing" of *kawwanah*. He also discusses in this essay the various ways in which the term was used by medieval Jewish philosophers and "the kabbalistic construction of kawwana."

183. Above, pp. 168–170.

Notes to Chapter VIII

1. M. Kadushin, *Organic Thinking* (New York, 1938), pp. 95 f. (this book will be referred to hereafter as *OT*).

2. M. Kadushin, *The Rabbinic Mind* (New York, 1952), pp. 124 f. (this book will be referred to hereafter as *RM*). On the hermeneutic rules, see *ibid.*, pp. 91, 123.

3. *Ibid.*, p. 126, and the references there.

4. Above, p. 36.

5. S. Schechter, *Studies in Judaism: First Series* (Philadelphia, 1919), p. 112. Naḥmanides' statement is found at the beginning of his commentary on Maimonides' *Sefer ha-Miẓwot*. See also Simon Greenberg, *The Multiplication of the Mitzvot, Mordecai M. Kaplan Jubilee Volume* (New York, 1953), p. 386 and n. 32 there. On the number 613, see Ginzberg's note, *ibid.*, p. 388, and the reference in the following note there.

6. S. Schechter, *Some Aspects of Rabbinic Theology* (New York, 1910), p. 141. See also his remarks on the homiletical character of R. Simla'i's statement, *ibid.*, pp. 138 f.

7. *Ibid.*, pp. 141 f.

8. *'Erubin* 54b. See Rashi, *ad loc.*

9. *Sifra* on Lev. 25:1, ed. Weiss (Vienna, 1862), p. 105a. At the beginning of his introduction to *Zera'im*, in his commentary on the Mishnah, Maimonides quotes this and the preceding statement as showing that the "explanations," namely, the details of a miẓwah, were given to Moses orally by God. He illustrates with an example of the miẓwah of the *sukkah* (the building and dwelling in a booth as ordained in Lev. 23:42).

10. *RM*, pp. 353 ff.

11. On the term "Midrash," see Bacher, ערכי מדרש (Tel Aviv, 1923), *s.v.* מדרש. See also *Ḳiddushin* 49b.

12. *Sifra* on Lev. 26:14, ed. Weiss, 11b. See also other such passages in *RM*, pp. 354 f.

13. כל מלי דרבנן אסמכינהו על לאו דלא תסור: *Berakot* 19b. See also I. H. Weiss, דור דור ודורשיו (4th ed.; Wilna, 1904), II, 49 f.

14. *Midrash Tannaim*, ed. Hoffmann (Berlin, 1909), p. 103, and the references there.

15. See, e.g., *Num. R.* XIV.4.

16. *Beẓah* 3b; cf. *Shabbat* 34a. See Ginzberg, *A Commentary on The Palestinian Talmud* (New York, 1941), I, 150 f.

17. Ginzberg's view (*loc. cit.*) is somewhat different.

18. *Yebamot* 20a. Similarly, in the case in *Ḥullin* 106a.

19. *Yer. Yebamot* II.4, 3d.

20. See G. Alon, מחקרים (Tel Aviv, 1958), II, 113. We are indebted to Alon for several references used in this discussion.

21. See also Greenberg's discussion on *miẓwot de-rabbanan—op. cit.*, pp. 386 ff.

22. See *Soṭah* 44b, and Rashi, *ad loc.*, who explains the term to refer to a transgression of "the words of the *Soferim*." Cf. *Menaḥot* 36a.

23. *Pesiḳta Rabbati*, ed. Friedmann (Vienna, 1880), p. 7b, and the parallels referred to there.

24. *Yer. Sukkah* III.4, 53d, על מצות הדלקת נר חנכה. See below, n. 27. We have discussed the shift from the second to the third person in the Birkat ha-Miẓwot elsewhere (*RM*, pp. 266 ff.).

25. *Yer. Sukkah, loc. cit.*

26. Cf. Babli *Sukkah* 46a. The words מצות לולב and מצות זקנים there refer to the endings of berakot, and hence not as Rashi interprets them (see שירי קרבן to *Yer. Sukkah, loc. cit.*).

27. *Num. R.* XIV.4; *Pesikta Rabbati*, ed. Friedmann, p. 9a–b. The authorities are changed around in this version but the text in the Yerushalmi seems to be correct; see R. Samuel Strashun's note to *Num. R.*, *loc. cit.* The norm has been established that in the berakot rabbinical ordinances, too, are to be characterized as miẓwot of God; see Maimonides, Hilkot *Berakot* XI.3, and the *Kesef Mishneh*, *ad loc.* But the rule is established on the basis of the discussion in the Babli, and that discussion is rather puzzling. In the Babli (*Shabbat* 23a; *Sukkah* 46a), the berakah on the light of Ḥanukkah ends with וצונו להדליק נר של חנוכה. According to that ending, kindling the light of Ḥanukkah is a miẓwah of God, even though this is not emphasized as strongly as in Rab's berakah. But the Babli continues by asking, "And where has He commanded us?" Two answers are given, one referring to Deut. 11:17 and the other to Deut. 32:7. The question and the answers by only associating the rabbinical ordinance with miẓwot qualify the berakah itself; indeed, on that basis, we should have expected the ending in the berakah to refer to *miẓwat Zekenim*, and not to the specific manner of kindling the light of Ḥanukkah.

28. Sifra, ed. Weiss, 23b; *Shebuot* III.6; *ibid.*, 21b. "On which he stands sworn from Mount Sinai" (*ibid.*, 22b; *Makkot* 22a).

29. Mekilta on Exod. 21:6, ed. Horovitz and Rabin (Frankfurt am Main, 1928), p. 253.

30. L. Ginzberg, *Legends of the Jews* (Philadelphia, 1911), III, 97 and IV, 39, n. 215.

31. *Shebuot* 39a. This section of the baraita is a distinct entity in itself, being another interpretation of Deut. 29:14. Cf. *Tanḥuma, Niẓẓabim*, par. 3. Other passages to the same effect—*Sifre* on Deut. 11:22, ed. Friedmann, p. 84b; *Tanḥuma*, ed. Buber, II, p. 58b, and the parallels there. ("Even what a faithful pupil will ask his master").

32. *RM*, pp. 341 ff.

33. *Ibid.*, p. 353, and the notes there.

34. Above, p. 170.

35. Greenberg, *op. cit.*, pp. 381–84, and the references cited there. As Greenberg indicates, it is not always easy to determine the meaning of the biblical term, since it may refer either to commands of God or of man.

36. The conceptual term is miẓwot, the plural; miẓwah (singular) usually refers to one of the miẓwot. There are instances, however, where miẓwah evidently possesses another connotation, but we shall not engage in an analysis of those instances now.

37. Above, Chaps. III–IV.

38. For example, *Lev. R.*, V.4 ed. Margulies (Jerusalem, 1958), p. 111, and the parallels referred to in the notes there. Men and women are described, in Aramaic, as lovers of miẓweta'; see S. Lieberman, *Greek in Jewish Palestine* (New York, 1942), pp. 71 f. and the notes.

39. *Lev. R.* XXXIV.4, ed. Margulies, pp. 779 f. See also *Deut. R.*, ed. Lieberman, p. 36 and n. 10, and the references there.

40. *Yer. Pe'ah* I,15b. See G. Alon, תולדות היהודים (Tel Aviv, 1953), I, 333, and see also, for a discussion of this law, above, p. 24. The Aramaic plural similarly may connote charity; see, for example, *Lev. R.* XXXIV.14, ed. Margulies, p. 806. Add to the sources in Alon, *loc. cit.*, n. 68: *Mekilta*, ed. Horovitz and Rabin, p. 78, and see the notes there.

41. *Tos. Pe'ah* IV.19, ed. Lieberman, p. 60. Lieberman, *Tos. Kif.*, I, 191, calls attention to Maimonides' statement (Hilkot *Mattenot 'Aniyyim* X.1) on the need for being

more careful with regard to "the miẓwah of *ẓedaḳah* than with regard to all the [other] positive miẓwot."

42. *Seder 'Olam*, Chap. V, and *Sanhedrin* 56a (baraita). These and other references are cited in Ginzberg, *Legends*, V, 92, n. 55, where there is a discussion of the subject. See also *ibid.*, I, 71. *Dinim*, here and elsewhere, are the laws according to which the courts render their decisions (Ginzberg, *Commentary*, IV, 62).

43. Above, pp. 42 ff.

44. Above, p. 56.

45. *Seder Eliahu*, ed. Friedmann (Vienna, 1900), p. 74, and see above, p. 43, where other formulations of universal ethics are also given.

46. The passage enumerates the wicked men who, because they engaged in these things, "were uprooted from the world."

47. See *Tanḥuma*, *Teẓe*, par. 2, ed. Buber (Wilna, 1885), V, 17a–b, and *OT*, pp. 111–12.

48. *Makkot* III.15.

49. *Baba' Meẓi'a* IV.3 ff., and the Babli, *ibid.*, 49b–58b, *passim*.

50. *Sifra* on Lev. 25:17, ed. Weiss, p. 107d; *Baba' Meẓi'a* 58b.

51. *Ibid.*

52. *Baba' Meẓi'a* IV.10. See above, p. 48.

53. *Baba' Meẓi'a* 58b. See the other examples at pp. 58b–59b; (also above, p. 60).

54. *Ibid.*

55. *Ibid.*

56. *Ibid.*

57. See, for example, the excellent discussion in M. Lazarus, *The Ethics of Judaism* (Philadelphia, 1901), II, 151–75.

58. *Ibid.*, pp. 167 f.

59. *Ibid.*, pp. 151 f., 155, note. He cites Lev. 25:14, 17; Exod. 22:20; Lev. 19:33; and Deut. 23:16–17.

60. On this point, see also the discussion on other rabbinic concepts above, p. 168. For a more extensive treatment, see *RM*, pp. 288 ff.

61. *Baba' Meẓi'a* 59a, for the latter example. *'Ona'ah*, *gezel*, *ẓedaḳah*, etc., are concepts that are concretized in acts or situations.

62. Above, p. 56.

63. In accordance with the quotation in *Yer. Berakot* V.3, 9c. As has been pointed out, the rendering of *Targum Jonathan* with respect to the halakah itself agrees with the view of the Rabbanan. See *Ḥullin* 68b, and the Sifra on the verse, ed. Weiss, p. 99b.

64. *OT*, pp. 192–96, and *RM*, pp. 110 f.

65. Above, p. 85.

66. Above, p. 128—the decision of R. Joḥanan.

67. See the quotations given by Albeck, *Commentary on Ḳodashim* (Jerusalem and Tel Aviv, 1956), p. 403.

68. For examples, see above, p. 80.

69. *Yer. Berakot* V.3, 9c; *ibid.*, *Megillah* IV.10, 75c, and cf. Babli *Berakot* 33b. We have rendered according to *Yer. Megillah* IV.10, 75c. The text in the Babli is מפני שעושה מדותיו של הקב״ה רחמים ואינן אלא גזירות, and the reading in *Yer. Berakot* seems to have been affected by that text.

70. *Berakot* III.1 (*Megillah* IV.9), and Rashi on the mishnah.

71. See Rashi, *loc. cit.*, and Maimonides, Hilkot *Tefillah* IX.7.

72. See the sources referred to in n. 69 above. Modern writers have assumed that R. Jose b. Bun's comment is of one piece with the rule in the Mishnah. See, for example, Schechter, *Some Aspects of Rabbinic Theology*, p. 10, n. 1, who also cites other scholars. It is true that the rule in the Mishnah is directed against several sectarian practices and doctrines, one of which we have discussed in an earlier work (*RM*, pp. 344 f.). But R. Jose b. Bun was among the last of the great Palestinian Amoraim (Z. Frankel, *Mebo ha-Yerushalmi*, [Breslau, 1870], p. 102a). His warning, if it was such, was certainly not directed against a sect which persisted, after all those hundreds of years, in praying in the synagogue. Actually, however, his statement was not directed against a sect at all, but consists of an objection to a *rabbinic* interpretation which differs from his, and his view therefore represents merely a personal predilection. It no more reflects a sectarian controversy than do the other amoraic interpretations of the rule in the Mishnah.

73. *Sifra*, *Ḳedoshim*, end, ed. Weiss, 93d.

74. Acceptance of *malkut Shamayim* is associated with *gezerot* in the passages cited above, p. 80. But there acceptance of God's kingship precedes acceptance of the decrees.

75. Above, pp. 43 f., and the discussion there.

76. See Rashi to *Yoma* 67b, *s.v.* השטן and תלמוד לומר.

77. See *Pesiḳta de R. Kahana* (Lyck, 1868), ed. Buber, pp. 40a–b, and the parallels there. The interpretation is based on *ḥuḳḳat*, a word taken to refer to *gezerah* (see the plural *ḥuḳḳotai* as used in the Sifra passage just discussed, and cited above, p. 44). The rabbis feel that there are reasons for the *ḥuḳḳim*, and that they will be revealed *le-'atid la-bo*, though not in this world, and that these טעמי תורה were revealed to Moses by God (see *Pesiḳta de R. Kahana*, ed. Buber, 39a–b, and the notes and parallels there).

78. See also Rab's statement in *Niddah* 35b.

79. גדול(ה) מצווה ועושה ממי שאינו מצווה ועושה; the references are given in the notes following.

80. *Ḳiddushin* 31a; *'Abodah Zarah* 23b–24a.

81. *Ḳiddushin* 31a.

82. Above, p. 207.

83. *Baba' Ḳamma'* 38a; *'Abodah Zarah* 2b–3a.

84. On the ethical concepts involved in the seven miẓwot, see above, p. 206.

85. It occurs once more in *Ḳiddushin*, *loc. cit.* (*Baba' Ḳamma'* 87a), where it is quoted with approval by R. Joseph (see Heinemann's discussion, טעמי המצוות, I [3d ed.; Jerusalem, 1954], 23 f.). Heinemann (*ibid.*, p. 24) points out that there are rabbinic statements which praise those who are not "commanded."

86. *Yer. Pe'ah* I.1, 15c; *ibid.*, *Ḳiddushin*, I.7, 61b. Dama's devotion to his parents, his probity, and even his character as a pagan (idol-worshipper) come out more clearly here.

87. מצות לאו ליהנות ניתנו: *Rosh ha-Shanah* 28a; *'Erubin* 31a; *Ḥullin* 89a.

88. Rashi to *Rosh ha-Shanah* 28a, *s.v.* לא ליהנות.

89. See R. Nissim to *Nedarim* 15b, *s.v.* שאין קיום המצות חשוב הנאה אבל מכל: והא מן מקום אי מתהני גופיה בהדי דמקיים מצוה הנאה מקרי. See also the next note.

90. *Rosh ha-Shanah, loc. cit.* Notice there also that only where enjoyment is forbidden because of a vow is the use of the fountain prohibited in the summer, and so similarly in the related case.

91. *Nedarim* 16b.

92. The application is not made specifically, to be sure. According to R. Joseph, the making of an *'erub* is permitted only for a *debar mizwah*, and going to a house of mourning and going to a wedding feast (*'Erubin* V.1) are taken by R. Joseph to be examples of his principle (*'Erubin* 82a). In a "defense" of R. Joseph in *ibid.*, 31a, the point is made that "all" hold both Raba's principle and R. Joseph's principle. In that case, Raba's principle thus applies to the going to a house of mourning and going to a wedding feast, acts of *gemilut ḥasadim.*

93. On these acts as *gemilut ḥasadim*, see above, p. 281, n. 147.

94. Lazarus, *op. cit.*, I, pp. 283 f.

95. A midrash beginning with a phrase reminiscent of Raba's principle—לא נתנו המצוות אלא לצרוף את הבירויות בהם—is nevertheless not germane to our thesis. It teaches that all the miẓwot are only a means. This midrash is found in *Bereshit R.* XLIV.1, ed. Theodor, p. 424, and has many parallels and versions (see the references and notes there). The meaning of the midrash hinges on the word לצרוף. Margulies has demonstrated that the word means "to test"—see his edition of *Lev. R.*, p. 277, n. 2. The parallel there (*Lev. R.* XII.3) also supplies the last part of the midrash. The passage, then, teaches that the miẓwot were given in order to test men for it makes no difference to God whether an animal be slaughtered at the throat or at the neck, and (*Lev. R.*) that when men meet the tests they are given reward. An unusual idea is thus contained in this midrash; in a related context above (p. 209), for example, it is taught that God has compassion on animals, is concerned for them. Furthermore, the phrase, "the miẓwot were given," refers, as in Raba's principle, to all miẓwot, and hence also to ethical matters, and both the Bible and the rabbis emphasize that these are indeed of concern to God. Medieval philosophers differ as to the meaning of לצרוף in this midrash. According to Heinemann, Maimonides interprets the phrase to mean that the miẓwot, when we obey them, prepare us for the world to come (*op. cit.*, I, 155, n. 124). Naḥmanides takes the word, apparently, to mean "to purify the soul" by teaching ethical modes or qualities; see his *Commentary on the Pentateuch*, Deut. 22:6.

96. *Yoma* VIII.6: וכל ספק נפשות דוחה את השבת. See also *Tos. Shabbat* XV (XVI). 16, ed. Zuckermandel and Lieberman, p. 134.

97. See *Yoma* 82a, and Maimonides, Hilkot *Shabbat* II.1.

98. In connection with this rule, Maimonides declares that the laws of the Torah are *raḥamim*, *ḥesed* (lovingkindness), and peace in the world (*op. cit.*, II.3).

99. *Nazir* VII.1. If there is no one else to attend to it.

100. *Berakot* 19b and Tosafot, *ad loc.*, and compare the parallels. See also *Sifre* on Num. 6:6–7, ed. Horovitz, p. 33 and n. 15 there.

101. *Berakot* 19b–20a, and *Megillah* 3b. In *Berakot* 20a, *s.v.* שב ואל תעשה, Rashi argues that whereas the case concerning the paschal lamb represents an instance of

superseding because of *kebod ha-beriyyot*, this is not true in the case of the high priest and the Nazarite. But see Tosafot, *ibid.*, on the same catchword.

102. *Ketubbot* 17a (*Megillah* 3b, 29a). A funeral escort in general, not a *met mizwah*; see Tosafot, *ibid.*, *s.v.* להוצאת. See also above, p. 29.

103. Above, pp. 176 f.

104. *Kelim* I.6–9. Cf. *Sifre Zuṭṭa*, ed. Horovitz, p. 228, and see the notes there. Although the versions differ, in both the number is actually eleven and not ten. See Albeck's discussion in his edition of *Ṭoharot*, pp. 508 f.; as he says, "ten" need not be taken literally.

105. *Sifre Zuṭṭa*, *loc. cit.* (*Num. R.* VII.8; *Yalḳuṭ Shime'oni*, Naso', par. 698).

106. *Mekilta*, ed. J. Z. Lauterbach (Philadelphia, 1933), I, 6; and see *RM*, p. 250.

107. Maimonides declares that the Temple and Jerusalem are permanently holy because of the *Shekinah* (Hilkot *Bet ha-Beḥirah* VI.16).

108. *Zebaḥim* V.1–5.

109. *Ibid.*, V.3, 5. In the Second Temple, the "enclosures" referred to the area within the Gates of Nicanor; see *Tos. Kelim, Baba' Ḳamma'* I.9, 12; *Zebaḥim* 116b. The word "curtains" refers to an analogous area in the period of the Tabernacle in the wilderness.

110. *Zebaḥim* V.6–8.

111. *Ibid.*, בכל העיר. A degree of levitical impurity is permitted in the city, and from that point of view only the *ḳodshe ḳodashim* are to be eaten in "a holy place." See *ibid.*, 55a.

112. *Zebaḥim* V.8. In the *Sifre* on Num. 18:20, ed. Horovitz, p. 142 (bottom), the first-born of the clean cattle is counted among the offerings which may be eaten by the priests outside the Temple and Jerusalem, the category we are about to take up. Lieberman explains this on the ground that the actual *mattanah* (see the next note) takes place wherever the animal is turned over to the priest, so that if the animal develops a blemish, the priest may eat it anywhere; if it is without a blemish and hence to be offered by the priest in the Temple, the animal thus offered is the priest's animal, since the *mattanah* had already taken place (see *Tos. Kif.*, II, 812, beginning אבל). But the criterion we speak of is reflected also in other examples. While the tithe of cattle may be eaten by any person, there are the portions of the thank offering, for example, that must be given the priests, yet both the tithe of cattle and the thank offering are *ḳodashim ḳallim* (*Zebaḥim* V.6, 8). Each of the first two grades has gradations of its own (*ibid.*, X.2–6; and cf. *ibid.*, I.2).

113. "Twenty-four *mattenot kehunah* [were given] to Aaron and his sons" by God (*Tos. Ḥallah* II.7 f., ed. Lieberman, p. 281 f., and the parallels there).

114. *Zebaḥim* V.1 f, 6 f.

115. *Tos. Ḥallah*, II.7, 9. For the term *ḳodshe ha-gebul*, see the reference in the next note.

116. See *Sifre* on Numbers, *piska'* 107, ed. Horovitz, pp. 134 (bottom)–136. Cf. *Tos. Ḥallah* II.10, ed. Lieberman, p. 282.

117. *Ibid.* See Lieberman, *Tos. Kif.*, II, 813, *s.v.* לחייב. The manner in which he quotes the passage in the Sifre enables the seriatim order and the hierarchical gradation to stand out.

118. Sifre on Numbers, *loc. cit.*

119. *Terumot* III.6, 7, and *Ma'aser Sheni* V.11. But compare *Sifre* Deut., *piska'* 303, ed. Friedmann, p. 128b.

120. See *Rosh ha-Shanah* 12b. During the seventh year, of course, the land was fallow.

121. *Ma'aser Sheni* V.10; *Sifre* Deut., *loc. cit*; *Sifra* on Lev. 27:30, ed. Weiss, p. 115a.

122. See the first two references in the preceding note.

123. *Ma'aser Sheni* V.3 (*Pe'ah* VII.6; *'Eduyyot* IV.5), and *Kiddushin* 54b. On נטע רבעי and כרם רבעי, see *Tosefot Yom Ṭob* to *Pe'ah* VII.6, *s.v.* כרם, and see Albeck's note in his edition of *Zera'im*, p. 404.

124. See Maimonides, Hilkot *Ma'aser* I.2, and the discussion there in the *Kesef Mishneh*. See also *Yebamot* 74a.

125. *Zebaḥim* IV.6: לשם השם. (See also *ibid.*, 46b; Sifra, ed. Weiss, p. 7c.)

126. *Ibid.* See also *ibid.*, 2b.

127. See Lieberman, *Tos. Kif.*, I, 479, n. 72, who cites *Ḥallah* II.3, Yer. *Ma'aser Sheni* V.7, 56c, and *ibid.*, *Ḥallah*, Chap. I, end, 58a.

128. Maimonides, Hilkot *Terumot*, IV.16, and the *Kesef Mishneh*, *ad loc.*, and see Lieberman, *Tos. Kif.*, II, 755, who cites these and other references in *ibid.*, n. 40.

129. The term *maḥashabah* is used with reference to sacrifices in *Zebaḥim* IV.6, but in the parallel, *Tos. ibid.*, V.13, verb forms of *kawwanah* are employed as well. See also *Menaḥot* XIII.11, and *ibid.*, 110a. *Maḥashabah* is used with reference to *terumah* in *Giṭṭin* 31a, and see also Maimonides, *loc. cit.*

130. This holds true of the manner whereby all the things in the hierarchy become *ḳedushot*. According to R. Jose, if a man sets apart *terumah*, the first tithe, and *ma'aser sheni*, the acts make the portions holy even if they have not been designated by name, although, as Lieberman points out, he is required to make these designations afterward (see *Tos. Ma'aser Sheni* IV.14, ed. Lieberman, p. 267, and *Tos. Kif.*, II, 775).

131. Above, p. 191. On the uttering of an intention in a context other than that of *ḳedushah*, see n. 142 on p. 291.

132. *Ma'aser Sheni* IV.7.

133. *RM*, p. 181.

134. *Rosh ha-Shanah* II.7 and III.1.

135. *Ibid.*, II.8–9.

136. *Yer. Rosh ha-Shanah* I.3, 57b.

137. *Mekilta*, ed. Lauterbach, III, p. 203.

138. See Albeck's discussion of this *bet din* in his edition of *Mo'ed*, pp. 305 f., and see also n. 2 there.

139. *Rosh ha-Shanah* 24a.

140. This is the way the rabbis interpret the verse, as we can see from the examples about to be given.

141. *Mechilta de-Rabbi Simon b. Jochai*, ed. Hoffmann, p. 107, and the parallels in the notes. Cf. *Mekhilta D'Rabbi Sim'on b. Jochai*, ed. Epstein-Melamed, pp. 148 f., and the notes. "To make it holy" means to make the entire day holy, and the day begins on Sabbath Eve. See Rashi to the parallel in *Pesaḥim* 106a.

142. *Mekhilta D'Rabbi Sim'on, loc. cit.*

143. *Ibid.*

144. *Mechilta*, ed. Horovitz and Rabin, p. 30 (*Pesaḥ*); Sifre, ed. Horovitz, p. 194 (*Pesaḥ*); Sifra, ed. Weiss, p. 102b (*Sukkot*).

145. *Rosh ha-Shanah* 32a, where this rule is applied to that day.

146. *RM*, p. 181.

147. *RM*, pp. 171 ff.

148. *Ibid.*, pp. 171, 178 (bottom), 180 f. On *tefillin* as higher in the hierarchy than *mezuzot*, see *Menaḥot* 32a (baraita) and Rashi, *ad loc.* On *sefarim*, see *RM*, p. 172, n. 24.

149. See Maimonides, Hilkot *Sefer-Torah*, X.1.

150. Maimonides, Hilkot *Tefillin*, Chaps. I–III.

151. Above, p. 219.

152. Maimonides, *loc. cit.*, I.15, and the *Kesef Mishneh* there. See also Lieberman, *Tos. Kif.*, I, 47 f.

153. On that dogma, see *RM*, pp. 348 f.

154. *Ibid.*, p. 350.

155. *Megillah* III.1, 3, and *ibid.*, 26a.

156. In *RM*, pp. 178 f., we discussed also the matter of the holiness transmitted by a *Sefer Torah* to its accessories, and concluded that such transmission does not imply the notion that a holy object possesses theurgical efficacy. In all these instances, *ḳedushah* has no other effect but that of transmitting itself; it is not regarded as having any physical effect, nor as a spiritual agency which, if properly applied, can affect the welfare of the individual or the community.

157. *Soṭah* 39a (*Num. R.* XI.4)—the berakah of the priests before they bless the people.

158. Above, pp. 217 f.

159. *Yebamot* XI.2.

160. ולא הוא לוי הוא ישראל: Yer. *Nazir* VII.1, end. On the ranking of the groups, see *Horayot* III.8; cf. *Yebamot* II.4.

161. Alon, מחקרים בתולדות ישראל, I, 148–76, especially pp. 158 ff.

162. *Ibid.*, p. 174.

163. *Ibid.* Both "the contrary tradition" and the tradition with which it is in conflict have their roots in the Bible (*ibid.*, p. 175).

164. *Seder Eliahu*, ed. Friedmann, p. 72; cited by Alon, *loc. cit.*

165. Alon, *op. cit.*, p. 176. He points out (*ibid.*, p. 161, n. 61) that those who organized themselves into groups whose purpose it was to observe the laws of levitical purity did so because they were thus able to help each other observe those laws. Their purpose was not to acquire additional *ḳedushah* for themselves through laws not incumbent on everyone, for they taught that such laws, and others not generally observed at the time, were nevertheless laws intended for all Israel.

166. *Ibid.*, p. 176, and nn. 114 and 115.

167. *Ḥagigah* II.5; just as the priest does before eating *terumah* (*ibid.*).

168. The stressing of a concept is apparent in most of the other hierarchies as well: In the case of the holy areas, the concept stressed is *gilluy Shekinah*; in the case of sacrifices and tithes, it is *kehunah*; in the case of holy objects, it is Torah. The holy

days involve a large number of concepts, and the problem of accounting for the hierarchy is too complicated to be taken up here.

169. It was this organismic quality of the value complex that sectarian thought apparently lacked. The Sadducees maintained that *ḳedushah* was limited to the priests, while the Essenes insisted on the application of the laws of levitical purity to all Israel and at all times. See Alon's remarks, *op. cit.*, p. 176.

170. *Horayot* III.8. This statement, be it noted, comes at the end of a mishnah ranking the various groups in the people.

171. *Ḳinyan Torah* (*'Abot* VI.5). See *OT*, pp. 49 f. and the notes there. On "thirty" and on "twenty-four," see *Maḥzor Vitry*, pp. 558 f.

172. See *OT*, p. 42.

173. In the discussion of these phases, soon to follow, we have drawn upon the material in Schechter, *Aspects*, pp. 199 ff., although our discussion also contains rabbinic material not given there. In the analysis we depart from Schechter in a number of respects. We ought to add that Schechter's analysis is the first modern treatment of *ḳedushah*, and that it is most suggestive.

174. *Sifra* to Lev. 20:7, ed. Weiss, 91d. See Schechter, *Aspects*, p. 208, n. 2.

175. *Num. R.* XVII.7. See the longer quotation in Schechter, *loc. cit.*

176. *Mekilta*, ed. Lauterbach, III, p. 157.

177. *Lev. R.* XXIV.8, ed. Margulies, pp. 562 f.

178. Margulies, *ibid.*, n. 7, and mark the reading in the conclusion of the parallel cited there, referring to the *ḳedushot*: והלואי יהיו כופין אותן.

179. *Tanḥuma*, ed. Buber, III, p. 37b. Cf. also *Pesiḳta' de R. Kahana'*, ed. Buber, p. 16a.

180. *Tanḥuma*, ed. Buber, III, p. 37a; Schechter, *Aspects*, p. 200.

181. *Mekilta*, ed. Lauterbach, III, 157.

182. Above, p. 203.

183. Schechter, *Aspects*, p. 201.

184. *Ibid.*, p. 200 and the note there. Source is *Sifra*, ed. Weiss, 86c.

185. *Ibid.*, p. 201, and the note. Sources are *Mekilta*, ed. Horovitz and Rabin, p. 127; *Shabbat* 133b.

186. *Sifre* on Deut. 11:22, ed. Friedmann, p. 85a. "Called"—since biblical verses speak of Him as merciful and gracious (Exod. 34:6), and as righteous and loving (Ps. 145:17).

187. *Seder Eliahu*, ed. Friedmann, p. 65.

188. See Schechter, *Aspects*, p. 202, and the reference to *Gen. R.* LVIII.9.

189. See also Schechter, *Aspects*, pp. 203 f.

190. Above, p. 99.

191. For example, *Kelim* I.1–4, and *ibid.*, I.5.

192. *RM*, pp. 180 f.: מעלין בקדש ולא מורידין.

193. *Pesaḥim* I.6 (*'Eduyyot* II.1) and *ibid.*, 14a. The rabbis were reluctant to add to the sphere of *ṭum'ah*: *Beẓah* 7a ('Abaye) and Rashi, *ad loc.*

194. Maimonides, Hilkot *Ṭum'at 'Okelin* XVI.8 and the commentaries and the sources and references there. Maimonides states this again in the *Moreh Nebukim*, Part III, Chap. XLII.

195. *Sifra* on Lev. 16:16, ed. Weiss, p. 81c.

196. Tosafot to the parallel in *Shebu'ot* 7b, *s.v.* דלאו טומאה ממש נינהו אלא בלשון: ויש טומאה נכתבו.

197. Above, p. 25. Malbim to Sifra, *loc. cit.*, attempts to work out categories of another kind, but in doing so he is obliged to put the cardinal sins and defiling the Temple into one category.

198. *Lev. R.* XXIV.4, ed. Margulies, p. 556. See the notes.

199. *Sifra* on Lev. 19:2, ed. Weiss, p. 86c: פרושים היו.

200. Cf. *Lev. R.* XXIV.6, ed. Margulies, pp. 559 f., and the parallel in the notes. See also Rashi on Lev. 19:2.

201. *Sifra* on Lev. 18:30, ed. Weiss, p. 86d, and the references there.

202. Schechter, *Aspects*, p. 206.

203. *Mekilta*, ed. Friedmann, 63a; (ed. Horovitz and Rabin, p. 209).

204. *Sifra*, 93b. Cf. *Num. R.* IX.7.

205. Schechter, *op. cit.*, p. 206 and the discussion following there.

206. *Sifra* on Lev. 11:43, and R. Abraham b. David of Posquière's first explanation. But notice that he gives a second, made by others, in which it is obvious that they take the Sifra statement to refer altogether to nonhierarchical *ṭum'ah*; and notice, too, how Schechter (*Aspects*, p. 207, n. 2) on the basis of this second explanation even suggests an emendation.

207. *Pesaḥim* 104a; '*Abodah Zarah* 50a, and Rashi and Tosafot, *ad loc.* In the version in *Koheleth R.* IX.9, R. Menaḥem is called נחום איש קדש קדשים.

208. *Makkot* III.15. See above, p. 207.

209. *Yebamot* 20a. (Cf. Sifre, ed. Friedmann, p. 95a): קדש עצמך במותר לך.

210. *Shebu'ot* 18b. For his sexual precaution R. Judah the Prince was called "the holy" (*Shabbat* 118b). See L. Epstein, *Sex Laws and Customs in Judaism* (New York, 1948), p. 147.

211. *Ta'anit* 11a, ed. Malter, p. 77 (ed. minor), and the sources referred to there.

212. Above, pp. 132 f.

213. Above, pp. 133 f.

214. Above, pp. 135 f.

215. See the discussions on the Ḳaddish (above, pp. 141 f.) and the Ḳedushah (pp. 142 ff.).

216. See Maimonides, Hilkot '*Abot ha-Tum'ot* VI.1, and the *Kesef Mishneh* there.

217. *Ibid.*, VI.2, and the sources in the commentaries.

218. *Ibid.*, VI.6, and the sources in the *Kesef Mishnah*, *ad loc.*

219. The acknowledgment by the individual Gentile was only a partial acknowledgment since it did not commit him.

220. *RM*, p. 289.

221. Holtz, "Kiddush Hashem and Hillul Hashem," *Judaism*, X, No. 4 (1961), 360 ff.

222. Above, p. 203.

223. Above, p. 186.

224. Above, pp. 197 f.

225. Above, p. 202 f. and p. 295, n. 27; Baer, סדר עבודת ישראל (Roedelheim, 1868), p. 439, and the notes and references there; Singer, *Daily Prayer Book* (London, 1890), p. 274. For the character of the objects employed in such acts, see the discussion in *RM*, pp. 170 ff.

226. For example, when putting on the *ṭallit* (*Berakot* 60b). See the following note.

227. For example, on the washing of the hands (*ibid.*), and on the taking of the *lulab* (*Sukkah* 46a). For the differences implied in these two usages, see *Pesaḥim* 7a–b, and the commentaries there, and see Lieberman, *Tos. Kif.*, I, 115 f., and his reference to the long discussion by Ibn Plat found in the *Sefer ha-Pardes*, ed. H. L. Ehrenreich (Budapest, 1924), pp. 195 ff.

228. כל המצוות מברך עליהן עובר לעשייתן—*Pesaḥim* 7b (and parallels). The exception is immersion (*ibid.*, and see Tosafot, *ibid.*, *s.v.* על הטבילה). For other occasions when the berakah is said after the act, and the reasons given therefor, see Lieberman, *op. cit.*, p. 113, *s.v.* המכסה, and pp. 116 f. R. 'Amram Gaon, quoted by R. Jonah to *Berakot* 60b, teaches that the rule in *Pesaḥim* 7b refers specifically to the Birkat ha-Miẓwot but not necessarily to other berakot. See also the discussion in *Sefer Abudraham*, ed. H. L. Ehrenreich (Cluj-Klausenburg, 1935), pp. 68 f.

229. We noticed above (p. 65) that there must be no interruption between the recitation of the berakah on bread and the eating of the first morsel. The rule that there must be no interruption between the berakah and the act to which the berakah refers holds with respect to all berakot. See Maimonides, Hilkot *Berakot* I.8 and the *Kesef Mishneh*, *ad loc.*

230. Above, pp. 108 ff.

231. *Mechilta*, ed. Horovitz and Rabin, p. 127, and the parallels there.

232. For the term *hiddur miẓwah*, see the halakah in *Baba Ḳamma'* 9b.

233. Above, p. 223, and the reference to Schechter in the note.

234. Above.

235. Maimonides, *Sefer ha-Miẓwot*, שורש רביעי, although his interpretation as a whole is not the same as ours.

236. שכל המצות טעונות ברכה (*Yer. Berakot* VI.1, 10a).

237. *Tos. Berakot* VI (VII).9, ed. Lieberman, p. 36— העושה כל המצות מברך עליהן.

238. Above, pp. 205 ff.

239. Lieberman, *Tos. Kif.*, I, 112, *s.v.* העושה.

240. *Ibid.*

241. See the *responsum* by Ibn Plat in S. Asaf, ספרן של ראשונים (Jerusalem, 1935), p. 200 ff. See also Lieberman, *loc. cit.*, n. 39, who refers to Asaf and others, and see also *RM*, p. 174, n. 31.

242. *Roḳeah*, 366 (cited by Lieberman, *loc. cit.*, text) lays down the rule that all the miẓwot to which non-Jews are also expected to conform—miẓwot having to do with charity, respect for the aged, and the like—do not require a berakah. But he does not take into account, as does Ibn Plat, the many other miẓwot which do not require a berakah.

243. Above, pp. 215 f.

244. Maimonides, Hilkot *Berakot*, XI.2.

245. *Kesef Mishneh* to *ibid.* Maimonides regards these two categories as basic general categories (see above, p. 250, n. 95, and the stricture there).

246. The law is in Deut. 22:8, and it adds the explanation, "that thou bring not blood upon thy house, if any man fall from thence." See *Sifre* Deut. to this verse, ed. Friedmann, p. 116a.

247. *Sefer Abudraham*, ed. Ehrenreich, p. 81, and the references given by Ehrenreich in n. 198 there. See also *Siddur R. Saadia*, p. 101.

248. See the explanation given by Ibn Plat, *loc. cit.*

Index

of universal concepts of, 53; interrelation of Haggadah and, 10; interrelation of worship and, 171ff.; philosophical approach misrepresents rabbinic, 8. *See also derek erez*; Ethical concepts; Morality
Ethics of Judaism (M. Lazarus), 241n., 296nn., 298n.
Exodus from Egypt, is *ge'ullah* (redemption), 93; felt as personal experience, 93f.; a rabbinic dogma, 94; recalled in 'Emet we-Yazzib, 92f.
Experience, mediated by concepts, 3; prayer is an incomplete, 14; Exodus from Egypt as personal, 93f.
Experience of God, in worship, 3; is an emphatic trend, 15, 35f.; mediated by concepts, 14f., 81; only partly communicable, 15; a paradox, 15; *gilluy Shekinah* as, 163f. *See also* Normal mysticism
Evil tidings, evoke berakah, 67
evil *yezer*, angels not subject to, 224; Israel exposed to, 279n.; *kedushah* as aid in overcoming, 224; raises objection to laws peculiar to Israel, 44f.
Ezekiel, "the son of righteous people," 112

Faith, see *'emunah*
Fearers of Heaven, non-Jews who rejected idolatry, 57
Festivals, 'Amidah on, 97
Finkelstein, L., 81, 100, 253n., 254nn., 255n., 256n., 259n., 261n., 262nn., 263nn., 264n., 267n., 270n., 272n., 274nn., 276n., 277n., 278n., 279n.
First Berakah of Birkat ha-Mazon, *see* Birkat ha-Mazon, First Berakah of
First Temple, locale of *gilluy Shekinah*, 163; *derek erez* practiced by those who lived in days of, 42
Folk, the, and normal mysticism, 13ff., 16f.; Halakah often reflects practice of, 25; interaction of rabbis and, in ethical sphere, 57ff.
Food, Gods' love as manifested in, 70
Forgiveness, 48
Form, in devices for emphasis, 37; in worship, 71ff., 76f., 77, 98 (the Daily Tefillah)
Fowler, W. W., 289n.
Frankel, Z., 297n.
Frankfort, H., 288n.
Friedmann, M., 245n., 249n., 256n., 259n., 271n.
From Religion to Philosophy (F. M. Cornford), 288n.
From the Stone Age to Christianity (W. F. Albright), 288n., 289nn.

Rabban Gamaliel, 98, 118, 240n., 262n.
Garfiel, E., 260n.
geburot, of rain and resurrection, 264n. *See also nissim*
Geiger, A., 265n.
gemilut ḥasadim (act[s] of lovingkindness), Birkat Ḥatanim and Birkat 'Abelim as, 5, 151ff., 281n.; Second Berakah in Birkat 'Abelim is, 155; Fifth Berakah in Birkat Ḥatanim is, 158; God's acts of, 34, 68, 281n.; imitation of God in *zedakah* and, 225f.; gladdening bride and groom is, 156; in comforting mourners, 153; specified acts of, 226; study of Torah may be interrupted for, 29; taking part in a funeral escort is, 29; taking part in a wedding procession is, 29; gradation in, 240n.; associated with *'erub*, 214, 298n.; may be overriding mizwot, 215; difference between *zedakah* and, 21; importance of *zedakah* and, 206; reflects emphasis on love and on individual, 27; a concept of *derek erez*, 42
Gentile(s), like high priest if he studies Torah, 29; Hillel's teaching to the, 35; *kiddush ha-Shem* in relations with, 133f.; who observed *kibbud 'ab wa-'em* (honoring of parents), 213; who rejected idolatry, 57; comforting of mourners of, 281n.; righteous of, 29, 250n., Second Berakah of 'Amidah refers also to, 267n.; recognition of legal institutions of, 30
Geonica (L. Ginzberg), 260n., 261n., 262n., 265n., 278nn., 279nn., 280nn.

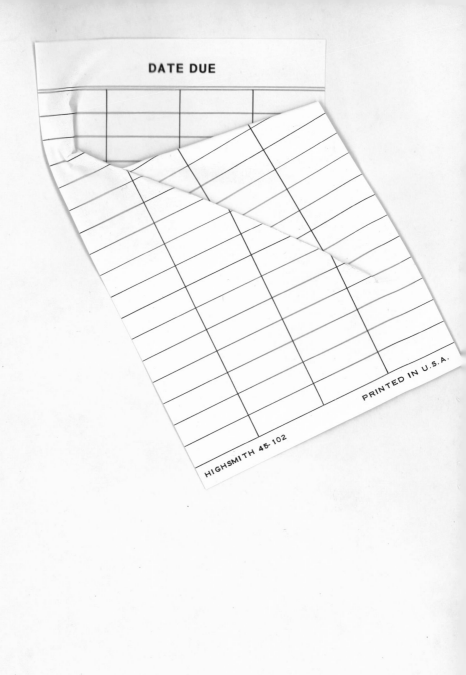

61518336R00171

Made in the USA
Lexington, KY
13 March 2017

RECIPE INDEX

For printable versions of the worksheets: please visit, www.biggirlsdoitrunning.com.

Positive mind,
strong body,
BEAUTIFUL LIFE

I CAN DO THIS!

Journal

Think Positive

Running Log

date	time	distance	walking speed	running speed	notes

get out and wog!

date:

How I'm feeling

place photo here

Hello beautiful!

Measurements

	arms	chest	waist	hips	thighs	" lost
JAN						
FEB						
MAR						
APR						
MAY						
JUNE						
JULY						
AUG						
SEPT						
OCT						
NOV						
DEC						
total lost						

You are doing fantastic!

Neutral Choices

FATS

nuts and nut butters
avocado
butter
cheese
cream
mayo
oils
whole eggs
full fat meats
chocolate
ice cream *
nut flour

*Bryers Carb Smart and no sugar added coconut dream

UNLIMITED/EITHER PLATE

spices
lemons & limes
berries
asparagus
broccoli
cabbage
cauliflower
celery
cucumber
egg plant
green beans
all greens
mushrooms
onions
peppers
sprouts
squash
tomatoes (salsa)
zucchini
Dreamfields pasta
Okios OOO yogurt
Low carb/Whole wheat Mission wraps

CARBS/STARCHES

sprouted breads
sprouted cereal
blue corn chips
old fashioned oats
apples
apricots
bananas
grapes
kiwi
melon
oranges/tangerines
peaches
nectarines
pears
pineapple
plums
popcorn
quinoa
rice (brown, wild)
beans
hummus
lentils
carrots
corn
potatoes (sweet)
WASA crackers (4)

The three possible plates for your meal

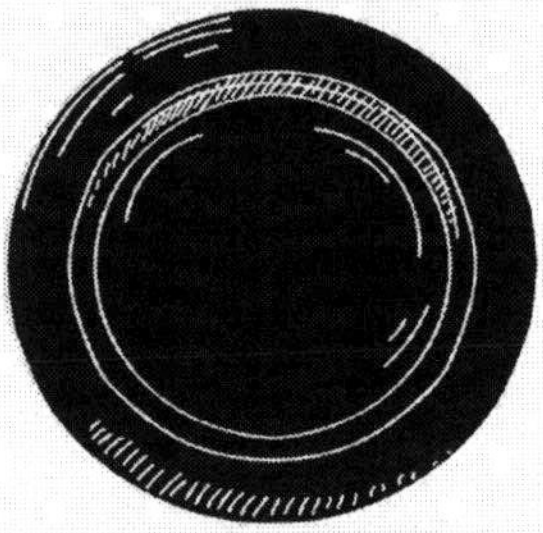

THE BLACK PLATE

Protein + Fat(s)

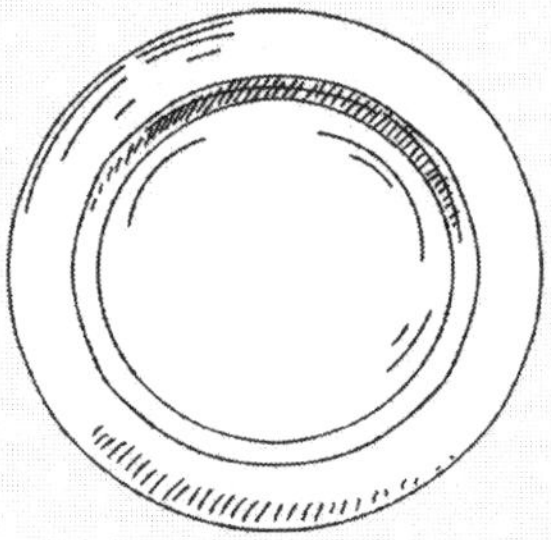

THE WHITE PLATE

Protein + Carbohydrates and starches

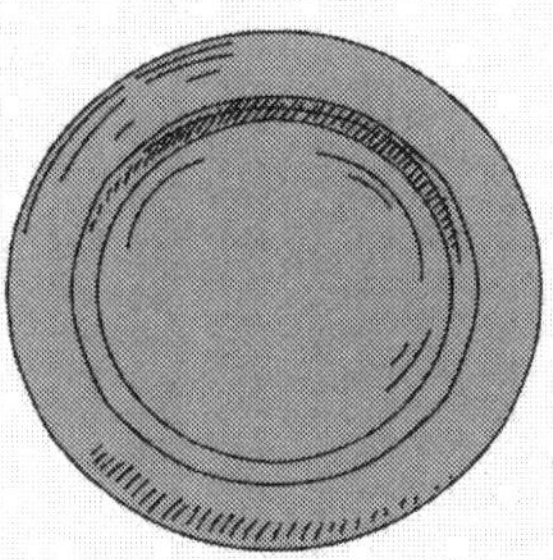

THE GRAY PLATE

Protein + Fat(s) + Carbohydrates/starches
(4-5 of these per week max)

Weekly Meal Planner

	breakfast	lunch	snack	dinner
SUNDAY	☐ white plate ☐ black plate	☐ white plate ☐ black plate	☐ white plate ☐ black plate	☐ white plate ☐ black plate
MONDAY	☐ white plate ☐ black plate	☐ white plate ☐ black plate	☐ white plate ☐ black plate	☐ white plate ☐ black plate
TUESDAY	☐ white plate ☐ black plate	☐ white plate ☐ black plate	☐ white plate ☐ black plate	☐ white plate ☐ black plate
WEDNESDAY	☐ white plate ☐ black plate	☐ white plate ☐ black plate	☐ white plate ☐ black plate	☐ white plate ☐ black plate
THURSDAY	☐ white plate ☐ black plate	☐ white plate ☐ black plate	☐ white plate ☐ black plate	☐ white plate ☐ black plate
FRIDAY	☐ white plate ☐ black plate	☐ white plate ☐ black plate	☐ white plate ☐ black plate	☐ white plate ☐ black plate
SATURDAY	☐ white plate ☐ black plate	☐ white plate ☐ black plate	☐ white plate ☐ black plate	☐ white plate ☐ black plate

Grocery List

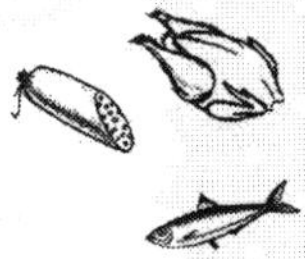

Grocery List

Oikos Triple 0 yogurt
Ezekiel brand breads & cereals – they even have English muffins
WASA brand crackers
Berries
Eggs – farm fresh are the best!
Applegate brand sausages (OMG, so good!)
Pancakes made from oats
Veggies – eat them in season to save. Local farmer's markets are the awesome.
Lily's brand chocolate
Dreamfields brand pasta
Meat & seafood – we try to do local, lean and grass fed. Laura's beef is a great brand
Almond milk – we love Califia Farms brand
Fairlife brand milk
Breyer's Carb Smart ice cream
Nuts – my family loves nuts, especially almonds and cashews
Baked blue corn chips
Mission brand low carb wraps (we use these for roll ups in place of sandwiches and for taco Tuesday)
Kerry's Gold brand butter
Sour cream – yep, the real stuff
Cheese – the real stuff, but nothing processed
Oils – I use mostly coconut and olive oil
Lots of herbs and spices. Don't think your kids won't like them, mine want everything seasoned now.
Quest brand protein bars – great after a run or workout
Lesser Evil brand popcorn – found on Amazon
Bai 5 brand drinks
Vitamin Water Zero

my goals

"God meant for my body to be healthy and strong.
I am worth the time it will take to make myself stronger and healthier.
It won't be easy, *but it will be worth it.*
Yes, it's okay to do this for those who love me as well, but this is for me.
I was beautiful then, I am beautiful now, and I will be beautiful tomorrow.

I CAN DO THIS.

I can do this despite feeling like I can't, or that I've been told I can't.
My body is beautiful at any size.
My body is going to be unstoppable when I'm healthier and stronger, so watch out!
NOTHING WILL DEFINE ME.
Nothing will stop me.
I CAN DO THIS!"

you are amazing

never stop

Chapter 1

BEING A FAT KID SUCKS

"TWO THINGS GET ME IN TROUBLE: FOOD AND MY MOUTH". If you've read my best-selling fiction series *Big Girls Do It,* then you're familiar with that opening line. What you may not know is that those books are partially autobiographical.

Before I wrote that series I'd read several romances and erotic romances and found myself struggling to identify with the female leads. They just…weren't people I could identify with. For one thing, they were all described as being thin and svelte, images of the way Hollywood and the marketing industry depicts the epitome of female beauty and perfection. And ladies...that ain't me. Never has been, and never will be. So I wrote *Big Girls Do It Better* in an attempt to write a story featuring a hot, sexy, self-confident female lead that also happened to be 'not skinny'. My heroine was a big girl, and she rocked it. Like just about every woman out there, she also had her self-doubts, her hang-ups and insecurities, but she didn't let them keep her down, and she didn't let them stop her from going after what—and whom—she wanted.

Now, if it were my mother telling this story she would say I weighed close to a hundred pounds at one year of age, and that she

was always worried about my size. But then, she also swears that I'm a MENSA level genius, so she probably shouldn't be trusted too far.

No, I didn't weigh quite *that* much at that age, but it is true that my weight is something I've always struggled with. But, the truth is, I can't really remember the first time I realized I was fat. What I actually remember more is thinking that something was wrong with me. It all started when I was around four or five years old—as I was getting ready to start school—and my mom told me I needed to go to the hospital for some "genetic testing." I wasn't really sure what that meant, exactly, but I was certainly aware that I'd been crowned the tallest four year-old in the state of Michigan—you can check it out, I'm in the medical books.

Our pediatrician told my mother that he was concerned I might be an actual, literal giant. At that age, one of my favorite things to watch on TV was wrestling. The only giant I knew was Andre the Giant, and I *really* didn't want to end up looking like him. At that age I couldn't even comprehend what actually having gigantism might mean for me, or what medical problems I might have as a result of it. All I knew was that I just didn't want it.

So I was taken to the hospital and they started doing tests on my growth. I was there for days, and they took vial after vial of my blood. After endless batteries of tests were completed, and I was poked and prodded until I felt like an alien abductee or some kind of medical experiment, we were told that they could find nothing wrong with me, I was just going to be a big girl, with big feet, big hands, a big head, and—as I would later discover—a really, *really* big booty.

Having a big booty wasn't a big deal when I was five years old, but as I continued to grow, so did my health problems. I developed asthma so severe I couldn't run or dance for very long without needing an inhaler. Despite my physical issues, I continued to be a very

active child. I danced, swam, played basketball, and softball.

But the real problem wasn't too much physical activity, it was food.

See, fat kids like cake. *All* kids like cake—okay, okay, *most* kids like cake, unless they're weird, in which case they probably prefer carrots or something. I was raised in an era when most birthday parties happened at McDonalds, when you tried all thirty-one flavors at Baskin-Robbins, and ate pizza at least once a week. As far as I was concerned, growing up in suburban Detroit was pretty great.

Then the pediatrician decided it would be best to shift our efforts and consult a pediatric nutritionist. What this meant was that I started going to Weight Watchers® with my mother.

And this is when things really took a turn for the worse.

Back in the 80s everyone was afraid of being overweight, and they were afraid of anything to do with the word *FAT*—that word represented everything that was big, bad and evil in our society. Anything that contained "fats" was taboo. Fats were declared to be the enemy. Real butter. Cheese. Cream. Nuts. Oils in food. These are all fats, and these were said to be the problem. Fats make you fat, right? That was the thinking of the day but, happily, we now know better.

I remember my nutritionist giving my mother and me a list of "free foods"—these were foods I could eat at any time, and I could have as much of them as I wanted. These foods were "free" because they were all "fat free." I distinctly remember angel food cake being one of the "free foods" on the list. I didn't even really *like* angel food cake, but since it was cake, and since I could eat as much as I wanted, I took full advantage. Meaning, I ate about half a cake per day. Free cake? Hell, yeah! And even though I was only in elementary school, I remember thinking this was really weird. How could *cake* be fat free,

and be good for me at the same time?

During that period my weight kept going up and my nutritionist was baffled. I was eating exactly what she had told me to eat; yet I wasn't losing any weight. When I noticed my weight wasn't going down, I started sneaking foods that were not on my approved list because what was the point? Why just eat shitty cake all day if I wasn't going to lose any weight?

I think the most weight I lost in the two years we attended those Weight Watcher® meetings was maybe five pounds. My mom stocked our fridge full of frozen diet meals and desserts, but if the package came with two portions, I would eat both. Why not? I mean, if you're ten years old and both Weight Watchers® *and* a nutritionist can't help you lose weight then why not eat two full meals and half an angel food cake every day? After all, it's diet food!

As you can see, my health and my mindset were both going straight down hill, *fast*. I think I gained about a hundred pounds during elementary school. The strange thing was, however, that even though my body was on a downward spiral, other things seemed to be okay. I was pretty funny, I had friends, I continued to dance and sing. Sure, I was the butt of some jokes, because not everyone could deal with me being 5'8" in 4th grade, or wearing women's size 11 shoes. I remember hearing people yelling out how much they guessed I'd weigh by sixth grade. I was well aware of the cruelty of it, keenly so, but I was also aware that everyone had some sort of trauma to overcome. To boost my confidence, I told myself I was going to rock this body, whether everyone was on board or not…

And then I'd secretly eat an entire box of Pop Tarts in my room after I got home from school.

One of my most vivid memories from sixth grade was being beaten up during recess by several of the boys in my class. Did they

think that because I was the biggest kid in my class it would be cool to take me on? I don't know, maybe they were all secretly hot for me? Yeah, let's just go with that. So, as if it wasn't bad enough getting thrown to the ground and having the shit kicked out of me by seven of the "cool guys", it was even more humiliating when someone told the principal what had happened. The result was that all seven of those cool kids had to personally apologize to me. God, that was awful. Now they all hated me, *and* they thought I had tattled on them to the principal. Later that day I was followed home from school by two of the boys who threw rocks at me the whole way. I'd officially been labeled a freak.

That event marked the first but, sadly, not the last time a boy would hit me—but more on that later.

In his goodness, God threw me a break even as I was experiencing these new terrible feelings about myself. I had a decent group of friends and I was getting positive attention for my singing voice, so I kept myself busy with singing and music.

Privately, however, my self-esteem was pretty much in the gutter. I'd had a few innocent pre-pubescent crushes but, overall, boys were just scary to me. Food was my coping mechanism. I ate away my problems and that helped to keep most of the bad emotions at bay. I made a fortress around myself with Twinkies and Ding Dongs and Pop Tarts.

Now, I'm not saying I didn't eat healthy stuff too; I never had any issues with vegetables, fish, or salads—I would eat almost anything. But my one true food friend, my one constant comfort was always sugar. Sweets were the friend that would never let me down. Part of the problem was that sweet, sugary treats were used as a reward in our family, so my father was always bringing home sweets of one sort or another. Case in point: the day my period started, my dad came

home with a cake to celebrate. Thank God it didn't say "HAPPY PERIOD!" on it, but it did have red roses made of frosting, and I ate most of that cake while thinking it marked the start of me becoming a woman. I was twelve years old, but even then I knew I'd need a lot more than cake to comfort me on the journey to womanhood.

Looking back, I wouldn't say I had a bad childhood. My family was middle class, we went on fun vacations, and we had a nice house and a pool. The only thing that makes the memories hard to look back on is the way I always felt about myself: something was very, very wrong with me. Something everyone could see. Something I couldn't hide, something the doctors, the nutritionists, and my parents couldn't fix...and it was getting worse every single day.

I think at some point I just accepted my new reality: I was always going to be fat—I was Fat Jasinda. So I made a decision: if I was always going to have this problem, then I'd better have smarts, talent, and humor to make up for it. So one day I started talking to God about how we could make this happen. I decided I was going to grow up to be a rock star, a chubby Tiffany or Debbie Gibson. It would be my destiny. So, in the name of taking charge of my life, that day I marched into my room with a box of Pop Tarts and started practicing.

Chapter 2

BEING A FAT ADULT ALSO SUCKS

"What can I say? I've never met a cupcake I didn't want to get to know better."—Anna, *Big Girls Do It Better* by Jasinda Wilder

I WAS ACTUALLY PRETTY POPULAR IN HIGH SCHOOL—I KNOW, I know, it was pretty shocking to me, too. I kept myself busy in band, choir and drama. I was a nerdy, academic, popular fat kid. I was in all the school plays and musicals—usually as the mom or the funny wife of a secondary character, but at least I got a part. I also helped with the production and choreography for the show choir, and I kept dancing through everything. During this time I was accepted to, and attended, a very prestigious summer arts program where I studied vocal arts.

At the time, I weighed over three hundred pounds, probably closer to three-thirty, but I managed to keep active and I stayed busy all the time. My grades were pretty good, and I was even in some honors classes.

Things were…survivable.

I had my first boyfriend around that time—I won't go into much detail to protect the innocent, but I will say things could have been

worse. He wasn't the type of boy your parents would pick out for you. He was rough around the edges, to say the least. Although that little relationship didn't last very long, it did give my self-esteem a tiny boost, and I was able to lose about forty pounds before my high school graduation.

I was kicking life's ass!

Then, near the end of my senior year of high school, I went to a party. I was a goody-goody, keep in mind, so I never really got into any trouble. That night, though, I decided to experiment with alcohol for the first time, and I ended up blacking out. I have no solid proof, but I believe I was sexually assaulted that night.

And, of course, I subconsciously blamed what had happened on my recent weight loss: I had let my guard down, I had been stupid—but I wouldn't be making *that* mistake again. I vowed I would only succumb to food in the future.

Cue the dramatic music.

I had applied to the music departments of several colleges even though I wasn't really sure where to go with my music. Ultimately, I attended the university that offered me a full ride. My parents told me that that sort of scholarship wasn't something you should turn down, so I agreed and packed my bags.

At the time, my music career was going very well; I was doing gigs and singing at weddings, funerals, and paid community events almost every weekend. I even talked with a record producer about doing a demo for a label but, in the end, I decided I was more of a teacher than a performer. Also, I wanted to have a fallback plan in place, since everybody knows you don't make money with an arts degree. So Michigan State's music education program seemed like a good choice.

Let me tell you, Michigan State University was a pretty crazy

place when I was there. Remember the riots? I was there when they were burning couches, and students were getting run over by fire trucks—those things happened literally right outside my dorm room window. I spent way too many nights hiding in my closet, either from the rioting or from the graphic sounds of my roommate and her boyfriend having sex.

Two very important events occurred that first year of university: I started dating a boy from my hometown who had graduated high school the year before me, so we had several mutual friends in common. And then, during my first year at MSU, right around Christmas, my parents called and told me they were separating.

My parents always seemed to have a wonderful relationship, so I didn't understand why they were separating, or how they could live apart. My dad was now living with my grandparents and my mom was "going away" for the holidays. My whole world spun upside down. My parents had always seemed happy. I never even saw them fight much. I couldn't comprehend what was happening. This news was a huge blow to me, leaving me in total shock.

So what did I do? I turned to my old friend Food for comfort. She had always been there for me before, and I knew she wouldn't let me down now.

In less than two months I had: a) quit school and transferred to a college closer to home, b) gained back all the weight I'd lost, and c) told the new boyfriend I would marry him.

Which decision do you think was the worst for me? If you guessed d) all of the above, you would be correct.

I'll spare you all the gory, painful details, but the relationship went downhill fast. I should have known it was a bad idea to get married when, on the day of the nuptials, the wedding arrangement that arrived at the church was, in fact, a funeral arrangement. True story!

Our relationship became physically violent very soon after the wedding. And shortly after that I became very, very depressed: my husband was never home, I was lonely, and my parents were still working on repairing their marriage. I was lonely and bored—I was still going to school and working part time, but I just wasn't fulfilled by any of those things.

So I started eating.

And I ate a *lot*.

I ate all the time.

I ate horrible, awful foods crammed full of sugar.

I quickly ballooned up to over 400 pounds, and was suddenly hit with a barrage of medical problems. Erratic periods, a resurgence of asthma, problems with my feet, skin rashes, problems sleeping, snoring…you name it, I had it. It was a dark and scary time for me. I quit my classes and my job. I stayed at home and sat in my house and ate. Food was my only friend.

I endured not one, not two, but *three* miscarriages in a very short space of time. The doctor told me the weight of my body was just too much for the pregnancies to be viable. It was quite possible I had PCOS, Polycystic Ovary Syndrome. I began taking anti-depressants just to make the anxiety manageable.

I'd given up.

Because all I did was watch TV, I dreamed of Jerry Springer having to cut me out of my house because I was getting so big, which wasn't too far from reality. While watching one of my mid-day shows, I saw a commercial for bariatric surgery. It sounded interesting. Maybe this was how I could solve all my problems at once. I was already suffering with an enormous amount of physical pain, so surely cutting myself open from top to bottom and radically changing the processes of my internal organs couldn't be that much more

painful, could it?

I figured if I had to choose between a quick death from surgery, and a slow death from eating too much, then it might be better to just try the surgery, right?

I picked up the phone and made the call.

At that point, I didn't think I had much to lose.

Chapter 3

WEIGHT LOSS SURGERY AND OTHER HUGE MISTAKES

AT THIS POINT I WAS 20 YEARS OLD WITH NO COLLEGE DEGREE, severe depression, an abusive husband, and I was morbidly obese. I felt as if the only way I could fix everything was to undergo gastric bypass surgery.

Before you start making any assumptions, let me tell you I investigated this surgery very thoroughly before I had it done. I researched online, joined a forum, talked to my doctors, went to a support group, and spoke with several different surgeons.

I was told my internal organs were beginning to shut down, one by one, because of my weight. I was also told I might never be able to have children, and that I was starting to show signs of diabetes—a condition I had watched my grandmother suffer from my whole life.

This surgery seemed like a magic solution to all my problems. If only I could get this weight off, everything would be better! I would want to live! I would have the will power to turn things around, this time for good! Food would no longer rule me!

It sounded like the perfect plan.

So, with a physiological evaluation under my belt, on the day before my 21st birthday I had a full RNY gastric bypass surgery. I

woke up in pain, and was given drugs. I don't remember much about the first few days after my surgery, but I do remember being given chicken broth, Jell-O and popsicles, but I didn't want any of them.

I now had a giant scar that went from just under my breastbone all the way down to my pubic bone. I couldn't look at myself in the mirror, because it all looked just too awful. My scars were more than just reminders of the surgery; they stood as stark proof of my desperation, evidence of so much emotional pain.

I lost two hundred pounds in what seemed like overnight, although it obviously took longer than that. I didn't really want to eat at all that first year, mostly because it was simply too painful; food had now become the enemy and my body was winning the war. I got down to a size fourteen, but I still felt sick inside. I still didn't like the way I looked. I still wasn't comfortable in my skin.

Shouldn't I be happier now?

I was still struggling emotionally, yet, because I was thinner, my confidence increased a bit. What a strange conflict, right?

So, with my newfound confidence I began singing again, and I began working as a karaoke DJ. As well, I taught vocal lessons on the weekend. Physically, I was starting to make tiny steps back into the world, but I was still completely lost mentally and emotionally. My husband grew more and more distant. He worked all the time and, when he was home, he was unhappy. The one small connection we'd shared was food, but I no longer wanted to eat. He became angry and suspicious of the people I was working with. He became increasingly violent towards me, and our relationship only ended when he went to jail. I can't really place all the blame on him, even though I probably should. I was a mess, and we both were very, very young.

My body had changed—*I* had changed.

I decided to have some plastic surgery done to remove my excess

skin. I thought that would help improve my self-image and make my clothes fit better; it seemed like a win/win to me. Yes, the physical pain from the surgery would be tough, but I had been through that before and I figured I could do it again. I had blocked out most of the memories of that experience anyway.

After this surgery, however, I ended up getting a horrible infection, which nearly killed me. I spent weeks in the hospital having the wound reopened over and over in an attempt to rid my body of the infection. When the hospital called my husband to ask him if he would come and be with me, he refused. He was done with my mess. Heck, *I* was done with my mess. It certainly doesn't excuse his physical violence toward me—nothing ever will—but in my mind it helps me understand, just a little.

Marriage is difficult enough to begin with, but when you don't love yourself it becomes almost impossible. I didn't see it then, but somewhere in all the mess and complications of life, I had stopped loving myself. I had given up. I was probably as close to death as you could be without actually dying.

I moved back in with my parents—who, thankfully, had reconciled by this point—got divorced, kept working, and started dating. I figured if I had this new body, I might as well use it, right? I really wasn't into having sex, but making out sounded pretty fun. I still had trouble eating and I was continuing to lose weight. I supported myself by working almost exclusively in bars, either singing or DJing.

And that's when Chase walked into the bar one night and began singing.

(As a quick aside, if you haven't read the *Big Girls Do It* series, you should probably put this book down real quick and pick that one up, just so you can get all the juicy details of my life at that time. Yes, Chase and Jeff are based on real-life love interests. I was just trying

to figure out whom I was and what I wanted to do and, at the same time, pay my bills. In the books, I rewrote history a little, and chose Jeff for Anna pretty much right off the bat, whereas in real life Anna was with Chase a bit longer.)

Okay, back to the narrative.

When I was pregnant with my oldest son, we found out when he was born that he'd suffered with IUGR (intrauterine growth restriction), and my daughter, who followed soon after, had the same problem. After the birth of my daughter I got so sick that I couldn't get out of bed, and I bled intensely for a long, long time, hemorrhaging from basically everywhere. I saw specialist after specialist, but no one could tell me what was wrong.

The diagnosis I received from the first two doctors was that I had leukemia, and a third doctor suggested colon cancer. I was horrified! Here I was, a mother with two little babies. I couldn't die! I went to the best hematologist-oncologist I could find, and when I met with him after having my blood tested, he told me that my hemoglobin was at a two—a normal hemoglobin result is between twelve and fifteen. Something was terribly wrong with me, but he didn't think it was leukemia, which gave me a little comfort at least, but not much. He took samples of my blood and sent it to the Mayo Clinic for analysis. They sent it back saying it wasn't real blood, so we took more samples and sent them in. Again, they said my samples couldn't possibly be blood: these samples had zero nutrients. Zip. Zero. None of the nutrients contained in normal blood were present in mine. I was walking death.

I remember calling my good friend after the appointment and telling her I was probably going to die. Not only was she a wonderful mentor, friend, and counselor to me, but she was also a prayer partner. We prayed together that night and in my head I started planning

my own funeral. I know this sounds grim, but that was how things looked at the time.

Together we prayed for a miracle.

This was a very difficult time for me, but I promise things are going to turn around with this story soon. Please stick with me—there's a light at the end of the tunnel.

Chapter 4

PREGNANCY AND OTHER WEIRD SHIT THAT REALLY EFFED UP MY BODY

I BEGAN TO REALIZE WHAT I'D DONE TO MYSELF, AND I BECAME angry. And this is where all that shit became horribly real.

By the time I finally received a correct diagnosis, I was virtually unable to leave my bed. I was weak to the point that I couldn't take care of my kids. I was pale, I was losing my hair, and I was continually bleeding. It was a nightmare. The diagnosis was a non-nutrient blood disorder caused by the gastric bypass.

I had tried to save myself...by nearly killing myself. Again.

The surgeon who performed the bypass admitted he might have removed too much intestinal and stomach tissue, figuring that because of my height more was better. At that point, however, it was too risky to fix the problems with my stomach and intestines, so my doctors decided to insert a medical port into my chest so they could infuse my blood with nutrients.

The surgery to insert the port didn't happen without its own complications, though, because this is *me* we're talking about here. The operating room was overbooked the day of the procedure so, to save time, they tried to give me a twilight sleep—a lighter anesthetic

that my body didn't accept. I woke up during the procedure and panicked, but I was physically immobile and unable to alert the surgeons that I was awake and feeling everything they were doing. Obviously I survived, but it's an experience I wouldn't wish on my worst enemy.

The port itself is still in place, eight years later, and it is still working. One of my goals for myself with this program is to become healthy enough so that I no longer need the port, and I can have it removed.

When I first had the port, I needed medication infused almost daily. Fortunately, I was able to get a home healthcare nurse who came and helped me with these daily infusions. It was amazingly helpful having her come to my house every day because, honestly, I was still feeling too weak to even leave my bed. She was a sweet, wonderful lady and she took great care of me. She really did help me heal both my body and my soul during an excruciatingly hard time in my life. I cried many tears as she listened and gave me my medicine.

My friends and my church group continued to pray for me, and soon I was feeling better and was able to get back to work teaching, leading worship, and being a wife and mother. My body was sometimes able to store enough nutrients that I could go days or even weeks without needing an infusion, but it was a constant balancing act between managing the frequent blood-work results and the medication.

I just want to take a moment here to say that my heart, and my thanks, goes out to all the nurses out there who take care of the hurting, the hopeless, and those in pain. Yours is not an easy job and it can be thankless at times, but I know I wouldn't be here without you. You inspire me with your kind, compassionate hearts.

In 2010 I got pregnant again and my doctors, now knowing what happens with my body during pregnancy, were very proactive about getting nutrients into my body. I had a high-risk specialist, constant ultra-sounds, and regular infusions to make sure both the baby and I were healthy. My pregnancy was very happy and I was healthy. I gained lots of weight, but my baby did too, and that was my primary concern. He came at the end of November, looking like a stuffed Thanksgiving turkey. I was so proud of what my body had accomplished!

And then, just a few months after having him, I got pregnant *again*, which came as a huge shock to me. Yes, I *do* know how babies are made—and I happen to enjoy that part, thank you very much! —but we were on birth control and I just wasn't expecting to have any more kids.

My body never really had enough time to recover between pregnancies, so that pregnancy was a rough one. Once again the doctors took great care of me and the baby. We had frequent ultra-sounds and I was still taking my medication regularly, but the simple fact was that I just wasn't ready to be pregnant again. My body was *so* tired. I know all you mamas out there who have had babies back-to-back will understand what I'm saying. Having a baby is like a marathon: if you don't get that recovery time after the birth, you just aren't going to recover properly.

It's weird, because even though those two pregnancies were so close together, the boys are so very different from each other. After my fourth child I felt so refreshed, energized, even, but after my fifth I felt as if I wasn't ever going to recover.

And then, two weeks after he was born, baby number five contracted RSV—respiratory syncytial virus. He was born a few weeks early, so the virus hit him hard. I knew something was wrong when

I saw him turn blue. We rushed to the hospital where they took one look at him and put him on a respirator. He was so small, and so sick. I can still see his tiny little hands and feet turning blue, and my husband holding him and praying to God, begging Him not to take our sweet baby that He let him stay with us.

Neither of us slept much while our son was in the hospital. I think I managed *maybe* five or six hours of sleep that whole first week. It got to the point that my father and husband had to haul me literally kicking and screaming from the hospital and put me into a car with my friend who took me home so I could rest. I was worried my son would die if I took even a few minutes to sleep. My friend came to pray over me while I slept, the same amazing friend who'd prayed with me after my plastic surgery, a time when I was sure I was going to die.

If you saw our CBS interview you know that at that time my husband was in an honors teaching program, which we had struggled for years to put him through. My teaching income barely kept us at poverty level, even after adding in his student loans, so needless to say things were tight. Jack had to take days, and then weeks, off from the program, some of which he had already missed because of the birth. While our son was in the hospital, Jack got a call from the university telling him that he had forty-eight hours to return to the program, or he'd be cut from it. We knew that based on how the classes were set up that if he left he might never get back into that program again. They were extremely selective, and even if he were re-accepted, we'd have to wait another whole year to reapply. That same night our son took yet another turn for the worse. We decided then that Jack just couldn't return to the program—he couldn't even bear to leave the hospital.

We weren't sure how we would move forward with this news but

we did know that we needed to focus on getting our son healthy and back at home. It was—and remains to this day—the most difficult time of our lives.

I still can't think about that time without choking up—my computer screen is blurring from tears as I write these words. Our son did recover and was able to come home with us after two weeks in the hospital. He's now healthy and happy, and he is our sweet but crazy little wild man, and we simply cannot fathom our lives without his cute, impish grin and devious ways.

So by now I'm sure you're probably thinking, "Gosh, these first few chapters have all been pretty depressing."

I promise you there's a silver lining in all of this.

Jack, who was no longer in the teaching program, had to come up with a way to help support our family, because without the student loans to supplement my income, things weren't just tight for us anymore, but completely unsustainable. We *had* to do something.

We happened to stumble upon an article about self-publishing and, as they say, the rest is history. We began writing and ended up with several *New York Times*, *USA TODAY*, and *Wall Street Journal* bestselling novels. I could easily spend a few chapters on this subject, but I think I'll save it for a book on my marriage with my husband somewhere down the road.

The important thing is that we survived, we thrived, and we got my health issues mostly under control. We got busy writing, attending signings, and raising our family.

Today, we wake up every single day feeling so blessed, not so much because we have enough money to feed everyone—which is both important and comforting—but more because we get to do what we love: tell stories, entertain, and inspire.

I believe all that struggle and pain has been for a reason. It might

have even have led me to be able to write this book, using my own experiences to inspire and help others going through similar situations. Sometimes, when I look back on those times and compare them to where I'm at now, it really does seem as if it was a different person who experienced all that pain.

Many of you reading this book have been following us since reading our first book, so you know our story. Heck, you could probably write it better than me! But these chapters are important because you need to know where I'm coming from, especially when we get into the next part of my story. You'll come to understand that I'm a woman just like you and, like many of you; I've been through some shit. I've put my body through so much stress and so much hell. I've tried everything to heal myself—and I mean *everything*—from nasty pills that made me poop raw fat to countless painful workout videos. I'm someone who has given up so many times, and who has been given countless second, third, and fourth chances. I've failed more than I've succeeded. But I'm a survivor.

Health wise, things began to change for me during my most recent pregnancy. I don't know how or why, but I started to *lose* weight, which was very, very strange. We also learned that two people in our immediate families had been diagnosed with diabetes. That was a HUGE revelation for me. I started getting really angry, and when I get angry, I do something about it.

I began to research like a madwoman. I've always read a lot of non-fiction, and health and wellness books in particular, but because of the revelations I was experiencing and the changes I was feeling in my body, my research really cranked up to a possibly obsessive level. I had to know why my body was acting so differently. Why did I feel so different during this pregnancy, and how could I continue to feel this way after the baby was born? I wanted to be healthy for my

husband, my kids, and myself.

I didn't want to continue to feel as if every day was a struggle. I didn't want to feel like I was dying inside.

I wanted to be truly healthy. I wanted to live, and live well!

PART 2:

My Favorite Part of the Story

Chapter 5:

OOPS, WE DID IT AGAIN!

MY HUSBAND AND I WERE TRAVELING A LOT DURING THE FALL of 2014. We were doing research for a new book on Mackinac Island, and we were also trying to schedule in some down time between releases and signings, and we had just come back from speaking at a writing and publishing conference.

I started to feel really, really sick on the plane, but I just chalked it up to stress and exhaustion. When we landed I wasn't sure I would be able to make the five-hour car journey home, so we stopped at a shopping plaza to get something to eat, thinking maybe some food would help me feel better. As we were sitting in the restaurant I thought perhaps the nausea could be related to the fact that my period was going to start. *Wait, when was my last period?* I couldn't remember. I started counting the weeks and then it hit me: a few weeks back Jack and I had had an *oops* moment after one too many Stella Artois while watching *The Fault In Our Stars*. Yep, it had been a kids-should-never-ever-die-of-cancer-so-let's-get-drunk-and-have-crazy-sex moment.

I started hyper ventilating—I was completely freaking out. There was no way in heck we could be having a baby! I literally ran

into Target, grabbed a pregnancy test, darted into the bathroom, and peed on the stick right then and there. After a few minutes of waiting and freaking out I got the results…and then I sent my husband a text message screenshot of the positive test.

HOLY SHIT! We were having a baby.

Now, please understand, I really do believe every child is a blessing, but I really only ever set out to have two…and now I was going to have *SIX*? Life can be pretty freaking crazy.

I spent the rest of the ride home sucking on peppermints, crying, and breathing into a paper bag. In the back of my mind I was sure this was God's way of slowing us down. I'd been feeling like all the business travel we were doing was worsening my health, and my lab results were proving me right. Maybe this news was an easy way for us to re-group and take some much-needed time to be with our family, and just relax for a change. Right? Um… if you know us, you're probably laughing (I'm sure my agent is) but, honestly, it was my happy thought to hold on to: a baby would bring downtime and rest. Ha!

Once we got home I called my OB/GYN because I knew she would want to see me right away, given my crazy health history. When I went to the appointment a few weeks later they wanted to weigh me. Now, what you have to understand is I had basically given up on weighing myself, to the point that I didn't even *own* a scale. I just didn't want to know, because I always ended up feeling sad and angry. There was no controlling my weight, just the depressing reality that the numbers would just keep going up no matter what I did. I wasn't even really trying to diet anymore. My weight would go up and down with my menstrual cycle, and arbitrarily, as well. I had been told that my blood nutrient disorder and the other nutritional issues that developed as a result of the bypass would make it nearly

impossible for me to lose any substantial amount weight. My body chemistry was behaving as if I was starving, so it would hold onto the bad stuff and release the good before I could absorb any nutrients from the food. I was trying to eat mostly healthy foods, but I did have sweets occasionally and I wasn't counting calories, or being very physically active. When we weren't at home, I was sitting most of the day while travelling, or sitting trying to finish whatever book we were working on. At home I sometimes used my walking treadmill desk, but it wasn't enough. I was mostly sedentary, apart from the occasional ride on my trusty horse Cowboy.

The nurse insisted she get a weight reading from me, and I grimaced at the *319* pounds that appeared on the readout when I stepped onto the scale. There was no way I could have gained that much! When the hell did that happen? Who had been stuffing all that fat into my ass? My OB said she wanted to keep a watch on my weight, and scheduled me for a few tests. I left feeling both excited and worried. I really needed my body to work well for this pregnancy, because I knew this was going to be my last baby, and I wanted to be as healthy as I could for him or her. I prayed that God would help me be strong through this pregnancy, both mentally and physically. I needed to find my health. I was on a mission.

That night, I dreamed of a laughing baby girl.

Most of my life hasn't gone as planned; in fact, it usually goes totally contrary to anything I plan. This pregnancy was unplanned, and the results of the pregnancy equally so. Initially, our older children weren't that excited about having a new sibling—remember, they

had to deal with two mischievous toddler brothers, and now we were having *another* baby. The first thing they said when we told them was that we would have to get a bigger car. This really upset them because we had just purchased a lovely 7-seat SUV that they all really liked. Nonetheless, the idea of another sibling seemed to grow on them, and by mid-pregnancy they were showing some signs of excitement.

My daughter requested the baby be a girl because we already had WAY too much testosterone in our house. There's a more equal gender ratio in the barn, so she likes to stay out there as much as she can. Don't get me wrong, she can hang with the boys, but she would much rather spend time with her pony, Shorty. She convinced the boys to start praying for a girl too, because they were already sharing a room and adding one more boy would mean fewer toys and less space for them. I just wanted a healthy, happy mama and baby. Since I'd had so many complications with my previous pregnancies, health was my number one goal for both of us.

Around the second trimester I started feeling pretty good. I wasn't overly exhausted and I was finally able to keep most of my food down. We were dealing with some work stress, which wasn't unusual, but overall I felt the pregnancy was going pretty well. At my 4th or 5th month appointment my OB remarked that I was losing some weight, and we both figured it was due to the fact that I had had so much nausea early on in the pregnancy. She told me not to worry too much about it, the baby was measuring normal, so I was just to continue eating as healthily as I could.

Once I reached the halfway point in the pregnancy, my entire outlook on food changed. It was sudden and it was drastic. Anything containing sugar immediately turned my stomach. It was a very strange reaction to what had been my comfort food, my long-time best friend. I remember our sweet nanny making the kids a special

after-school treat and she asked me to try it. I took one bite and spit it out; I just couldn't tolerate the sweetness even though everyone else raved about it. Weird things were happening to me.

The second odd thing that happened was my reaction to my normal morning breakfast. For about three years my breakfast has consisted of toast and yogurt—a peach Chobani yogurt to be exact. As the pregnancy went on I started to get light headed after eating. This really became a problem when I would try to shower after breakfast and would have to get out of the shower and sit down, trying to not pass out.

It took me weeks to figure out that what I was eating was somehow connected to how I was feeling.

I'm sure moms out there are wondering about gestational diabetes. I had done a fasting blood work panel and all of my levels had come back totally normal, so this dizziness was really bizarre. Again, as I have previously stated, *nothing* about my body has ever made sense and nothing ever goes as planned. At my next checkup, the scale once again revealed that I was continuing to lose weight. We had another ultrasound planned for the baby, and as long as that looked okay my OB said things would be fine. Everything looked good on the ultrasound with Baby Wilder, so we just chalked the dizziness up to my weird nutrient levels and the pregnancy.

By springtime, my family and friends were starting to notice that I was losing weight. The difference in my face was pretty drastic—the previous roundness was now more sculpted, and my eyes looked bigger. My clothes were starting to get baggy, and the only way to tell I was pregnant was to look directly at my belly with my shirt pulled up. This was unlike every other pregnancy. What was going on with my body? It was a mystery.

Right around that same time, two people in our immediate fam-

ilies were diagnosed with diabetes. My husband had already been dealing with some blood sugar issues at his young age of 33. Diabetes ran on both my side of the family and his which meant our kids had an even greater chance of developing it, as well.

I began a quest for answers and started doing some research. Now, I know it's common knowledge that I'm a pretty fast typist, but I'm not sure how much I've spoken about how fast I read. Well, I started devouring one or two non-fiction books per day on diabetes, nutrition, exercise, and overall health. I was also Googling like mad, trying to figure out if the changes to my body were mental, emotional, chemical, or just physical. Maybe, after 35 years, my body was just done with the way I had been eating, and maybe it had decided to take things into its own hands?

My research kept bringing me back to one primary culprit: my good old friend sugar. I started thinking back on my childhood and those damn angel food cakes. Apart from those cakes, what *had* I eaten back then? Weight Watcher® meals, Healthy Choice pre-packaged meals, diet bars, diet soda… I started to take a closer look at those things.

Man, I had been eating *junk*!

It was almost too depressing to even think about. But my mindset was changing. Now I was really focused on the idea of food being fuel. It was no longer working as simply a comfort or a friend to me. I wanted/needed the right fuels to keep my sweet baby and myself going strong. So what changed? What was so different now? I asked myself these questions and made a list:

- I didn't want to die prematurely. For me, this had always been a frightening and constant reality simply because of my weight alone. Yes, weighing 430 pounds was actually slowing

killing me. And then, once I had the bypass and lost some weight, the blood disorder I developed became a constant threat to my life. Despite my infusions and medications, and the fact that I was usually able to keep a good handle on things, it was still very scary for my family and me.

- I was done dieting—I was *beyond* done dieting.
- I was done being unsuccessful. I hated being a bad example for my kids, and I hated being so negative about my body and my health. Yes, I tried to keep a positive self-image and body-image both at home and professionally but, let's face it, it's hard not feeling well *all the time*. I was often tired, and I wanted to be active and to just, basically…*feel good*.
- I was thinking about my body differently.
- Things just didn't taste the same. I know you've heard the old saying "nothing tastes as good as skinny feels." Well, for me it had become "nothing tastes as good as healthy feels." I had reached a point where my health had become my main priority.

My own health and the health of my family became my primary focus. I was determined to turn things around and I knew it would all start with food. I have more on the specifics later in the book, but there were two things that I think made the biggest impact on my health and body during my pregnancy: cutting out sugar, and starting my day with protein—specifically farm fresh eggs.

Sounds fairly easy right?

Well, during my pregnancy it sort of was. I think most people would think that cutting out sugar would be the hardest part, but because I was feeling such adverse affects from sugar during my pregnancy, it was pretty easy for me to eliminate it. All in all I lost about

30 pounds during my pregnancy. It was both strange and beautiful, and I embraced the ease of my weight loss…and then the baby came and all hell broke loose.

Chapter 6

AND THEN CAME JOYFUL NUMBER SIX

I'VE REALLY GOT TO COMMEND OUR NEW SWEET BABY GIRL FOR really rolling with the punches, because she was born into a crazy circus of a family. Most babies probably wouldn't choose to join a household with five other kids, two crazy *New York Times* bestselling workaholic parents, and 100 farm animals. Well… maybe they might. We do have some pretty cool mini-donkeys.

All joking aside, sweet Ree came into the world on June 30, 2015, right when she wanted to, the only one of my children to ever go past their due date. She came out smiling and hasn't stopped since. She loves to eat and sleep, and smile and smile and smile. Sometimes I worry that her poor little face is going to crack because she is always smiling so big. Had all of my babies been like her, we would probably have a dozen.

We had about one hour of peace with her before all hell broke loose. First, someone hit our car in the parking lot of the hospital while I was giving birth, a hit and run. Then we got an email from our editor informing us that our edits needed to be turned in to Berkley, our new traditional publishing partner, within a week's time, which was a lot sooner than we'd thought. And *then* we found out we were

being audited by the IRS! Yay!

No kidding—this was all within days of bringing our new baby home from the hospital.

Can you guess what happened? The stress of it all caused me to spiral downwards, and *fast*. I ended up depressed and comforting myself with food. Yep, my old friend was back. Within a few weeks I had put on ten pounds. Here I was with this beautiful, perfect, smiling baby and I was feeling like a bloated, stressed out bag of mommy poop.

Who's got the wine?

I spent a good week or so wallowing in my own self-pity and more than a few bottles of wine. We got the car fixed, the edits done, a CPA dealing with the IRS, and I was looking forward to seeing some of my author friends who were coming into town for a signing. As good as it would be to see them, I was still feeling really crappy, and if you know my beautiful and amazing friends Tara Sivec and R.K. Lilley, you know they are as sweet as they are gorgeous. Well, hanging around those two beauties only ended up making me feel even angrier with myself. I was *done* with the way things were going.

Let me just say, as an aside, that post partum depression is no joke. Ladies, if you are feeling down for any reason after giving birth to your precious little baby PLEASE talk to someone, although it probably shouldn't be your mother or your husband, but rather a friend or a medical professional who can be more objective, someone who can help you get perspective, or help, and/or medication. There is such a stigma regarding mental health in general and depression in particular in our country. Postpartum depression a very real thing, and left untreated it can ruin mothers, and fracture families. Please get help when you need it, because that new little life needs you happy and healthy.

Ok, now that I've gotten that out of the way, back to my story.

The Monday after my friends left, I took a picture of myself in the mirror, wearing only my bra and underwear. It was a "come to Jesus" moment for me, let me tell you. I realized I had only two choices: either I could continue on as I had been for the past 30 years, or I could fight back. For the second time in my life I knew I didn't have much to lose; I was going to fight.

My precious baby girl had been the key to weight loss during my pregnancy, and I was going to use her as my motivation again—I wanted to live a long and healthy life with her. I didn't want to feel sick anymore. There *had* to be a way to get this shit under control.

So I pulled up my good friend Google and got to work trying to figure out a plan I could manage long-term which would also be successful for my whole family. I knew that if I was going to be healthier we would all need to do this together, which meant that somehow I had to get everyone on board with it. All five of the older kids *and* my husband would need to see why these changes had to happen, and understand why I needed them to support my plan.

I had been blind for so long to many of the health issues in our family, and my research was telling me they were all being aggravated—if not outright *caused*—by the food we were eating. My family has ADHD, autism spectrum disorder, asthma, food allergy and sensitivity, and constipation, just to name a few. I came up with an action plan.

I sat down with my family and I laid it all out for them.

We were going to eat as healthily as possible, and we were going to be more physically active. I wanted to teach them how to decide day by day, meal by meal, what the best foods were to put in their bodies, and I would teach them by example. I was doing it for them, but I was also doing it for myself and maybe even for future gener-

ations.

See, when I was a child I was fed a steaming load of bullshit about what I should be eating, which has negatively affected me my whole life. I believe now that what I had been told to eat were actually the things that made me so unhealthy. These same foods had actually *caused* the majority my heath problems, directly and indirectly. I'm not trying to shift blame—I know my parents did the best they could to help me, I just think the so-called "experts" they had trusted were flat-out wrong. I think the diet and the food industry were wrong, and I believe that my desperation was fueled by those bad eating decisions. It had been a perfect storm and now I was determined to do everything I could to steer my kids away from that.

I was jumping on the bandwagon of parents who made family health a priority. Yeah, I admit it; I sometimes rolled my eyes at those moms who went around requesting "healthy snacks" for their kids at school. Those crazy, homemade-baby-food-making, grain-grinding mamas who got up early in the morning to prep meals. Yeah, *those* crazy mamas. I was turning into one of them.

I just *knew* my family would love this idea.

Chapter 7

MAKING THE PLAN

"I am a better person when I have less on my plate."
— Elizabeth Gilbert, author of *Eat, Pray, Love*

IF YOU WERE TO GO A BOOKSTORE OR DO A SEARCH ON AMAZON right now, you'd find roughly three trillion books on diet, health, and fitness by a variety of so-called and self-proclaimed "experts". As I pointed out in the foreword at the beginning of this book, I am not in any way, shape, or form an expert—I just want to share with you the things that have worked fairly easily and quickly for my family and me. Now, "easily and quickly" is a relative term, and I certainly don't want to market this book as some sort of magical get-skinny-quick scheme. If anything, nothing could be further from the truth.

What I'm going to lay out for you is what worked for us. It might work for you, but it might not, or not in the same way it did our family. From my research, though, my guess is that our plan will help more people than I could even begin to estimate at this moment.

My plan is fairly straightforward, even allowing for the fact that our family has children from under one year of age to twelve years old, with very picky toddlers in the mix. I had to make sure the

plan allowed every member of my family not just to survive and be healthy, but to thrive, enjoy life, and enjoy food.

As I mentioned, the first thing I did was call a big family meeting. I should point out before we go any further, however, that my biggest worry when calling this meeting was actually my husband. If you know Jack at all you know he is very vocal about his hatred of all vegetables. So much so, in fact, that if you ever get him drinking he'll tell you about the time he held lima beans in his mouth for several hours rather than swallow them. It was only after his mother discovered them still half-chewed inside his mouth *three hours* after he left the table that she sent him to go and spit them all out. Obviously, Jack *hates* lima beans, but he also shudders with disgust when I bring up nasty words like broccoli or cauliflower. The struggle is real—just ask his mother.

Jack's aversion to vegetables led to the crux of the problem: I knew for this plan to work, we needed to incorporate a lot more leafy greens and veggies into our diet. I can almost hear mothers everywhere laughing as they are reading this: yeah, right—mothers have been trying to get their families to eat vegetables since the beginning of time. Well, I was going to give it my best shot…I had to either get them past Jack or hide them so he couldn't figure out what he was eating.

But first I got everyone into the family huddle and talked to them about my health, and how I had decided now was the time to choose health, and that I was going to make as many healthy choices in my life as I could. My sweet little three year-old just kept nodding his little head, and my nine year-old daughter was rolling her eyes and thinking, "Oh boy, here we go. Mom's lost her mind."

I explained the basics of diabetes to them, and told them the disease ran on both my side of the family *and* Daddy's, and that two

of our family members were already struggling to manage it. I told them I felt it was my responsibility as their mother to help them be as healthy as they could be. I told them I loved them, and that I wanted them to live long and healthy lives.

I could tell about half the group had totally tuned out and were thinking about which TV show they were going to watch after dinner, but at least two of the children were at least somewhat interested in what I was saying. Jack was playing his usual supportive husband role, but I hadn't got to the part about vegetables.

The kids wanted to know what this would mean, and how would it change the way we actually ate. Would there be gross stuff? Would we have to stop going out to dinner? Could they still have cookies?

I answered their questions as best as I could, but I didn't want to drop too many bombs on them right away—I knew from experience it was best to ease them into things. No need to scare them, right?

So, when they woke up the next day, instead of their usual breakfast of toast, cereal, or granola bars, I told them they could have either some Greek yogurt or some eggs. I hadn't picked those items at random, however; there was a reason behind these choices. I'd been researching a lot and really felt that if we were going to kick our sugar habit, then we needed to start the day off loaded with protein. My plan was to start by changing our breakfast choices, and then I would change dinner, and then hopefully lunch would come on its own.

The first two days were a bit rough. The younger ones weren't sure about the options I'd given them; they really wanted their usual cereal—which weren't even the really bad sugary ones like Lucky Charms or Cap'n Crunch—rice puffs and Cheerios, mostly. They weren't necessarily horrible, but they weren't the best choices either.

I know, I know. Cheerios? How can Cheerios be bad for you? Keep reading and you'll see what I'm talking about.

By the end of week one I was already starting to see changes in everyone. Real, noticeable changes! I had so much more energy than before, my clothes were feeling looser, and I wasn't bloated, two of my kids noticed a decrease in their constipation and insomnia… and this was *week one*. Things were changing just from switching up our breakfast options! I knew was on to something. If just this small change could have such a huge impact, what effects would other changes have?

Next, I was going to get rid of all the juice and pop in the house. I just *knew* my family would be on board enthusiastically with that too, right? Seriously, I knew it wouldn't be easy but I had to try, because soda, diet or regular, is a killer, no exaggeration. My older kids only had soda on rare occasions, maybe two or three cans a week at most, but after all of my research I knew any at all was terrible for them. What about juice? Well, the amount of sugar in things like apple juice is much less than in soda, but even too much fructose can be bad.

I had to find a way to lure them into creating healthy habits.

I decided to find fun replacements for the bubbly, sugary drinks they wanted. My first pick was LaCroix brand naturally flavored water. The great thing about LaCroix is they aren't much more expensive than soda, they have a really wide variety of flavors, and the cans come in really bright, bold colors—which may seem silly, but it's a well known fact in the marketing industry that colorful packaging is extremely important. I bought a couple of different flavors, and I was honestly surprised at how easy it was to get them to drink those.

We also bought a few different flavors of Stevia-sweetened "soda"—which is really just sparkling water with a bit of added sweetness to it, so it tastes closer to real soda. Those went over even better; my kids really enjoy the orange, grape, cream soda, and root

beer flavors. These beverages are also free of the added colors and dyes regular sodas contain.

Finally, we bought True Lemon and True Lime—don't worry about taking notes just yet, I'm going to list our favorite grocery items later in the book. True Lemon and True Lime come in a variety of flavors, but those are our personal favorites. They're simply packets of flavored powders, and they come in larger sizes for making pitchers as well as small packets for flavoring individual glasses or bottles of water. They're great to put in your purse for when you're going out and you're just not in the mood for water or iced tea.

It took way less time than I thought for all of us to completely abandon our favorite drinks in favor of healthier options; my kids were reaching for the healthy stuff without any complaint. I was continuing to see radical changes in my kids just from a protein-centered breakfast, reducing sugar/artificial sweetener consumption, and a major increase in water intake. Major changes were happening just from a few small adjustments. I was thrilled!

I'm sure there are a few people out there who are outraged that my kids were drinking soda or eating white toast and cereal in the first place. Hey, I knew then that those things weren't great for us, but I also know our conveniently packaged American lifestyle is really hard to fight. We're a very busy family: Jack and I work all the time, our kids each have busy schedules, and we have a farm that requires constant attention and work. We're not the only busy family, either. Most families have one, if not two, parents working a minimum of forty hours a week, plus after school activities for kids, church commitments, sports… the list is endless. Which makes it all too easy to just pick the easiest, quickest food option, even if we know, intellectually, it isn't the best choice.

I think that for many of us, especially working mothers, food

and nutrition can take a back seat to the host of other things on our proverbial plate. Just yesterday I was at the dance studio with my daughter watching a mom run in with McDonalds for her daughter to eat between classes. It's not ideal, but guess what? It happens. And I'm certainly not one to judge because I've done it, too. Haven't we all?

But here's the thing: I really, truly believe that so many of the physical, emotional, and mental issues we're seeing in our kids are caused by poor nutrition. Here's just one example: My oldest son is wonderful, handsome, inspiring…and he's also on the autism spectrum. He's very high functioning, so most people would never even be able to tell without having personal experience themselves with high-functioning autistics. In just a few months on our adjusted diet, my son's grades went up, his sleep habits improved, his fidgeting lessened, and he was able to stop taking his medications on the weekends. He lost weight because he started running regularly with us; he's completed several five-kilometer runs now and he's always the one who finishes first—this is a child who just a few short months ago couldn't run a mile without stopping.

Having shared this, I have to say that I don't think my family is that uncommon. My kids are not the exceptions.

I think changing what we eat might even be easier than we think. I believe we've made this hard on ourselves. The collective "we" I'm speaking of here isn't just the average person, but also the food industry, and the diet-and-exercise industry, too. Whoever "we" is, whoever decided this is how we should eat and how we should live, is about to be challenged by me. I'm going to use my children, my life, and my home as an example. We'll be a case study.

As scary as that statement is for me, I feel it's my duty to lay it out there for you. I'm actually a very private person—surprising right?

I just keep thinking that if I can help one family, one mother, one child who's struggling with weight and health issues, I know it'll be worth it. Just stay with me. I've got so much to say and so many more examples to give. We can do this!

Once my family had eliminated our major food crutches, I started thinking maybe this was a little *too* easy. Why was I taking baby steps with this? I was seeing such amazing results—none of the kids were crying about eating more veggies (notice I'm not mentioning Jack), and we were all looking and feeling so much healthier. Even our skin was clearer. I mean, really, this was going pretty darn well.

So, naturally, I decided to jump straight off the cliff—I grabbed some trash bags and entered my pantry. I should mention we are very blessed to have an amazing pantry in our home. With so many kids, one of the major features of our house is an amazing kitchen with a walk-in butler's pantry, which is seriously a *dream* for a mom of six. We had a lot of food in that pantry which, I was realizing, was not the best or healthiest choices for us. So, I gave it all away. Every single last cereal box, granola bar, and packet of fruit snacks, even the Cheez-Its! It was all gone, and it felt both scary and awesome at the same time. I still wasn't exactly sure at that point what we *were* going to eat, but I knew it wouldn't be any of that crap.

Then I did something extreme: I ordered every cookbook in the Amazon Top One Hundred. Yes, it cost me a small fortune, but my family's health was worth it.

I had more studying to do. (More on that later).

My kids were already telling me how they were trying to make the healthiest choices they could at lunch. A few of them had even talked to their teachers and the school lunch providers about the sugar in the snacks and lunches they were eating. I was so proud of how proactive they were being! I never pushed them or told them

what they could or couldn't eat; we just discussed the nutritional values of different food items, and we told them to always try to make the best choice at each meal.

I never wanted them to feel the pressure of making food choices that were off limits or wrong, because I knew from long, painful personal experience how demoralizing that can be. I didn't want them to walk around feeling guilty or ashamed if they had a bagel or a slice of pizza now and then. I just wanted them to be informed. I wanted them to see the results of good nutrition, and the changes in their bodies when they made healthy choices. Heck, that's what I wanted for myself! I just wanted to see our whole family reap the rewards of being as healthy as we could.

Which gave me another great idea that both scared me and excited me: I wanted us all to start running together. I was sure I could get the kids on board.

I just had to convince Jack.

Chapter 8

MOM FIGURES IT OUT: SUGAR IS THE ENEMY, FATS ARE YOUR FRIEND

So back when I was a kid you'll remember I was told *ad nauseam* that fat was bad. Fat was the enemy. Fat was horrible. Don't ever eat Fat. This was so ingrained in my head that, without even thinking, I always grabbed whatever product was labeled "fat free" at the grocery store. It made me a fatty-food bigot and, as an adult, I still carried that bias. But as I was investigating different diet books and health plans and reading scientific studies, I was quickly realizing that all the understanding regarding fat and its effects had changed.

Fat wasn't what was made me fat—it was all the sugar.

The collective wisdom from decades of scientific study is that some fat in your diet is okay, and even necessary. Fats just aren't as bad for you as we once thought them to be, and they're certainly not the be-all and end-all cause of obesity.

My number one goal is to make this book as easy to understand and helpful as possible, because after reading the top one hundred health and diet books, my head was spinning. Most of them are com-

pletely contradictory and over half weren't at all family-friendly.

I kept thinking how hard it was to wade though the vast amount information that's out there. I won't share all of the science behind my plan, but please know everything I'm telling you is based on both science and research. You can find this research for yourself if you're interested. I am lucky I'm both a speed-reader and a person who likes to consider all the information available before making a decision about which way to go. I'm a studier, and I never do what people tell me—my husband says it's both a blessing and a curse to be married to such a hardheaded woman.

All of my reading was making me angry. Why is it so hard for us to get healthy? Why are there so many gimmicks and unnecessary costs associated with being healthy? Why is health so damn hard for us as Americans? I think a huge part of it is that there are just too many people looking to make a quick buck, and too many people desperate to lose weight, which has lead to this constant stream of next "hot diets" or "easy weight loss systems."

What follows is the truth I've gleaned from all those contradictory studies and how, as a result of a lot of trial and error, it has worked for my family and me.

Every other diet book is going to tell you that carbs are bad for you. Paleo, Ketogenic, and Atkins all have their place on the top 100 health charts. But let me tell you why I still eat healthy carbs—note the phrasing, it's an important distinction: *healthy carbs.* First, I've lost a lot of weight while still eating them and second, I don't think that eliminating any of the God-created food groups is necessary or healthy. If you have a legitimate, food-specific allergy, then that's a whole different story. One of my very best friends has Celiac Disease and I'm not going to debate food elimination in those cases; it's necessary and non-negotiable.

But in the case of carbs, especially when it comes to feeding my children, it's best not to throw out the baby with the bathwater. I think the way companies process grains is harmful to us, but whole, unprocessed foods like oats, flax, sweet potatoes, quinoa, brown rice, and breads made from sprouted grains are both healthy and necessary, and can actually aid in weight loss.

Again, this is contradictory to most of the books I read, but I want you to know about *my* personal experience. I believe carbs are very important for kids, because they give them energy and aid growth. My kids love to add some rice to their dinner, or start off the day with old-fashioned oats with some yogurt and berries mixed in.

One of the main reasons I think so many of us have failed diet after diet is that it becomes unmaintainable in the long-term. We lose those last few pounds and then we go right back to business as usual. And then guess what happens?

Vrrrroooooooot! Our weight balloons right back up to where we were, if not even higher. Right? I know you've experienced it, too.

So when I set out to create a whole new system of healthy eating for my family, I knew we needed to make it something we could all live with long-term. I didn't want anyone to feel deprived; I wanted us to be excited about the food we ate. I also wanted them to have a voice in what we decided to eat, and why. My older three kids now read the labels even when they're at school; I started getting emails from teachers telling me they heard my kids questioning some of the snacks they were offered at school, and suggesting healthier alternatives...and their peers and the school staff were listening! This was honestly surprising to me—my kids were taking their nutrition seriously, all on their own! It blew my mind.

As time went on, and my family continued to feel better and look better, I decided to be a bit bolder in what I asked of them. On

Halloween we decided we would still go trick or treating, but we would donate our candy. We dressed up in our costumes and went downtown to see all the fun costumes and to take part in the annual parade. Then we went home and I made them special treats: sugar-free donuts, flavored popcorn, and dark chocolate.

I'm sure there are people out there rolling their eyes and shouting about how I ruined Halloween, so let me give you another reason to write me angry emails. We all ran a 5k race that day, and here's the crazy thing: my kids said it was the best Halloween they'd had ever had. They loved the 5k and the special treats I had made, and no one, not even the three and four year-olds, asked for sugary candy. They didn't even miss it!

How crazy is that?

I think we often underestimate our kids—I know I do. I also know it's sometimes hard to find a good balance between when to really push them on something and when to just let them coast. I think in terms of nutrition and health we always need to push. We need to help them understand the importance of being in control of what goes into their bodies, especially when they are preteens as my older three are. Become informed, mama. Tell them *why* certain things aren't a great choice and see what they do on their own. Above all, if you are a good example, your kids will rise to the occasion, too.

I've listed below what we *don't* eat because it's a much shorter list than what we *do* eat. Also, I've given you some great resources for finding family-friendly recipes that your husband and kids will *rave* about (Pinterest is your friend). We never focus on weight in my family; our conversations are about health, how we feel, our strength, and our energy levels. Yes, there are very noticeable physical differences in my family that I want to share with you, but our number one goal has been and always will be health and wellness.

Strong is the new sexy; healthy is the new black.
Being healthy is the new American dream!

FOODS WE AVOID, AND WHAT WE BUY INSTEAD:

- **No to sugar.** Yes, all sugar. Did you know sugar is also the main cause of heart disease? Get rid of the sugar! Be aware that many packaged foods contain sugar, ketchup for example. Read the labels and try to choose something different. We use natural Stevia instead, and sometimes xylitol or erythritol. If you use xylitol be careful that your dog doesn't get it, as it can be lethal to them. My kids LOVE True Lemon and True Lime sweeteners. You can buy them at your local store and they are usually found near the powdered, packaged drinks.
- **No to most cereals and granola.** We substitute these with the Ezekiel and Uncle Sam brands which we love. We often add them to our yogurt for some crunch. A little goes a long way!
- **No to anything you would get from a bakery.** Yes, even cupcakes…especially cupcakes!
- **No to whole-wheat pasta.** Instead, we eat brown rice and Dreamfields pasta in place of regular pasta. Dreamfields is especially good for replacing that macaroni and cheese your little ones insist on.
- **No to regular bread**—white or wheat, or even "whole wheat". My family eats only Ezekiel and/or other sprouted grain breads. You can find them in the freezer section of your grocery market, and my local Target even has a brand that is kid-approved.

- **No to all the "normal" American snack foods.** We don't do granola bars, crackers, cookies, chips, or pretzels. My kids do like to snack, so it was important to find good substitutions. One of our favorites is WASA crackers; we do so much with these! They're a low glycemic, low sugar cracker which we slather liberally with Laughing Cow cheese, cream cheese, or natural peanut butter and low sugar jelly for a PB+J snack. My kids like them topped with almost anything, even cucumbers. I will say that the longer they've been off sugar the better they like them. We also add them to soups and chili. My kids also *love* nuts! I try to keep a tray out in the kitchen at all times filled with almonds, pistachios, and cashews, which all have good healthy fats and proteins that will help curb hunger. Nuts and veggies are sometimes a bit more expensive, but we try to shop local and use lots of farmers markets and farm stands. If you are able to access those, it can mean great savings on your food bill. Your health is worth it!
- **No to ice cream, sorbet, popsicles, and yogurt with added sugar.** This can be difficult for kids, and parents too. The great thing is that we live in a day and age where there are lots of alternatives. I took my kids shopping with me and we found some things that they liked that were good for them. We all eat Bryers Carb Smart Ice Cream topped with some Fat Free Reddi Whip, or a few Lily's stevia-sweetened chocolate chips. Yes, those chocolate chips are expensive but it's worth it. Because you only need a few, a package can last a long time. We also indulge in Halo Top brand ice cream for very special occasions. We also make our own shakes with fresh berries, almond milk, ice, yogurt, and stevia. Jack and I often add whey protein powder to a shake after we've done

a run or a workout. We only use Greek yogurt, mostly the Oikos Triple Zero brand as they have great flavors my family loves. When it goes on sale we often buy out the store's entire supply—if you ask, some stores will even sell you the wholesale box they received. Just as an FYI, the banana flavor is wonderful to use for making pancakes. And now I'm hungry.

- **No to soda and juice.** We don't drink soda or juice, as I've already mentioned. Did you know one can of soda per day increases a child's risk of becoming obese by 60 percent? *One* can. Our drinks of choice are mostly sparkling water and tea. Other great options are Zevia, Honest Fizz, and Blue Sky Zero. These are all pop alternatives sweetened with Stevia. They're basically sparkling water, but they have a sweeter taste, and they have great flavor choices—we're huge fans of the Vanilla Cherry Crème from Blue Sky Zero, which you can find on Amazon. Jack and I also drink the occasional light beer or dry red wine. I know that's also contrary to many current health and diet ideas out there, but I think wine has many health benefits (more on that later).
- **No to anything that has a ton of unpronounceable ingredients.** If we do buy prepackaged foods, we make sure they have a minimal list of ingredients; if we can't pronounce it and the list is more than five or so items long, we probably won't eat it. Yes, we do make exceptions, but that's our general rule. Don't eat something if you can't figure out what's in it. Eat as many natural, God made, whole foods as possible. Fresh is best!

FOOD MY FAMILY LOVES:

- Oikos Triple Zero yogurt.

- Ezekiel brand breads and cereals—they even have English muffins for making a little pizza or breakfast sandwich!
- WASA brand crackers
- Berries, fresh and frozen
- Eggs—farm fresh are the best!
- Applegate brand sausages (OMG, so good)
- Pancakes made from oats
- Veggies—eat them in season to save money. Local farmers markets are awesome.
- Lily's brand chocolate and Dr. John's candy (Ahhh-mazing)
- Dreamfields pasta
- Meat and seafood—we try to do local and grass-fed when we can. Laura's Beef at our local store often goes on sale and I stock up when it does.
- Almond milk—we love Califia Farms brand
- Fairlife brand milk
- Breyer's Carb Smart ice cream (yes, this has a bit of Splenda in it, but not enough that I'm going to lose sleep over it.)
- Nuts—my family loves nuts, especially almonds and cashews
- Baked blue corn chips
- Mission brand low carb wraps (we use these for roll-ups in place of sandwiches, and for "Taco Tuesday", and for lots of other things listed at the end of the book)
- Kerry's Gold brand butter—yep, the real stuff
- Sour cream
- Cheese—the real stuff, nothing processed or fake
- Oils—I use mostly coconut oil and olive oil
- Lots of herbs and spices. Don't think your kids won't like them. My kids have really grown to want everything seasoned.

- Simple Girl BBQ sauce (can be found at Amazon)
- Quest brand protein bars—great after a run or a workout
- Jay Robb brand and Quest brand protein powders. Again, great after a workout
- Lesser Evil brand popcorn—found on Amazon (be careful, that stuff is addictive!)
- Bai 5 brand drinks
- Vitamin Water Zero

Most of these items *are* more expensive than their counterparts. It's stupid and it sucks, but nothing is more important than your health. I'm a bargain shopper ninja, so I shop sales and stock up in mass quantity whenever I can. When our local co-op puts Lily's chocolate bars on sale I've been known to buy them in embarrassing quantity, but my family *loves* them for treats and, hey, half-off is half-off. When you find things you know your family loves, keep an eye out for when the prices go down and stock up big time. Some stores will give you a nice discount if you buy in bulk quantities, so ask!

Will what worked for my family work for you exactly the same way? Probably not, but I think making the healthiest choices you can for your family is vitally important. I believe the diseases plaguing our kids, and us as adults, at increasingly high rates, are intrinsically related to what we put inside our bodies, often without thinking about it. So start thinking! Read the ingredients. Look and see if you recognize the things in the ingredient list of the foods you buy.

Below is the ingredient list, taken from Wikipedia, for a popular breakfast product. Do you know which cereal it is?

"Oats (Whole grain), Oats (flour), marshmallows (sugar, modified starch/modified corn starch, corn syrup, dextrose, gelatin, calcium carbonate, yellow 5 & yellow 6, blue 1, red 40), artificial flavor, sugar,

corn syrup, corn starch, salt, calcium carbonate, food coloring/artificial color, trisodium phosphate, zinc, iron, vitamin C (sodium ascorbic), niacinamide (a B vitamin), vitamin B2 (riboflavin), vitamin B1 (thiamin mononitrate), vitamin A (palmitate), folic acid, vitamin B12, vitamin D, vitamin E (mixed tocopherols)."

What the hell is niacinamide? Palmitate? Thiamin mononitrate?

Do you recognize that product? It's Lucky Charms. The manufacturers say those things are "vitamins", but why do you need to add them in the first place? Fresh whole foods have all the vitamins and minerals you'll ever need.

Pro tip: if you can't find some of these recommended items in your local store, check Amazon—they almost always have them in stock and some are even available for auto delivery, bulk quantity, or pantry boxes for an even better discount. You can also use the website "store locator" for hard-to-find items. Asking your grocery store to order them for you might also be an option; mine gives a discount for special bulk orders.

Chapter 9:

KEEPING IT SIMPLE: LET'S START IN THE KITCHEN

MY HUSBAND AND CHILDREN DON'T REALLY NEED TO SHED any weight, as they've all reached a place where they're within the normal range for their height and age. Two of my children lost about ten pounds each that had them close to an unhealthy weight according to their doctor. This weight loss was due to the changes we had made in terms of food intake and activity levels. My other kids had issues that were not at all connected to weight, and these all improved once we changed our diet. They've since maintained their new, healthier weights, and our doctor is pleased with their overall health progress.

My weight had always been at the root of my long laundry list of health problems and I felt I was basically becoming carbohydrate-intolerant. Virtually any sugar made me feel yucky, my blood disorder and the lack of nutrients in my blood was also causing some issues.

I believe that balancing your blood sugar levels is key to your overall health and I knew I'd have to start managing my blood sugar and insulin levels. At this point, I decided to include several superfoods to my diet (see the list of superfoods in Chapter 11), as well as some additional vitamin supplements. I also read a handful of books

on the concept of food cycling, and I immediately decided that it made sense and I wanted to try it.

In a nutshell, food cycling is eating certain foods together at the same time and cycling carbs in and out of your diet, so that you can burn off body fat more easily. There are several different ways to do this, and I found lots of contradictory information on the subject. Some books suggested eating carbs one week and not eating them the next, while other books recommended having carbs with every other meal, and still others said to rotate a few days on and a few days off.

Needless to say, all this new information seemed very complicated, and the rules were very confusing to me, so I set out to come up with a plan that would be easy for me and my busy schedule. And…I had to create meal plans that would accommodate my eating preferences with those of my family members.

My solution? I let my family lead the way. I knew from my research that I wanted to try and keep healthy, carb-friendly meals separate from meals with fats, so I would plan meals for my entire family and then structure my specific plan around that. What does that look like? Well, if my family has Taco Tuesday with low carb Mission wraps, I'm going to skip the cheese and do a low fat sour cream or tacos on lettuce wraps. Sometimes I'll have oatmeal for breakfast three or four days in a row, and then when my whole family decides they want omelets I'll join them, and add some turkey bacon or chicken sausage. My kids will usually add toast with some low sugar jelly.

For lunch Jack and I almost always eat a chef's salad. It is loaded with protein and it fills us up for the whole afternoon. My go to snack is yogurt—I *love* yogurt, and sometimes I'll add some Ezekiel cereal for crunch in the morning, or mix in a few chocolate chips and freeze it for a bedtime snack. It's actually really funny because as much as I

love yogurt, Jack hates it. He won't even touch the container. He says he has some repressed childhood memories. He's so weird. ;-)

I do track my calories with a fitness app just so I'm sure I'm staying within range, and I don't go crazy with any one particular food group. Protein and greens are daily staples, and I try to make sure I'm always getting enough fluids. Drinking all day is tough, though, because I have to pee all day, but I've also come to realize I'm often dehydrated, which can cause false hunger, so make sure you're drinking enough. Tea—both iced and hot—is what I try to go for during the day. We have a whole cupboard containing many different types of tea. Jack and I both keep a big thermos of hot tea on our desk, so we keep drinking throughout the day. I'm sure you can find some sort of tea you like—I've seen everything from watermelon tea to chocolate tea. It's great for your body, too!

As far as developing family recipes of our own, I've found a few great cookbooks we use on a regular basis, and we also use Pinterest a lot—we have a Pinterest board only we can see and we pin things we think the family might like. My amazing nanny helps with meal planning and shopping, and we often modify recipes that have things we are trying to stay away from, substituting the bad ingredient for something healthier. If you find a sweetener you really like—we love Swerve brand—you can just use that if the recipe calls for sugar. I even came up with a corn casserole modification for Thanksgiving that my kids thought was decent.

There *is* a bit of a learning curve to all this, but there are amazing bloggers, vloggers, and moms out there working on family-approved, low-sugar, low- or no-carb meals. Be confident, you can do it.

Let's just be honest for a minute, here: I'm a mom of six, a best-selling author, and I run a 50-acre farm—I don't have the time to make gourmet meals for my kids. The few recipes of my own I'm

including in this book come from a busy woman who just wants to give her kids healthy foods they'll actually eat, enjoy, and gain nourishment from. If you're looking for fancy, you won't find it here.

GET READY AND STOCK UP!

I've included a list of things that are great to have in your pantry, and I bet you have many of these things in your kitchen already. These are my regular go-to utensils and products. But, please, let me say it is not necessary to run out and buy everything to start with. Just add these things gradually as you go.

Let me say again that your health is an important investment. Fresh ingredients make good foods; they will always taste better than things that come in a package.

Let food be thy medicine and medicine be thy food. – Hippocrates

KITCHEN UTENSILS:

- A good set of knives
- A good set of pans (these don't have to be expensive). I really like the Stone Earth pans by Ozeri. Stainless steel or cast iron are also both great choices.
- Stainless steel measuring cups and spoons
- A nice 9-inch ceramic baking dish—I have an enameled cast iron dish by Cuisinart and I love it!
- A large skillet
- Nice, sturdy mixing bowls
- A good blender. Ninja, Vitamix, or Blendtec are all great. But a blender doesn't have to be new or top of the line to get the job done; my mom still uses the one she bought in the 70s.
- I love a good wok for preparing stir-frys. Meat, veggies,

some coconut oil, and spices make a quick and yummy dinner.

- I also love the new multi-cookers, a newer take on a regular old crockpot. If you haven't seen those yet, check them out. They make cooking so much faster and easier, and busy moms always need more convenience, right?
- A few pretty plates and mugs are always nice to have—don't save all the nice dinnerware for holidays! We eat our morning omelets on really cute Pioneer Woman plates I got at Walmart. I always feel special in the morning when we use them. There is a truth to the saying that "we eat with our eyes"—make every meal a reason to get out the good dishes. Fueling your body is important so, take your time, enjoy the process, and make it pretty!

FOR YOUR PANTRY:

- Old-fashioned oats—I use these for so many things!
- WASA crackers are so versatile! Use them with Laughing Cow cheese, veggies, berries, and even chocolate!
- Nuts, nut butters, and nut flours
- Brown rice
- Quinoa
- Coconut oil. This oil is amazing! Pour it in your mouth, on your skin, and all over your food. Honestly, where has coconut oil been all my life? It's ahhhh-mazing!
- Extra virgin olive oil (for low and medium temperature cooking only)
- Spices—my favorites are ginger, cinnamon, cayenne pepper, pink sea salt (pink sea salt is wonderful for you. We buy it in bulk on Amazon. Amazing health benefits!),

pepper, chili powder, oregano, garlic, turmeric, and basil

- Sugar and chemical-free protein powder
- Mustard
- Apple cider vinegar—add this to your LaCroix sparkling water with some True Lemon. This is a tasty combo, sweet like soda but good for you; the health benefits of apple cinder vinegar are listed in the supplements section.
- Sugar-free pasta sauce; we *love* the Classico Riserva
- Dark chocolate (70% cocao or higher), or stevia sweetened
- Pyure or Swerve stevia
- Seeds such as hemp, chia, buckwheat
- Cocoa powder
- Coffee and tea
- LaCroix sparkling water
- True Lemon or True Lime

FOR YOUR FRIDGE:

- Power greens such as kale, Swiss chard, spinach, dark green lettuce. Salads are wonderful for lunch.
- Eggs—give us this day our daily eggs! These are the perfect food; so don't leave them out of your diet!
- Almond milk
- Cream cheese
- Oikos Triple Zero Greek yogurt
- Sour cream
- Cottage cheese
- All non-processed cheeses
- Mayonnaise (we really like the Just Mayo brand)

- Real butter
- Veggies
- Fresh salsa
- Lots of low sugar fruits: lemons, limes, and berries are great for infusing into your water.
- Meat—I prefer to eat meat that is still on the bone. It has nutrients that boneless cuts do not have. Get some wings, thighs, and even whole chickens. My kids *love* wing night and we feel really wild and primal ripping that juicy meat off the bone.

FOR YOUR FREEZER:

- Meats of all kinds—it's really your choice. We stock up when things go on sale. Check your SAM's Club and Costco for good prices on organic meat. My freezer is currently full of grass-fed beef because I saw it for a steal of a deal at Meijer. Wait for a sale and buy all you can; healthy doesn't have to mean expensive. Also, you will eat less of the good stuff. Good organic meat does not have added fillers, and it allows you to stay full longer.
- I *always* keep frozen berries to add to smoothies and our morning oatmeal mush.
- Spinach is always great to keep frozen. Spinach is loaded in protein and iron and you won't even taste it in your smoothie—even Jack adds it to his post-workout smoothies, and I told you how he feels about veggies.
- We also buy sprouted-grain bread and keep that in our freezer. Yes, these are expensive but I also buy in bulk when I see a good sale price.
- Frozen organic veggies (often cheaper than the fresh, but

still good)

FRUIT AND SUGAR:

Yes, fruit has natural sugars, but some affect your body more than others. I'm not okay with cutting all fruit from your diet, because I believe God gave us these tasty treats for a reason. Just know that some fruits are going to be better and easier on your body than others. Below is a list of fruits that include the best and the worst at keeping your insulin levels in a good place. And remember: all things in moderation.

- The best fruits: blueberries, raspberries, lemons, limes, avocado and tomatoes. Two servings per day of these is fine.
- Okay-but-not-great fruits: green apples, kiwi, grapefruit, honeydew melon, mandarins, plums, peaches, pears, nectarines, strawberries and oranges. If you do choose these fruits try to limit them to one per day.
- On occasion fruits: grapes, cherries, red apples, pineapple, papaya, mangoes, and bananas. Because of the high fructose levels in these fruits they should be eaten very rarely.

BE CHOOSY WITH YOUR GRAINS:

Not all grains or carbohydrates have been created equally; some have a very negative impact on your body, and others are good for you. Most people are aware that things like regular factory-processed bread, cakes, cereals, cookies, and crackers are bad for you, but did you know barley and rye could have similar damaging affects on your body?

- The best grains: buckwheat, millet, oats, quinoa, brown

rice and flax

- Sprouted breads are always the best choice. You find these in the freezer section of your grocery store.

Pro tip: Shop the perimeter of your grocery store: they usually put all the food you don't want front and center by the entrances, and in the middle! Also, eating a protein bar before you shop will help you avoid making impulse purchases—shopping when we're hungry can be dangerous! Stalk the sales, and buy in bulk! If you keep your pantry stocked with all the good stuff you will be less inclined to go for that no-no on the back shelf. Also, really examine the ingredients lists for things like salad dressing, pasta sauce, peanut butter and flavored water, because they often include sugar.

Chapter 10

MY DIVORCE FROM SUGAR; DETOX IS HELL

"One cannot think well, love well, sleep well,
if one has not dined well."
— Virginia Woolf

I RECENTLY READ THAT THE AVERAGE AMERICAN EATS OVER A hundred and fifty *pounds* of sugar each year, *triple* what we consumed just a hundred years ago. That sort of increase is causing not just obesity, but all the related illnesses that come along with it.

Sometimes it is hard to avoid sugar altogether. It's amazing how many different foods have a high sugar content; start looking, and you'll see what I mean. Sugar is in *everything*! If the second ingredient is sugar, put it down and walk away.

THE MANY NAMES FOR SUGAR:

- Agave nectar
- Barbados sugar
- Barley malt
- Barley malt syrup
- Beet sugar

- Brown sugar
- Buttered syrup
- Cane juice
- Cane juice crystals
- Cane sugar
- Caramel
- Carob syrup
- Castor sugar
- Coconut palm sugar
- Coconut sugar
- Confectioner's sugar
- Corn sweetener
- Corn syrup
- Corn syrup solids
- Date sugar
- Dehydrated cane juice
- Demerara sugar
- Dextrin
- Dextrose
- Evaporated cane juice
- Free-flowing brown sugars
- Fructose
- Fruit juice
- Fruit juice concentrate
- Glucose
- Glucose solids
- Golden sugar
- Golden syrup
- Grape sugar
- HFCS (High-Fructose Corn Syrup)

- Honey
- Icing sugar
- Invert sugar
- Malt syrup
- Maltodextrin
- Maltol
- Maltose
- Mannose
- Maple syrup
- Molasses
- Muscovado
- Palm sugar
- Panocha
- Powdered sugar
- Raw sugar
- Refiner's syrup
- Rice syrup
- Saccharose
- Sorghum Syrup
- Sucrose
- Sugar (granulated)
- Sweet Sorghum
- Syrup
- Treacle
- Turbinado sugar
- Yellow sugar

Detox from sugar can be actual hell. The average American is addicted to both sugar and carbs, and it's a very hard addiction to break. You can experience flu-like symptoms. You might even ques-

tion your sanity. And it may take days or even weeks to kick the addiction.

Here's why: sugar is a drug.

For many of us, even if we refuse to admit it, sugar has a hold on us and, in my case, a near-fatal hold.

Before my last pregnancy and my detox from sugar, I would crave things *so* badly—I would lose focus just *thinking* about a sweet treat. I would often go out of my way just to pass the bakery. This is not just a "fat kid" thing, this is more normal than abnormal, I think. I could see the same thing happening to my kids, and I could really see it in my borderline-diabetic husband. His cravings and low and high sugar spikes turned him into another person. He would be irritable, sleepy, and angry from the sugar rollercoaster.

If there is one piece of advice you take away from this book, it needs to be this: CUT OUT THE SUGAR. It's nasty stuff. Elevated blood sugar levels are now known to be toxic to the brain. I truly believe the increase in neurological disorders in our country is directly linked to the food we are eating. Things like ADHD, depression, chronic headache, insomnia, autism, anxiety, epilepsy and schizophrenia have all been directly correlated to diet.

Our bodies are just not equipped to handle these kinds of foods and in the quantity we as a culture are consuming them. People are eating too many processed foods, foods that are virtually devoid of any nutrients and that are jammed full of chemicals.

Cute little things like animal crackers, pure sugar shaped into little fruits, cereals liberally sprinkled with marshmallows, and ultra-processed grains shaped into flakes literally *coated* in frosting… these kinds of things are seriously harming our children.

They're not just *bad* for us, they're *killing* us.

It seems every new scientific study reveals another illness caused

by poor nutrition. Even cancer has been directly linked to diet! But don't just take my word for it—I'm not a doctor, I'm just an angry mom. Please read *Always Hungry* by Dr. David Ludwig, *Grain Brain* by Dr. David Perlmutter, or watch the Internet video *The Skinny on Obesity* by the University of California with Dr. Robert Lustig.

Please become aware of the crap we are being fed—and I mean that literally—in terms of the way the effects of highly processed, high caloric and low nutrient foods are being downplayed. I believe these kinds of foods are harmful at worst, and are doing nothing good for us at best. I believe we need to take a stand and demand that the food industry make changes, and start giving us more options. We've reached epidemic levels when it comes to the number of people affected by metabolic syndromes—currently over 60% of all Americans are affected by a metabolic syndrome of some kind.

How many people do you know with heart disease, hypertension, type 2 diabetes, dementia, cancer, PCOS or liver disease? How many kids do you know with ADD or ADHD? We now have scientific studies that make a direct correlation between these things and what we're eating.

Is it any wonder we are seeing such an increase in neurological disorders, seeing that our culture is consuming *more* sugar each year?

Once my family broke free from sugar and were past the detox phase, we honestly began to feel like different people. We had crazy energy, and I'm not talking about something like a sugar-high or a caffeine-buzz energy spurt—this new sugar-free energy is constant and steady. We don't have the afternoon crash. We feel stronger, and we sleep better, too. I can point to each one of my children and say they've had a dramatic change in their physical wellness just from consuming less sugar.

And, by the way, artificial sweeteners like aspartame count as sugar, and are even *worse* than sugar. So switching to "diet" soda doesn't count. Sorry! Those artificial sweeteners are awful for you, too.

Even though I have said previously that our way might not work for every family, I *do* firmly and passionately believe that cutting out sugar will make *everyone* feel better. It may take some adjustment, there will be a detox phase, and it might take weeks or months, but it *will* be worth it.

My dear father came to visit us when we were just beginning to make these changes. After eating the dinner I'd made, he told me it tasted like wood. If you know my dad, then you know that comment was actually pretty kind. But then, this past Christmas, when he was up visiting I made a cheesecake he raved about, and he wanted more to take home. What he didn't know was that I had sent my mother some of the stevia sweetener I use, and she'd been using it in her cooking and baking as well, and he didn't even realize it! This is just further proof that, yes, it does sometimes require baby steps to make changes.

Baby steps are *fine*! None of us got healthy in a single day, or with a single meal. The journey to becoming strong and healthy can take some time. Give yourself that time and grace. Don't give up. Keep moving forward—you're worth it!

Life without sugar can look weird to some people. Some of my friends poke fun at my family. I'm often seen passing out True Lemon packets to my kids when we're out to eat. I'm the mom that packs Ziploc bags of nuts and handfuls Quest bars in my purse. I've been known to send my kids to school with a snack of colorful sliced bell peppers. Hey, it's cool to be weird, right?

I think that for many of you reading, this all sounds a little crazy.

If you had told me a year ago that I would lose over 100 pounds—again—and write a family health book, I would have laughed at you…but crazier things have happened. It's okay to do this your way. It's okay for your family to find things that work for you and you alone.

For example, my family doesn't really like avocado. I'm sure many of you want to throw this book across the room just because of that fact alone, but we really don't. We've tried. I know there are many awesome things that can be done with avocado and I hope your family adopts them as new favorites.

This book isn't a one size fits all. But it is about what it takes for your family to be healthy and strong. What does health look like to you? Just take that first step to find out.

QUICK AND EASY TIPS FOR CUTTING OUT SUGAR:

- Start with one meal at a time—breakfast first
- Don't dump your whole pantry if that doesn't work for you or your budget; slowly make changes in the things you buy, phase things out. This isn't all-or-nothing—look at the big picture.
- What are your go-to staples? Do you love popcorn and wine at night? What's the healthiest way to do that? Maybe change the sugary, sweet wine for something dry and red? How about a Skinny Girl 100 pack of popcorn instead of the butter flavor you usually buy?
- Increase your water intake. This is a detox, so we need to flush this junk out. Make sure you stay hydrated. Not to be gross, but pee shouldn't be bright yellow or orange, and it shouldn't smell super pungent. If it does look and smell like this, then you are dehydrated.
- Focus on your proteins. I make my kids do something I call

> the "meat challenge." It's just a fun game for them to try and eat all of their protein first. At each meal they try to eat all the protein first and then go to the other things on the plate: this is the meat challenge. We've found that protein fills them up and keeps them that way—which means they snack less, we spend less on snacks and we eat better foods as a result! This has been wonderful for my two younger sons who always get excited when they complete the "meat challenge." We make it a big deal for them. Before our dietary changes, they would sometimes refuse to eat the main course or maybe even dinner itself. Now, they are eating healthy at every meal. It's really wonderful for me to see everyone satisfied at each meal. I can't tell you how stressful it was when my kids didn't want to eat for whatever reason. I think it was often because they "craved" bread and sugar. Now that they are off the sugar, I'm seeing them eat a variety of foods that I wouldn't have imagined possible before.

The great thing about detox is that it doesn't last forever. It might be rough for a few days or weeks, but once you've come out of the sugar-fog you'll feel like a million bucks! My sugar detox wasn't as bad as some I've read about, as I didn't get crazy headaches or feel achy all over. If anything, I just felt "weird." I did immediately feel a change in my body, though—it really felt like someone had flipped a switch. I'm not really sure why, because I've tried cutting out sugar before. I think my resistance was just better this time. I didn't have an urge to cheat at all. Once I had passed a certain point, sugar didn't even look appetizing anymore.

Jack and I were at a signing right after the baby was born, and a reader brought some of the best looking cupcakes I had ever seen

from a fancy bakery in New York. The smell was intoxicating and they were a work of art. Did I eat one? Nope, sure didn't. I really wasn't even tempted. I had my Lily's chocolate bar in my purse and I was going to have it as a treat once we were done. I ended up giving the cupcakes away and I know they were thoroughly enjoyed. Would I have beat myself up had I had some? No. But I just didn't *want* them. I made a choice and I was proud of myself.

The food choices I made on that trip were so shocking to my mother that it started her on her own health journey. Now, at age sixty-five, she's also down several pounds, feeling better, and recovering from the chronic stomach pain and irritable bowl syndrome she's struggled with for many years. Until she tried my plan, she hadn't been able to lose any weight at all in fifteen years! I don't think age or stage of life play any part in this, either. If my three year-old and my mother can see amazing results just from cutting out sugar, you can too! I would love to see mothers, daughters and grandmothers all doing this together. We need to encourage and inspire the best health for the ones we love. It's so important.

If sugar has been a friend to you like it's been to me, then this stage might be emotional. It's okay to miss your friends and it's okay to grieve. I'm not even being funny about this. Breaking up with my favorite foods was hard. Cupcakes were like a BFF to me, but I found other things that satisfied me even more.

Cheesecake and cookie bars are two of my most favorite holiday treats, and I was able to find two amazing recipes that surpassed my expectations this year. My kids loved it and raved that it was the best cheesecake they'd ever had. Did it take planning and time to find something I thought would take the place of our previous treats? Yes. Did it end up being a bit more costly to use the more expensive sweetener and sugar-free chocolate? Yes.

My family doesn't eat these sorts of treats on a daily basis, but for special occasions it's okay to go all out making treats everyone will enjoy. Life is about living, and being happy. Sharing a meal is part of that; especially when it comes to birthdays, holidays and other special days in the year so go all out! The best part will be that you won't feel sick or sluggish afterwards. No food comas! You will have energy to laugh and play together. Trust me on this!

Maybe there is a certain soda that you just can't live without, Diet Coke for example. I believe diet soda was a huge contributor to my weight gain and becoming bloated and inflamed. I was a Diet Sunkist addict for ten years, but I found an orange flavored Zevi that is a great replacement. Not as sweet, but it does the trick. The weird thing is that I don't even want that daily anymore. I have one maybe every few days when I think something would go well with it. But I'm not attached to it like I was with the Diet Sunkist drink. Surprising, but true.

Now, wine is a totally different story. You won't ever get me away from my wine. Please...bury me with a fancy bottle of Cabernet Sauvignon. Ha!

Honestly though, don't doubt your body's ability to roll with these changes.

One day at a time; you can do it! Start slow and don't go overboard. We want this to stick and we want it to work. If you want a lifestyle change to be sustainable, then it has to be able to be maintained long-term. Keep experimenting and find replacements for things containing sugar and I promise you it will continue to get better. If Jack can do it, you can do it. Just don't ask him to eat cauliflower...that's a hard limit for him.

Chapter 11

SEEING FOOD IN A WHOLE NEW WAY: FUEL VS. COMFORT

About three weeks into making these healthy changes, your weight is going to go up, or you're going to get stressed out, or just hit a wall. It's bound to happen. Don't give up; you've got it!

My body chemistry and hormones were working in sync while I was pregnant with baby Ree, so the weight came off pretty easily and steadily, but after I had her my body was no longer with the plan. And, to this day, I'm not sure why. I just know my weight started to creep back up. There were a few days when I swore a lot and wanted to chuck my newly acquired scale out the window and then run it over with my truck a few times. Why the heck couldn't my body ever get with the freaking program? The more upset I got, the more I would use food as a comfort.

I was getting sucked right back into the old cycle.

I remember listening to Oprah talk about her battle with her weight and food, hearing her say she used food as a comfort as well. For me, though, I think the comfort was mostly out of habit; I knew my body didn't *need* the food to feel better, and I knew the food wouldn't even really make me feel better. In fact, the food usually

just ended up making me feel worse. The issue was, comfort eating is what I always did, going back to my childhood when I would sneak snacks up to my room just because I was bored. There isn't really one specific thing I can point to as the single major contributor; it was just everything about Food, with a capital 'F'.

So what changed this time?

Well, I think I was finally at the point where I wanted to fight back, and fight *hard*. I was sick of the way I felt all the time. I hated the stigma of illness: asthma, bad knees, blood disorder, morbid obesity—my whole self, basically. I was finally at a point where I wasn't going to take it anymore. I knew there was no quick fix to this. There was no surgery, no pill, and no magic potion. This had to be a body, mind, and spirit change. I asked God to change my heart about food.

Now, I have to admit, I've been praying this prayer my whole life, but I just figured God was too busy with other stuff to deal with it. But, in all honesty, God *had* been giving me answers—I just didn't want to hear them.

This time, however, I felt like everything was laid out in front of me, obvious and undeniable.

First, I had to pick different foods. The ones God created, not man. Food that would nourish, heal, and fuel my body, not control it and drag me down. I also knew I had to get moving and get physically active.

That was it. I could see it as clear as day: healthy calories in, and constant physical movement.

It wasn't going to be easy, but that was the clear and direct answer from God Himself. Nothing in life worth having comes easy. That's been the theme of my life, and it might be yours, too. We have to want health over other things: over money, over time, over leisure. This isn't an easy pill to swallow, I know, but it's actually quite em-

powering.

I know there are going to be many times during the remainder of my life when I'm going to need comfort, when I'm going to need to be consoled, when I'm going to weep. I refuse to let food be the illusion of real comfort. Real comfort is my husband's arms, my friend's ear, or my child's laugh. Food will only mask or distract you from what you really and truly need. Don't give it that power over you. It's only fuel; you deserve real comfort.

POSTIVE SUBSTITUTIONS FOR COMFORT EATING:

- Sex—burns two hundred calories in thirty minutes when done correctly. Dude, that's a whole yogurt! Just sayin'.
- Exercise—I know it sounds crazy but you might actually grow to like it. I know I have!
- Turn on the music and dance. I've found some great YouTube videos featuring short dances set to my favorite songs. I've broken up my afternoon with one of those and felt so much better.
- Go for a short walk
- Read—may I suggest you read my books and then re-visit suggestion number one?
- Call a friend—yep, I said *call*, not *text*. Talk to an actual person with your actual voice.
- Express your creativity—paint, sing, play an instrument, dance, write, whatever gets your creative juices flowing!
- Drink some tea—oolong tea actually burns calories and revs up your metabolism.
- Pray—I mean that. If cake is calling to you, maybe Jesus can help. It's worked for me!
- When all else fails, eat a handful of nuts—try it, it really works. Fats stop hunger.

- And perhaps most importantly: learn to be okay with being hungry for a bit.

I know that last one sounds crazy, but one of my biggest victories was simply learning how to cope with my hunger. It actually goes away if you just ignore it for a while, which I didn't know until I was thirty-five years old! Hunger will wane; you should be able to go every three or four hours without a meal. And it's okay to take the time to figure this out for yourself. Feeling hungry doesn't mean you are about to die; it's just a reminder that you will need to eat at some point in the near future.

IMPORTANT TIPS TO BUYING THE BEST FUEL:

- Stay away from anything processed and packaged containing unnatural chemicals—if you can't pronounce the ingredients, don't buy it.
- Farm fresh food is best—try to find a local farmers market you can visit, and don't be afraid to negotiate on the price, especially if you are buying in bulk.
- Customize a meal plan that works best for your family. You'll find you save money by not shopping every day, and sticking to a food plan means you don't have to worry about meal planning until your next shopping cycle.
- Keep an eye on sales of your favorite food items. I know when Zevia goes on sale at my store each month I stock up.
- Try some superfoods! Even your picky eaters might like a few of these, and they are good for you! Some of our favorite superfoods include eggs, walnuts, apples, salmon, canned pumpkin, cauliflower, brown rice, strawberries, black beans, broccoli, sweet potatoes, flaxseed, Greek yogurt, dark chocolate, dried

tart cherries, tea—green and black, natural peanut butter, blackberries, grapes (wine!) and blueberries.

- You don't have to buy *everything* organic, but be aware of the "dirty dozen"— foods that have the highest pesticide residue: peaches, apples, sweet bell peppers, celery, nectarines, strawberries, cherries, pears, imported grapes, spinach, lettuce, and potatoes; you should always buy these organic.
- Always check out the labels of your favorite foods. Is there a better alternative? My youngest son *loves* catsup, so I've switched to one with no added sugar and he likes it just the same—he never even noticed a difference.
- Low-fat, non-fat, and fat-free aren't always a better choice, and sometimes they are actually worse for you, so we usually prefer the full fat and organic options; they taste better, and are better for you.
- I try to use coconut oil whenever I can, as it really is the best and safest option for high heat cooking. The refined version has no coconut taste at all, and you can buy it in spray, liquid, or solid forms to suit your cooking needs. I still use locally made olive oil for lower temp cooking—375 degrees or less to be safe.
- When buying meat, grass-fed or wild is best, and farm fresh is always a wonderful option. Look into farm co-ops near you for great deals on local meat, and check your SAM's Club and Costco for great deals on organic meat.

A quick note about Stevia. When I first started looking into sugar alternatives fifteen or more years ago, there just wasn't much out there. I tried all the alternatives and they all either left me running for the bathroom, bloated, or gassy. I felt pretty awful after several of the protein bars I tried, and don't even get me started on the "di-

abetic" prepackaged items—they were honestly just gross, and that's putting it nicely.

Now, however, we have stevia, which is 100% natural and comes from the stevia plant. It's one hundred and fifty times sweeter than sugar and it has a negligible affect on blood glucose levels. This sweetener has been a true game changer for me. I've done a lot of research on this, and I believe it to be safe for the whole family—I wouldn't give it to my kids if I thought otherwise. I think this is the best and safest alternative to sugar that we currently have; I've even talked to my doctor, and she agrees. So if your family has a genetic pre-disposition to diabetes, this could be a lifesaver. I use it to modify recipes for baked goods and treats for my family—to rave reviews. Some of my kids even like my baked goods better now than when I made them with regular sugar.

One caveat, however, is that not all stevia sweeteners are created equal. You will even find some "stevia" out there that contains actual sugar in the blend. So beware, that stuff isn't the real, all-natural stevia so don't buy it! I prefer to buy brands that I know and love. We do use a few blends that have xylitol and erythritol in them, but if you use those please be careful with it around your pets, as it can be lethal to dogs if they ingest enough of it. I highly suggest trying the Pyure and Swerve (granular and confectioner type) brands first; my baked goods were greatly improved by the Swerve confectioner's stevia product. But if you don't like those, keep trying until you find one you do like.

A one-to-one to sugar conversion makes things pretty easy to start off with, but your tastes will change the longer you go without sugar, so you might need to keep adjusting the sweetness levels. I'm often scaling back, because things are starting to taste *too* sweet. It's amazing how great these sugar-free treats can be once you find the

sweet spot for your family, and if you don't tell your kids it's stevia sweetened, they probably won't even notice! Don't be afraid to take one of your family favorites and give it a go—I think you'll be surprised!

THE NEXT STEP

Once you've finished this book, you're going to start my full eight-week health plan—The Wilder Way. Why eight weeks? Because I believe your body needs time to adjust to the changes you're going to make.

I don't want you focusing on counting calories, points, numbers, or portions. I want you to learn about your body, and discover what *true* health looks and feels like. I'm honestly not sure that the average American even understands what true health means anymore, because we've moved away from natural foods and regular exercise to lead lives that are sedentary and that are fueled, primarily, by processed foods. To compound this issue, we are all confused by what we're being told.

Information has changed so often over the last thirty years that my head has always been spinning: don't eat fat…do eat fat; don't eat carbs…do eat carbs; don't eat eggs…do eat eggs; don't eat red meat, don't ever eat bacon…real meat and bacon is just fine; orange juices causes cancer…orange juice *cures* cancer. Where's the moderate voice in our food culture? And who can be trusted?

Even as I was pouring over recipes, trying to modify them for this book, I ended up throwing many of them out, because either everything was so fancy that none of my kids or my husband would even touch it, or so full of junk that by the time I finished revising the

recipe, there was nothing left! Who the hell can get their kids to eat water chestnuts and tofu?

I'm going to show you a new way of eating which at first might sound like nothing you've heard before, something new, something fresh, but I honestly think it's super easy, and makes a whole lot of sense. It might sound a bit overwhelming; I know most of you have a whole family to consider; so winning everyone over can be tough.

I want you to really focus on one meal at a time. That's it. Just focus on that next meal, and make the healthiest choices you can each and every time you sit down to eat. I want this to be fun for you. I want your family to enjoy doing this together. I want them to feel better.

I believe we are on the verge of a food revolution. There's going to be a tipping point where the people suffering from a plethora of food-related diseases will demand change. I think it's coming sooner rather than later, so take the first step with me.

THE BASIC PRINCIPLES OF THE WILDER WAY:

- Eat real foods with minimal ingredients—shoot for five or fewer. If you can't pronounce an ingredient without sounding it out, don't eat it.
- No sugar. None. Nada—Sugar is a killer. No, not even donuts. Say it with me: "SUGAR IS A KILLER!" We'll talk about doing this gradually later on, so for now just keep reading. Don't be scared, you won't even miss it, I promise!
- No processed foods or refined carbohydrates—you only want the real stuff!
- Cycle your food combinations for weight loss—if you want to lose weight, keep your body guessing. More on this later.

- Mindful eating, not mindless eating
- SLEEP—your body needs regular sleep. This is vitally important, so don't skip this one.
- MOVE! Our bodies were made to move. If you want to feel good and look smoking hot, *get moving*! Get up, go outside, and start doing your thing, whatever it may be. More on this later, as well.
- As always, be sure to stay hydrated!

So why isn't my program complicated? Aren't diets supposed to be complicated? Don't we need to suffer? Why aren't there little boxes to measure your serving sizes? Why don't you have to count calories?

Why?

Well, I think that's all bullshit. Sorry if that's a little blunt, but I've been counting calories my whole life. I've counted points and calories, I've used boxes and pre-packaged servings, and all of this got me exactly nowhere. It didn't accomplish one thing. So, if none of that worked, why are those methods still out there? Why are we still gaining weight? Why is our health crisis getting worse each day? Why are there more and more obese Americans every year?

We need to stop focusing on another weight loss program or exercise gimmick. Instead, we need to focus on something totally different: our food choices. It's really that simple. All it really takes is reading labels, and a little knowledge. My plan is for busy women—and men too!—who just want to be able to spend their precious time with their kids, and not measuring, boxing, or counting bullshit points systems or calories.

My plan is taking us back to the basics. Nourishing food, physical movement, and health. That's it! Sit back and relax. If a mom of six with a farm and a publishing business can do this, you can too!

Pro tip: I never leave my house without filling my purse with snacks; now I never get sidetracked by the pastry window at Starbucks. I don't leave home without some nuts, a Quest bar, or some dark chocolate...or all three!

Chapter 12

THE WINE DIET: CHOCOLATE, WINE, AND SEX... ALL IMPORTANT FOOD GROUPS

"All you need is love. But a little chocolate now and then doesn't hurt."
— Charles M. Schulz

THIS IS A SPECIAL LITTLE CHAPTER FOR ALL THE COUPLES OUT there. If you aren't married, or in a committed relationship, move on to the next chapter. Move on, move on, there's nothing to see here.

If you are married or committed, then grab a glass of your favorite wine and let's chat for a moment.

My husband and I *love* what we do. We have a passion for reading, writing, marriage and sex. Luckily for us, all those things go together and, from chatting with many of our readers, it does for them too! We hope to share more of our marriage wisdom in its own full book one day, but for now I just wanted to add a special chapter on how food, marriage, how we feel about ourselves and life in general all seem to interconnect for so many women. After I wrote *Big Girls Do It Better*, I was literally overwhelmed with emails from women who told me they were having sex with their husbands regularly after

a long period of going without it. That was so exciting to me!

There are many reasons you might experience a sexual drought in your marriage. Maybe you had a new baby, or one of you is struggling with illness. Maybe one or both of you are under a lot of stress from work. Maybe finances have you in knots. Maybe you just feel like shit about yourself, and simply don't have the desire.

The really worrisome thing about many of the emails I received is how women just felt too bad about themselves and their bodies to enjoy sex with their husbands—they were ashamed of their bodies. Ladies, this is unacceptable! If there's one thing that'll put a marriage at risk for divorce, it's that.

I'm sure if you asked your husband right now, he would be up for sex with you no matter what state you are in. Heck, I once went to the bathroom post-sex to find mascara smeared all over my face and I looked like a raccoon. My husband didn't seem to mind at all—I'm not even sure he noticed! My body is covered in scars from surgery, I've lost and gained a few hundred pounds, and my breasts have fed five babies. I'm sure you get the picture.

My point is you need to get your sexy back!

Your husband *needs* sex with you, and you *need* sex with him! Sex is incredibly important to your overall health, on top of just being fun, so grab a glass of red wine (lots of wonderful antioxidants!), some dark chocolate (superfood!), and get into the bedroom for some "exercise" with your husband. I even read recently that some studies have been done showing wine can actually help with weight loss—yippie!

I can honestly say I've never laughed as much or come as hard as after a nightcap of good wine and a few bites of dark chocolate shared with Mr. Wilder. Sometimes we get really crazy and challenge each other to planking or push up contests and then jump into bed.

The best part about this is that you are also going to burn some calories having sex—up to two hundred calories when you have a *really* good time! Now, if I was worried about how I looked, or if I didn't feel sexy, or how I looked or felt inside, I would miss out on all that marital fun.

If that's you, then you need to listen up.

Mama, you *deserve* that love and attention from your man. My goal is to get you feeling better about yourself, so you'll want it, and know deep down that your man thinks you're sexy. Little steps will make all the difference in how you feel, so start eating better, get moving, and take good care of yourself. All of these things are connected.

When you feel better inside, you'll want to show that on the outside. Don't miss out on life, don't let it pass you by because you think you can't do this—you can! Sex is a part of the whole program. Regardless of what size you are today, or how you're feeling about your body just remember, tomorrow is a new day. Being relaxed and having fun with your husband will only make this journey so much better for *both* of you.

Personally, I'm not in favor of depriving myself in any way. There are days where I'm just pushing through to get to the wine and chocolate part of the night. With six kids and a hundred farm animals all running amok, those treats are sometimes what helps me keep hold on my sanity; this is something that took me a long time to figure out. What's on the outside reflects what's inside, and what's inside you is reflected outside, so fake it till you make it, if that's what it takes. On the days when I'm feeling down, or I just feel like crap, I put on some lipstick and sexy panties. I know it sounds crazy and almost *too* simple, but those two things can help you get into a slightly different frame of mind. Maybe paint your toenails or wear your

favorite color, or put that lipstick and those panties on, take a photo and send it to your hubby. Whatever it takes! Just don't let yourself think you aren't a sexual being—*you are*. Marriages need sex. Daddy needs sex. Mama needs sex… and maybe some wine and chocolate too. Don't worry: you don't even have to report back to me on this one. Just do your thing, and maybe name the baby Jasinda.

I'm kidding…mostly. If Lily's chocolates wanted to change the name of their sea salt chocolate to the Jasinda Bar, I would totally understand. Eat one and you'll see what I mean. They're that good!

MY FAVORITE WAYS TO INDULGE AND FEEL SEXY:

- A nice hot bubble bath—add a LUSH bath bomb for extra luxuriousness. Those things are magic!
- A nice box of Dr. John's chocolates. These things are sugar-free and you'd never know it. Give them a try and thank me later: www.drjohns.com
- LELO brand personal pleasure products. No need to thank me if you don't already know about these. Wow. Just…*wow*.
- Oil candles. We just got some of these as a gift and the wax actually dissolves into a massage oil. Very sexy and really sets a sultry mood.
- Spanks. Yep, I know. I might get some backlash for this, but I actually love my Spanks. I've been known to wear them to bed for sexy time. They help me feel good and tuck in my mommy belly—I think they put the hole in the crotch for multiple reasons. There's no shame in putting those on for a night out if you want to get everything pushed up and held in so you feel good for yourself and look good for your man.
- Music or audiobooks! Sex is all about the senses, so put on

your favorite sexy tunes, or make your husband a playlist and send it to him. Maybe you like to listen to your favorite hot book before bed. Hey, the couple that listens together gets busy together!

- Speaking of which…read any of our Jack and/or Jasinda Wilder books to get in the mood. We love it when you invite us into your bedroom…metaphorically speaking.

Chapter 13

BIG GIRL PSYCHOLOGY 101

BEFORE WE GO ANY FURTHER, I THINK IT'S IMPORTANT WE TOUCH on some "Big Girl" thinking. I've been morbidly obese for nearly twenty-five years. That's a very long time to deal with everything that goes along with being a big girl. And let's just put it all out in the open: there's a lot that comes with being overweight. I believe it's one of the last things that people will still publicly ridicule and mock.

I follow a very successful plus size model that I've seen called every single nasty name in the book, *publicly*, on her professional social media pages. It's honestly disgusting. Why do people think this is okay? It's not! We are more than our bodies. We are also souls, sometimes delicate and always beautiful, souls. You never know what someone has gone though, or is going through, because of their weight.

Shame on our society for taking their own pain, anger and frustration out on people with weight issues. We've heard all the jokes and names and none of it was ever funny, so just stop already.

I believe this shaming has put women—especially women in the public eye—into one of two categories: one group are the women who say, "Eff you, I'm going to look however I want to look. I'm big

and I'm proud of it!" Category two is the group that says, "Let's not talk about the elephant in the room that is my weight."

As a woman, it's very difficult not to let yourself be defined in some way by your body, regardless of your size, but it's exponentially harder for women who are curvy or plus-sized. Some of the questions I've been asked about my books tip toe around the idea that I wrote a "BBW" series. Honestly, I hate categorizing my books and I'm not a huge fan of the BBW title. When I wrote the *Big Girls* series, I was honestly just writing my own story. It didn't even really occur to me that Anna was a "plus sized heroine" until people pointed it out to me. I just wanted to tell that particular story about that particular girl at that moment in time. Who knows what she looks like now or what she's doing now? Hopefully, she's happy and feeling good.

I'm not sure which side of the coin most of my readers are on, so my reason for writing this book is to share where I've been, what I'm going through, and where I hope to end up. At this point in my life, my happiness has very little to do with looks. I figure I'm a bit past my prime and too happily married to worry about it. My focus at this point in my life is my health.

As a society, I would love to see us make peace with our bodies and make peace with each other.

I know that some of my readers have been pretty vocal to me about their success with gastric bypass and band surgeries, so I'm going to address that as well. I found lots of staggering statistics while I researching this book. The truth is, less than 20% of people who undergo those procedures keep the weight off for more than a few years. Many of them have additional health problems arising from the surgery, and more than 10% require additional operations after the first surgery. A recent study by the National Institutes of Health showed almost 40% end up having serious complications or nutri-

tional deficiencies.

I know there are exceptions to every rule but in my mind, surgical procedures are just putting a Band-Aid on a gaping wound. Simply cutting people open and removing part of their intestines can't solve our nation's obesity problem. Why aren't we more successful with those procedures? Well, I believe that the body, mind and soul are all connected, and those surgeries only address a single aspect of the weight problem, and not even permanently or safely for that matter. Surgical procedures that modify our bodies won't change our brains, our habits, the way we think about ourselves, or what we eat.

When I volunteered at a well-known bariatric hospital after my surgery, I saw a lot of horrible things, like people trading food addictions for addictions to alcohol, drugs, and sex, and I saw people coming in for their second or *third* bypass or banding. People who are so desperate for health end up more frustrated, without hope, and in worse shape than they were before their surgeries.

I believe eating right and dealing with our emotions and connections to food is critical for success. You *must* break the chains food has over your body and mind. Success comes through strength. If you've had bypass surgery and gained the weight back, it's okay, that doesn't define you! If you plan to undergo that surgery, I wish you the best of luck with it but, *please,* do the research and understand it's just a tool and, in my opinion, an unsafe one. There is a better, safer, long-term solution. Not all doctors will tell you that, either—mine didn't. Bariatric surgery is an extremely lucrative business, one which doctors and hospitals make enormous profits from.

Love your body the best you can. Give it a chance to get healthy without putting it at even greater risk. Please keep reading this book. I would love to show you a safer way. Let's heal from the inside out. If you've already had a surgical intervention and still need help to feel

good and healthy, please join me.

We can do this!

In the next chapter of this book I'm going to focus on physical strength, wellness, and health. I want to be very clear though, and say that none of the things I have accomplished changes the fact that I will always be a Big Girl who puts on her big girl panties every single day. I'm a touch under six feet tall and I have a size twelve and a half shoe. My frame just isn't tiny, and that's how God made me. It's part of who I am—heck, it is *who* I am.

But, regardless of my weight, I'm a woman, and one with serious health issues, some which stem from my own poor choices, but still more from being misinformed. The last year was an epiphany for me; I've learned so much, not just about myself, but also about the human body. I want you to know that no matter what your weight may be; you can *always* be healthier by making positive food choices, engaging in physical movement and getting enough rest. We are all works in progress. Yes, I've lost a significant amount of weight making these changes, but even more importantly, I've found my strength and my health. I've discovered pride in my body.

I recently ran five miles without stopping… *five* miles! Can you believe that? I honestly couldn't believe it even while I was actually doing it. It's *nuts*! I've always had asthma and bad knees, even as a child. How the hell could I run that far —albeit slowly—without stopping?

What I realized was that I've been lying to myself my whole life. I just assumed I couldn't do it. Fat kids can't run, and fat adults certainly can't, so how could I do it now? Thirty-six years old, mother of six children, countless health issues; there's just no way, right? Well, what if all those lies are silenced once I clean the toxins out my body? What if my body starts working in concert with my mind, and I start

to believe I *can* do it? What then?

That's where this is headed.

So, get on your running shoes and take my hand. This isn't just *my* moment, it's also *yours*. There's a reason I'm writing this book right now: it's for *YOU*. Today is the day, *NOW* is the time. You are going to get moving with me. We've been fed a bunch of bullshit and told a lifetime of lies, and now it's time to fight back. We've been abused, made fun of, yelled at, and looked down upon. Not anymore, my friend. This is when our tiger comes out and we stop letting this abuse go any further.

I don't care if your whole closet is full of BBW pride T-shirts and you're standing strong for the positive body image cause—that's wonderful, but don't let your health suffer for it. Let's continue to fight for *all* women, but for ourselves first.

Good health and change starts with *you*. You have more power than you think! Mama, you've got the power to change the course of the rest of your life.

If you are hearing lies in your head, stop now and say this out loud with me—yes, actually say it out loud. If your family is home and you are embarrassed just go into your bathroom.

Stand in front of the mirror and say this out loud:

"God meant for my body to be healthy and strong.

I am worth the time it will take to make myself stronger and healthier.

It won't be easy, but it will be worth it.

Yes, it's okay to do this for those who love me, but this is for me.

I was beautiful then, I am beautiful now, and I will be beautiful tomorrow.

I can do this.

I can do this despite feeling like I can't, or that I've been told I can't.

My body is beautiful at any size.

My body is going to be unstoppable when I'm healthier and stronger, so watch out!

Nothing will define me.

Nothing will stop me.

I can do this!"

PART 3

Running Wild!

Chapter 14

THE CHALLENGE

"Run when you can, walk if you have to, crawl if you must; just never give up." — Dean Karnazes, ultramarathon runner

I'M ABOUT TO CHALLENGE YOU. ACTUALLY, I'M GOING TO FULL-ON *double* dare you to run with me, and by run I mean walk, wog, jog, wobble, hobble, whatever you it takes to get to the finish line. I'm not kidding; I'm not even sort of joking about this. I want you to get on Google *right now* and find a 5k race in your area. Maybe there's one coming up in a few weeks, maybe there's one happening in a few months. Either way, I know you're laughing and thinking, "There is *no* freaking way I'm going to do this! Jasinda Wilder has obviously lost her mind."

Truth be told, I lost it long, long ago, but I'm not joking about this. This is a real, honest to goodness, throw-down challenge. I want you to do this. Not because I told you to, but because there is a tiny little speck of "*just maybe I can*" hiding inside you somewhere.

Don't worry about being ready, because you never will be. You just have to do it, ready or not.

So go ahead and sign yourself up for your very first 5k.

Yes, right now.
I'll wait.

Still waiting.

This is not a joke; and, yes, your friend can come too.

Sure, sign up your whole family without asking them, like I did.
They'll love you for it…I promise.

What are you waiting for? You can do this. Come on!

Whew, I'm so glad you did that! I was worried we would lose time on this.

Now I can officially say you're in training with me. This is the blind leading the blind, the wogger leading the woggie—"wog" is what I call my "walk-jog." It's a low impact run I do to protect my knees. I'll explain more about that later, the important part is that now you're ready for some serious training.

The next few chapters are basically going to be an idiot's guide to getting moving. Registering for a 5k is half the work, so consider yourself half done. Now, let's get to the really fun stuff!

I know, I know, right now it might actually feel like suicide to attempt this. Me? Run five kilometers? That's like…three miles! Three point one, to be exact, but I know you can do this, and I know when you reach the finish line you'll go home and sign up for the next chance to reach the finish line. You may never have thought of yourself as a runner, but guess what? You are, now! Your body was built to move. It was built to run, jump, dance, and walk. It's part of the design. You are, in fact, a born runner.

When my family started feeling better, we decided we wanted to create some memories doing physical things together. We had seen on Facebook that a local running club was sponsoring several 5k runs to benefit charities throughout the upcoming fall and winter holidays. One of the wonderful things about our local community is that most of the runs sponsor a local charity, so not only are you helping yourself get stronger and healthier, but you're also helping a local charity, so it's a win/win!

I know a lot of people think these events are only for the uber-athletic, but let me tell you; those types blaze to the end as soon as the gun goes off. Like, they're done and home having a snack by the time I reach the finish line. The people I roll with are moms with

strollers, senior citizens, and fat dogs. In fact, during one race a very fat dog with a limp jogged right past me—honest-to-God truth! My point is, you don't have to be the fastest. You don't even have to be in the top fifty percent. Everyone gets a shirt or a hat, and everyone can have whatever time he or she needs to finish. I'm sure someone out there is thinking they'll be dead last. So what? At least you did it! You're doing more than someone who's at home in front of the TV. What did they gain that morning? Nothing! But you…you're a finisher! You are one badass mother runner! You did your first 5k!

Your first one is going to be special and maybe a bit crazy, because you don't know what to expect. The wonderful thing is that there will be other first-timers there, too. You won't be the only one and you certainly don't need to be embarrassed. You'll be able to tell the real athletes from the…not-athletes, trust me on this one. All sorts of different people will be there, and there'll always be someone there to cheer you on.

I'll never forget our Jingle Run, a 5k we did around Christmastime. I was pushing our baby in a stroller while dragging my four-year-old who was in desperate need of a nap. We were nearing the end of the race—thank God!—when a person on the side of the road watching the race yelled, "Wow, she's jammin'!" They were talking about me! I was jammin'! He may have been talking about the fact that I was blasting "Turn Down For What" on my phone's speakers as loud as it would go, but I prefer to think he was talking about my amazing 16 minutes per mile pace.

Please don't worry about your time for your first race, or doing too much training—I don't want you to worry about that at all, in fact. Just commit to doing it, even if you have to walk the whole thing. My older daughter sometimes walks while I wog and she finishes before I do! Do this at your pace and no one else's. The only

person you're competing against is yourself. There's no shame in getting there when you get there, whether it's in thirty minutes or two hours! If you can do short bursts of speed to pick up the pace, hey, that's great. I just want you to get out there and *do it*. Don't get overwhelmed and don't go overboard.

Don't get ahead of yourself. This is important to understand. Don't make this yet another New Year's resolution to change your life. I want you to stick with this for more than a day or a week or a month, or even a year; this is your new forever. We're going to take this one step at a time. Maybe you want to work on your food plan first and get things going there. My mom has been doing that for months without really increasing her exercise at all, and she's had amazing results. I didn't start moving until I felt better and knew it was time to move.

So what does that look like for you? This isn't one size fits all. Maybe you need to move first and then adjust your food plan. In my experience, though, cutting out the worst enemies to your health is a great place to start, and then gradually make other changes.

Physical exercise and strength training *is* important; I do want to make that very clear. I read several diet books that basically said exercise was optional and not that important. I don't buy that for a second.

Why?

Because of what I've seen and experienced with my own body.

I really believe nutrition and physical fitness go hand and hand with feeling great and looking great. Could we probably excel in one without the other? Yeah, sure. I just heard about a trainer with an amazing body and huge social media following who says she eats almost only fast food. Hmmmm…that doesn't make much sense to me. Why trash the inside of your body and then work so hard on the

outside? Let's find a balance and love both the inside *and* the outside. They both deserve your attention, right? I want you healthy—body, mind and soul!

So how do we really get started on a lifestyle of physical fitness? I'm not talking about becoming a gym rat or running in circles all weekend, I'm talking about adjusting your life in increments to make your exercise and physical wellness a priority as well as something fun. How does that look for you? For me it means a few things. I spend half of my day on my feet—at least 8,000 to 10,000 steps every day however I can get them in, and I do some sort of fun exercise for thirty minutes, four to five days a week.

This can take the form of a bunch of different things—a fast paced walk or run with my kids, a YouTube video with some cardio dance moves to a popular song, working a simple Kettlebell circuit, hell, even just walking up and down my stairs a few times. I do whatever I can, each and every day, to get my body moving.

If you have a home office or have any influence at work, I highly suggest either a standing desk or a walking desk. I have a walking treadmill desk I use every single day. If you see me on social media, it's almost always when I'm on my treadmill desk, because it's a great way to kill two birds with one stone. I get my steps in, keep my back in good shape, answer emails, and even edit my books while at my treadmill desk. Those steps each day really hold me accountable to staying on track with my work while benefitting my health.

A quick aside to all of my author friends who might be reading this—get a walking desk, PLEASE. A sedentary life spent sitting down all day every day is not good for your body. I do a fast walk or wog while I'm doing my social media and emails, and then a nice slow stroll while I am writing. You'll be surprised how quickly that will get you off

social media, and how many miles you'll be walking in a day. Hell, I challenge you to sprint with me! Message me and we can word-sprint while physically challenging each other to see who can walk the farthest or fastest. All that hard work won't be worth much if you're sick, so please take care of yourself. Please move, and eat well. Our profession worries me, because we're all too isolated and stationary. Get moving! Let's be leaders in our industry. Let's get ourselves in fighting shape! We need you to be healthy so we can keep reading your books.

Sorry, but that needed to be said.

Now, I know a walking desk is specific to my life and job, but I bet you can find ways to make double tasking work for you. The other day I came across a group of mommy fitness bloggers who incorporate their kids' play time with their workouts. They hold their kids while doing squats, and/or use them as extra weights for pushups. I don't know if that would work with my crazy kids, but I might just give it a try when I'm in a pinch for some extra free weight—gotta put those kids to use somehow! My point is, there *has* to be some extra things you can do to stay active. You'll be surprised at how much extra energy it gives you, and how much better you'll sleep at night. Also, don't underestimate those bathroom break squats.

I signed up for my first 5k not long after my oldest daughter was born. My friend, who's super athletic and has been running her whole life, told me to do a training program first, but of course I didn't listen. Why would I? I never do what anyone tells me...just ask Jack! I think I'd run a total of two times for five minutes at most before driving to downtown Detroit for the 5k run I'd promised my friend I would do with her.

I wasn't in any kind of shape to do it, but I was sure as hell going to pretend. As soon as the race started I *blazed* to the very start of the

pack. It may have been more of a hobble, but it felt like I was blazing. I got about a mile into the race when I started to realize this might actually be the day I died.

I tried to slow down, but when you're in the middle of a pack of actual runners, people who know what they're doing, people who can actually run faster than a stroll, it's kind of hard to stop, or even slow down. You'll get trampled like the running of the bulls in Pamplona. So, of course, I did what any self-respecting person who's trying not to die during a race would do: I pretended I had a horrible cramp. Actually, I didn't have to pretend… I did have multiple cramps…shit, my whole body was one giant cramp, and I couldn't breathe. It was a bitterly cold November day in Detroit, so my lungs hadn't adjusted, and I was literally hyperventilating.

What the blue fuck had I been thinking? I'm pretty sure I actually saw Jesus for a minute; I was *that* close to death. So I collapsed to the ground and just stayed there for a couple of minutes and tried to catch my breath. After a while I was finally able to get some oxygen into my lungs, at which point all the normal, non-running people were starting to appear at the rear of the pack. These were *my* people, I realized. The great thing was that there were people doing a brisk walk and others who were just strolling—*this* I could handle. I ended up finishing that race with a grand time of 58 minutes.

Here's the deal, though. Someone out there may have been laughing at me, but I was pretty proud of that finishing time. I had actually finished! I conquered those three point one miles, and I did it in the freaking cold and snow no less! And I hadn't even trained! Just imagine what I could have done had I actually taken some time for preparation.

Now, you might think that experience would have inspired me to continue on doing more 5ks. Well…it didn't. I was happy just to

still be alive. I thought, "Wow, God kept me here on the Earth, so I probably shouldn't attempt anything that dumb ever again."

It wouldn't be until years later that I even *thought* about doing another one. Why? Because it's easier not to—and that's the honest to goodness truth. It's much easier to stay home in a warm bed and just relax on a Saturday morning, whereas it takes real effort to wake up early, get suited up, and actually run a race.

Let's go back to what I was saying earlier about what you're eating. A good portion of my life was spent struggling against a food haze. Even when I was trying to eat right, things I didn't even know were bad for me were causing so many problems. I was in a constant food coma, and didn't even realize it. Most people are in that same place right now, I think. Just floating along in an impenetrable food coma caused by a lifetime of poor nutrition, simply because they don't know any better.

Imagine spending years eating a whole-wheat bagel with low fat cream cheese, fruit, and fruit-on-the-bottom yogurt, only to find out those foods are actually doing *serious* damage to your body. That was my problem, that's your problem...that's our whole nation's problem. Once I changed the way I ate and the order in which I ate food—BAM! I had *unbelievable* energy. I was doing things that "those people" did, those athletic go-getter lunatics I've always hated! Running five or six miles, lifting kettlebells, jumping rope, doing interval sprints... and best of all, I didn't feel as if I was about to die afterwards.

We've all heard the stereotype that fat people are lazy. Man, I've always hated that crap. Because you know what? I wasn't *lazy*, I was being *poisoned*. I know that might sound shocking or melodramatic, but it's true. Take away all that sugar, all that processed, mutated, and refined carbohydrate crap and *WHAM*! You're gonna to feel like a new person!

This is vitally important, supremely important. You *have* to kick that poisonous bullshit to the curb before you're going to see real success with your walking, moving, and running.

I have energy to do things I never thought was possible, and I believe you do, too!

So, how do we get started? Well, you could download one of those running apps, or you could hire a personal trainer, or any number of other possibilities, but what I think you should do just *start moving*. That's it. Just move. Five minutes a day, if that's all you can handle at first. Whatever, however long. It doesn't matter. Just *move*.

Ideally, you should be moving for thirty consecutive minutes, three to four times a week. I started with walking. Please, don't go crazy and hurt yourself! Remember, your body is still healing and we don't want to derail that, so start with something you like, something basic and fun, and over time your body will start telling you when it's ready for more.

I spent weeks just strolling slowly while answering emails at my walking treadmill desk. Sometimes I would increase the pace for a while and then slow it back down. I would make it a game to see how much walking I could do in thirty minutes. How far could I go, how fast could I go? Then I started gradually increasing the pace until I reached the max the treadmill would allow, but this happened about two months after starting my new nutritional program, not in the first week, or even in the first month. I just knew my body felt stronger and I felt ready to push a bit more, so I started wogging.

Wogging is just a low impact walk, but at a slightly faster pace. Sort of a combination between walking and jogging. I try to hit the ground with the middle of my foot and not raise my legs very high so I can protect my knees, which aren't in the best shape.

Listen to your body. Set goals and select races you would love to run. You'd be amazed what a powerful motivation it is to know you've committed to a race. I really believe that *everyone* can finish a 5k. For example, this past New Year's Day, my entire extended family ran one together. My sixty-year-old in-laws both beat me to the finish line! And you know what? I was as proud as I could be! Running that race with their grandparents is a great memory my kids will have forever.

Now, get out there and move!

FROM COUCH TO 5K IN 20 DAYS:

Day 1—locate several pairs of yoga pants

Day 2—put on your best pair of yoga pants

Day 3—locate your running shoes

Day 4—realize you don't own running shoes

Day 5—go to a good retailer or get on Amazon and buy some good running shoes; don't skimp on the shoes, because taking care of your feet is key to consistent running.

Day 6—put on yoga pants, running bra, a shirt, new running shoes, and take a sexy selfie. Now take a nap, because that shit was exhausting.

Day 7—it's raining and you don't want your hair to get wet. Not running.

Day 8—get suited up and run one block. Almost die. Go home.

Day 9—get suited up and run two blocks. You're going to need headphones to do this again.

Day 10—get on Amazon and one-click some Beats headphones—so worth the price!

Day 11—block one actually didn't seem all that bad! I'm killing it!

Day 12—block three killed me. I'm dead. Walk home and take a nap.

Day 13—run four blocks without stopping! YES!

Day 14—run six blocks without stopping!

Day 15—take a day off. Running is hard.

Day 16—take another day off because it's hard to get upright after all that stupid running.

Day 17—run eight blocks and pass the neighbor's fat dog that's out for a walk.

Day 18—run nine blocks at a speed *almost* faster than walking. Almost, but not quite.

Day 19—run ten blocks with only two stops to stave off imminent death.

Day 20—run the full ten blocks without stopping even once. If you can do that, you'll totally kill a 5K. You're always allowed to walk if you need to, and there are usually snacks at the end. You've got this!

That was a joke, but not really—any effort put into being healthy is worthwhile. Each day you try do something, *anything*, in an attempt to be healthier is a step in the right direction. No one expects you to become an ultra-marathoner, or try out for the Olympics. I just want you to *make the effort*. Your body was made to move. You're strong and you're ready, *right now*. There's nothing more important than your health, so even if it's just a walk from the far end of the parking lot into the store, take it. Think of each step as a step in the right direction. Take that extra time and do something good for yourself. You'll never know what you're capable of until you try, and my guess is if we give you one 5k, you're going to want at least four more to go with it. Once we have the ball rolling, you're going to be unstoppable.

So, lace up those cute running shoes and let's get moving.

You've got some races to run!

Chapter 15

YES, RUNNING SUCKS BUT IT'S ALSO SORT OF AWESOME

I HATE RUNNING. HONESTLY, I DO. I HATE HAVING TO PUT ON ALL these stupid special clothes and shoes. I mean, running requires wearing pants! Who wants to wear pants? There's no part of me that really ever feels *excited* about going out to run. The entire time I'm getting ready I'm thinking, "Why the hell am I doing this to myself?" Well, maybe there *is* a tiny part of me that gets excited when I run with my husband; it is fun to watch his cute little butt running up the hill in front of me. But, other than that, it never seems like a great idea.

When I'm actually running, or "wogging", I hate it even more. I'm sweaty, I'm out of breath, cars full of people who might know me are passing by left and right, and body parts I didn't even know I had are chafing.

Even though our ancestors have been running for ages, running for exercise still seems about as logical as juggling porcupines naked…while walking a tightrope. Maybe not *that* bad, but still pretty awkward.

The key to learning how to do anything is to take it slow and build up your awesomeness in stages. The first time you run, liter-

ally just try to walk a block to get warmed up to the idea, and then wog until you can't wog anymore. For me, that stage went on for weeks. My nanny would send me texts at least once a day asking if I was okay because apparently she thought I was dying, based on the noises I was making. Even if you sound like a donkey in labor, the chances of you actually dying are actually pretty slim, so just trust me when I say that if *I* can do it, you can too!

You'll be cursing me for the first few weeks, I'm sure, but I'm also willing to wager you'll start feeling better and stronger, and that your endurance will increase with time and effort. It's amazing how quickly we can stop feeling like crap and start feeling like Wonder Woman once we put our mind to it.

If you're only able to walk, just try to increase your walking pace a little. Maybe you start with trying to do a twenty-minute mile and in the first few weeks make it your goal to get that down to seventeen or eighteen minutes. That's great! When you walk, jog, or run, the only person you are competing with is yourself.

When I first started running, I made notes on my iPhone to keep track of my progress; each day I would note the day, time, and how far and how fast I walked or wogged. And in just in a few weeks I could see a *huge* improvement. I also started to notice the shape of my body changing, and I knew I was getting stronger. I could pick up my son more easily, and I wasn't out of breath walking up a flight or two of stairs. I was even sleeping better!

The increase in energy was remarkable right off the bat. Being able to exercise was a direct, immediate result of hauling my ass out of the sugar haze. I was a better wife, mother, and writer because my mind and body just simply *felt better*.

This is really important; because I think as women we can easily get sucked into a pretty vicious cycle. If we don't feel good, we

take even worse care of ourselves, which leads us down a rabbit hole of eating more, and eating nasty, unhealthy crap, because what's the point, right? If we're gonna feel like shit and look like shit, why bother? Sometimes we feel like we won't ever get back to where we once were. We can't seem to break the cycle, and that donut or that ice cream bar makes us feel a tiny bit better for a few minutes. But then, almost immediately, it makes us feel worse physically and we get down on ourselves mentally for being weak. Then we're right back into the cycle again.

Our American life often makes it hard to recover from these things. We watch *The Biggest Loser* or *Extreme Weight Loss*, which leads us to think the only way we can break out of the cycle is to throw our whole life at it, to sign up for the gym and lift weights and shake ropes and flip tires and eat nothing but celery and tofu and water chestnuts.

Well, I don't know about you, but the thought of that seems pretty freaking exhausting to me. I get tired and hungry and irritable just *watching* those programs. What I think is missing in so many of these approaches is the idea of taking things slow and steady. Taking things one day at a time, one meal at a time. Rome wasn't built in one day. Your body didn't get this way in one day, and it certainly won't get healthy again in one day…or even in one week, or one month!

The good news is that even if you lose just *half* a pound each week, that's twenty-five pounds lost in a year. Lose a whole pound a week and you've just kissed fifty pounds goodbye in a year. With that weight loss will come increased strength, wellness, mental clarity and increased energy. You're going to *feel* like getting up and getting moving, and you will feel as if you've actually, finally, got a handle on things.

I've learned that most good things in life are worth waiting for,

worth working for, and that anything worth having usually doesn't come overnight, so start small. List your goals and cross them off one by one, day by day.

You're *worth* it. You're worth the time it will take to make this happen. Your health is the most important thing in your life, so take the time and make the effort, every single day.

I know moms out there are asking, "What about my family? What about my kids?" And my response is, how can you take care of those precious babies if you aren't feeling well all the time? You can't! So take some time out for yourself, get your health in order, get yourself feeling great and looking great.

As far as running goes, I've got lots of goals. I want to finish my first 10k with my three oldest kids and my husband, running my fastest time ever. The thought of running six point two miles scares the literal poop out of me but, damn it, I'm determined to try! Second, I want to continue to get better at this. I want to be a positive example for my kids. I want to show them that even Mom can get into "beast mode" at the end of a race, and sprint that last tenth of a mile. I want them to see that health is a priority for me and, by extension, a priority for them.

If you're a mom and you're reading this, I encourage you to get your kids out there with you. These are family memories they'll have for their whole lives. You'll laugh, wog, and cry together. Even my little kids talk about how awesome our "turkey race" was last Thanksgiving. (I haven't heard a single mention of the yummy sugar-free pie I made that day, but the race itself is brought up in family conversation all the time). These are things they won't forget, and you're leaving them a legacy of health, too. A healthy mom is more likely to have healthy kids who, in turn, become healthy adults. Plus, it's just plain fun to run together.

Here's something that I don't hear people talk much about either: when you finish a run—I don't care if it's a community 5k or just a run around your neighborhood—you're going to feel *good*. And not just sorta good, a million bucks good! The more you do it, the better it feels. It's almost like good wine, or sex. Regular physical activity will give you have a stronger mind and an increased sense of wellbeing.

My kids keep telling me how much better they feel, how much more soundly they sleep. Even on days when they kick and scream about it, as soon as we get out there they talk about how much they love it when we run. If you don't have kids, take your husband, or your boyfriend, a friend, your dog, your mom, or heck, even drag a second cousin along with you—having a pal when you run always makes it more enjoyable.

When my family runs, we break off into groups, and those who reach the finish line first cheer on the stragglers. The weekends when we have a run are always so much fun. My kids fight less, they are more focused and they are kinder to each other.

Go ahead and test me on this. You can thank me later. Maybe one day we can all race together. Wouldn't that be fun?

Another benefit from this increase in health and stamina is in the area of marital relations. I'm sure I don't have to spell it all out, but once you become more physically fit that part of your marriage will be…healthier, let's say. So let hubby in on that little secret when he starts complaining that you signed the whole family up for a run. There are benefits for all! Trust me!

Below are few other benefits of running and overall physical fitness:

- You'll sleep better.

- You'll be happier. You'll feel amazing, even after a short run. Try just doing twenty minutes and see if you don't feel better, even if you've had a rough day. I would bet money you'll want to do it again tomorrow. There's science behind this—it's been proven that running releases dopamine.
- Your body will be leaner. It may take some time, but you'll see your body start to change. It will make you stronger and you'll add muscle one step at a time. And, you can burn eight hundred and fifty calories per hour!
- Increased strength and endurance. If you have bad knees, walking and wogging will make them stronger. I know that many of us bigger people worry about our knees, so trust me when I say that even if your knees make lots of strange noises, like mine do, it will get better as you run more—I can't believe how well mine have held up.
- Reduced risk of cancer. There's scientific proof of this, too. Don't believe me? Google it! Why wouldn't you want to get moving if it could aid you in the fight against cancer?
- You'll live longer. Again, science!
- Relief from anxiety and depression. For some it's almost like meditation, and it's certainly better than medication. I know this sounds weird, but it does put you in a chill mind space.
- Stronger lungs and heart. Yes, I was the fat kid with asthma, but running has actually helped my lung strength and increased my stamina.
- Increased confidence and body image. You'll feel more badass with every mile you put under your feet. There's no better feeling than crossing a finish line, or meeting a goal you've set for yourself.

Chapter 16

SO YOU STILL THINK YOU CAN'T RUN?

"*What if I fall? Oh but my darling, what if you fly?*" — Erin Hanson

I CAN ALREADY HEAR YOU INSISTING YOU CAN'T DO IT. IN FACT, I hear it when I'm running, too. If you put a hundred women in a line-up and asked them to step forward if they think their body is banging, I'd be surprised if more than a handful take that step forward. I think our society places value on things most women can never live up to. We're constantly being told we have to be shredded, that we should be tiny in some places and unnaturally large in others. We see entertainers shot full of Botox and silicone and think we're less beautiful and badass than them because we sag and have wrinkles and cellulite, and they don't. How do we turn this around? How can we empower our daughters and sons to look elsewhere for standards of true beauty? How can we display better values?

Ladies, this revolution starts at home. It starts with you. It starts with me. It starts with your mom, your aunt, your daughter, your best friend and your neighbor. It starts here and now.

I just want to digress for a moment. My family watches very little TV. We have one television in our home, and it's in a family area

where we all have to agree on one program. It's also way upstairs, a bit out of the way, so we have to actually get up and move if we want to watch something. This was a conscious choice for us. Why? Because we want to see what our kids are watching. Does that mean we're constantly helicoptering over every single thing they are exposed to? No. But it does put us within earshot if they see something depicting women, relationships, or life in a way we don't agree with and then we can start a conversation about it.

This isn't the perfect solution, but it does keep conversations with our kids open and honest about things like how people look and how they are perceived, what people think, what they say, and why. Talking with your kids is important. I don't really try to hide things from them—I want them to form their own opinions and not be negatively influenced by society's views, especially TV and Hollywood's depictions of female beauty.

Moms, I urge you to monitor what your children see and hear. We expose them to too much. If you're a mother of boys, please influence them about their views regarding women, how they view them, how they talk to them, how they treat them. It's far too easy for little boys to become men who think it's okay to treat women like objects, or like a set of body parts and nothing else. It's too easy for them to think it's okay to talk down to women or to catcall and objectify women. Raising boys who treat women with respect starts with you, and it also starts with monitoring what they see on TV.

The same goes for raising little girls, but in a different way. It only takes a couple of negative experiences to make a girl ashamed of her body, or make her think she has to be skinny to be beautiful. We need to offer positive experiences so our children can feel good about their bodies. Sometimes I wonder if the dance classes, football fields and baseball diamonds are cutting it.

So how does this play into how *you* feel about *your* body? What can we do as families to place a different value on our bodies? Running 5k races is a great place to start.

Yes, back to this.

First, it's a great bonding experience for your family. Second, it really isn't a team sport, so the whole family can have different goals, competing *together* rather than against each other. My husband and oldest son blaze to the finish, with my second oldest son not far behind, and my daughter and the younger three bringing up the rear with me. It doesn't really matter where we are in the race, only that we all finish.

I can't tell you how often I struggle near the end of the race, and then I see my husband and two boys at the finish line, cheering me on. Honestly, it's brought me to tears a few times. A year ago I'm sure they wouldn't have ever guessed I could run that far at all, much less without stopping to gasp for breath. It wasn't that they didn't believe in me—I didn't think I could do it either!

I'm sure you're sitting there thinking the same thing about yourself: running is for skinny people, for weird, preppy athletic people, it's for someone who needs a horde of zombies chasing them to be motivated to run. I get it, really I do. I can't tell you how many times I've joked that I don't run unless something is chasing me. Are there hungry bears? No? Then guess who's not running?

When I was a kid I always felt like I was going to die if I even tried to jog a block. Looking back on it though, it wasn't like anyone was really trying to teach me about running. I took dance classes several days a week and I swam like a fish, but I just never thought I could run. I'm not even sure why I thought that. I guess, in my mind, running had to do with aerodynamics and my big butt. I just wasn't ever going to get any speed going because I had too much dragging

me down. I was partially right, but mostly I was wrong. I think we should teach every child that he or she *can* run, no matter what their body type, that running equals stamina, health, and energy. Plus, there's so much you can learn about yourself while running, because you have so much time to think.

I'm going to use my daughter as an example. I'm usually pretty private about my kids, but I know her story will inspire you, so I got her permission to share this. My daughter is ten years old and incredibly beautiful. She has one of those rare smiles that lights up a whole room. She's been a performer since she danced out of the womb. She's was born a star, in every way, so you'd think a child like that would have lots of self confidence but, in reality, it's something she really struggles with. She's very hesitant to engage in most physical activity, so when we decided to do our first family 5k, she was the one who said she couldn't do it. The morning of the run she actually thought she was going to puke; she just didn't believe she could do it. Well, her brothers insisted she could, and promised to stay with her the whole way, so she took off with them.

Later on, when we caught up to her brothers, she was nowhere to be seen. We eventually found her walking with friends from school. She did end up running with me a little near the end, but she felt pretty defeated. So before the next race we did a few training runs with the kids at home, so they could practice. Our "block" around the farm is three and half miles, so it makes a pretty good practice course for a 5k. This time I got right behind her and told her how strong she was every single time she wanted to quit. I told her God gave her muscles and strength for a reason. I played her favorite songs and cheered her on. As always, it was just she and I dragging behind the big boys, but you could tell she was beginning to feel more confident.

The next race we entered was attended by three times the number people as our previous race. It was a qualifying event for the Boston marathon, so people came from all over to do it. These were *serious* runners we were with, so why the hell were we doing this?

My daughter took off like a rocket! I didn't see her again until we reached the end and I found he eating her fruit and drinking water at the finish line. That girl soared to the end and beat her best time by fifteen minutes! I can't even tell you how proud of her I was. It's amazing what having her family by her side did for her self-confidence. It's a huge boost when she hits a new personal best and then gets to celebrate with the family. She's still running, and the confidence she's gained from that experience shows in her dance classes as well. She holds herself with more confidence, and you can see she has more respect for her body.

Let's tell our kids how strong they are, *show* them how strong they are, and then stand back and watch how far they can go with it. You'll be surprised!

Inspire each other.

Do healthy, challenging activities together as a family. There's no better way to spend time together. It certainly beats sitting on your butt watching TV!

I'm talking to you specifically, Mama, because I'm hearing you say your husband wouldn't do this with you, or that your kids would cry and complain the whole time, or that you'd embarrass them just by going out in your gym clothes. Stop that negative bullshit RIGHT NOW! Ain't nobody got time for that! You aren't going to get this time back, so don't waste it lying to yourself. Your body is able to walk, crawl, run, jog, or wog to the finish line. It might take you a solid hour, and that is totally fine. Maybe your husband won't join you, or maybe he'll tell you it's a total waste of time and money. Fine!

Let him think that. But when you come home with your participant's T-shirt, looking all healthy and hot, and he might be inspired to try it with you next time. There's pride in wearing a shirt you can only get by running a 5k. You can't buy it; you can't get it in stores or on Amazon. You only get that shirt by running the race. That shirt? It's a point of pride. Your kids will notice, I promise you. They'll say "Hey, Mom, can you sign me up for the next one?"

I'm not a doctor, and I'm not a life coach, but I *am* a mother of six, so I think I have a pretty firm grasp on kids and family life. I know it's hard, but I also know our nation is full of physically, mentally, and emotionally unhealthy children. It's up to us as parents to change the status quo, for them, for ourselves, and for future generations. Change starts at home.

The idea of "running with your tribe" has serious merit; even a hundred years ago families worked, played, and explored together in a way we simply don't do anymore, at any level. Life was active. If you wanted something, you worked for it. Our day-to-day lives are so dominated by convenience and ease that if it isn't right in the palm of our hands we can't be bothered to make the effort, and our kids are picking up on that. We've become complacent and lazy as a culture. I'm sorry if that's offensive, but I'm just being honest, and I'm including myself in this.

Have you ever seen the Pixar film *WALL-E*? Those giant slobs incapable of walking on their own two feet? That will be us in a few generations if we don't start making changes. We are becoming less and less physically active as a culture; because every new device and piece of technology is aimed at making everything easier, more convenient, requiring less work and less effort. Even when I watch my kids play soccer I find myself thinking about how little effort so many kids are willing to put in. Unless the coach is yelling at them to

run, they're standing around idle, or even sitting down.

So, I'm challenging them on it now. I'm challenging myself. I'm challenging you and your family. I'm reaching out to all you ladies between twenty and fifty years old who are my core readership. You've really poured your hearts out to me about your struggles with weight. I know how hard it is. I know it seems hopeless. I know what I'm asking of you right now feels utterly daunting. You feel like you've failed before you've even begun.

You haven't!

You can do this!

Put the book down, *right now*, and get on your gym clothes.

…I'll wait.

Still waiting…..

I'm not even kidding about this. Get those gym clothes on! Whatever you've got that even remotely resembles workout clothes, get 'em on!

I want you to stand in front of the mirror and say this out loud.

Yes, this again.

Say it like you really mean it. Say it for yourself, and for your kiddos.

They need a strong, healthy mama; they deserve it! They, and you, deserve the best version of you!

So say it with me, one more time, with bone-deep conviction:

"God meant for my body to be healthy and strong.

I am worth the time it will take to make myself stronger and healthier.

It won't be easy, but it will be worth it.

Yes, it's okay to do this for those who love me as well, but this is for me.

I was beautiful then, I am beautiful now, and I will be beautiful tomorrow.

I can do this.

I can do this despite feeling like I can't, or that I've been told I can't.

My body is beautiful at any size.

My body is going to be unstoppable when I'm healthier and stronger, so watch out!

Nothing will define me.

Nothing will stop me.

I can do this!"

Now I want you to run around your block. One block. I don't care if you have to stop and walk for a while.

You aren't even allowed to turn the page until you've run that one block. I mean it! I'm from Detroit and I will kick your ass if you don't run around that block. Don't make me show up at your house. I will.

I'll be right here when you get back.

Ready…set…go!

Race Day pro tip: Make sure to pack snacks and extra water. A healthy breakfast of egg whites and toast with some turkey bacon or sausage or some oatmeal is my go-to pre-race breakfast.

Chapter 17

LET'S TALK RUNNING GEAR!

NOW WE GET TO TALK ABOUT ONE OF MY VERY FAVORITE PARTS of running: getting suited up! Let me start by saying you really don't *need* anything special to run, not even shoes—there are even whole groups dedicated to running barefoot! I don't really advise that unless you're seriously committed to running, though. You can buy some cheap shoes at Wal-Mart or Target, if you are on a budget; I'm currently in love with my size thirteen NYC edition ASICS Gel Nimbus 17s I got from Amazon for a steal of a deal. They feel like heaven on my feet and are so easy on my knees.

That being said, when I started this journey I really wanted to discover what I liked to wear, and what worked best for my body, so I tried countless different brands and styles. When you're bigger it can be hard to find clothes you feel comfortable working out in and that fit well, so I applaud a lot of the big-box stores and mall clothing lines for adding these items in their stores.

I like to browse Amazon and compare prices to what is available in the stores—you'd be surprised how much of a price difference you might find on certain items. Old Navy also has a much better sizing selection online than in stores; I've found things up to a 4x on Old

Navy's website, and those are usually hard to find in a retail store at a decent price. I also really, *really* like the Calia by Carrie Underwood workout clothes. They're higher in price but the quality is great, and they also have plus sizes.

We have a small, local running store in town that we really love. Employees at your local running store have a wealth of knowledge on anything from fitting a good running bra to testing your feet for which shoe fits best, so make sure you check yours out if you have one local.

Running as a big girl can add some additional challenges. When I first started running I noticed my body was fighting me in certain areas. Now, I'm going to get a bit personal here, but I'm sure some ladies reading this will find this information helpful, so I'm not holding anything back. I've got a big chest, butt, and thighs so I knew, after running for a few weeks, that I would need extra support in those areas. As I continued to run I lost weight and I noticed my belly skin getting a bit looser, so it was easy to see I needed some help there, too. This is totally normal and okay!

Wearing support garments when you run will help you run longer, farther, and faster. You have to know and understand your body—this might be an issue for you, and it might not, it just depends on your body. You may start with no hanging skin and then find that with exercise and weight loss you need to tuck and compress in some places. I believe in doing anything necessary to be comfortable while exercising.

A few months ago I started testing different types of clothing to see what I felt worked best. In terms of sports bras, I think you really should invest in a good one if you've got a larger chest. If you're a B cup it might not be a problem, but if you're a DD, you're really going to want to strap those puppies down tight. I like Panache or

Under Armor bras, sized down a little so I'm absolutely sure nothing is gonna pop out. Yes, these are a bit expensive, but this is something worth investing in. You don't want to give yourself a black eye while running.

Another thing that's really helped me is a Squeem tummy supporter, and I also like the Sweet Sweat brand. I wear them over a tank or running shirt and it helps me keep my stomach in place while I'm running. Now, I'm not sure it would work for everyone but, after being pregnant so many times, having that extra stomach support is great—it actually helps me run faster.

I also make sure to wear high quality compression tights or pants, and now I'm often running with wraps around my thighs as well. Again, all this does is give me extra support and it makes me more aerodynamic. If you've lost a lot of weight, these things can really help, so don't be afraid to try them. I think it's much better to invest in good support garments than to just quit running because your skin is in the way. This is nothing to be embarrassed about! Your body is getting lean, mean, strong, and sassy; so don't let anything hold you back, literally or figuratively.

I also think you need music. If you're walking or wogging with a friend, then this might not as important. I know, for me, when Jack and I run together he ends up way ahead and then my mind starts to wander, so music helps me to keep going; I've actually plotted out two books while running! It's a great time for inspiration, prayer, focus, and meditation. These things are important, so why not have a good soundtrack to go with them?

There are some amazing playlists out there—I'm a pretty lazy person when it comes to making my own playlists, so I usually just buy those cheesy "workout mixes" and run to those. Hip Hop is awesome to run to—check out my playlist at the end of the book for

some of my favorites. My husband prefers to listen to death metal when he runs, but he's a weird one. Just find something you like and get moving!

When I first started running I wanted those cute in-ear buds I saw everyone wearing at the races but, guess what? They just didn't work for me. I would be running and then one would literally fly out of my ear. I must have odd shaped ears or something, because I would put them in and go on my merry way, and then *bam*, they'd fly out again. I was worried one was going to hit some other poor runner in the eye.

I use some pretty sweet Beats By Dre when I write but they have a cord that gets in the way when I'm running, so finally, after months of headphone drama, I broke down and bought some wireless over-ear Beats that stay on my head and sound amazing. Yes, they're pricy, but *dude*, I'm not scrambling all over the road trying to find those stupid buds that kept shooting out of my ears. It was so worth it!

You may feel a bit self-conscious when you run outside the first few times. It's weird, because I only feel that way in high traffic situations, like suddenly there's a bunch of cars zipping past, and I freak out a tiny bit. They're staring at me! Do I look okay? This is totally normal, so if you have the funds, go and get a few sets of exercise clothes you feel sexy in. I personally love pink and other bright colors, so I have a whole bunch of pink running gear—it makes me feel badass and sexy—and it gives me a bit of comfort in the knowledge that drivers will see me when they drive down our main road where I run; it's pretty hard to miss a six-foot-tall lady in bright pink from head to toe.

Another item I stumbled upon and fell in love with was the running skirt or tutu. These skirts are so darn cute and so comfortable to run in! When it's warm out you'll see me running in a super cute,

limited edition Cupcake running skirt. Mine even has pockets! It doesn't ride up and will keep you cool when you walk, wog or jog. They also hide any extra movement you might have in the rear, if you have a bit of junk going on in your trunk.

I really think it's the little things that keep you going. Consider making this running skirt a reward for meeting a goal or besting your previous record. They come in all sizes, colors, and shapes, so I'm sure you'll find one you like. If you need help picking one out, just let me know, because I love shopping for this stuff!

I also sweat a *lot,* so I wear a lot of fun headbands that keep my hair and sweat from being all in my face. This stuff will make you feel sporty and super cute! A word of caution, though: you should *NOT* do crazy makeup on a race day. It's only going to stay on your face for about two seconds, and then it'll be running down your face and stinging your eyes and getting in your mouth and it'll taste nasty and you'll look like a bedraggled raccoon, so no to the make-up. However, I do make sure my nails are painted, and I always wear sunscreen and some lip-gloss.

If you're running in the cold like I am *ALL THE TIME,* then make sure to keep some lip balm or gloss with you—good running pants will have a little pocket you can stick it in. I love my Graced By Grit running jacket because it also has awesome arm pockets for my phone and other things I might bring with me, and you can also get some really cheap running belts that will hold your phone, keys, gloss etc. Just don't forget to remove your belongings before you wash your stinky running clothes!

I also want to talk a bit about running tech. There are so many awesome wrist gadgets on the market that I think it's important to touch on this topic for a moment. I've tested the FitBit, Garmin and the Apple Watch while I've been running. For me, it's a toss up be-

tween the FitBit and Garmin wearables. Both of them have a heart rate monitor, and I also like their social media notifications.

All of these options have great apps that will track your progress and help motivate you on a daily basis, and you can even challenge your family and friends, especially with the Garmin. The Apple Watch is awesome if you have the budget for it—I've actually called my husband from my watch while running. It's great for emergencies too, like the time a wheel busted off the jogging stroller and Jack was a mile ahead of me.

We really like Apple products in our family: we all work on Macs, even the kids, and neither Jack nor I can go anywhere without our big iPhone 6 Plus. The Apple Watch health app is really cool because it sort of learns your habits and challenges you to push harder. It's sort of like having a personal trainer on your wrist—my watch will prompt me to get up and move every hour, which actually does make me think about standing up and moving around when I've been on my butt working for too long. It always pushes me to work out harder and longer, and prompts me to beat my last time.

The other really cool thing we've found is a weigh scale that connects to our health apps; it's nice to be able to see a graph of your health stats all in one place, right on your cell phone. I've seen these scales priced from between $50 and $200, so if this is something that might really help you, go for it!

In no way are any of these things necessary, but they are cool and they provide added incentives. Knowing the cycle of your body and being able to see each morning if those pesky weight fluctuations are muscle, water, or hormone cycles is useful knowledge to have. Because we waste so much time guessing, having the real info in the palm of your hand can be a relief and a blessing.

Just don't become obsessed with the numbers. Your body needs

grace and time.

Pro Tip: When looking for shoes it's a great idea to get fitted at your local running shop. Many of them will have you step on a machine that can figure out which particular shoe will be best for you. You'll need a half to full size larger than your normal sneaker for running, so it's a good idea to be professionally fitted. Get the pink, orange, or purple ones! Stand out in the crowd!

Chapter 18

RUNNING FUN VS RUNNING FAR!

So, you just finished your first 5k and now you think you want to do a full marathon. Let's put on the brakes for a moment—I'm not at all against long distance running, and I'm not going to tell you not to do it, but I am going to offer a word of warning. I want this to be fun for you and your whole family. I want this to become a part of your lifestyle. Wouldn't it be cool to pick a vacation destination because there's a fun themed 5k or 10k race, or maybe your whole family did your local Turkey Trot every Thanksgiving? That's what I hope you do with this. I want you to get moving. I want running to become something you look forward to, maybe even crave.

What I don't want is for it to become a pressure for you, or to cause injury.

Long distance running isn't for everyone—I get that. I think a fun 5k or 10k is healthy and can be super fun for the whole family. You aren't taxing your body too hard, you can walk if you have to, and you can have a great time while getting in some good exercise.

Remember, we're looking for *long-term* health and moderation. We want to give your body time to heal, recover, and strengthen. Please continue to see your doctor during this time and take it easy.

If you want to run a marathon next year, then let's get you healthy and as strong as possible first, because a marathon is no joke. Even a 10k is something to work up to gradually. There's a lot of evidence that says that the more quickly we jump head first into things, the less likely we are to stick with them.

So my challenge to you for this first year as a runner—or for those of you getting back to running after being away from it—is to do four races max, maybe one 5k each quarter. Pick some really fun ones so you can laugh a lot and enjoy yourself. Make this about celebrating your body and your health, which is what this is really all about. The truth is, running is going to become addictive. Once you get started, you're really going to love it. I want you walking, running, jogging, or wogging three to four times a week for about thirty minutes. I think that is really all you need.

I only want about an hour and a half each week from you. And since I'm so nice, I'm even going to allow you one day of whatever kind of exercise you want—Zumba, baseball, half an hour of sex are all great!

This might sound too easy but, actually, it really is just that simple. You have a total of 168 hours in your week; so just give me one and a half hours of fun, physical movement. You should enjoy your life, so I want you to have fun with this. If it's a little hard sometimes and you hate me while you're running, that's fine. I'm okay with you hating me as long as you're moving. But you hating it so much you never do it again, that I'm not okay with! I want you to be physically active for the rest of your life. I want you on your feet using the beautiful body God gave you. There are some weeks I even count dancing in my kitchen as my workout. Kitchen dancing is so much fun, and it's something the whole family can do together, too.

What, you don't kitchen dance? Well, you should totally start.

Pro tip: wine helps.

If you're at the point where you're still unable to walk, run, or wog a 5k, don't beat yourself up, or injure yourself trying. You might need a few extra months of training, and that's fine too! You'll get there! Remember, my first 5k was almost my funeral! Just keep challenging yourself in positive ways. You can always do short bursts of fast walking or wogging and then go back to walking. You *will* get to that 5k, just keep going.

So, I'll stop proselytizing for a minute and ask you a few simple questions: What's going to be your first 5k? Your second? Where would you like to run? Who would you like to run with? Who could you inspire with your running? Who could you run in memory, or in honor of?

These are things I really want you to think about. Everything we're doing is supposed to be fun, and all about you. This isn't a one-size-fits-all program—this is *your* plan for *your* health, so there are no boundaries, no limits, and no minimum requirements. Give yourself time to heal and strengthen, so you can really soar! Once we get you going, there will be no stopping you! Just have fun. Keep pushing yourself and enjoy the ride. I'm already proud of the things you're going to accomplish.

If you find yourself in need of support on your journey to health, please know you can contact me on Facebook. I've set up a group called BIG GIRLS DO IT RUNNING on Facebook that is there to motivate and inspire you, and to answer any questions you may have. Please feel free to join us, because you are *not* in this alone. This is a revolution of health and wellness. All are welcome!

Pro tip: It's a great idea to keep a journal to record your journey to health and wellness. Track your progress, set new goals, and note

the details when you reach a goal, or set a new record. You will feel so good about yourself when you read back on your early entries and realize how far you have come.

Chapter 19

CHAFING, RUNNER'S ITCH, AND STUFF I PROBABLY SHOULDN'T MENTION

"Runner's itch sucks." – Jasinda Wilder

I DON'T WANT TO DISCOURAGE YOU IN ANY WAY WHEN IT COMES TO being more active. Getting your body moving and building up strength and endurance is awesome! Remember weeks ago when it was difficult to even get up the stairs? It's a breeze now, right?

I do want to touch on some of the possibly not so good things that might crop up for you. If you're a bigger girl—or guy—you might encounter some chafing and rubbing issues, particularly on your thighs. Remember when I talked about having the right garments? Well, it really is very important. If you're wearing some old, ratty gym shorts you borrowed from your husband, it's only going to make chafing and rubbing worse. Wearing some good compression tights or support pants will help a lot. You can also try powder or lotions to keep any problem areas dry or lubricated as needed.

In my experience, running in the cold it seems to make the itching and chafing worse, so I'm a *huge* fan of coconut oil. I also really like the Naturewell Extra Virgin Coconut Oil Moisturizing Cream…

that stuff is actual magic for your skin. I rub some into my skin before I put my tights, and it really helps alleviate the effects of chafing.

You also may want to have lots of lubrication under your bra if you're going to be wogging or jogging. You may encounter some pretty serious redness and rubbing where the bra straps touch your skin, so don't be afraid to use some oil or lotion in those areas too—the last thing you want is scratching or chafing all over the girls.

I've noticed my bra seems to get tighter as I run, and I have no clue why. Maybe my skin expands? I don't know. I'm sure there's a scientific explanation for it, but all I know is that it happens. If you're going to be running a long distance—anything over three miles, for me—I would suggest loosening the straps a little. I once tried to adjust my bra while running and that was a big mistake; the driver of a big truck that was going down the street saw me and, well, I can tell you how well *that* went. It may even be worth a trial run if the bra is new, since it's not fun to get half way through your run only to find yourself fighting tears because your bra is digging into your skin somewhere. My advice is to spend some money on a good sports bra. The girls need your support.

Winter running isn't for the weak up here in northern Michigan. When we first started running this winter I developed a crazy itch—it felt as if my legs were on fire and tiny ants were having a dance party on them. I finally talked to my doctor and she said there's an actual thing called "runner's itch" which can cause your body to itch like mad. She said that, basically, my body was becoming allergic to exercise! Isn't that just hilarious? Ha…ha? Yeah, *not* so funny.

After the appointment I did a bit more investigation and discovered it's very common to have an allergy-type reaction to running, depending on the environment. The extreme cold was already making my skin dry, and the running was just aggravating the condition.

If this does happen to you, don't freak out. It isn't ants, bugs, or a deadly flesh-eating virus. If I survived runner's itch, you can too. Just don't do what I did one time. I went for a run, took a shower, forgot to put on lotion, and then put on tights, and then tried to sit still for a three-hour movie date with my husband. I do NOT suggest that... *at all.*

I have another important PSA I should probably put out there. Are you ready for it? Gosh, it's so embarrassing that I'm not sure I can type it!

Running makes you poop!

I didn't even know about this until I decided to take a long run with my husband, only to find myself making a mad dash for the toilet as soon as we got home. Don't worry though; you *probably* won't poop your pants. I mean, you might, and I'm sure it will happen to someone, but hopefully it won't happen to you. Fingers crossed. (I'm likely just giving you more reasons not to run, but it's just I want to make sure you're fully informed before you start. The best surprise is no surprise.)

Running really is amazing, once you get started. I really, truly, deeply believe you're going to love it...just get ready to shit your brains out afterward. The great thing is that pooping is good for you. A healthy body and a healthy metabolism will promote regular, healthy bowel movements. Just know going in that it's totally normal and you shouldn't be embarrassed.

The final thing I want to cover in this chapter is stinking. I mean, since we talked about pooping, we may as well talk about body odor, too. When we first started on our health journey, I switched to a more natural deodorant. I'd tried them before and never had much luck, but since I was sweating and working out I decided now was a good time to test a few more out; I wanted to minimize my body

odor in a more natural way. I tried a few different products but none of them would go on well or stay on, and if they did they didn't minimize the smell very well.

I finally found a lavender-scented deodorant I really liked, but it wouldn't last very long. And then, while browsing our local farm co-op, I spotted a few natural body odor sprays and tried a few of those, but they didn't last very long either. I was getting frustrated. Then, one morning, out of sheer exhaustion and caffeine-deprived desperation, I put them both on and guess what? I had forty-eight hours without stinking! No joke! Something about layering the stick and the spray gave me some superhuman B.O. coverage. Now that's all I use, and even Jack is doing the same thing. There were a few days where I had some weird detox thing, but now I almost never have any body odor, even after a long run or workout session.

Jack and I will do kettlebell workouts together once in a while, and I always sweat so much more during those sessions. I'm always so surprised that I never need to worry about body odor. I'm a human daisy!

I do think it's worth looking for deodorant products that are more natural, and there are many good products out there these days. Jack even found one he likes that makes him smell like "the woods". I think it's a guy thing.

Chapter 26

SUPPLEMENTS, BEAUTY AND FASHION, OH MY!

MY MATERNAL GRANDMOTHER DIDN'T SEE A DOCTOR FROM the time she had my uncle at forty years old until the day she died at eighty-five. She didn't believe doctors had any medicine for her that she couldn't find at the health store. I thought she was crazy—I mean, I loved her dearly but I think there's a middle ground between modern medicine and simply eating well and taking supplements. I don't take a ton of supplements, but I do think there are a few worth taking to promote overall good health.

- You need a good multivitamin. Make sure if you choose a chewable that has no added sugar. My kids love the Smarty Pants No Sugar Added with Fiber. Lots of bang for your buck.
- I put integral collagen and MTC oil in my coffee each morning. The MTC oil helps with my blood and nutritional deficiency, and collagen is wonderful for your complexion, among other benefits. I haven't had a single breakout or skin issue since I started taking it. It also helps promote healthy lashes, nails and hair!
- I also put Bragg Apple Cider vinegar in my morning LaCroix. It's really helped me curb sugar cravings, and it also has many

other health benefits: prevents stomach illness, dissolves kidney stones, regulates PH balance and blood pressure, lowers glucose levels, and provides relief from nausea, heart burn, acid reflux, asthma, allergies, and gout, migraines, sinus pressure and infections, inflammation, bug bites, rash, warts and acne! Just mix it into water with lemon and drink it in the morning. Why would you pass up all those health benefits?

- Vitamin C. I use it on my face. I know it sounds gross, but go check out the Amazon reviews for the Foxbrim brand (I really like that whole line of products, so check them out), and you'll find that huge numbers of people are seeing some great results from it. I swear, the day I turned 35 my face started looking older. Not that aging really bothers me, but I want to take care of my skin, so I use a good face lotion and vitamin C, and people have said they have noticed a glow. I'm a mom of six, I'll take whatever I can get!
- Probiotics are important. Why? They help with your immunity, assist with bowel issues, and will also help keep good bacteria in your body. Take a probiotic especially during the detox phase to make sure the good stuff is staying in and all the bad stuff is going out!
- I take Cod Liver Oil and Vitamin D every day. It helps with my immunity, inflammation, and nutritional issues, and they've also been shown to help with depression. As always, talk to your doctor about your vitamin and supplement needs.
- Getting enough fiber is vital. My little boys had terrible issues with constipation, so I make sure everyone stays regular with a fiber supplement—I use PGX Fiber by Webber Naturals. We also use a powder for the kids that's totally invisible and tasteless, made by Renew Life. It's great because they don't even

know they're getting it. It is also available on Amazon. Fiber is so, *so* important for a healthy diet, but don't overdo it...you don't want to poop lava.

- Bathe and shower with Epsom salts. Release those yucky toxins! I buy giant bags from Amazon and add some coconut oil to make a salt scrub. You can also add a bit of an essential oil and fancy it up a notch—works as a scrub or a soak.

You'll start seeing changes almost overnight. Some weeks the changes will be numeric and you'll see the pounds melt away. Other weeks you'll go down a clothing size, but your weight will stay the same. My mother, several friends, and a beta testing group will all tell you that if you do everything I'm laying out for you in this book you'll start dropping excess weight immediately.

For me this was both a blessing and a curse. Most of you probably know that over the past three years I was traveling several weeks each month for book tours, speaking events, and signings. I'd built up a pretty kick-ass wardrobe—in size twenty-two. I'd been wearing so much maternity clothing over the years that those items were extra special to me. Alas, I shrunk from a twenty-two to a size eighteen in the blink of an eye, and then down to a fourteen! These changes happened over a matter of months. None of my clothes fit anymore!

So, what do we do about clothes that no longer fit? We give them away. I found lots of special ladies to bless with those clothes—some were even brought to tears. You can also find a consignment or resale store where you can swap or donate clothes. It's a very real possibility that you won't be wearing new clothes for very long. I suggest going for leggings, or anything with some stretch to it. Also, there are fun online boutiques like The Zig Zag Stripe and Lu La Roe that have been a huge blessing for me as I constantly change sizes. They have

one-size-fits-most clothing, which will stretch and shrink with you, so I can hold on to my new items for a little longer. It's just so much more economical as you don't really know where you're going to end up size-wise, so try to buy on the smaller size and wear those clothes as long as you can. It's a good problem to have.

I believe you need to find a goal outfit. I know I've already said it isn't about the numbers, and I just want to reiterate that. It's not about the numbers on the scale, or the numbers on the tag! It's about feeling good and looking good, so find something in your closet that's a little tight, something you've wanted to wear but couldn't because it's been too small. Maybe it's even your wedding dress, or a sexy little black dress from college. Whatever it is, pick something that will motivate you on your journey to wellness, something that shows where you came from and where you're headed. Take that dress or outfit out of your closet and put it somewhere where you can see it all the time.

You're worth it! Don't let that goal out of sight.

You're going to be wearing that outfit before you know it!

Chapter 21

THE WILDER WAY FOR THE PREGNANT MAMA

I WAS HALFWAY THOUGH MY MOST RECENT PREGNANCY WHEN WE started making health changes. My doctor was thrilled with what I was doing and the positive effects it was having on my pregnancy. It's critical that you discuss what's best for you with your doctor. I do know whole foods free of chemicals and additives are going to be wonderful for you and the baby, and that stabilizing your blood sugars and insulin levels will help prevent gestational diabetes, which is something so many women deal with during pregnancy.

Be sure that if you do lose weight you discuss the weight loss with your doctor; my OB felt that as long as the baby was measuring normal my weight loss was a good thing. Your OB might not want you to lose too much weight during the pregnancy, depending on where you were before conception. You can always eat more good carbs for extra energy, and there's nothing wrong with eating any good, nutritious, whole foods while pregnant.

Running during pregnancy isn't something I personally would want to do, but some women do it. Again, this is something you should talk to your doctor about. I didn't start running until Ree was about two months old. By that time I didn't feel like a total zombie,

and I actually wanted to get out there and move. I did walk a lot when I was pregnant with her, and unless you have some issue or condition during your pregnancy I would think most doctors would be totally fine with the idea of you walking three or four times a week, even pretty far into your pregnancy.

Actually, the closer we got to my due date the more we walked. I've always had very long and complicated deliveries, and the only thing that was different with Ree was that my health and eating habits had changed drastically in comparison to my other pregnancies and deliveries. I believe being more physically fit at the end of my pregnancy made my delivery so much easier.

The awesome thing about pregnancy is that it will help you tune into your body in a way you might not when you aren't pregnant. I'm so grateful that my pregnancy and baby Ree helped me finally understand what was going on with my blood sugar. I was able to make much-needed changes to my health—my body was demanding these changes, and I finally *had* to listen. I've never in my life craved bacon and eggs like I did when I was pregnant: my body needed fat and protein for the baby, and those cravings were my body's way of informing me.

If you are pregnant, I suggest keeping a journal to write down what you're experiencing—this is important information that you might want to refer to in the future. Pregnancy is an illuminating time. I really wish I'd kept better records of my health during my first two pregnancies, as it would be great to compare the differences.

I recently watched a video about infants becoming obese; the doctors said they believe the health of the mother during pregnancy was the causal factor in the strange phenomenon. The baby's glucose levels are being set in the womb and the baby will start demanding similar levels after delivery. The nutritionist in the video said the best

way to prevent this decline in babies' health is to advocate for prevention of obesity in the mother prior to her childbearing years.

As women go from being adolescents to teenagers and adults, it's important they focus on their health for the wellbeing of their future children. This struck me so hard: I have a 10 year old daughter, and I want to teach her to be healthy and strong *now*, while she's young enough to make it a lifestyle. Me teaching her healthy living habits won't just affect her, but it will also affect my future grandchildren and *their* children.

The last thirty years of American culture has had drastic affects on us, and not necessarily for the better. Now is the time for us to start showing our kids a better way to eat, a better way to view their bodies. I'm not talking about size or numbers; I'm talking about positive nutrition and strength.

If you're a mom, pregnant, or thinking about becoming pregnant, I urge you to take a look at the quick-start guide at the back of my book, and talk about healthy eating with your doctor. The food we eat while pregnant has a massive, long-lasting impact on our children as they develop in utero and as they grow after birth. Motherhood is both an honor and a responsibility, one we *have* to take seriously. I know this might sound like a lot to think about, especially if this is your first child, but you won't get this time back. Being a mother is the greatest and most difficult job you'll ever have; if you focus on your health first, your child will be better for it in the long run. Get healthy now, mama. Make it a priority! Kids keep you on your toes, and sometimes bring you to your knees, so you're going to need every healthy molecule and burst of energy you can find!

Chapter 22

YOU FINISHED THE BOOK...NOW WHAT?

"The most difficult thing is the decision to act, the rest is merely tenacity." – Amelia Earhart

Now that you've reached this point in the book I hope you've found it both educational and fun to read; I know I really enjoyed the process of writing it. Honestly, though, this book isn't about me, it's all about *you*.

What follows is The Wilder Way, an eight-week health plan and 25 of my favorite family recipes. You might not even get to those, you might close the book right now and never take a step toward improving your health; you may be thinking it's too hard, or it won't work for you, or that you're not worth the time and effort. I disagree. I don't think there's anything else *more* important than your health, and by health I mean everything—your body, spirit and mind.

Yes, I'm gonna get all hippie and metaphysical on you. You aren't just the sum of your parts—you are an amazing woman designed to be healthy, strong, and bold. Ponder all the times you've been excited about something only to fail—I get it, I've been there a thousand times myself, from that first time I put my Teen Steam dance video

in my VCR to the last time I tried a fancy new diet. Nothing ever worked for me. So I understand the fear all too well—I know that fear far too intimately.

Stay strong; *this* will work, I promise.

I want you to close your eyes and imagine yourself healthy and fit. What that looks like is different for everyone. I know what that looks like for me: I want this port out of my chest; I want to finish a 10k in an hour and fifteen minutes; I want my belly to be full of healthy fuel, and my muscles to be beautiful and strong; I don't want to worry about diabetes looming; I don't want to be nutritionally deficient; I want to look *damn* good in my size twelve dress and sexy heels. That's what health looks like to me, and for the first time in my life, I feel *so* close to having just that. I've got it within my grasp, ladies. I'm almost there! And you can be, too.

Look at the cover of this book; do I look healthy and happy to you? Through all the trials and tribulations, through all the false starts and failures, I've learned that my body *does* work. Right now, my body's fat mass is within a healthy range for the first time in my life! My legs are strong. I've got powerful biceps. My back doesn't hurt anymore.

What about you? What's your story? What's your final goal, and how are you going to make that vision in your head become a reality?

All you need is eight weeks to change your life; I don't think eight weeks is a long time, do you? Yes, there are things that might be difficult in those weeks. In fact I'm pretty sure people will send me nasty emails around week five. I'm okay with that! You can even email Jack about how horrible I am for putting you through this, but I know that by week eight, I'll be getting an equally awesome apology email. One that says your inflammation is now gone, that you finally have a normal blood sugar level, and maybe there will even be a

photo of your face looking years younger. You'll tell me that not only did you lose weight but also, for the first time in your life, you have self-confidence and strength and you feel sexy in your skin.

I want those things for you! I want you to learn what I've learned on this journey: most of us weren't born with something wrong with us. Most of us aren't genetically challenged. We don't lack will power, we don't need to cut ourselves open and remove portions of our intestines, we don't need to sleeve, band, or starve ourselves to be healthy.

It's about food combinations. It's about moving. It's about kicking sugar to the curb and never looking back.

Please believe me when I say that if this hot mess mother of six can do it, you can too. I know it!

What I would love for you to do is read through the start-up plan and the recipes that follow—all the way to the very end—and then I want you to take some time and think about why you want this. Why is this your moment? Why are you finally done with all the diets, the workout fads, and gimmicks. Why is *now* the moment when true health is going to be your goal?

Before I even started writing this book, I knew it would be the most important book I ever wrote. I feel a responsibility, an obligation, to use my story to help people. Even if only a few people pick it up, I know I can change those lives forever. I have the ability to reach people who would *never* pick up a health book unless it was written by me. What an honor! If you've never read any other health or fitness book before, then you picked the right one! This is going to be a system you can live with, and it will allow you to enjoy life as never before.

Take it one day at a time, one meal at a time. Stick with me even when it gets hard, even when you see the scale creep up during the

challenge weeks. It's okay, it happens, and it will come back down. Give your body grace and time—you deserve that. Your body needs time to heal from the lifetime of damage that sugar and chemicals and refined carbs have done to it. Detox is a gift to your body, but you have to give it time.

If I could talk to you right now, I would ask which race will be your first—I'm so excited for you to cross that finish line! I can see it in my head, and it makes me want to cry for you, for *all* of us who never thought we were capable of running, for those of us who never believed our bodies could cross a finish line without being dragged across by paramedics. You—yes *YOU*—will finish that race, and it will be glorious.

Then I would tell you to take this one week at a time. Follow the plan I've laid out. Yes, you could take a short cut, but it won't do any good in the long run. This is four weeks of detox and four weeks of learning how to create your meals; that time is crucial, so don't skip it.

The last thing I would do is tell you this is a journey you should enjoy. The year or two it will take to transform your health is a blessing. How many people will you inspire? How many lives will be changed watching you take control over your health and your life? Just remember, I'm going to be here cheering you on the whole way! I hope you connect with me on social media and share your progress—I can't wait to watch you run wild!

Please remember to consult with your doctor before starting any new health plan. If you are already being treated for diabetes or blood pressure, talking with your doctor regularly is very important.

PART 4

The Wilder Way

MY 8-WEEK GET-STARTED GUIDE

WELCOME!

I am so glad you're here.

This is the first step on the journey to reset your health. If you've been feeling tired, depressed, fat, and lazy, leave that all behind and get ready for one hell of a *WILD* ride. Don't think about other plans you've tried in the past, this one is totally different. We're going to get your body in fighting shape and moving like a warrior in just 8 weeks.

When I first began eating in this new way, I would either pull back on my carbs or my fats depending on my needs for the meal; I was trying to replicate the way my body naturally wanted to eat when I was pregnant with my last child. After that pregnancy, and when I was going to have a workout day, I would do a meal or two with carbs for more energy and pull back on the fats for those meals. It was just the easiest way for me to do it—I didn't have to count anything and there were no carb caps or measuring or portions to worry about. Just mixing things up kept my body guessing and then adding in regular exercise was really all I needed to get my body in better health.

When my beta group began testing this 8-week plan, the carbs and fats got a bit confusing to them, so I told them it seemed black and white to me—and the idea of the black and white plates that you will read more about coming up emerged from there.

For black plates, the idea is to reduce or eliminate carbs, and for white plates carbs are included but fats are reduced. Protein is always the number one focus, regardless of plate color.

This 8-week plan is set up to gradually reduce your dependency on sugar in a slow, sustained detox, and then slowly ease you into an easy carb cycling lifestyle. This is NOT a diet; this is a new way of life, a new way of eating, and a new way of thinking about food. Try to take it one week at a time and don't overwhelm yourself. Slow and steady wins the race.

You can do this! How do I know? Because if I can do it, anyone can.

On your mark, get set…

GO!

WEEK 1

WEEK 1 CHALLENGE

This is a slow and steady, from-the-inside-out approach. No quick fixes. We're retraining your body and mind, and that takes time. I don't want you to ever feel frustrated or deprived. I've made these challenges doable for any fitness level, age, or overall health condition.

The first step is to detox your body from the biggest culprits behind the majority of health issues:

First, no sugar at breakfast. None. Focus on protein-rich foods, and completely cut out all sugar before noon. There are sixty-one names for sugar, so please make sure nothing you eat has it hidden in the ingredients. Yes, honey and agave are sugar. You can use stevia as a sweetener—my favorite brands are Pyure and Swerve. You can get them at the grocery store or on Amazon. Try eggs, bacon (remember, fats *ARE* your friend), oatmeal, yogurt (Greek without any added sugar), cottage cheese, toasted Ezekiel brand bread, or cereal with unsweetened almond milk. Berries are great too, so you can load up on those for some natural sweetness. Coffee can be creamed with half and half or heavy whipping cream.

Second, find a 5k to run in the next six months. There are tons

of great races out there, so I'm positive you can find one near you. Ask, beg, or coerce a friend or family member to do it with you. If you have kids, I encourage you to include them too—a 5K is fun, healthy, and a great motivator to get moving. Walk if you're not there yet. Or you can try wogging. A 5K is three point one miles from start to finish, so it will take you about an hour, max. You don't even need to start training right now, just commit to running one 5K in your near future. You are *going* to cross a finish line!

WEEK 1 ENCOURAGEMENT

I've studied my ass off trying to figure out why so many of us struggle with excess weight and poor health. I think we fail because we are set up to fail. Why can some people eat whatever they want yet never gain weight, while some of us eat normal amounts and still gain weight? Why won't our bodies work right?

Some of us have had our metabolism literally shut down because of what's being put in our food. We've been eating food we think is healthy, food we're being *told* is healthy, but it's killing us, causing illnesses like diabetes and cancer.

Here's the deal—your current health and weight have nothing to do with your will power or lack thereof. Our bodies are being poisoned to the point of shut-down. Losing weight becomes fairly easy when we cut out chemicals, sugar, fillers, and processed carbohydrates. If you feel an increase in energy by the end of week one, it's a sure sign you were being affected by the sugars in your morning breakfast. Your body is at its most vulnerable in the morning, so it's easy to cause an all-day fog eating the wrong things in the morning. You might not even need as much coffee once this phase is complete and the sugars have been filtered out.

These first six weeks are going to be all about healing; you may

not lose ANY weight during this time—none. Why? Because your body is literally turning back on and resetting, and this takes *time*… four to six weeks, in my experience. You may notice a change in your face almost immediately, however, and your pants may get a bit looser. This is because inflammation tends to fade immediately.

YOU CAN DO THIS! Your health is now up to you, but I promise I'll give you all of the tools you'll need to succeed.

WEEK 2

WEEK 2 CHALLENGE

This week we're getting the sugar out of our system completely, all day, past dinnertime. This is going to be tough, but you can do it!

Week 2 has two parts: eating and moving. So, with no further ado:

Part One: Eating

Below are my favorite go-to lunches (see my sample diary for more suggestions). Focus on protein, and try to fill up on veggies, nuts, and berries. You can add yogurt too; you have lots of options.

- Salad piled high with meat, cheese, and veggies. We usually do a big chef salad two or three times a week—they're super filling and give you lots of good protein. Remember, lean meats are best but any meat is fine. Heck, throw some bacon in there if you want. It's okay! FAT IS GOOD FOR YOU! Make sure your dressing is low sugar without any crazy additives. Regular old ranch or Italian, things like that. Check your labels!
- Soup. Progresso Lite soups are quick and easy choices for lunch, especially when you throw some WASA crackers in there, or include some Laughing Cow cheese on crackers as a side.

- Mission brand low carb wraps can be used for a rollup sandwich, a quesadilla, or even a pizza—just throw on some tomato sauce, cheese, turkey, pepperoni, and BAM, you've got a healthy pizza! Delicious. Veggies are always great, whether as a side, on a pizza, or however you want to eat them.

Part Two: Movement.

I want you to start moving this week, three times for thirty minutes. I don't even care how you do it. Dance naked in your living room if you want. The only requirement is that you move non-stop for thirty minutes three times this week. Walking is a great option. Don't overwhelm yourself—slow and steady wins the race. This is a change for your whole life, so no need to go crazy. If you love to dance, then I highly suggest Dance Fitness with Jessica. She's got free routines on YouTube that are really fun, so check them out!

WEEK 2 HOMEWORK

You are going to start to documenting your changes this week.

Daily: weigh yourself each morning immediately after your first pee. Write down anything specific you notice about how you are feeling or looking.

Weekly (yes, each week): I want photos. Take some "before photos" from the front and side, and then just your face. These are great for encouragement when the scale isn't moving. Sometimes things are changing shape when your weight stays the same. I also want a waist measurement at the very least. If you want to do more measurements, fine, but I need to have waist measurement. I know this is a lot, but this is a big week and I know you can do it.

Go get 'em!

WEEK 2 ENCOURAGEMENT

This is an 8-week, slow-and-steady plan. I am not expecting any weight loss at this stage and neither should you. In fact, your weight may even go up! That's fine, don't worry! The first four weeks is focused on cleaning up what you eat, and the next four are all about adjusting those foods to get your body into the weight loss mode. I want your weight loss to be for your whole life, not just for a few weeks or months. I want you living and eating in an entirely new way. You didn't become unhealthy over night, and you won't become healthy overnight, so please, please, *PLEASE* give this time. You need your body and mind working together. It's scientific fact that the more quickly you lose weight the less likely you are to keep it off, so let's do this right! Don't freak out and sabotage yourself and the plan.

We'll get there!

WEEK 3

WEEK 3 CHALLENGE

This is a big week. I know this challenge is going to be tough, so it's the *only* thing I'm asking you to do this week.

Cut out *all* non-stevia-sweetened soda and sugary drinks. You don't need them and they're doing incalculable harm to your body. The good news is; I have a few fun beverages for you to try this week.

I know you can do this!

Just say no to junk!

Stick with no sugar until dinnertime—after dinner it is all yours…this week.

Stick with thirty minutes of movement three times a week.

Keep tracking your weight every day.

You've got this! Lots more to come. We've only just begun.

WEEK 3 ENCOURAGEMENT

Do you drink Green Tea? If not, you should! But drinking any tea will be great for you. Add some cinnamon and ginger to help with the detox and to keep your blood sugars level. I usually have some green tea about three in the afternoon, with a few nuts to keep me satisfied until dinner.

My afternoon tea treat, Wilder Tea:

- Steep your favorite green or black tea (make sure it doesn't have added gluten)
- Add some unsweetened vanilla almond milk
- Sprinkle on some cinnamon (this is going to help you fight sugar cravings)
- Add some ginger (so good for you! I buy it in both liquid and powder forms)
- Add a little Stevia if you are craving some sweetness.

Pro Tip: Don't forget to drink lots of water. Drinking water when you wake up in the morning will jump start your metabolism; add some lemon to get that fire burning!

WEEK 4

WEEK 4 CHALLENGE

This is a big one, so hold on to your Spanx!

This week we are cutting out ALL sugar and refined carbs. Kiss them all goodbye, because you don't need them—they're killing you! That's a bold statement, but it's the absolute truth. They're hurting you and you no longer want that, you want to be healthy and strong. This week you should see a pretty big difference in your face, so make sure to take a photo or two. All your inflammation is going to go away pretty quickly once we get all the junk out of your system. Get excited! Big things are about to happen.

The second part of the challenge this week is about movement. I'm not changing the three times a week movement rule, but I do want one of those days spent either walking, wogging, or jogging. Thirty minutes of your feet hitting the pavement. I don't care how fast or slow you go, just get out and do it. Even short bursts of wogging and getting your heart rate up is great for you. Try it!

You've got this!

WEEK 4 HOMEWORK REMINDER

Daily: I want you to weigh yourself each morning right after

your first pee. I also want you to note anything specific about how you are feeling or looking.

Weekly: I want photos. Take some "before photos"; front and side views, and then also just your face. These are great for comparison and encouragement when the scale isn't moving. Sometimes things are changing shape when your weight stays the same. Remember to take your waist measurement. If you want to take more measurements, go right ahead, but make sure you do that waist measurement.

WEEK 4 ENCOURAGEMENT

Don't cry into your Wilder oats just yet! There are so many good things you can have this week! Low carb mission wraps, brown rice, sweet potatoes, sprouted breads, Dreamfields brand pasta, oats, quinoa, nut flours, and carbs that naturally occur in fruits, nuts, veggies and beans. You'll get the hang of this. It's okay for progress to take some time. It *will* happen and you *will* get there. Just stick with me and don't give up.

WEEK 5

WEEK 5 CHALLENGE
BLACK PLATE WEEK

Remember, black plates are for proteins and fats; white plates are for proteins and carbs.

As I already said, our bodies have difficulty keeping our metabolism running steadily when we consume both high fats and high carbs in the same meal. So, this week and next week we are in fats and carbs boot camp. This week is the harder of the two, since it's BLACK PLATE WEEK. This means you won't be eating ANY carbs for the next week—your *only* bread choice is Mission brand low carb wraps.

No other grains.

AT ALL.

I'm watching you.

The only fruits allowed are berries, lemons and limes. Don't cry, though, because you can load up on cheese, sour cream, meats, nuts, and Lily's chocolate. Please be sure to take a look at my ***BLACK PLATE WEEK SHEET on page 287** for full food options.

KEEP MOVING

You also need to walk, run or wog for as long as you can this week. If possible, I want you to try my Wilder Wog, described in the FAQ section. Journal about it at home, and then let me know how it went. I want specifics like, "I walked for twenty minutes and I wogged for ten. It was really hard and I almost died and I hate you."

You can do this.

Be prepared to kick some serious ass.

Keep up on your daily weigh-ins and measurements! Change is a-comin'.

It's going to be worth it, I promise!

WEEK 5 ENCOURAGEMENT

My dream is to start a revolution, one in which we all stop dieting and begin a new regimen of eating that we will stick to for our whole lives. One where we start feeling good about our bodies, where we have positive self-images and we walk with our heads held high, proud of what we've accomplished. In this health and wellness revolution, everyone believes they can run—and they even get excited about it. I long for the day when we aren't suffering from horrible diseases like diabetes, PCOS and ADHD. I want the whole world to know that if *I* can do it, they can do it, too.

WEEK 6

WEEK 6 CHALLENGE
WHITE PLATE WEEK

Remember, black plates are for proteins and fats; white plates are for proteins and carbs.

This week is the same concept as last week, except we're changing plate colors; get out your white plates, girls, because this week the carbs are in the house!

Carbs have a bit of a bad reputation, but they aren't the bad nutrient everyone makes them out to be. You just need to find the *right* carbs to put on your plate—that's what we're doing this week, focusing on *healthy* carbs. Which means all other kinds of carbs are dead to you...FOREVER!

The stars of the show this week are sprouted breads and cereals, old-fashioned oats, fruit, brown rice, beans, and potatoes. These are the good carbs; please be sure to check my graphic on *white plates, on page 287, for the full list.

This week you need to stick to *lean* meats and proteins. What does that mean? Chicken and turkey breast, fish, venison, lean

ground turkey and chicken (96% protein or higher), lean deli meats and ground beef—85% lean or better (drained). Make sure you stick to low fats in your food this week because we don't want to have any of our black plate friends accidentally turn your white plates gray—that is *not* allowed.

This week might seem hard, but I know you can do it. Just focus on lean protein and don't forget your veggies, as you'll need lots of fiber after the full week of fats last week.

Yes, you can still have Progresso light soup.

It will be okay, I promise!

You've got this!

WEEK 6 HOMEWORK:

Keep taking photos and measurements, and don't forget to journal. This is your health journey, so we want good records to show how far you've come!

This week we're also going to amp up your training. I need you to step it up…literally. Continue with the three movement sessions of at least thirty minutes each this week. Two of those *have* to be walking/wogging/jogging for as long as you can, as far as you can. I don't care what those numbers are, but you HAVE to try. You're going to be running a 5k soon, so we need to get you ready. Now get going! Get on your workout gear, ladies, because it's time to get moving!

WEEK 6 ENCOURAGEMENT

Are you starting to feel the changes in your body? Maybe your weight has gone down a bit, or maybe it's gone up. Regardless of the number, you're seeing and feeling *something*. This week and next week we're setting the metabolic pendulum into full swing. Think of

your body as a beautiful beach: the black plate and white plate weeks will put the waves into motion. It's okay if you see your weight start to creep up a bit, that's normal. Just look for an overall, long-term downward trend. As we get into the next few weeks you'll see that now that your metabolism has been jump-started, keeping it revving will become easier and easier. Just keep on keeping on, have faith in your body and in the plan, and don't stop moving!

WEEK 7

WEEK 7 CHALLENGE
MIXING UP YOUR PLATES!

Remember, black plates are for proteins and fats; white plates are for proteins and carbs.

This is the week you've been waiting for! Now we start to mix up your plates. Throughout the last two weeks you've probably been able to see how your body responds differently to the protein plus fats combination, and the protein plus carbs combination. Now we're going to keep mixing it up so your body never knows what's coming.

An important note before we get started, though, is that you can't do this halfway. This *isn't* Atkins. Think about these two different plates like a swinging pendulum. As far as you swing in one direction, you need to swing just as far in the opposite direction. Don't be scared of good carbohydrates! Your body needs them. Swinging back and forth will keep the waves of your metabolism moving.

Try these daily plans this week and find out which one works best for you. Next week you'll be totally freestyling your plates, and even mixing them up a bit.

So, for Week 7, your job is to adhere to the following in terms of your food intake:

Day 1: Black only all day

Day 2: White only all day

Day 3: Black, Black, White—breakfast, lunch, dinner

Day 4: White, White, Black—breakfast, lunch, dinner

Day 5: Black, White, Black—breakfast, lunch, dinner

Day 6: White, Black, White—breakfast, lunch, dinner

Day 7: White, Black, Black—breakfast, lunch, dinner

As well, I want you wogging three times this week, for as long as you can. Stop and walk if you have to, but I want you to really push your limits this week.

Don't forget, your body was made for greatness!

WEEK 7 ENCOURAGEMENT:

Can you see the finish line? You're *so* close to reaching your goal! Your metabolism is running full force this week, you're wogging and starting to get strong. This is the time to journal. Remember how you're feeling, and don't forget it's only been less than two months. Can you believe how far you have come? Remember where you started, and keep an eye on where you're going! That 5k will be here before you know it!

WEEK 8

WEEK 8 CHALLENGE

PLATES YOUR WAY!

Remember, black plates are for proteins and fats; white plates are for proteins and carbs.

Eating:

Congratulations! You made it to Week 8! Four weeks of detox, three weeks of learning plate styles and combinations, and now this final week where we get your metabolism revving high and on fire—not just for a few weeks or months, but for the rest of your life!

This week is all about learning how to keep it going on your own.

All you need to do is pick your plate for each meal; ask yourself which plate do you want for this meal? Which color will you do for breakfast tomorrow, or dinner on Thursday? This is the easy part, really, because you are totally in control. You can mix it up however you want!

A word of caution, though: don't devise your meal plan to include fifty plates of gray! Gray plates are, of course, plates that com-

bine carbs, fats, and proteins. You don't want too many gray plates in your weekly plan—I try to limit mine to about three or four per week, max. Gray plates are totally fine in moderation, and they will help keep you on the right path, just don't get too dependent on them. We need to keep that pendulum always moving, those waves always crashing.

Now that we have your body working *for* you rather than against you, you have to keep working for your body. How many black plates and how many white plates should you do per week? Well, that depends on you; your body will tell you what it needs. I try to get in one white plate each day, usually for breakfast, as I've found this the best way to keep my metabolism humming at a nice pace. You may find yourself needing more white plates or fewer, depending on how your body responds.

I do think, however, that the more you increase physical activity the more white plates you'll probably need, since they're a great energy source. If you're doing a long or strenuous run, I would make sure you have a white plate dinner the night before and then again for breakfast that morning—you'll need those carbs! I do average more black plates than white, and more white than gray, but that's just what works best for me as a borderline diabetic. Everyone is different; so let your body dictate what's best for you.

If you stall in terms of weight loss, my best advice is to mix things up. Keep changing up the plate colors and that'll get things moving. Don't worry when you have those stalls, though—your body just needs time to adjust. I hit a plateau about every fifteen to twenty pounds I lose.

Don't forget to hydrate.

Eat your veggies.

EAT! Not eating enough, regardless of plate color, will only slow

your progress. Try to get to a place where you're neither under-eating nor over-eating, and don't forget that protein is *always* the focus.

These basic principles will keep your body moving and healthy.

Movement:

Your movement this week is easy: Three days of wogging, working up to a 5k!

- Day 1: one easy mile. Walk first and then try to move into a wog and keep wogging as much as you can.
- Day 2: two miles. Start with a nice brisk walk and work into your wog. Wog to the end. Don't forget to "beast mode" those last few minutes!
- Day 3: three miles! Yes, *three*. You can totally just walk the first one, nice and easy. Mile two, get into a comfortable wogging pace. Bring it back down to a walk whenever you need. Mile three is for beast mode: push yourself hard! Find out how much wogging you can do all the way to the finish line. You've totally got this 5k in the bag!

I knew you could do it, even when you didn't!

Now, just keep it up on your own.

Keep training and keep moving your body.

You're kicking ass!

WEEK 8 HOMEWORK:

Keep documenting your changes.

Daily: Keep weighing yourself each morning right after your first pee. I also want you to note anything specific you noticed about how you're feeling or looking.

Weekly: I want photos. Take some "before photos"; front and side, and then also just your face. Use these photos for comparison

purposes when the scale isn't moving. Sometimes things are changing shape when your weight stays the same. Keep up with those waist measurements and if you want to do more measurements, fine, but don't stop putting that measuring tape around your waist. I would love to hear your story and see your photos! Please consider emailing them to me, or sharing on social media. www.jasindawilder.com **#biggirlsdoitrunning**

WEEK 8 ENCOURAGEMENT:

Give your body as long as it takes to reach a place of strength and health. How long will that be? Eight more weeks? Eight more months? Eighteen months? It doesn't matter! The only goal is good health. If there's anything I've learned on this journey, it's to give my body time and grace: this isn't a sprint, it's a marathon. Don't worry if you trip up a few times along the way—just pick yourself up and keep on wogging. You've made all the right steps toward good health, now keep focused on the next meal, the next day, and the next run.

I'm so proud of you!

Pro tip: I tend to "Suzan Sommersize" my fruit, meaning eating it in moderation and eating it alone, unless it's berries, lemons, or limes. I've found loading fruit in with other carbs is just too much sugar for me, and I suspect you may find the same thing to be true for you.

PART 5

Additional Info to Keep You Motivated

Jasinda's Reset:

FOR THOSE TIMES WHEN YOU JUST NEED A KICK-START.

If you feel as if you just can't get the hang of which order to do your plates in, below is a version I think works well for the long term. If you're struggling with not getting your metabolism moving as fast as you would like, or if you just aren't feeling so great, this combination might be helpful to you.

I like to do this combination with as little dairy on my black plates as possible—think a sprinkle of cheese instead of a full cup. You can still have it, just cut back on your cheese, cream, and any other dairy for one week and see how you feel. I also try to limit myself to just one snack a day when I'm doing this little reset. If I get the munchies, I'll snack on some non-starchy veggies or berries. Keep your movement normal and don't forget to drink lots of water; I like to infuse mine with some lemon and lime.

- Day 1: B-B-B
- Day 2: B-W-B
- Day 3: B-W-B
- Day 4: W-B-B
- Day 5: B-W-B
- Day 6: W-B-B

- Day 7: B-B-W

You can come back to this whenever you need a week of reset. Sometimes we can get too much dairy, which can block us up or slow us down, and I think this is a nice little break for our body. I know mine really likes it.

FAQS

What happens if I mess up? Why will it be different this time?

"I can't do this."

"I messed up."

"I'm a failure."

"I ate a cupcake."

"I didn't run this week."

"This can't work for me."

"I'm hopeless."

I've said all those things to myself at some point on this journey.

Here's the reality.

So what if you ate something you shouldn't have? So what if you skipped a whole week of working out! So what if you're sure when you step on the scale tomorrow you'll have gained twenty pounds? This kind of thinking is something we need to toss out the window, *permanently*.

Let me fill you in on a little secret: you aren't perfect. Why are you expecting yourself to be? You *are* going to mess up. Everyone does, at some point. You might have a bad day, or even a bad week, but that doesn't mean you give up! Dust yourself off and try again. Don't even dwell on the failure, because that isn't going to help any-

one, least of all you. When's your next meal? Focus on that! Do that one right. This is a day-by-day, meal-by-meal plan. Ignore minor slip-ups; focus instead on all the amazing things you're accomplishing, focus on everything you're doing right.

You're going to finish a 5k! You're going to work your body and get stronger and healthier. This isn't a "maybe", this is fact. Pay no attention to unimportant hiccups and focus on your future. Remember why you are doing this. Think about the people you are going to inspire. It's okay to mess up every so often, just keep your eyes on the prize.

Food combinations and carb cycling: Why does it work?

When I was pregnant with my daughter I had a come-to-Jesus revelation. As I explained earlier, my body was literally prego-craving food combinations. I would eat eggs and bacon for breakfast, a big chef salad for lunch, and maybe some whole grains at dinner. I never ate fats and carbs together because it literally made me feel ill. I have no explanation for this phenomenon. I had huge bursts of energy, which was also odd because I was pregnant. And perhaps most important, I didn't want sugar *at all*—even the thought of sugar nauseated me. I started wondering what was going on with me. I didn't realize it at the time, but I was food combining and it was making me feel good.

I searched Google for recipes that were low-carb and no-sugar, and I kept hitting on Trim Healthy Mama recipes. Do yourself a HUGE favor and get that cookbook, it's amazing. They talk about food combining and cycling, too. And then I read several more books that each confirmed what I was starting to believe: eating fats and carbohydrates in the same meal makes it difficult to lose

weight—in fact, I believe eating those two things together frequently makes it nearly impossible. The problem is with the fact that we've created foods that are impossible to digest. The result is that many of us have slow, lagging, messed up metabolisms. By eating foods that are over processed and full of unnatural, inedible chemicals we've clogged up our systems. Giving your body similar natural foods in logical groupings will turn on your metabolic engine.

I don't believe in taking away an entire food group—like a carb-free diet for example. I just don't think it's sustainable or smart. But I *do* believe in jumpstarting your metabolism with food combinations that will make it dramatically easier to lose weight. Along with making some other adjustments and changes in your life, food combining will help you win the impossible weight loss struggle you've fought against your whole life.

It's a light bulb moment.

Yes, you can eat pasta, rice, and the occasional potato. You can have meat. You can have cake and ice cream—as long as it's made with stevia. I don't want you to be deprived; I want you to be healthy and smart. If you don't believe me, read some of the books written on the subject by actual doctors, who know much more than I do and can explain it more thoroughly. There is a list of these books at the end of this book.

Or, you can give me eight weeks and see what happens.

What results can I expect if I follow your 8-Week Plan?

Here's what will happen if you follow my program:

- Normal, stable blood sugar levels
- Increased energy
- Better complexion

- Better sleep patterns
- Increased strength (both mental and physical)
- Better focus
- Reduced inflammation
- Weight loss
- Self confidence

I know these are bold statements to make.

I know I might even sound crazy.

I've tested my plan with objective groups of women who were as frustrated as I was with continuing to fail at successfully completing weight loss plans. I also recruited friends, my family, my children and my husband, not to mention myself. Every single person who tried my method experienced the benefits listed above.

Why is my plan different?

Because it works.

Because combining the body and mind is just as important as combining foods.

Just try it for 8 weeks—don't rush and don't skip any steps. You won't figure this all out overnight. Give your body the grace and time it needs. You're in this for life. I'll be here with you!

Why the different plate colors?

It's the best way I've found to make the plan easy to understand.

It's simple: black plates are for proteins and fats; white plates are for proteins and carbs. Gray plates contain carbs, fats, and proteins, but use them in moderation.

And no, you don't need to go out and buy all new dishes and only use black, white, or gray plates. I simply devised this as an easy way to visualize the different meal options and combinations.

Why aren't there any fat or carb limits on these plates?

Because only you know your body, and I believe in listening to what your body is telling you, and eating until you are full. Your build, gender, age, and exercise level can also affect the amount your body may need, so setting generalized limits doesn't work; just don't over eat. You don't need to eat everything on your plate; enjoy your food, eat until you're full, and try to keep your body guessing. Which plate is coming next? Only you know; there are no rules.

What do I eat when I'm at a restaurant?

Don't worry! We eat out all the time, so I've got you covered. You can eat almost anywhere and find something that will leave you feeling satisfied and proud of yourself for not eating something harmful to your body. I can even find something at the bar to eat! Imagine it, a mother of six hanging out at the bar and sticking to her health plan.

Below is a quick list of ideas to help you be successful wherever you dine:

- Focus on protein—just about every restaurant is going to have meat. What's your favorite? Beef, chicken, seafood? Figure out a way to have it prepared the way you want it. Talk to the server and explain your needs. Most chefs are hip to the needs of their customers, and most of them have no trouble adjusting a dish to suit you. If a Starbuck's barista can pull off a Grande, Quad, Nonfat, One-Pump, No-Whip, Mocha then I'm pretty sure a chef can wrangle a no-carb or a no-sugar meal.
- Even at a drive thru or a deli counter, don't be afraid to ask for things to be prepared the way you want them; you're paying for this food and you should be able to order it the way you like it. Don't be embarrassed to ask for a lettuce wrap for your burger

instead of a bun. It's okay; you aren't the only one doing it! We have two restaurants in our town that are now doing a burger lettuce wrap option because of us! Start a trend, be cool!

- Start with a side salad
- Forget the chips and salsa, and order some veggies and guacamole instead
- Grilled fajitas without the tortillas
- Taco or grilled chicken salad—just pick a dressing that isn't too sweet; creamy is best, or just oil and vinegar
- Tacos in a lettuce wrap, or just eat the filling.
- A burrito in a bowl without the wrap
- A big bowl of chili
- Omelets with bacon or sausage
- Plain chicken wings—always ask for sauce on the side, as you don't need as much as you think
- Grilled salmon with brown rice—always ask if it's really brown or just white rice colored to look brown, or choose a sweet potato instead of the rice
- Lettuce wrap or unwich—ask your favorite burger joint or deli to wrap with lettuce: most will gladly do this for you.
- At a pizza place? Go for the wings, or get a salad and throw the entire pizza toppings, cheese and all, on top. You won't believe how yummy that is!

Pro tip: You don't need bread, and you don't need croutons, but if you are anything like me you NEED some wine. That's okay! Just pick something red and dry. Don't like it dry? Throw some stevia in it when the waiter isn't looking—he'll never know. Don't like wine? Have a low carb beer or two. Vodka and La Croix is also a great choice, and whiskey is Mr. Wilder's favorite.

Isn't it more expensive eating this way?

Yes and no. Yes, your food bill might go up a tiny bit, but not as much as you might expect. When you aren't buying all the highly marketed, packaged junk, you'll find your family is eating a smaller quantity of the nutrient-packed good stuff, which means the kids won't be asking for snacks every thirty minutes. You'll stay full longer and you'll have more energy so you won't need the quick fix from sugar and carbohydrates.

I did see a slight increase in our food bill during the first few weeks because we did a lot of stocking up on new ingredients. Once we had completely changed over into the healthier eating pattern, we didn't see much change in our grocery bill.

Shopping is actually *much* easier because I know all the items we eat and I just load up on those when I see a good price on them. There aren't any impulse buys, and I'm no longer tempted by slick marketing and packaging—even my kids can see right through that crap, now. The other huge money savings comes from better health: being sick is expensive! My family is so much healthier since we've started eating this way, and our overall quality of life is just better. We eat better food, feel better, and live better.

So even if there is a small monetary increase, I believe it is well worth it. I'd rather invest in my health than anything else.

Why does my weight keep going up and down?

I wish I had a really smart and savvy scientific answer for that. The truth is I can only link the weight fluctuations to water weight and your monthly cycle. So, to me, this is very, very normal. My best suggestion is to keep close track of your weight; I highly recommend using an app that will show you the overall downward trend of your loss. I like the Happy Scale app for that because it clearly shows that

even if you go up by a few pounds this week or that, your overall weight loss is still trending down.

I really wish I'd had a better grasp on all of this when I first started my new plan—I'd gain five pounds in the middle of the month, every single month, and it drove me *crazy*. Once I really started paying attention and tracking it, however, I found out it was just water weight associated with ovulation. I know some people will tell you not to weigh yourself every single day, but I believe the scale is simply a tool we can use to better understand our bodies. It's important to keep in mind the number on the scale is just that, a number, but what those numbers can tell us may actually help us feel better.

Everyone is different. I now know that each month my weight loss is part of a cycle I can predict: week one, I'll go down maybe a pound or two; week two, my weight usually goes up; week three, I'm down four pounds; week four, I'm going to lose a few more pounds. This is a consistent cycle for me. On average I lose about a pound or two a week. If I was on week two and I saw that gain I might even give up—don't do it! Weight fluctuations like that are absolutely normal, so don't freak out. We're looking for a downward trend over the *long* term.

Just keep doing what you're doing. You're making great progress! This is NOT a quick loss program; this is slow and steady, these are healthy changes for the rest of your life. One pound a week is great! That's fifty-two pounds a year! Don't get caught up in the numbers; get caught up in taking control over your health and how you feel. Don't let anything steal the joy of your success.

You're doing great!

What is Wilder Wogging, and how do I do it?

Wogging is my low impact version of running—I would almost

call it a shuffle. I try to land flat on the middle of my feet to make sure that my whole foot is taking the impact rather than just my heel. My feet stay low to the ground and I make sure to tighten my stomach and butt as much as possible, which has the added benefit of really helping to tighten and strengthen those areas.

You can wog as fast or as slow as you want, just take it one step at a time and gradually increase your speed. If you do have bad knees, please remember to reduce the impact by keeping your feet low to the ground—meaning, don't lift your knees or feet too much, which is why it feels more like a fast shuffle than anything else. You might feel a bit like you're falling forward, but that assist from gravity will actually make it easier for you to keep going.

Don't worry if you need to slow to a walk for a minute and then pick it back up; my kids can actually walk faster than I wog, and that's just fine. The wog part just adds to the cardio aspect and helps my momentum. Check out YouTube for a video about how to wog, or find me online if you need more help!

Happy wogging!

What happens when I reach all my goals?

First, congratulations! Next, I would challenge you to set new goals! If you feel happy with the weight you're at, great! Do you feel physically fit and strong? Awesome! If you're getting to the point that you're worried about losing *too* much I'd start adding in more whole grains and good carbohydrates with your high fat meals. It's okay! My husband and children always do a side of brown rice, whole grain bread, whole grain pasta or a potato to maintain their size and energy. Once you feel like you're in a good place, those carbs will help maintain your weight—just don't add in added sugars, those will *always* get you in trouble.

What do I do with all this skin?

That is an excellent question! If you figure it out, let me know! My best advice is to get a good pair of Spanx; those things work wonders. I have tried a few other things like skin brushing and cellulite lotions, but none of them did much for me. I think if you lose a significant amount of weight, skin is just going to be an issue for you unless you're blessed with some miracle genetics.

There are surgical options for skin removal, but those also come with risks. I can't say I haven't thought about having surgery, because the excess skin on my thighs rubs a lot and I do find it really makes running more difficult. At this point, though, I'm not sure I'm willing to undergo another surgery. In the end, I think you need to do what makes *you* feel good. You've come a long way, and you deserve to feel as good as you can in your skin.

Have you only tested this plan on your family?

No, I would never publish a book like this without doing objective testing to make sure my plan can help a wide variety of people. A beta test group worked with me over the course of several months helping me to tweak my health plan. These ladies did a phenomenal job with my program, so please be sure to read their testimonials at the end of the book.

My testers came from different backgrounds and ages, and they all had different reasons for wanting to change their health. They all saw positive results from the changes they made on my program. One of my beta group ladies hadn't seen a normal blood sugar reading since she was thirteen, but after only three weeks on my program she was seeing normal numbers. Another found relief from issues with her period, and another saw better overall energy with her struggles with MS. Most of these ladies also included their chil-

dren in the new healthy eating plan and they saw great results, too.

I'm positive my health plan will bring about positive results for anyone who does the full eight weeks as I've laid them out. Cutting out added sugar and refined carbohydrates along with eating healthy and whole foods will do wonders for everyone.

Why is it okay for me to eat fruit and dairy?

Well, maybe it is and maybe it isn't—I think that's something you need to really watch and figure out while doing my 8-week plan. Are you sensitive to dairy? If so, limit how much you have, or cut it from your diet entirely. If something makes you feel bloated, gassy, or in pain, then stop eating it! I think for most of us a moderate amount of cheese, sour cream, or yogurt is going to be okay. Just pay attention to own body and make adjustments if you feel better without a certain type of food.

Fruit is the same. Personally, I can't eat too much fruit; I *love* my berries, but a banana will make me feel yucky if I have it with too many other healthy carbs. I know that several people in my BETA group were able to enjoy apples, bananas, and even other fruits with no issue at all. If you have pre-diabetes or diabetes, then I would caution you to really watch the fructose. A steady insulin level will ensure the best health for you. Moderation and self-evaluation is key here.

Should I add other forms of exercise?

I think walking/wogging and jogging are the best exercises start out with. I would try my gradual approach with the eight-week plan and then see how you feel. You could add a few other forms of cardio; jump rope is a killer workout, and I love to challenge my sons with it. Aerobic dancing is also really fun—my daughter and I to do it

together. You could do some kettlebells or light weights for strength training if you feel like it. I don't think strength workouts will contribute to weight loss, but it's all about how you feel. Listen to your body and add things when you are ready. This is a marathon, not a sprint. Take your time and find your own health groove.

How do I make peace with my body?

Focus on all the good things it's done for you. It's time to love yourself and your body. You've come such a long way! Be proud of yourself and all the things you've done with your body so far. Comparison is the thief of joy. This is your journey, your race. Take it one day at a time, one meal at a time, and one wog at a time. You'll get there!

DAILY MEAL SUGGESTIONS

Keep it simple! One day at a time, one meal at a time.

Day 1: (Black, Black, Black)

Breakfast: Cheese and salsa omelets with a side of bacon or sausage.

Lunch: Chef salad with no-sugar-added dressing.

Dinner: Cheeseburger without a bun and a side of broccoli and/or green beans.

Snacks: Almonds or WASA crackers with laughing cow cheese, Oikos Triple Zero Yogurt

Day 2: (White, White, Black)

Breakfast: Old Fashioned Oats with unsweetened almond milk and Greek yogurt and berries. (Wilder morning mush—see recipe)

Lunch: Quesadilla with a Mission low-carb wrap, lean meat, peppers and Laughing Cow cheese . A few blue corn chips and fresh salsa

Dinner: Burger or Salmon over salad. (If your kids don't like salmon you can also use plain chicken strips. My kids love to make their own bowls, so don't toss your salad; let them pick what they want for toppings. You'll be surprised what they might pick. I often do some berries as a side, and maybe some rice, too.)

Snacks: protein shake (I love Jay Robb with some Greek yo-

gurt, stevia, integral collagen, and berries—see recipe); almonds and cheese

Day 3: (Black, White, Black)

Breakfast: Breakfast burrito on Mission low carb wrap. Eggs, bacon or sausage, cheese, peppers or onions, or just some *pico de gallo*.

Lunch: Light soup (we love Progresso Lite) and some WASA crackers, and a Triple Zero yogurt

Dinner: Spaghetti with Dreamfield's pasta. I use spaghetti sauce made with ground turkey but with no added sugar, and we top it with cheese. We include a side of vegetables. Let your kids pick which ones they want. Also add a side salad and eat that first.

Snacks: Berries, Quest bar, some Lily's chocolate

Day 4: (Black, Black, Black)

Breakfast: Cheese omelet seasoned with sea salt and some cayenne pepper. Side of Applegate chicken sausage.

Lunch: Large Chef Salad

Dinner: Wilder Wings, salad, and veggies

Snacks: Quest Bar, almonds and cashews

Day 5: (White, White, Black)

Breakfast: Protein loaded pancakes (see recipe). You can leave out the chocolate chips.

Lunch: Mission wrap sandwiches with lean meat and Laughing Cow cheese

Dinner: Homemade pizza using Mission low carb wraps (Fat Head low carb crust is another great option)

Snack: sugar free Cheesecake (see recipe)

Day 6: (White, Black, White)

Breakfast: Scrambled egg whites and toast

Lunch: Chili (see recipe)

Dinner: Loaded sweet potato and/or grilled chicken kabobs

Snack: nuts, Nanny Karri cookies

Day 7: (White, Black, Black)

Breakfast: Triple Zero yogurt, berries and toast (mix some Ezekiel almond or flax cereal into the yogurt for extra fiber)

Lunch: Lettuce wrapped burger (so yummy!)

Dinner: Pizza cups (see recipe)

Snack: Quest bar

Pro Tip: White plates are MADE for wogging. If you're going to be doing a big run or workout, a white plate meal is a great idea because it's fast burning. I love having oatmeal or pancakes made with oats for some extra pep in my step.

SAMPLE RUNNING DIARY

Day 1: Today I didn't really want to run but I got out there and ran a whole mile. I only stopped twice. My pace was 17 minutes per mile and I felt pretty good when I was done. Go me!

After run snack: Quest bar

Day 2: Today I ran a bit further than yesterday, but I stopped three times. One time I actually thought I might die. The middle of my run felt best. Tomorrow I'm going to rest.

After run snack: protein shake

Day 3: Rest Day. (Yes, Rest days and weeks are important—your body needs the rest to rebuild those muscles)

Day 4: Didn't have time to run.

Day 5: I RAN TWO MILES! Not full-out running, but not as slow as a walk. I felt great when I was finished. I only stopped once.

After run snack: Triple Zero yogurt

Day 6: Rest Day

Day 7: I took the dog and kids for a nice 30-minute walk. I told the kids I wanted to see them run and we wogged for about half of it. It was so much fun to exercise with them! I'm feeling better and stronger every day!

Snack: Mixed berries topped with Fat Free Reddi whip (one of my very favorite snacks).

Pro Tip: It doesn't matter if you run or walk outside or inside. All that matters is that you did it. Figure out how you like to move and get moving!

Jasinda's Jams

WORK MY BODY WORKOUT PLAYLIST

I LOVE TO LISTEN TO MUSIC AS I WALK, WOG, OR JOG. BELOW ARE some great tunes that get me motivated and moving.

"Levels"—Avicii
"Till the World Ends"—Britney Spears
"Chasing the Sun"—The Wanted (Hardwell Radio Edit)
"Don't Wake Me Up"—Chris Brown (Panic City Remix)
"Stronger" —Kelly Clarkson (Nicky Romero Club Mix)
"The One That Got Away"—Katy Perry (R3had club mix)
"Hey Mama"—David Guetta (Club Killers Remix)
"G.D.F.R." —Flo Rida (Nolaswift Remix)
"Time of Our Lives"—Ne-Yo & Pitbull (DJ Noodles Remix)
"Where Are U Now"—Skrillex and Diplo with Justin Bieber (Kaskade Remix)
"Outside"—Calvin Harris feat. Ellie Goulding (Hardwell Remix)
"Shut Up and Dance"—Walk The Moon (Jason Nevins Remix) *
"Something Better" —Audien (feat. Lady Antebellum) *
"Love Myself"—Hailee Steinfeld *
"Turn Down For What"—DJ Snake & Lil John

"Work"—Iggy Azalea (Gregor Salto Radio Edit)
"Fireball"—Pitbull feat. John Ryan (Jump Smokers Remix)
"Stay With Me"—Sam Smith (Soul Clap Remix)
"Work Work"—Britney Spears *
"Lose Yourself"—Eminem
"Black Horse"—Katy Perry
"Burn"—Ellie Goulding (Mat Zo Remix)
"Neon Lights"—Demi Levato (Country Club Martini Remix)
"I Cry"—Flo Rida *
"Must Be Love"—Christina Grimmie *
"WTF (Where They From)" —Missy Elliott
"Light It Up"—Major Lazer (feat. Nyla & Fuse ODG)
"Work This Body"—Walk The Moon
"Drop It Low"—Kat DeLuna

*ONE OF JASINDA'S FAVORITES – A MUST HAVE!

Pro Tip: The Spotify and Rock My Run apps will use your smart phone to monitor your running pace and suggest music to match your pace. Rock My Run has really improved my run time. It's also a great way to find new running music that will keep in rhythm with your own movement.

BUSY MOM AND WILDER KID APPROVED RECIPIES

MY KIDS ARE ALWAYS GIVEN THE OPTION OF A HEALTHY CARB as a side with dinner. They're growing so they need those good, healthy carbs for energy! I know you're busy too, so you don't need a bunch of fancy recipes to keep your family healthy and happy, you just need a few dozen tried-and-true recipes your whole family will love. Figure out what they like and modify them to be healthy. It'll be easier than you think, trust me on this. You're laying the health groundwork for your child's entire life—making these changes now will improve their health forever.

For full-color recipe photos, please visit www.biggirlsdoitrunning.com.

Wild(er) Monkey cakes
(White/Gray Plate)

These are our Saturday or Sunday morning go-to special treat for our kids. I won't even tell you how long it takes to make pancakes for eight people, but it's worth it to see the smiles on their faces. My kids look forward to waking up on the weekends now, because they smell breakfast and come running. We pair these with some turkey bacon.

Ingredients:

2 cups of oats, blend well in a blender or food processor and set aside

Blend together separately:

1 cup low fat cottage cheese

1 5.3oz container of Triple Zero yogurt (banana)

2 cups liquid egg whites (one large carton)

1 teaspoon vanilla extract

1 teaspoon banana extract

4 teaspoons baking powder

4 tablespoons stevia sweetener (Pyure or Swerve)

(You can also add a scoop of protein powder for added protein and a thicker texture).

Coconut oil (to grease the pan)

Method:

Blend all ingredients together, including the oats, and then let it sit for a while to thicken up. This is an important step, so don't skip it!

Heat your griddle or pan and lightly coat the surface with some coconut oil and cook on low heat.

I make these in four small frying pans. They are a bit thin—something between a crepe and a regular pancake.

Added notes:

Feel free to adjust the extract and yogurt flavors.

For the kids top the pancakes with fat free Redi whip, and/or sprinkle them with Lily's chocolate chips.

Keep them white plate for the adults.

Make sure you coat the pan with coconut oil, and cook on low heat.

Wild(er) Nachos
(These can be modified for any plate color)

My family LOVES nachos. My recipe is a worry-free way to enjoy an old favorite—I use sliced peppers instead of tortilla chips. Adjust the quantities to suit your needs.

Ingredients:

Bell peppers sliced into nacho-chip sized strips.

Sautéed ground beef, pork, turkey, or chicken. The seasoning is up to you.

Shredded cheddar cheese

Lettuce, hot peppers, salsa, onions, sour cream, green onions, tomatoes. Your choice.

Method:

Pre-heat the oven to 350 F

Place the peppers in an ovenproof baking dish

Place the cooked meat on top of the peppers

Sprinkle everything with the shredded cheese

Bake at 350 F for 5–10 minutes, or until the cheese is melted

Top with the lettuce, hot peppers, salsa, sour cream etc.

Option:

Make a cheese sauce by combining:

- 8oz grated sharp cheddar cheese
- 8th tsp cayenne pepper
- salt ¼ tsp
- ½ cup almond milk
- ½ cup cream cheese

- 1 tablespoon butter

Pour over the nachos and enjoy!

You can do these so many different ways. If I'm really in a hurry I'll throw the sliced peppers in the oven with just seasoning, salsa, and cheese. You can top them with so many fun things. Get creative!

Nanny Karri Cookies
(Black Plate)

I found this recipe online and our nanny was super bummed because she couldn't eat them—she's allergic to almonds, the poor thing! She tried modifying the recipe so she could enjoy them, and ta-dah… Nanny Karri cookies! These cookies are soft and tasty and totally hit the cookie spot; you won't even miss your old sugar-filled cookies anymore. I promise!

"These cookies are so good, it makes me angry"- Jack Wilder

Ingredients:

8 oz 1/3 fat cream cheese (softened)

2 Tbsp butter

1 Tbsp natural peanut butter

1 cup stevia or stevia blend

1 tsp vanilla extract

Method:

Pre-heat the oven to 350 F

Line a cookie sheet with parchment paper

Whip everything in the above list until well combined

Then add:

Add 3 eggs

Keep whipping until the eggs are well combined

Then add:

½ tsp sea salt

½ tsp xantham gum (can be found online); it makes the cookies thick and chewy

1 tsp baking powder

2/3 cup peanut flour

1 scoopful whey protein powder (we use either vanilla or peanut butter—Jay Robb and Quest are my two favorite brands)

1½ cups Lily's brand sugar-free chocolate chips (you could also use the 70% dark cocoa variety)

Chopped nuts (these are optional)

Place spoonfulls of the batter on the cookie sheet

Bake at 350 degrees for 10 minutes.

This recipe makes about 50 cookies, but don't eat them all at once!

Wilder Mush
(white plate)

My kids *loved* the sugary, pre-packaged oatmeal—the kind with the dinosaur eggs that melt into dinosaur shaped sugar flakes was their favorite. I know, I know…*so* bad for them! Which meant, of course, that I had to find something to replace those little sugar bags of death. When I first started playing around with this recipe, I would add a few pinches of stevia to it in order for them to really like it, but now they don't miss the sweetener at all. Even if you aren't a kid—even if you don't really like oatmeal—give this a try. I've already converted most of my northern Michigan friends to this—it's perfect for those cold winter mornings. It'll hit the spot and keep you full till lunch.

For a single serving:

Ingredients:

1 to 1 ½ or 2 cups of old fashioned oats (you decide how hungry you are); Jack always needs two cups

Unsweetened vanilla almond milk

Frozen berries

Okios Triple Zero yoghurt (single serving size)

Method:

Place the oats in a bowl and pour over the almond milk until it covers the oats (you don't want too much or it will taste watery—yuck)

Microwave on high for 2 or 2 ½ minutes

Top with some frozen berries and microwave for another 30 seconds.

Remove from microwave and mix in the container of Oikos Triple Zero yogurt.

Enjoy!

Note: Mix up the yogurt flavors and change the berries for different flavor combinations. We like the blueberry, raspberry, strawberry, blackberry and cherry flavors. Our favorite combos are raspberry vanilla and blueberry banana.

Jack and Jasinda's Chef's Salad (Black Plate)

Jack and I eat a chef's salad almost every day; there are some days when we might have a tin of Progresso soup, or a rollup, but most days we do a salad. Jack usually has some WASA crackers with his, and I'll add some almonds or cashews as my side.

Ingredients:

A mixture of greens
Sliced meats: ham, turkey, chicken—whatever you like
Hard-boiled egg
Avocado
Tomatoes
Onions
Cheese
Salad Dressing of your choice

Method:

Layer everything into a pretty bowl and top with the dressing.

Notes:

We use a super-food greens mix available from our farmer's co-op that's got everything in it *except* iceberg lettuce. Branch out and try all the great greens that are out there like spinach or kale. Just try adding a bit more variety in terms of greens to your normal salad… you'll like it. Also, they have *way* more nutrients than iceberg lettuce.

Sometimes we'll add cheese crisps instead of regular cheese. Cheese crisps are made from baked cheese—sorta like a crouton without all the nasty crap. Yum! You can find them at your grocery

store, probably in the produce section.

Right now we're really into the yogurt or salsa ranch dressings.

Some days I add a few squirts of lemon flavor fish oil when Jack isn't looking. Please don't tell him!

If you wanted to get really crazy, you could fold your salad inside a Mission Low Carb whole-wheat wrap.

It's such a quick and easy lunch—there's not a ton of prep and it fills us up for a long time. We're even lucky enough to have a local deli that knows our salad preferences, and they start making those salads for us as soon as we walk in!

Wilder Wings
(Black plate)

My kids *love* chicken wings! We usually go to Buffalo Wild Wings after church on Sunday because KIDS EAT HALF OFF! Do you know what a deal that is for parents with six kids? It's basically like winning the chicken wing lottery.

Well, my crazy kids kept hounding me to make my own wings, so I said, "Fine, I'll try." These are what I came up with. My family tends to like things a bit spicy, with lots of flavor, but you can adjust the spiciness to satisfy your little wild ones.

Ingredients:

40-50 chicken pieces: wings, thighs or strips. (For the health benefits, I prefer chicken on the bone, but little ones might prefer the strips).

6 tbsp Baking Powder

4 tsp salt

Method:

Preheat oven to 250 degrees

Wash and dry the chicken and place on a baking sheet lined with aluminum foil

Combine the baking powder and salt and then sprinkle over the chicken

Place the chicken on the middle or lower rack and cook for 30 minutes.

Then, while the chicken bakes, mix together in a small dish:

1 cup mayo

1 big spoonful of Greek yogurt

1 tbsp lime juice (bottled is fine)

½ cup to1 cup (depending on spiciness preference) Frank's Red Hot Original Cayenne Pepper Sauce

½ tsp onion powder

½ tsp chili powder

½ tsp turmeric

A generous dash of Worchester sauce

½ tsp minced garlic

1 tbsp blackstrap molasses

pinch of pepper

Remove the chicken from the oven and turn up the oven temperature to 400 degrees.

Brush the chicken generously with the above mix. Bake for another 30 minutes at 400 degrees.

Pass the napkins!

Mere's Mixed Berry Muffins
(White plate)

Meredith started helping me at home when we first moved up north and were further away from our parents; she's a real life Mary Poppins! She helps with everything from booking my hotel rooms to picking up kids from school, so when we started making our big health changes, she helped me by grabbing things at the grocery store and preparing meals. She's amazing, and so are her muffins!

These muffins freeze well and they are great to have on hand when you're having a hectic morning.

Ingredients:

1 cup oat flour
½ cup coconut flour
3 tsp baking powder
1 cup Swerve
6 tbsp water

1¾ cup egg whites

¼ tsp sea salt

¾ cup berries of your choice (we like blueberry and raspberry)

¼ tsp powdered glucomannan (you can find this on Amazon or at your health store)

¼ tsp vanilla

Coconut oil for spraying the muffin tins

Method:

Pre-heat oven to 350 degrees

Spray your muffin tin with coconut oil

Combine everything but the berries in a mixing bowl. Whisk everything together until combined well.

Fold the berries into the batter

Spoon batter into muffin tin and bake at 350 for 20 minutes

Enjoy!

Wicked and Wilder Meat Lover's Crock Pot Chili **spicy!** (Can be modified for either plate)

My whole family *loves* chili, especially Jack. I like to pair it with WASA crackers for my kids because they can each have their crackers the way they want; some crumble their crackers into their chili, others keep them out and spread Laughing Cow cheese on them.

We live in northern Michigan where it's -2 degrees for half the year, so we need chili to keep us warm. I usually just throw it in the crock-pot before church so we have something quick and easy when we get home. I know the chicken *and* the beef might sound weird, but just try it, you might like it!

This recipe is just right for all five of my big kids—it's not *too* spicy and it has just enough kick.

Ingredients:
1 lb boneless skinless chicken breast
2 lbs ground beef

1 small onion, diced

1 tbsp minced garlic

A bit of oil for frying

1 can lime LaCroix (tap water is also okay)

1 tsp red pepper flakes (optional)

1 can drained beans—my family likes pinto beans

2, 14oz cans of diced tomatoes—I like Rotel

1 cup plain Greek yogurt

½ block cream cheese

½ tbsp chili powder

½ tbsp cayenne

1 tbsp ground cumin

2 tsp sea salt

Juice of one lime (bottled is fine)

Method:

Pre-cook the ground beef and chicken, along with the onion, in a bit of oil. Then place in your crockpot.

Add remaining ingredients to the crockpot and mix everything together.

Turn the crockpot onto low for eight hours, or high for four hours.

Notes:

When serving add: sour cream, white cheddar cheese, and chopped cilantro.

YUM!

Perfect PB & J Smoothie
(Even the kids love it)

This is the perfect post-workout smoothie. It's so good we sometimes have it for dessert with just a touch of fat free Redi Whip on top. (I'm lazy, so I use the empty yogurt cup to measure).

In a blender mix together the following:

1 scoop Jay Robb Whey Isolate Strawberry protein powder

1 cup of Okios Triple Zero yogurt (Jack likes Strawberry or banana)

1 empty Triple Zero cupful frozen strawberries

1 empty Triple Zero cupful frozen blueberries

2 empty Triple Zero cupfuls unsweetened vanilla almond milk

1 small spoonful of natural peanut or almond butter

1 generous spoonful Pyure or Swerve

Pinch of sea salt

A few pieces of frozen spinach for extra protein (optional)

One scoop of collagen (optional)

Wilder Sangria

Start with your favorite dry red wine. If you don't like dry wine, just work with me here and try this anyway. All wine-lovers: TRY THIS!

1 large glass of wine
1 tsp Pyure (organic stevia sweetener)
½ cup frozen fruit or berries
A few splashes of lime juice
(mix or shake)

I know it isn't exactly real Sangria, but it will work in a pinch, and it's delicious. Once you've had one, the second one will taste even better.

Wilder Margarita

Fill a cocktail shaker with ice, and then add:

3 oz tequila
1 squirt lemon juice
1 squirt lime juice
1 packet, or to taste, True Lemon (flavored stevia)
1 packet, or to taste, True Lime (flavored stevia)
1 pinch salt
(SHAKE IT UP)
Serve with a slice of fresh lemon or lime. **#fancy**

Note:
Don't get too crazy, people. This is a family show!

French Toast Sticks
(Black Plate)

Traditional French toast was something my kids really missed, especially my littlest guys. I searched high and low until I figured out a way to make something even mom and dad could enjoy. The kids love having French Toast Sticks as a special treat on weekends,

This recipe makes 16 sticks, so big families like mine should double the recipe. These are so easy to make even the kids can help!

Ingredients:

1 package Mission low carb whole-wheat wraps (contains 8 wraps)

2 eggs

Granulated and powdered stevia

Spreadable cream cheese (1/3 fat type)

Butter for frying

1/4 cup unsweetened vanilla almond milk

Sugar free syrup (optional)

Separately mix together:

Microwave heaping three tablespoons of butter

3 tbsp granulated sugar

1 tbsp bootstrap molasses (adjust according to how much of a molasses taste you like—a little goes a long way)

1 tbsp cinnamon

Set above mixture aside.

Method:

Spread cream cheese on the inside all 8 of the wraps

Spread the molasses mixture on top of the cream cheese—I like to use a pastry brush

Roll up and cut each wrap in half to make 16 pieces.

Mix the eggs and almond milk in a wide bowl

Dip the rolled up and sliced halves into the mixture, and turn them so the eggs and milk soak in

Place 3 tbsp butter in a large pan and fry those puppies up.

Notes:

We serve them topped with the Swerve brand powdered stevia!

You can also dip them in sugar free syrup, but it isn't really needed as they're plenty sweet as is. (Our little boys love to dip them, so we go with it!)

These are the perfect morning breakfast sweet treat. I like them with a small bowl of berries. **#Fancy**

Perfect Chicken Strips
(Black Plate)

If your kids are like mine, they're going to want some good, old-fashioned chicken strips. I serve these with sweet potato fries for them and salad for mom and dad—Jack and I often just the lay the chicken strips right onto our salads. You really can't go wrong with this recipe. If you want to give them a bit of a zing, just add some cayenne.

Ingredients:
2 lbs boneless chicken, cut into strips
¾ cup almond flour
1 cup grated parmesan cheese
¼ tsp paprika
½ tsp chili powder
a dash of black pepper
1 tsp Italian herb blend
¼ teaspoon sea salt

1 tsp garlic powder
2 large eggs, stirred
½ stick butter, melted
Olive oil

Method:

Preheat oven to 400 degrees

Line a baking sheet with parchment paper.

Combine the flour, spices and cheese and place on a plate

Combine eggs and melted butter and place on a plate (a pie plate is perfect)

Dip the chicken in the eggs and butter and then roll them into the flour, spice, and cheese mixture.

Place chicken on the baking sheet and lightly drizzle with olive oil

Bake for 30-35 minutes or until golden brown.

Traverse City Cherry Lime Cheesecake

I buy premade whole-wheat crusts at my local farmer's co-op, and Whole Foods should have them, too. You can create several different flavors combos with this recipe, so experiment! We've done lemon with dark chocolate, and a peanut butter version—it depends what you're in the mood for.

Ingredients:

Filling

1/6 oz softened cream cheese

1/3 cup sour cream

½ cup heavy whipping cream (sour cream and heavy whipping cream can be substituted for each other, or use cream cheese for an even denser cake)

½ cup Swerve sweetener

1 tbsp tart cherry concentrate

2 tsp Watkins cherry extract

2 tsp vanilla extract

3 tbsp of Real Lime

pinch of salt

3 large eggs

Premade whole-wheat crust

Method:

Preheat oven to 350 degrees

Grease a springform pan with coconut oil

Place whole-wheat crust in the springform pan

Whip or mix the filling ingredients together and pour onto the piecrust.

Place the cheesecake in the preheated oven and bake for 45 – 50 minutes. It is done when the top is just slightly jiggly.

Notes:

Keep a close eye on it at the end as it can burn.

I like to drizzle some melted Lily's chocolate on top after it's cooled. My dad likes his topped with some pecans and Fat Free Reddi Whip, too. It would also be good with a side of fresh berries.

This is a special treat my family really enjoys. I hope yours does, too.

Low Carb Cheddar Biscuits (Black Plate)

My kiddos love these family favorite biscuits. There are lots of other low carb options out there, but we really like this one that I made up. I hope you like them too!

Ingredients:

Biscuit Mix

2 cups almond flour

2 cups coconut flour

2 tbsp baking powder

4 oz shredded cheddar cheese

1 cup water

3 eggs

½ cup cream cheese (soft)

A pinch of salt

1/3 cup milk

4 tbsp butter (melted)

Method:

Preheat oven to 375 degrees

Line a baking sheet with parchment paper

In a mixing bowl combine the ingredients listed above and mix well. I like to use my big pink Kitchen Aid mixer.

Scoop the batter by the spoonful onto the baking sheet and shape into a biscuit form

Bake for 10-12 minutes.

Topping Mix

While the biscuits are baking, mix together:

1 cup melted butter

½ teaspoon salt

¼ teaspoon onion powder

¼ teaspoon dried parsley

Once the biscuits are done, brush the topping mix generously over the tops.

Enjoy!

Mom's Famous Mac & Cheese (Black Plate)

I started making this Mac & Cheese for Easter when my firstborn was a toddler. He was obsessed with mac & cheese, and probably ate it way too much. Well…he's 12 and he's still obsessed with it; he calls this recipe my "famous" Mac and Cheese.

We only make this for special occasions—in fact, it should come with a warning label because even though the Dreamfields pasta is a great choice, the fats in this one are pretty heavy. Don't eat it too much or too often.

Ingredients:

2 boxes of Dreamfield elbow macaroni

8 tbsp butter

2 cups Half and Half

2 eggs

1, 8 oz. package of cream cheese

4 cups of your favorite cheese, shredded. (We like equal parts of Muenster, Cheddar, Monterey Jack and Colby)

S & P to taste

Cayenne pepper, garlic powder and/or dry mustard to taste

Method:

Preheat oven to 350 degrees

Coat a casserole dish with coconut oil

Cook the pasta as directed on the box, and then drain.

Combine all ingredients except the pasta in a large bowl.

Add the cooked pasta to the wet ingredients and mix well.

Pour the pasta mix into your casserole dish and place in the

oven.

Bake for about 20-25 minutes. It's done when you see it start to bubble.

Top it with a tiny bit more cheese—we REALLY like cheese—and serve with a nice green salad.

Pro Tip: make sure not to eat reheated Dreamfields if you are working on achieving your goal weight. The protective coating won't be the same once it's reheated with the result that it causes a higher insulin reaction.

Cheesy Pizza Cups
(Black Plate)

Okay, I'll admit that at one point in our lives my family was eating pizza every week. Usually on a Friday or Saturday night when I just didn't have any time to plan a meal or the energy to cook one. One of the first things my kids complained about missing, after we changed the way we ate, was pizza.

As you all know, necessity is the mother of invention. I wanted to come up with some sort of pizza my family would enjoy and something that would meet our dietary requirements. I saw something online about making cheese taco shells and this idea just came to me; I merged one of our old favorite pizza bake recipes with this, and *BAM*! Pizza magic.

The result is Cheesy Pizza Cups—they are individual pizzas made in muffin pans that kind of look like muffins, but taste like heaven.

For the crust, we often use a large Joseph's low carb flat bread, a

Mission Wrap, Ezekiel English muffins, or an egg-and-cheese pizza crust (try the Fathead low carb version—you can find the recipe online), but the version below takes the prize for my family. Yes, it takes a bit more time and prep, but the result is amazing. I serve this with a side salad and my kids gobble it right up.

Get out your muffin tin and get ready to make pizza like you've never dreamed of.

Ingredients:

(This recipe will make 8 pizza cups, but I double it for my family. Most of my family members can eat two with some sauce on the side).

Part 1:

Ingredients:

For the cheese liner shell:

One bag of grated mozzarella cheese

One bag of grated Parmesan cheese

Italian seasoning to taste

Method:

Preheat the oven to 350 degrees

Spray the muffin pan(s)—I use coconut spray, but anything will work

Next, heat up your small frying pans—I've got lots of people to cook for, so I usually do four at time.

Combine the cheeses and seasoning (only you know how much seasoning your family likes. My kids love lots of flavor, so I throw in a bunch).

Place a spoonful of the cheese and seasoning mix into a heated fry pan and fry up the cheese—It'll cook like a pancake.

Don't take your eyes off them as they can easily burn. When the edges get brown, get them into the muffin pans one at a time. Tamp them down with a spoon, so the tops come above the top of the muffin tin.

Once all eight are done, just let them sit for a few minutes and harden up.

Part 2:

Ingredients:

Combine the following:

1 lb of ground turkey, beef or even sausage, **browned** in a skillet

Minced onion to taste (optional)

1 egg

¼ tsp of pink sea salt

A bit more cheese

A tiny bit of your favorite marinara sauce—make sure the sauce is sugar-free!

Method:

Mix the filling ingredients together

Place a scoop of the mixture into each of the cheese crusts

Top each with more sauce, more mozzarella cheese, and a slice or two of pepperoni. (You can use turkey pepperoni if you prefer). **#fancy**

Bake in your preheated oven for 20 minutes!

Enjoy!

Big Bird!
(Black Plate)

When I make roasted chicken, my kids EAT. By the time we're done with this dish, the carcass looks like velociraptors have been at it. This one is super easy to make and tastes great! Buy as many chickens as it will take to feed your family, and follow the recipe below for each one. My family can easily eat three chickens at one meal! I look for these on sale, or grab them when my farmer's co-op has some fresh ones in.

Ingredients:

Whole chicken(s)—as many as you need
Soft butter
S & P
Garlic powder
Fresh cloves of garlic, whole
An onion, quartered

Paprika

Method:

Preheat oven to 425 degrees

Rinse your chicken(s) under cold water and pat dry

Place your chicken(s) in an oven roaster; I use cast iron.

Coat the bird(s) with butter—I rub them with the stick of butter, but you can also use your hands or a fork. I don't mind getting my hands dirty, but do whatever works for you. Coconut oil is also okay here.

Sprinkle the birds with salt, pepper, garlic powder and paprika. Massage to get all the spices rubbed in.

Shove a big chunk of butter inside the bird with a few cloves of garlic and a quarter of an onion. Yes, stick it right up inside; just don't forget to wash your hands afterwards.

Roast the birds for approximately 60–75 minutes, depending on the size of the bird. Use a meat thermometer to check the internal temp of the birds: it should read at least 165 degrees before you take it out of the oven. (If you don't have a meat thermometer insert a paring knife into the thigh when you think it is done. If the juices run clear you know the bird is cooked).

Wait 10 minutes before carving and serving.

Enjoy!

Jack's Meatloaf Gone Wilder (Gray Plate)

You just can't go wrong with meatloaf. I like to use ground turkey and serve the meatloaf with either some garlic green beans or mashed cauliflower on the side. And, yes, you can always use a no sugar added or reduced sugar ketchup. It tastes just as good!

Ingredients:

3lbs of ground turkey (or other ground meat)

2 bell peppers (finely chopped)

1 small onion (finely chopped)

3 tsp minced garlic

2 large eggs

1 cup grated cheddar cheese

1 tbsp cayenne pepper (depending on your preferred level of spiciness)

½ tablespoon black pepper

A few red pepper flakes (optional)

1 can tomato paste

2 tablespoons heavy cream

3 toasted and crumbled slices of Ezekiel bread

Your favorite tomato sauce

Method:

Preheat oven to 375 degrees

Mix all of the ingredients with your hands in a large bowl. I know it's gross but you'll survive.

Divide the mixture into two loaf pans.

Top with your favorite tomato sauce

You can also top it with some WASA cracker crumbles and cheese. Mmmmmm!

Bake for between 60 and 75 minutes.

Wine and Chocolate Cake
(Gray Plate)

I know you might be scared to try this, but please just give it a try; it's pretty darn good. Just trust me on this. My kids eat this up and ask for more.

Cake:

Ingredients:

15 oz tin of Black Beans (drained)

6 eggs

½ cup red wine (substitute with almond milk if desired)

1 tsp vanilla

½ tsp almond extract

6 tbsp butter (melted)

½ cup cocoa powder

3 tbsp coconut flour

1 cup Swerve

1 tsp baking powder

1 tsp baking soda

½ tsp salt

Method:

Preheat oven to 350 degrees

Lightly spray a 9” square baking pan with cooking oil

Blend all wet ingredients together.

Blend all dry ingredients together.

Combine everything together and pour the batter into the pan.

Bake at 350 degrees for about 45-50 mins, or until a toothpick inserted into the center comes out clean.

Icing:

Ingredients:

1 8oz package cream cheese, softened

2 cups heavy whipping cream

3 tablespoons cocoa

4 tablespoon Swerve (confectioners style)

A pinch of salt

A dash of red wine (optional)

Method:

#WHIPITGOOD

Frost the cake when it has cooled.

Spicy Shrimp
(WHITE PLATE or BLACK PLATE)

My husband isn't a huge fan of seafood, but he does like salmon and shrimp, and my second oldest son *loves* shrimp, so this is a recipe they are always asking me to make.

I get a pound or two of large, peeled, and deveined from our small town meat market. In the summer we grill it on the BBQ, in the winter we fry it up!

Ingredients:
1 or 2 lbs of large, peeled, and deveined shrimp
Chopped bell peppers, grilled
Garlic, minced if fresh, or powdered, to taste
Oil for frying (I prefer using liquid coconut oil)

Seasoning Mix: (adjust the quantities to suit your family)
Sea salt

Black pepper
Paprika
Cayenne pepper
Onion powder
Garlic powder
A pinch chili powder

Method:

Place seasoning ingredients, along with the shrimp, into a Ziploc plastic bag and give it a good shake.

Prep the frying pan with a bit of liquid coconut oil and heat the pan

Place the grilled bell peppers and garlic in the frying pan and heat for a few minutes

Then add the bag of seasoned, uncooked shrimp to the fry pan and cook until the shrimp are nice and pink.

Notes:

Serve with a salad and a side of sprouted rice. You can also add some tomato sauce as well. You can also prepare this recipe using chicken breast instead of the shrimp

Super quick and easy!

My Kids' Favorite Veggie Dip

This dip is so good and so easy! I love to have it ready for my kids when they get home from school. I serve it with a big tray of bell peppers, carrots, cucumbers or whatever's in season and they dip like crazy. You can make this with your favorite cheese; we like it with cheddar or Parmesan. Making a veggie tray with this dip and keeping it in the fridge is a great way to get my kids to choose healthy veggies as a snack.

Ingredients:

1 cup sour cream (we use full fat and usually organic, depending on the price)

1 tbsp dried minced onion

1 tsp onion powder

¼ tsp garlic powder

¼ tsp salt

¼ tsp dried or fresh parsley—you can also use chives

¼ cup or more of cheese

Method:

Mix all ingredients together in one bowl and serve with veggies of your choice.

Note:

I usually double the recipe so I can keep the extra in the fridge for a few days

Enjoy!

Ru's Fruit Dip

My older daughter is *obsessed* with fruit—she eats at least one apple every day. I came up with a healthy dip to replace the old one. Now she doesn't even miss the old stuff!

Ingredients:

Half a container of your favorite Triple Zero yogurt
Quarter scoop of favorite protein powder
One spoonful of peanut butter
A dash of cinnamon.
A dash of vanilla bean powder (optional)
Sliced fruit of your choice

Method:

Blend everything except the fruit. Then get dipping with the sliced fruit.

Notes:

You could also add some almond milk to the above mix for a yummy smoothie.

Don't be shy about trying different flavors and variations; Ru's favorite is strawberry yogurt and vanilla protein powder.

Mom's Fancy Spinach Omelet
(Black plate)

I think we've already established how much I love eggs—they are my number one superfood of choice, and I think you should eat them every day. No, your cholesterol won't go up, I promise.

Below is the recipe for the omelet I make if I have a few extra moments in the morning to get fancy. I always keep frozen spinach in my freezer because I like to sneak it into things whenever I can. It's also great with chicken, in your smoothie, with eggs, and it's *loaded* with protein. Heck, let's just add spinach to my favorite superfood list too, it's that amazing. Make one of these omelets and then try to disagree with me.

Ingredients:

Frozen spinach, or fresh. Use as much as you like.

3 eggs, well whipped. Really whip the hell out of those eggs; we want this omelet to be fluffy and perfect.

1 large spoonful of cream cheese (I usually use 1/3 fat because it's just as tasty as the regular kind.

¼ cup of salsa (I like things spicy, so I use the Field Day Organic Jalapeno Lime—you can thank me later for telling you about that stuff—but use whichever salsa you prefer).

Method:

Heat the spinach in a frying pan in a tiny bit of oil (coconut oil is best!) and some pink salt.

When the spinach is cooked, add a nice big spoonful of cream cheese and tiny bit of the salsa.

Place the whipped eggs in a separate frying pan and cook until the omelet is done on the underside.

Flip the omelet and cook the other side. Doesn't it look great?

Place the spinach mixture and the rest of the salsa in the center of the omelet—and, because I'm crazy about cheese, add even more cheddar cheese—then fold the omelet in half.

Note:

Be careful about sharing this with your kids, because they're going to want one for breakfast too, and nobody has time to make eight fancy omelets for breakfast!

Roasted Broccoli and Green Beans

Broccoli and green beans are my two favorite vegetables; if you don't eat them, you're missing out! As I've probably established by now, I like mine a bit spicy and full of flavor. If the vegetables don't have *lots* of garlic Mr. Wilder won't even touch them. I love these served with salmon. Get ready for a vegetable explosion in your mouth!

Ingredients:

Fresh broccoli florets

Green beans, trimmed

¼ cup of olive oil

Sea salt (to taste)

Red pepper flakes (to taste)

Cayenne pepper (to taste; yes, I put cayenne on everything)

2 tbsp minced garlic

Method:

Preheat oven to 375 degrees

Place the fresh broccoli and green beans on a baking sheet coated in coconut oil.

Combine remaining ingredients and brush liberally onto the veggies.

Bake for about 5 minutes, turn them over, and then cook for another 5 minutes—you can add another 5 minutes or so of cooking time if it looks like they need it.

Pro tip: You can do this with almost any veggie! Try it with some zucchini or squash too.

Loaded Baked Potato with Chicken (White Plate)

I think only the girls in my family like sweet potatoes, which is fine because it means more for us! Most people only think of loading up a regular potato, but I like to load up a sweet potato for a quick dinner—it's filling and *so* good! I serve it with a salad bar.

Ingredients:

1 large sweet potato per person

Cooked and shredded chicken

Black pepper and salt to taste

Veggies (I like broccoli and/or a tiny bit of corn—whatever you want!)

1/3 fat cream cheese, or Laughing Cow cheese

Method:

Preheat the oven to 400 degrees

Place the sweet potatoes on a baking sheet and bake at 400 degrees for about 50–60 minutes.

Once the potatoes are cooked, slice them in half; (I scoop a little out of the center to give me more room to add the fillings.

Layer on the fillings

Pop the potato(s) back in the oven for 10–15 minutes.

Once done, top with your favorite salsa, or some low-fat cheese.

Yum!

Meat Bowl is the new Taco Tuesday!
(White Plate)

On one of our road trips, Jack and I stopped at a chain burrito place and tried to figure out the best way to eat healthy, which is how our obsession with the meat bowl was born.

We make this buffet bar style for our kids so they can choose their own veggies and other items to make it the way they like it best.

This layout is also very colorful and a great way to impress your guests. Plus, it is very simple to pull together.

Ingredients:

Lean meat such as shredded, cooked chicken
Cooked brown rice
Shredded lettuce
Salsa
Corn kernels
Sliced or diced bell peppers

Beans: kidney, pinto, chickpeas—whatever you like
Low fat sour cream
Low fat cheese, shredded
Berries of your choice
Blue corn chips
Mission low-carb, whole-wheat tortillas

Method:

Place each ingredient in a separate bowl or dish and let everyone help themselves!

Notes:

Choose lean meat; my family *loves* shredded chicken, so that's our usual. I usually offer some berries, because my kids like a tiny bit of sweet with their meals. My kids ALWAYS want some blue corn chips. If your kids really need a wrap, you can use the Mission low carb whole-wheat tortillas.

MISSION LOW CARB WRAPS

I can't say enough about these things. Mission low-carb whole-wheat wraps are the BOMB! Yes, they cost a bit more than traditional wraps, but my local store often puts them on sale and then I stock up. These things are *so* versatile and so good for you. Their texture and softness makes me prefer them over the regular wraps. We use them at nearly every meal, since they're neutral, which means you can use them on either a white or black plate.

Breakfast:

Breakfast burritos. We use bacon or sausage, cheese, and scrambled eggs in our breakfast burritos. If you want to get really fancy you can bake some cheese on top, and add some salsa. If you need a quick grab-and-go breakfast, make up a batch and freeze them for easy reheating!

Another way to serve these wraps is to coat one with cream cheese, layer on your favorite fruit and then top it with a second wrap. Lightly fry in a pan for a few minutes on each side. Our favorite filling is cream cheese and strawberry. To serve, top with powdered Swerve or sugar-free syrup, and a side of vanilla Triple Zero yogurt. It's amazing, delicious and **#fancy**.

Lunch:

Quesadillas. The kids add different meats and cheeses to their wraps, and then dip them in salsa and sour cream. So easy, quick and yummy!

Use them for any and all types of sandwiches. My little boys will even eat a PB&J on them. You can also make rollup sandwich wheels with cream cheese or Laughing Cow cheese. Just spread the wrap

with the soft cheese of your choice and then roll them up like a cigar. Slice into wheels and you've got lunch!

Dinner:

We use these wraps for tacos, burritos, and enchiladas. They bake well, so you can use them in almost any dish that calls for a traditional tortilla.

You can also use them to make personal pizzas. These are super fast to make and it keeps the kids happy—they choose their own toppings, and they bake very quickly. They're surprisingly tasty. Even Mr. Wilder likes these.

WASA crackers

I've referred to these crackers many times in this book. Let me just say that the WASA cracker is an incredible thing. You've probably passed them in the grocery store without even knowing what they were. These little crackers are so versatile I've used them for breakfast, lunch, dinner, snacks, and treats! We use them so much I buy them by the case from Amazon!

WASA crackers are packed with fiber, which is vitally important for a healthy body. They have minimal carbs, and they fill you up. Whether you're craving something hearty or sweet, we can find a way to smash that craving with a WASA cracker.

Don't take my word for it, just try them!

Some of our favorite WASA cracker combinations:

- Rye WASA with natural peanut butter and all fruit jelly
- Cream cheese and all-fruit jelly and/or berries
- Any and all flavors of the Laughing Cow brand cheese with various toppings: veggies, salsa, meats
- Pizza WASA: tomato sauce, mozzarella cheese, and pepperoni (a great late night snack)
- Tomato, fresh mozzarella, and balsamic
- Sourdough WASA and your favorite cheese
- Cream cheese, nuts, and drizzled chocolate—oh yeah, I went there!

Pro tip: Throw WASA crackers into your soup and forget about croutons or other crackers. You can also crumble these into your salad for added crunch instead of using croutons.

AUTHOR NOTE

Dear Reader,

You've made it to the end of this book, and I wish I could give you a great big hug! I wrote this book for *you*. I know that for so many of us, our weight has been a life long struggle. It's personal, and often painful. It often represents a lifetime of failure, and it feels like a curse.

But things *can* be different for you.

You *can* do this! It's your time. You *WILL* succeed! You're going to KICK ASS! You have the knowledge to succeed, and I'll be right here with you every step of the way. We're going to do this together.

You ARE strong.

You ARE worthy of this positive change, and you are worthy of good health.

Don't dwell on the pain of the past; look instead toward the sweetness of the future.

Good things await you. Each new day is another chance to change the rest of your life.

Please feel free to reach out to me via social media; I would *love* to hear from you. You're in my heart and in my thoughts every day. My prayer is that women will start to make changes for their families and themselves, amazing, positive changes which will eventually end the cycle of obesity and its long list of devastating diseases.

We can do it, one mom at a time, one meal at a time.

God bless you,

Coach J

Hebrews 12:1

COOKBOOK RECOMMENDATIONS:

- *100 DAYS OF REAL FOOD* by Lisa Leake—a wonderful education about food.
- *TRIM HEALTHY MAMA* by Pearl Barrett and Serene C. Allison—my kids' favorite! These ladies are amazing at modifying family-favorite recipes. Check out THM blogger websites, too.
- *THE WHOLE 30* by Dallas Hartwig and Melissa Hartwig — perfect if you want to for start off with clean eating
- *WELL FED* by Melissa Joulwan—great ways to modify menus to include healthy Paleo options.
- *THE KETOGENIC COOKBOOK* by Jimmy Moore and Maria Emmerich—this book is just beautiful, and has some great recipes in it.
- *PRACTICAL PALEO* by Diane Sanfilippo—even though I'm not technically paleo, I love her recipes. It's a great, informative book.
- *THE PIONEER WOMAN* by Ree Drummond—I adjust these recipes to suit our needs, but they are still some of our favorites.
- *THE GRAIN BRAIN* by David Perlmutter and Kristin Loberg—fancy but solid
- *THE SEXY FOREVER RECIPE BIBLE* by Suzanne Somers—enough said.
- PINTEREST—Yes, the app. Pinterest is almost always my go-to when I want to try something new. It's an amazing resource if you want ideas or want to find a way to modify your favorite recipes. I'm sending a huge shoutout to all the bloggers who put their talents into that site for us. Some of these recipes can make a huge difference to those of us who get a hankering for something, but just can't figure out how to make it. Check Pinterest if you can't find what you're looking for in one of your cookbooks.

ADDITIONAL RESOURCES AND READING SUGGESTIONS

Always Hungry by David Ludwig MD, Ph.D.

The Body Book by Cameron Diaz

Grain Brain by David Perlmutter MD and Kristin Loberg

Why We Get Fat and WhatTo DoAbout It by Gary Taubes

Eat Fat, Lose Fat by Dr. Mary Enig and Sally Fallon

100 Days of Real Food by Lisa Leake

Choose To Lose by Chris Powell

Trim Healthy Mama Plan by Pearl Barrett and Serene Allison

Running Like A Girl: Notes on Learning to Run by Alexandra Heminsley (I *love* this book!)

Run Like A Mother by Dimity McDowell and Sarah Bowen Shea

Women's Running Magazine

www.nutritiondata.com is a great website for checking the nutritional values on your favorite whole foods.

8-WEEK CHALLENGE TESTIMONIALS

Below are testimonials from several people who've tried my plan. They inspired me and I know they will inspire you, too.

I have struggled with my weight for nearly 20 years. I was recently diagnosed with hypothyroidism and knew I was ready for a lifestyle change rather than just a new diet. I've been following Jasinda's program faithfully and have found it very easy to stick with. The first thing I noticed was I didn't miss the sugar and that I was never hungry; in fact, I ate until I was full. There was no counting calories or points, which made things stress free. Food actually tastes so much better and my energy level is through the roof! I am confident I will continue with "The Wilder Way" for many reasons. I'm no longer lethargic, and my stomach issues have disappeared. I feel good and have no problem making the best choices for my meals. I can't wait to share what I've learned with my family and friends. This experience has truly changed my life! — *Heidi M, 43*

This was the simplest change I could ever make. It was super easy to do and I really didn't have to think about it at all. All you do is eat, walk/wog, and you lose weight. It cannot be simpler than that. — *Jennifer O, 34*

I was so frustrated with my weight, so when I saw Jasinda's post asking for volunteers for a beta group for weight loss, I almost didn't care what we were going to have to do. I couldn't have imagined that

eight weeks on this program would've brought so many changes. The first thing I noticed after just three days was a slight increase in energy. Nine days in and I noticed a significant decrease in heartburn. About two weeks in, I (and others) noted positive changes in my complexion (coloring and condition).

These changes have continued throughout the entire eight weeks. I've also noticed increased confidence and overall just feeling better.

One of my favorite things to come out of this experience has been that my whole family got involved. We're in the kitchen together most nights cooking dinners, and we eat out a lot less, but I love that it is not difficult at all to stay with our lifestyle changes on evenings we choose to eat out. I don't feel deprived; I can still have chocolate and ice cream. I don't have to weigh out perfect portions; I don't have to leave the table hungry or unsatisfied, no calorie counting, none of those things that made me give up on past attempts at weight loss.

I never imagined that eight weeks after starting on these changes that I would be prepping for my first 5k. The results I've achieved with minimal changes are more than I could have hoped for. I am so grateful to have been a part of this. This is not a "diet" to me. I have negative associations with that term and it sounds temporary. This is truly a lifestyle change and I have no problem staying on this track. **#WoggingWilderWay4Life** — *Andrea G, 40*

I was so excited to be chosen for this journey. The process has been empowering and easy to follow and understand. I have tried and failed many other diets before, mostly because I never really understood what to do correctly, despite reading things over and over.

With *Big Girls Do It Running*, not once have I felt hungry or

deprived. I have had no cravings for any bad food. The recipes are all delicious and I love the variety. My favorite is the cheesecake. I thought I would have to just say goodbye to cheesecake in my life! I have more energy and I look forward to getting out and moving.

I take things day by day and am glad there is no true end in sight. It's the first time I am not worried about getting to the end of a diet and then messing up on the maintenance.

This is how I want to eat for the rest of my life! I have found my inner athlete. Finally, for the first time in my life, I am not defining my success as a number to reach at the end of all this. Friends and family have already noticed changes in my skin and body. Many have commented that I am happier as well. I do smile more!

The *Big Girls Do It Running* revolution has truly saved me. At the start of this year I was frustrated and didn't know where to turn or what other diet I could possibly try. I truly think Jasinda is an angel. This process is successful since she herself has experienced the struggles so many of us have. Thank you, Jasinda, for being such a light in my life. I am so grateful for you and your guidance. I feel my life is being transformed. I feel I am discovering my true self!

Thank you from the bottom of my heart! — *Donna K, 38*

This woman and her program have saved my life. A few weeks before being selected for this wonderful journey I was told I was going blind because of my diabetes. My blood sugars have always run in the 300s, even with up to six injections of insulin a day. I had given up in life.

This program has gotten me off insulin in four weeks. For the first time in 15 years my blood sugar is normal. Jasinda has helped me be able to see for many years to come. — *Sara W, 28*

I am one of the many people in this world who has tried many diets—some with great success—only to find myself eventually gaining back the weight I lost. Whether it's because I stopped counting points, or ate a bread and potato-heavy meal, one misstep would spiral out of control and the next thing I knew, all my hard work would disappear.

With the Wilder Way things have been different. For starters, the things Jasinda has asked us to cut out: sugar, bad carbs like non-sprouted bread and white potatoes, are things I don't miss. Not only do I not miss them, I feel better without them. I think that's the key to the Wilder Way success. You aren't cutting out things without a purpose or just for weight loss.

The weight loss is a pleasant side effect of your body getting the nutrition it craves. I feel better having done this plan for the past eight weeks than I have felt in years. Removing sugar from my diet has improved how I sleep and how I feel throughout the day. The food I eat tastes delicious and I enjoy eating. And because I'm eating the right thing, I get full faster and feel more satisfied longer.

If that's not enough, I'm JOGGING! Even at my lightest weight the thought of any thing close to a run would make me shudder.

As more and more people start to notice that I am looking physically better, it's hard not to want to tell them about everything I'm doing because I'm so excited about it. I truly believe this way of eating, the Wilder Way, is what is going to change my life.

As a single girl living in a big city, it's important that I am able to eat meals out, and this plan not only lets me do that, but it makes it easy to do!

The Wilder Way does take some adjustment, but once you get used to it, it feels natural and easy. It's something you can live with for the rest of your life and never feel deprived. I will always be grateful

to Jasinda for inviting me to be part of this process and for helping me change my health and my body for the better. — *Michelle K, 32*

The Wilder Way has been life changing for me! It's amazing to think that eight weeks can change your life, but it completely has! Jasinda has given me the tools I need to be healthy and strong for a lifetime. Now, I can teach my children how to be healthy and strong before they become adults.

I look at things differently now, I think more about what my body needs, I read labels, and I am more knowledgeable and informed. It hasn't even been difficult; I had full faith in Jasinda, and she really came through! I was wearing a size 24 when we started this journey, and after eight weeks I have lost 18 pounds and I am now comfortably wearing a size 18! I have lost over five inches on my waist and my skin even looks healthier!

And I know this is not a temporary loss like I've had with other diets and programs, because this is NOT a diet, this is a whole new outlook on food and getting healthy. I'm getting the physical movement that my body needs, something it has not had for so long.

Thank you Jasinda for changing my life and my family's lives for the better. And I'm proud to be a part of the start of a REVOLUTION! — *Tracie W, 46*

This journey has changed my life in so many ways. The way I look at food and my body will never be the same. I've learned that I don't need a magic pill to lose weight or become healthy. Just changing the food I eat and adding FUN exercise will get me there.

I've learned that giving my body time to change is okay, and

that it's okay if it doesn't happen right away. Support is number one; I wouldn't have made it this far without it. I am so grateful for this opportunity to learn a new healthy way to live my life.

My family and I are forever changed. Thank you, Jasinda, for being so unbelievably brave and for sharing your life with us. — *Chandra T, 34*

Let me start by saying that Jasinda has changed my life in so many ways! I have struggled with my weight my entire life, and I'd gotten to the point were I honestly wanted to give up. I gained 75 lbs in 2015 and was diagnosed with Polycystic Ovary Syndrome. I felt like that was the end for me. How was I ever going to defeat that? How was I going to manage losing weight with not only a broken back but with this new diagnosis?

I remember praying so hard that Jasinda would choose me when I read her post for volunteers for the beta group, but I never even dreamed I would get chosen out of the hundreds of messages she got. I cried so hard when she added me to the group, and I remember thinking, "Please God, let this be the change for me because if something doesn't give I'm not going to be around for my babies."

He answered my prayers: I truly believe Jasinda is the best thing that has happened to me in years! I went from a size 3x to a plus size XL; I was 260 pounds in December and now I'm at 238 and feel fantastic! I can exercise and not be in excruciating pain. I can eat amazing food and not feel deprived, yet I'm losing lots of inches.

I can never thank Jasinda enough for what she has done for me. Coach J, you have changed my life and I thank you from the bottom of my heart! — *Amber F, 29*

I couldn't feel more privileged to be part of this test group. The last eight weeks have taught me so many things about my body, my health, and the fact that junk is hiding in our everyday food.

I never thought I'd be able to give up sugar, soda and chips and never miss them. This isn't a diet; it's a lifestyle change that I can stick to. I'm eating well *and* losing weight! No starving. Not only am I losing in a healthy way, but also I *feel* healthier. I have energy, I'm exercising, and I'm not feeling like I'm about to quit any minute.

This program isn't hard and it's not depriving me of anything. I can have cookies and cake if I want it! They just don't have all that bad for you "death-dough" in it.

I will be forever thankful to Jasinda Wilder for inviting me on this journey to better health. I never thought I'd eat real food, not starve, *and* lose weight. I can't wait to be skinny, hot, and healthy just like Jasinda.

If I can do this, I know anyone can. — *Erecia C, 33*

When I agreed to start this program, I thought, "I cannot *wait* to change the lives of my children!" I was hopeful that I could change their eating habits and overall health. With four young children I often worry whether I am making the right decisions. Now I know for sure that I am!

My family is eating healthier and still indulging in all the things we want to eat. Jasinda has a beautiful way with words, and I have always admired her ambition and tenacity. She has truly gone above and beyond to help me, to take the time to listen to my questions and concerns, to guide my journey.

Shortly after starting this program, I realized I should be doing this program for my children. I needed to lead by example, I needed

to show my family the way. And I have. I have lost weight and inches, and that makes me proud. I know this would not be possible without Jasinda's program!

The program was easy to follow, slow to start, but steady throughout. No matter what food we wanted to eat, whether it was chocolate or salad dressing, there was an alternative that was not only healthy, but it tasted good. I fully believe in the Wilder Way.

The Wilders have changed my life, changed the lives of my children, and changed my future. I am so blessed that I was chosen to help pilot this program. — *Amy B, 33*

Being 29 with PCOS has been difficult. It has been hard to find a diet and exercise program that worked. I needed to find a lifestyle change for my overall health and wellness. When Jasinda began looking for people to join her trial…I was very excited. Jasinda has inspired me for many years as an author, and now as my friend.

I trusted her with her program and she has inspired me to begin my new life. She gave me the tools to succeed with her program. My family also benefits from Jasinda's program with every meal I prepare for them. I myself am down 15 pounds and counting! I couldn't be happier with my progress. I have never felt this good and have never been happier in my life! — *Alysa D, 29*

Have you ever felt like all of the cards in the deck are stacked against you? That you feel like you don't know how much more you can take? That's where I was before this journey with *Big Girls Do It Running* began.

I had a very bad lifestyle that wasn't healthy for me, and most importantly it would end up costing me my life if I continued down

that path. I was blessed enough to be selected by Jasinda for a small group to test her program before the release of this new book.

I have to say that not only am I blown away by the support I've received, but also how lucky I was to be personally coached by Jasinda. My whole outlook on food, my body, and lifestyle is completely turning around. I know changing my ways is a life-long process, but these 8 weeks have shown me I can do this for my family and myself.

Besides the weight loss, I feel like a completely different person. During my journey I experienced some life-shaking and soul-changing realizations: first, I was diagnosed with PCOS, and second, my son was going to need a very serious spinal surgery this year. I need to make myself stronger and healthier so I can face anything for him. And I will do it! **#TheWilderWay #BigGirlsDoItRunning** — *Tara R, 29*

Although I haven't lost as much weight as some of the other wonderful women in this group, I feel better than I have in a very long time. I got my ass off the couch and into the gym three days a week in spite of my hectic schedule. I have kicked my addiction to sugar, which I know now is truly evil. I never in a million years would have dreamed I would be able to do that! Diabetes runs on both sides of my family, and I'm sure I was on my way to that diagnosis…until Jasinda changed that for me.

I have learned to make the healthiest choices possible for each meal, and to plan ahead to prevent myself from failing. The dedication you have shown to me and the other women in this group is remarkable. I owe you a lot and feel a deep admiration for you. Your kindness and drive to give us the gift of health is beyond heartwarming. I love your heart, your sense of humor, your compassion, and

your need to help others. I honestly don't know how you have been able to give us so much of yourself almost 24/7 for the past eight weeks.

Thank you from the bottom of my healthier heart. — *Diana K, 51*

On January 5, 2016, Jasinda Wilder asked me if I was ready to be part of The Wilder Way. Was I ready to see if eight weeks could change my life?

Eight Weeks…56 days. Could I really do this? Could I take my body, which I had been abusing for years with unhealthy habits, and completely turn things around in eight short weeks? I made a decision that day when I stepped on the scale and saw, staring back at me, a number that scared me to death; I *had* to say YES! Changes needed to happen, and *fast*. As a wife, mom, and woman I had completely lost my zest for life, as well as my confidence. It was time to put in the work and make the changes necessary for creating a healthy lifestyle for my family and me!

I knew by saying yes to The Wilder Way that I had to be 100% committed to making a huge lifestyle change. I also knew that saying no wasn't an option, this was it. If you are reading this and thinking, "Been there, done that, tried every program," believe me, I have too! And with every other thing I tried, within days, I was back to my old habits.

But, what I would come to discover is that the way Jasinda Wilder's program is laid out makes it easy for the average person to follow.

The beginning of the program made all the difference to me sticking with it. I was able to ease my body and mind into it, really taking the time to learn about food and exercise, and what they

can do to fuel my body to success. Other plans I've tried in the past meant quitting cold turkey on everything, and exercising to death, which was just so hard for me to do, so I would give up! This plan had me gradually making the changes, making it much easier to keep up with.

After the first few weeks into Jasinda's program, it wasn't just the number on the scales that kept me motivated; it was the changes taking place right before my eyes that completely had me hooked on The Wilder Way lifestyle change!

Taking pictures of myself really helped me notice those everyday changes that were happening. I started to notice huge differences: my eyes were more defined, I had clearer skin, a smaller waist, no more swollen ankles, my chin and neck were shrinking, and I had a brand new energy for life! I actually *wanted* to work out, something that was completely foreign to me!

Worried about what you will eat on this plan? DON'T! Before this, my day consisted of things like frozen pizza, soda, and candy bars to get me through, but I never felt full. I cannot believe all the food I can eat in a day now. I'm eating more than I ever have before and, with Jasinda's recipes along the way, my meals are not only delicious, but nutritious, too!

If you want your life back, I urge you to try Coach J's plan. Give yourself eight weeks on The Wilder Way. It will change the way you live for the rest of your life! — *Jen G, 44*

Jasinda Wilder's plan, The Wilder Way, is educational and easy to follow. You don't have to count calories or measure out everything you eat. There are no bland, prepackaged meals, no chalky shakes to

choke down, no starving yourself; you eat *REAL* food. Not only does The Wilder Way provide you with delicious new recipes to try, but also healthier versions of old favorites like cookies and cake! This is not a diet, a fad, or a gimmick, it's a plan you will want to continue for life.

I have accomplished some amazing things in just eight weeks: I've lost pounds and inches, I've gone from a sedentary lifestyle to participating in a 5K, I've kicked my pop habit (I never in my life thought I would be able to go five weeks without a soda and not miss it!). I've been able to stop taking one of my daily medications and, most importantly, I feel better physically and mentally than I have in YEARS.

I don't feel weighed down—literally and figuratively—after eating. My whole relationship with food has changed and I no longer feel guilty about eating. Not only has Jasinda changed my life, but she has given it back to me. Don't think eight weeks can change your life? Think again! — *Kerry G, 44*

I have struggled with my weight for most of my life. There have been more highs than lows, literally. I did my best on a popular, commercial weight loss regimen, losing 30 pounds in two years and three months. The trouble was I felt like I was competing, even if only with myself. If there was no change on the scale, I was a failure.

Then there was a new way, a sensible way, a Wilder Way! Nothing crazy, just smart eating, better planning, and more effective movement. I felt confident and competent; championed, and challenged.

In eight weeks, I lost 13.2 pounds, and inches off of every stubborn spot on my body. I also found a community of similar weight-worried and weary women who knew my tale all too well.

Long story short…I have pride, I have purpose, and I have power. Who would expect to gain so much from losing?

Thank you, Coach J! — *Wendy K, 48*

Eight weeks ago I pled my case to Jasinda, requesting a place in her beta test group. I had high blood pressure, skin issues, kidney issues due to weight, and overall poor health. The day I found out I was chosen, I cried. Being a single mom of two, I knew I had to give my all to this program.

Jasinda is someone I admire; and I thought if Jasinda decided that this was her calling, then I knew that this was it, my chance to take my life back. This plan is so easy. Not only for me, but my children. My daughter has severe allergies and asthma, but since making simple changes to our diets, her asthma has become virtually non-existent.

Jasinda dedicated her time, knowledge, strength, and courage to create this program, and she gave me the opportunity to take back my life, just by changing my eating—I eat real food all the time now. Then I added in running or wogging and now I can run three miles. Me! Three miles! Crazy, I know.

If you want to change your health, life, and overall outlook on your life, then join this journey. The Wider Way is the only way.

It works, and I AM PROOF!!! — *Debbie B, 43*

Blind faith is never easy, but Jasinda's passion for not only weight loss but also life-change is infectious. Paving her own path down an already well-traveled road, Jasinda is pioneering a new lifestyle. It's more than weight loss. More than a lifestyle change. Jasinda's plan

may very well be your last stop on the weight loss roller coaster.

We own our weight. The world may have you thinking differently, but your weight and the reason(s) you hold on to it is personal. Whatever your struggle may be, Jasinda's plan will have you reevaluating everything you think you know about weight loss. Week by week you will learn that you're strong enough. That you have the determination. That you're worth it.

Why buy a book about a topic that has been worked and reworked? Well, actions speak louder than words. Jasinda has proven this process works. She is talking the talk and walking the walk. She is a talented author who has documented her personal journey and has chosen to share that journey with the world. Her hope is to better the life of at least one person, but I feel she will help change the world.

Am I a believer? Well, 40 pounds down, my migraines are at a minimum, my skin looks great, I have tons of energy, and no more airplane seatbelt extensions! Is this a quick fix? No. I didn't put this weight on overnight, and I won't lose it overnight. It's a lifestyle, not a diet. A way of life that not only betters me, but the people around me. I am a work in process. I will never give up on myself. Even when I was at my heaviest there was always a part of me that kept trying, in some way.

You have nothing to lose but weight, right? What better way to learn than with someone who has been in the trenches, put in the work, done the research, and has found a solution that works? I believe in Jasinda as a friend, an author, and now as a pioneer. You will too! — *Pamela C, 37*

Upon joining *Big Girls Do It Running*, I was depressed, unmotivated, and complacent. When I thought about going to the gym, or start-

ing a new diet, I always told myself, "there is always tomorrow," but tomorrow always came and went, and led to constant excuses and giving up. I was torn between wanting to be healthy but feeling like I didn't know where to begin.

Then I was chosen to be in this revolution, and little did I know it would be life changing! It sparked a motivation in me. For once in my life I had an "I *can* do it" attitude! I felt stronger, energized, healthier, and more alive.

Jasinda introduced us to wogging and, at first, I got scared and didn't think I could hit the pavement, and that my body wasn't made to run. Little did I know the opposite was true, and I pushed myself to see if I could go farther, faster and to see if I could run without stopping to catch my breath.

With this program, I have achieved more in eight weeks than with any other program I've tried. I also feel the best I have in my entire life! My relationship with food and my body has changed, which I never thought was possible…and it was all due to Jasinda's constant support, and her program. — *Kelly L, 28*

Thank you, Jasinda Wilder, for deciding to share what you learned with other women, thank you for picking me to join this amazing group of women who were all ready to change their lives.

I have been talking for the last few years about losing weight, but it never happened. I was determined this year that I was going to make it happen, and then you, Jasinda, appeared!

My mom died of breast cancer at age 46. I just turned 44. The closer I get to 46, the more fearful I become. I have so much life to live and so many things I want to do. While I can't prevent breast cancer, I can do something about heart disease, diabetes, and other

health issues I'm at risk of because of my genetics.

This plan has given me the strength to fight hard for my body and my life. I now know I can do this! Are there days when I want to throw in the towel and give up? Yep! But I see the bigger picture, and I pull up my big girl panties and I keep going, because I'm down 11 pounds and I can see it working.

I look at all the other ladies in this group, and I'm motivated. Thank you all so much for helping me get back to the me that's not ashamed of looking in the mirror. The me that isn't ashamed to take pictures. I didn't really take a full body picture in the beginning because I was ashamed and embarrassed of what I had let happen to my body. I'm working my way back to me, and I'm so very thankful to you, Jasinda. I'm still scared some days that I'm messing up, but I won't quit! — *Camisha C, 44*

This 8-week program has educated me more than anything else I have tried. There are so many lies in the food industry and, sadly, most companies don't care about our health. Jasinda's book has educated me on how to read labels and what to look for. Before taking part in this trial, knowing what to eat was very confusing. But having her support and motivation through these eight weeks has been like nothing else. She is hardcore, but in a fun way!

Thank you for teaching me about health and about myself, Jasinda, and thank you to all the other ladies in this 8-week group. We rocked it! — *Ashlee B*, 31

I have not battled with obesity my whole life; in fact, I was the quintessential skinny girl growing up. "Bean Pole and Olive Oil" is what

they used to call me. I could pretty much eat anything I wanted.

The battle started when I got to college. You know the "Freshman Fifteen" everyone talks about? Yeah, mine was more like the "Freshman Fifty." I was working at McDonald's and I thought I could eat anything I wanted and not gain a pound. I was wrong—I gained *lots* of weight. I eventually drifted to my second fast food job, Hardee's. I continued the same terrible eating habits and eventually ballooned to around 350 lbs. I was shocked because I weighed 195 lbs in high school.

At first you don't think about how much of an impact weight has on your body, but eventually many ailments came with the excess weight I was carrying. I developed varicose veins in both legs and when I had my first child, I developed preeclampsia and the fear of diabetes.

I almost lost my child and my life because my weight was out of control. Thankfully, however, both of us survived and I vowed to be healthier. Well, that didn't last too long, and before you know it I was having my second child and I still had the same health issues; this time my leg had swollen to twice its normal size. I was confined to bed because they feared I had a blood clot and they didn't want it to travel. I had a healthy baby, but momma wasn't healthy.

I struggled with my weight fluctuating for years. I've tried Weight Watchers, diet pills, and many other programs that were quick fixes but weren't long term. Each time I gained the weight back fast, plus more.

When Jasinda posted that she was looking for women to join her *Big Girls Do It Running* group, I said to myself, "What the hell, I've tried everything, so why not try this too?"

I was skeptical when I started this journey. Jasinda's advice and support is truly valuable. She and the amazing group of women in

the group helped me celebrate my successes, and kept me focused on my goal. Jasinda didn't let me beat myself up when I had a slip up, and she helped me remember how far I had come at each step of the journey. Her loving words are what kept me going. "Focus on the next meal," she would say.

Her plan didn't have me completely cutting out everything I loved; instead it had me finding healthier, alternative choices. I was excited about what I got to eat, and I didn't feel deprived because of what I couldn't eat. She challenged me to slowly introduce exercise and eventually she had me wogging two miles! I found myself accomplishing things I'd never done before.

This entire process made me realize that weight loss is not a quick fix. No, *wham, bam, thank you ma'am*. It takes time—it is a complete life change, a happy shock to your heart, body and mind. I now have more confidence than I've had in years, and I finally feel comfortable in my clothes.

I'm still learning, growing, succeeding, and failing. And that's okay because I know there is an amazing group of woman there to support me along the way. I am completely grateful for Jasinda's passion to help others lead healthy lives. Thank you. I will forever be indebted to you. — *Monique W, 30*

Beta Test Group Results:

Upon completion of the 8-Week trial, members of the group experienced the following:

- Normal blood sugars
- Improved skin condition
- Improved sleep
- Increased energy
- Increased libido
- Improvement with anxiety and depression
- Improvement with lethargy
- Total weight loss of 365 pounds and 130 inches around the waist, across 25 participants from all ages, races, and socio-economic backgrounds.

PART I:

My Backstory

Contents

Acknowledgements

This book would not have been possible without the support from so many special people in my life.

Thank you to my dear friends Karri and Meredith, who fill in all the gaps in my life and our crazy schedule, from testing recipes to picking up the slack around the house and folding laundry. You ladies are the best. Thank you from the bottom of my heart.

To my amazing photographer Leah, and my graphic designer Sarah: Thank you so much for working so hard to give this book a special look and feel. You drip talent and I'm so grateful to be able to work with you both.

To my editor Valerie, who didn't balk when I told her I wanted to do a non-fiction project: thank you for believing in me and in this body of work. You are invaluable in our writing process. Thank you!

To my agent Kristin Nelson, who is always willing to help me with my indie projects when she gets paid almost nothing to do so. Thank you! Your support and constant help and guidance with this project has been nothing short of amazing. The team at Nelson Literary Agency is simply the best of the best.

And last but certainly not least, I would like to extend a special and heartfelt thank you to the twenty-five brave, beautiful, and kick-ass warrior women who volunteered to be my beta test group for The Wilder Way. You amaze me, and you inspire me. Thank you so much for trusting me with eight weeks of your lives, and for taking this incredible step toward health with me. Let's start a revolution, ladies!

Dedication

First, this book is dedicated to my husband, who sees me as beautiful on my best days as well as my worst: I couldn't do this life without you. TODAAT-CWM

Second, this book is for my children who inspire me every single day to be the best I can be. You are my heart and soul. Don't forget to beast mode at the end—you won't regret it. I'm so proud of you!

And finally, this book is for my parents, who always tried so hard to help me find health; I've finally found it. Thank you for never giving up on me and pushing me to always be my best. I wouldn't be who I am today without your love and guidance.

Foreword

First, let me thank you for picking up this book. I hope if you or someone you know are struggling with the same issues I have struggled with, namely maintaining a healthy weight and lifestyle, that *BIG GIRLS DO IT RUNNING* will offer insights and encouragement to help you move forward.

But, before you begin reading, I want you to know that I am *not* a health expert. In fact, I'm about the farthest thing from an expert you could imagine. I'm just a mom, a wife, and a daughter with a little bit of wisdom and a lot of personal experience to share. I truly hope that by sharing my journey I will be able to help anyone who is trying to look at their health and their life in a different way.

This book is written from my personal perspective only, and the information contained herein should by no means be considered a substitute for the advice of a qualified medical professional.

Always consult your physician before beginning any new exercise or health program. Every effort has been made to ensure the accuracy of the information contained in this book as of the date of publication. The author and publisher (that's me!) expressly disclaim responsibility for any adverse effects arising from the use, or application, of the information contained herein.

Jasinda Wilder
February 2016

Cover art and Worksheet Graphics by Sarah Hansen of Okay Creations. Cover art © 2016 by Sarah Hansen.

Formatting by Champagne Formats

Photos by Leah Renee Photography

For full-color recipe photos and printable versions of the worksheets please visit, www.biggirlsdoitrunning.com.

This woman and her program have saved my life. A few weeks before being selected for this wonderful journey I was told I was going blind because of my diabetes. My blood sugars have always run in the 300s, even with up to six insulin injections a day. At this point I had given up in on life. This program has gotten got me off insulin in four weeks. For the first time in 15 years my blood sugar is normal. Jasinda has helped me to be able to see for many years to come. — *Sara W, 28*

As a single girl living in a big city, it's important that I can eat meals out, and this plan not only lets me do that, but it makes it easy to do! *The Wilder Way* does take some adjustment, but once you get used to it, it feels natural and easy. It's something you can live with for the rest of your life and never feel deprived. I will always be grateful to Jasinda for inviting me to be part of this process and for helping me change my health and my body for the better. — *Michelle K, 32*

Jasinda Wilder's plan, *The Wilder Way,* is educational and easy to follow. You don't have to count calories or measure out everything you eat. There are no bland, prepackaged meals, no chalky shakes to choke down, no starving yourself; you eat *REAL* food. Not only does *The Wilder Way* provide you with delicious new recipes to try, but also healthier versions of old favorites like cookies and cake! This is not a diet, fad, or gimmick, it's a plan you will want to continue for life. I have accomplished some amazing things in just eight weeks: I've lost pounds and inches, I've gone from a sedentary lifestyle to participating in a 5K, I've kicked my pop habit…and I've been able to stop taking one of my daily medications. Most importantly, I feel better, physically and mentally, than I have in YEARS. — *Kerry G, 44*

Praise for Big Girls Do It Running

You have nothing to lose but weight, right? What better way to learn than with someone who has been through the trenches, put in the work, done the research, and has found a solution that works? I believe in Jasinda as a friend, an author, and now as a pioneer. You will too! — *Pamela C, 37*

This was the simplest change I could ever make. It was super easy to do and I really didn't have to think about it at all. All you do is eat, walk or jog, and you lose weight. It couldn't be simpler than that. — *Jennifer O, 34*

One of my favorite things to come from this experience is that my whole family has become involved. We're in the kitchen together most nights cooking dinners, and we eat out a lot less. But I love that it is not difficult at all to stay within our lifestyle changes on evenings when we do choose to eat out. I don't feel deprived; I can still have chocolate and ice cream. I don't have to weigh out perfect portions; I don't have to leave the table hungry or unsatisfied, and there is no calorie counting. There are none of the things in this program that made me give up on past attempts at weight loss. —*Andrea G, 40*

The *Big Girls Do It Running* revolution has truly saved me. At the start of this year I was frustrated and didn't know where to turn, or what other diet I could possibly try. This process is has been so successful for me because Jasinda herself has experienced the same struggles so many of us have. Thank you, Jasinda, for being such a light to in my life. I am so grateful for you and your guidance. I feel my life is being transformed. I feel I am discovering my true self! Thank you from the bottom of my heart! — *Donna K, 38*

Big Girls Do It Running:

Health, Fitness, and Kicking Life's Ass!

My journey from 430lbs to fit AND fabulous

Jasinda Wilder